Henry Kiddle, A. J. (Alexander Jacob) Schem

The Dictionary of Education and Instruction

A Reference Book and Manual on the Theory and Practice of Teaching

Henry Kiddle, A. J. (Alexander Jacob) Schem

The Dictionary of Education and Instruction
A Reference Book and Manual on the Theory and Practice of Teaching

ISBN/EAN: 9783337172572

Printed in Europe, USA, Canada, Australia, Japan

Cover: Foto ©Paul-Georg Meister /pixelio.de

More available books at **www.hansebooks.com**

THE DICTIONARY OF EDUCATION AND INSTRUCTION;

A REFERENCE BOOK AND MANUAL ON THE
THEORY AND PRACTICE OF TEACHING,

FOR THE USE OF
PARENTS, TEACHERS, AND OTHERS;

BASED UPON THE
CYCLOPÆDIA OF EDUCATION.

BY
HENRY KIDDLE AND A. J. SCHEM.

NEW YORK:
E. STEIGER & CO.
1881.

SANTA BARBARA. CALIF

Special attention is invited to the following publications:

The Cyclopaedia of Education. *A Dictionary of Information for the use of Teachers, School-Officers, Parents, and Others.* Edited by HENRY KIDDLE and ALEXANDER J. SCHEM. One large volume, 8vo. In Paper Cover, uncut edges, $4.00 (also in 4 divisions at $1.00 each); bound in Cloth $5.00 — and uniform with the volumes of *Appleton's American Cyclopædia*, in Library Leather $6.00; in Half Morocco $7.00; in Half Russia, extra gilt $8.00; in Full Morocco, or Full Russia, with gilt edges $10.00.

The Year-Book of Education for 1878. Being an Annual Supplement to the *Cyclopædia of Education*. Edited by HENRY KIDDLE and A. J. SCHEM. 8vo. Cloth $2.00.

—— —— **for 1879.** Edited by HENRY KIDDLE and A. J. SCHEM. 8vo. Cloth $2.00.

In addition to editorial matter on the progress of education in America and foreign countries, each of these two volumes contains a list of Collegiate and Private Educational Institutions in the United States and Canada, and other Catalogues and Lists of value and interest.

Steiger's Educational Directory for 1878. 326 pp. 8vo. Limp cloth $1.50.

Contents: Lists of Collegiate and Private Educational Institutions (United States, British Dominions, Germany, Austria). — Catalogues, etc.

☞ A new edition for 1881–82 is in preparation.

Education and General Philology. *A Classified Descriptive Catalogue of American, British, German, French, and other Foreign Publications on Education and General Philology; together with Works of Reference, Teachers' Hand-books, etc., exclusive of Text-books.* Edited by E. STEIGER. 48 pp. 8vo. Paper 10 Cts. net.

NOTICE.

Desirous of securing for the *Dictionary of Education and Instruction* the widest possible circulation among teachers, school-officers, parents, and all progressive persons, the undersigned publishers invite propositions from booksellers, agents, and others intending to thoroughly canvass certain limited territory.

E. STEIGER & CO.

PREFACE.

The *Cyclopædia of Education*, the only publication of the kind in the English language, has now been before the public about four years, during which time this work has secured the unqualified approval of the most eminent and experienced educators and official authorities both in America and abroad. This is all the more satisfactory, as much of the commendation bestowed has resulted from a careful study and constant use of the *Cyclopædia* as an educational guide.

But while the *Cyclopædia* has been thus cordially welcomed and commended, a demand has been expressed, with increasing urgency, for a smaller work of a similar character, that, excluding matter of only occasional interest and value to the professional teacher, may contain solely what is of every-day need; and which may be obtained at a moderate cost, and yet supply a large amount of information on a great variety of subjects, such as could be obtained only with considerable difficulty from large and expensive works.

To meet this demand the *Dictionary of Education and Instruction* is now offered to teachers and all others interested in education and instruction, — school-officers, parents, and the public in general.

The *Dictionary* is, in the main, a compilation of the articles embraced in only one of the eight departments contained in the *Cyclopædia*; namely, those on the *Theory of Education and Instruction* (Pedagogy and Didactics) which are designed to comprehend a consideration of the principles of education, in each of its departments, with practical suggestions as to the best methods of applying them both in training and instruction. To adapt this class of articles, thus reproduced from the *Cyclopædia*, to the wider use now intended, they have been, as far as seemed necessary, abbreviated, extended, or otherwise modified. In this way it is expected that the *Dictionary* will supply a convenient manual for study and reference not only to teachers engaged in professional work, and in teachers' institutes, but likewise in normal schools in which it is designed to serve as a text-book on Theory and Practice.

To facilitate the use of the *Dictionary* for this purpose, all the longer articles have been supplied with indented sub-titles so as to enable the instructor to conduct recitations on the subject, either by interrogating the student, or by requiring full statements from him on any of the topics thus indicated.

The special objects designed to be attained by the publication of the *Dictionary*, more specifically stated, are: (1) to supply a brief compendium of the theory and practice of education in a series of clear and definite articles, alphabetically arranged so as to be easily referred to, or systematically studied; (2) to encourage in this way the study by teachers of the principles and practice of their profession, thus giving to the work of education a greater degree of intelligence and efficiency; (3) to afford a convenient class manual of pedagogy for use in normal schools and teachers' institutes as the basis of a course of instruction in principles and methods, not necessarily superseding other valuable manuals differently arranged, but accompanying and strengthening them; (4) to supply, at a small cost, to every teacher that portion of the *Cyclopædia* which is of especial value in practical education, reserving this larger work for occasional reference, particularly when information regarding educational history, biography, and statistics is needed; and (5) to supply a useful hand-book to parents in the home education of their children.

Of the character of the articles contained in this work but little need be here said, as they have already secured the highest encomiums for their philosophical and professional correctness, practical character, and literary excellence. This indeed was to have been anticipated, the writers being all practical educators of long experience and distinction in their profession. Among the contributors to the *Cyclopædia* whose articles have been drawn upon for use in this volume the following may be especially mentioned: Professors EDW. OLNEY, of the University of Michigan; FRANCIS A. MARCH, of Lafayette College; DAVID B. SCOTT, of the College of the City of New York; E. H. DAY, of the New York Normal College; CHARLES T. HIMES, of Dickinson College, and J. M. D. MEIKLEJOHN, Professor of Education in the College of St. Andrews, Scotland; also JAMES DONALDSON, LL. D., Rector of the Edinburgh High School; THOMAS F. HARRISON and NORMAN A. CALKINS, Assistant Superintendents of Schools in the City of New York; and also the editors, HENRY KIDDLE, for many years chief Superintendent of the schools of the City, and for several years principal of the Normal School in the city of New York; and Professor A. J. SCHEM, also one of the Assistant Superintendents of the New York City Schools, and long and favorably known for his extensive scholarship, literary attainments, and numerous encyclopædic, statistical, and other works.*

Special attention is invited to the valuable list of educational works for professional study and reference prepared especially for the *Dictionary* by W. H. PAYNE, M. A., Professor of the Science and the Art of Teaching in the University of Michigan.

The hope is here expressed that this book will be favorably received, and that it will prove the instrument of much good in elevating the teacher's profession, and in disseminating correct information in regard to the principles of education and instruction.

NEW YORK, July 1st, 1881.

---

* Prof. SCHEM deceased May 22d, while this work was passing through the press.

ABACUS (Gr. ἄβαξ, a slab or board), a piece of school apparatus, used to facilitate the teaching of children to count, and perform other simple arithmetical operations. Various forms of the abacus are employed as counting or adding machines.

A-B-C BOOK, a primer, or little book used to learn the alphabet and its simplest combinations, with the most rudimental lessons in reading. (See HORN-BOOK.)

A-B-C METHOD. See ALPHABET METHOD.

ABECEDARIAN. This word, formed from the names of the first four letters of the alphabet, is generally used to denote a pupil who has not advanced beyond the most elementary stage of school or book education, that is, who is learning A B C, or the alphabet. The name has been sometimes applied to one engaged in teaching the alphabet. (See READING, and WORD METHOD.)

A-B-C SHOOTERS (Germ. *ABC-Schützen*), pupils of those scholastic vagrants who, during a certain period of the middle ages, and even later, used to wander through many parts of Germany, giving instruction to such pupils as they could pick up, who accompanied them in their journeyings. These pupils were often obliged to purloin food, fowls, etc., to supply their masters' wants, and hence were called, partly in derision of their elementary knowledge, A-B-C Shooters — *shoot*, in their parlance, being the slang word for *steal*.

ABSENTEEISM is opposed to regularity in the attendance of pupils belonging to a school. The number of school sessions from which a pupil was absent, as compared with the number at which he was present, during any particular period, gives the absenteeism of the pupil for that period. The average daily attendance of pupils divided by the average daily enrollment — the "average number belonging" — shows the percentage of attendance; and this subtracted from 100 gives, of course, the percentage of absenteeism. Within certain limits, this is a criterion of efficiency of management and instruction, since teachers who interest their pupils necessarily secure a more regular attendance than those who fail in this respect. Where the basis for computing the degree of absenteeism is the average enrollment, and where regularity of attendance is made a test of efficient management, teachers will be more careful to keep the number of pupils on the rolls as little as possible above the average attendance. Hence, to render this test reliable, a uniform rule should be followed in the discharging of pupils for non-attendance. Such a rule has been adopted in many cities of the Union, any pupil's name being invariably dropped from the roll after a certain number of days of absence, however caused. This is based on the principle that irregular attendance is not only of no profit to the pupil concerned, but a positive injury to the other pupils of the school or class, and is, moreover, a serious hindrance and embarrassment to the teacher.

How found.

Test of efficiency.

Uniform rules.

ABSTRACT AND CONCRETE. These terms have a very important application in many departments of practical education. *Abstract* has reference to general ideas, or the ideas of qualities considered apart from the things to which they belong; *concrete*, to those which are only conceived as belonging to particular objects or substances. Thus, if we speak of a man, a horse, a tree, etc., we use abstract or general ideas; for we are not thinking of any particular object of the class, but only of the assemblage of qualities or characteristics that especially belong to all the members of the class. But when we mention such names as Cicero, Washington, John Smith, etc., we have in our mind a conception of the characteristics that distinguish those persons from all other men. Thus, the expressions *five pounds, a true statement, an honest man* represent concrete ideas; the words *five, truth, honesty,* abstract ones.

Definition.

Distinction in education. The immature minds of young children employ to a great extent concrete ideas, and hence the instruction addressed especially to them should deal principally with these. As the mind advances, it becomes more and more occupied with abstract conceptions, which constitute the material for all the higher forms of thought and ratiocination.

ACADEMY (Gr. Ἀκαδήμια or Ἀκαδήμεια) was originally the name of a pleasure ground near Athens, and was said to be so called after Academus, a local hero at the time of the Trojan war. Its shady walks became a favorite resort for Plato: and, as he was accustomed to lecture here to his pupils and friends, the school of philosophers which was founded by him was called the *Academic School*, or merely the *Academy*. During the middle ages the term was but little used for learned institutions; but, after the revival of classical studies in the 15th century, it again became frequent. In a wider sense, it was sometimes applied to higher institutions of learning in general. Gradually, however, its use was, in most countries, restricted to special schools, as academies of mining, of commerce, of forestry, of fine arts, and, especially, of music. In England and the United States, the national high schools for the education of military and naval officers are called academies. Thus, England has the Naval Academy at Portsmouth, and the Royal Military Academy at Woolwich; and the United States, the Military Academy at West Point, and the Naval Academy at Annapolis. In the United States, the name has also been assumed by a large number of secondary schools, which are designed to prepare their pupils for colleges, or to impart a general knowledge of the common and higher branches of education.

Origin.

Academy of Plato.

How applied.

Applied to learned societies. The name *academy* is also employed to designate an association of learned men for the advancement of science and art. Some of these associations are of an entirely private character, others have been founded by the state. The first academy of this kind was the Museum of Alexandria, in Egypt, which was founded by Ptolemy Soter. The academies constituting the Institute of France are among the most important of the kind in the world. The *Académie française* is the highest authority upon every thing relating to the niceties of the French language, to grammar, and the publication of the French classics. The *Académie des inscriptions et belles lettres* embraces among the objects of its attention comparative philology. Like the French Institute, the academies in the capitals of Spain, Portugal, Sweden, Russia, and other countries, have gradually become great national centers for the promotion of science and art; but no such centralization has been effected in Italy, Germany, England, or the United States. In the United States of America, there are also a number of learned societies to which the name *academy*, in the sense used on the continent of Europe, has been applied.

ACCOMPLISHMENTS. This term, as contrasted with *culture*, refers to those educational acquirements which fit a person for certain special activities, while culture has reference to the general improvement of the character or mental faculties. Hence the expression "external accomplishments," or "ornamental accomplishments," such as skill in foreign languages, music, drawing, painting, dancing, etc. (See CULTURE.)

ACQUISITION. The acquisition of knowledge must be, to a certain extent, the scope of every process of teaching. Sometimes it is the primary object; but, in the earlier stages of education, it is generally secondary, the educative value of the process taking precedence of the practical importance of the knowledge communicated. The acquisition of new ideas must always, more or less, improve the mind by affording additional material for the exercise of its various faculties; but, in education, what particular faculties are concerned in the study of any subject or branch of knowledge, is a matter of paramount importance, and therefore should never be lost sight of by the teacher. Where this is disregarded, instruction is apt to degenerate into mere rote-teaching; and the teacher will often rest satisfied when his pupil can repeat the formulæ of knowledge, without evincing the acquisition of new ideas, on which alone the improvement of the mind depends.

ACROAMATIC METHOD (Gr. ἀκροαματικός, to be heard, designed for hearing only), a name originally applied to the esoteric teachings of Aristotle and other Greek philosophers, to designate such as were confined to their immediate hearers, and not committed to writing. Later, the term has been applied to a system of instruction in which the teacher speaks and the pupil only listens. A method of this kind, of course, presupposes scholars of a certain maturity of age and of considerable progress in intellectual culture. It forms the basis of the lecture system.

AFFECTATION, as opposed to what is real, genuine, and natural, is carefully to be guarded against in the education of the young. In certain peculiarities of character, there is a proneness to the formation of habits of affectation in manners and speech. This tendency, however, rarely shows itself at an early age. Children generally yield to their natural impulses, and do not assume or reign what they do not feel, or, to use a common expression, "put on airs". Their mode of training, however, may tend to this, particularly if they are forced to assume an unnatural mode of expression in phraseology or pronunciation, in the attempt to make them excessively precise in such matters. Some styles of reading and elocution may lead to this characteristic; and hence the importance of adopting methods that, in all respects, correspond to the prevailing usage. The standard of the educator should, in every respect, comport with the ease, grace, simplicity, and beauty that belong to what is natural; and every tendency to the contrary, in his pupils, should be promptly and sternly repressed. Locke (in *Thoughts concerning Education*) says: "Plain and rough nature left to itself, is much better than an artificial ungracefulness, and such studied ways of being ill-fashioned. The want of an accomplishment, or some defect in our behavior, coming short of the utmost gracefulness, often scapes observation; but affectation in any part of our carriage, is lighting up a candle to our defects, and never fails to make us to be taken notice of, either as wanting sense or wanting sincerity."

AGE, in Education. The life of man has been variously divided into periods, or ages. Thus Pythagoras assumed four, Solon and Macrobius ten, different ages, while others have preferred a division into five, six, seven, or eight. With regard to the education of man, one great turning-point stands forth so conspicuously, that teachers at all times have chosen it as a broad line of demarcation, into whatever number of periods they have thought it proper to divide human life. This turning-point in life is the period when man passes from the age of youth into that of virility. The physical development at this time has become complete; in social life both sexes have attained majority; and the education of the young man or woman for the career that has been selected, is, in the main, concluded. Up to this time, the education of man is conducted by others, chiefly parents and teachers; henceforward, he is expected to educate himself, and to assume the education of others.

Periods of life.

Turning-point in life.

During the period of life when man is dependent upon others for his education, three different ages are broadly distinguished, — childhood, boyhood or girlhood, and youth. These are marked, in the physical development of the body, by the shedding of teeth, the entrance of puberty, and the setting in of virility. The process of mental development in these three ages is as different as the physical basis; and, accordingly, each of them demands a peculiar pedagogical and didactical treatment.

Different ages.

Childhood, which embraces the first seven years of life, is characterized by the rapid growth and development of the organs of the body. At the age of seven a child weighs about six times as much as at its birth, and it has attained one half of the stature, and about one third or one fourth of the weight of the grown man. The mind is, during this period, more receptive than self active; the only manifestations of self-activity being found in the efforts to retain and arrange the impressions which have been received. All pedagogical influence upon the pupil in this age can be only of a preparatory character. The body must be guarded against injuries, and must have opportunities for a vigorous and manifold development. The mind must be preserved from debasing, weakening, or over-exciting influences, and must be kept open for any thing that is conducive to the development of its faculties; and, in order not to become sated and confused, it must learn to distinguish what is important from what is unimportant. As the child is thoroughly dependent upon the educator and unable to direct its own exertions, it should be made to understand as clearly as possible, that any opposition of its own will to that of its educators can be followed by only evil consequences. It should,

Childhood.

therefore, be taught obedience, but not obedience through fear, for fear has a repressive influence upon the development of the mental faculties, but an obedience springing from confidence in the superior wisdom and experience of the teacher, and from love produced by his kindness. The natural educators of the child are the parents, especially the mother; but, toward the close of this age, systematic teaching by a professional teacher begins. Legislation in regard to the school age differs considerably in different countries. In some, children are sent to the public schools when they are four years of age; in others, not until they are seven. Of course, instruction at such an age must be limited to the most elementary rudiments, such as reading, writing, and arithmetic. The method should be thoroughly adapted to the mental condition of the child, and modern educators are agreed in recognizing the importance of object teaching for the first stages of a child's instruction. A novel mode of instruction, specially intended as introductory to the regular primary school, is the kindergarten, founded by Froebel. The astonishing rapidity with which it has spread through all the countries of the civilized world, and found admission into educational systems otherwise radically at variance, seems to prove it to be a great improvement in elementary education. (See KINDERGARTEN.)

Boyhood or girlhood. Boyhood or girlhood embraces the time from the 7th to the 14th year of age. In the development of the body, this age is characterized by the appearance of the permanent teeth, by the completed growth of the brain, and by the first consciousness of sexual difference. Boys and girls long for the free and frequent exercise of their muscular systems. At the beginning of this age, girls like to take an active part in the plays of the boys; but they soon show a preference for more quiet occupations and less publicity; while, on the other hand, boys manifest an increased interest in noisy and wild sports. It is among the prime duties of the educators of this age, to keep the development of the natural desires and aspirations of the two sexes within the right channels. The minds of boys and girls afford many proofs of independent thought and activity. The company of adults is not sought for by them as eagerly as before, but they feel entire satisfaction in the society of children of their own age. They think, as yet, little of the realities of life and of their future careers; but their plays give more evidence, than before, of plan, serious thought, and perseverance, and generally indicate the faculties with which they have been most strongly endowed; each child, in this way, foreboding to some extent its future career. It is of great importance that the educator should not only understand the peculiar nature of this age in general, but that he should thoroughly know the character of each individual; for the faults which are peculiar to this age are best overcome in individual cases, if the educator knows how to make the right kind of appeal to those good qualities of his pupils which are most strongly developed. In arranging a course of instruction for this age, it must be specially remembered that the minds of boys and girls are predominantly receptive. The memory readily receives and faithfully retains impressions; and this, therefore, is the right time for learning a foreign language and geographical and historical facts. The independence of mind peculiar to this age shows itself at the same time in the growth of imagination, which awakens in the boy a lively interest in all that is great and extraordinary in history. On many questions relating to the education proper for this age, educators still differ. Prominent among these questions, are, whether the two sexes should be educated separately or conjointly, to what extent the same course of instruction should be prescribed for both, whether special studies should be begun at this age, or whether the entire course should be obligatory upon all the children of a school.

Youth. The age of *youth* extends from the beginning of puberty to the complete development of sexuality, or from the fourteenth to about the twenty-first year of age. At this time the growth of the body is completed; young men and women become aware of their special duties of life and of the difference in the careers upon which they are respectively to enter. The time of study is drawing to its close; the entrance into active life is at hand. Among the lower classes of society, this transition occurs at the beginning of this age; and the only increase of knowledge that is accessible to most persons of these classes must be derived from evening schools, public lectures, and reading; while those of the wealthier classes, and all who wish to fit themselves for any of the learned professions, now enter upon the special studies of those professions, or finish the general studies of the preceding age. Toward the close of this period, if not earlier, the preparation for entering public life is completed, or an actual entrance into life begins.

AGRICULTURAL COLLEGES. It is only within the last fourteen years that any general and systematic effort has been made *Congressional provisions.* in the United States to furnish facilities for acquiring a thorough scientific and practical education in agriculture. In 1862, Congress gave to the several states and territories land scrip to the amount of 30,000 acres for each senator and representative, on the condition that each state or territory, claiming the benefit of this act, should, within five years from its passage, "provide not less than one college, which should receive for its endowment, support, and maintenance the interest of all moneys derived from the sale of the aforesaid scrip or lands." It was further required that "the leading object" of these colleges "should be, without excluding other scientific and classical studies, and including military tactics, to teach such branches of learning as are related to agriculture and the mechanic arts, in order to promote the liberal and practical education of the industrial classes, in the several pursuits and professions of life."

Up to 1865, the agricultural college of Lansing, Mich., was the only one in *Colleges founded.* the United States in which students could pursue a college course arranged and adapted to meet the wants of those who might desire, in after years, to engage in agriculture. Since that time, some colleges have been organized — a large proportion of them from parts of universities — which are largely devoted "to teaching such branches of learning as are related to agriculture and the mechanic arts." As a general *Organization and equipment.* rule, no pains have been spared by these colleges to furnish all the facilities for pursuing a college course at the least possible expense. Manual labor is required in many of the colleges; in others, it is optional. Students' labor is paid for at various rates. Liberal state appropriations have been made, which have been largely expended in erecting buildings. The amount of private donations is very large. The late Ezra Cornell gave $700,000 to the university that bears his name, and the total amount of private donations to this single institution is not less than $1,400,000, of which the colleges of agriculture and the mechanic arts have received their due proportion. The equipment includes laboratories, workshops, etc., serving, directly or indirectly, to illustrate and teach all the subjects relating to agriculture, as follows: mechanical laboratories or workshops, furnished with tools for working in iron and wood, and sometimes with engines, planers, turning-lathes, drilling-machines, saws, and other necessary but less expensive tools; physical laboratories, most of them furnished with apparatus for illustrating the subjects of mechanics, electricity, magnetism, heat, acoustics, and optics. Nearly all these colleges have well equipped chemical laboratories; and several of them furnish excellent facilities for instruction in chemistry. There are also anatomical, geological, and botanical laboratories equipped for student practice in these institutions, and several have greenhouses; also drafting-rooms with the necessary tables and models for illustrating the subjects taught. A large amount of practice in drawing is, moreover, required in several of the branches related to agriculture. Free-hand drawing, also, has been to some extent introduced. Several colleges have large collections of models of farm implements and machinery; engravings, photographs, charts, and drawings; together with numerous specimens of grains, grasses, and other plants; geological and mineralogical specimens; collections of insects and skeletons of domestic and other animals; all constituting what might be called an agricultural museum, though usually kept in separate rooms for the sake of convenience. For a fuller treatment of this subject, see *Cyclopædia of Education*.

ALGEBRA (Arab. *al-jabr*, reduction of parts to a whole). For a general consideration of the purposes for which this study should be pursued, and its proper place and relative proportion of time in the curriculum, the reader is referred to the article MATHEMATICS. It is the purpose of this article to indicate some of the principles to be kept in view, and the methods to be pursued in teaching algebra.

The Literal Notation. — While this notation is not peculiar to algebra, but is the characteristic language of mathematics, the student usually encounters it for the first time when he enters upon this study. No satisfactory progress can be made in any of the higher branches of mathematics, as General Geometry, Calculus, Mechanics, Astronomy, etc., without a good knowledge of the literal notation. By far the larger part of the difficulty which the ordinary student finds in his study of algebra proper — the science of the *equation* — and in his more advanced study of mathematics, grows out of an imperfect knowledge of the notation. These are facts well known to all experienced teachers. Nevertheless, it is no unfrequent thing to hear a teacher say of a pupil: "He is quite good in algebra, but cannot get along very well with literal examples!" Nothing could be more absurd. It comes from mistaking the importance and fundamental character of this notation. It is of the first importance that, at the outset, a clear conception be gained of the nature of this notation, and that, in all the course, no method nor language be used which will do violence to these principles. Thus, that the letters a, b, x, y, etc., as used in mathematics, represent pure number, or quantity, is to be amply illustrated in the first lessons, and care is to be

Why it should be specially studied.

taken that no vicious conception insinuate itself. To say that, as 5 apples and 6 apples make 11 apples, so $5a$ and $6a$ make $11a$, is to teach error. If this comparison teaches any thing, it is that the letter a in $5a$, $6a$, and $11a$, simply gives to the numbers 5, 6, and 11 a concrete significance, as does the word *apples* in the first instance; but this is erroneous. The true conception of the use of a, to represent a number, may be given in this way: As 5 times 7 and 6 times 7 make 11 times 7, so 5 times any number and 6 times the same number make 11 times that number. Now, let a represent any number whatever; then 5 times a and 6 times a make 11 times a. The two thoughts to be impressed are, that the letter represents some number, and that it is immaterial what number it is, so long as it represents the same number in all cases in the same problem. Again, the genius of the literal notation requires that no conception be taken of a letter as a representative of number, which is not equally applicable to fractional and integral numbers. Thus we may not say that a fraction which has a numerator a and a denominator b, represents a of the b equal parts of a quantity, or number, as we affirm that $\frac{3}{4}$ represents 3 of the 4 equal parts; for this conception of a fraction requires that the denominator be integral; otherwise, if b represent a mixed number, as $4\frac{2}{3}$, we have the absurdity of attempting to conceive a quantity as divided into $4\frac{2}{3}$ equal parts. The only conception of a fraction, sufficiently broad to comport with the nature of the literal notation, is that it is an indicated operation in division; and all operations in fractions should be demonstrated from this definition.

Illustrations.

Application to fractions.

So also to read x^m "x to the mth power", when m is not necessarily an integer, is to violate this fundamental characteristic of the notation. In like manner, to use the expressions *greatest common divisor* and *least common multiple*, when literal quantities are under consideration, is an absurdity, and moreover fails to give any indication of the idea which should be conveyed. For example, we cannot affirm that $2ax^2 - 2bxy$ is the *greatest* common divisor of $2a^3x^4 - 2a^3bx^3y + 2ab^2x^2y^2 - 2b^3xy^3$ and $4ab^2x^3y^2 - 2ab^2x^2y^3 - 2b^4xy^4$; since $ax - by$ is a divisor of these polynomials, and whether $2ax^2 - 2bxy$ is greater or less than $ax - by$ cannot be affirmed unless the relative values of the letters are known. To illustrate, $2ax^2 - 2bxy = 2x(ax - by)$. Now suppose $a = 500$, $b = 10$, $y = 2$, and $x = \frac{1}{10}$; then $ax - by = 30$, and $2ax^2 - 2bxy = 6$. Moreover, it is not a question as to the value of the divisor that is involved; it is a question as to the *degree*. Hence, what we wish to affirm is that $2ax^2 - 2bxy$ is the *highest common divisor* of these polynomials, with respect to x.

Other expressions.

In order that the pupil may get an adequate conception of the nature of the literal notation, it is well to keep prominently before his mind the fact that the fundamental operations of addition, subtraction, multiplication, and division, whether of integers or fractions, the various transformations and reductions of fractions, as well as involution and evolution, are exactly the same as the corresponding ones with which he is already familiar in arithmetic, except as they are modified by the difference between the literal and the Arabic notations. Thus, the pupil will be led to observe that the *orders* of the Arabic notation are analogous to the terms of a polynomial in the literal

Literal and Arabic notations.

notation, and that the process of "carrying" in the Arabic addition, etc., has no analogue in the literal, simply because there is no established relation between the terms in the latter. Again, he will see that, in both cases, addition is the process of combining several quantities, so that the result shall express the aggregate value in the fewest terms consistent with the notation. This being the conception of addition, he will see that for the same reason that we say, in the Arabic notation, that the sum of 8 and 7 is 5 and 10 (fif-teen), instead of 8 and 7, we say, in the literal notation, that the sum of $5ax$ and $6ax$ is $11ax$. In fact, it is quite conceivable that the pupil, who understands the common or Arabic arithmetic, can master the literal arithmetic for himself, after he has fairly learned the laws of the new notation.

Positive and Negative. — Although the signs $+$ and $-$, even as indicating the affections positive and negative, are not confined to the literal notation, the pupil first comes to their regular use in this connec-

How to illustrate the notation.
tion, and finds this new element of the notation one of his most vexatious stumbling-blocks. Thus, that the sum of $5ay$ and $-2ay$ should be $3ay$, and their difference $7ay$, and that "minus multiplied by minus should give plus," as we are wont to say, often seems absurd to the learner. Yet even here he may be taught to find analogies in the teachings of the common arithmetic, which will at least partially remove the difficulty. When he comes to understand, that attributing to numbers the affection positive or negative gives to them a sort of concrete significance, and allies them in some sort to denominate numbers, he may at least see, that $5ay$ and $2ay$ do not necessarily make $7ay$; for, if one were feet and the other yards, the sum would not be $7ay$ of either. If, then, he comes to understand that the fundamental idea of this notation is, that the terms positive and negative indicate simply such opposition in kind, in the numbers to which they are applied, as makes one tend to destroy or counterbalance the other, he is prepared to see that the sum of $5ay$ and $-2ay$ is $3ay$; since, when put together, the $-2ay$, by its opposition of nature, destroys $2ay$ of the $5ay$. The ordinary illustrations in which forces acting in opposite directions, motion in opposite directions, amounts of property and of debts, etc., are characterized as positive and negative, are helpful, if made to set in clearer light the fact, that this distinction is simply in regard to the way in which the numbers are applied, and not really in regard to the numbers themselves.

So, also, in multiplication, the three principles, (1) that the product is like the multiplicand; (2) that a multiplier must be conceived as essentially abstract when the operation is performed; and (3) that the sign

How applied in multiplication.
of the multiplier shows what is to be done with the product when obtained, remove all the difficulty, and make it seem no more absurd that "minus multiplied by minus gives plus," than that "plus multiplied by plus gives plus": in fact, exactly the same course of argument is required to establish the one conclusion as to establish the other. When we analyze the operation which we call multiplying $+a$ by $+b$, we say "$+a$ taken b times gives $+ab$. Now the sign $+$ before the multiplier indicates that the product is to be taken additively, that is, united to other quantities by its own sign." So when we multiply $-a$ by $-b$, we say "$-a$ multiplied by b (a mere number) gives $-ab$ (a product

like the multiplicand). But the — sign before the multiplier indicates that this product is to be taken subtractively, *i. e.* united with other quantities by a sign opposite to its own." This, however, is not the place to develop the theory of positive and negative quantities; our only purpose here is to show that the whole grows out of a kind of concrete or denominate significance which is thus put upon the numbers, and which bears some analogy to familiar principles of common arithmetic.

Exponents. — One other feature of the mathematical notation comes into prominence now for the first time, and needs to be clearly comprehended: it is the theory of exponents. Here, as well as elsewhere, *Special difficulties pointed out.* it is important to guard against false impressions at the start. The idea that an exponent indicates a power is often so fixed in the pupil's mind at first, that he never afterwards rids himself of the impression. To avoid this, it is well to have the pupil learn at the outset that not all exponents indicate the same thing; thus, while some indicate powers, others indicate roots, others roots of powers, and others still the reciprocals of the latter. Too much pains can scarcely be taken to strip this matter of all obscurity, and allow no fog to gather around it. Nothing in algebra gives the young learner so much difficulty as radicals, and all because he is not thoroughly taught the notation. Perhaps, but few, even of those who have attained considerable proficiency in mathematics, have really set clearly before their own minds the fact that $\frac{2}{3}$ used as an exponent is not a fraction in the same sense as $\frac{2}{3}$ in its ordinary use; and hence that the demonstration that $\frac{4}{6} = \frac{2}{3}$, as given concerning common fractions, by no means proves that the exponent $\frac{4}{6}$ equals the exponent $\frac{2}{3}$. Other principles bearing on this important subject will be developed under the following head.

Methods of Demonstration. — It requires no argument to convince any one that, in establishing the working features, if we may so speak, of a science, it is important that they be exhibited as direct out*Elementary conceptions to be addressed.* growths of fundamental notions. Thus, in giving a child his first conception of a common fraction, no intelligent teacher would use the conception of a fraction as an indicated operation in division, and attempt to build up the theory of common fractions on that notion. It may be elegant and logical, and when we come to the literal notation it is essential; but it is not sufficiently radical for the tyro. It is not natural, but scientific rather. So in the literal notation, the proposition that *the product of the square roots of two numbers is equal to the square root of their product,* may be demonstrated thus: Let $\sqrt{a} \times \sqrt{b} = p$, whence $ab = p^2$; and, extracting the square root of each member we have $\sqrt{ab} = p$. Hence $\sqrt{a} \times \sqrt{b} = \sqrt{ab}$. Now, this is concise and mathematically elegant; but it gives the pupil no insight whatever into "the reason why." What is needed here is, that the pupil be enabled to see that this proposition grows out of the nature of a square root as one of the two equal factors of a number; *i. e.*, he needs to see its connection with fundamental conceptions. Thus $\sqrt{ab}$ means that the product ab is to be resolved into two equal factors, and that one of them is to be taken. Now, if we resolve a into two equal factors, as $\sqrt{a}$ and $\sqrt{a}$, and b into two equal factors, as $\sqrt{b}$ and $\sqrt{b}$, ab will be resolved into four factors which can be arranged in two equal groups, thus $\sqrt{a} \sqrt{b} \times \sqrt{a} \sqrt{b}$. Hence $\sqrt{a} \sqrt{b}$ is the square root of ab because it is one of the two equal factors into which ab can be conceived to be resolved. In this manner, all operations in radicals may be seen to be based upon the most elementary principles of factoring. Again, as another illustration of this vicious use of the equation in demonstrating elementary theorems, let us consider the common theorems concerning the transformations of a proportion. As usually demonstrated, by transforming the proportion into an equation, and *vice versa*, the real reason why the proposed transformation does not vitiate the proportion, is not brought to light at all. For example, suppose we are to prove that, *If four quantities are in proportion, they are in proportion by composition,* i. e., if $a:b::c:d$, then $a:a+b::c:c+d$. The common method is to pass from the given proportion to the equation $bc = ad$, then add ac to each member, obtaining $ac + bc = ac + ad$, or $c(a+b) = a(c+d)$, and then to transform this equation into the proportion $a:a+b::c:c+d$. No doubt, this is concise and elegant, but the real reason why the transformation does not destroy the proportion, viz., that *both ratios have been divided by the same number*, is not even suggested by this demonstration. On the other hand, let the following demonstration be used, and the pupil not only sees exactly why the transformation does not destroy the proportion, but at every step has his attention held closely to the fundamental characteristics of a proportion. Let the ratio $a:b$ be r; hence as a proportion is an equality of ratios, the ratio $c:d$ is r; and we have $a \div b = r$, and $c \div d = r$, or $a = br$, and $c = dr$. Substituting these values of a and c in the terms of the proportion which are changed by the transformation, we have $a + b = br + b$, or $b(r+1)$, and $c + d = dr + d$, or $d(r+1)$; whence we see that $a:a+b::c:c+d$ is deduced from $a:b::c:d$ by multiplying both consequents by $r+1$ (the ratio $+1$), which does not destroy the equality of the ratios constituting the proportion, since it divides both by the same number. Moreover, this method of substituting for the antecedent of each ratio the consequent multiplied by the ratio, enables us to demonstrate all propositions concerning the transformation of a proportion by one uniform method, which method in all cases clearly reveals the reason why the proportion is not destroyed.

Special value of this method. This choice of a line of argument which shall be applicable to an entire class of propositions is of no slight importance in constructing a mathematical course. It enables a student to learn with greater facility and satisfaction the demonstrations, and fixes them more firmly in his memory; while it also gives broader and more scientific views of truth, by thus classifying, and bringing into one line of thought, numerous truths which would otherwise be seen only as so many isolated facts.

Range of Topics to be Embraced. — We may distinguish three different classes of pupils, who require as many different courses in this study. *First,* there is a very large number of our youth who, if in the city, never pass beyond the grammar school, or, if in the country, never have any other school advantages than those furnished by the common or rural district school. Nevertheless, many of these will receive much greater profit from spending half a year, or a year, in obtaining a knowledge of the elements of algebra (and even

Wants of different pupils.

of geometry) than they usually do in studying arithmetic. (See ARITH-
METIC.) For this class the proper range of topics is: a clear exposition of
the nature of the *literal notation;* the *fundamental rules*, and *fractions*,
involving only the simpler forms of expression, and excluding such abstruse
subjects as the more difficult theorems on factoring, the theory of lowest
common multiple and highest common divisor; *simple equations* involving
one, two, and three unknown quantities; *ratio* and *proportion;* an elementary treatment of the subject of *radicals* with special attention given
to their nature as growing out of the simplest principles of factoring; *pure*
and *affected quadratics* involving one or two unknown quantities. The
second class comprises what may be called high school pupils. For this
grade the range of topics need not be much widened, but the study of
each should be extended and deepened. This will be the case especially
as regards the *theory of exponents, positive and negative quantities, radicals, equations involving radicals*, and *simultaneous equations*, especially
those of the second degree. To this should be added the *arithmetical* and
geometrical progressions, a practical knowledge of the *binomial formula*,
and *logarithms*, and a somewhat extended treatment of the application of
algebra to the business rules of arithmetic. A wide acquaintance
What should be omitted. with the results attained in our high schools in all parts of the
country, and an observation extending over more than twenty
years, satisfy the writer that time spent in these schools in
attempts to master the theory of *indeterminate co-efficients*, the demonstration of the *binomial* and *logarithmic formulas*, or upon the *higher equations, series*, etc., is, if not a total loss, at least an absorption of time which
might be much more profitably employed on other subjects, such as, for
example, history, literature, or the elements of the natural sciences. The
course taken by such pupils gives them no occasion to use any of these
principles of the higher algebra; and the mastery of them which they can
attain in any reasonable amount of time is quite too imperfect to subserve
the ends of good mental discipline. This second course is entirely adequate
to fit a student for admission into any American college or university. The
third course is what we may call the college course.

Class-Room Work. — It is probably unnecessary to say, that a careful
and thorough study of text-books should be the foundation of our class-
room work on this subject; nevertheless, so much is said, at the
Utility of text-books. present time, in disparagement of "hearing recitations" instead
of "teaching," that it may be well to remark that, if our schools
succeed in inspiring their pupils with a love of books, and in teaching how
to use them, they accomplish in this a greater good than even in the mere
knowledge which they may impart. Books are the great store-house of
knowledge, and he who has the habit of using them intelligently has the
key to all human knowledge. But it is not to be denied, that there is an
important service to be rendered by the living teacher, albeit that service,
especially in this department, is not formal lecturing on the principles of
the science. With younger pupils, the true teacher will often preface a
subject with a familiar talk designed to prepare them for an in-
Examples of oral lessons. telligent study of the lesson to be assigned, to awaken an interest
in it, or to enable them to surmount some particular difficulty.
For example, suppose a class of young pupils are to have their

ALGEBRA 13

first lesson in subtraction in algebra; a preliminary talk like the following will be exceedingly helpful, perhaps necessary, to an intelligent preparation of the lesson. Observe that, in order to benefit the class, the teacher must confine his illustrations rigidly to the essential points on which the lesson is based. In this case these are (1) *Adding a negative quantity destroys an equal positive quantity;* (2) *Adding a positive quantity destroys an equal negative quantity;* (3) *As the minuend is the sum of the subtrahend and remainder, if the subtrahend is destroyed from out the minuend, the remainder is left.* Now, in what order shall these three principles be presented? Doubtless the scientific order is that just given; but, in such an introduction to the subject as we are considering, it may be best to present the 3d first; since this is a truth already familiar, and hence affords a connecting link with previous knowledge. Moreover, this being already before the mind as a statement of what is to be done, the 1st and 2d will follow in a natural order as an answer to the question how the purpose is accomplished. To present the 3d principle, the teacher may place on the blackboard some simple example in subtraction as:

$\begin{array}{r}125\\-74\\\hline 51\end{array}$ He will then question the class thus: What is the 125 called? What the 74? What the 51? How much more than 74 is 125? If we add 74 and 25, what is the sum? Of what then is the minuend composed? What is $51 + 74$? If we destroy the 74, what remains? If in any case we can destroy the subtrahend from out the minuend, what will remain? Having brought this idea clearly before the mind, the teacher will proceed to the 1st principle. If $- 3ab$ be added to $7ab$ how much of the $7ab$ will it destroy? (Here again we proceed from a fundamental conception — the nature of quantities as positive and negative, thus deducing the new from the old.) Repeat such illustrations of this principle as may have been given in addition. If several boys are urging a sled forward by $7ab$ pounds, and the strength of another boy amounting to $3ab$ pounds is added, but exerted in an opposite direction, what now is the sum of their efforts? What kind of a quantity do we call the $3ab$? [Negative.] Why? How much of the $+ 7ab$ does $- 3ab$ destroy when we add it? If then we wish to destroy $+ 3ab$ from $+ 7ab$, how may we do it? Proceeding then to the 2d principle, it may be asked, how much is $6ay - 2ay$? If now we add $+ 2ay$ to $6ay - 2ay$, which is $4ay$, what does it become? What does the $+ 2ay$ destroy? What then is the effect of adding a positive quantity? Such introductory elucidations should always be held closely to the plan of development which the pupil is to study, and should be made to

Teacher and text-book to agree. throw light upon it. It is a common and very pernicious thing for teachers to attempt to teach in one line of development, while the text-book in the pupil's hands gives quite another. In most cases of this kind, either the teacher's effort or the text-book is useless, or probably worse — they tend to confuse each other. Such teaching should culminate in the very language of the text; and it is desirable that this language be read from the book by the pupil, as the conclusion of the teaching. Moreover, there is great danger of overdoing this kind of work.

Special hints. Whenever it is practicable, the pupil should be required to prepare his lesson from the book. A competent teacher will find sufficient opportunity for "teaching" after the pupils have gathered all they can from the book. Another important service to be rendered by the living teacher is to emphasize central truths, and hold the pupils to a constant review of them. So also it is his duty to keep in prominence the outlines of the subject, that the pupil may always know just where he is at work and in what relation to other parts of the subject that which he is studying stands. All definitions, statements of principles, and theorems should be thoroughly memorized by the pupil and recited again and again. In entering upon a new subject, as soon as these can be intelligently learned, they should be recited in a most careful and formal manner; and, in connection with subsequent demonstrations and solutions, they should be called up and repeated. Thus, suppose a high school class entering upon the subject of *equations*. Such a class may be supposed to be able to grasp the meaning of the definitions without preliminary aid from the teacher, save in special cases. The first lesson will probably contain a dozen or more definitions, with a preposition or two; and the first work should be the recitation of these by the pupils individually, without any questions or suggestions from the teacher. Illustrations should also be required of the pupils; but neither illustrations nor demonstrations should be memorized, although great care should be taken to secure a good style of expression, modeled on that of the text. To this first recitation on a new subject all the class should give the strictest attention; and every point in it should be brought out, at least once in the hearing of every pupil. In the course of subsequent recitations in the same general subject, individuals will be questioned on the principles thus developed. For example, what algebra is will have been brought clearly to view in this first recitation; but when a pupil has stated and solved some problem, and has given his explanation of the solution from the blackboard, the teacher my ask, Why do you say you have solved this problem by algebra? The answer will be, Because I have used the *equation* as an instrument with which to effect the solution. Can you solve this problem without the use of an equation? What do you call such a solution? What is algebra? Again, suppose the solution has involved the reduction of such an equation as the following: $2x - \frac{1}{2} = \frac{1}{2}(3x - 1) + \frac{1}{3}(x + 1)$. In the first place the pupil will solve the example and give a good logical account of the solution; but the teacher will make it the occasion for reviewing certain definitions and principles with this particular student, in such a practical connection. Thus he will ask, What is your first equation? What is your last? [$x=2$.] Do you look upon these as one and the same equation, or as different equations? In how many different forms have you written your given equation? What general term do you apply to these processes of changing the form of an equation? What is *transformation?* Similarly, every principle and definition will be reviewed again and again in such practical connections. But mere statements of processes should not be allowed to pass for expositions of principles. To illustrate, the pupil has placed the following work upon the board:

$$7x^2 - 28x + 14 = 238$$
$$7x^2 - 28x = 224$$
$$x^2 - 4x = 32$$
$$x^2 - 4x + 4 = 36$$
$$x - 2 = \pm 6$$
$$x = 2 \pm 6 = 8, \text{ or } -4.$$

He is then called upon to explain his work. Something like the following is what we hear in the majority of our best schools:
"Given $7x^2 — 28x + 14 = 238$, to find the value of x.
"Transposing, I have $7x^2 — 28x = 224$.
"Dividing by 7, $x^2 — 4x = 32$.
"Completing the square, $x^2 — 4x + 4 = 36$.
"Extracting the square root, $x — 2 = \pm 6$.
"Transposing, $x = 2 \pm 6 = 8$, and $—4$."

And the pupil turns to his instructor in the full consciousness of duty nobly done. The fact is, all that he has said is useless, nay, worse than useless. He has simply intimated what processes he has performed. That he could solve the problem was sufficiently apparent from his work. There was no need that he should tell us what he had done, when he had performed the work before our eyes. What is wanted is a clear and orderly exposition of the reason why he takes every step. This involves two points, since he is to show (1) that the step taken tends to the desired end, that is, the freeing of the unknown quantity from its connections with known quantities so as finally to make it stand alone as one member of the equation; and (2) that the step does not destroy the equation.*) Something like the following should be the style of explanation: "Given $7x^2—28x + 14 = 238$, to find the value of x. In order to do this, I wish so to transform the equation that, in the end, x shall stand alone, constituting one member of the equation, while a known quantity constitutes the other member. Hence I transpose the known quantity 14 to the second member. This I do by subtracting 14 from each member, which may be done without destroying the equation (or the equality of the members) since, if the same quantity be subtracted from equals, the remainders are equal. I thus obtain $7x — 28x = 224$. I now observe that the first term of the first member contains the square of x, while the second contains the first power. I wish to obtain an equation which shall contain only the first power of x. In order to do this, I make the first term a perfect power by dividing each member of the equation by 7, which does not destroy the equality, since equals divided by equals give equal quotients, and I have $x^2 — 4x = 32$. Now, observing that $x^2—4x$ constitutes the first two terms of the square of a binomial of which the square of half the co-efficient of x, or 4, is the third term, I add 4 to this member to make it a complete square, and also add 4 to the second member to preserve the equality of the members, and have $x^2—4x+4=36$. Extracting the square root of $x^2—4x+4$, I have $x—2$, an expression which contains only the first power of x; but to preserve the equality, I also extract the square root of the second member, obtaining $x—2= \pm 6$. Finally, transposing $—2$ to the second member by adding 2 to each member, which does not destroy the equation, I have $x=8$, or $—4$." If it is desired to abbreviate the explanation, it is far better to make it simply an outline of the reasons, than a mere statement of the process. In this case, an outline of the reasons may be given thus: The object is to disengage x

---

*) "Destroy the *value* of the equation," is an absurd expression which we frequently hear. An equation is not a quantity, and hence has no value. The equality of the members is meant.

from its connections with the other quantities so that it shall stand alone, constituting one member while the other member is a known quantity. The first process is based upon the principle that equals subtracted from equals leave equal remainders, the second, upon the principle that equals divided by equals give equal quotients," etc. Again, while it is admissible, when the purpose is to fix attention upon any particular transformation, to omit the reasons for some of those previously studied, it is far better that these be omitted *pro forma* than that something which is not an exposition of reasons be given. Thus, if the present purpose is to secure drill in the theory of completing the square, after having enunciated the problem, the pupil may say: " Having reduced the equation to the form $x^2 - 4x = 32$," etc., proceeding then to give in full the explanation of the process under consideration. But it is well to allow no recitation on such a subject to pass without having at least one full explanation. These remarks apply to study and recitations designed to give intelligent facility in reducing equations. In what may be called "Applications of equations to the solution of practical problems,' the purpose is quite different, and so should be the pupil's explanation. In these, the *statement* is the important thing, and should be made the main thing in the explanation. In most such cases, it will be quite sufficient, if, after having given the reasons for each step in the statement, thus fully explaining the principles on which he has made the equation, the pupil conclude by saying simply: "Solving this equation, I have," etc. Outlines of demonstrations and synopses of topics are exceedingly valuable as class exercises. For example, it requires a far better knowledge of the demonstration of Sturm's theorem to be able to give the following outline than to give the whole in detail: (1) No change in the variable which does not cause some one of the functions to vanish, can cause any change in the number of variations and permanences of the signs of the functions; (2) No two consecutive functions can vanish for the same value of the variable; (3) The vanishing of an intermediate function cannot cause a change in the number of variations and permanences; and (4) The last function cannot vanish for any value of the variable; and, as the first vanishes every time the value of the variable passes through a root of the equation, it by so doing causes a loss of one, and only one, variation. We, therefore, have the theorem [giving the theorem]. Finally, no subject should be considered as mastered by the pupil until he can place upon the blackboard a synoptical analysis of it, and discuss each point, either in detail or in outline, without any questioning or prompting by the teacher. The order of arrangement of topics, *i. e.*, the sequence of definitions, principles, theorems, etc., is as much a part of the subject considered scientifically as are the detailed facts; and the former should be as firmly fixed in the mind as the latter.

Blackboard analysis.

ALMA MATER (Lat., fostering mother) is a name affectionately given by students of colleges and universities to the institution to which they owe their education.

ALPHABET. The alphabet of any language is the series of letters, arranged in the customary order, which form the elements of the language when written. It derives its name from the first two letters of the Greek alphabet, which are named *alpha, beta*. The letters in the English alphabet have the same forms as those of the Latin language, which were borrowed from the Greek. The Latin alphabet, however, did not contain all the Greek letters. The letters of the Greek alphabet were borrowed from the Phœnician, which was that used by many of the old Semitic nations, and is of unknown origin. It consisted of 22 signs, representing consonantal sounds. Into this alphabet the Greeks introduced many modifications, and the changes made by the Romans were also considerable. Its use in English presents many variations from its final condition in the Latin language. Thus, I and J, and U and V, instead of being merely graphic variations, were changed so as to represent different sounds, during the 16th and 17th centuries. W was added previously, in the middle ages. The twenty-six letters of our alphabet have been thus classified with regard to their history: (1) B, D, H, K, L, M, N, P, Q, R, S, T, letters from the Phœnicians; (2) A, E, I, O, Z, originally Phœnician, but changed by the Greeks; (3) U (same as V), X, invented by the Greeks; (4) C, F, Phoenician letters with changed value; (5) G, of Latin invention; (6) Y, introduced into Latin from the Greek, with changed form; (7) J, V, graphic Latin forms raised to independent letters; (8) W, a recent addition, formed by doubling U (or V), whence its name.

Alphabets compared.

The imperfections of the English alphabet are manifold: (1) Different consonants are used to represent the same sound; as *c* (soft) and *s*, *g* (soft) and *j*, *c* (hard) and *k*, *q* and *k*, *x* and *ks*. (2) Different sounds are expressed by the same letter; as *c* in *cat* and *cell*, *g* in *get* and *gin*, *s* in *sit* and *as*, *f* in *if* and *of*, etc. (3) The vowels are constantly interchanged, as is illustrated in the following table of the vowel elements of the language and their literal representations, the diacritical marks used being those of Webster's Dictionary.

English Alphabet imperfect.

Long.			Short.		
ā e	" "	ape, they	ĕ	" "	end
â ê	" "	care, ere	ă	" "	hat
ä	" "	art	ȧ	" "	ask
ạ ô	" "	all, orb	ǫ ŏ	" "	what, not
ē ï	" "	eve, pique	ĭ	" "	sit
ê î ŷ	" "	her, sir, myrrh			
ō	" "	old			
ọ u o͞o	" "	do, rule, too	ọ u o͝o	" "	wolf, put, book
ü	" "	urn	ȯ u	" "	love, luck
ū	" "	use			
ī ŷ	" "	ice, my			
oi oy	" "	oil, boy			
ou ow	" "	out, owl			

From this table it will be seen that the letter *a* is used to represent seven different sounds; *e*, *five* sounds; *o*, *six* sounds, etc. (See PHONETICS.) The names given to the letters are not in conformity with a uniform principle of designation. Thus, the names of *b, c, d, g, p, t, r*, and *z* are *be, ce, de, ge*, etc.; while the names of *f, l, m, n, s*, and *x* are *ef, el, em, en*, etc.; and the names of *j, k*, are *ja, ka*. The heterogeneity of these names and of their construction will be obvious. It is important that the teacher should take cognizance of these incongruities in giving elementary instruction, as they dictate special methods of presentation. (See ALPHABET METHOD.)

ALPHABET METHOD

ALPHABET METHOD, or A-B-C Method. This has reference to the first steps in teaching children to read. According to this method, the pupil must learn the names of all the letters of the alphabet, either from an *A-B-C book*, from *cards*, or from the *blackboard*; that is, he must be taught to recognize the various forms of the letters, and to associate with them their respective names. The method of doing this, once very general, was to supply the pupils with books, and then, calling up each one singly, to point to the letters, one after the other, and to pronounce the name of each, so as to associate arbitrarily the form with the name; or, in simultaneous class instruction, to exhibit the letters on separate cards, and teach their names by simple repetition. This process must, of course, be not only long and tedious, but exceedingly dry and uninteresting to a child, since it affords no incentive to mental activity, — no food for intelligence. By a careful selection and discrimination, however, in presenting the letters to the attention of the child, its intelligence may be addressed in teaching the alphabet by this method. The simple forms, such as I, O, X, S, will be remembered much more readily than the others; and these being learned, the remainder may be taught by showing the analogy or similarity of their forms with the others. Thus O becomes C when a portion of it is erased; one half of it with I, used as a bar, forms D; two smaller D's form B; and so on. This method is very simple, and may be made quite interesting by means of the blackboard.

Method described.

The letters which closely resemble each other in form, such as A and V, M and N, E and F, and C and G, among capitals, and *b* and *d*, *c* and *e*, *p* and *q*, and *n* and *u*, among small letters, should be presented together, so that their minute differences may be discerned. When the blackboard is used (as it should always be in teaching classes), the letters may be constructed before the pupils, so that they may perceive the elements of which they are composed. Thus the children will at once notice that *b*, *d*, *p*, *q*, are composed of the same elements, differently combined, — a straight stroke, or stem, and a small curve. By an appropriate drill, the peculiar forms, with the name of each, will then be soon impressed upon the pupils' minds; and, besides that, their sense of analogy, one of the most active principles of a child's mind, will be addressed, and this will render the instruction lively and interesting. In carrying out this plan, the teacher may use the blackboard, and as a review, or for practice, require the children to copy, and afterwards draw, from memory, on the slate, the letters taught. Cards may also be used, a separate one being employed for each letter. With a suitable frame in which to set them, these may be used with good advantage, the teacher making, and the children also being required to make, various combinations of the letters so as to form short and familiar words. A horizontal wooden bar with a handle, and a groove on the upper edge in which to insert the cards, forms a very useful piece of apparatus for this purpose. *Letter-Blocks* may also be used in a similar manner by both teacher and pupils. These blocks are sometimes cut into sections so as to divide the letter into several parts, and the pupil is required to adjust the parts so as to form the letter. This method affords both instruction and amusement to young children, and at the same time, gives play to their natural impulse to activity. These various methods will be combined

Comparison of letters.

Apparatus.

and others devised by every ingenious teacher. In some schools a piece of apparatus, called the *reading frame*, is used. This is constructed like a blackboard with horizontal grooves, in which the letters can be placed so as to slide along to any required position. By the use of assorted letters, the teacher can construct any word or sentence, building it up letter by letter, as types are set. Many interesting exercises in reading and spelling may be given by means of such an apparatus, the children being required to construct words and sentences themselves, as well as to read those formed by the teacher. The A-B-C method of teaching the elements of reading has now, quite generally, been superseded by the word method. Bain, in *Education as a Science* (1881), remarks in relation to this method: "Much stress is now laid by teachers on the point of beginning to pronounce short words at sight, without spelling them; and a strong condemnation is uttered against the old spelling method. The difference between the methods is not very apparent to me; after a few preliminary steps, the two must come to the same thing." (See ORTHOGRAPHY, and PHONETICS.)

ALUMNEUM, or **Alumnat** (Lat., from *alere*, to feed, to nourish), the name given in Germany to an institution of learning which affords to its pupils board, lodging, and instruction. The first institutions of this kind arose in the middle ages in connection with the convents. Among the most celebrated are those founded by Maurice of Saxony, in the 16th century, at Pforta, Meissen, and Grimma. When the pupils were received and instructed gratuitously, they were expected to perform various services for the school and church, such as singing in the choir. The pupils of these schools were called *alumni*. (See ALUMNUS.)

ALUMNUS, pl. *Alumni* (Lat., from *alere*, to feed, to nourish) originally the name of a student who was supported and educated at the expense of a learned institution (see ALUMNEUM), now generally applied to a graduate of a college or similar institution. The graduates of higher seminaries or colleges for females are sometimes called *alumnae*.

ANALYSIS, Grammatical, or Sentential. — By the analysis of a sentence is meant a decomposition of it into its logical elements. Every sentence must either be a single proposition, or be composed of propositions more or less intimately related; and every proposition must contain a *subject* and a *predicate*, the former expressing that of which we speak, and the latter, what we say of it. The entire or logical subject must contain a noun or pronoun, either alone or with related words called *modifiers* or *adjuncts*, or it may be a phrase or a clause. The entire or logical predicate, in the same manner, must consist of a verb with or without adjuncts. These constitute all the parts, and all the relations, involved in the construction of a sentence. A few words, such as interjections, may be used independently of them. Grammar has been defined as the "art of speaking and writing correctly," or as the "practical science which teaches the right use of language"; and for general purposes this account is, perhaps, sufficiently explicit. It does not, however, truly distinguish grammar from the other arts concerned in teaching the "right use of language," and hence does not correctly point out its peculiar province. From a want of precision in defining the limitations of any art or science, there must necessarily follow a corresponding inaccuracy and looseness in its treatment; since, before we can reason properly as to

Explanation of the analysis.

the best methods of attaining any object, we must clearly conceive what that object is, and carefully distinguish it from all others.

The special province of grammar does not extend beyond the construction of sentences; but it is quite obvious that to use language correctly, *Province of* those principles and rules must be understood which underlie *grammar.* the proper method of combining sentences so that they may constitute elegant and logical discourse. A person may be sufficiently familiar with grammatical rules to construct sentences with perfect correctness, but may so arrange them as to express only nonsense; and such a person could scarcely be considered as understanding the "right use of language." The sentence being the peculiar province of grammar, it follows that the only subjects of investigation embraced within it are words, their orthography, inflectional forms, and pronunciation, and their arrangement in sentences. All grammatical definitions and rules are founded upon the relations of the parts of a sentence to each other; and, therefore, these relations should be first taught. It is with reference to these relations, that words are classified into parts of speech, or, as they might properly be called, parts of the sentence. To define or explain these parts of speech before giving any definition of a sentence, is, therefore, clearly illogical; yet this has been the method of many grammarians, words being explained and *parsed* as if they had only individual properties. It is in this that the distinction between parsing and grammatical analysis consists. Both are, in fact, only different kinds of analysis, and are based on precisely the same relations, — those in which the words stand to each other as parts of a sentence.

Parsing and analysis. Parsing, as uniformly employed by grammarians, is a minute examination of the individual words of a sentence, with the view to determine whether the rules of grammar, proper to the particular language in which the sentence is written, have been observed or violated. Analysis, on the other hand, deals with the relations upon which those rules are based, and which are common to all languages. Thus, in parsing, the pupil is obliged to scrutinize all the inflectional forms in which the words composing the sentence are used; and, in order to determine whether they are proper or not, must not only know the rules of syntax, but the relations of the words to each other, so as to be able to apply those rules. The relations are invariable in all languages, but the rules which refer to the inflections are founded on particular usage, and hence are in no two languages exactly alike. On this account, since the *general* logically precedes the *special*, the treatment of sentential analysis should precede any exercises in parsing. Otherwise, how, for example, could a pupil be required to distinguish the cases of nouns and pronouns, and the person and number of verbs, before being taught the relations of the words to each other?

Advantages of the analytical method. By means of the analytical method, when rightly applied, the study of grammar is made clear, logical, and easy from the very beginning. The pupil is first taught the nature of the sentence, its essential parts, and their relations to each other, and is shown how to analyze sentences of a simple character. He is troubled with but little phraseology; for all the terms that are essential to the complete distinction and designation of the parts of a sentence are *subject, verb* or *predicate, object, attribute,* and *adjuncts.* These being defined, and the pupil taught how to distinguish them, a complete foundation has been laid for the intelligent study of all other grammatical terms and distinctions; and this being the foundation, should, of course, be the first thing done. Those who oppose the analytical method assert that words are the real elements of a sentence, and that any consideration of these involves, therefore, an exhaustive analysis of the sentence itself. With the same propriety might it be said that pieces of iron of various shapes are the elements of the steam-engine. They indeed compose the machine, and it can ultimately be resolved into them; but could its structure and workings be explained by taking these fragments of metal in a hap-hazard way, and noticing how they are related to others in immediate juxtaposition, without regard to the general structure of the machine, and the dependence of its operation upon a few elementary or primary parts, as the cylinder, piston, condenser, etc.? Words are not necessarily the real elements of a sentence. These are the subject and predicate and their adjuncts; and, unless these component parts of the general structure be first observed, the relations of the separate words cannot be understood. Hence, we find that those writers who have ignored a definite consideration of these logical elements, have fallen into many errors and inconsistencies.

The real elements of a sentence.

The various systems of analysis in use differ in no essential respect, the chief variation being in the nomenclature employed to designate the elements of the sentence. The name generally applied to a proposition forming a part of a sentence is a *clause,* and any group of related words not making a proposition is called a *phrase.* The modifying elements are by some called *adjective* or *adverbial,* according as they perform the functions of adjectives or adverbs. Instead of the term *adjective, adnominal* is sometimes employed. The term *adjunct* is generally employed to designate an element subordinate to either subject or predicate. Such adjuncts may be *modifying, descriptive,* or *appositional.* A modifying adjunct changes the meaning of the element to which it is applied, generally, by making it more specific, or by restricting the class to which it belongs. Thus *animal* is a more general term than *four-footed animal;* hence, *four-footed* is a modifying adjunct. But the term *man* is no more general than *man that is born of a woman,* or *mortal man;* the adjuncts, *that is born of a woman* and *mortal* being only descriptive, not modifying. Appositional adjuncts only explain; as: *He, the chieftain of them all,* in which the phrase, *the chieftain, etc.,* is only explanatory, or appositional. Adjuncts may be single words, phrases, or clauses; and one of the chief advantages of sentential analysis is to show the pupil that groups of words are often used so as to perform the same office as single words. In teaching this subject, a proper gradation of topics should be observed; and much caution exercised to avoid the perplexing of the young pupil by presenting to his mind distinctions too nice to be discerned by his undeveloped powers of analysis. Various methods have been devised in order to present to the eye of the student the analyzed sentence, so as to show clearly the relation of its parts; and, in the rudimental stages of the instruction, these are, without doubt, of considerable utility; but they should not be carried so far as to present to the student a confused

Different systems.

mass of loops, lines, curves, or disjointed phrases, far more difficult to disentangle than to analyze, without any such aid, the most involved sentence. All such devices, it must be remembered, are only auxiliaries to the mind's natural operations, and cannot at all supersede them. Neither should the exercise of analyzing sentences be allowed to degenerate into the mechanical application of its most simple requirements. As the student advances, he will be able to omit more and more of the routine, until he reaches a stage of progress, at which the general structure of the sentence — its component clauses and their relations, will be all that he need observe or state. When judiciously and rationally employed, sentential analysis must engender a very important quality of mind, and greatly conduce to clear thinking, intelligent, critical reading, and accurate, terse expression.

Limits of the analysis.

ANALYTIC METHOD OF TEACHING. This is the method used by the teacher when he presents to his pupils composite truths or facts, and by means of analysis shows the principles involved, or leads the mind of the pupil to an analysis of them for himself. In this way he teaches principles which the pupil is to apply to the elucidation of many diverse problems. In the synthetic method, the teacher begins with principles, explains their meaning, and shows how they are to be applied. Thus, suppose the pupil is to be taught how to add and subtract fractions. According to the analytic method, the fractions to be operated upon are presented to the pupil's mind, and he is shown, first the difficulty involved, and secondly, how to surmount this difficulty, by (1) finding a common denominator, and (2) by changing the numerator so that the fractions with the common denominator may have the same value as the given fractions. Then the method of addition or subtraction becomes obvious. In this way learning the principle himself by analysis, the pupil is enabled to construct a general rule, and apply it to any given case. In the synthetic method, the pupil would be taught in the first place the nature and use of a common denominator, then the method of reducing fractions to a common denominator, and then to add or subtract fractions by finding a common denominator. If the object of the instruction given were, exclusively, to make the pupil expert in adding and subtracting fractions, the synthetic method would perhaps have some advantage over the analytic; but, since an important part of this object is to train the mind, the analytic method is greatly to be preferred; for (1) it stimulates the mind to greater activity, (2) it teaches it how to investigate for itself, and to discover truth, and (3) it gives it a much clearer knowledge of the fundamental principles involved in the subject taught. Whether the analytic method should be employed and to what extent, is to be determined by a consideration of the nature of the subject taught, and the degree of advancement of the student. In the higher stages of education, much time would be lost by rigorously following this method; and if, in the more elementary stages, the pupil's mind has been thoroughly trained in this way, it will not be necessary to adhere to it when he comes to study the higher branches. At every stage, however, there will be occasion for the use of both analysis and synthesis; and the judgment of the teacher must be exercised, at every step, to determine which is the appropriate method to be employed.

Described.

Illustrated.

Advantages.

Limits of its use.

ANGLO-SAXON. There are no persons to whom this study is more important than to teachers of English grammar. The explanations of the forms of words are all to be sought in it. The origin and meaning of the possessive ending 's, of the plural endings, of the endings for gender, of the tense forms and other forms of the verb, the adverbial endings, the prepositions, may at any time be demanded of the teacher. Pupils will ask him whether *John's book* is a contraction of *John his book*; how comes *geese* to be the plural of *goose*, and *men* the *plural* of *man*; how comes *lady* to be the *feminine* of *lord*; how comes *I have loved* to express the perfect tense; what does the *to* mean when you say *to be*, or *not to be, that is the question*, and so on without end. But such questions cannot be answered without knowing Anglo-Saxon. It is the same with questions of syntax. Almost all difficulties grow out of Anglo-Saxon idioms, or find their solution in the forms of that speech. Teachers who know nothing of the history of the language puzzle themselves infinitely with subtle reasonings to prove that expressions must be parsed in one way or another, when a glance at an Anglo-Saxon grammar would settle the matter in a moment. No teacher can safely pronounce on any such mooted questions of our language without knowing the Anglo-Saxon forms. No normal school ought to send out graduates from its grammar department wholly ignorant of this study. A lesson a day during the last school term skillfully directed to the most frequent examples in which this knowledge comes into use, would perhaps answer the most pressing necessities of the common school teacher. Twice that time would be a meager allowance to lay the foundation of the education of an accomplished high-school teacher in this department. For this study may be used MARCH's *Comparative Grammar of the Anglo-Saxon Language* (New York); — this contains a full syntax; R. MORRIS's *Historical Outlines of English-Accidence* (London); HADLEY's *Brief History of the English Language*, in Webster's Dictionary (1865). For a full consideration of this subject, see *Cyclopædia of Education*, and *Year-Book of Education* for 1878.

APPARATUS, School. — The work of instruction in school is very greatly facilitated by sufficient and appropriate apparatus, such as blackboards, slates, globes, maps, charts, etc. This is especially required in the teaching of children in classes, as in common schools. By this means, the sense of sight being addressed, the impressions made are clearer and more durable. Besides, the concrete is made to take the place of the abstract, by the use of suitable apparatus; and, in the first stages of education, the former is almost exclusively to be employed since abstract principles or truths are not comprehended by the young mind, except upon a sufficiently extensive basis of concrete facts. Thus by means of the numeral frame, the various rudimental combinations of numbers are presented to the mind of the young pupil, in connection with actual objects; and in this manner a clear idea is given of those processes which, merely by abstract statements of the truths, or by mere verbal repetition, however long continued, would scarcely be apprehended at all. Of course, the teacher should be careful not to carry the use of such apparatus beyond its proper limits; since the pupil's mind is gradually to be accustomed to conceive clearly the truth of abstract propositions without regard to their concrete applications.

Utility.

Limits.

Every stage or grade of school instruction must have its appropriate apparatus. Infant instruction requires a great number and variety of simple apparatus *(gifts)* in order, by natural methods, to aid the development of the child's mind. (See KINDERGARTEN.) The primary school should be supplied with a numeral frame, blackboards, slates, and pencils for the use of the children, a box of forms, spelling and reading charts, color charts, pictures of animals, etc.; and, when elementary geography is taught, simple maps and a small globe. For this purpose, one that may be divided into hemispheres (Hand-Hemisphere Globe) is best; since by means of it the relation of the planisphere maps to the globe may be clearly shown. (See GLOBES.) A simple relief globe is also of great service at this stage. Other ingenious and attractive apparatus has been devised to aid the work of the primary school teacher, to which a special reference is not needed. In the more advanced stages of instruction, the use of any other than the ordinary apparatus, such as the blackboard, maps, globes, etc., becomes less and less necessary, except in the teaching of certain special subjects; as higher arithmetic, mensuration, astronomy, and other departments of natural science. For such purposes, the cube-root blocks and other geometrical solids, a tellurian, an orrery, etc., will be of great value. Charts of physiology, history, etc., are scarcely to be dispensed with. In the teaching of natural science, very expensive and complicated apparatus is not at first required. Indeed, the simpler it is, the better; since the use of such appliances will incite the pupil himself to experiment with those simple contrivances which his own powers of invention will enable him to devise. Thus the use of the lever may be just as well explained by means of a pen-holder or a pointer as by a polished steel rod specially constructed for the purpose. Nothing marks more fully the ability of the teacher than adroitness in availing himself of all common resources for the purpose of illustration. Some of the most important discoveries in physical science have been made with very rude apparatus. In the use of apparatus to illustrate scientific facts, as of the globe, tellurian, or orrery for the purpose of teaching astronomy, it should always be borne in mind that such contrivances cannot supersede the study of nature itself. Cumbrous and complicated machinery, without an attentive observation of the natural phenomena which they are intended to explain, rather serve to give false notions than to impart correct ideas of the actual facts. The latter must be clearly grasped by the mind as facts before their illustration is attempted by means of artificial contrivances. This depends upon an important principle which the teacher should be careful to recognize and apply. (See BLACKBOARD, and NUMERAL FRAME.)

Different kinds.

Only simple apparatus needed.

ARCHÆOLOGY (from ἀρχαῖος, *ancient*, and λόγος, *knowledge*, *science*) denotes properly the science of antiquities. In the widest sense of the word, it would embrace the history, mythology, political institutions, religion, commerce, industry, literature, and fine arts of ancient times, but it is now used in a more restricted sense, as treating of the remains of the primitive inhabitants of a country. Thus, while it is an important handmaid of history, it is widely distinguished from it. To the teaching of history, even in the most rudimental form, this subject is not to be dispensed with.

ARITHMETIC

ARITHMETIC (Gr. ἀριθμητική from ἀριθμός, number), the science of numbers. This subject occupies a prominent place in the curriculum of all elementary schools, both primary and grammar, as well from its educational or disciplinary, as from its practical value. In the practical consideration of this subject, the first topic that presents itself is:

What should constitute the course in arithmetic. — In the first place, there should be a thorough unification of the processes of mental and written arithmetic. There is but one science of arithmetic; and everything that tends to produce the impression in the pupil's mind that there are two species, the one intellectual and the other mechanical, is an obstacle to his true progress. What is valuable in the methods now peculiar to mental arithmetic, needs to be thoroughly incorporated with what is practically convenient or necessary in written arithmetic; so that the whole may be made perfectly homogeneous. The basis upon which this is to be effected is, that principles should be discussed first by the use of small numbers which can be easily held in the mind, and which do not render the difficulty or labor of combination so great as to absorb the attention, or divert it from the line of thought; and that we should pass gradually, in applying the reasoning, to larger numbers and more difficult and complex combinations, in which pencil and paper are necessary. The rationale should be always the same in the mental (properly, oral) arithmetic and in the written, pencil and paper being used only when the numbers become too large, or the elements too numerous, to render it practicable to hold the whole in the mind. For example, suppose the pupil to be entering upon the subject of *percentage*. The first step is to teach what is meant by *per cent*. In order to do this, small numbers will be used, and the process will not require pencil and paper, nor will such numbers be selected at first, as will cause difficulty in effecting the combinations. Thus, the first questions may be, "Mr. A had 300 sheep and lost 5 out of each hundred; how many did he lose?" "What phrase may we use instead of '5 out of each hundred?'" "Mr. B had an orchard of 400 peach-trees and lost 6 per cent of them; how many did he lose?" "What phrase may we use instead of '6 per cent?'" To assign as the first example, one like the following would be a gross violation of this principle: "Mr. A put out $759 on 7 per cent interest; what was the interest for a year?" After the principle to be taught is clearly seen, larger numbers should be introduced, and such as require that the work be written. But the same style of explanation should be preserved; and great care should be taken to have it seen that the method of reasoning is the same in all cases. To illustrate still farther: as, in practice, the computer ordinarily uses the rate as the multiplier, the form of explanation, when the whole is given orally, should be adapted to this fact. At first, such an example as the first above will naturally be solved thus: "If Mr. A lost 5 sheep out of 100, out of 3 hundred he lost 3 times 5, or 15 sheep." But before leaving such simple illustrations, the reasoning should take this form: "Since losing 1 out of 100 is losing .01 of the number, losing 5 out of 100 is losing .05 of the number. Hence, Mr. A lost .05 of 300 sheep, which is 15 sheep." Thus, in all cases, the form of thought which will ordinarily be required in solving the problem, should be that taught in the introductory analysis. A farther illustration of this is furnished by *reduction*. At first, the question, "How many ounces in 5 lb.?" will naturally be answered, "Since there are 16 oz. in 1 lb., in 5 lb. there are 5 times 16 oz., or 80 oz." But in practice the 16 is ordinarily used as the multiplier, and it is better that the introductory (mental) analysis should conform to this fact. Hence, the pupil should be led to see, at the outset, that, as every pound is composed of 16 ounces, in any given weight there are 16 times as many ounces, as pounds; and he should be required to analyze accordingly.

Use of mental processes. Apart from this use of what are called mental processes, there is no proper well-defined sphere for their employment. In practical applications, it is quite unphilosophical to classify the examples, by calling some *mental* and others *written*. We do not find them so labeled in actual business life. The pupil needs to discriminate for himself as to whether any particular example should be solved without the pencil or with it. It should also be borne in mind that business men rely very little upon these mental operations. They use the pen and paper for almost every computation. In the second place, in constructing our course in arithmetic, we need to give the most careful attention to the condition and wants of the youth found in our public schools. Perhaps it is no exaggeration to say, that from eighty to ninety per cent of the pupils disappear from these schools by the close of the seventh school year; and not more than one in one hundred takes a high school course. Since all pupils of the common schools have need of the rudiments of number, as counting, reading and writing small numbers, the simple combinations embraced in the *addition, subtraction, multiplication, and division tables*, the simpler forms of *fractions*, and the more common denominations of *compound numbers*, an elementary text book is deemed to be needful for many schools. The objections often urged to having these primary lessons entirely oral are, that it makes an unnecessary draft upon the time and energy of the teacher, renders the pupils' progress very slow, does not so readily supply the means of giving them work while not actually under instruction, and more than all, begets in their minds a dislike for study and self-exertion, and a disposition to expect that the teacher must do all the work, and thus carry them along. But whatever disposition may be made of *primary arithmetic*, as usually understood, there is an imperative demand that the course in arithmetic for the masses should be so arranged that the more important practical subjects can be reached and mastered by a majority of our youth during the comparatively short time which they can spend in our schools. In order to effect this, three things will be found necessary: (1) a rigorous exclusion of all topics relatively unimportant, (2) a judicious limitation of the topics presented, and (3) care that, in the laudable desire to secure facility in fundamental processes, — adding, multiplying, etc., the teacher does not consume so much time that the great mass of the pupils will never advance beyond the merest rudiments of the subject. The range of topics to be included in the common school course, will be the *fundamental rules*; *common* and *decimal fractions*; *denominate numbers* (care being taken to reject all obsolete or unusual denominations, and to give abundant exercises calculated to insure a definite conception of the meaning of the denominations);

percentage, including *simple*, *annual*, and *compound interest*, with *partial payments*, *common* and *bank discount*, and some of the more common uses of *percentage*. If, after this, the course may be extended, the next subjects in importance are *ratio*, *proportion*, and the *square* and *cube roots*; and in treating these, constant care will be necessary to introduce problems which occur in actual life, and as far as possible to exclude all others. Something of common *mensuration* should be introduced in connection with the *tables* of measures of *extension*; and the more common problems in *commission*, *insurance*, *taxes*, *stocks*, etc., will be readily introduced in *percentage* without occupying either much space or time.

Extended course. For the few who can take a more extended course, a thoroughly scientific treatment of the subject of arithmetic is desirable; and this quite as much for its disciplinary effect, in giving breadth and scope to the conceptions, and inducing a disposition to systematize and generalize, and thus to view truth in its relations, as for the amount of mere arithmetical knowledge which may be added to the pupil's stock. Here we may introduce an analytical outline of the subject,

Analytical outline. presenting the topics in their philosophical relations, rather than in their mere practical and economic order and connection. Thus, in treating *notation*, the various forms of notation can be introduced, as of simple and compound numbers, other scales than the decimal, various forms of fractional notation, the elements of the literal notation, etc. Then, as *reduction* is but changing the form of notation, this topic will come next, and will embrace all the forms of reduction found in common arithmetic, as from one scale to another, of denominate numbers, of fractions common and decimal, etc., showing how all arithmetical reductions are based on the one simple principle: *If the unit in reference to which the number is to be expressed is made smaller, the number must be multiplied, and if the unit of expression is made larger, the number must be divided.* Passing to the combinations of number, under *addition* all processes thus designated in arithmetic will be treated, and the general principles out of which they all grow will be developed. In this method of treatment, the pupil will not find himself merely going over the elementary subjects through which he plodded in the days of his childhood, but new ranges of thought will be presented, at the same time that all the principles and processes of the elementary arithmetic are reviewed; the very first sections, even those on *notation*, *reduction*, and the *fundamental rules*, bringing into requisition most of his knowledge of arithmetic, and giving vigorous exercise to his mind in grasping new truth. But in addition to all this, which pertains to the method of presentation,

Business rules. there will be much of practical arithmetical knowledge to be gained. In the business rules, *discount* needs a much fuller treatment than it has usually received in any of our text-books. Many problems, of frequent occurrence in modern business circles, are not provided for in these books; and, in fact, some of the most common have had no solution at all which has been made public. The wonderful development of the *insurance* business demands that its principles and methods receive a much fuller treatment than they can have in an elementary course: this is especially true of *life insurance*. *Foreign exchange*, *customs*, *equation of payments*, etc., are other topics suitable for this advanced course, which are quite impracticable in an elementary course, within the reach of the masses. Two other ends will be subserved by this method: (1) It will be a leading purpose *to teach the pupil how to investigate*, and to this end he should be put in possession of the great instrument for mathematical investigation, namely, the *equation*.

The equation.

Of course, only the simpler forms of the equation can be introduced; nevertheless, enough can be given to enlarge very greatly the student's power to examine new questions for himself. By means of the equation, he may be taught the solution of such problems as the following, which would be quite out of his reach without this instrument:

To find what each payment must be in order to discharge a given principal and interest in a given number of equal payments at equal intervals of time.

To find the present worth of a note which has been running a certain time, and is due at a future time, with annual payments on the principal, and annual interest; so that the purchaser shall receive a different rate of annual interest from that named in the note.

These and many other important business problems are quite within the reach of the simple equation, and are scarcely legitimate questions to propose to a student who has not some knowledge of this instrument. (2) The second general purpose which we shall mention as being subserved by this course is, that by grouping all the arithmetical processes under the fewest possible heads and showing their philosophic dependence, the whole is put in the best possible form to be retained in the memory. Thus, if it is seen that a single principle covers all the cases in reduction, that another simple principle covers all the so-called "*problems in interest*," that all the common intricate questions in *discount* are readily solved by the simple equation, etc., these processes will not be the evanescent things which they have often been.

Principles and maxims to be kept in view while teaching arithmetic.
— I. There are two distinct and strongly marked general aims in arithmetical study: (1) To master the rationale of the processes, and (2) To acquire facility and accuracy in the performance of these operations. The means which secure one of these ends are not necessarily adapted to secure the other. Thus, to secure the first for example, in reference to addition, the steps are, learning to count, learning how numbers are grouped in the decimal system, learning how to make the addition table, and, finally, by means of a knowledge of the sum of the digits taken two and two, learning to find the sum of any given numbers. In regard to the latter process, the pupil needs to know why we write units of a like order in the same column, why we begin at the units' column to add, why we "carry one for every ten," as the phrase is, etc. But all this may be known, and yet the pupil make sorry work in practical addition. In order to secure a knowledge of the rationale, each step needs to be clearly explained and fully illustrated, and then the pupil must be required to repeat the whole, "over and over again," in his own language. For this purpose, much class drill on the blackboard, in having each pupil separately explain in detail the reasons for each step of the work which he has before performed, will be necessary. Pupils may be required to bring into the

Principles and processes.

ARITHMETIC 29

class practical exercises solved on their slates, and then sufficient time be given to explanation from the slates. These three things repeated in about the same way,—(1) a clear preliminary explanation of principles either given in the text-book or by the teacher, (2) a thorough mastery of these principles by the pupil so that he can state them in a general way, and (3) a careful and continued repetition of them in the class, in application to particular examples,—will secure the first of these general ends of arithmetical study. To secure the second, namely, facility and accuracy in applying these principles, so as to be able to add with ease, rapidity, and accuracy, long continued drill, with the mind quite unencumbered by any thought of the reasons for the processes, will be indispensable. It will not be sufficient that pupils solve accurately numerous examples, in the slow plodding way to which they are accustomed in their private study, but large numbers of fresh problems should be furnished in the class, which the pupils should be required to solve with the utmost promptitude, and with perfect accuracy. In respect to all mere numerical combinations, as addition, subtraction, multiplication, division, involution, evolution, etc., oral drills like the following will be of the greatest use and should be continued until the combinations can be made as rapidly as we would naturally read the numbers: Teacher repeats while the pupils follow in silence, making the combinations, "5 + 3 ÷ 2 * + 3, squared, — 7 ÷ 7 × 3 + 7, square root, etc." These oral drills may be commenced at the very outset in regard to addition, and extended as the other rules are reached, and should not be dropped until the utmost facility is secured. A similar drill exercise can be secured by pointing to the digits as they stand on the board, or on charts, and simply speaking the words which indicate what combinations are required. Any figures which may chance to stand on the board may be used in this way to secure an indefinite amount of most valuable drill. This latter exercise, — making the combinations at sight — is of still greater practical value than the former, in which the ear alone is depended upon; for it is a singular fact that facility in one method does not insure it in the other, and the latter is the form in which the process is usually to be applied. Again, in the *business rules*, the principles underlying the processes must be clearly perceived, and the pupil, by continued practice in explaining solutions written upon the board, must become able to give in good language the reason for each step. But when all this is secured, there will be found need of much drill on examples to the answers of which he cannot have access, and which he must take up and solve at the moment. In this department, much valuable exercise may be given by handing the pupils written notes or papers in due form, and requiring them to compute the interest, or discount, or make the required computation at sight. But the illustrations now given will suffice to show that there are, as above stated, two general purposes — the theoretical and the practical — which must run parallel

Oral drills.

---

* The signs of division, multiplication, etc., are not used with strict propriety in this specimen exercise; they are applied to the result of all the preceding operations in each case as though all before them had been included in a parenthesis. Thus in this case it is 5 + 3, or 8 which is meant to be divided by 2 giving 4, to this 3 added, giving 7, this squared, giving 49, etc, through all good teaching in arithmetic, and that they are generally to be attained by different means.

How and why. II. In order to realize the above, a careful discrimination needs to be made between simply telling *how* a thing is done, and telling *why* it is done. Very much of what we read in our text-books, and hear in class-rooms, under the name of *analysis*, in explanation of solutions, is nothing more than a statement of the process — a telling *how* the particular example is wrought. This vice is still so prevalent as to need the clearest exposition and the most radical treatment. Indeed, it has become so general as to be mistaken by the masses for the thing it purports to be; and pupil and teacher frequently seem to think that this parrot-like way of telling *what has been done* is really a logical exposition of the principles involved.

Pure and applied arithmetic. III. There should, also, be a careful discrimination between *pure* and *applied* arithmetic, in order that they may be so taught as to secure the proper end of each. Pure arithmetic is concerned solely with abstract numbers, and the breadth of discipline to be secured by its study is not great; but the applications of arithmetic are almost infinitely varied, and give a far wider scope for mental training. In the latter, the questions are not *how* to multiply, add, subtract, etc., but *why* we multiply, add, or subtract. Thus, in solving a problem in interest, it would be quite out of place to cumber the explanation with an exposition of the process of multiplying by a decimal, but it is exactly to the purpose to give the reason for so doing. The most important object in applied arithmetic is to acquaint one's self so thoroughly with the conditions of the problem — if in business arithmetic, with the character of the business — as to discern what combinations are to be made with the numbers involved. Many of these applications are quite beyond the reach of the mind of a mere child. Thus, to attempt to explain to very young pupils the commercial relations which give rise to the problems of *foreign exchange*, or the circumstances out of which many of the problems in regard to the value of *stocks* grow, would be perfectly preposterous.

Problems. IV. In teaching applied arithmetic, it is of the first importance that the problems be such as occur in actual life, and that in expressing them, the usual phraseology be employed. For example, compare the following:

(1) What is the present worth of $500 due 3 yr. 7 mo. 20 da. hence, at 6 per cent per annum?

(2) I have a 7 per cent note for $500, dated Feb. 6th, 1873, and due July 10th, 1876. Mr. Smith proposes to buy it of me Sept. 18th, 1874, and to pay me such a sum for it as shall enable him to realize 10 per cent per annum on his investment. What must he pay me? In other words, what is the present worth of this note Sept. 18th, 1874?

The first supposes a transaction which could rarely, if ever, occur, and even disguises that. Most pupils who have gone through discount in the ordinary way, if asked, "What interest does the $500 bear, in the first example?" would answer, "6 per cent." Of course, it is understood that the money is not on interest. Moreover, we find no such paper — no notes not bearing interest — in the market. Again, the assumption seems to be that the note — if even a note is suggested at all — is discounted at the time it is made. Thus, it is obvious that the first form is calculated to give the pupil quite erroneous impressions; whereas the second brings a real transaction into full view.

V. From the beginning to the end of the course, it should be the aim to teach a few germinal principles and lead the pupil to apply them to as great a number of cases as his time and ability may permit. *Principles to be taught.* Thus, at the very outset, a good teacher will never tell the child how to count; but having taught him the names of the numbers up to *fourteen*, will show him the meaning of the word fourteen (four and ten); then he can be led to go on to nineteen by himself. No child ought to be *told* how to count from fifteen to nineteen; and after twenty, he needs only to be shown how the names of the decades, as twen-ty, thir-ty, for-ty, and fif-ty are formed, to be able to give the rest himself; nor does he need to be told how to count through more than one deca-de. In reference to the fundamental tables, it may be suggested that no pupil should be furnished with an addition, subtraction, multiplication, or division table ready-made. Having been taught the principle on which the table is constructed, he should be required to make it for himself. As preliminary to practical addition and subtraction, the combinations of digits two and two which constitute any number up to 18 (9 + 9) should be made perfectly familiar. Thus the child should recognize 1 + 4, and 2 + 3, as 5; 1 + 5, 2 + 4, and 3 + 3, as 6 etc.; and this should be made the foundation of addition and subtraction. He should be taught, that if he knows that 3 + 4 = 7, he knows by implication that 23 + 4 = 27, 33 + 4 = 37, etc. Passing from the *primary arithmetic*, he should be taught *common fractions* by means of the fewest principles and rules consistent with his ability. Thus in multiplication and division, *To multiply or to divide a fraction by a whole number*, and *To multiply or to divide a whole number by a fraction*, are all the cases needed; and these should be taught in strict conformity with practical principles. Thus, to multiply a whole number by a fraction is to take a *fractional part* of the number; and to divide a number by a fraction is to find how many times the latter is contained in the former. To cover all the forms of *reduction of denominate numbers*, nothing is needed but the principle or rule, that to pass from higher to lower denominations, we multiply by the number which it takes of the lower to make one of the higher; and to pass from lower to higher we divide by the same number. These simple principles should be seen to cover all cases, those involving fractions as well as others.

In like manner, by a proper form of statement of examples, and an occasional suggestion or question, most of the separate rules usually given under *percentage* may be dispensed with. In dealing with the cases usually denominated *problems in interest*, all that is needed is the following brief rule: *Find the effect produced by using a unit of the number required, under the given circumstances, and compare this with the given effect.* This should be made to cover the cases usually detailed under six of eight rules.

Stages of mental de-velopment. VI. There are *three stages* of mental development which should be carefully kept in view in all elementary teaching: (1) *The earliest stage*, in which the faculties chiefly exercised are observation, or perception, and memory, and in which the pupil is not competent to formulate thought, or to derive benefit from abstract, formal statements of principles, definitions, or processes; (2) *An intermediate sta,e,* in which the reasoning faculties (abstraction, judgment, etc.) are coming into prominence, and in which the pupil needs to be shown the truth, so that he may have a clear perception of it, before he is presented with a formal, abstract statement, the work, however, not being concluded until he can state the truth (definition, principle, proposition, or rule) intelligently, in good language, and in general (abstract) terms; (3) *An ultimate stage,* or that in which the mental powers are so matured and trained, that the pupil is competent to receive truth from the general, abstract, or formal statement of it. At this stage, definitions, principles, propositions, and statements of processes may be given first, and illustrated, demonstrated, or applied afterward. (See ANALYTIC METHOD, and DEVELOPING METHOD.)

ART EDUCATION. Every complete system of education must provide for the culture of all the varied faculties of the human mind, physical and intellectual, moral and spiritual, esthetic and emotional; and must, besides, supply the means necessary for the development of those practical capacities upon which the social and national progress of every civilized people depends. Among the agencies required for this purpose, art education claims profound attention. The element of beauty, which exists in the human mind, when made the subject of progressive cultivation, and applied to the various industries of social life, becomes a thing of pecuniary as well as esthetic value. The training of the hand and eye, which is obtained by drawing, is proved by experience to be of very great advantage to the operative in every branch of industry; indeed, in many occupations, drawing is indispensable to success. But the value is still greater if to this simple training, the culture of the perception and conception of forms and their combinations is added, leading to skill in designing — a branch of art of the highest value in very many departments of manufacturing industry. "Art education," says an eminent authority, "embraces all those appliances and methods of training by which the sense of form and proportion is developed. It is successful when the student unerringly discriminates between what is ugly and what is beautiful, and expresses his ideas of form in drawing as readily as ideas of other sorts on the written page." (See DRAWING.)

ARTS, Liberal. The term *arts,* or *liberal arts,* was, during the middle ages, applied to certain studies which constituted an essential part of a learned education. The full course of study, at that period, embraced "the seven liberal arts," three of which — grammar, logic, and rhetoric — composed what was called the *trivium* (the triple way to eloquence); and the remaining four — music, arithmetic, geometry, and astronomy — constituted the *quadrivium* (the quadruple way). The term *faculty of arts* denoted, in the universities, those who devoted themselves to philosophy and science, in contradistinction to the faculty of theology, of medicine, or of law. *Master* (Lat. *magister*) was used to designate one who taught the liberal arts; and *doctor* one who taught or practiced divinity, law, or medicine. The first degree *(gradus)* of proficiency in the arts, instituted, as it is said, by Gregory IX. about the middle of the 13th century, was that of *bachelor* (Lat. *baccalaureus*); and the second that of *master*, which originally conferred the right, and indeed imposed the duty, of teaching one or more of the liberal arts. This title, in the colleges and universities of the United States, England, and France, is now merely honorary. (See DEGREES.)

ASSOCIATION OF IDEAS. By this is meant that relation or connection which is formed between ideas, so that one immediately suggests *Definition.* the other, hence called by Dr. Brown the *principle of simple suggestion*. This law of mental operation demands a most careful consideration in both moral and intellectual education. Feelings of pleasure and pain are often associated with certain ideas or objects in the minds of pupils at school, and thus control their whole after life. Antipathies, prejudices, or predilections are thus so firmly fixed, *Application in teaching.* that they can never be eradicated. The law of association, rightly applied by the teacher, may thus be used to establish in the minds of his pupils an abhorrence of meanness and wrong, of falsehood and dishonesty which will go far toward forming a thoroughly virtuous character. This law has a very important application in the intellectual training of the young, and in the general cultivation of the mind. The power to control the succession of our ideas or thoughts very much depends upon the habits we may have formed in establishing these associations. If the ideas with which a person's mind is stored are connected only by arbitrary or accidental associations, he will find it difficult to arrange his thoughts on any subject in a regular, logical order. On the other hand, there are minds so trained as to be able, at any moment, to command their ideas upon any subject with which they are acquainted, so that they flow forth in an unintermitting logical stream. This is the intellectual quality to be aimed at by the teacher, in connection with the association of ideas. It follows, too, from this that the law by which ideas become permanently associated by means of repetition, should have a most important place in the consideration of the teacher. Certain branches of knowledge require the special application of this law; such as arithmetical tables, grammatical paradigms, and all other things that, having no logical relations, are to be arbitrarily associated. The point to be gained in such acquisitions is to connect these ideas in the mind in such a way that one will instantly, and, as it were, automatically, suggest the other. The perceptions of sight and hearing may both be brought into play in accomplishing this. Hence the use of the blackboard and slate, particularly the former; also the importance of repeating aloud from the printed page.

ASTRONOMY (Gr. ἄστρον, a star, and νόμος, a law), the science which treats of the heavenly bodies, has peculiarly strong claims to a *Place in education.* place in every educational scheme of study, both as a means of intellectual training, and on account of the practical value of the class of facts which it embraces, as well as its ennobling influence upon the mind of the student.

In teaching this subject, the order of investigation — the analytic method, should be at first adopted, for two reasons: (1) because in this *Analytic method required.* way we are able to impress upon the mind of the pupil clearer conceptions of fundamental facts, and (2) because he will thus form the habits of thought which are particularly needed in the study of this science. We should insist upon his observing for himself all the more obvious phenomena, and then stating, as fully and accurately as possible, the result of his observations. It is astonishing how many persons go through the world, filling the measure of a long life, without casting anything but an indifferent, uninquiring, and uninterested glance at the glories of the stellar firmament. So it is also with children, before their attention is attracted, and their interest aroused, to observe the wonders of the heavens. The teacher, therefore, should lead his pupils, by questioning them, to notice some of the most ordinary phenomena; as the rising and setting of the sun and the moon, the phases of the latter, the apparent diurnal revolution of the stars, the positions and apparent movements of the larger and more conspicuous planets among the stars, the ebb and flow of the tides, the solar and lunar eclipses, etc. Finding, from such questioning, that they have really been inattentive to what they might readily have observed, the pupils will strive to see these things for themselves, and will thus, in a short time, acquire such an experience of their own, as will enable them to pursue the study with interest and success. As soon as they have acquired a clear conception of these natural appearances, their attention should be called to the explanation of them; and in this, for a short time at least, it would be well to let the pupils try to think out for themselves some hypothesis to account for what they have seen, and not to give them the correct scientific explanation until they have exhausted their own conjectures. For, it is not so much facts that we desire to communicate as mental habits; and, by the process here recommended, whatever facts are finally imparted, though they may be few, will be indelibly impressed upon the memory. This process is, however, strictly in accordance with the educational axiom, that the pupil should be told nothing which he may be made to discover for himself; to which may perhaps be added, that he should be told nothing until he has endeavored to discover it for himself, and has failed in the effort. (See SCIENCE.)

Observation and inference.

After this preliminary instruction, an elementary course in astronomy should embrace the following topics arranged in the order of presentation: — (1) The *earth* — its form, magnitude, motions, etc., with the phenomena connected with it, and arising from its relations to the sun, such as day and night, and the seasons; (2) The *solar system* — its general arrangement, the bodies of which it is composed, with their magnitudes, distances, periodic times, the position of their orbits and axes, and their apparent motions; (3) The *circles etc. of the sphere;* as equator, equinoctial, ecliptic, meridians, tropics, polar circles, longitude and latitude, both terrestrial and celestial, declination and right ascension, the horizon, vertical circles, altitude and azimuth, etc. If the preliminary instruction has been correct and thorough, these various tropics can be taught in such a manner as, at every point, to appeal to the learner's intelligence, and, not as a mass of arbitrary facts, encumbering his memory for a while, to drop out afterward as useless lumber. For example, if we would lead his mind to a clear idea of the use of longitude on the surface of the earth, we ask him to locate, that is, to describe the location of, any point on the surface of the globe. He will soon be led to perceive that this cannot be done without some standards of reference; and thus

Elementary course.

the use of the equator and meridians will become obvious, and, in a similar manner, that of altitude and azimuth, in locating the positions of stars and planets in the visible heavens, or right ascension and declination, in fixing their places in the celestial sphere.

No part of this science need be taught arbitrarily. Even the numerical facts, as distances, magnitudes, periods of revolution, etc., should, in part at least, be worked out, however rudely, for the student from the data of observation; or he should be required to work them out himself, after being taught the principles and methods involved. Thus, the teacher may begin with the diameter of the earth, and show how this has been determined; then the distance of the sun from the earth, explaining in this connection the nature and use of parallax; then the linear diameter of the sun from its apparent diameter; then the sidereal year of the earth, and the sidereal periods of the planets from their observed synodic periods; and next the distances of the planets from an application of Kepler's third law, etc. In this way, the whole subject will be so woven together in the pupil's mind, that it will be impossible for him to forget its fundamental principles, however few of its facts of detail he may retain. After such a course it will be a very simple matter to present for his study the other important topics comprehended in the general subject.

Not arbitrary.

The use of diagrams and apparatus should be constantly resorted to in giving the instruction here marked out; but great care should be observed to prevent the use of apparatus from superseding or obscuring the ideas obtained from the observation of nature itself. The student must come down to the apparatus from a clear conception of the actual phenomena, using the machine to apprehend the manner in which the phenomena occur. Very simple apparatus is much to be preferred to cumbrous and complicated machinery,—admirable, perhaps, as pieces of ingenious workmanship but of little value for the purpose of illustration. The student should, however, be thoroughly practiced in the use of the globes, as a very essential part of the training comprehended in this branch of instruction. The use of a telescope, of at least moderate power, is also a valuable means of augmenting both the interest and information of the student, especially in connection with the study of uranography, which is certainly one of the most useful as well as entertaining departments of astronomical science. In this part of the study, a good planisphere will prove a valuable adjunct.

Diagrams and apparatus.

ATHENEUM, or Athenæum (Gr. 'Αθηναιον, a building dedicated to Athena, or Minerva, the tutelary goddess of Athens), was the name applied to a temple at Athens, in which poets and scholars used to meet and read their productions. In modern times, this name is frequently used to denote a scientific association or the building in which such an association meets. In Belgium and Holland, it is used to designate a school of a higher grade, ranking next to the university.

ATLAS is the name applied to a collection of maps, first thus used by Mercator in the sixteenth century, the figure of Atlas, bearing the globe on his shoulders, being on the title-page of his book of maps.

ATTENTION (from the Latin *tendere*, to strain, implying a strained effort of the mind) is perhaps the most important of the minds activities, since the quality and duration of the intellectual impressions depend upon

Why important. the degree of attention with which the faculties have been exerted in acquiring them. There is no point of difference between the trained and the untrained intellect so striking as the voluntary power of fixing the mind for a continuous period of time upon any given subject. Hence, to discipline this power becomes, in an especial manner, the office and duty of the educator. Commencing with the most rudimental exercise of the observing faculties, he passes on, step by step, to the process by which, through the entire and determined giving up, as it were, of the whole mind to the contemplation and study of any given class of facts or ideas, the student learns to evolve new truths, or analytically to explain the intricacies of abstruse problems. When the attention has become obedient to the will, this branch of mental training is complete; and, therefore, the aim of the educator should be to instill habits of controlling the attention, and rigidly preventing those of desultory, wayward application, or listlessness. This power of continuous attention is, without doubt, the most valuable result of intellectual training. To produce this result, it is of the first importance to interest the pupils, especially in the earlier stages of instruction. Young minds have an intense desire to know—not words merely, but things. They have a strong craving for new ideas, and take the deepest enjoyment in the exercise of the perceptive and conceptive faculties. Hence the importance of object-teaching. The perceptive faculties are exercised in the observation of the sensible qualities of all the different things with which the child is surrounded, or which may be presented to its view by the teacher for the purpose of attracting its attention; and these objects should be diversified as much as possible, so as to appeal to the child's love of novelty. Hence, there are three things especially needed: (1) Constant change of exercises; (2) Short and well adapted lessons; and (3) The presentation of ideas before words, objects before names.

How trained.

On other accounts, the attention should not be exercised for long periods of time. When the teacher perceives that it is flagging, it is best to stop the exercise; for all that is done while the child's attention is relaxed, is worse than fruitless. It is from an inattention to this truth that children are often made incurably listless in school. They are set at exercises which awaken no interest in their minds, and, consequently, acquire ineradicable habits of superficial, careless attention. In all the subsequent studies of the pupil, it is essential that his interest be awakened as much as possible; but it will be found that there is a reciprocal action of interest and attention. The pupil having acquired in the first stages, in some degree, the habit of voluntary attention, will, as a matter of duty, apply his mind to the studies prescribed for him; and this very application, if earnest and diligent, will soon excite the deepest interest in the subjects of study. The dependence of memory upon attention is well known to all who have observed, however superficially, the operations of the mind; and the power to recall at will our mental impressions and acquisitions is perhaps directly in proportion to the attention with which the associations binding them together were formed. When these are feeble, loose, accidental, or formed with little volition, the mind will have but an imperfect control of its thoughts, and, consequently, will be wanting in the chief quality of a sound intellectual character.

Memory and attention.

Attention requires a vigorous exercise of the brain, and, therefore, is, more or less, dependent upon the physical condition. When this has been exhausted by labor, either bodily or mental, or weakened by disease, attention is scarcely possible; and the effort to give it is injurious, because it induces still farther nervous prostration. Neither should deep attention be exerted or attempted immediately after a hearty meal. The nervous energy is then directed to the digestive functions, which active cerebration will greatly disturb. Hence, the diet of a student should be light, but nutritious. The brain should also be supplied with thoroughly oxygenated blood. No one can think well in an impure atmosphere, especially if it is contaminated by the breathing of many persons. In this way, children often suffer a serious loss of health. They are crowded in apartments too small for the number to be accommodated and very imperfectly ventilated; and, at the same time, are expected to give close and earnest attention to the subjects of instruction. This is a physical impossibility, and the attempt to do it must always be followed by disastrous results. In no respect has the aphorism, "A sound mind in a sound body" a more forcible application than to the exercise of attention. For what contrast can be stronger than that presented by the poor wretch whom disease has bereft of every mental state but wandering thoughts or absolute vacuity, and the man of sound health and a well-trained mind, who is ready at will to concentrate all his intellectual energies upon a given subject, and to keep them steadily fixed upon it until the object of his investigations has been attained! (See INTELLECTUAL EDUCATION.)

Relation to physical health.

AUTHORITY (Lat. *auctoritas*), the right to command, or the persons or body by whom the right is exercised; sometimes also, in matters pertaining to the intellect, the power to influence or exact belief. In education, the term has especially this twofold application: (1) to the discipline, or management of children; (2) to their instruction. The primary authority, both in respect to time and importance, to which the child is subjected is that of the parent; and for several years no other can be exercised over it, except *in loco parentis*. It is true, the state extends a protecting c re over the child; but only by an exercise of its authority over the parents, requiring them to perform their proper duties as the natural guardians of their children. When the parents neglect or repudiate these duties or are guilty of acts in contravention of them, the state interposes its authority, but not even then directly, upon the child, but only to place it under the authority of those who will better care for its interests, and perform for it the natural duties of its parents. The right exercise of parental authority is, therefore, one of the most important elements in the education of the child. (See HOME EDUCATION.) If the child from its earliest years has been accustomed to recognize and submit to the authority of its parents, firmly but judiciously exercised, there will be ordinarily, but little difficulty, on the part of the teacher, in making his authority effective. The child, on entering the school, feels for the first time that it is under an authority different from that of its parents, to which it has previously learned to submit with unquestioning obedience. Its first impulse is perhaps, to refuse submission to this new authority; and the influence

How applied in education.

Parental authority.

of the teacher over the child will greatly depend upon the manner in which obedience is enforced. (See DISCIPLINE.) In the authority of the teacher, as well as in that of the parents, two elements are combined, — one that attracts and encourages, and one that curbs and subdues. Without the former, authority is arbitrary and violent; without the latter, it is feeble and often powerless. In other words, the authority that truly educates should be founded not alone upon fear, but upon love and esteem as well. The authority of the teacher is not, like that of the parents, based upon a natural law, but is delegated either by the parents or by those who stand in the parental relation to the child. This is what is meant when it is said that the teacher is *in loco parentis*; not that he has exactly the authority of the parent, but only so far as it is not limited by the general usages of society, or by special contracts. The conscientious teacher cannot, for a moment, doubt that it is his duty strictly to observe these limits; since, by willfully overstepping them, he must either break a contract, or violate a most sacred trust; and, in either case, his authority will be either weakened or destroyed.

Authority of the teacher.

Many cases will arise, both in the family and in the school, in which children will refuse submission to the authority of their educators; and hence the mode of enforcing authority becomes a matter of serious importance. Authority, of course, implies a control of the will of those over whom it is exercised; and the means by which this is to be obtained will differ according to the disposition and habits of the child, and, to a considerable extent, also according to the character of the educator himself. A violent, irascible, morose, or capricious parent or teacher will have a constant conflict with the child, and will never be able to establish his authority, to whatever extent, for the time being, he may compel a seeming obedience. Authority should not be exercised as such; "the right-feeling parent," says Herbert Spencer, "like the philantropic legislator, will not rejoice in coercion, but will rejoice in dispensing with coercion." (See MORAL EDUCATION.) In this connection, arises the question of the propriety of corporal punishment to enforce authority in the family or school. All educators are agreed, that the use of physical force, if at all sanctioned, should be only, as a *dernier ressort*, brought in when every other means of coercion has failed; some, however, condemn the "use of the rod" utterly. Locke assents to it only in cases of extreme obstinacy.

Enforcement of authority.

The principle of authority has an important application to the mental as well as the moral education of children. In the earliest stages of intellectual instruction, the child must receive most of the information imparted to it on the authority of its teacher; but modern principles and methods require that, even from the first, as far as possible, the child should learn for itself by the exercise of its perceptive and conceptive faculties, and not merely on the authority of its teachers. Much, however, must be imparted, that is beyond the scope of the child's understanding and experience; and, consequently, there will be a wide range for the operation of the teacher's authority. It will, of course, be greater or less in proportion to his personal influence in other respects, and particularly in proportion to the confidence

Authority in mental education.

felt by his pupils in his wisdom and attainments. The teacher should infuse into the minds of his pupils an intellectual independence, — not a skeptical questioning of everything, but a thoughtful investigation of the *why* and the *wherefore*, a diligent balancing of the weight of testimony, and a habit of inquiring into the ultimate reasons of things, as far as they can be adduced. This will impart concentrativeness and activity of mind, and call into exercise the judgment and reflection upon whatever is presented to the attention, whether in study, reading, or conversation. Rousseau severely criticised the pedagogy of his time, for basing the science of education on the principle of authority. He demanded that the pupil should not know any thing merely because it was told him by the teacher, but because he understood it. He should not learn the science, but discover it. "If," said he, "you give him an authority instead of a reason, he will never think independently, but will always be the football of the opinions of others." This is an extreme view, as every teacher of experience must know. The authority of the teacher cannot be eliminated in intellectual education; since to do so would put the undeveloped understanding of the pupil on an equality with the mature and developed intellect of the instructor; neither can its just limits be definitely fixed. The disposition to accept the statements of the teacher as truths, when not fully understood, should be cultivated. Modesty is often as requisite and as becoming in thought as in morals. The great principle to be kept in view is, that authority should not have its aim within itself, but that its object should be to develop the faculties of the pupil, so that he may fully understand as true and right, what he has received on the authority of the teacher.

The following practical principles are enjoined in a recent publication of great merit: "(1) Restraints should be as few as the situation admits
Practical principles. of. (2) Duties and offenses should be definitely expressed, so as to be clearly understood. (3) Offenses should be graduated according to their degree of heinousness. (4) The application of punishment should be regulated according to certain principles. [See PUNISHMENT.] (5) Voluntary dispositions are to be trusted as far as they can go. (6) By organization and arrangement the occasions of disorder are avoided. (7) The awe or influence of authority is maintained by a certain formality and state. (8) It is understood that authority, with all its appurtenances, exists for the benefit of the governed, and not as the perquisite of the governor. (9) The operation of mere vindictiveness should be curtailed to the uttermost. (10) So far as circumstances allow, every one in authority should assume a benign character, seeking the benefit of those under him, using instruction and moral suasion so as to stave off the necessity of force. (11) The reasons for repression and discipline should, as far as possible, be made intelligible to those concerned; and should be referable solely to the general good." See BAIN, *Education as a Science* (N. Y., 1881).

BACHELOR (Lat. *Baccalaureus*), a term applied to one who has reached a certain grade in a college or university education; as, *Bachelor of Arts* (A. B., or B. A.), *Bachelor of Civil Law* (B. C. L.), *Bachelor of*

Divinity (B. D.), etc. The word as thus used is of uncertain etymology. It was introduced into the University of Paris by Pope Gregory IX., in the 13th century, and applied as a title to those students who had passed certain preliminary examinations, but were not prepared for admission into the rank of master, teacher, or doctor. Afterward, it was adopted by other European universities, to indicate the lowest academical honor, as now used in this country and Europe. (See ARTS, and DEGREES.)

BELLES-LETTRES is a French expression for *polite literature, i. e.,* books and language in so far as they are shaped by the idea of beauty. It has been used in English to designate a somewhat vague class of studies connected, more or less, with the mastery of literature on its esthetic side. Some of the colleges in the United States have had a professor of *belles-lettres*, who has taught rhetoric and elocution mainly: but also poetry, prose fiction, criticism, classical philology, and the humanities in general.

BENEVOLENCE, good-will, general and habitual kindness of disposition in our feelings, not only toward each other, but toward the lower animals, is a trait of character which should receive a careful cultivation in the education of the young. Children, in general, are not naturally benevolent. Their undeveloped sympathies, their active propensities and love of sport, and their proneness to what is called by phrenologists "destructiveness", incline them to acts of selfishness and cruelty. In order to check this tendency, their sensibilities should, as much as possible, be aroused; they should not be subjected to harsh or inconsiderate treatment, and they should not only read and hear stories that awaken their sympathies, but should be made to observe objects of compassion that require their active aid; and they should be incited and encouraged in every possible way to self-sacrifice in relieving the sufferings of others. In their conduct toward each other, they should be habituated to lay aside their resentments, to forgive injuries, to put the kindest and most considerate construction upon the acts of their companions, and to dismiss from their minds all suspicions and jealousies, as well as all distrust that is not based upon indisputable facts. The quarrels of children may for this purpose become the means of wholesome discipline in instruction; since the disputants themselves may be made to feel the desirability of mutual forbearance, and their associates, by being brought in to aid in reconciling them, may be impressed with the beautiful character of the peace-maker. In the treatment of the lower animals by children, there is much occasion for this kind of training; and the skillful teacher will not fail to make use of the numerous incidents of school life to impress this virtue upon the child's character. (See MORAL EDUCATION.)

BIBLE (Gr. τα βιβλία, the books), the book which contains the sacred scriptures of the Jews and Christians. The use of the Bible in schools has been for some time a subject of earnest and often heated discussion. Some regard this use as a necessary adjunct to every system of education, secular as well as religious, inasmuch as they consider the Bible to be the basis of all religious truth or spiritual knowledge, and consequently indispensable to the complete development of the mental and moral character. Moreover, it is the view of this class of educators that secular and religious education should be always intimately conjoined. Others, who uphold state or common school education, which they regard as necessarily unsectarian, deem it impracticable to use the Bible in schools, either by study or simple reading, without trenching upon their unsectarian character, and hence relegate its use to the Church and Sunday school. Still others, who regard the Church as the divinely constituted and inspired source of all religious instruction, oppose the use of the Bible on the ground that it constantly requires the special exposition which only the Church can give, or authorize to be given. For a full account of this agitation, see *Cycopœdia of Education.*

BLACKBOARD, an important piece of school apparatus now in use in all classes and grades of schools. It is generally constructed of wood, and is either attached to the wall of the room, or made to stand on an easel or to revolve in a frame.

The blackboard for the use of the teacher in giving his instruction or explanations to the whole school or class, should, for the sake of convenience, be placed near his desk and in front of the pupils. It is a great advantage also to have sufficient blackboard surface to admit of its use by all the pupils of a class, or by sections of it. This is especially desirable in higher instruction; but even in elementary district schools will be found to be quite desirable. Some of the pupils of a school can be employed in writing, drawing, or working out arithmetical problems on the blackboards, while others are engaged in oral recitation. There is scarcely any branch of instruction, or any kind of teaching, from the object lesson of the primary school to the lecture of the college professor, in which the use of the blackboard is not found to be almost indispensable. In teaching mathematics, it has an especial value. Scarcely a teacher, at the present day, in the most remote country schoolhouse, would think of teaching arithmetic without a blackboard. But it is a most important aid also in teaching writing, drawing, geography, grammar, composition, history, and music; indeed, in every thing that admits of, or requires, an ocular demonstration addressed to a large number of pupils. Blackboard drawing can be made very instructive and interesting, particularly when crayons of different colors are used. In some schools this kind of drawing is carried to great perfection. Map-drawing, or rapid map-sketching, on the blackboard, is also very useful in teaching geography. Recitations on this subject may be conducted by this means. One of the pupils draws the outline of the state or country which is the subject of the lesson; another fills in the rivers; the next, the cities, etc., till the map is complete. As the study of maps depends so largely on the proper and attentive use of the eye, this method of blackboard instruction cannot fail to be quite effective.

How to be used.

Blackboard illustration will also prove very effective in the oral teaching, by a series of lessons or lectures, of abstract subjects other than mathematics, such as logic, metaphysics, mental and moral philosophy, etc. By this means the divisions and subdivisions of the subject, with their exact logical relations, are presented to the mind through the eye, and a much stronger, clearer and more durable impression is thus made. For an excellent example of this kind of teaching, see MARK HOPKINS, *An Outline Study of Man* (New York, 1876).

Its use in oral teaching.

BLIND, Education of the. The blind constitute. in every country, a numerous class of afflicted persons for whom *special instruction* is needed. An institution for the blind should comprehend three schools, or departments; namely, the *literary department* or school proper, the *school of music*, and the *industrial school*. This organization is essential, in order to give the general instruction which every child needs, and also such special training as blindness renders necessary. In the literary department, the course of instruction includes the branches which are usually taught, in the common and high schools, to the seeing; the principal difference being in the apparatus and methods of teaching employed. Instead of the blackboard, wall-maps, slate and pencil, and pen and ink, there are employed topographical maps, embossed books, slates with movable type to represent numerals and algebraic signs, geometrical cards with figures in relief, metal tablets for tangible writing, according to the New York point system,—also for the New York system of alphabetic writing and musical notation.

Organization.

Appliances.

The first efforts to instruct the blind found expression in an attempt to teach them how to read by means of the fingers. Many alphabets in relief have been devised, but all may be included in two classes: (1) Those composed of lines, forming the ordinary capital or small letters in their original form, or in some modification of it; (2) Those in which the letters are formed of raised points, or dots, in no respect resembling the ordinary letters, and called the *point alphabet*. These can be both printed and written in a tangible form. The use of line letter text-books in classes is very limited, from the fact that a classification according to reading ability differs entirely from that based upon mental capacity and attainments. For this reason, the instruction in each of the departments is chiefly oral. The instruction of the blind in music is of paramount importance. It develops and refines the taste, promotes general culture, affords constant and inexhaustible enjoyment, as well as the means of respectable support. The musical course of instruction comprises voice lessons, part and chorus singing, lessons and practice in piano and organ playing, and a thorough course of teaching and training in the tuning of pianos. Blind organists, teachers of the piano. and piano-tuners may be found in all parts of the country. Heretofore, this department of instruction has been exclusively oral; but there is now a piano instruction book, in the *New York point system of musical notation*, by which the blind pupil may learn by finger-reading from the printed or written page.

Music.

The importance of *mechanical training*, in comparison with other branches of instruction, in the education of the blind, is a matter of vital interest. Some are of opinion that instruction in trades is of the first importance; others give it simply a place co-ordinate with other departments of teaching; while still others attach the chief importance to such branches as lead to those employments in which skilled manual operations are required. The latter position cannot be maintained, since in all such operations the guidance of the eye is more or less essential to perfection and dexterity of manipulation; from which fact it is obvious that purely mechanical pursuits are not necessarily the best adapted to those who are deprived of sight. This being so, it is a great mistake to rest the education of the young blind, and the prospects of their future

Mechanical training.

usefulness and welfare, exclusively upon such employments. The true plan is to give manual pursuits such a place in the scheme of education as is required by the conditions which blindness imposes. The training of the young blind in one or more industrial occupations should be rigidly enforced, not because such employments furnish the only, the best, or the most available means of future support, but because such training and discipline of the head and the hand in work are necessary to the proper education of every pupil. Thus, manual training is made the means to an end, but not the end itself. Male pupils are taught to make brooms, mats, mattresses, and brushes; to put cane bottoms into chairs; and to perform other handicraft labors. Female pupils are taught to sew, knit, and crochet, to use the sewing and knitting machine, and to work a great variety of articles useful and ornamental.

BOOK-KEEPING, a system of recording the transactions of a business so as to exhibit, in a plain and comprehensive manner, its condition and progress. The usual method of such a record comprises *Mode of record.* (1) a history of the transactions at the date and in the order of their occurrence, in a book, called the *day-book*, and (2) the classifying of results in a book called the *ledger*. This classification consists in arranging upon opposite sides of separate statements, or *accounts*, all items of purchase, sale, receipt, expenditure, investment, withdrawal, production, cost, etc., which, in any way, affect the business. The accounts taken together should thus be adequate to express all that one may need to know of the progress of the business and its *Single entry.* condition at any time. The simplest form of record, by day-book and ledger only, here explained, is applicable merely to a very limited business. In the more extended and complicated enterprises, various concurrent or auxiliary books are required, their number and character depending upon the nature and peculiar operations of the business. In even the simplest kinds of book-keeping, it is customary to use an intermediate book between the day-book and ledger, called the *journal*, the office of which is to state, or separate, each transaction so as to simplify its transfer to the ledger.

Double entry. The only competent system of book-keeping is that known as *double entry*, so called from the fact that the complete record of any transaction requires at least two entries in the ledger — one on the debit or debtor side of some account, and one on the credit or creditor side of some other account. The terms *debit* and *credit* (meaning *debtor* and *creditor*, and usually marked *Dr.* and *Cr.*) are, for the most part, used arbitrarily. They are really significant only when applied to personal accounts; but their uniform application to all accounts is a matter of great convenience. The charm and utility of the double-entry system consist in the philosophical adjustment of mathematical facts to the most exacting requirements of finance, and in the tests afforded of *Underlying principles.* the correctness of the work at any point. The simple principles underlying the system may be succinctly stated thus: (1) All financial resources, or items of wealth, are measurable by the money standard; (2) The sum of all the resources of a concern, thus measured, less the sum of all its liabilities, is its real or present worth; (3) All increase or diminution in wealth comes from one of two sources:

namely, the receiving of more or less for an article than its cost, or the appreciation or depreciation of the value of an article while in possession; (4) The immediate result of all gains or losses is the adding to, or taking from, the net worth of the concern; and, consequently, the net gain or net loss of a business during any specified time must agree with the increase or diminution of its net worth for the same period. The foregoing propositions may be said to be self-evident facts; but they are important facts nevertheless, and such as any competent presentment of business affairs must recognize and enforce; and this is just what double-entry book-keeping does.

The science, or philosophy, of the system is shown in the *ledger*, which, as before stated, consists of *accounts*. An account is a collection of homogeneous items pertaining to some part of the business, such as the receipt and disbursement of money *(cash)*, the purchase and sale of goods, the issue and redemption of notes, the incurring and liquidating of personal indebtedness, etc. All accounts are alike in their structure, each having a title, more or less significant, and two sides, with the items on one side exactly opposite in effect to those on the other; and, like *plus* and *minus* quantities, each canceling the other to the extent of the lesser side, the preponderance, or excess, of either side being the true showing and significance of the account. Thus, the debit or left-hand side of the *cash* account contains the items of cash *received*; and the credit or right-hand side, the items of cash *disbursed*; the difference or *balance*, which, if any, must be in favor of the debit side, will be the amount of cash *on hand*. Again, the debit of *merchandise* account contains the items of the cost of goods purchased; and the credit side, the items of avails of goods sold, or what the separate sales have produced; the difference or *balance*, when all the facts are shown, being the preponderance of production over cost, or of cost over production, as the case may be — in other words the *net gain* or *net loss*. All transactions which mark the progress of the business, having in them the element of gain or loss, must occur between the two classes of accounts represented by *cash* and *merchandise* — the one taking cognizance of measuring financial worth, the other indicating its increase or diminution. (The mere exchange of one fixed value for another, such as the canceling of a personal indebtedness by receiving or paying cash, should be called a *liquidation* rather than a *transaction*; for although it requires a complete record, the same as the buying and selling of goods, it has nothing to do with the progress of the business, having in it no element of gain or loss.) The real transactions of the business being, therefore, divided between these two classes of accounts, we have in the one class — such as *merchandise* — the indication or statement of all the separate gains and losses which have occurred, and in the other — such as *cash* — the complete measure of the net resources, or real wealth; the two together establishing the satisfactory concurrence of cause and effect, or assertion and proof. Thus, the accounts of assertion or cause indicate a net gain or net loss, while those of proof or effect show correspondingly increased or diminished net worth.

The peculiar methods or forms of recording business affairs are so various — owing to the great variety of manipulation or processes, as also to

Accounts described.

the difference in the estimates of a competent record, that they cannot be pointed out. The general conception of the purpose and sphere of book-keeping, however, may be stated as compassing such a record of affairs as will enable the proprietor to know, at any time, the extent of his wealth and of what it consists. Of course, if the real worth of a business man can be ascertained at any time, the increase or diminution between any two periods may readily be obtained.

Purpose of book-keeping.

BOTANY (Gr. βοτάνη, herb, plant), the science of vegetable life, treating of the elementary composition, structure, habits, functions, and classification of plants, in which are included herbs, shrubs, and trees. This is a branch of that general descriptive, or empirical science, called *natural history*; being based upon the facts of observation. The educative value of botany, especially in the early stages of the mind's development, is very considerable,—far more so, indeed, than its usual place in the curriculum of school education would indicate; since it is generally superseded by subjects which seem to be of more practical importance to the pupil in his after life. In the more modern systems of elementary education, both in this country and in Europe, particularly in Germany, the training of the perceptive faculties by the systematic observation of objects holds a very prominent place, indeed is considered the basis of all sound mental culture; and among all the objects of nature, none can claim precedence in point of variety, beauty, and interest, for this purpose, over those of which botany treats. The facility with which plants may be collected, handled, and analyzed, as well as their general attractiveness, makes them peculiarly well adapted for object teaching. Bugs and beetles are often quite repulsive to a child, but where is the girl or boy who is not pleased with the contemplation, or the manipulation, of leaves and flowers?

Definition.

Educative value.

For the purpose of this kind of instruction, and as an introduction of the subject to young minds, the chief point is to direct the attention of the child to the most obvious characteristics of plants and of their parts, as leaves, stems, roots, flowers, seeds, etc. They should be set at once to collect specimens for themselves, and be shown how (1) to observe them, (2) how to state and record the results of their observations, so that they may acquire a knowledge of the words used to express the characteristic peculiarities of different objects. Here will be afforded a wide range for the exercise of *comparative observation*, in the perception of both resemblances and differences, but particularly the latter. It is not requisite, nay, it would be injurious, to teach anything of classification at this stage; nor indeed is it necessary that the child should know the name of any plant the whole or part of which is under observation. Some prefer to teach the names; since the child's mind has a craving for the names of such objects as interest it. When, therefore, the name is asked for by the pupil, there can be no objection to the teacher's telling it. The observation and description of the characteristics are, however, the essential points to be insisted upon. For this purpose, no plan can be better than the "Schedule Method," invented by Prof. J. S. Henslow, of Cambridge, England. According to this method, the pupil starts with an observation of

How applied.

Schedule method.

the simplest characteristics, as the parts of the leaf — its blade, petioles, stipules; its venation, margin, etc. The general appearance of these may be at first represented by pictures, but only to enable the learner to study the natural objects, which he carefully observes, and writes the characters in his schedule, attaching each specimen to it, as a verification to the teacher of the accuracy of his observation. (See YOUMANS's *First Book of Botany*.) It will be easily seen that by a continuous application of this plan, the pupil will acquire a considerable knowledge of the characteristics of plants, as well as of the nomenclature of the science; and, moreover, that at every step his observation, and his judgment too, will be thoroughly exercised and trained, in order to be able to describe the minute distinctions of form, structure, color, etc., that are subjected to his discriminative attention. This process harmonizes entirely with the following just view of a distinguished educator: "The first instruction of children in the empirical sciences should mainly consist in exhibiting to them interesting objects and phenomena; in allowing them to look, handle, and ask questions; and in giving opportunity for the free exercise of their youthful imaginations. A teacher may guide them in their explorations of the neighborhood, direct their observations, make inquiries, give explanations, conduct experiments, call things by their right names; but he must be careful to do it in such a manner as not to check their play of fancy or chill their flow of feeling." (See WICKERSHAM's *Methods of Instruction*.) But the young pupil is not to be kept constantly at mere observation, or the comparison of the form, structure, color, etc., of leaves, flowers, and other parts of plants; his attention may be called to the simple facts of vegetable physiology, and thus shown "how plants grow" and "how they behave," as well as what they are. Such information as the circulation of the sap, its use, the functions of the leaf, the root, the flower, and the seed, communicated in an appropriate style and explained by their analogy with other things, familiar to the mind of every child, will properly supplement the knowledge gained by the pupil through his own observations. If, after this elementary instruction, it is deemed important that botany should be studied as a science, the pupil must be gradually trained in classification, for which the foundation will have been laid. In this branch of study, as in all other departments of natural history, the mental processes to be successively performed are: (1) Observation, with the view to comparison and analysis; (2) Classification; (3) Induction, or the discovery of principles, so as to embody the observed facts into a science; and (4) Application of the scientific principles to new facts. The elementary exercises already described conduct the pupil through the first stage only; but the scientific study does not begin until the third, and is not completed till he has become practiced in the fourth. The observation of common characters in plants will necessarily lead the mind of the pupil to perceive the method and the value of classification; but such exercises need not be very protracted, since it is natural even to a child to generalize and classify. He will soon be prepared for the methodical

Systematic botany. study of systematic botany; and then very properly may be supplied with a good text-book. But the pupils must only use it as an auxiliary or instrument, in the study of nature. Let them still be encouraged to collect specimens, to notice as fully and accurately as possible their peculiarities, and to describe them by the proper terms. Some simple means of drying and preserving plants will be very serviceable, so that the school at least may possess a tolerably complete herbarium.

BOYS, Education of. In the education of boys, the same general principles are to be applied as in that of girls; and, up to a certain age, in their school education, the same arrangements for discipline and instruction will answer. Education, however, rightly considered, has for its object to aid and guide the development of the powers or faculties, both generic and specific, of the individuals who are subjected to its ministrations; and, consequently, its processes should vary with the character of the faculties which are to be developed. And this is by no means the whole. Education is to be addressed to all the elements of character, — physical, mental, and moral. There are propensities to restrain and subdue as well as powers to bring out and direct. There are tendencies to good to cultivate and encourage; and there are, from the first, those of an opposite character to repress or extinguish. There is not only the intelligence to be stimulated and guided, there is the will to be subdued, — to be made subject, not only to the authority of the educator, but to the conscience of the educated. Doubtless, there are principles sufficiently comprehensive to embrace all these considerations, and to afford a safe foundation for practical methods and rules sufficiently minute to reach every case, however peculiar or eccentric; but what we wish here especially to lay down, is the important, fundamental law, that education, claiming to be scientific, and not a mere mechanical empiricism, must take cognizance of all these elements of human character, not only in their average condition and degree, but in those marked diversities which constitute individual character. (See EDUCATION.) According to this principle, boys and girls can never properly be subjected to precisely the same processes of education, because their natures are very different,—physically, mentally, and morally. This fact is, however, not necessarily in conflict with *co-education*; indeed, it may be an argument in favor of it. Children of both sexes may be trained in the same family, and instructed in the same school or class; but the wise parent and the skillful teacher will often have to make a careful discrimination in his treatment of them as boys or girls.

Objects to be kept in view.

Discrimination needed.

BRAIN, the principal organ of the nervous system, and the fountain of nervous energy to the whole body. It is the seat of consciousness, feeling, and intellect, and also the recipient of all impressions made on any part of the nervous system. The brain being the organ especially concerned in education, its hygiene is an important subject for the attention of the teacher. The development of this organ is very rapid. The average weight of the brain in adults is about 48 ounces, and this limit is generally attained at the age of thirteen years. No organ is, from the time of birth, so regularly and so incessantly exercised as the brain. During the period of infancy, nature herself superintends this process; and unless her care is interfered with through the ignorance, folly, or neglect of the mother or nurse, it results in a healthy growth and development. When the age of infancy is passed, and the child is surrendered to the educator, intelligence and skill may

What is the brain.

Development.

accomplish much benefit in regulating the cerebral development; or a want of skill and intelligence may do, and often does, very great injury. Exercise is the natural instrument by which all the bodily organs are brought to a maturity of growth and strength, and by which they are kept in a condition of health. In applying this principle, the teacher should see that the exercise be proper, (1) as to its kind, (2) as to its degree, (3) as to its direction; and in all these respects, that it is adapted to the age and peculiar physical condition of the child to be educated. The same process will not answer for all. The teacher who wishes to do good, whose aim is really to educate, will study the external indications of temperament, of bodily health and disease, and also of cerebral structure; and will, as far as possible, regulate his operations accordingly. The brain is exercised both by thought and feeling; being the seat of various faculties, both mental and moral, its activities are aroused by whatever is addressed to the intellect, the conscience, the emotions, or the propensities. "The first step," says Combe, "towards establishing the regular exercise of the brain, is to educate and train the mental faculties in youth; and the second is to place the individual habitually in circumstances demanding the discharge of useful and important duties." The healthy development of the brain may be prevented (1) by wrong exercise, (2) by being overtasked, (3) by bad physical conditions, (4) by bad moral conditions. Overstrained or too long continued attention, excessive tasks from books, committed to memory under the pressure of fear, long confinement in close rooms, and hence the want of properly oxygenated air, will impair the functions of the brain, and lay the foundation, not only of future disease, but perhaps of future imbecility. So, too, when subjected to harsh discipline, to unkind treatment, to a moral atmosphere vitiated by the irritability, ill-humor, and moroseness of the parent or teacher, the brain of the child loses even its natural or normal physical condition, and its growth is necessarily morbid. (See PHYSICAL EDUCATION.)

How regulated.

BURGHER SCHOOL (Ger. *Bürgerschule*), a name given to many public schools of a higher grade in the towns of Germany, designed to educate the children of citizens for a practical business life.

BUSINESS COLLEGES, as distinct institutions, are the outgrowth of the past thirty years, although schools and private classes for instruction in the commercial branches—particularly book-keeping and penmanship—have been in vogue for a much longer time. Formerly, most of this kind of instruction was given by a few private teachers in the large cities (who generally united the duties of teacher with those of public accountant), and by itinerant professors who traveled from place to place, teaching special classes for a limited number of lessons at low rates. The utility of this practical training was readily apparent, and as a matter of self-protection no less than of self-respect, the established schools, public and private, were induced to recognize the importance of these useful branches, and to supply instruction therein in more liberal measure. There sprung up also, in the large cities and villages, schools, making the practical studies a specialty, and calling themselves *commercial* or *mercantile colleges*. Some of them were organized under state charters and authorized to issue diplomas in due form. These institutions placed themselves before the public as professional schools, assuming the same relations to the future business-man as those which already existed between the medical, law, and theological schools, and the members of those various professions. See *Cyclopædia of Education*.

CALISTHENICS (Gr. καλός beautiful, and σθένος strength), a system of physical exercises for females, designed to promote strength and gracefulness of movement; or, by assisting the natural and harmonious development of the muscular system, to improve the health, and add to the beauty of personal appearance. Calisthenic and gymnastic exercises are based on the same principle,—that exercise is essential to the proper development of the physical as well as mental faculties, and to the maintenance of their healthy condition; and that, in education, it is requisite that suitable exercises should be systematically employed. The only difference between calisthenics and gymnastics consists in the adaptation of the former to the physical education of girls; and, of course, the exercises employed require a less violent muscular action. These exercises may be practiced with or without apparatus. The latter, which should be employed first, consist in such movements as bring into regular and systematic operation all parts of the body. The movements are neither violent nor complicated, being in fact only such as are required in the ordinary exercise of the limbs. Their advantage over those required in the common active sports of girls consists in their systematic regulation so as to insure an equal and regular action of the muscles; while long continued sports of any particular kind, such as trundling the hoop, using the skipping-rope, etc., have the reverse effect. Calisthenic exercises should, however, be so varied as to exhilarate the spirits as well as task the muscles, or they will lose much of their beneficial effect; since while the body is exercised, the mind must be interested. The simplest apparatus used consists of wands or poles, dumb-bells, backboards, elastic bands with handles, light weights, etc. With such instruments, a great variety of beneficial, graceful, and interesting exercises can be performed; and when whole classes are exercised simultaneously, there will necessarily be a healthful mental excitement mingled with the physical training, particularly when the movements are regulated by the rhythm of music, which is usually the case in modern schools. The utility of such exercises, when properly and judiciously employed cannot be doubted, especially after the age of 12 or 14 years, before which they should rarely, if ever, be resorted to. Numerous ailments to which females are peculiarly liable are due to the neglect of proper physical training, and may be prevented or cured by a judicious employment of calisthenic exercises; but in resorting to them, certain general rules and directions are to be kept steadily in view. They should never be practiced immediately after meals, nor very near the time of eating, as digestion cannot be properly performed when the system is in an exhausted condition. The best time for exercise is early in the morning or toward evening. In school, these exercises, being of a moderate character, may come after the mind is wearied with

On what principles based.

Peculiar value of.

How used.

Utility.

Rules and directions.

protracted intellectual work, for then they will prove a relief; but intellectual efforts cannot effectively be put forth after the physical system has become jaded and fatigued by protracted exercise. Calisthenic exercises should always be commenced and finished gently; indeed all abrupt transitions from gentle to violent exertions, or the contrary, should be avoided. It is by moderate and prolonged or repeated exercise that the physical organs are to be developed or improved, not by violent and fitful efforts. The weaker organs should receive the most attention, so that the whole system may receive a harmonious development. The dress should be light and easy; and the department in which the exercises are taken should be spacious, cool, and well-ventilated. All such exercises require to be practiced with many precautions and with a due regard to the condition of the individual. Teachers may be the means of doing much injury by indiscriminately requiring all their pupils to go through the same amount of exercise. The effect upon every pupil should be carefully watched; and, in some cases, the advice of a careful physician should not be dispensed with.

CALISTHENIUM, a newly coined term, applied to an apartment or hall in which calisthenic exercises are practiced. It has been formed after the analogy of *gymnasium*.

CATECHETICAL METHOD, the method of instruction by question and answer, according to which the pupils are required to answer *Limita-* the questions of the teacher, so as to show what explanations *tions.* they particularly need in order to obtain a correct knowledge of the subject; or sometimes they commit to memory and recite answers to set questions from a text-book. There are but few subjects, however, which can be properly taught in this way; since, in training the intellectual faculties, the sequence of facts, thoughts, or ideas, is more important than their clear apprehension or expression singly and disconnect-*Objections* edly. On this principle, there are several objections to the *to the* catechetical method as one of general application: (1) The *method.* pupil is deprived of a proper exercise of the expressive faculties, being required only to repeat what has been enunciated in the language of others; (2) The logical relations of the facts learned are apt to be unnoticed by the pupils, from the absence of those intermediate connective words and phrases by which ordinarily those relations are indicated; (3) The pupil, by learning merely the answer to a question, fails to obtain a full idea of the truth, a part of which, and sometimes the most essential part, is expressed in the question itself. Thus, if a pupil is asked, *What is an island?* and he answers, *Land surrounded by water*, he does not entirely express the fact, but only a disjointed fragment of it. Many text-books constructed on the catechetical plan are liable to this objection; others, however, obviate it by invariably making the answer a complete statement, the gist of the question being repeated. Thus, the answer of the question, *What is an island?* would be, *An island is land surrounded by water*. When the catechetical method is employed in giving oral instruction, the teacher should be careful to keep this principle in view. A skillful use of this method will always be found effective in opening *How made* up to the mind of the pupil the fundamental ideas and prin-*effective.* ciples of a subject previous to its formal study by the pupil himself, or, when difficulties arise, in leading the pupil's mind, by an adroit series of interrogatories, to such an analysis of the statement or problem in question as will enable him to apprehend the elementary facts or principles involved, and thus to solve the difficulty without further aid. This, however, is not so much an application of the catechetical method as a skillful use of interrogation, one of the most valuable and indispensable means of imparting information. (See INTERROGATION.)

Why abandoned. The catechetical method was formerly very popular in schools, and almost universally employed; but, in proportion as mechanical methods of recitation and rote-teaching gave place to such as appealed directly to the pupil's intelligence and powers of expression, the mere question-and-answer system of instruction became discredited and was abandoned. In its place, the *topical method* is now in quite general use. This requires that the pupil shall give a connected statement, not simply as an answer to a question, but as logically expressing the knowledge which he has acquired in regard to the topic assigned by the teacher.

CATECHISM (Gr. κατηχισμός, instruction), an elementary work containing a summary of principles, especially of religious doctrine, reduced to the form of questions and answers. The name catechism for a religious work of this kind was probably first proposed by Luther, whose two famous catechisms appeared in 1529. The use of catechisms in formal religious instruction is very general, the object being not only to present to children, in the most lucid form, the tenets of the religious communion of which they are expected to become active members in after life, but to impress these doctrines indelibly upon their minds.

CATECHUMEN (Gr. κατηχούμενος, instructed by word of mouth), the name given, in the early Christian church, to a convert who was receiving catechetical instruction preparatory to baptism. The catechumens were divided into different grades or classes according to the degree of their proficiency, only those of the highest grade, who had been pronounced fit for baptism, being permitted to be present at the administration of the Lord's Supper. This appellation was afterward given to the younger members of any Christian church who were undergoing instruction to prepare them for the rite of confirmation, or for the Communion, in which sense the term is still used.

CHARACTER, Discernment of. The perception of the peculiarities of individual character by its external manifestations constitutes an essential preliminary to all sound and judicious educational treatment.

Its importance in education. There is an endless diversity in the natural inclinations and capacities of children; and, therefore, no system of education can claim to be scientific that fails to recognize this fact, and to supply (1) the principles and rules that should guide the educator in discerning these individual peculiarities, and (2) the practical methods of treatment best adapted to each. Generally, however, education is carried on with but little or no such discriminations; pupils, whatever may be their temperament, physical condition, state of health, mental capacities, or moral proclivities, are treated according to the same system or plan. It is true, there is in every mind a kind of instinctive perception of the peculiarities of character, either the result of an inexplicable impression or prejudice, formed with little observation, or a positive

Neglect of.

judgment derived almost unconsciously from an attention, more or less superficial, to the person's appearance, actions, and words on different occasions. A systematic study of the external indications of character has not, however, been generally, or usually, enjoined upon the teacher as a preparation for the work of training and instruction. Nevertheless, the most distinguished educators have fully recognized the principle. "Let him that is skilled in teaching," says Quintilian, "ascertain first of all when a boy is entrusted to him, his ability and disposition."

When children are educated at home by private teachers, and, indeed, always in that part of education which belongs to the family or home circle, there is a wide scope for such discrimination; but when large masses of children are taught together, as in public schools, a discrimination of *Basis of classification.* individual traits, and a corresponding adaptation of method and requirement becomes, except within quite narrow limits, impracticable; still, it has been questioned whether, in the organization of such schools, the classification of the children should not be based upon other considerations than merely their apparent proficiency in a few elementary branches of study. If to secure these intellectual acquirements be the exclusive end of the teaching to be given, the usual classification is, of course, proper; but, even then, it should be constantly corrected according as individual capacity unfolds itself. Some *Consequences of disregarding it.* pupils will make much more rapid progress than others; and if these are kept back in order that the general or average progress of the class may be brought up to a given standard, their future progress will be greatly obstructed; their mental activity and elasticity will be impaired by the want of due exercise; and their interest in study will be more or less extinguished. Moreover, not finding the natural craving of their minds for exercise gratified, their sensuous nature will be unduly developed, and they will be inclined to plunge into frivolous and idle amusements. In large schools, conducted almost entirely without any of the discrimination here referred to, the individual is sacrificed to the mass; and many a bright youth loses not only the best hours of his life, but, by untoward habits and a want of due training, the very spring of his intellectual nature. The moral influence of such indiscriminate treatment is still worse; since there is nothing that requires so delicate and careful a consideration as the proper methods of guiding, controlling, and training the dispositions of children.

CHART (Gr. χάρτης, Lat. *charta*, a leaf of paper), a large sheet generally of pasteboard, containing a synoptical exhibit of letters, words, colors, plants, etc., to be used in giving instruction, particularly to classes. This is a very useful piece of school apparatus, since by means of *Its utility.* it the eye is addressed, and large numbers of pupils may be taught simultaneously; while the teacher is relieved from the trouble of writing out or drawing on the blackboard what is to be presented. In teaching *color* by object lessons, a chart is indispensable, as it exhibits, in a methodical way, the objects themselves. Several excellent charts for this purpose have been constructed. Charts are also very useful in teaching phonics. In higher instruction, there are many subjects in which the use of charts affords an important means of illustration; and, hence, we find in school rooms charts of botany, physiology, **chemistry,**

astronomy, etc. While the rapid sketching of an illustration on the blackboard has many advantages for certain kinds of illustration and teaching, the more accurate delineation of objects by charts is often to be preferred, and, therefore, no school room can be completely furnished without sets of these articles.

CHEMISTRY, although one of the youngest branches of physical science in its development, is one of the most important from an educational point of view. But the attention may be so readily arrested by its many easily recognized points of contact with the individual and society, in its numberless applications in the household, the shop, the farm, etc., as well as in the industrial processes on a grander scale, that any value it may possess, as a purely disciplinary agent, may be overlooked, even by teachers of it, and it may be regarded too much, simply as a low utilitarian element in an educational course, however valuable it may be admitted to be. It is, nevertheless, true that, in recent years, much that had contributed a peculiar attractiveness to chemistry as a branch of instruction, seemed inextricably involved in discussion. The perspicuity of its nomenclature, the precision of its statements, the simplicity and comparatively limited number of the laws involved in its most complex phenomena, were all apparently affected. But it has at last emerged from this formative condition, so changed to be sure, that many well educated in chemistry a few years ago may be obliged to recast their knowledge in new moulds, but with a system of philosophy which has much clearer and more comprehensive generalizations. It has, moreover, lost nothing of its peculiar character as perhaps the most sharply defined branch of physical science. The changes have not been so much those of abandonment of views formerly held, as of their expansion, to provide for the wonderful accumulation of facts since the science first took form about the beginning of the century. The old nomenclature survives only in a few general principles. The names, being out of accord with established and accepted facts, were too precise, and expressed too much.

Its educational value.

In teaching chemistry, three methods readily suggest themselves: (1) By text-books; (2) By lectures, accompanied by experiments; and (3) By experiments or investigations performed by the pupil. These methods are so different in themselves and in the end to be accomplished, that they cannot be compared as to effectiveness; but they so fully supplement each other, that they should as far as possible be employed together. The tendency, at the present time, is to undervalue the text-book. Whilst there can be no doubt that, by itself, it yields the least return for the time, attention, and drudgery of both teacher and pupil, as an adjunct to either of the other methods, it not only imparts fullness to the knowledge, but also renders it more precise. Another incidental advantage of the highest character consists in a certain facility for reference, which its study imparts; and, in many cases, an ability to make use of the literature of the science, and, by means of it, to study up a subject, or investigate a particular case, may be of far more value than a memory thoroughly crammed with facts.

Methods of teaching it.

Lectures accompanied by illustrative experiments are generally conceded to be valuable, and to some extent indispensable, aids in teaching physical science. Text-book study, however faithful and earnest, must be supplemented by them. The facts formulated in words must be vitalized, and re-enforced by their objective reproduction. Presented thus directly to the senses, they not only become more intelligible, but possess a peculiar charm, that impresses them upon the memory, and renders the whole study more profitable, as well as more attractive. But lectures are more particularly adapted to teach the general principles of the science, and to develop to its fullest extent the disciplinary value of the mode of reasoning employed in the investigation of the truths of nature, and also to cultivate the faculty of observation. They are, however, not at all adapted to displace the text-book. They are feeble in teaching details. Simple statement and re-statement, and illustration combined, will not impress these upon the memory. If the pupil be required to take full notes, or indeed be allowed to take any notes at all, it will be at the loss of much that is peculiarly valuable in such lectures. With the faculty of observation in the pupil generally untrained, any division of attention between writing, and listening, and observing will greatly reduce the proper effect of the lecture. Great pains should be taken to arrange the matter, and bring it before the pupil so that the salient points may impress themselves upon the memory; and the lecture should be filled in from memory afterward, or it may be a still better plan, in many cases, to furnish, on the blackboard, a very brief syllabus of the lecture. But much of the effectiveness of a lecture is lost in attempting even incidentally to teach numerous details by means of it. It cannot be expected, nor is it at all necessary, to reproduce all, or indeed a very large proportion, of the facts and processes of the text-book, in order that it may be fully comprehended. There are many facts and processes in chemistry that possess a typical character, aiding directly in the comprehension of many others, and these are the ones most likely to be drawn upon by the lecturer. There is no branch of physical science that admits of a fuller illustration and verification of its facts with comparatively limited and inexpensive apparatus, nor any in which the want of thorough practical knowledge and skill on the part of the experimenter is productive of less damage to the apparatus employed. Up to a very recent date, simple entertainment and amusement have been regarded, almost equally with instruction, as the objects of such lectures. The most sensational experiments that the science and the means at command could afford, were impressed into service; and these, too, often loosely connected, or arranged in the order of the text-book. There is still unfortunately a residuum of expectation of something of this kind. The apparatus and experiments with it are apt to be made the display features of the instruction. Whilst simple entertainment, or even amusement, may sometimes legitimately accompany lectures on chemistry, it should be only as a natural incident; and even then, should not occur too often, since it is apt to create an expectation of, if not a desire for, such features; and this will seriously divert the attention of the pupils from the line of thought which should always connect the experiments. Every experiment should come upon the scene like a well-trained servant, just at the right point of time to add its proper effect to the total effect of the lecture; and, in no case, should it control the lecturer. An experiment without such a subordinate relation is as much out of place as a word without proper connection in a discourse. As the text-book is largely a compendium of details, its somewhat arbitrary plan of arrangement, and its formal, systematic, didactic treatment must give way to the more instructive, as well as more attractive, Baconian method of insinuating knowledge into the mind of the pupil in the manner in which it was discovered. Topics should be taken up, discussed, and illustrated. The most familiar phenomena should be noticed, and the lecturer should place himself, with his appliances, in the position of an investigator,—an interrogator of nature, and an interpreter of her replies. The point of attack, and the line of investigation should be carefully determined upon and wrought out, so as to evoke the most valuable information, and exhibit the logic of facts inductively employed. The pupil will readily follow the investigator in his alternate inductions and deductions, as he "guesses and checks his guesses." He will thus not only learn the subject, but acquire, in a measure, the attitude of mind by which facts are discovered, judged, and arranged, and by which also they may be turned to practical account. To take a very simple case: carbonic acid being selected as the subject, a burning candle may suffice to start the inquiry which will lead up to it, and far beyond it. Then, out of the numerous questions that suggest themselves, the chemist might ask whether, as the material of the candle evidently undergoes a radical change, the air surrounding it is affected? It is placed in a jar, and covered; it goes out. Is the air changed? Test with lime-water. Yes. Will a splinter change it in the same way? Try. Yes. It is then allowable to guess that all burning bodies affect the air in the same way. The guess may be checked by employing a wax taper; then an oil-lamp; then a gas-jet. The inference then becomes the very plausible hypothesis, that burning bodies invariably affect the air surrounding them in such a way, that it will render lime-water turbid. All would be satisfied to stop at this conclusion; but a jet of burning hydrogen is at hand, and on repeated trials, each time with greater care, it fails to give the result predicted from the hypothesis. The many facts only led up to that degree of certainty; the one discordant fact shakes the whole fabric. The case is now looked at anew. What have these bodies in common so as to produce this identical result in burning, which hydrogen has not? Carbon. A piece of charcoal is tried. It confirms the conjecture which led to the experiment with it. More cautiously than before, the hypothesis would then be modified to suit the new fact,—bodies containing carbon in burning modify the atmosphere in a certain way. From this point, all the leading properties of carbonic acid could be developed, with but little more apparatus than may be found in any household: its specific gravity, by pouring it from ordinary pitchers, or running it off by means of a syphon, by weighing it in a paper bag on ordinary scales, etc.; its solubility in water, and the solvent properties it imparts to the water, by passing it through lime-water, until the precipitate is re-dissolved, then re-precipitating it by boiling the solution, etc. The other constituents of the atmosphere are, in a similar way, readily brought within the range of inquiry. Such a mode of treatment has for the pupils all the freshness of an original investigation. It arouses a spirit of inquiry, and quickens observation; since they will be far more apt to observe closely when they are to discover what is to be seen, than if required

Topical method.

Illustration.

Effects of this method.

simply to see what is described. There will, moreover, be a pleasing surprise at the evolution of clear general principles from apparently confused inquiries. In such lectures, a sensational experiment without a direct bearing upon the subject, would be entirely out of place. Humble and apparently trifling experiments are frequently found to present the truth in its simplest, clearest, most intelligible form. In all cases the chemical *Notation to be used.* notation should be freely employed. All reactions should be expressed by symbols upon the blackboard. One fact, however, should be continually kept in mind in arranging such a lecture, and bringing the phenomena before the pupils; namely, that in pupils of all ages, without any previous training in this direction, the power of observation is generally exceedingly feeble, and that they can follow the lecturer but slowly. They are very apt to overlook or mistake the feature to be observed, or to be misled by some unavoidably prominent accessory. An examination upon a lecture of the simplest character will reveal this fact. The most salient points, even, will often be found to be wanting. A great part of the value of the illustrations of scien- *Experiments by the student.* tific lectures in our higher institutions, and of the highly elaborated popular lectures is lost for the same reason. This difficulty may be remedied in a great measure by adding the other method of teaching suggested; that is, by allowing the pupil, under the direction of the teacher, to perform the experiments and conduct the investigation, requiring him to keep accurate notes, and, in some cases, to reproduce the results in the form of a lecture. Chemistry is peculiarly adapted to this mode of instruction. A few test-tubes, flasks, corks, etc., and very little material will put it into the power of the pupil to reproduce the explanation of many facts. He will learn more by a few failures than by a whole series of experiments successfully exhibited in a lecture, and will realize how much of care and painstaking accuracy must be expended in the preparation of every successful experiment. He will appreciate the importance of the most trifling essential condition, and will find that here no oversights, no mistakes, no negligence can be condoned; but that failure follows them as inexorably as effect follows cause. He will be surprised to find how apparently trifling an oversight often lay between him and success, and will learn to estimate conditions by other standards than their apparent magnitude or importance. He will thus form the habit of observing closely, and of noticing every thing exhibited in the course of lectures, and will carry this habit into all the affairs of life.—See DAUBENY (Prof. Charles G. B.), *On the Study of Chemistry as a Branch of Education*, in *Lectures on Education* (London 1855).

CHRIST CROSS ROW, or **Criss Cross Row**, a familiar designation formerly applied to the first line, or row, of the alphabet, as arranged in the old horn-books, or primers. In these books, which consisted of only a single page, the letters were printed in the following manner:

+ A a b c d e f g h i j k l m n o p q r f s t u v w x y z etc
a e i o u A B C D E F G H I J K L M N O P Q R S T U V W X Y Z.

The first line commencing with a cross was called the *Christ cross row*, or briefly the *cross row*.

CHRONOLOGY. See HISTORY.

CLASS (Lat. *classis*, from Gr. κλᾶσις, from καλεῖν, to call, because applied to an assembly of the people when called together), a number of pupils or students in a school or college, of the same grade of attainments, receiving the same instruction, and pursuing the same studies. When large numbers of pupils are to be taught, a careful distribution of them into classes becomes requisite; indeed, nothing is so important, previous to the work of instruction, as an accurate classification. Heterogeneous masses of children cannot be instructed simultaneously. They may be made to perform mechanically certain school exercises,— may, perhaps, be taught to read, to spell, to write, and to cipher to some extent; but it can only be by rote, without the due exercise of their intelligence, and, hence, without proper mental development. A poorly classified school can never be really efficient, whatever talent in teaching may be brought to bear upon it. There is no doubt that individual teaching has many advantages over the teaching of classes; since there is a better opportunity to observe the pupils' peculiar traits of character, and to adapt the instruction to them; but class teaching approximates to individual teaching in proportion as the classification is so accurate as to bring together under the influence of the teacher pupils of a like grade of attainments, and of similar disposition, temperament, and mental constitution. Such a degree of accuracy in classification is ordinarily impossible; but this is the ideal standard to which the teacher must always endeavor to approximate in organizing the classes of his school, or he cannot anticipate success.

Definition.

Need of classification.

A proper limit as to the size of classes should be carefully observed. This is difficult to fix by the statement of any particular number, since the number of pupils that may be properly placed under the instruction of a single teacher will vary with the age and character of the pupils, the evenness of the grade, and the skill and experience of the teacher himself. When the number is between 50 and 100, or over, as it sometimes is in large city schools, of course no proper result can be effected. "In a large class," says Reid (*Principles of Education*), "each of whom seldom, and at best only for a short time, receives individually any attention from the teacher, the progress is slow, the faculties little developed, and the education altogether very imperfect." The danger inseparably connected with the indiscriminate treatment of pupils of different characteristics has been often referred to by experienced educators. Thus, we find in a work designed to aid practical teachers, the following important admonitions: "In every class, however well graded, the pupils will differ much in age, health, mental capacity, and home advantages. A correct and judicious classification will reduce this inequality to a minimum; but there will still remain a wide field for the exercise of discrimination, care, and caution on the part of the class-teacher. The lessons should, in all respects, be adapted to the average ability of the pupils of the class; but, even beyond this, some allowance will often have to be made in the case of pupils of quite inferior mental capacity or opportunities for home studies;" and further. "Teachers are especially admonished to be considerate toward pupils of a delicate constitution, an over-excitable brain and nervous system,

Size of classes.

Discrimination necessary.

or in temporary ill health. Many children of this class are precocious in mental activity and exceedingly ambitious to excel; and the greatest care is required to prevent them from injuring themselves by an inordinate devotion to books and study." (See *How to Teach*, N. Y., 1873.) The comparative advantages and disadvantages of home (individual) instruction, and school (class) instruction are quite fully discussed in Isaac Taylor's *Home Education*. "A principal and necessary distinction," he remarks, "between the two systems is this, that while, in the one, all methods of instruction and modes of training are or may be, with more or less exactness, adapted to the faculties, tastes, and probable destination of the pupils singly, and may be accommodated to the individual ability of each; in the other system, that is to say at school, it is the mass of minds only, or some few general classes, at the best, that can be thought of.... And yet even this undistinguishing mechanism, which is proper to a school, and which carries all before it with a sort of blind force, is in itself, in some respects, a good; and if some are the victims of it, to others it may be beneficial. There are children who are not to be advanced at all, except by the means of a mechanical momentum; and such might well be sent from home to school, on this sole account, that they will then be carried round on the irresistible wheel-work of school order.... But although in a large school, even when broken up into classes, little regard can equitably be paid to individual peculiarities of faculty or taste, the principle which is characteristic of home education, may readily be extended to schools not much exceeding the bounds of a numerous family. In fact, it is only the personal ability of the teacher, his tact, his intelligence, and his assiduity, that can fix the limits within which the principle of adaptation may be made to take effect." The number of pupils that should be placed in a class is, therefore, a matter requiring the utmost exercise of good judgment, taking cognizance of all attending circumstances.

Home and school instruction.

What should constitute the *basis of classification* is also a matter requiring a careful consideration. The several grades of the course of study should, of course, be exactly defined, and all the subjects, or parts of subjects, prescribed, should be carefully adjusted, so that the various requirements of the grade may be accomplished simultaneously, and a due proficiency in each may constitute the basis of distribution or promotion at every reorganization of the classes. Still, let the adjustment be as nice as practicable, some diversity will be found at the end of each period of instruction. One pupil, for example, will have made good progress in arithmetic, but very little in reading, writing, grammar, etc. What, then, is to be done? If the average progress is taken, pupils of such unequal attainments in particular studies may be brought together, that the teacher will find it impossible to give instruction to one portion of the class without neglecting the other, or will be obliged to divide his class into sub grades, and thus sacrifice much time in attending to each separately. This difficulty is often, measurably, obviated by selecting some one branch of instruction, as arithmetic, and basing the classification upon the pupils' attainments in this subject, working constantly thereafter to bring the pupils, as far as may be necessary, up to the same standard in other subjects.

Basis of classification.

Whether a school is best taught by classes or by subjects, is a question that has received much attention from educators; that is to say, whether *Classes and* each teacher shall instruct a particular class in all the branches *subjects.* of study which the pupils are required to pursue; or whether each class shall be taught in succession by several teachers, each one taking a particular subject or class of subjects. The diversity of attainments, mental tastes, and special skill among teachers, would seem to dictate the subject system rather than the class system; since, were certain branches assigned as a specialty to each teacher, there would be more time for the careful study by the teacher, not only of the branches themselves, but of the proper methods of teaching them; and, of course, better work would necessarily be done. Other considerations, however, seem partially or wholly to neutralize this apparent advantage. The success of a teacher, especially of young pupils, depends upon his thorough knowledge of their disposition, and also upon their familiarity with his characteristics; and this knowledge it would be difficult to acquire if the teacher were required to spend but a short time with each class, and his means of acquiring it were distributed over a number of classes. Some educators, however, take a view directly opposed to this. "If the pupil," says Wickersham, "recite always to the same teacher, he may become familiar with certain lines of thought, but he will most likely be confined to them. He might be trained by a more unvaried discipline, but it is a discipline in one direction. He becomes imbued with his teacher's peculiar opinions, acquires his manners, and is apt to create a little world in which his teacher is the reigning sovereign and himself the most conspicuous citizen of the realm. It is much better for all pupils to have different teachers, with different tastes, talents, and opinions; but it is very important that this should be the case with advanced pupils." Nevertheless, it has generally been found that much better discipline, — a firmer control, prevails in schools conducted under the class-teaching plan than in those taught on the subject or departmental system; and, consequently, the former is the prevalent mode of organization in large public schools. In district or private schools consisting of but few pupils, and in institutions of a higher grade, as high schools, colleges, and universities, the other system is invariably, and of course necessarily, employed.

Instead of requiring all the members of a class to study the same branches, some schools are so organized that pupils recite different studies *Loose classi-* in different classes. This method has sometimes been denomi*fication.* nated a *loose classification*. It encourages unequal attainments, the pupil being stimulated to do his best in each study without any regard to his progress in other studies. This is, of course, a great disadvantage. Besides, it requires a constant change of classes in the working of the school, and, consequently, makes the discipline more difficult. "I recommend," says Wickersham (*School Economy*), "a close classification, with such departures from it as overruling circumstances may make expedient." — See WELLS, *Graded Schools* (N. Y., 1862); WICKERSHAM, *School Economy* (Phil., 1864); ISAAC TAILOR, *Home Education* (London and N. Y., 1836); BALDWIN, *Art of School Management* (N. Y., 1881).

CLASSICAL STUDIES, a term denoting the study of the Latin and Greek languages and literatures. The word *classical* is derived from the Latin word *classicus*, that is, relating to the classes of the Roman people, especially to the first class. The best authors known to the Romans, both Latin and Greek, were rated as *classici*, that is, *of the first class*, or *classics*. The expression is sometimes used to designate the standard authors of any nation, but it is chiefly applied, as it was originally, to the standard Latin and Greek writers.

Meaning of the term.

The method of teaching and studying the classical languages and literatures must, of course, vary according to the object or purpose for which they are taught or studied. In some schools, the study of these languages (particularly Latin) has been adopted for the sole or chief purpose of showing their relation to the English language, and of giving a clear insight into the meaning of English words derived from them. Where this is the exclusive object, a comparatively small amount of time will be found sufficient for this study. In classical schools, colleges, gymnasia, etc., classical studies are generally pursued for the purpose of cultivating and developing the mental faculties, and introducing the student to the literary treasures of which they are the keys. It is obviously of the greatest importance, that the teacher should be fully conscious of the precise aim that is to be attained, and that the pupils themselves should, as soon as possible, be made to understand the objects and advantages of the study. The first reading exercises will, of course, serve chiefly to familiarize the pupil with the grammatical rules; but, as soon as he understands the peculiar structure of the language, the teacher should strive to unveil, as much as possible, what is beautiful and excellent in the classic authors selected for study. Both translation and explanation should aim not only at increasing a knowledge of the vocabulary and the grammar, but at the training of the mind to comprehend, to appreciate, and to admire these beauties and excellencies. The finer parts of a classic author will, of course, require the greatest and most concentrated attention of the pupil; and, therefore, the greatest possible exclusion of mere grammatical explanations. It is evident that none but teachers of the best skill and attainments are competent to give this kind of instruction. The college graduate who has just completed his course, however well he may have been taught, cannot be expected to make the impression, and accomplish the success, by his teaching, which can spring only from a professor of ripe scholarship, cultivated taste, and experience in giving instruction. There is no doubt that classical studies have suffered in repute as the agencies of a higher education, by the mechanical methods employed by teachers. The letter, and not the spirit, has been taught; and the consequence has been, that the perusal of the sublimest masterpieces of ancient history, oratory, and poetry has commonly degenerated into the study of petty grammatical subtleties, only puzzling the mind of the student without informing or elevating it. Next in importance to the employment of competent teachers, is the selection of proper text-books, in order to produce the best results in this department of instruction. The books at first needed by every pupil are a grammar, a dictionary, and books for translation. The grammars and dictionaries used should be those specially prepared for pupils; for the wants of pupils are different from those of teachers and scholars. As regards the editions of classic authors, some teachers prefer

Methods of teaching and study.

Grades of instruction.

Text-books.

texts with notes, others those without notes In the former case, the notes should be exclusively calculated to promote the pupil's knowledge of the language and a clear understanding of the writer's meaning. The use of translations is generally discouraged by teachers, though all know that "ponies" are great favorites with students. There are some educators who regard a judicious use of translations as not only not hurtful, but commendable. When a knowledge not only of the classic language but also of its literature is desired, the use of the entire work of an author is preferable to that of selections, such as are found in reading-books. An introduction, giving the pupil information in regard to the author of the work, facilitates a correct understanding of the work itself, and increases the pupil's interest. Geographical and historical explanations should be given wherever they are needed. The translations should be at first literal, but should, invariably, be converted into good English, and should reproduce, as much as possible, the excellencies, as well as interpret the meaning, of the original. Of course, the pupil should not be discouraged by too harsh and minute a criticism of his efforts. Minor faults should, at first, be passed over, and the pupil's mind gradually trained to facility, accuracy, and elegance of expression. — See BAIN, *Education as a Science* (N. Y., 1881).

Translations.

CO-EDUCATION of the Sexes, a term used to denote the system of educating males and females together, that is, in the same institution, school, or class, and by means of the same studies and methods, pupils of each sex receiving the same school training and culture. See *Cyclopædia of Education*, and *Year-Book of Education*.

COLLEGE (Latin *collegium*, originally meaning any kind of association) is a name given to large classes of educational institutions, especially in the United States, England, and France. The academic use of the word *college* began about the beginning of the 13th century, and originated in the following manner. The students who flocked to the university towns often came into collision with the citizens, and frequent brawls resulted. In order to protect the public peace, as well as to watch over the students, lodging-houses were provided in which the students were under the charge of a superior. These houses were called *colleges*; and this name was afterwards applied to any academic institution of a certain grade, whether connected with a university or not. Colleges appear to have been first established in Paris; and soon afterward in Oxford and Cambridge, in Bologna and Padua, and in Prague and Vienna. They were richly endowed by popes and other dignitaries of the church, princes, and powerful families; and, in some of the university towns just named, they became so numerous in the 15th century, that almost every student of the university was a member of some one of the colleges.

COLOR, as a branch of object instruction, is of great interest and value; since, at an early age, children take particular notice of colors, and, hence, lessons upon this subject furnish an excellent opportunity for training them to distinguish resemblances and differences, and for encouraging the formation of those habits of attention and comparison which are necessary to the successful study of other subjects. From the fact that many persons are found to be color-blind, it is of great importance that suitable lessons should be given children to enable

Utility of lessons in.

teachers and parents to ascertain whether this defect exists in any under their care, before they become old enough to engage in any occupation in which color-blindness would be an insurmountable defect. Besides, by the early training of children to observe colors, much of the inability to distinguish them, which is commonly not discovered until later in life, may be overcome by education. Furthermore, a general knowledge of colors, and of their relations to each other, is of importance in nearly every avocation of life. This becomes especially apparent when it is remembered how much depends upon color in the manufacture of materials for dress, furniture, household decorations, in the work of artists, and in various other kinds of employment.

Since a knowledge of color can be gained only through the sense of sight, the methods for teaching it in school should be so arranged that the *Methods.* pupils may have abundant exercise of this sense in distinguishing colors. For the first lessons, place before the pupils the *best colors* that can be procured, in order that they may obtain correct conceptions as to what are good *reds*, *yellows*, *blues*, *greens*, *purples*, etc. Commence with showing a single color, as red, and leading the pupils to compare red cards, paper, silk, worsted, etc., with it, and thus to notice resemblances and differences between the true red and the several objects compared with it. Give similar exercises, with each of the primary and secondary colors, singly; then place two of these colors before the pupils, and let them select articles to match each of the given colors. Proceed in a similar way with the other colors; and, finally, place several or all of them before the pupils at the same time, and require them not only to point out the colors as named, but to select colored articles to match each.

Frequent changes in the mode of giving these exercises on color will increase the interest of the children in the subject, and add to their knowledge of it, especially when each one has something *to do* in the *Varied exercises.* exercise. After the pupils have learned to know each of the six colors used in the previous lesson, fresh interest may be given to the subject by supplying each child with a piece of colored paper, taking care that those who sit side by side shall, as far as possible, hold different colors. When the papers have been distributed, the teacher may say, "Now, look at your paper, see what color you have, then fold your arms so as to hide your paper. Now, look at the color which I show you; all who know that they have a like color may hold it up.—Right.—Now, look at this color,—all who have one like it, hold it up." Proceed in the same manner with each color;—to close the lesson, request one pupil to collect all the red papers, another all the blues, another the greens, etc. Similar lessons may be given for the purpose of teaching children to distinguish shades of colors, as dark and light reds, blues, greens, etc.

If it be desired to continue these lessons, and teach that the six colors previously shown may be divided into two groups—primary and secondary *Primary and secondary colors.* —procure artist's paints: red (carmine), yellow (chrome), blue (ultramarine); also a small palette, and a palette knife. Place a little yellow and blue on the palette, side by side, requesting the pupils to notice what colors are used. Then, with the knife, mix these two colors together until *green* appears in place of the yellow and blue. Then ask the pupils what color has been produced by mixing the yellow and the blue. Proceed in a similar manner to mix red and blue, to produce purple; red and yellow, to produce orange. The teacher may now write on the blackboard for the pupils to learn: *Mixing yellow and blue will produce green. Mixing red and blue will produce purple. Mixing red and yellow will produce orange.* Then pupils may select the two primary colors that will produce given secondaries, also the secondary that may be made from two given primaries. Show the pupils also that light and dark colors may be formed by mixing white or black with other colors. Provide exercises by which the pupils may do something to indicate that they know each fact taught.

In order that children may understand *harmony of colors*, they must be led to observe that to produce harmony, the three primary colors must be grouped together; that if two of them exist in a given secondary, the other primary will harmonize with that secondary. To accomplish this result by teaching, arrange colored paper, or other material, so that *red* and *green, yellow* and *purple, blue* and *orange, pale green* and *violet*, may be compared, and the sensation noticed. Request the pupils to tell what colors are compared in each instance; also whether the *three* primaries exist in each group; as well as to observe that the colors of these groups harmonize. Next, compare red and orange, blue and green, yellow and green, requiring the pupils to observe the effect on the sense of sight; also to state which primaries exist in each group, and to notice that the colors of these groups do not harmonize. These lessons will be more or less useful in proportion to the amount of exercise which the pupils have in distinguishing and comparing colors, and in observing their relations. (See SENSES.)

Harmony of colors.

COMMENCEMENT denotes, in the United States, the occasion on which degrees are conferred by colleges and universities upon their graduates. This takes place in June or July, and closes the scholastic year, so that the name in this respect appears to be a misnomer. It refers, however to the beginning of the student's independent career after being released from tutelage. The life of school ends, but the school of life *commences.*

COMMON SCHOOLS, the name given in the United States to schools maintained at the public expense, and open to all. These schools are public elementary schools, although the common-school system of any state or city often includes schools of several grades, as primary, grammar, and high schools, besides normal schools for the special instruction and training of teachers. Common schools in the rural districts are called *district schools*, being under the supervision and control of the officers of the school district. For the history and description of the common-school system of each State in the Union see *Cyclopædia of Education.*

COMPANIONSHIP, as one of the necessary conditions of a child's life, is an important element in education; indeed, the influence of a child's companions, either for good or evil, is often far greater than any that can be exerted by parents or teachers. The social nature of a child is stronger than that of an adult; and, therefore, to educate it by itself, excluding it from all intercourse with children of its own age, would result not in a natural or normal development, but in a kind of monstrous distortion. The selfish principles of its nature would attain a disproportionate growth and strength; and it

Why an important element.

could have neither sympathy nor self-control. Hence, companionship is necessary for several reasons: (1) To develop the social sympathies and affections of the child; (2) To cultivate properly its moral nature; (3) To bring into play its intellectual activities, and to accustom it to their ready exercise. Besides, without suitable and congenial playmates, it would not be properly or sufficiently stimulated to bodily exercise, and its physical growth and development would be incomplete.

Companionship, therefore, being indispensable, it is of the greatest importance that it should be of the right character. It is particularly true *Caution required.* of children, that "evil communications corrupt good manners," and not only manners, but morals; indeed, the society of the debased will inevitably undermine the whole character, leaving it but an example of incorrigible depravity. Nevertheless, a youth must gradually be accustomed to the exercise of considerable freedom in selecting his or her associates, since the circumstances of after life will necessitate this independence of choice. The great *desideratum* is, that the child's mind should be so impressed with right principles, that it will avoid the companionship of those whose conduct and language it perceives to be vicious. There is, however, always need of great vigilance in order to prevent corrupting companionship, even when the greatest care has been *Parental companionship.* exercised in the previous moral training of a youth; for the stronger will must always control the weaker will, when brought together, and children learn much faster from each other than from their elders. To influence a young person, so as to form his character in a particular direction, or fully to control his actions, it is requisite to cultivate a certain degree of companionship with him. Parents who pursue this course,—fathers making companions of their sons, and mothers, of their daughters, are the most successful in establishing the character of their children. To a limited extent, the same principle may be applied in school education. The austere teacher who never strives *Companionship of the teacher.* to cultivate any other relation between himself and his pupil than that of authority, will never exert any considerable influence over his moral character; while, on the other hand, he who is easy and familiar, who cultivates the friendship, esteem, and confidence of his pupil, will find the latter always glad to be his companion, and will be able to control his conduct to an almost unlimited extent.

COMPOSITION, as the formal expression of thought, and as a branch of school exercise, has usually been confined to that which is writ*Definition.* ten; but by some the signification of the term has been so extended as to embrace also the oral use of language in the expression of a logically connected series of ideas. Thus, it has been said that *"oral composition* may be cultivated from a very early period, indeed from the beginning of the pupil's school education; and whatever degree of facility he attains in it will secure his more rapid advancement when he enters on the study of written composition;" which is undoubtedly true. At the same time, as nothing is gained by extending the application of a term beyond the limits of ordinary usage, it would seem best to restrict the word *composition* to the written expression of thought; more especially as this requires a somewhat diverse training from that which is needed in oral discourse. Of course, the habit of using language correctly in all the

COMPOSITION

oral school exercises, as well as in ordinary conversation, is not only useful but essential as an antecedent preparation for written composition; and in view of this, it is important that pupils should be accustomed, in all their recitations, to be accurate in expression and not only to use the proper forms of words, but to construct complete sentences, instead of such fragmentary phrases as are very often made use of in answer to the questions of the teacher. Moreover, in all recitations which do not absolutely require a *verbatim* repetition of the language of the text-book, the pupil should be accustomed to use his own language as far as possible, thus drawing upon the resources of his own vocabulary, and his constructive power in expression. But all this is only auxiliary to written composition, which requires special and peculiar exercises, beginning almost as soon as the pupil has learned to write simple words and sentences; indeed, rudimental exercises in composition may constitute an essential part of object lessons, the teacher writing on the blackboard instead of requiring the pupils to write on the slate or on paper. For example, in the description of an object, the pupils observe and state each quality successively, and the teacher writes each separate statement on the blackboard, observing strictly the rules for punctuation and the use of capitals; and then the pupils are required to put the whole into a connected statement, which the teacher also writes on the blackboard. Thus, suppose the object is a piece of *glass*. The pupils say, and the teacher writes, *Glass is hard. Glass is solid. Glass is brittle. Glass is transparent.* Then the whole is formed into a connected statement; and the teacher writes, *Glass is hard, solid, brittle, and transparent.* Such simple exercises are susceptible of a very great variety, and, consequently, may be made to afford a great deal of valuable training both in thought and language. Reading also may be made available in training pupils in the ready and correct use of language, by requiring them constantly to reproduce, in their own modes of expression, the substance of the lessons read; and, as soon as they have learned to write with sufficient fluency, to set down on paper, or on the slate, portions of these statements. Akin to this kind of exercise, is the reading of simple narratives by the teacher, and requiring the pupils to give the substance of them in their own language.

Use of language.

Exercises.

In all these cases, the pupils are trained chiefly in the use of words and the construction of sentences; but the teaching of composition requires, (1) a cultivation of thought; and (2) a cultivation of the faculty of expression. Thought implies ideas and their logical arrangement according to certain laws of association. The mind must recall all that it has learned upon the subject under consideration, — ideas, facts, propositions, opinions, etc., and arrange them into a symmetrical whole. To do this well requires not only maturity of mental culture, but much practice in the use of language, filling the memory not only with a vocabulary of words, but a large accumulation of phrases, and other forms of expression, associated regularly with certain recurrent ideas. The difficulty experienced by pupils in writing compositions is proverbial; and to a considerable extent, it is to be hoped, obsolete; since modern methods of instruction have gone far toward eradicating many of the

Teaching composition.

Writing compositions.

absurd educational practices of by-gone times, one of which was to require young pupils to write formal compositions upon difficult abstract themes without any, or with very inadequate, preliminary preparation and training. The necessity of such training is now pretty generally recognized, and suitable graded exercises are employed; such as the following: (1) Conversations upon familiar objects, such as usually engage the attention of children; (2) Sentence-making, in various forms, and affording practice in the application of grammatical rules; (3) Formal descriptions of objects; (4) Simple narratives; (5) Didactic essays, graduated from the simplest composition upon such subjects as *a horse, a cow, a flower*, &c., up to those upon complex abstract themes; (6) Argumentative compositions, in which the principles and rules of logic and rhetoric may find an application and illustration. Each of these classified forms of exercise needs much continuous practice; and the pupil should not be required to write miscellaneous compositions until he has been successively trained in those of the first four classes, and has acquired a fair degree of readiness at each stage of his progress.

In all the exercises, however, of whatever grade or kind, it is very essential that the pupil should, as much as possible, be induced to make use of his own experience in selecting subjects for compositions writing of what he has himself seen and heard, and using the simplest and most direct language he can command. Mere grammatical exercises are of little use in teaching composition; perhaps, they are rather a hindrance, since the exclusive attention to the construction of sentences without regard to their meaning or logical coherence, tends to the formation of habits that are directly opposed to success in actual composition. The great point is to accustom the pupils, by constant daily practice, to the free expression of their thoughts in writing. Let them have something to say, and then require them to write it in the most natural way, employing their own modes of thinking and of using language, and thus, in the course of time, developing a style; since style is only the peculiar impress of a writer's individuality upon his forms of expression. Paraphrases and translations, however, afford a very valuable kind of exercise in composition; but should not be employed except in the more advanced stages of the instruction, since to reproduce exactly the thought of a foreign writer requires a great command of language.

Subjects for composition.

In the correction of compositions, the teacher should exercise great prudence, so as to impart the kind and degree of instruction adapted to the pupil's progress; and, at the same time, not discourage his efforts by too minute criticism. If a class is under instruction, the prevailing errors of the pupils, as discerned on a perusal of the compositions, will suggest certain topics on which instruction is needed; and this may then be illustrated by examples culled from the compositions without referring to them individually. Especially should the teacher avoid holding up any of the pupils' efforts to ridicule or severe rebuke, unless the inaccuracies are such as result from sheer carelessness. A pupil's whole intellectual career may be vitiated by an imprudence of this kind; since, in general, there is nothing in respect to which persons, whether adults or children, are so sensitive as in regard to their efforts in written composition.

Correction.

When the compositions have been carefully read, and the errors pointed out by suitable marks, the pupils should be required to transcribe them, so that they may be presented for further revision. The study of grammar and composition should be pursued together in the early stages, and rhetoric and composition in the later.

Transcription.

CONCENTRIC CIRCLES, System of. Among the new methods of instruction which have recently been extensively employed in schools, that of teaching on what has been called *Concentric Circles* deserves to be specially mentioned. According to this method, a subject which is to be taught in several grades or classes, is not distributed into a number of consecutive sections of which the lowest class studies the first, the following the next, and so on, until the last section is reached by the highest class; but the most elementary points — forming an outline — are selected for the lowest class; and in the following class or classes, this part of the work is reviewed, and the review is combined with additional selections still covering the entire extent of the subject, but with greater detail, until, in a number of such *concentric circles*, the information of the scholars is extended to the limit which the course of study prescribes.

In Germany, this plan has been quite extensively adopted in the teaching of history, geography, natural science, and language, as well as in arithmetic (see DEVELOPING METHOD). See *Year-Book of Education* for 1878.

CONCEPTION, or the **Conceptive Faculty**, the faculty of the mind which retains past perceptions, and forms from them general ideas, or notions, sometimes called *concepts*. In this manner, the individual impressions obtained by perception are associated in the mind, according to their resemblances and analogies, and become the materials of thought; for without general ideas thought is impossible. Thus, the child perceives a horse, but the concept in its mind as the result of the perception, is not of that particular horse, which it will remember to have seen at a particular time and place, but of the horse as one of a class of animals resembling the one seen; and to each one of this class it is at once prepared to apply the name *horse*. As, if you ask a child, How many legs has a horse? he answers, *four*; because such is his concept or notion of a horse, formed from all the perceptions which he has had of this animal. "Nature," says Isaac Taylor, "for purposes which it is not very difficult to divine, has allowed an absolute predominance to the conceptive faculty during the season of infancy, and has granted it a principal share in the mental economy during the succeeding years of childhood." Hence, it is with this faculty that early education has principally to deal. At this period, the mind is to be stored with ideas— images, or mental pictures of past perceptions, which it is to employ as the material for the exercise of the other faculties,—imagination, judgment, reason. "A rich and ready conception," says Currie, "is the soil out of which grows a sound judgment. The cause of error in our judgments lies as frequently in the want of materials on which to base them as on the want of power to compare them when required." He also judiciously remarks, "It is a great mistake to hasten on the child to use the

Definition.

Illustration.

Conception in childhood.

forms of judgment before his mind is stored with the materials to which to apply them, under the impression that we are teaching him to think." The faculty of conception is most active in relation to the objects of sight, that is, the perceptions derived from that sense give rise to the strongest or most vivid conceptions; hence, indeed, the word *idea*, meaning *image* or *picture* in the mind. To those who are deprived of the sense of sight, the perceptions produced by the sense of hearing stimulate, perhaps, with almost equal force the conceptive faculty. "The furniture of the conceptive faculty, as derived from the objects of sight," says Isaac Taylor, "constitutes the principal wealth of the mind, and upon the ready command of these treasures, with some specific end in view, depends in great measure its power." The cultivation of this faculty should aim, (1) To give clear, definite ideas of objects and their properties; (2) To imprint them deeply upon the mind, so that they may be permanently retained, and readily recalled; and (3) To associate them, as far as possible, according to their intrinsic or logical relations. It is a well-understood fact that the clearest and deepest conceptions are obtained by a close and accurate observation of the objects from which they are derived. Clearness and strength of perception are followed by the same qualities in conception. Hence the value of object teaching, the best results of which are the effects produced upon the conceptive faculty. In training the perception, we are, indeed, training the conception; and it is the latter process that is especially valuable, not the former. This training can only be carried on by means of language. No idea can be fixed in the mind to be of any practical value, unless there is linked with it its proper verbal designation. Words as well as ideas are the elements of thought. A large part of elementary teaching consists in analyzing the parts and properties of objects, and, after leading the mind to form concepts of them through sense-perception, applying to them the names by which they are commonly known. As examples of lessons of this kind, the following are given from Currie's *Early and Infant School Education:*

Visible objects.

Cultivation and conception.

Language.

TREE.
PLACE—in the ground, in fields, gardens, etc.
FORM—upright, bending, wide-spreading above, with waving motion, etc.
PARTS—Root, below ground, branching, etc.
    Trunk: round, solid, pillar-like, firm, dark, rough, knotty, etc.
    Leaves: heart-shaped, oval, etc.; soft, green, yellow, etc.
    Blossom and fruit in their seasons.
SOUND *(in motion)*—rustling, gentle, violent, etc.

GLASS.
COLOR—light, stained, clear, transparent, obscured, etc. } *Sight.*
FORM *(in windows)*—square, round, oval, lozenge-shaped, etc.
    Thin, light, hard, brittle, cold, sharp, etc.   *Touch.*

SEA.
TASTE—salt, unpleasant, cold, etc.   *Taste.*
SIZE—large, broad, deep, etc.
COLOR—green, blue, clear, sandy, etc. } *Sight.*
FORM—Surface: plain, wavy, billowy, foaming, etc.
SOUND *(in motion)*—dashing, murmuring, gentle, violent, etc.   *Hearing.*
    cool, refreshing, cold, etc.   *Touch.*

    Such lessons admit of an endless variety, and may be either entirely objective, that is, given with the objects placed before the pupils, or purely conceptive: such as those above on the *tree* and *sea*. Both kinds, however, have the same primary object in view, — to train the conceptive faculty in connection with expression. Observation is also greatly stimulated and guided by such lessons. Thus, to take so familiar an object as the *sky*, of which every child must necessarily have a multitude of conceptions, although perhaps indefinite and almost useless, because not associated with any names. How much would his real available knowledge be increased by an exercise enabling him to enumerate the various appearances of the sky by proper designations. Thus: — THE SKY may be *serene, stormy, clear, overcast, misty, hazy, foggy, gloomy, lowering, bright, resplendent, brilliant, deep, dull, brazen, red, gray, azure, starry, dark, lurid,* etc., etc. In a similar manner, the sensible properties of a great variety of familiar objects may be recalled and named, and in this way the attention of the pupils to minute characteristics may be cultivated, and their command of language much increased.

The conceptions of the mind are greatly influenced by the feelings. An indifferent, apathetic mental mood will effectually preclude the formation of any deep or durable impressions; on the contrary, the con- *Influence* ceptions of objects and scenes with which the mind has been *of the* brought into contact under circumstances causing deep emotion, *Feelings.* either of pleasure or pain, are ineffaceable. "The cherished and imperishable recollections of childhood, often as bright and clear at eighty as they were at twenty, are those treasures of the conceptive faculty which have been consigned to its keeping under the influence of vivid pleasurable emotions." There is no principle which the teacher should more earnestly consider than this, prompting as it does to the effort to associate with the scenes of the child's school life every possible object which may excite its interest, awaken its delight, and lend a charm to its intellectual acquirements. — See ISAAC TAYLOR, *Home Education;* CURRIE, *Early and Infant School Education.*

CONCERT TEACHING, a mode of instruction in which the pupils memorize what is to be learned, by simultaneous repetition. It is thus a kind of rote-teaching, and is subject to all the disadvantages and liable to all the objections incident to that system. In large *What it is.* schools, in which very many pupils are taught together in a single class, this has been a common and favorite practice with teachers; because it has been found a ready way to fix in the memory of children the rudimentary principles of reading, spelling, arithmetic, etc., and to impart to the pupils the ability to repeat, in answer to set questions, *Value* what has been thus mechanically learned. The arbitrary associa- *of it.* tions established in this way are very strong and durable; and, as some things are to be taught arbitrarily, and others to be associated in the mind so that they may be arbitrarily suggested, that is, recalled without any effort of reasoning or other mental process, the method of concert repetition, has a place in teaching that is useful and important. For example, the multiplication table would be of little value if it were so learned, that the pupil would require to reason out, or reckon up, the result of each required combination; the associations must be of such a character, that thought is unnecessary to recall them, the process of simple suggestion being alone required. Hence, in memorizing such things as arithmetical tables, grammatical declensions, conjugations, etc., concert teaching is valuable, on the principles, (1) that all repetition is valuable in order to impress the mind; and (2) that, the sense of hearing being strongly appealed to, the mental impressions and their associations are more durable, and more easily recalled. Besides, by such exercises, the young pupils are constantly employed; their minds are kept steadily upon their school work, and a strong social or collective sympathy is established, which would not be possible by the exclusive employment of individual exercises. In this connection, Currie says, " By this oft repeated simultaneousness of thought, action, and emotion, the mass becomes welded together, takes on one stamp, breathes one spirit.... Such is the foundation of that simultaneous action with which, under the name of *collective lessons* or *gallery lessons*, we are so familiar in the infant school." So strongly is this writer impressed with its usefulness, that he styles it " the very essence of the infant-school system, springing immediately from the root of it, and embodying a first principle of its existence."

The exercise of intelligence is, however, to be considered the chief instrument of education; and this is so much an individual matter, that *Limits of its use.* the limits within which concert or simultaneous repetition is proper, are quite narrow; and the tendency with most teachers is to transcend them. Consequently, the intelligence of many pupils, instead of being properly addressed and exercised, is kept in a kind of stagnant condition, and is thus impaired rather than benefited. The teacher, in giving simultaneous instruction, must endeavor to prevent this. The pupils will have different temperaments and different degrees of mental power; and, consequently, cannot all perform the same work. The questions, when addressed to the whole class, will not be adapted to all the pupils; and if the teacher should depend upon a mere simultaneous response, only a part of the class would be benefited by the teaching. A show of hands is a ready and useful tentative means of ascertaining the condition of the class in this respect; and thus the advantages of the simultaneous and individual plan of teaching may be combined, the teacher selecting from all who raise their hands those who are to answer, and, at the same time, observing carefully who do not raise their hands. Then, when the teacher wishes a certain answer to be repeated for the purpose of impressing it upon the pupils' minds, the class may be required to repeat it as often as may be necessary in concert. Tact and skill on the part of the teacher will make this method of elementary instruction very effective.

In the simultaneous responses, the tones of the voice should be as natural as possible. Without great care on the part of the teacher, concert exercises *Tones of the voice.* are very apt to degenerate into a sing-song monotonous drawl, which undermines or prevents all proper habits of reading and speaking. The pupils, too, are very apt to pitch their voices too high, or to use a kind of shouting tone, which no intelligent teacher would, for a moment, permit. Under the limitations referred to, and with all proper efforts to guard against the abuses to which this system of teaching is peculiarly liable, it is of great value; but should never be employed, except when the common nature and common intelligence of the children are to be brought into play.

CONSCIENCE, Culture of. The feeling of moral obligation, the conviction that certain actions are right and others wrong, the sense of duty, the moral principle, or by whatever other phrase of similar signification we may define *conscience*, is the most important object of culture in every department and stage of moral education. The strength of this principle, as an active element of character, differs greatly in different individuals, whether children or adults. As a general fact, however, children are influenced but very slightly by a sense of right or duty; they are acted upon by a different class of motives. The desire of sensuous enjoyment, the love of approbation, emulation, self-will, the hope of reward, and the fear of punishment, are the usual means by which youthful minds are swayed, and their actions controlled. The appetites are strong; the moral sentiments, weak. Hence, to address the conscience of a child as a ruling principle would be a great error; perhaps, a disaster. Still, children should be treated as possessing at least the germ of conscience; and they should early be habituated to scan their own conduct as well as that of others, and apply to it a certain standard of moral rectitude. However imperfect this standard in a child's mind may be, much will be gained when we have induced him to ask, in regard to any of his actions, "Is it right?" The enlightenment of conscience is much easier than its development; to one who is deeply impressed with a sense of duty, a knowledge of specific right and wrong will be very readily acquired. It should be borne in mind that, while the child is really restrained by the lower motives of conduct, such as those above enumerated, the conscience is to be steadily but carefully addressed. Thus, if a pupil, whose love of approbation is strong, has learned a difficult lesson simply to please his teacher, it is right to accord him all the praise which he craves as the reward of his conduct; but let not the teacher fail to impress upon his mind, at the same time, that this praise is given because the action performed is good — is right; so that his mind may be drawn from his overweening desire for the approbation of others, and gradually led to appreciate more highly the approbation of his own conscience; and so in respect to all the lower incentives. If the child is punished for a fault by an angry teacher or parent, he will rather dread the anger than be impressed with the wrongfulness of his conduct; and, if sly and deceitful, the only result of the punishment will be to render him more careful to conceal than to avoid similar wrong-doing in the future. Hence, the interposition of the teacher's personality in connection with either reward or punishment is an obstacle to the moral improvement of the pupil; because it diverts his attention from the character of his conduct, as good or bad in itself, to an exclusive consideration of its effects upon the mind of the teacher, as producing praise or censure. Some thoughtless teachers punish their pupils for not telling of each other's offenses; when they should be glad to perceive an exhibition of such a sense of honor, and should rather encourage and commend it. Of course, if a pupil who is strenuous in his refusal to act the part of a tale-bearer, as being mean and wrong, could be convinced that his duty demanded that he should make known the wrong-doer, he would at once yield; but, after a simple statement of the case, he should be permitted to exercise his conscience, without any violence or threats being brought against it. A high standard of moral excellence in a child is just as striking an instance of precocity, as great intellectual power and attainments; and is, *Precocity.* perhaps, as much to be discouraged. "Be content," says Herbert Spencer, "with moderate measures and moderate results. Constantly bear in mind the fact that a higher morality, like a higher intelligence, must be reached by a slow growth; and you will then have more patience with those imperfections of nature which your child hourly displays."

The conscience is not to be cultivated by simply giving moral precepts. "Moral education," says Dymond, "should be directed, not so much to informing the young what they ought to do, as to inducing those moral dispositions and principles which will make them adhere to what they know to be right." The highest success in this is achieved when the pupil is seen to be willing to make self-sacrifice, to practice self-denial, in order to do what he feels to be right. This point of moral excellence having been reached, the individual may, with entire safety, be allowed to control his own actions, with the assurance that he will not, in any circumstance of life, go far astray.

Value of moral precepts.

The basis of moral rectitude has not here been considered; nor is it necessary to plunge into any speculations as to what constitutes that discriminative power between right and wrong which is a part of the original constitution of the human mind. It may undoubtedly be strengthened by religious training of a proper character; and hence, such training constitutes a very important agency in the culture of the conscience. "Parents," says Hartley, "should labor, from the earliest dawnings of understanding and desire, to check the growing obstinacy of the will, curb all sallies of passion, impress the deepest, most amiable, reverential, and awful sentiments of God, a future state, and all sacred things." (See MORAL EDUCATION, and RELIGIOUS EDUCATION.)

Basis of morality.

CONVERSATIONAL METHOD. This refers to the mode of giving instruction, in which the lessons, instead of being formal recitations, exercises, explanations, or lectures, consist of a familiar discourse by the teacher, interspersed with questions or remarks by the pupils; that is to say, in which the lessons partake of the character of conversations, both as to the manner of presenting the subject and the style of language employed. This mode of teaching is especially adapted to young children, because it affords the teacher a constant opportunity to appeal to their intelligence and experience, and to employ the simplest colloquial expressions. Besides, the utmost freedom being given to the pupils, they are enabled to show by their questions and remarks to what extent and in what respect they need special instruction and information. In order to arouse and sustain the pupils' interest, their attention is called to such facts in connection with the subject as, although quite obvious when shown or explained, are usually overlooked by children, who are generally but superficial observers before being trained to close attention and careful investigation. In object teaching, the lessons should always be conversational, the teacher saying only enough to lead the pupils to observe, and to talk freely about what they notice.

CORPORAL PUNISHMENT. See PUNISHMENT.

COURSE OF INSTRUCTION

COURSE OF INSTRUCTION, or Course of Study, is a series of subjects of instruction or study, arranged in the order in which they should *Definition* be pursued, and grouped or divided into grades, each to be *and des-* completed in a certain time. Such an arrangement of studies *ignations.* is sometimes called a *graded course*, and, especially in superior instruction, a *curriculum*. When these various subjects are arranged in the form of a daily order of exercises, showing the time, or the number of lessons, to be given to each subject, it constitutes the school *programme*.

In order that the objects of intellectual education may be fully attained, it is of the greatest importance that the course of instruction should be *Require-* judicious in respect to several points: (1) The selection of sub- *ments.* jects; (2) Their order or arrangement; (3) The number prescribed for simultaneous study; (4) The division of the course into grades, with a definite time assigned for the completion of each. The first of these considerations is of paramount importance; since the subjects of study constitute not only the basis of intellectual culture, but the source *Points to* of necessary information. Two points, consequently, are to be *be consid-* considered in this selection: (1) The value of the subjects as *ered.* means of culture; (2) Their importance as sources of information. In the early stages of education, the first of these considerations should, without doubt, have the preference; but, as education advances, the second claims an increasing degree of attention, until in the sphere of technical and professional education, it becomes almost the exclusive aim. We cannot, therefore, decide upon a course of instruction, without considering the nature of the mind to be educated as well as the objects for which it is to be educated. In elementary or primary education, *Grouping* the necessary subjects of instruction may be grouped into the *of subjects.* following: (1) *Language*, including reading and elocution, spelling, the analysis and definition of words, grammar, and composition; (2) *Rudimentary Mathematics*, including arithmetic, mental and written, algebra, and geometry; (3) *Elementary Science*, or a knowledge of *things*, graded from the simple perceptive facts of object instruction up to the rudiments of geography, natural history, physiology, physics, astronomy, etc.; (4) *History*; (5) *Graphics*, — writing, drawing, etc.; (6) *Athletics*, — gymnastics or calisthenics. To these may be added music, vocal or instrumental, which constitutes a part of *esthetics*. In addition to these branches of study, in some cases, the rudiments of a foreign language are also taught. The distinction between primary and secondary instruction not being definitely fixed as to subjects, some of those mentioned above may be deemed exclusively appropriate to the higher grade. For proper mental discipline, there must, however, be instruction in things as well as words, — the perceptive and conceptive faculties must be trained as well as the expressive faculties, so that the mind may be stored with ideas and their *Primary* representatives in language. A proper discrimination between *and secon-* primary and secondary instruction depends upon (1) the kind *dary in-* of instruction, and (2) the subjects of instruction. Science *struction.* taught in the high school is a very different thing from science in the primary school; in the one case we address to a much greater extent the higher faculties, — abstraction, generalization, reasoning, etc.; in the other, chiefly the perceptive and conceptive faculties. The subjects of elementary instruction have been classified by an eminent educator as follows: "(1) *Reading and Writing*—the mastery of letters; (2) *Arithmetic*—the mastery of numbers; (3) *Geography*—the mastery over place; (4) *Grammar*—the mastery over the word; (5) *History*—the mastery over time."

In schools of secondary instruction (high schools, academies, etc.), the course includes also language—the vernacular, and one or more modern languages, and also the rudiments of Latin and Greek, particularly in preparatory schools; mathematics, including algebra, geometry, trigonometry, mensuration, etc.; science (taught as such), including physics and chemistry, astronomy (descriptive, at least), physiology, etc.; to which are usually added English literature, rhetoric, the elements of mental and moral philosophy, etc. What properly belongs to a high school or academic course is, however, far from being settled; indeed, to fix the line of demarcation between primary and secondary instruction has scarcely been attempted; hence, what should constitute the course of study in schools of this grade is an open question, which is usually determined by the circumstances and special aim of the school. Thus, the course for a business college, for example, is very different from that of a collegiate or preparatory school. The theory of the common-school system in the United States requires that the pupil should enter the high school with a good knowledge of the studies already mentioned;—at least, reading, writing, arithmetic, geography, English grammar, and the history of the United States; but it is a great error to suppose that these subjects can be fully mastered by an immature mind. "Until all educators," says a thoughtful teacher, "shall agree as to the precise culture power of each study, as well as to the exact value of its imparted information, and shall determine, to the satisfaction of all, what particular faculties each calls into activity, and just how the calling into action of these faculties educates a man, it will be impossible to establish a course of study which all shall acknowledge as absolutely the best."

Higher course.

Basis of graduation.

The division of the course of instruction into grades is sometimes made by *topics*, and sometimes by *text-books*; and each method has its advocates. The former, it is claimed, gives more freedom to the teacher — more scope for the exercise of intelligent discrimination and original treatment; the instruction proceeds to a greater extent from the living teacher, since there is less inducement to confine it to a mere hearing of recitations. The subject is the paramount consideration; the text-book, the secondary. The teacher, and the pupil also as far as possible, is required to consult various books, to compare their statements, to correct their errors; and thus, while perhaps a particular text-book is used as a basis for the instruction, a more general knowledge of the subject is imparted than is contained in any single work. Thus, if the study is the history of the United States, to one grade is assigned the *Colonial History;* to another, the period of the *Revolution* and the *Establishment of the Federal Government*, etc.; while, if the division were by book, it would be necessary that all the schools should use the same, and a certain number of pages would be assigned to each grade. For absolute uniformity, of course, the second plan is preferable; but some educators claim that uniformity may be carried too far, constituting a Procrustean standard, and tending to deprive the instruction of one of its most essential qualities, —its adaptability to different minds. Evidently the topical system makes more demands upon the teacher; and this, it is claimed, constitutes its great advantage, since it necessitates better information, higher culture, and more real teaching ability. What kind of development, it is asked, can result from the mere hearing of recitations? And what kind of influence can be exerted by a teacher that never goes beyond the narrow scope of the school text-book? Not that the legitimate use of text-books is to be discouraged, but only a servile dependence upon them; and it is claimed that the prescribing of topics rather than books, tends to prevent this. Says D. P. Page, in *Theory and Practice of Teaching*, "A teacher who is perfectly familiar with what is taught, has ten times the vivacity of one who is obliged to follow the very letter of the book." See THOMAS HILL, *The True Order of Studies* (N. Y., 1876).

Topical system.

CRAMMING, a term used in regard to education, to denote the fault of filling the mind with facts, without allowing it sufficient time to arrange and generalize them, to compare them with its previous acquisitions, or to determine their real significance, as related to general principles. It is thus a kind of mental stuffing, and, consequently, is opposed to the true object of education, which, as the word etymologically considered implies, is not to pour something into the mind, but to bring out, by appropriate exercise, its latent faculties. In college phrase, students are said to *cram* for an examination, when they make preparation with undue haste, impressing upon their memory by repetition a mass of things about which they expect to be questioned, but which, when the examination is over, they immediately forget. Such a process is exceedingly injurious to the mind, since it is a misdirection of its powers, wasting them at a time when they should be all steadily employed in the formation of those habits of acquisition and thought, which constitute the basis of a sound intellectual character.

In elementary education, cramming is, therefore, especially pernicious; and it is at this stage that it is the most likely to occur. It may assume various forms, but chiefly the following: (1) Crowding the memory with verbal *formulæ*, — definitions, rules, statements of facts, names in geography, dates in history, etc.; (2) Overtasking the powers of the mind with a multiplicity of studies, or with such as are not adapted to its immature condition, and, therefore, cannot be comprehended; (3) Undue haste in instruction, so that the pupils are compelled to commit to memory what they have had no time properly to digest in their minds. Cramming may be the result either of the ignorance of the teacher, or of circumstances which compel him to violate the correct principles of education for some special end, as the preparation of pupils for a public exhibition in which they may make an imposing display of their superficial acquirements. Such a sad perversion of the teacher's work as this implies is of too frequent occurrence; for parents and patrons are too fond of witnessing such displays, and there are teachers whose eagerness for praise or patronage is sufficient to overcome their sense of the true object of their vocation.— See BLACKIE, *On Self-Culture* (Edinburgh, 1875).

CRECHE, a french word signifying a *crib* or *manger*, but used in France, Belgium, and some other countries in Europe to designate a kind of infant asylum.

CRUELTY (to Animals) is often a prevailing trait in the characters of children who have not been specially trained to habits of kind, considerate, and humane feeling and conduct. The activity of a child's nature, its love of sport, and its undeveloped sympathies predispose it to acts of inconsiderate cruelty. The need of educating the sympathetic affections in order to counteract this tendency in youthful minds has been very generally recognized by educators. Habitual training, not mere precepts, can alone effect this. Locke is very earnest on this point. "Children," says he, "should be accustomed from their cradles to be tender to all sensible creatures." See *Cyclopædia of Education.*

CULTURE, a term used to denote the improvement of the human character by means of discipline, training, or self-exertion. It is used in *Definition.* both an active and a passive sense; in the former, implying the use of all necessary means and agencies to cultivate the human faculties, and in the latter, the result of their operation. Culture comprehends both development and refinement; that is, not simply bringing into active exercise the latent powers of the mind or body, but adding thereto a nice and careful discrimination as to their proper or improper exercise, with a due regard to the circumstances which require their employment. Thus a man of culture not only is able to express his thoughts in suitable and impressive language, but knows how to adapt his language to the persons, the place, and the occasions which call for this expression; nor does he give utterance to his thoughts except when it is proper to do so. Hence, culture, in its mature stage, not only implies power, but restraint, both belonging to the inner nature of the individual. There are as many *Different kinds.* kinds of culture as there are departments of human nature, or special faculties, to be cultivated and improved. Thus, culture may be physical, intellectual, moral, spiritual, and esthetic, according as its scope is the improvement of the powers and susceptibilities of the body, the intellect, the moral sentiments, the soul, or the taste. General culture implies that everything constituting the character of the individual has been brought to as high a degree of improvement as is possible. Special culture has reference to a particular department of human nature, or to the development of power in a certain direction. Thus, the culture of the poet, the painter, the orator, the teacher, the lawyer, or the clergyman is special, developing faculties needed in the particular vocation of each. Special culture, however, does not exclude general culture; for no man need be merely a practitioner, or worker in any narrow sphere of effort. The object of higher education is to give this general culture as a basis for that which is necessarily special, or technical.

The real instrumentality, — in a certain sense the only one, by which culture can be effected, is self-exertion. None of the faculties, whether of *Self-exer-* the spirit, mind, or body, can be cultivated except by exercise. *tion.* Thus a person can never learn to compose by studying grammar and rhetoric, nor to think and reason by committing to memory the rules of logic. If he would learn to write, or to think and reason, he must write and think and reason, on the same principle and in the same way as a person learns to swim, or a child to walk. This exercise is the individual's own work; but the exercise may be unsuitable and injurious, and, therefore, needs, at first, the careful guidance of experience. Hence, the need of an educator, until the individual has acquired sufficient knowledge and experience to direct the exercise himself. This shows the relation of education and culture, the one being the handmaid of the other. The instruments of culture vary with its special scope. For those of physical culture, we must learn what a knowledge of physiology and experience in gymnastics dictate; those of intellectual culture can be judiciously selected only by studying the laws which regulate the operations of the mind. But we are particularly to be on our guard in supposing that intellectual culture can spring from the mere study of other persons' ideas. True culture of this kind can alone come from (1) a patient, laborious, and diligent acquisition of ideas of our own, by observation and reflection; and (2) the study of the experience of other minds, and its verification, as far as possible, by that of our own. "The original and proper sources of knowledge," says Professor Blackie, "are not books, but life, experience, personal thinking, feeling, and acting." And again, "All knowledge which comes from books comes indirectly, by reflection, and by echo; true knowledge grows from a living root in the thinking soul; and whatever it may appropriate from without, it takes by living assimilation into a living organism, not by mere borrowing." (See *Self-Culture*, Edinburgh 1875.) This is simply an emphatic and illustrative expansion of the general principle above stated; namely, that to cultivate our faculties we must properly exercise them. No moral culture can be secured by the study of ethics; legitimate objects for the exercise of the moral feelings must be sought for and discovered; and, more especially, the will must be trained so that it will obey the voice of reason and conscience, even amid the mightiest tempest of passion and desire. Related to this, is the culture of the soul — a culture which is paramount to all, and to which every other species of culture is subservient; and just as one can learn to walk only by walking, to think only by thinking, and to live nobly only by acting nobly on every occasion, so one can advance in spiritual culture only by communing, by prayer and contemplation, with the Great Spirit, the Father of mankind, and the Creator of the universe. True Christian culture comprehends the development of a capacity to do right, and to be right, in every relation which we bear to each other, and to our Maker, simply by applying the general principle herein enunciated, of active beneficence, based upon the simplest principles of moral and religious truth. (See EDUCATION.)

Instruments of Culture.

Moral Culture.

Soul Culture.

Christian Culture.

CURRICULUM. See COURSE OF INSTRUCTION.

DACTYLOLOGY. (Gr. δάκτυλος, a finger), a method of communicating ideas by means of signs made with the fingers, composing what is called the manual or finger alphabet, and employed by the deaf and dumb. There are two alphabets of this kind: the single-hand alphabet, and the two-hand alphabet.

DEAF-MUTES, or **Deaf and Dumb,** a class of persons, scattered throughout every nation in a greater or less proportion, who cannot hear the sound of the human voice, and, consequently, lose that sympathetic association which exists between the organs of hearing and speech, so that the latter are rendered inactive. Two methods or systems of teaching are in use (with some modifications) in nearly all the institutions in the world. *Method of teaching.* One is that of *articulation* and *lip-reading* (sometimes called the German method, because used in most of the German schools), the other that of *writing,* or the *sign language.* Both have their special advocates; and each it is claimed, possesses superior facilities for educating the deaf and dumb. In teaching articulation, the pupil is placed before the teacher, who begins with the vowels, and requires the pupil to watch the motions he makes with his mouth, lips, and throat; he places the pupil's hand upon his own throat, so as to feel the different movements, and then imitate them himself. When he has succeeded in some degree, the consonants are introduced and practiced for a longer or shorter time, according to the ability or aptitude of the pupil. Simple words are then introduced, and their meaning illustrated by pointing out the object, action, etc.; and as progress is made in this, qualities and actions are introduced. This course must be continued, and the lessons repeated, till the pupil can read the lips of the teacher, and communicate his own thoughts, in questions and answers. Reading must then be taught; and the knowledge of language already acquired aids the pupil in understanding what he reads. It will be apparent that this is a work requiring much time and patience on the part of the teacher as well as of the pupil, merely to acquire the meaning of the words and their proper pronunciation. Most *Articulation system.* of the institutions in the United States give more or less instruction in articulation, generally in special departments. The Clarke Institution, the Boston Day School, the N. Y. Institution for Improved Instruction, and Whipple's Home School make articulation a specialty. This mode of teaching is especially adapted to the condition of *semi-mutes,* who still retain some remnant of the ability to use spoken language. Experience has shown that children deprived of the sense of hearing can learn by means of sight and feeling, to distinguish the various elements of speech, to read them from the speaker's lips, and to imitate them in articulation.

The other method, writing and sign-making, is substantially taught in the following manner: An object is shown to the pupil, as for example, a *cat,* and the natural sign made for it, an outline is then drawn on the slate, *Writing and sign-making.* and c-a-t is written in the outline; the same sign is applied to the name as was applied to the object and the outline; and the pupil thus learns the word. The object is removed and the outline rubbed out; the same sign is used for the word alone, and the pupil soon associates it with the object. Other objects are presented, and the same process repeated. The color of the cat is then taught; as, if black, that is joined to the name, and *black cat* is learned; then action is represented, as *black cat eats;* and then the object follows, *black cat eats meat.* The phrases are lengthened as the pupil proceeds, and short stories are related by signs, and written down by the pupil, the proper distinctions being made at the time, so that the pupil, in a short time, is enabled to use language properly. An important feature of this method is, that the pupil begins at once to learn words which convey meaning, without the slow process of learning the alphabet, the single letters of which convey no ideas; and in this manner the mind is quickened, and incited to redoubled activity by the knowledge gained. As this proceeds, the pupil becomes familiar with the printed as well as the written characters, and soon understands short simple phrases; and then only a few months are required to enable the pupil to understand clearly what is related to him. For further information, and statistics, see *Cyclopædia of Education*.

DECIMAL NOTATION, the ordinary method of expressing numbers on a scale of ten, ten units of any order being equal to one unit of the next higher order. The first lessons in arithmetic should give the pupil a clear idea of the principle of this notation. This can be done by means of the *numeral frame* (q. v.).

DECLAMATION, or the formal delivery of set speeches or of memorized pieces of oratory, is a school exercise of considerable importance, when conducted in a proper manner and with a due regard to its special uses and limitations. The objects chiefly to be gained by exercises of this kind are the following: (1) The training and culture of the voice; (2) Practice in elocution; (3) The habit of speaking in public with confidence, ease, and grace; (4) The cultivation of a taste for public speaking; (5) An improvement of the pupils' style of composition. In the education of boys and young men particularly, these are all points of great importance, inasmuch as the ability to speak effectively in public is of great value in all civilized communities.

Objects to be kept in view.

The following points should be carefully attended to in giving elementary instruction in declamation: (1) The piece to be declaimed should be well studied, not only in its language, but in regard to the thoughts, emotions, reasoning, etc. which it may involve, and the circumstances under which it was originally spoken, as well as the character of the speaker; (2) Minute rudimentary criticism should be rendered unnecessary by sufficient preliminary training in enunciation and other departments of elocution, as well as in the use of gesticulation; (3) The various kinds of gestures having been taught, the pupil should be allowed great freedom in respect to their use; (4) The spirit, and not simply the form, should be the object aimed at in the instruction; and no piece should be assigned to a pupil to speak which is beyond his capacity to understand and appreciate. The pupils of the common schools are generally not advanced sufficiently to receive theoretical instruction in rhetorical delivery; but this should find a place in the course of instruction of colleges, academies, and schools of a higher grade in general. Even the pupils of elementary schools, however, may be benefited by appropriate exercises in recitation and declamation; thus, the speaking of easy and interesting dialogues by two or more children will be found one of the best methods to impart to young pupils a practical knowledge of the elementary rules of declamation, besides cultivating a natural style of speaking.

Points to be attended to.

DEFINITION. In giving instruction upon any subject, the need of defining terms constantly arises, in order (1) that the mind may clearly conceive the object to which they are intended to apply, and (2) that the mind may understand what that object is as distinguished from all others. Hence, clearness of ideas and precision of thought depend upon accuracy of definition; for without this there must be a confusion of language which will preclude the possibility of correct thinking or reasoning. This may arise either from a dim conception of the thing spoken of, or from a misapplication of the term used to denote it. It is a part of the fundamental work of the teacher to instill the habit of accurately defining the terms employed in every subject taught. This is generally recognized, but the principle is not always correctly applied. It is customary with many teachers, and most writers of elementary text books, to begin with definitions, because this seems to be the most logical in the formal treatment of any subject; but this practice is opposed to well-established principles of pedagogy. Definitions are dependent upon abstraction and generalization; and, without a knowledge of the concrete details from which they have been deduced, they often convey no distinct ideas to the mind. Definition should not be confounded with description: the former includes only what is required to distinguish the objects referred to from other objects; the latter should comprehend all that is required to convey to the mind a complete and vivid idea of the thing described. In teaching, we should rather begin with description and end with definition; and, when, by this twofold process, the idea of what we wish to convey to the pupils' mind has been made distinct in itself and distinguished from all other things, the proper term should be associated with it. This is in accordance with the requirements of the *developing method (q. v.)*.

Object of.

Relation to clearness of ideas.

Place of, in teaching.

DEFINITIONS, a branch of elementary education, usually having reference to instruction in the meaning of words. The operations of a child's mind naturally lead to a knowledge of words as representatives of ideas; and, at quite an early age, a child acquires a very extensive vocabulary of terms and the ability to apply them properly, since they are learned not by formal statement or definition, but by hearing them used, and by subsequent practice in using them in connection with the actual objects or conceptions which they represent. In this way, the words which young children learn make but little impression upon their minds as *words*; but they are so intimately associated with the objects, actions, and qualities which they represent, that they convey to the mind the same ideas as the objects, actions, etc. themselves. The school exercises or lessons designed to increase the child's vocabulary, or to teach the meaning of words found in books, often disregard this natural method of acquisition, and attempt to teach the meaning of individual words by means of their approximate synonyms, without any regard to their application, or use in phrases and sentences. Without an embodiment of words in actual speech the recitation of formal definitions is of no use. After sufficient illustration of this kind, the pupil should be required to tell, in his own language, the meaning of the word in question, which the teacher can then correct. No exercise in synonyms is of any value, but on the contrary, rather injurious, until the meaning of words has been thus explained. In

A child's vocabulary.

Proper method of teaching.

oral lessons in definitions to classes, one pupil may be required to use the given word in a phrase or sentence, another to explain its meaning, and another to give a brief definition by a synonymous phrase or word. Very simple words, the meaning of which is already known to the child, should not be given for formal definition; since properly to define such words, requires a nice discrimination in the use of language, and a minuteness of analysis beyond the capacity of a young child. A full exercise of this kind should comprise the following: (1) To pronounce the word; (2) To use it in the construction of a phrase or a sentence; (3) To define it; (4) To write a sentence illustrating its meaning and use. [A written exercise for the whole class, each pupil writing a different sentence.] Instruction in the derivation of words and the meaning of the common prefixes and suffixes should be commenced at an early stage.

DEGREES are titles of rank conferred upon students in colleges and universities, as evidence of their proficiency in the arts and sciences, or upon learned men as a testimony of their literary merits. At first, the terms *master* and *doctor* were applied indifferently to any person engaged in teaching in the university. In process of time, the term *master* was restricted to teachers of the liberal arts and the term *doctor* to divinity, law, and medicine. When regulations were established to prevent unqualified persons from teaching, and an initiatory stage of discipline was prescribed, these terms became significant of a certain rank, and of the possession of certain powers, and were called *gradus*, — steps or degrees. Below is given a list of the various degrees usually conferred in this country, with the usual abbreviations employed to designate them.

The colleges for females confer, in the place of the title Bachelor (of Letters, of Arts, of Liberal Arts), the title Graduate, though they retain the abbreviations L. B., A. B., and B. L. A.

A. B., Bachelor of Arts.
A. L., Laureate of Arts.
A. M., Master of Arts.
A. S., Sister of Arts.
B. A., Bachelor of Agriculture.
B. Arch., Bachelor of Architecture.
B. C. E., Bachelor of Civil Engineering.
B. L A., Bachelor of Liberal Arts.
B. M. E., Bachelor of Mining Engineering.
C. E., Civil Engineer.
C. & M. E., Civil and Mining Engineer.
D. B , Bachelor of Divinity.
D. C. L., Doctor of Civil Laws.
D. D., Doctor of Divinity.
D. D. M., Doctor of Dental Medicine.
D. E., Dynamic Engineer.
D. Sc., Doctor of Science.
L. B., Bachelor of Letters.
LL. B., Bachelor of Laws.
LL. D., Doctor of Laws.
L Sc., Laureate of Science.
M. B., Bachelor of Medicine.
M. D., Doctor of Medicine.
M. E., Mining Engineer.
M. F. L., Mistress of English Literature.
M. L. A., Mistress of Liberal Arts.
M. L. L., Mistress of Liberal Learning.
M. Sc., Mistress of Science.
Mis. Mus., Mistress of Music.
Mus. B., Bachelor of Music.
Mus. D., Doctor of Music.
Ph. B., Bachelor of Philosophy.
Ph. D., Doctor of Philosophy.
Sc. B., Bachelor of Science.
Sc. M., Master of Science.
S. T. D., Sacrae Theologiae Doctor.

DEPARTMENTAL SYSTEM, or **Subject System**, a method of school organization in which each department of instruction or subject of study is assigned to a particular teacher, instead of requiring each teacher to give instruction to a particular class in all the branches of study pursued. This system is rarely employed in schools for primary instruction; but, in those of a higher grade, is nearly universal. In regard to its advantages and disadvantages, as compared with the class system, many considerations are urged; and the experience of instructors seems to be quite diverse as to its success. The chief argument in its favor is, that it would narrow the range of subjects required to be mastered by a single teacher, and, in this way, improve the character of the instruction imparted. For other considerations in regard to this question, see CLASS.

DEVELOPING METHOD (in German *entwickelnde Methode*) is a term introduced into the science and practice of pedagogy through the philosophy of Herbart, and popularized among European teachers through its greatest followers, Beneke and Diesterweg. It means an education of the natural endowments of the individual according to the psychologic laws of human development, and to the exclusion of all purposes foreign to such development. The term, in some respects, is a misnomer, as it implies far more than it expresses. It means a system, realized in, or applicable to, a variety of educational methods, and based on the fundamental principle, that human nature alone, as developed and shown in its best products through a long historical period, should be the guiding star in all educational efforts. Herbart, who was the first among the German philosophers, in opposition to the prevailing speculative philosophy, to apply the method of induction to philosophy, and who based his system on inductive psychology, and treated the latter mathematically, wrote, as early as 1806, a work on pedagogy in which the new drift of educational ideas inaugurated by Rousseau and Pestalozzi, was reduced to logical principles. He was the first in history to render intelligible the processes in the human soul which lead to memory, comparison, the distinction of impressions and their growth into mental images, notions, judgment and reason, disposition and will; and, in so doing, he reasoned from the established facts of consciousness, and developed a long series of mathematical *formulæ* as evidences of his correctness in interpreting the facts. Beneke, more straight-forward than Herbart, gave, in his *Lehrbuch der Psychologie als Naturwissenschaft* (1833), and *Erziehungs- und Unterrichtslehre* (1835), a very lucid and common-sense exposition of this new system of psychology, in its application to pedagogy, which, through Diesterweg's practical treatises and school books, grew almost universally popular among the German teachers. The founders of this system did not go so far as to reach all the legitimate conclusions which may logically be derived from its principles, and which were drawn by the succeeding generation of teachers.

Definition.

Herbart's system.

Beneke and Diesterweg.

Improvements.

The system, as now taught and practiced by men like Dittes and some of Froebel's followers, has undergone a series of gradual improvements, and seems capable of many more; since human nature itself is a subject that receives, through the constant improvement of all the natural sciences, a daily increasing illustration. Nor is there, as yet, a complete agreement among the foremost pedagogical writers upon what may be considered the genuine development of human nature; but the principle itself, that the spontaneous growth of all the faculties of the mind into the greatest possible harmony should be facilitated according to the laws of normal development, which are to be faithfully followed, not counteracted; guided, but not curbed — and all this in the order which is indicated by nature herself — this principle seems to be so well established, that, henceforth, only its interpretation can be doubtful.

This new psychology sails clear of all the rocks of preceding systems and of the maelstrom of party strife; it deals with none but demonstrable

DEVELOPING METHOD

Foundation facts. facts. Such facts are, that the unfolding of intelligence and mental activity in the newborn child is caused by impressions from without; that the latter, called *traces*, cannot grow into distinct images without a grouping of the traces in an order corresponding to the outward objects; that we can verify by actual experiment, both with animals and men, the laws according to which equal traces strengthen each other, and similar ones aggregate and form opposites to dissimilar groups of traces; that fugitive impressions have obscure traces, lasting or often repeated impressions, clear traces; that one trace or set of traces is for a time obscured by new ones, and that the consciousness of an image is the effect of either pleasure or pain of the mind in consequence of the impressions, etc., etc.

Mental processes. The theory goes on to show that all the higher mental processes are repetitions of the photographic action of the first traces, in a higher order, and follow with mathematical exactness their laws. A normal pedagogy is, therefore, possible, independent of philosophical systems. Disputed questions of physiology and psychology concern only unimportant topics, and, therefore, may be ignored and left to the future development of science; but it is all-important in pedagogy to demonstrate clearly all the conditions without which no mind can grow, whatever the nature of mind itself may be.

It is, therefore, of the first importance to cultivate the action of the senses, the gates to all mental development, in such a way as to render them self-active by their appropriate combination with pleasure *Progressive steps.* and pain; next, to offer to their self-activity a succession of outward impressions which will leave distinct and, by repetition, lasting traces and the most complete images of objects, accompanied by sensations and impulses. The first consciousness being thus awakened, it follows that a comparison and distinction of the representations once produced must lead to both clear notions of their single features and clear consciousness of the mind, without which the origin of *self-consciousness* would be retarded, and its growth stunted. The latter taking its start from the first efforts in speaking, language becomes the chief means of education, and its proper use on the part of the educator, in connection with the objects designated, the way to the subsequent normal development. The gap in this system left between this stage and the first school age was not filled until Froebel, starting from a somewhat different stand-point, invented his kindergarten plays.

Great stress is, in this system, laid on the gradual progress of education, which, after all, is little more than instruction, a somewhat one-sided culture of the intellect, the imagination, and the memory. The *Practical rules.* teacher is to proceed from the *simple* to the *compound*, from the concrete to the *abstract*, from *perception* to *reflection* in the pupil, from *examples* to *rules*, from *facts* to *laws*. He is to be more a guide than a teacher; he is not to tell his pupils any thing which they can be led to find out themselves. He is to present them just mental food enough, and no more, at a time, than can be fully digested; and that food ought to be adapted to the age and degree of development. Every kind of mental food ought to be so fully digested as to contribute to the strengthening of every mental faculty. The pupil is to be rendered his own teacher; his self-activity is to be fostered first, last, and at all times.

The cultivation of the memory at the expense of observation and reflection, which, in all *routine* teaching, plays so prominent a part, is made unnecessary by stimulating the mental appetite and digestive power of the pupil; whatever is fully understood will forever remain mental property. All mechanical drill, and all moral preaching, is more hurtful than useful, because skill in the learner is to grow out of repeated self-appropriation connected with that pleasure which accompanies the satisfaction of every mental appetite; and because an appropriate mental food is conducive to moral power. Development means self-development, guided by well-developed educators.

Routine teaching.

It is evident that this new system exacts a far higher standard of abilities and attainments in the educator than ever before had been deemed necessary. This necessity led to a considerable improvement in the course of training of pupil teachers in the German and other normal schools. "The teacher is the school," was the maxim inculcated there. If he be the proper person destined by natural gifts and prepared for his calling by a careful study of mental phenomena and a long theoretic and practical training, he will make up for the shortcomings of text-books, apparatus, and previous education. If he be full of enthusiasm for his sacred task of forming minds, and patient in all his laborious methods, he will mould his pupils' minds and morals by means of their self-development. The rational sobriety of this system was greatly aided by the marvelous spirit of self-devotion and educational enthusiasm which had been engendered in the teaching fraternity by Pestalozzi; and it may be called a fact, that hardly ever, or anywhere, was there done such intelligent and faithful work in thousands of schools, and for so scanty a remuneration, as in the *developing-method* schools up to the period of the "School Regulations."

Teacher's requirements.

Among the reforms in special methods that followed in the wake of this system, must first be mentioned the introduction of phonic or phonetic reading. Spelling was altogether superseded, and orthographical writing exercises substituted, based on a few rules which the pupils had to deduce for themselves from a comparison of examples. Gräser and Vogel improved this method, which is liable to be too mechanically applied, by combining it with the *writing-reading* and the *synthetico-analytic* methods. The former begins with analyzing the single sounds of which the words consist and teaching the written signs for them, and continues with writing these and other words; printed words, or rather sentences, are introduced when the pupils can read all written letters, and thereafter all that has been read must be faultlessly copied. The latter begins with sentences that must be analyzed into their component words, and the words into their component sounds; the corresponding signs (letters) are then given, either in written, or in printed form, or in both (as in Douai's method, exemplified in his *Rational Readers*) and then synthesis-reading begins, accompanied with constant copying exercises, which must be carefully regulated. Another improvement has been effected by connecting penmanship exercises with the first writing exercises by means of time-beating (*Taktschreiben*). The object is to prevent the formation of careless habits instead of weeding them out when formed, which is still further aimed at by reading *in concert*, alternately with indi-

Reforms in special methods.

DEVELOPING METHOD

vidual reading. In arithmetic, the beginning was made with mental exercises in the analytic method; but there is a great variety in the methods of connecting analysis with ciphering, and in the extent to which it is carried. Great importance, however, is universally attributed to a full understanding of the value of numbers, both single and in their decimal orders. Some methods, progressing through concentric circles of 1—10, 10—100, 100—1000, etc., involve, within each circle, all the four ground rules; some, only addition and subtraction together, and, later, multiplication and division together; some, only one at a time, with larger concentric circles, etc. Some introduce the elements of fractions at a very early stage, dividing them also into concentric circles; some introduce decimal fractions even before common fractions. Object lessons in special branches, according to the older (Pestalozzian) process, were to some extent crowded out when all teaching became *object teaching*; yet special object lessons in zoölogy and botany, geometry and geography, remained favorite branches in most plans of teaching. The method of teaching the mother-tongue is also very variable; but, through all the variety, a tendency is conspicuous to make the most of the pupil's self-activity by guiding him to form sentences orally and in writing, whether for orthographical, grammatical, rhetorical, or elocutionary purposes. Grammatical analysis with parsing occupies far less time than synthesis. It is a strange fact that the study of Latin and Greek has, only recently and to a very limited extent, been subjected to the same method; but the modern languages were treated in the analytico-synthetic way (not to be confounded with the Ahn or Ollendorff method, from which it is distinguished by its scientific, pedagogic spirit, and far greater efficiency). There is an endless variety of special methods in all branches of primary and secondary instruction, which it is not necessary here to explain.

Methods not to be stereotyped. It is useless to discuss the merits and shortcomings of special methods, since any one of them that has passed the ordeal of a practical application in the school room may be called good, because adapted to the genius both of the teacher and his particular class of pupils. No single practical method can claim universal applicability; since every one will need to be modified in order to be adapted, not only to the teacher's peculiar development, but also to that of the class or pupil. He is a bad follower of the *developing method* who treats, year in and year out, every new class of pupils according to a stereotyped manner for each branch of instruction, instead of accommodating himself to the wants of the class. The *developing method* means nothing more nor less than that there shall be *method* in all the teacher's doings, — a well-concerted plan, calculated to develop every gift of each pupil by educating him to self-activity in every branch of the curriculum, and to produce a certain degree of uniform general development without neglecting either the forward, or the backward portion of the class. And high as this standard of effectiveness may be, experience proves that it will be almost universally realized, if the position of the teacher be sufficiently remunerative, independent, and honored, to attract to the profession all persons born to be teachers. This realization has, moreover, been considerably facilitated by the preparation for primary classes, obtained from Froebel's kindergarten.

DIARY, School, a daily record of the lessons, recitations, deportment, etc., of pupils, kept in a small book which is taken home each day, or each week, to be exhibited to the parents, whose inspection is attested by their signature previous to the diary's being returned to the teacher. Thus, a constant correspondence is kept up between parent and teacher, the former being continuously informed of the child's progress, merit or demerit, and behavior; and thus enabled intelligently to co-operate in his school education. Instead of the diary, some teachers prefer the monthly report.

DICTATION, a school exercise in which the teacher reads or speaks (dictates) to the pupils what is to be written by the latter for practice in writing, spelling, etc. Such exercises are very useful, not only to give accuracy and expertness in writing words and sentences, but to train the ear to the ready apprehension of spoken language. In this respect, it supplements *copying*, which exclusively disciplines the eye.

DIDACTICS, the theory of instruction, as distinguished from that of education in its narrower sense, implying simply moral education. It is commonly treated under two heads: *general didactics*, which exhibits *Definition* the philosophical principles of teaching, and the conditions of *and* its success; and *special didactics*, or *methodics*, which applies *division.* the general truths to the several branches of instruction, the different ages to be instructed, and the various individual characters and their treatment. The distinction between didactics and pedagogy in the narrower sense is made only for the sake of separate scientific treatment, as it is universally conceded that all instruction can be rendered *All* a means of moral education, and that no instruction deserves *instruction* the name, or can be truly successful, without a corresponding *moral.* development of moral power. In any branch of instruction, the very first beginning presupposes *attention* on the part of the pupil, while the progress made will depend on his *self-activity*, and his ultimate mastership on his full appropriation of all the *moral power* inherent in the branch of art or science concerned. On the part of the teacher, moral power, engendered by such mastership, must be presupposed, if he is to impart to his pupil attention, self-activity, and love for the *Consid-* subject. In regard to the age of the pupil, instruction and *eration of* moral education bear to each other a changing proportion. *age.* During the first age,—from earliest infancy up to the eighth or tenth year, the so-called *formal purpose* of education prevails in importance; the several functions of the youthful mind must be made self-active, and the *material purpose* of didactics,—the acquisition of knowledge or positive learning, must be made a mere means to the former, so that no more of each concentric circle of facts be given to appropriate than can be digested for the benefit of each function. The second age, which extends to the beginning of sexual maturity, is the one during which instruction and education should be, as it were, in equipoise; while, in the period after sexual maturity, the material purpose, that of the acquisition of knowledge and skill, may preponderate. In regard to the branches of instruction, general didactics shows which of these are adapted to the several stages of the mental and moral development of the three ages, and which concentric circle of facts and truths of every science and art may be introduced at the time when it can serve as wholesome mental and moral food. A most important distinction is made between the pedagogical and the scientific treatment of every subject of instruction, *Pedagogi-* the latter being of necessity *systematic* and *synthetic*, while the *cal and* former should be *methodic* and *analytic* first, *synthetic* last; *scientific* that is to say, should introduce every object of learning at *treatment.* such a time, and in such a manner, that it may be mentally and morally appropriated.

Special didactics, commonly designated as *methodics*, treats of the pedagogical means proper in each branch of instruction, at each age and stage of development. An explanation of the more important *Special* methods of didactics will be found under the titles of the various *didactics.* branches. In general, however, we may state that all prominent educators concur in holding that the teacher is every-where the best method, as he is in fact the school itself, if he be a true teacher. It would, however, be a dangerous error to suppose, on that account, that every teacher should be left free to invent his own methods, or could be expected to be successful without an acquaintance with the best methods in use. This error will be avoided by those who, on the one hand, are so deeply imbued with the great responsibility of their calling, as to feel that the wisdom of the preceding generations of great teachers cannot be neglected, and, therefore, that the methods devised and practiced by them should be made a subject of faithful and conscientious study; but who, on the other hand, realize the principle that the most approved methods cannot benefit a teacher who has not mentally so appropriated them as to reproduce them according to his own individuality, and to be able to adapt them to the peculiar wants of his pupils, as well as to all other circumstances in which he is placed. All teaching should be methodical in every aspect; it should be based on the thorough appropriation of a proper system of pedagogy; and it should be a natural outgrowth of the teacher's personality, if it is to perform its proper office in the work of real education.

DILIGENCE, the virtue of constancy in labor, is an important, though not the sole, means of success in any branch of human calling. It is a function of the will power, as distinguished from intellect and sensation, and is of spontaneous growth, wherever the occupation is akin to the inclination and productive of pleasure. It can, therefore, artificially be engendered only by connecting the occupation with pleasurable emotions that are not foreign to the subject. Where the latter are missing, only dire necessity can keep diligence alive, — either some necessity from natural, or from positive law. But then diligence has ceased to be a virtue, though it may continue as a habit, mechanically as it were. In education, diligence is more powerful than natural adaptation, as all the experience derived from the history of great men shows. It is the office of pedagogy to promote diligence in the pupils by spontaneous growth, as is done in the kindergarten system of education. Where such spontaneous growth has not been effected by early influences, an artificial growth must be cultivated; but the pleasurable emotions to be connected with the occupation, should be prompted as little as possible by means foreign to the subject, such as, for instance, outward punishments, rewards, purely mechanical discipline, or the stimulus of ambition. Whatever the occupation or study in which pupils are required to engage, they should, as soon as possible, be induced to take a lively interest in it for its own sake; because such an interest will arouse into active exercise all the best powers of their minds, and thus lead to the most effective and salutary educational discipline. Besides, the habit of depending upon external incentives,— the love of distinction, of praise, of pleasure, or of gain, must necessarily engender selfishness, and thus narrow and debase the mind which a generous, earnest zeal in the pursuit of a praiseworthy object would expand and ennoble.

DIPLOMA (Gr. δίπλωμα, any thing doubled, or folded), a term anciently given to a formal certificate of authority, because such documents were usually written on double or folded waxen tablets. In more modern times, the term was applied to a royal charter or to any governmental testimonial of authority, privilege, or dignity. (Hence the science of state documents is called *diplomatics*.) The term is now chiefly confined to a certificate given by a university, college, or other literary institution, as an evidence that the person upon whom it is conferred has attained a certain degree of scholarship; or, in the case of professional schools, as a license to practice a particular art.

DISCIPLINE (Lat. *disciplina*, from *discere*, to learn), a term which, according to its literal acceptation, means the condition of a disciple, or learner; that is, subordination requiring strict obedience to certain directions or rules, or conformity with a system of instruction, having for its object some kind of training. Hence the word *discipline* is sometimes used in an active sense as synonymous with training or culture, as in the expression *intellectual* or *moral discipline*. Sometimes it is employed to denote school government; and, frequently also punishment for the commission of offenses. The word, however, should, particularly in education, be confined to its strict meaning as above defined. In all teaching, there is need of attention and obedience on the part of the pupil; and as an important aim of education is to instill certain habits as a basis for the formation of character, the learner must be required constantly and punctiliously to conform to certain rules and general precepts; and the discipline of the teacher is good or bad in proportion as he succeeds in enforcing obedience to these necessary rules. In large schools, the system of regulations becomes more complicated, and a habitual ready attention to them on the part of the pupils produces what is technically called *order*. (See ORDER.) This kind of discipline assimilates to what is required in an army, with the special object of so unifying a large number of men that they may be moved as a single person. In military discipline, the individual is sacrificed to the general object to be attained by its enforcement; indeed, he has no claim to consideration, except what is secondary and subordinate. The danger, in the management of large schools, is that the same principle will be applied, the interests of the pupils as individuals being lost sight of in the endeavor to enforce mere discipline for the purpose of general management or show. In education, however, the interests of the individual should never be disregarded. School machinery, — marching and countermarching, simultaneous movements, the motionless gaze, or the dead silence of multitudes of children, all perhaps trembling under restraint, certainly constitutes a kind of discipline, but a kind, if not absolutely pernicious, of

Definition.

Need of discipline.

Order.

but little educational value. Order is indispensable to the proper working of a school; but it has been well remarked that "good order involves impression rather than repression; it does not consist in a coercion from which result merely silence, and a vacant gaze of painful restraint; but it proceeds from the steady action of awakened and interested intellect, — the kindling of an earnest purpose and an ambition to excel." Hence, the discipline that is necessary to produce order in a school or class, is of secondary importance, in comparison with that which has for its object to train the intellectual and moral nature of the pupils as individuals. "By discipline", says Currie, "we understand the application of the motives which prompt the pupil to diligent study and to good conduct"; that is, such motives as the desire of the approbation of teacher or parent, emulation, or the desire of distinction, the hope of reward, and the fear of punishment. To what extent these motives should be resorted to, and their comparative efficacy in dealing with children of different temperaments and traits of character, constitute important subjects for careful discussion. (See GOVERNMENT, and REWARDS).

Motives to be cultivated.

All moral discipline must be directed to the training of the will; and it is in this connection that the consideration of motives becomes of primary importance. Educators are at considerable variance as to the proper methods of controlling the will of children. Some advocate, in all cases, an application of the law of kindness, and contend that physical force should never be brought in to coerce or restrain even the most self-willed pupil; others are of the opinion, based on experience, as they claim, that, in some cases, physical punishment is indispensable. The best training is, without doubt, that which brings into play the pupil's higher nature, and leaves him habitually actuated by motives derived from it. The child cannot be always restrained by fear, — that is, the fear of immediate physical pain; and, hence, the discipline to which he is to be subjected, should be such as will implant motives and principles of conduct that will be effective as a means of permanent self-control. The mere subduing of the will of children is not sufficient; indeed, it may be injurious. The aim of the teacher should be to bring the will into subjection to conscience and a sense of right: in the words of a distinguished educator, "to discourage the child in the proper development of its nature has a tendency to crush out the life of the child rather than to cultivate that life into better methods of thought and action". The motives brought to bear in the school-room should, as far as possible, be those which will be operative in after life. Special school incentives, such as merit marks etc., are useful and proper within certain limitations; but the great aim should be to dispense with them, and substitute natural for artificial motives — motives that will cling to the child during his whole after life.

Moral discipline.

Subduing the will.

Incentives.

Unnatural discipline.

Unnatural, overstrained discipline, that is, the exaction of a precise conformity with the minor regulations of a school, not only crushes out the individuality of the child for the time, but in its reaction engenders a feeling of resistance in his mind, which, having no outward demonstration, naturally results in a habit of deceit. Nothing is so baneful to the nature of a child as an atmosphere of tyranny and arbitrary power; and any system of discipline that is founded exclusively upon it, must produce the worst effects possible. After all, the best discipline, even if the outward *order* should not be so exact, is that which is brought to bear upon the pupils through the consistent example, and the kindly heart-felt sympathies, of the living teacher, whose very presence is sunshine to his school, and who quells waywardness by the sublimity of his patience, firmness, and perfect self-control. "The discipline of a school", says Baldwin, in *The Art of School Management* (New York, 1881), "should be intrusted to no one unfamiliar with the science of duty, for everything of value to human beings is involved in this science" (See CONSCIENCE, CULTURE OF.)

The teacher.

DISGRACE. See PUNISHMENT.

DIVERSIONS. An important part of the education of youth consists in affording them an opportunity for natural, unrestrained diversions, in which they may have free scope to exercise mind and body, particularly the latter, according to their inclinations. During the early period of childhood, no tasks can be or need be imposed to guide or accelerate the natural development of the mental and physical faculties; the buds of humanity open of themselves, if their condition is normal, and their growth is not arrested by injudicious interference. At first, nature, as a wise educator, trains through the pleasurable emotions; for the impulses which she inspires are all to varied activity, and activity is delight when nerves and muscles have the spring of health and vital energy. A few lessons in conscious restraint are all that this period requires or admits. They are purely negative, checking the violence of natural impulse, not urging the child's activity in any particular direction. This is the education of home and parents, when presided over by love and good sense, during the first years of the child's existence,—a period of continuous diversion. When the age for serious application begins, — the season for labor, or occupation under restraint, the educator should strive to make the transition as easy and gentle as possible. Frequent diversions should be intermingled with formal exercises; and much will be gained if those exercises be made to partake of the nature of diversions, by having the characteristics of novelty and variety, and by stimulating the child's curiosity. As the age of the child increases, passing into youth, the times for regular occupation and for recreation, or diversions, become more distinctly separated. The boy or the girl is gradually led to feel that there are duties to be performed, as well as sports to be enjoyed; and that the pleasure received from the latter will be greatly increased by the feeling that it has been earned by a conscientious devotion to the former. Hence, under no circumstances, should youth be deprived of their opportunities for free and innocent recreations, except as a penalty for misdoing or neglect of duty. The office of diversions is twofold, — recreation and exercise. The former is absolutely essential after studious employment. to refresh the mind; and the latter is needed to give health and vigor to the body. Those sports are the best, therefore, which combine cheerful relaxation of the one with the due employment of the other. Boys, if left to themselves, will take violent exercise, and thus develop their physical powers and promote their growth; and girls will select sports of a lighter

Scope to be given to natural impulse.

Home education.

Diversions in youth.

Office.

Treatment of boys.

character, — such as are adapted to their different physical constitution. It is a serious error on the part of parents to keep their boys under painful restraint, and, from solicitude for their safety, to debar them the enjoyment of diversions common to their age, because attended with some degree of danger. Excessive maternal tenderness and care thus exercised must result in rendering boys effeminate, and unfit to cope with the dangers and trials of subsequent life. The only need of restraint is to keep boys from vicious actions, low company, petulance and a contentious spirit in their sports, and from too daring and perilous feats of agility and strength. Gymnastic exercises may also be made a recreation, and, when carried on with some system, they constitute an important part of a regular physical education. (See GYMNASTICS.) What has been called *athletics*, — rowing, swimming, riding, ball-playing, cricket, etc., are greatly to be encouraged in the maturer periods of youth, not only on account of their effect in developing physical vigor, but because they keep those who actively engage in them from those vicious indulgences which constitute the great peril of that age. As for the more quiet in-door pastimes, they should be encouraged with moderation. Chess and draughts may be permitted; but, in these games, particularly in the former, there is great danger of excess; and it has never been demonstrated that a good chess-player is, on that account, good for any thing but to play chess. The game of billiards gives training to the hand and the eye, and involves considerable exercise, moderate but healthful: yet it may be doubted whether youth should be encouraged to engage in it, because of its fascinating character and its tendency to draw their attention from more useful and necessary employments, not to mention the dangerous associations of the billiard room.

DRAWING, may be divided into two distinct departments, instrumental and free-hand, the former being principally employed in the mechanical, engineering, and architectural branches of industry; the latter, *Divisions.* by artists, designers, and others. The two divisions are sometimes referred to as scientific and artistic, because the subjects coming under the first group, are based on scientific principles, and the results obtained are capable of demonstration by geometry; whilst free-hand work, either in imitation or original design, employs the perceptive rather than the reasoning faculties, and its results have to be judged by the standard of taste, in all the features which do not involve a question of fact.

Instrumental Drawing. — The group of subjects which come under this division may be classified as *elementary* or *applied*; the first teaching methods of obtaining accuracy of form, and its appearance under given conditions; the second applying this power of drawing to practical purposes, in the arts of planning, construction, and design. — The *elementary Subjects.* subjects are: (1) plane geometrical drawing; (2) projection of solids, *(a)* radial or perspective, *(b)* parallel or orthographic; (3) projection of shadows, *(a)* radial or perspective, *(b)* parallel or orthographic and isometric. — The *applied* subjects are: (1) architectural drawing and building construction; (2) machine drawing, construction, and design; civil and military engineering; (3) surveying and topographical drawing; and (4) ship draughting, and marine architecture. — The elementary subjects teach the student how to draw the forms of lines, planes, or solids, either as the eye sees them by perspective, or as they actually exist, by orthographic or isometric projection. The forms usually employed *Forms.* in teaching, are regular geometric planes and solids, conveying, by the instruction given, the principles of representation by lines, on planes of delineation, when the objects are seen in space, or in a defined position in relation to the eye. The study of the elements of instrumental drawing is necessary, therefore, because by it we learn how to draw, as a science, which is obviously required before we can apply it to *Element-* purposes involving a knowledge of the science. The elementary *ary* branches may thus be considered purely educational, whilst the *branches.* advanced or applied divisions may be described as industrial. — In the applied subjects, a knowledge of plane and solid geometry prepares the architectural draughtsman to make working drawings for the builder, *Applied* the carpenter, the mason, and other mechanics employed in the *subjects.* erection and construction of buildings; displaying, by geometrical drawings made to a regular scale, the true forms and dimensions of all parts of the fabric; enabling the builder to calculate exactly the quantity of materials required in its construction, and each artisan to prepare his share of the work, so that it shall truly fit its place. The science of projection and perspective is the basis of the language by which the architect expresses his design for the whole structure, displaying his arrangement of the plan, his design for the elevation, the true form of the building in its several aspects, and the appearance of the whole by means of a perspective view. — Again, in mechanical engineering, the designer *Mechan-* of a machine must be thoroughly acquainted with projection *ical engin-* as a science, before he can express on paper his devices for *eering.* securing the speed and power required for his purpose. Working drawings have then to be made of the several parts and details, to furnish accurate information to the model maker, by which he may make each part of the machine in wood, to the moulder who has to cast it in metal, and for the guidance of the finisher and fitter who complete the work and erect the machine. So, also, in surveying and topographical drawing, the *Surveying,* actual features of a country or an estate are ascertained through *etc.* the application of plane and solid geometry, and reduced from the natural size to a plan which is, in all respects, like the true plan of the original, although on a different scale. By the use of such scale drawings, railways are planned and executed, cities and towns are laid out; and, by civil and military engineers, who employ the same means of delineating their work, cities are drained, supplied with water, or fortified and protected, bridges are built to span the river, and piers made to encroach upon the sea, tunnels made to cut through hills and mountains, and embankments and viaducts to fill the inequalities of valleys. — The *Naval con-* marine engineer or naval constructor is equally dependent upon *struction.* his knowledge of projection, in laying out the lines of his ship or boat, in displaying its capacity for freight, and modeling its shape for speed. All these features of his design are expressed by means of drawings, which are the application of plane and solid geometry to a special industrial purpose. It will be evident, therefore, that the constructive arts, which bear so important a relation to modern civilization, and employ so vast a number of persons, are all dependent upon drawing for the initiation of their schemes. At the foundation of successful work, in any and all of their departments, lies a knowledge of elementary drawing, which, regarded as a language, is of such a character, that it may be efficiently taught in the elementary schools by the regular teachers employed to give instruction in general subjects, as soon as this practically useful subject forms a part of all normal-school education. Pure *Application of* geometry may be considered the study of all these sciences in *geometry.* the abstract, and this is successfully pursued in the schools and colleges; scientific or instrumental drawing, under the headings called elementary subjects, would be the concrete application of geometry to the needs of practical education, to be applied at a future time to actual industry.

Free-Hand Drawing. — As the name implies, this kind of drawing is the expression, by the unassisted hand, of what the eye perceives, or the *What it is.* mind, or imagination, conceives. Its results, therefore, are dependent upon the truthfulness of observation or power of conception possessed by the draughtsman, and, in some measure, upon his manipulative skill as a workman. As a rule, however, the power of drawing, or expression, is equal to the perceptive power, and imperfect or faulty work proceeds generally from a lack of clear understanding of the subject rather than want of hand skill. — As in instrumental drawing, free-hand *Divisions.* drawing consists of two groups of subjects, — elementary and applied, the first being educational, and the second, industrial or professional. In the elementary division, are all those branches of study or exercises which develop the imitative faculties, embracing all kinds of *Elementary, and* copying from flat examples or round objects, including also the subjects of geometrical drawing and perspective, by which alone *applied.* the truthfulness of expressed form can be tested. In applied drawing, the language of form is employed to embody new ideas, either as original designs for industrial art and manufactures, or to express the ideal of fine art, the work of the imagination. It will be seen, therefore, that both scientific and artistic drawing, by instruments or by the free hand, have a common characteristic; they both involve a knowledge of, and skill *Drawing* in, drawing as a language, before the language can by employed *as a* for original purposes. To continue the analogy, and regarding *language.* drawing as the language of form, its alphabet consists of two letters, the straight line and the curve. Simple combinations of these, by elementary practice, produce, as it were, words of one syllable; the grouping of several objects in a drawing, may be described as a sentence; and an original design is the same as a composition or essay on a given theme. The artist uses the expression "out of drawing" in precisely the same sense as a scholar employs the term "ungrammatical", and (other terms being substituted) the criticism which has been made on a poem or a work of fiction, might apply exactly to a historical picture or an ideal *Condition* figure, possessing similar characteristics. To ensure success in *of success.* teaching the subject in the public schools, the following conditions are necessary : (1) Only those elementary branches should be taught which are educational in their influence, and the knowledge conveyed by them of general use (such as have been described as being at the foundation of all constructive industry). (2) Instruction in drawing should begin with school life, and end only when school, college, or university education is completed. (3) At the basis of all instruction is geometrical drawing, which illustrates the facts of regular forms; and perspective, which determines the appearance of those facts. (4) Original design, either elementary or applied, should form a part of the regular exercises required from pupils, alternating with other exercises, such as drawing from memory, and dictation, in order to give variety to the study. (5) The principles of drawing, and of shades and shadows, should first be taught from regular forms, and with scientific method and accuracy, before the pupils are allowed to draw and shade irregular forms, with no guide but their own observation. All practice should proceed from the simple to the complex, from the regular to the irregular, from the fact to its appearance.

The following is suggested as a *course of instruction* for elementary schools:

1st year. — The names of geometric forms and lines; drawing straight lines and their combinations into simple forms; also, the same forms from memory. (All work on the slate.)

2d year. — Dictation and memory drawing of geometric patterns; simple designs composed of straight lines and simple curves. (Slate work.)

3d year. — Practice on paper of what has been previously learned; also in drawing, with readiness, from memory and dictation, forms previously drawn from copy. Designing new combinations from copies.

4th year. — Free-hand outline design, geometrical drawing, model drawing of both curved forms and objects bounded by right lines.

5th year. — Drawing ornaments and objects of historical character, as Egyptian lotus forms, Greek vases, etc.; the same to be drawn also from memory; geometrical drawing of a more advanced character.

6th, 7th, and 8th years. — Free-hand drawing and design, geometrical drawing, model drawing (from the solid object), and free-hand perspective (developing ideas in preparation for advanced work), dictation and memory drawing; design with half-tint back grounds. Botanical names and forms. Colors and the first principles of their harmony. See *Cyclopædia of Education.*

DRILL, a term used in education, particularly in school instruction, to denote the strict routine of exercises required either to train pupils to the ready performance of mental or physical processes, or to impress upon their memory those arbitrary associations of facts or words which are required in many subjects of study. Thus, a certain amount of drill is required in teaching the arithmetical tables, the paradigms and rules of grammar, the spelling of words, and those facts of geography that pertain to the location of places (memorizing maps). Drill requires definite exercises and regular practice in them, continued a sufficient length of time, in order to impart a kind of automatic force to the recollection. Both mind and body, by repetition, acquire fixed habitudes, by means of which thought and muscular action may be accommodated to the performance of acts which at first might have seemed impossible. This is the foundation principle of drill.

DULL SCHOLARS, or Dullards, a class of pupils found in every school and class, whose perceptions are deficient in rapidity, and whose mental powers are sluggish. Such pupils need especially the spur of encouragement, and should never be subjected to blame or derision on account of their slowness. Many teachers often greatly err in dealing with this class of pupils, applying to them such epithets as *blockhead, dolt, numbskull, simpleton, dunce,* etc. They are, moreover, sometimes neglected by the teacher, who naturally prefers to give attention to those bright, precocious pupils who need but little instruction. The best powers of the teacher, however, are displayed in developing the latent capacities of these dull scholars; and very often it has been found that those who bore the character of dullness in school have risen to great eminence in after life. The great English poet and novelist, Sir Walter Scott, and the illustrious German chemist Liebig are often mentioned as examples of this fact.

EAR, Cultivation of the. Recent physiological researches appear to leave but little reason to doubt that, at birth and for months afterward, the organs of the special senses exist in only a rudimentary form, and that they owe their gradual development entirely to the external influences exerted upon them by nature and society. It is, therefore, not only probable, but experimentally demonstrable, that the education of the senses is more or less efficient according to the time at which it begins after birth. In the light of modern experience, it is considered by some extremely doubtful whether there is really any case of actual congenital blindness or deafness. The tendency to these defects, doubtless, often exists as an hereditary imperfection, but is scarcely ever of such a nature as to be incurable, if discovered and treated properly soon after birth. Hence, except when an organic malformation exists, it follows that a systematic and judicious training of the senses, from the earliest infancy, may remedy most, if not all, cases of such defects as color-blindness, weakness of sight and hearing. etc. Such indeed is the conclusion derived from the experience gained in infant asylums. kindergartens, and intelligent families. This is an important fact, since it serves to correct the notion, so generally entertained, that good speakers and singers must be born such, and that there are but few persons thus naturally endowed. There is, without doubt, considerable diversity in the sensuous endowments of different individuals; but, at the same time, it is impossible to fix a limit to the improvement of which every organ of sense is susceptible by continuous and proper education, and particularly by a cultivation carried on through several successive generations. As regards the ear, this may be considered as historically established; since, three centuries ago, there were but an exceptionally few persons who showed any ability to appreciate, and a still smaller number who were able to reproduce, musical melody and harmony. The progress of musical art among modern civilized nations, and particularly the diffusion of musical taste among the people, are striking illustrations of ear culture, since this progress could not be effected without an organic as well as an esthetic improvement.

The sense of hearing is the earliest to be developed in infancy, and, at the approach of death, seems to be the last to be extinguished; it is also the last to be overcome by sleep, and the first to be aroused on awakening. In reaching objects at a distance, its power is next to that of sight. In the earliest stages of intellectual development, the sense of hearing performs a most important office, since language, the most efficient means of all education, depends upon its exercise. Moral education, no doubt, also begins with the genial accents of the maternal voice, both in speech and song, as heard by the infant; so that even the lullabies which soothe it to slumber constitute an agency in its development. While, therefore, loud and explosive noises may injure the physical organization of the ear of a child, harsh and angry tones will affect injuriously the development of its affections and sentiments. All disagreeable sensuous impressions are deeper and more durable than those of an opposite character; and, hence when often repeated, they tend to destroy the capacity of the ear for the appreciation of beautiful sounds. Otherwise, variety of sound is not detrimental to the infant's ear, but on the contrary, beneficial, especially when the source of each sound is, at the same time, presented to the sight, or touch, or both these senses. From the time the infant begins to understand simple language, — usually after the fourth month, especially if the words are accompanied with mimicry or gesticulation, care should be taken to articulate distinctly. In families in which there is a negligence in this respect, it will be found that the children either never, or with very great difficulty, acquire a distinct articulation. It is a great error, quite common in some families and communities, to repress the natural vociferations of children, and to insist on the constant use of low tones in speech. Nature dictates a great deal of crying, shouting, etc., in order that the lungs and vocal organs may be fully developed; but, of course, all excess should be restrained, since the habit of yelling and shouting in the open air will not only injure the delicate organs of the voice, but will have a bad effect upon the moral development of the child, besides incapacitating him for the perception and appreciation of those delicate distinctions of sound upon which musical harmony and melody depend. (See SENSES, EDUCATION OF.)

Practical suggestions.

EDUCATION (Lat. *educatio*), a general and comprehensive term, including in its signification every thing that pertains to the bringing up of children, and the operation of influences and agencies designed to stimulate and direct the development of the faculties of youth by training and instruction, and thus to control the formation of their character. Hence, education has been divided into several departments, according to the class of faculties to the development and improvement of which it is directed, including (1) *Physical Education* (q. v.), or the education of the bodily powers; (2) *Intellectual Education* (q. v.), that of the mind or intellect; (3) *Moral Education* (q. v.), — of the propensities, sentiments, will, and conscience; (4) *Esthetic Education*, — of the taste, musical, artistic, or literary, that is, comprehending the sphere of the imagination (see ESTHETIC CULTURE); and (5) *Religious* or *Spiritual Education*, — of the religious sentiments, the spiritual instincts; that is, those which concern the soul as an immortal essence, and its relations to the Infinite Spirit. (See RELIGIOUS EDUCATION.)

Definition.

Classification.

Education is also distinguished into *home* or *domestic education*, and *public* or *common-school education*, or, considered as a means for the general enlightenment of the people, *popular education*; also into *private education*, that is, supported by private funds, and *national education*, — provided for by the state.

School education, generally called *instruction*, on account of the more limited character of its scope and the sphere of its operations, is distinguished, according to its grade, into (1) *primary instruction*, that is, the instruction given in elementary schools (such as the common schools, — the primary schools of cities representing only

School education.

a lower subdivision of primary instruction); (2) *secondary instruction,*— as given in academies and high schools (middle schools); (3) *superior instruction,* — as given in colleges and universities; (4) *special instruction,* — as of the blind, the deaf and dumb, and the imbecile; (5) *professional and technical instruction,* — as in art schools, law schools, medical schools, military schools, theological seminaries. schools of architecture, etc.

Education is to be carefully distinguished from instruction, the latter being only a subordinate part of the great schemes of controlling and guiding the development of a human being. To this department of education the term *didactics* (from the Greek word δ.διδάσκειν, *to teach*) is often applied. (See DIDACTICS and INSTRUCTION.) Instruction is addressed to the intellect or understanding; while education comprehends the whole nature of man and the various agencies by means of which, in its formative state, it may be effected. Its primary object is to form the character either by stimulating its development in the normal direction, or correcting tendencies to morbid growth. In respect to the scientific principles by which its practical operations should be guided, education is a science; in the relation to the proper mode of performing those operations so as to render them as effective as possible. it is an art.

Instruction.

The science of education is a very complex one, inasmuch as its principles must be drawn from many different departments of science; superadded to which, as its own peculiar sphere of investigation, there is the great body of truths which concern the growth and development of mind and body, and which especially constitute the *theory of education,* or *pedagogics,* as sometimes called. A distinction is now plainly drawn in the minds of professional educationists between the *old* and the *new education,* the former referring to the system of verbal memorizing, of which there are so many relics at the present time; and the latter, to the development system (*q. v.*), by which a constant appeal is made to the intelligence of the child, in the exercise of its observing and conceptive faculties. Hence the term New Education is often applied to Froebel's kindergarten. A recent writer remarks : —" The old education was painful and repulsive: the new education inspires voluntary and glad effort. Adaptation and interest are cardinal. The old education consisted largely of unmeaning task-work, which tended to discourage and repress. The new education leads the pupil to discover and apply, and inspires boundless enthusiasm". BALDWIN, *Art of School Management* (1881).

Science of education.

The old and new education.

EDUCATION, Theory of. The word *education* is derived from the Latin verb *edŭco* which is properly used to designate the sustenance and care bestowed by a nurse on a child; and it is, no doubt, connected etymologically with the Latin verb *edūco,* to lead out; but it never has this literal sense, and it is extremely unlikely that the Romans connected the idea of *drawing out* with that of *educatio.* In order to get a true idea of education, we must look at the circumstances of the case. We proceed by way of analogy. We know in regard to the seed of a plant that it contains a peculiar and special power within it. Place it in the proper soil, with the proper temperature, and it will burst forth into active life. It will gather from earth and air the means of support and increase. It

Meaning and aim of education.

Illustration.

will fashion the elements which it lays hold of into a definite shape, and it will pass through various stages of progress until it withers away, leaving, however, behind it the means of continuing the species. Within certain limits, the plant has a definite form of its own, and its mode of life is also uniform; and, within these limits, there lies a perfect form and a perfect life for the plant. It may not be easy to say what is that perfect form and perfect life, but it is plain to every observer, that it, as it were, strives after an ideal form and an ideal progress, to which it approximates more or less closely. Man is like the plant. The living power within him strives to attain a particular form, and to go through a particular progress, and it continually strives to attain an ideal of these, within certain limits. The difference between the plant and the man is, that the limits of his condition and progress are much wider, and that he can consciously form an ideal for himself, and strive after it. Now education, in its proper sense, is the deliberate effort on the part of one conscious being to clear the way so as to enable another to attain this perfect condition of life and this normal progress. It is assumed that the man naturally strives after perfection. It is assumed that he must move in some direction, whether forward, or zigzag, or backward; and the educator endeavors to keep the movement in the right direction.

The word *education* is used in a variety of senses, connected but not always compatible with the true idea. Thus man is viewed as being, in his earliest stage, a kind of compressed mass of faculties, and education is the drawing out of these faculties. Again, every thing that acts on man's nature is sometimes said to be educative, whether the result is beneficial or not. Other instances could be adduced of the use of the word in the vaguest manner; but by stating the true idea we oppose ourselves to the vague uses of the word. It is enough, therefore, to state first that man must be viewed, not as passive but as active, not as being drawn out, but as striving to act, and that no act is truly educative which does not help him to strive after actions that are becoming to his nature, or, to express it objectively, to strive after what is good, beautiful, or true.

Various uses of the word.

But, in thus stating the work of education in a general proposition, we have done very little toward explaining its true nature. Education sets before it an ideal. How are we to form anything like an adequate conception of this ideal? Only by a minute and careful study of human nature; and, therefore, every educator must necessarily devote a great deal of his attention to the phenomena of body and mind, and to man, the combination of both. The ideal is a unity, but it is a composite unity, made up of the perfect accomplishment of endless detailed actions, and we must, therefore, examine all the details before we can attain to a clear notion of the whole.

The ideal.

The subject may be viewed in another light. Every portion of man is made or preformed for a special function or functions. Thus the eyes are made for seeing, the hands for grasping, the skin for touch. For what is the whole body made? For what is man, body and soul, made? It is the work of the educator to help him whom he educates to discharge the functions for which, as man, he has been made or preformed. Accordingly, most of the definitions of education

Another view.

which have been given, have been based on the answer to the question, what is the chief end — the *summum bonum* — the destiny of man? This was a question which occupied the attention of the ancients much, and Clemens Alexandrinus has gathered together a large number of the answers which ancient philosophers gave to the inquiry. These are interesting to the educator, because they suggest different points of view from which to look at the problem. In more modern times, the form which the answer has most frequently taken is the statement that it is the work of education to produce, as far as it can, an equable and harmonious development of all the powers of man. Herbart and his school object to this way of expressing the aim of education. The term *powers* is apt to mislead. There are no separate and special faculties in man's mind. All the best psychologists admit that these faculties are fictions; and therefore, the aim of education must be defined apart from these. Herbart himself defined the aim of education to be morality; but he used the word in a truly philosophical sense, in which it is not understood by the masses, and, therefore, he preferred to state the object of education to be, to produce a well-balanced many-sidedness of interest. The emphasis laid on *interest* has been productive of much rich fruit in educational investigation and experience; but, practically, Herbart's definition comes to the same as the other. Man is viewed as destined to a series of activities closely connected the one with the other. These activities may be in harmony with his nature, or his ideal nature, as we may call it, or they may be more or less aberrations from it. The business of the educator is to prevent the aberrations, and to help those activities which are in harmony. Those activities which are in harmony find their sphere in nature, in man, in God. It is important that all these activities come into play. Man does not pursue his ideal course, if they do not come into play. He must be fully developed. But if his activity comes into play on these subjects according to the right method, his interest in them is awakened and becomes stronger and stronger; for all pleasure is the accompaniment of the vigorous discharge of some function, and all pain is the accompaniment of the weak discharge or hindrance of some function. If the organ which discharges the function is exercised too powerfully, as may be the case with our bodily powers and lower mental energies, there is first intense pleasure; but the over-tension impairs the healthiness of the organ temporarily, or it may be permanently, and then the impaired activity is followed by pain. And the pleasure that may arise, may arise from the exercise of what we call the lower functions, when the higher are neglected. Thus the lazy man desires true pleasure, as far as it goes, from the vigorous exercise of his vital or vegetative powers. But, whatever pleasure does exist, exists from the efficient discharge of function, or in other words from healthy activities of body or of mind. This pleasure may not be consciously before the mind, as in the highest intellectual operations when the student does not feel how intense has been his enjoyment, until the enjoyment is over. This accompaniment of all our healthy actions is cumulative. It grows in degree, in proportion as the actions are repeated in a healthy or proper manner. And, hence, our interest increases with the healthy repetition of the activities on the objects. Herbart's definition becomes, therefore, nearly synonymous with the other, but directs the attention to the external

Aim according to Herbart.

side of man's activity, to the objects on which the mind works. Both sides must be carefully considered by the educator; for, in the activity of man, they are invariably conjoined. The distinction between *formal* and *material* in education has to be made with great caution; and it has always to be remembered that form is impossible without matter, and matter impossible without form, that while there can be no right activity, if the mind does not act in a right manner, it is equally true that there can be no right activity, if there is not a right object for the mind to act upon.

After having thus generally discussed the aim of education, we should now enter minutely into particulars, for the general is of slight use with-
Particulars. out the particular; but this would be to write a treatise on the laws of the activity of the human mind, and the modes to be adopted by men to direct these activities aright in the young. We must, therefore, confine ourselves to hints which may suggest to the reader the subjects which deserve his careful and minute examination.

A child gazes at an apple on a tree. What are the operations of the child's mind? First, we have the exercise of the bodily organ. Then the apple produces an impression on the child's mind. This im-
Phases of activity. pression we call a sensation. The child feels something. Some change has taken place within him. But, if this is not the first impression which the apple has made on the child, we can observe that the sensation has attained in its complexity to three phases: First, the child has the feeling of pleasure in seeing the apple; second, he sees that there is an object before him which he calls an apple; and, third, if, on a previous occasion, he has tasted apples and enjoyed them, the recollection of that enjoyment comes back, a desire arises within him, and he is under an impulse to make an exertion to obtain the apple. In this one instance, we have the various phases of man's activities. He is, first of all, a physical being; then he is capable of feeling, — has an emotional nature; then he is capable of perceiving, — has an intellectual nature; and, finally, he is capable of desiring, of striving after, and, thus, has a practical and moral nature. Though we speak of him thus as if he had four natures, he really possesses but one. All the distinctions, except perhaps the first, are distinctions made by the mind, but the facts do not exist separately. The emotional, intellectual, and volitional are blended with each other in the actual human mind. The mind cannot exist without them. There can be no absolute separation of them, since they stand in the closest relation to each other. Yet it is essential to separate these elements in our discussion of them, for they may blend with each other in different degrees. The one phase may predominate to the injury of the others. A man may have a clear head, but a hard heart and a stubborn will. Another may be too emotional, ready to melt before the slightest distress, and yet possessing almost no capability or inclination to relieve the distress. The true aim of man is to bring out all the elements in harmonious proportion, and the work of the educator is to help each child to accomplish this difficult task for himself.

The aim and end of physical education is to produce health, not strength in particular organs, but a general healthiness of all the organs.
Physical education. This aim is accomplished by a careful examination into the nature of the human body, an exposition of the laws of health which arise from this study, and the exhibition of the reasons

which ought to lead us to give all due care to the body. Intellectual education is based on a careful investigation into the laws which regulate the gradual progress of the mind from its earliest weak state of mere sensation till it reaches the power of dealing with the most abstract ideas. But when we come to the *education of the emotional nature*, we enter upon a more difficult sphere — one in which the educator has often to grope in darkness; for the emotions are not directly under his control, and the movements of the mind in regard to them are hid in such secrecy, that sometimes an influence which seems to us likely to produce one emotion, actually produces the opposite; as, for instance, efforts to beget love may have for their result the production of dislike. We can here take but a short glance at this important subject.

Intellectual education.

Education of the emotions.

The first point to which the attention of the educator may be directed is a general result at which he may aim. The broadest division which can be made of the feelings is into those of pleasure and those of pain. The mind assumes a particular attitude in consequence of its experiences of these. We shall take a case. A child performs a mental act. He does it successfully. He feels pleasure. He performs another successfully. The recollection of the past pleasure unites with the present feeling, and the feeling is stronger. Others thus blend until the child has a permanent state of feeling; or, as we may call it, a mood. He looks forward with hope; he expects to be successful; but he may fail. A failure takes place; he feels pain. The feeling of pain now acts antagonistically to his feeling of pleasure; and, if these painful feelings recur, the one set strive for the mastery over the other; and the result will be, that the mind will ultimately be in a bright and cheerful mood, or in a dark and gloomy one; it will either be full of hope or be given to despair; or, at the least, have a tendency to go in the one direction or the other. There can be no doubt that it is the business of the educator to produce the bright, cheerful, hopeful mood. This is the natural mood, if we use the word natural as expressive of the ideal after which nature strives. This mood is the result of the successful discharge of all the functions; and it is of immense consequence for the child to have this mood. The mind communicates its tone to every thing around it; and so the cheerful mind sees good in every thing, catches the bright side, and strengthens all the powers; for the cheerful mind becomes the strong mind. Obstacles, pain, failure are sure to come; but the cheerful mind casts them all aside, rises superior to them, and, after temporary depression, sees again with the same clearness, and hopes with the same steadfastness. The methods by which the educator can help to produce this state of mind in his charge are various, and must all be used. First of all, he must himself be of this cheerful and hopeful mind. There is no direct teaching on excitation of the emotions; but they are often produced, in the proper circumstances, by what we may call infection. Love begets love; we catch admiration from those who have felt the admiration before us; and, no doubt, the sweet, gentle, loving smiles of a mother who is uniformly kind to her child, have a powerful influence on his whole destiny, a more powerful influence than they are generally believed to exert. Secondly, health is a mighty agent in the earliest stages

Pleasure and pain.

The natural mood.

Methods.

of life, before it can be expected that the mind should triumph over bodily evils: and, therefore, special care should be taken to render the infant healthy. And, thirdly, after a certain stage has been reached, some truths reached by the intellect can come powerfully to the aid of the emotional nature; such, for instance, as a belief that the arrangements of this world are in favor of man, that the amount of happiness in the world is much greater than we may suppose, that God is working all things to wise and noble ends, and that man's destiny is for virtue and love.

When we pass from this general consideration to the particular feelings, we find ourselves in a labyrinth. A feeling is a phase of mind which arises from the consciousness of having passed from one state into another; and, accordingly, no mental act can take place without a feeling. Hence, we have feelings connected with the body, feelings connected with the intellectual operations, and feelings connected with the practical and moral nature. Or we might speak of the feelings according to the objects which give rise to them; as those that arise in connection with nature, with one's own self, with man, with God. We select out of these, two classes of feelings that especially deserve the attention of the educator. The first class deserve attention principally because they are in danger of being neglected, owing to the character of the present age. The educator should awaken and keep alive the feelings of admiration and mystery. A child naturally wonders and admires, and these feelings must not be allowed to die out. Moreover, the sense of mystery, closely connected with these, will be a source of great blessing to him. The practical man is apt to look on all things as definite and fully known; but the fact is, that nothing is completely known. We know neither the beginning nor the end of any thing. The smallest object and the largest are equally invisible to us. Our knowledge is limited by a boundary that lies far within the infinitesimally great and the infinitesimally small; and so all knowledge attained points to an infinite region the depths of which we have not sounded. A consciousness of this is closely connected with a humble spirit, and true humility generally allies itself with love. The second class of feelings is that which relates to the beautiful.

Particular feelings.

Mystery.

The beautiful.

The sense of the beautiful is the power to feel the loveliness of symmetry, of proportion, of harmony. This power is to be acquired only by the exercise of it. The symmetry and loveliness exist in nature. They are calculated to produce an effect on the soul of man, but the soul of man must be brought into contact with them, before it can feel them. Therefore, in regard to the cultivation of the feeling for the beautiful, the one essential condition is, that beautiful objects be placed before the person in whom the sense is to be awakened and strengthened, and that they be placed frequently and at proper intervals; because the sense of the beautiful is awakened only by slow degrees, and it expands, passing from the external and simple to the harmonies which prevail amidst the grandest spheres of thought and intelligent existences. But it can be brought before the pupil in every form at an early stage, in beautiful pictures, in beautiful rooms, in beautiful landscapes, in order, in gentleness of tone, in noble action, and in many other ways, so as to induce within himself a love of all that is orderly, harmonious, and peaceful.

Two cautions may be specially urged in connection with the cultivation of the feelings. The first is, that it is possible to render a human being too sensitive, — to give feeling too great a preponderance in the individuality of the person educated. Such a person becomes sentimental, is easily moved to joy or tears, is sympathetic in the highest degree, but the sympathy does not lead to action. The educator has to take care that every train of feeling be strengthened and guided aright by clear and well-reasoned convictions, and be followed by appropriate action. The second danger is, that the feeling of self may become so strong as to harden every other. Naturally, every one bestows a great deal of attention on himself, and there is a tendency to feel only when the circumstances relate to one's self. Here, again, what has to be done is, to prevent the mind's being occupied too much with self, and to interest it in the thoughts and circumstances of others. Both these cautions point to the next division of the sphere of education — that of the will or of the practical powers. The exercise of these is closely connected with the intellect and the feelings, and indeed ordinarily results from them. Man is naturally a striving or desiring being. He is a force, and by a force we mean something that strives to exert itself. Accordingly man's first act is an effort. And the powers which he at any time possesses strive for spheres of action. But these spheres are in the main determined by the results of the action of his intellect and the motive power of the feelings. A child does something which gives him pleasure. He has finished the action. He turns to something else. What remains of the previous action? A recollection of something pleasant; but the recollection of something that is pleasant excites the desire to enjoy it again. Thus arise desires in the mind; and as these desires arise again and again in connection with objects belonging to separate classes, groups of desires or inclinations arise, and we call these groups by general names, such as the love of money, the love of honor, the love of fame. These desires grow in intensity according to the amount of time during which they are allowed to continue in the mind, and the amount of space they are allowed to occupy in it. Add to this fact that we naturally put a value on the things which we desire, and regard some as higher than others, and we enter the region of morals. Two or three functions of mind lie before us which we are able to discharge at the time. We weigh these functions in the balance. We pronounce one of a higher nature than the others. This is the one which we feel bound to perform. Thus the function of the eye is a nobler one than that of the nose or the taste; and, hence, the educator who trains the child to see is performing a nobler function than he who indulges a child's taste for sweets. All functions may be necessary, but each must have its own place in a well-arranged and systematic order of gradation.

The first essential, then, to a good practical training is to impress on the pupil the true value of all actions and things. He is enabled to attain to this only by having a clear intellect and a right state of feeling, and, therefore, it cannot be too strongly urged, that a thorough intellectual education is an important element in the attainment of a sound moral character. But, besides this, we learn to act by acting. There is a natural instinct to act, and this instinct must not be resisted or blunted. It is by one action that we rise to the power of doing a greater. Here the same kind of fiction as that which we have noticed in the case of the mental faculties is apt to mislead. Man is often spoken of as possessing a will; but man has not one will, but many wills. The word *will* is used to denote the complicated power which man possesses, through his original faculties and the exercise of them, to will for the future. But, if this be the case, the strength of the power to will in any particular case depends upon the previous exercise which the mind has had in willing similar actions; and so a man may have a strong will in one direction, and a weak will in another. Hence, the educator must take care to bring into activity the willing power of his pupil in as many directions as he can, without impairing his strength of will in the most important directions. Moreover, in action, we are influenced strongly by the action of others, just as in feeling by the feeling of others. The teacher who wishes to lead his pupils to action, must himself act first. The influence of example is all-powerful in this matter. And, finally, as willing depends first upon fixing an appropriate aim, and, secondly, on selecting the right means, the pupil must be trained, in all cases, to use the right means. The clear insight into the true value of actions, that is, into the aims which should guide us, may be of comparatively little use, if we have not the good sense to employ suitable means for our purposes. These are the general rules which regulate practical education. It would be impossible in an article like this to go into the particular phenomena which must be investigated before the educator can have a proper grasp of the subject. Just as in the case of the feelings, desires and inclinations arise in connection with all the activities of man, — with the physical, the intellectual, the emotional, and the practical forms of man's energy; and they embrace the same extent of objects. They connect themselves with nature, with one's own self, with other men, with God. But, they have wider ramifications, and a more potent influence than the feelings, and open up, therefore, a wider field for investigation; and, in this subject, aberrations demand the closest attention. The educator has continually to guard against the formation and strengthening of inclinations which imperil the well-being of the individual and the race.

Means of guidance.

Lastly, there is religious education, embracing within it intellectual, emotional, and moral aspects. Religion may be said to arise in a feeling. We feel our weakness and littleness. We feel that we are limited in power, in knowledge, in vital energy. We feel surrounded, on every hand, by powers that are stronger than we are, and hemmed in by irresistible forces. If this, however, were the only feeling, despair would lay hold of us. But, we come to feel that the irresistible forces are not antagonistic to us, that we can come into harmonious relations with the supernatural, that, to use the Christian mode of thought, we can trust in a God of justice and love. It is when we gain this feeling of trust that we attain to a religion. But, a religion advances beyond the mere feeling; it sets down God or gods, as possessing a certain character, and, therefore, enjoining a certain kind of worship. Especially does the Christian religion present definite conceptions as to the character of God, and enjoin, as the first condition

Religious education.

of worship and as the great law of life, love to God and love to man practically exhibited. The Christian religion thus brings into play the feelings as the foundation of religion, the intellectual powers in apprehending its great truths, and the inclinations and practical powers in carrying them out.

The subject of education is discussed in a great variety of treatises. The most satisfactory discussion, in our opinion, is contained in the works of Herbart and Beneke. Herbart's educational writings *Literature.* have been collected and published recently in two volumes (Leipsic, 1873—1875) under the editorship of Otto Willmann. Beneke's great work on the subject is *Erziehungs- und Unterrichtslehre* (2 vols., third edition, Berlin, 1864). The first volume is devoted to *Education*, the second to *Instruction*. Of the followers of Herbart, Ziller's works deserve special mention; and of those of Beneke, the works of Dittes and Dressler. The educator will also derive much good from the study of the best works on psychology. Both Herbart and Beneke have written hand-books of psychology; and, in English, special mention, may be made of the writings of Sir William Hamilton, Dr. Morell, Prof. Bain, and Mr. Herbert Spencer, the last of whom has a work specially devoted to education (*Education: Intellectual, Moral, and Physical*). For other references, see *Cyclopædia of Education*.

ELABORATIVE FACULTY, a term often used, at the present time, to indicate that function of the mind by which it employs the materials supplied by sensation, perception, conception, and consciousness (or the inner sense), and builds them up into systems or chains of thought and reasoning. The different processes that, according to this nomenclature, are elaborative, are comparison, abstraction, generalization, judgment, and reasoning. To these particular processes the term *thought* is now often restricted, instead of being, as formerly, applied indifferently to every intellectual operation. Dr. Hopkins, in *An Outline Study of Man* (N. Y., 1876), thus describes this faculty and its functions: "The processes of the elaborative faculty hold the same relation to the materials brought into the mind that the processes of building and repairing hold to the materials which are brought into the body. The building and repairing systems take hold of that which is brought into the system and elaborate it; they transform it, and make of it another thing. The elaborative system does the same thing in the mind. It takes the material given by the presentative faculty [sensation, perception, etc.], and performs the operations of comparison, abstraction, etc." Dr. Porter, in *The Human Intellect* (N. Y., 1869), thus defines the office of the elaborative faculty: "The thinking power has been treated as twofold, and been subdivided into two: the *elaborative faculty*, as performing the processes, and the *regulative*, as furnishing the rules, or more properly as prescribing the sphere and possibility of thought. These are named also the *dianoetic* and the *noetic* faculty. By some writers they are distinguished as the understanding and reason, in a usage suggested by Kant, but deviating materially from his own. Milton and others call them the discursive and instinctive reason". (See INTELLECTUAL EDUCATION.)

ELOCUTION, the utterance or expression of thought in reading and speaking, is an important part of a scholastic education, because of the constant need of such vocal utterance in the ordinary circumstances of both private and public life. The departments into which this subject naturally divides itself are the following: (1) Articulation, or the proper and distinct enunciation of the elementary sounds as usually combined in words; (2) Pronunciation, as dependent upon a knowledge of the various sounds represented by letters and their diverse combinations in words, and upon accentuation; (3) Emphasis, or the placing of a stress of the voice upon a particular word or words of a sentence, so as to bring out the meaning fully, and to give life and spirit to the delivery; (4) Voice inflections, — upward, downward, or waved, as a means of giving a particular significance to words or sentences, and as auxiliary to emphasis; (5) Tones, or those variations of the voice in pitch, force, and quality, by which it is modulated to the expression of particular sentiments and emotions. (See READING, and VOICE, CULTURE OF.)

EMPIRICAL METHODS, those methods of instruction or education which are based not on theoretical principles, but on the effects of practical operations as learned by experience. Hence the term (from Gr. ἐμπειρία, experience). When the application of scientific methods, or those derived from general principles, is possible, the use of empirical methods becomes a cause of reproach, and is to be condemned. The science of education is, however, too unsettled and incomplete to justify such condemnation, except to a limited extent. Methods that have stood the test of actual experiment, and have proved effective, are not to be discarded merely because the principle underlying them is not understood, or because they seem to contradict some favorite theory. Such experimental processes are the source of much valuable experience, and the facts thus obtained should be generalized so as to supply additional scientific principles, or correct those already deduced. In this way, the practical experience of educators may be employed to improve and extend the science of education. On the other hand, it is undoubtedly true that teachers are too apt to follow empirical methods blindly, without concerning themselves with principles. The complaint is often and justly made that education is not scientific; and, that, consequently old methods and processes are often employed, when the circumstances render them entirely inapplicable. This would naturally be the result of adhering to empirical methods, since principles alone can guide to a just discrimination as to practical processes. The "rule of thumb" may answer when the operator is confined to a very narrow sphere of his art, and is never obliged to depart from it; but it is entirely inadequate to grapple with the difficulties presented in a varied and enlarged sphere of practical effort, whatever the art or profession may be. This is particularly true of education, since the elements with which it has to deal are as innumerable in their combinations as the phases of human character. In proportion as education emerges from this condition of empiricism, and assumes a settled scientific status, its practical operations will rise to the dignity of a profession, and those engaged in it will receive the consideration which appertains to the professional character.

Definition.

Utility.

Not to be used blindly.

Principles needed.

EMOTIONS are those conditions of the mind in which the sensibility is excited, so as to act upon the will, and with the tendency to outward

manifestation in bodily acts. The difference between emotions and passions is rather quantitative than qualitative; the former, while character-
Emotions and passions. ized by an intensity of feeling, still leave a considerable scope for the exercise of reason and judgment; the latter, for the time being, disturb the equilibrium of self-consciousness, and produce a condition in which the mind is overmastered and controlled by the particular feeling, and is borne along by its force, helpless and suffering (hence the name *passion*, meaning *suffering*). Of this, we have illustrations in the effects of extreme anger, love, hatred, or revenge. Emotions are
Sentiments. also to be distinguished from *sentiments*, the latter being to a greater extent based on mental discriminations, and more steady and durable in their nature. Thus, he who has cultivated the sentiment of patriotism, cannot but feel an emotion of joy at a victory gained by his country over her enemies. Emotions are likewise to be distinguished from
Feelings. *feelings*, or the immediate sensations of the physical organism, giving rise to mental perceptions, or to bodily pleasure or pain. The nature of children is more emotional than that of grown persons, because the restraining principle of the mind is less active, and the sensibility more fresh and more acute. This is particularly true of certain kinds of temperament and mental constitution. The office of education is to recognize every principle of the human being, and to employ it or appeal to it in the educative processes. An emotional nature should be cherished; inasmuch as one who is deficient in this respect is apt to be cold, selfish,
Culture of the emotions. and unsocial. The emotions are not only compatible with, but necessary to, the best elements of man's moral nature; and the educator should strive to connect them with moral motives. The attempt to awaken emotion in the minds of children by mere sentimentality is futile and ridiculous. Stirring stories of heroism, endurance, patriotism, generosity, self-denial, filial affection, etc. will awaken corresponding emotions; and when properly applied constitute a means of emotional culture; but youth should, as far as possible, be permitted to yield to the natural emotions to which the ordinary circumstances of their lives give rise; they should witness emotion in others, under restraint, but still expressed; and by imitation, as well as instinctive impulse, be habituated to ardor in their feelings toward all that is beautiful, true, and good in natural objects, historical incidents, or the conduct of those with whom they meet in their daily lives.

EMULATION (Lat. *æmulatio*, from *æmulus*, a rival), the desire to excel, is a principle of action which has had a very general application in
Use of in education. practical education, being one of the most common incentives brought to bear upon children and youth to induce exertion in study. The various systems of merit marks, prizes, etc., are based upon this principle, inasmuch as they definitely recognize and reward superiority or excellence.

Scarcely any subject has been more thoroughly discussed than the propriety of resorting to emulation as a school incentive. On the one
Arguments for its use. hand, it has been held that the human mind, particularly in its immature state, needs the stimulus of secondary motives to awaken its dormant energies, especially for the accomplishment of tasks in which it takes only an imperfect interest. Naturally, children

are but little prone to study, their fondness being rather for active sports and amusements; and, hence, the awakening of an interest in the studies themselves, while an important object of the teacher's efforts, cannot be depended upon to incite the pupil to continuous industry. While there are some minds and temperaments that feel an almost innate desire for the acquisition of knowledge, and hence a love of study, on the other hand, the great majority of children have no such desire until it is engendered by the force of secondary motives, that is, by holding out inducements to study based upon the attainment of things in which they do take an interest. All children are, more or less, prone to emulation; they love to excel others, particularly in things that bring commendation and honor, in this respect resembling those of maturer years; for this principle of action has been recognized as leading to eminence in every department of human effort. Hence, in schools and colleges, emulation is an important and valuable incentive which the educator may, by no means, cast aside. Of course, it is not to be allowed to degenerate into personal strife, animosity, or jealousy; nor is it to be indulged in such a manner as to obliterate the pupil's real interest in the study pursued. It is always to be impressed upon the student's mind that he is working in a good cause, and that he should strive to attain to the highest possible degree of excellence in it,—higher, if he can, than that which he sees has been attained by any of his fellow students. Thus what others achieve becomes the measure of what can be done by him if he exerts himself to the utmost, and also the standard beyond which he is to go in order to obtain the prize of excellence. For a fuller treatment of this subject see *Cyclopædia of Education*.

Cautions.

ENCOURAGEMENT, as an educational incentive, is of indispensable importance in dealing with a certain class of minds, particularly with those characterized by an excess of caution, timidity, and diffidence. Many teachers repress the exertions of their pupils by failing to discern their true character, so as to be able to ascertain the amount of effort they may have put forth in order to accomplish an assigned task, or to avoid a temptation to do wrong. Adopting an arbitrary standard, they sometimes condemn alike all who fail to attain it, making no allowance for diversity of talent, opportunity, or the power of will; whereas the true test of a pupil's merit is not the accomplishment of the task, but the exertion put forth and the self-control exercised in the endeavor to comply with the teacher's precepts or directions. Encouragement consists in adjusting the standard of success to the peculiar circumstances and traits of the pupil. If the latter is dull, indolent, self-indulgent, feeble in will, and yielding easily to temptation, the educator who recognizes these traits, accepts with satisfaction the feeblest efforts at amendment which he sees have been put forth, and by judicious commendation induces stronger and more persistent ones, until the foundation of moral or intellectual strength has been safely laid. Timid children must be encouraged to lay aside their fears by being shown that they are groundless. They must not be repressed by harsh words of censure, or by those forms of punishment which should be the exclusive penalty of willful wrong-doing. On the contrary, they should be made to feel that, even if they have failed, they have won their teacher's approving smiles by their

Impor-tance.

How to be applied.

honest efforts. All the various forms of encouragement, within the power of a teacher of skill and experience, will find occasions for employment in dealing with the endless diversities of character presented by the pupils of a large class or school. Some minds, on the other hand, need rather urging than gentle encouragement; and the latter, in the form of excessive praise, to talented pupils is often a means of flattering their vanity, and thus operates as a kind of moral poison, destroying the force of every true stimulus to activity.

ENGLISH, the Study of. The mother-tongue has peculiar relations to education. Language has a twofold nature,— on the one side, *Relations voice, on the other, thought.* Early thought is almost all stimu-*to educa-* lated, guided, and supported by the mother-tongue. All early ac-*tion.* quisition of knowledge may be regarded as the study of the mother-tongue; and, even in civilized nations, few persons ever advance beyond the knowledge stored up for them in their native speech. The mother-speech is also the means of communicating with others, and of influencing them; so that the study of it as an art includes the study of rhetoric and oratory, and of the art of poetry.

It would seem then that there are four chief direct uses in studying English: (1) To understand what is spoken or written in that language; (2) To speak it well; (3) To write it well; and (4) To master *Uses.* English literature. And there are three remoter ends: (1) To master the language scientifically; (2) To acquire the knowledge of language in general; and (3) General culture.

Early study, in infant schools, kindergartens, and primary schools. — The *meaning of words* is the first thing children learn of languages. The names of a few familiar objects and acts are repeated in connection with the objects and the acts themselves so often, that the infant's *Meaning* thought passes promptly from the sound to the thing. Thus, *of words. papa, mamma, kiss, laugh,* make the child think of the person or act before it can speak any words. Many words are also attached to thoughts by being often heard connected with other words in discourse. Such knowledge, caught by the child rather than taught to it, is for the most part very indefinite and inexact, but no part of education is more important.

The objects named should be objects worthy of thought. Good and bad qualities should be marked by such tones and manner as will give their names correct and powerful associations. The means of *Names of* expressing the affections should be carefully taught. In the *objects.* kindergarten or other infant school, care should be methodically taken to teach the words which accurately name the objects and processes that the children learn; unnamed objects and processes, however amusing or ingenious, enter little into thought and contribute little to culture. A leading purpose in all object teaching should be to give valuable ideas; but that is the same as giving familiarity with good words. Teachers of infant schools need good books, containing classified lists of important words, with directions how to teach them by means of well-chosen object lessons, and amusing occupations. (See KINDERGARTEN, and OBJECT TEACHING.) For children of a larger growth, we have a great number of *Spellers* and *Definers,* and small dictionaries which teach the meaning of English words. The latter should be constantly used.

The study of meanings in such manuals is, however, of little worth, unless supplemented by object teaching on the one hand, and by the study of discourse on the other. Manuals of object teaching arranged for the purpose are wanting. Object teachers often contrast the study of words with the study of things, and condemn the study of words, instead of teaching them through their exercises. There are many books made up of progressive selections of discourse, intended to introduce young pupils to words. Most *Primers* and *Readers* attempt something in this way, and some are skillfully prepared with notes and exercises for this purpose.

Object teaching.

To speak well requires a knowledge of the meanings of words and of the combinations in which they are actually used, of the meanings and uses of grammatical prefixes and suffixes, and of the exact sounds which are made by good speakers. Speaking must go on at a certain speed; and, therefore, thoughts, words, and the movements of the vocal organs must be closely associated, so as to follow one another without effort and with great rapidity. Much practice in speaking is necessary in order to speak well; and, in general, practice in the very kind of speaking in which the excellence is desired. In the early stages of education, this must be almost wholly imitative practice. Children catch and use the sounds and forms which make the liveliest impression on them, and which they hear oftenest; to use a form or sound once, makes it most likely to occur to the mind again. Teachers should, therefore, train by inducing imitation of their own speech. Exercises may be used in repeating after the teacher the elementary sounds, and afterwards difficult words, and then familiar dialogues, and finally passages of poetry, or elevated prose, which the teacher likes and can repeat with feeling. Incorrect articulation and bad grammar should be constantly corrected, not by repeating and caricaturing what is faulty but by substituting the correct expression. Children should also be encouraged to talk, at proper times, to repeat the explanations of the teacher, not *verbatim* throughout, but yet with a constant, close, and correct use of the technical terms or important words; nor is it unscientific to commit to memory formulas of permanent importance, to be fully comprehended afterwards; such as the multiplication table, catechisms of moral and religious truth, and noble utterances which it does men good to have fast in the memory. The youth should be led on by language faster and farther than his own thoughts could have gone alone. Practice of this kind will naturally go along with reading.

How to cultivate correct speaking.

Learning to read should begin early. The monstrous spelling of the English language makes this much more difficult than to learn to read German; and teaching the names of the letters, and the sounds of the syllables as if made up of them, has a mischievous effect on the reason of the learners. Several methods are used in our schools to overcome the difficulties. The word-method (q. v.) is one. In this, children are taught to recognize words as wholes before learning the letters. In skillfully prepared books, with pictorial illustrations, children learn to read very rapidly by this method, but not so accurately; and it is very hard to teach them to spell. Skillful teachers will use a judicious combination of the two methods. Books are also prepared with an

Methods.

alphabet in which each letter has always the same sound, a proper phonetic alphabet, and with classified examples of words, and reading extracts, spelt in the phonetic alphabet wholly at first, and gradually passing to our standard spelling. These have been used for some years in New York, Boston, St. Louis, and elsewhere, and are reported to save one half of the time usually devoted to learning to read. There is now an active movement for the reform of our spelling which it may be hoped will save the next generation much time and toil. (See ORTHOGRAPHY, and PHONETICS.) Books of this kind are LEIGH'S edition of various elementary reading-*Books.* books; also DAVIS'S *American Primer*, DOCAI'S *Rational Phonetic Primer*, LONGLEY'S *American Phonetic Primer*, SHELDON'S *New Phonetic Primer*, SHEARER'S *Combination Speller*, VICKROY'S *Phonetic First Reader*. Primary cards and charts to aid in this early instruction are to be had in good variety. Practice in writing is one of the best aids in learning to read and spell, and hence, copying choice extracts, and then writing them down from memory, is quite useful. Soon after lessons in penmanship begin, grammar should be taken up.

Grammar is often used as a name for the whole science of language and the art of using it; but by masters of the science of language, it is now confined to the classification of words into parts of speech, *Grammar.* according to their uses in discourse, the description and exposition of the changes of form called inflections, and the uses of these in the correct construction of sentences. There would be some advantage in dropping the old traditional definitions, which lead teachers and pupils to expect that the study of English grammar will make them able to speak and write the English language correctly. It is only one of the helps to correctness in speaking and writing. The attempt by makers of school grammars and by teachers to do too much is one reason why the study is so much neglected and abused. Descriptive grammar consists of definitions of the parts of speech, paradigms, and rules of syntax. With children, a careful selection of simple and typical matter should be made, just as in botany or in any other science. This matter should consist of definitions and rules, stated in accurate scientific language, but simply and briefly; and of selections of words and sentences, also simple and clear, and suited to illustrate the definitions and rules. This matter should be managed by the teacher so as to use mere verbal memory as little as possible, and to train the pupil to see, hear, and think as much as possible. The definitions and the rules should be learned like rules in arithmetic, but the main work should be the application of them to examples. The scholar should every day hand in written grammar work on the slate or on paper, like sums in arithmetic; and the preparation and explanation of this work should be the main grammar lesson in the early years. This method needs some system of notation by which any sentence may be put on paper or on the blackboard with its words so designated by signs, or by an arrangement in diagrams, that the analysis and parsing of it may be made plain to the eye. Such systems are found in several books. A considerable number of our best teachers use substantially this method, many of them, without a book, dictating, day by day, definitions which the pupils are to remember, and giving out words and sentences to be classified and analyzed, also proposing trials in collecting and inventing words and sentences of the kind to be studied. Books are often wholly condemned by these teachers, who collect, year by year, in their own note-books, or memories, a store of happy questions and examples, as well as carefully considered definitions and rules; and it would obviously be a great help to young teachers, as well as to pupils, to get a good note-book of this kind, neatly printed, and there are some books for beginners which are, in substance, such note-books. For a full treatment of this subject, with directions as to advanced instruction, see *Cyclopædia of Education*.

ENGLISH LITERATURE. This is a very important, but an enormously extensive subject for school instruction. The whole cycle of literature is no more to be known by one person than the whole circle of the sciences, still less by young people at school. The impossibility of achieving the whole task being seen, two questions at once arise:

Questions to be discussed. (1) What shall we teach and what leave untaught? and (2) How shall we teach it?

In attempting to answer the first of these questions, we can find some guidance from analogy; and the school subject which appears, in its vast size and the enormous contents of its wealth, to have the closest resemblance to literature is the subject of *geography*. Now, in geography, we do not burden the attention and overload the memory of our pupils with the infinite number of names of small towns, insignificant rivers, diminutive lakes, and unimportant headlands; but we take only the most prominent and, as it were, the central features of the world, and round these we group the knowledge which is intended to abide with the pupil, and to serve as a nucleus for his subsequent accumulations. In the same way, there are certain names which the sifting of time has caused to stand out with always increasing clearness; there are certain books which have been, and which continue to be, *forces* in the development of civilized humanity; and it is with these authors and with these books that the teacher should make the pupil acquainted. Thus stated, the path seems to be plain — so plain that no good teacher can miss it. But there are two dangers — two besetting sins, which await the teacher in his attempts toward the systematic treatment of a subject so large; and

Details to be avoided.

Encyclo-pædism and abridg-ment. these are the vices of *encyclopædism* and *abridgment*. Looked at more closely, both these vices are seen to be only two sides of the same central error — an error which pervades all kinds of teaching, and which is, indeed, the most prevalent educational error of the present day. By *encyclopædism*, is meant the desire to include too many facts — and, in the present instance, too many authors — within the range of the pupil's mental vision; and the consequence is a pressure which results in an *abridgment* of the closest kind — an abridgment in which nothing is said of — no facts are given about — the author, but when he was born, and when he died, and the name of his best-known book. It is plain that such knowledge is no knowledge at all, and is of no more value than an acquaintance with the street directory. The desire to teach too much ends in achieving too little; the attempt to learn everything results in nothing. Besides, the pupil must have a *living* and *interior* knowledge of English literature, and not a dead and external acquaintance with its mere husk, appendages, and circumstances; and the question which presses upon the teacher is therefore: How is this to be done? Before answering this question, the teacher must have settled with himself *what* is to be done.

(1) Let us suppose that, seeing the impossibility of embracing all the details of so large a field, he has resolved upon making a selection of the best writers in prose and verse in each epoch. Round each of *Selection of* these he will then collect the most able of his contemporaries, *authors.* and explain to his class their relations and the influence which each had upon the other, and which the requirements and spirit of the period had upon them all. The teacher will then, probably, select *Chaucer* — as the type of the chivalric period of English Literature; *Mandeville* — as the "Father of English Prose"; *Spenser* — as the richest poet of the Elizabethan era; *Shakespeare* — as the greatest dramatist of the period when the *drama* was at its highest; *Hooker* — as the type of the ornate and elaborate prose style of the sixteenth century; *Bacon* — as the most compact and thoughtful English essayist; *Milton* — as the poet of the Reformation, and the master of the most sublime rhythms in the language, and in his prose works the most elaborate of sentence-makers; *Butler* (in parts) — as the antipode of Milton; *Jeremy Taylor* — as the sweetest prose-writer of the seventeenth century; *Dryden* — as the herald of a new and more "popular" style; *Pope* — as the culmination of the most polished, clear-cut, and sparkling English; *Swift* — as the most powerful intellect of his time; *Johnson* — as the representative of the massive common-sense of his country, too ponderously, though characteristically, expressed; *Goldsmith* — as the most charming writer of his generation; *Burke* — as the most brilliant rhetorician that the modern world has seen; *Cowper* — as the transition and the link between the age of Pope and the nineteenth century; *Wordsworth* — as the dawn and the bright shining of the new day of English literature, and *De Quincey* — as the most wonderful prose-writer of the nineteenth century.

(2) But it is evident that all the works of these writers cannot be read in school; and a selection from them is, therefore, necessary. Here again common repute comes to our aid, and maps out our course for *Selection of* us. In Chaucer, we should probably find it sufficient to read *works.* the *Prologue,* or the *Knightes Tale,* or the *Man of Lawes Tale;* in Mandeville, a few chapters of his *Travels;* in Spenser, a book or two of the *Faerie Queene;* in Shakespeare, one or two plays, such as the *Merchant of Venice,* or *King Lear* (*Hamlet* is too difficult and super-subtle, while the subject of *Othello* must always keep it out of schools); in *Hooker*, the First Book of his *Ecclesiastical Polity;* in Bacon, twenty of his best *Essays*, such as those on *Envy, Great Place,* or *Travaile;* in Milton, the *Lycidas,* the *Comus,* the *Hymn to the Nativity,* and his other minor works, with perhaps one book of the *Paradise Lost;* in Butler, one or two Cantos of the *Hudibras;* in Jeremy Taylor, a few chapters of the *Holy Living* and perhaps a *Sermon;* in Dryden, the *Absalom and Achitophel* and the *Mac Flecknoe;* in Pope, the *Rape of the Lock* and the *Essay on Criticism;* in Dr. Johnson, two or three of his *Lives of the Poets* and the *Preface* to the *Dictionary,* with perhaps *Rasselas;* in Goldsmith, the *Vicar of Wakefield,* the *Traveller* and the *Deserted Village;* in Burke, the *Reflections on the French Revolution* and one of his speeches; in Cowper, the *Task,* the *Progress of Error, Truth,* and some of his minor poems, while his *Letters*

should be read, were it only for their style; in Wordsworth, the best of his *Sonnets*, the *Lines on Tintern Abbey*, *Laodamia*, and many of his minor poems; and in De Quincey, his *Suspiria de Profundis*, his *Vision of Sudden Death*, and some of his criticisms.

But, even after all this has been done and well done, there are still two things to do. The first is to give the pupil an intelligible and striking view of our literature before Chaucer — that is, from the *Beowulf* of the 5th century — a poem which, like the Iliad, existed only in the memory and not in a written form, for several hundred years — down to Caedmon, Beda, and King Alfred, to the Saxon Chronicle and Chaucer. This ought to be done orally by the teacher, who should, at the same time, write upon the blackboard short characteristic extracts from the works of these authors, and explain and illustrate the growth of the oldest English, with its highly inflected forms, into our present English. The second thing to be done is, to connect every-where the appearance and the work of a writer with the social condition and the political events of the age in which he lived, and to show — as far as this can be shown to a young audience — how these influenced the character and the feelings of the writer. Nothing, for example, can be clearer or more easy to explain than the influence of the two opposite views of politics upon the writings of the two contemporaries, Milton and Butler.

Growth of English.

The writer and his age.

The standing difficulty and perpetual temptation — a difficulty with which the teacher will have constantly to fight, and a temptation which he will have at every moment to resist — is to present to his pupils conclusions the data for which have not been given, and critical results the steps to which have never been taken by the pupils themselves. There is nothing more prejudicial to the young mind — nothing so fatal to its kindly and harmonious growth, as the presence within it of ready-made thoughts, of alien ideas, and of too easily accepted results. The pupil may seem to be in possession of such ideas and conceptions, but he is not; they may seem to be the fruit of his own mind, but they are really dead artificial apples — the witnesses, not of a vigorous, spontaneous life, but of mental poverty and death. The *second-hand* is the deadly foe of original life.

Arbitrary conclusions.

A large part of the benefit of a course of literature will be lost to the pupils, if they are not required, always and every-where, to react with their own mind upon the material they receive, and the forms which they are asked to contemplate. This view demands that, accompanying every step of the course, there should be a well-selected and judiciously chosen set of exercises. Such exercises might include the following:

Proper exercises.

(1) An account of a poem such as Chaucer's *Prologue*, in the pupil's own words, — always avoiding the vile practice of "paraphrasing." (2) A short life of an author, from memory. (3) An abridgment of an important chapter from some prose work. (4) The turning into modern English of a passage from a writer of the 11th or 12th century. (5) A critical comparison between the treatment of the same subject by two different writers. (Thus *Autumn* has been treated both by Keats and Shelley; the *Nightingale* by Milton, Keats, and Matthew Arnold; the *Death of a Friend* by Spenser

— in his *Astrophel* — and by Shelley — in his *Adonais;* an *Escape* by Shelley — in his *Fugitives,* and by Campbell, in his *Lord Ullin's Daughter.*) (6) The discussion of separate literary dicta — like the following by Russell Lowell: "Style, like the grace of perfect breeding, makes itself felt by the skill with which it effaces itself, and masters us at last with a sense of indescribable completeness". (This might be at first discussed in the classroom; and then the line of argument and the results would be given in the form of an essay or paper.) (7) The story of a play of Shakespeare. (8) The analysis of some character in a play. There are many others which will naturally occur to the teacher in the course of his work.

The steady purpose to be kept in view in this instruction is to deposit in the pupil's mind a few nuclei of thought, and to collect around these *Aim.* nuclei as large an accretion of cognate ideas from different writers and from different ages as possible. The existence of these nuclei will enable the teacher to preserve unity in his teaching — to link together his lessons with bonds of "natural piety"; and thus to make the thoughtful child the father of the wise and instructed man. And, from the point of view of intellectual training, they will enable him to keep true to the central principle of *repetition without monotony.*

The study of English literature is incomplete unless it include a view of the works of American authors, by whom many departments of the literature of the English language have been greatly enriched. *American* Thus, in poetry, the chief productions of Poe, Whittier, Long-*writers.* fellow, Willis, Bryant, etc., should be classified and criticised, and compared also with the productions of English poets in the same departments. In history, due attention should be given to Prescott, Hildreth, Bancroft, and Motley; and, in general literature, including essays, fiction, etc., Irving, Poe, Hawthorne, Emerson, Tuckerman, Whipple, and a host of others, claim attention. The principles and methods suggested in regard to English authors, in this article, are equally applicable to the American literature of the English language. For a list of books of reference, see *Cyclopædia of Education.*

ESTHETIC CULTURE. Esthetics (Gr. αἰσθητικός, from αἰσθάνεσθαι, to perceive), the science which treats of taste and its object, the beautiful *Esthetics.* in nature and art, has been recognized, since the middle of the last century, as an independent branch of philosophy. Depending, as it does, upon the exercise of a special faculty of the mind, it forms a part of the basis of a complete and harmonious education. However well the intellect, the will, or the conscience of an individual may have been trained, if esthetic culture is wanting, he must continue rude and unrefined; and, hence, in a comparison of nations which are esthetically cultivated with such as are deficient in this respect, we find a marked difference in the degree as well as in the general character of the civilization which they respectively present. The esthetic element, however, cannot be wholly wanting. Even the rudest nations or the most barbarous tribes manifest delight in those objects which satisfy their natural sense of the beautiful. Like children, they feel an intense fondness for showy ornaments, uncouth pictures and images, harsh and discordant music, and grotesque dances. The love of these things springs from the esthetic principle in their minds, in its uncultivated and partly undeveloped condition. Their perceptions of the beautiful are, like their thoughts and their reasonings, processes unregulated and misdirected. They have, also, the moral sense — the sense of right and wrong, but not knowing how to distinguish right from wrong, they often conscientiously perform acts which, judged by a proper standard of rectitude, are reprehensible in the highest degree; for conscience is only the general impression that a distinction between right and wrong exists, not a power to discriminate between specific right and wrong. In the same manner, the esthetic principle is the sense by which the mind, in a general way, distinguishes between what is beautiful and what is ugly; but it does not teach specifically what objects are beautiful.

Taste. Hence, however advanced persons may be in esthetic culture, they will still differ to some extent in this specific discrimination. This difference we attribute to a diversity of taste, the word *taste* being used to designate the esthetic principle or faculty of the mind. We find, also, the same diversity in the exercise of the moral sense, in the absence of a settled standard, some persons regarding as worthy of approbation the same act that others look upon as decidedly sinful.

The aim of esthetic education must, therefore, be to cultivate the sense of the beautiful, *i. e.*, the taste, (1) by showing what the elements of beauty are, and thus establishing in the mind a proper standard of the beautiful; (2) by presenting to the mind simple forms of beauty, for the purpose of illustrating this analysis of the elements, and also impressing them deeply upon the mind, as the foundation of esthetic culture; and (3) by practice in criticism, so that the mind may be trained to judge whether in any complex object, either of nature or art, the elementary principles of beauty are present, and in their normal or proper combination. The elements of beauty are to be sought for in the constitution of the human mind; and, therefore, our knowledge of what they are and how they are to be combined must be derived from experience and observation, upon the results of which *esthetics* as a science must be based. The educator must, antecedently to the exercise of his professional skill, have acquired a knowledge of this, just as the teacher of mathematics or of physics must be versed in those branches, before he learns how to teach them; but with this difference, that in esthetic culture, it is the faculty that is immediately addressed, the primary object being disciplinary; while in most other departments of instruction, discipline is a secondary object, the primary aim being to impart a knowledge of the subject taught. To illustrate, we do not, in elementary schools, teach *esthetics* as such; but we strive to cultivate the esthetic faculty by instruction in drawing, painting, music, etc. In this department of teaching, the practical value of the subjects themselves is a consideration of great importance, but the development of the pupil's taste is indispensable to any true progress, and, therefore, during the earlier stages at least, must be the primary aim of the educator. When the mind has become enriched with varied forms of beauty, the mechanical skill will soon advance to the degree requisite to give them expression. This work commences in the kindergarten, and is

Practical sug-gestions. continued in the object lessons of the primary school, by means of varied exercises in *form* or *color*. The most rudimental exercises in drawing should have a strict reference to this principle; that is to say, the pupils should be required to delineate not uncouth figures, but simple forms of beauty. The hand and the eye may be trained, it is true, by practice in drawing any forms, whether beautiful or not; but the taste is to be developed and cultivated as well; and, therefore, only such forms as appeal to the esthetic sense should be. at first, presented. The elementary forms of the script letters are illustrative of the esthetic principle; and, hence, writing is a means of esthetic culture. The letters themselves, however, being complex forms, it is held that rudimentary drawing should precede writing.

Esthetics is not only concerned in the beauty of forms; it embraces the objects of every bodily sense, and also of what may be called the inner *Applica-* sense, — a discriminative consciousness of the beautiful in *tions.* thought and action, which the rhetorician, the poet, and the orator recognize and address in their several spheres of activity. That part of esthetics which depends upon the objects of hearing is cultivated by means of music, which is the expression of the beautiful in sound. The same guiding principle is applicable to instruction in this as to the teaching of form. Simple melodious combinations, regular and beautiful in themselves, should be constantly employed; all that is harsh and dissonant should be avoided. The beauty of composition, that is, rhetorical beauty, depending upon subtler principles, requires a more careful treatment in education. Habit and association, however, play an important part in this branch of esthetic culture; and, therefore, the child, even from its earliest years, should be accustomed to hear only chaste, pure expressions; and the most familiar colloquialisms should be entirely free from what is coarse and vulgar, and especially from slang. The esthetic element in *Poetry.* poetry cannot be addressed until an advanced stage of culture has been reached. Poetry is the expression of the beautiful by means of words; it embraces rhetorical beauty, and the beauty of thought and action, as well as of external forms.

ETYMOLOGY (Gr. ἐτυμολογία, from ἔτυμον, the true meaning of a word), a department of philological science which explains the derivation of words and their literal meaning. This is historical etymology. (See ENGLISH, STUDY OF.) The term *etymology* is also applied to that part of grammar which relates to the classification of words as parts of a sentence, and their various inflections, used to indicate their relations to one another, or modifications of the general ideas which they express. This is grammatical etymology. (See GRAMMAR.) As a branch of elementary instruction, it teaches the component parts of words, — root, prefix, and suffix, and by explaining the primitive meaning of these parts in the language from which they are derived, shows the exact literal meaning of the words. (See WORDS, ANALYSIS OF.)

EXAMINATIONS constitute an important part of the educator's work in order to test the result of what has already been accomplished, and to incite his pupils to additional efforts. While it is perfectly true that the best effects of educational training can be but imperfectly, if at all, tested by any personal examination: yet, there is no other ready and definite method of ascertaining the efficacy of the teacher's work and the proficiency of the student. Examinations, moreover, are of great educative value, if they are conducted on sound principles. The judicious examiner who is master of the subject, while ascertaining what the student has learned, necessarily, to some extent, shows him what he has failed to learn, either in consequence of an imperfect method of study or a lack of attention to certain important parts of the subject. Thus he is taught how to make his future efforts more successful; and, further, by coming in contact with a mind more mature in its operations and attainments, he obtains views of the subject which no amount of study of his own could impart. On this account, examination and recitation should go hand in hand, the student showing, in the first place, what he has learned of the lesson assigned to him, and the teacher then, by skillful examination, demonstrating to him his ignorance on certain points, and in this way instructing him in such things as may be beyond the grasp of his unaided research. Examinations of this kind form an indispensable part of instruction itself; those which occur at the end of certain periods, either for promotion, or for graduation, have in view the exclusive aim of testing the actual progress of the pupil. Indirectly, however, such examinations being anticipated by the student, guide and stimulate his efforts, both in acquiring and remembering. — See *Cyclopædia of Education*.

EXAMPLE, the Influence of. This depends upon imitation and sympathy, two principles of action which are exceedingly potent in the minds of all persons, but particularly in those of children. Its influence among men is shown by the existence of national customs, prejudices, vices, fashions. etc., and by the use of language, which would be scarcely possible without the force of imitation or example. In infancy and early childhood, this principle is the almost exclusive means of education, and the impressions which it makes are so strong and durable, that they are hardly ever obliterated in after life. Parents very rarely appear to realize that they are, by a kind of "unconscious tuition", educating their children simply by what they say and do in their presence. The power of example has an important application in the education of the intellect; since, in giving instruction in any department of science or art, the illustrative power of the teacher, in showing to the pupil what it is desired that he should accomplish, has great efficacy in stimulating his efforts, and more especially in fixing in his mind a definite standard to the attainment of which he may direct his aim. Indeed, in every branch of instruction, imitation is one of the most important principles for the teacher to recognize and employ. But it is in moral education that the force of example has its chief sphere of activity. In it is comprehended all that we mean by the *personal influence* of the instructor. His manners, his modes of action and speech, the expression of his countenance, and the tones of his voice, all are constituent elements of this influence. This personal power, it has been well said, is an "emanation flowing from the very spirit of the teacher's own life, as well as an influence acting insensibly to form the life of the scholar". — See *Unconscious Tuition*, by Prof. Huntington.

EXPULSION is often resorted to in schools in the case of pupils who, by their willfulness, insubordination, reckless and disorderly conduct, or general depravity, cease to be amenable to the ordinary regulations of the school, or are likely to contaminate the manners and morals of the other pupils. It is an extreme measure, which, in public schools, should not be taken until all other proper means to control the pupils have been employed; because it generally deprives these pupils of all opportunity of receiving the education for which the laws of the state provide. Two circumstances can alone justify it: (1) That the pupil is utterly uncontrollable by any of the ordinary means of school government; (2) That the depraved character of the pupil is such as to imperil the welfare of the other pupils. Expulsion, in some places, is used as a substitute for corporal punishment; but the propriety of this has been called in question. In view of the fact that the expulsion of incorrigible pupils must be occasionally necessary under all circumstances, it would appear that a reformatory institution constitutes an essential part of every public-school system.

EYE, Cultivation of the. The sense of sight is capable of an almost incredible improvement by culture; of this, modern scientific investigations leave no doubt. We see improvement in this respect not only in individuals but in the general visual capacity of whole nations. There can be no question, for example, that, 3,000 years ago, when the civilization of the Chinese came to a stand-still, they were very deficient in the power of seeing perspectively; so that, in spite of all their skill in drawing and painting, their pictures show all objects on the same plane, without any variation of size, or of light and shade, in order to represent the distances and relative positions of the objects depicted. Many proofs might be adduced to show that, in the course of centuries, the human eye has improved in power. The aim of education in this respect is twofold: (1) To improve the physiological conditions of sight, by removing any causes of a morbid state, or by strengthening the physical organ of vision; (2) To cultivate, by judicious practice, the sense of sight, so as to render it more observant, and able to receive more full and accurate impressions of the objects which pass before it. This is of special importance, as of all the senses that of sight is, without doubt, the most far-reaching, and leads to the most numerous and vivid conceptions.

Capability of culture.

The cultivation of the eye should begin soon after birth, and, for a few weeks, should be confined to keeping the infant from all excessive glare of light; but, at the same time, allowing it sufficient light properly to excite the nervous activity. Children, like plants, need a great deal of sunlight, which, provided it is not dazzling, is the most important agent of both bodily and mental growth. At the first, it should be a reflected, diffused, and mild light, direct sunlight being admitted only after several weeks, and then gradually. Weak eyes may also be caused by surroundings of but one color, particularly if decidedly brilliant. Hence, it is well to relieve the impression made by a single color, by alternation with its complementary. Red or blue curtains should be never allowed continuously to throw their tinge upon the infant's eye; but, as a rule, subdued colors should be preferred. The power of distinguishing both outlines and shades of color is susceptible of cultivation by means of the slow movement of bodies of different hues before the child's eyes. This is an exercise which is employed in Froebel's nursery education, and is very properly accompanied by singing, because the sense of hearing, having an earlier development, is well adapted to excite the action of sight. After the second or third month, when the infant can wield its hands and arms, the sense of touch should be called into activity in order to correct the impressions made on the eye. Various contrivances may be resorted to for this purpose, among them

When to commence.

Methods.

the suspended wooden globe and colored balls which Froebel suggests for use at this stage of education. As the child learns the meaning of simple language fully one or two years before it is able to repeat the words, it is safe to let it hear the names of the things which it sees and handles, but always in connection with the objects themselves. Thus language fixes, at the age of infancy, the various impressions of the senses, which impart a definite meaning to every word, and thus secure the proper expressions when the child begins to speak. When language has been acquired to some extent, the teacher should, by means of skillful questioning, attract the child's attention to those visible properties and peculiarities of things which, without a trained observation, are generally passed by without notice. It is surprising how much may be instantaneously perceived by a trained eye, and how delicate and far-reaching the sense of sight may become, under circumstances requiring its constant exercise. Thus the practiced astronomer is able to notice the most minute points of light, which the ordinary observer utterly fails to detect. On the other hand, the eye is, of all our organs of sense-perception, the most delusive if it is permitted habitually to gaze at objects without any comprehensive or discriminative view of their peculiarities and less obvious details. It is on this account, that Froebel invented that well-arranged system of kindergarten occupations, by which the free self-activity of the child, stimulated by agreeable intercourse with those of his own age, learns how to employ his sense of sight in an endless variety of pleasurable work, that never ceases to educate both mentally and morally. (See KINDERGARTEN, and OBJECT TEACHING.)

Without any special or technical aid, the teacher may readily discover whether any of his pupils are color-blind, by a proper use of color-charts or color-tablets. Every child that cannot select from among the tablets the exact color which is pointed out on the chart is, of course, more or less color-blind, and should have the benefit of frequent exercises with (1) the three primary colors, and (2) with their double and triple combinations. By using very strong and brilliant colors alternately with those complementary to them, this kind of defect in sight may be, in part at least, removed. (See COLOR.)

Color-blindness.

Teachers should not permit their pupils to stoop while engaged in reading, writing, or drawing; since this tends to injure the sight. It is also advisable to accustom the pupils to use their eyes at changing distances of the object with an equal degree of perfection, especially in reading, writing, and drawing. Then, if the eye be tired at a given angle of sight, it may continue its work, without injury or discomfort, at a smaller or larger angle, and thus be enabled to do more work without detriment to the sight. Many of the ordinary school arrangements are more or less injurious to the organ of sight. "Short-sightedness", says Liebreich *(School Life in its Influence on Sight,* London, 1872), "is developed almost exclusively during school life; rarely afterwards, and very rarely before that time. Is this coincidence of time accidental, — *i. e.*, does the short-sightedness arise at the period at which children go to school, or has school life caused the short-sightedness? Statistical inquiries prove the latter to be the case, and have shown, at the same time, that the percentage of short-sighted children

Caution.

Short-sightedness.

is greater in schools where unfavorable optical conditions prevail". There are, according to this writer, three changes in the functions of the eye, which are immediately developed under the influence of school life: (1) Decrease of the range of vision — short-sightedness (*myopia*), (2) Decrease of the acuteness of vision (*amblyopia*), and (3) Decrease of the endurance of vision (*asthenopia*). These are chiefly caused by such arrangements as afford either insufficient light, or admit it in an improper manner. The following is an important practical direction in this respect: "The light must be sufficiently strong, and must fall on the table from the left-hand side, and, as far as possible, from above. The children ought to sit straight, and not have the book nearer to the eye than ten inches at the least. Besides this, the book ought to be raised 20° for writing, and about 40° for reading. — See FAHRNER, *The Child and the Desk*. (See HYGIENE, SCHOOL, and SENSES, EDUCATION OF.) See also *Year-Book of Education for* 1878, art. HYGIENE.

Effects of school life.

FACULTY (Lat. *facultas*), a term originally applied to a body of men to whom any particular privilege or right is granted; hence, in a college or university, the *faculty* consists of those upon whom has been conferred the right of teaching as professors of specific subjects *(facultas profitendi et docendi.)* The faculties of a university are subordinate corporations, each consisting of a body of teachers, or professors, in some particular department of knowledge. At first the European university (that of Paris) comprised but two faculties, — that of arts (q. v.) and that of theology, to which, in the 13th century, those of canon and civil law and of medicine were added. The division into four faculties was transferred from the University of Paris to the German universities; the faculty of arts was afterwards named the philosophical faculty. Many changes have been introduced in this part of university organization since that time. In American universities and colleges, the faculty consists of the body of professors, with the president at its head, and has the power of conferring degrees.

FAGGING, a peculiar custom which has existed, from the earliest times, in the great public schools of England — Eton, Harrow, Rugby, etc., according to which boys of the lower forms (classes) perform certain personal services, for those of the higher. These services are either due to a particular student — the special master — or to the whole higher class. The former are such as carrying the master's messages, preparing his breakfast, waiting upon him at dinner, stoking his fire, etc.; and the general duties are to attend at the games, in cricket, for example, standing behind the wickets to catch the balls, and other such minor services. While many of these services appear to be of a menial character, they are not considered such, inasmuch as, without a fag, the boy would be obliged to perform them for himself. The system of fagging, like *pennalism*, in the German universities, has been the means of great abuse and tyranny exercised upon the younger students, yet it has strenuous defenders, as being, on the whole, beneficial.

FEAR, a sense of danger, the apprehension of coming injury, or the anticipation of pain, is an emotion of the mind which the educator often finds it necessary to excite, in order to control the actions of his pupil, but which he should address with extreme care and only after other means of persuasion have failed. There are two kinds of government, — that of influence and that of force; and the former should always be preferred to the latter, because it addresses the inner nature and produces a permanent effect upon the character, while the latter can be only temporary. By the one, the will of a child is trained, and a self-controlling power is fixed in the mind; by the other the misdirected, perverted will is still left a prey to vicious propensities, the operation of which is checked only as long as the external restraint continues. Some dispositions, however, need to be restrained by a sense of fear before other influences can be brought to bear upon them. Many children are inconsiderate, rash, and impulsive, and accordingly yield at once to their propensities. Physical punishment seems to be needed in order to produce any conscientious observation of their own conduct; but, without great care on the part of the educator, in inflicting pain for this purpose, much injury may be done to the child. Unless the educator's personality in this infliction can be subordinated, in the child's mind, to the sense of deserved punishment for wrong-doing, he will antagonize the child, and destroy all means of controlling him by personal influence. "The moment a child's mind is strongly affected by fear", says Horace Mann, "it flies instinctively away, and hides itself in the deepest recesses it can find, — often in the recesses of disingenuousness and perfidy and falsehood. Instead of exhibiting to you his whole consciousness, he conceals from you as much of it as he can; or he deceptively presents to you some counterfeit of it, instead of the genuine. No frighted water-fowl whose plumage the bullet of the sportsman has just grazed, dives quicker beneath the surface than a child's spirit darts from your eye when you have filled it with the sentiments of fear". This is especially true of certain dispositions; and, hence, this appeal to fear should not be made without very careful discrimination. Hecker, in the *Scientific Basis of Education* (N. Y., 1868), says, " If *cautiousness* is too large, seek to influence the child through his affections. Fear will paralyze such a mind. To make this faculty useful where it is predominant, the teacher must get the affections of the child, and he can then, by proper direction, make fear an intelligent restraint". No school government can be approved that is not intended to amend as well as to control. Children should be made to fear to do wrong; and this should be brought about as much as possible by what Herbert Spencer calls the *method of nature*, that is, by making punishment the necessary consequence of the wrongful act, on the principle involved in the maxim, "The burnt child dreads the fire". This eliminates the personal element in the fear implanted in the mind of the child. He does not fear the teacher, but he fears to offend, — to do wrong. The same consideration excludes from discipline all threatening, scolding, and harsh words, for the purpose of engendering fear, and, especially excludes anger in punishment. The fear to be excited in the mind of the child should not be an apprehension of personal safety, leading to meanness, cunning, and deception as a means of self-protection, but should be akin to that feeling which Solomon referred to when he said, "The fear of the Lord is the beginning of wisdom". This is not inconsistent with a constant appeal to the higher motives and finer feelings of human nature, but may be made a means of their development.

FEMALE EDUCATION. This is a subject which, especially in recent years, has very greatly engaged the attention of practical educators, scientific educationists, physicians, and all others who have either written or spoken on questions concerning the present condition and future prospects of human society and human welfare. The proper education of woman has been recognized as an important, perhaps the chief, factor of social progress. In ancient times, woman in general, occupied a secluded state; and it was only in the privacy of the home circle that she exerted the potent influence inseparable from her sex, whether as daughter, wife, or mother. The Roman matron, within this narrow limit, was an educator of her daughters always, and sometimes partly of her sons, as in the case of Cornelia, illustrious as the "mother of the Gracchi".

Importance of the subject.

History affords many examples of women who, breaking through the barriers of social custom, became illustrious for their learning and eloquence. Such were Aspasia of Athens, and Hypatia of Alexandria. The career of such women illustrated the intellectual capacity of their sex under circumstances permitting or encouraging its culture. Female education, however, has always been viewed as radically distinct from that of males, — as presenting entirely different aims, and requiring different processes of training and instruction, and a widely different curriculum of study. Much has been said and done in recent years to modify very greatly this view; but it is still generally entertained, and is, at the present time, the principle on which most schemes for the education of females are based. "A system of education", says Maudsley, "adapted to women should have regard to the peculiarities of their constitution, to the special function in life for which they are destined, and to the range and kind of practical activity, mental and bodily, to which they would seem foreshadowed by their sexual organization of body and mind". "From the beginning of the eighth year", says Schwarz, "the two sexes require, in almost every respect, a different education". "The culture of girls", says Von Raumer, "commonly requires a process of instruction entirely different from that of boys". Alonzo Potter, in the *School and the Schoolmaster* (N. Y., 1842), emphasizes this principle, and argues that "there should be, in the education of females, a special reference to their sex and condition of life". "The best educational training for a boy", says Dr. Clarke, in *Sex in Education* (Boston, 1873), "is not the best for a girl, nor that for a girl best for a boy". Such are the views upon which the education of females has been based. Arranged, as it has been by the other sex, the only considerations that have dictated its methods and processes have been the average physical weakness of women as compared with men, and the accomplishments they might need as wives and matrons. It is not difficult to perceive that were the education of men arranged by the other sex from an analogous ·stand-point, it would also be narrowed in its scope and processes. During the last few years, the questions pertaining to female education have been vigorously discussed by writers of both sexes; and much experience has been gathered, which appears to show that the necessity for a modified system of education for females is by no means so great as has been supposed and asserted. See *Cyclopædia of Education.*

Education of males and females.

FICTION, Works of, constitute an important part of the literature used in the education of children. The young mind delights in interesting tales, and receives impressions therefrom, deeper and more durable perhaps than those derived from any other source. While it instinctively perceives what is fictitious in the scenes and incidents of the story, it imbibes as true the characters of the personages and their relations; that is, it feels that such characters and relations may, possibly or actually, exist in real life.

Use in education.

By means of suitable works of fiction, the minds of children and youth may be cultivated in several respects; (1) By imparting vivid conceptions of persons and things; (2) By impressing upon them sentiments of virtue, courage, and patriotism; (3) By developing and training the imagination and the taste. Such were the reasons which prompted Fénélon to write *Télémaque*, and probably Xenophon in the composition of the *Cyropædia*; and this office of fiction as a vehicle of instruction and moral elevation has been recognized by most, if not all, great educators. Pestalozzi selected it as the most effective means of reaching the popular mind. In his *Leonard and Gertrude* (1784), he laid the foundation for a national pedagogical literature. There are, however, dangers to be avoided in using fiction as an educational agent, which we may thus briefly summarize: (1) By its exciting character, it may so occupy or intoxicate the mind, as to destroy the taste for more solid and useful reading. Such is uniformly the result of permitting children to read the wild, romantic, and startling stories, with which some of the juvenile periodicals of the day are filled. The constant perusal of such narratives is baneful; like ardent spirits, it intoxicates but does not nourish. (2) In the case of narratives which present instances of suffering, the sympathies are expended upon fictitious objects, and pity thus becomes habitually a mere sentiment, instead of prompting to active beneficence. "In the healthy state of the moral feelings", says Abercrombie, "the emotion of sympathy excited by a tale of sorrow ought to be followed by some efforts for the relief of the sufferer. When such relations in real life are listened to from time to time without any such efforts, the emotion gradually becomes weakened, and that moral condition is produced which we call selfishness, or hardness of heart". (3) By presenting to the young mind fictitious scenes of immorality, vice, or crime, it becomes familiar with their associations, and is thus depraved. (4) By impressing upon the mind false conceptions of the enjoyments, duties, and objects of life, it may be the means of producing a kind of infatuation, unfitting for every sphere of useful employment. Johnson, in *Rasselas*, well describes this mental condition: "The mind dances from scene to scene, unites all pleasures in all combinations, and riots in delights which nature and fortune, with all their bounty, cannot bestow. In time, some particular train of ideas fixes the attention; all other intellectual gratifications are rejected; the mind, in weariness or leisure, recurs constantly to the favorite conception, and feasts on the luscious falsehood whenever she is offended with the bitterness of truth. By degrees the reign of fancy is confirmed; she grows imperious, and in time despotic. Then fictions begin to operate as realities, false opinions fasten upon the mind, and life passes in dreams of rapture or of anguish". (See IMAGINATION, CULTURE OF.)

Dangers.

FORM, one of the most important branches of object teaching, since, from the first dawn of intellect, the endless variety of forms presented to the child's sight constitutes perhaps the most effective means of awakening and exercising its perceptive faculties. The first comparison which the young child makes between the objects of its perception must be based upon their resemblances, the conscious perception of differences occurring somewhat later. This arises from its need of forming general ideas as preliminary to the exercise of its thinking powers. The diversity of forms, like that of color, as seen by the child, very greatly interests it and attracts its attention; and, hence, when formal education begins, the child has already accumulated in its mind, in a rude and indefinite way, many materials which the expert teacher will use, in guiding his pupil to more exact knowledge. The untaught child's vocabulary of terms to denote the various forms which it has seen is very meager; and, hence, its conceptions are too indefinite to form the materials for conscious thought. They are, as it were, only embryotic thoughts, to be developed by the power of language. Hence, an important office of the instructor is to teach the proper term, or word, by which each particular object of the child's attention is to be designated, and in this way clearly individualized. For example, a young child intuitively perceives the difference between the form of a round object and a square one; but before the terms *round* and *square* have been learned as the names of these forms, they cannot be used by the mind in any process of thought. Besides, the young mind, in the exercise of its unaided powers, is chiefly occupied with the observation of resemblances and analogies, and only after the guidance of the teacher, comes to recognize clearly points of difference, the *sense of analogy*, as it has been called, taking the lead in the first stages of mental development.

Why an important branch.

In making use of *form* as a basis for training the observing faculties the teacher should be guided by the following principles: (1) Resemblances are perceived before differences; (2) The concrete precedes the abstract; (3) Every object is perceived as a whole before its component parts are noticed; (4) Every idea must have its proper verbal designation to be clearly and permanently fixed in the mind. The teacher should, therefore, begin with simple regular forms, such as the cube, prism, parallelopiped, pyramid, sphere, cone, and cylinder. These, at first, should be all alike in material and color, and about the same in size, so that the teacher may clearly develop the idea of *form*, as the rudimental step in the instruction. At first the process should be very slow. Thus the teacher holds up to the view of the pupils a cubical block of wood [one of the box of solids usually employed in such lessons], and asks, "What is this?" And the children probably reply, "A piece of wood". Then the teacher presents successively the sphere, cone, cylinder, etc., asking the same question and obtaining the same answer. The teacher then says, "Each of these is a piece of wood; are they all alike?" To which the children answer, "No". "Do they differ in color?" "No". "In size?" "No". This leads the teacher to show, in a very general way, not by giving names at first, but by directing the pupils' attention, that the objects differ in *form*; that is, each has its own peculiar form. The teacher may then go back to the *cube*, and ask the pupils to

Guiding principles.

Processes.

mention any other things they have seen which have the same form as the block of wood; and so on with the other forms. This exercise being a perfectly natural one will awaken interest, besides familiarizing the children with the particular forms presented. The next step will be to lead the children to observe the points of difference between these forms; and, in order to do this, the analytic process must begin. Thus, the teacher develops the idea of *side* or *face*, and the pupils perceive that the *cube* has six *faces*; the *edges*, *corners*, and *equality of faces* and *edges* may then be observed. When the pupil has perceived the distinctive characteristics of the form, its name, as *cube*, *prism*, etc., may be taught. This method requires the teacher to begin with solids (as the *concrete*) and to deduce from the observation of them, the ideas of *surface*, *line*, and *point* (as the *abstract*), in accordance with the principle (2). After these ideas have been thus developed, and the method of representing lines and figures on the black-
Varied board shown to the pupil, he is prepared for varied slate and *exercises.* blackboard exercises on the positions and combinations of lines both straight and curved, to be followed by similar exercises on plane figures. The study of *form* thus passes into that of *drawing*, in connection with which inventive exercises of a simple character may be employed, the children being shown how to combine lines and figures into simple patterns or designs. Of a similar but more elementary character are block combinations, which will serve to interest and instruct very young children. Boxes of blocks made for this purpose, with designs for construction, can be readily obtained. Charts containing diagrams of plane figures will also be found very useful in giving lessons on form. These lessons should be systematic, not desultory, but regularly arranged, with the underlying principle kept steadily in view. Especially should the teacher guard against requiring the pupils to commit to memory formal geometrical definitions, the chief point to be attained being the discipline of the observing faculties.

FRENCH LANGUAGE. The French language is universally recognized as standing, with the English and German, at the head of the lan-
Place in guages of the civilized world. Wherever a knowledge of any other *education.* than the native language is valued, French always has its claims considered. Hence, in the schools of the English-speaking world, it usually occupies, with the German language, a place in the course of study.

Instruction in French, as in every other foreign language, begins with the acquisition of a correct pronunciation. Next to English, French is
Methods. the least phonetic of all languages; and, therefore, a large number of rules must be learned before the pupil is able to pronounce ordinary words. It is important that this pronunciation should be learned, partly at least, by means of an imitation of the teacher's pronunciation. Memorizing lessons, before the correct pronunciation has been acquired is positively injurious. The French grammar offers but few peculiarities and difficulties. The absence of case-endings and of many other inflections, and the paucity of simple tenses and of changes in the radical part of irregular verbs, facilitate the reading of a French author at a very early stage of instruction. The chief peculiarities, such as the interrogative and negative form of sentences, ought to be frequently practiced. Attention should be called to the relationship which the Latin and the Norman elements of the English

language bear to both English and French. Simple exercises in etymology may greatly facilitate the early acquisition of a sufficient number of words, to enable the pupil to read easy writers without a too frequent use of the dictionary. If French is studied by pupils who possess some knowledge of Latin, this knowledge can be used to great advantage in etymological illustration, and in giving a clear view of the peculiar character of the Romanic languages. The understanding of French authors can be made quite easy for most pupils, who soon find that the majority of the words have equivalents from the same roots in their own language. The reading should, therefore, be rapid and not too much interrupted by grammatical or literary remarks. The aim, at first, should be to make the language familiar to the pupil; as he advances, it will be easy, without any sacrifice of time, to call attention to the rhetorical excellencies of the French classics. Classic prose should precede poetry, and should be read to a much larger extent. The great prose writers of the 17th and 18th centuries have some claims to the privilege of being read first; at all events, they should not be neglected. French literature is exceedingly rich in works suited, in every respect, for beginners; and there is no reason why modern writers should deprive Fénélon's *Télémaque* and Voltaire's *Charles XII* of the deserved popularity which they have so long enjoyed. — There is, generally, too little time in English and American institutions for the study of French literature. In most cases, the time devoted to it may be more profitably spent *French literature.* in improving the pupil's technical knowledge of the language. Of course, advanced pupils should become acquainted with the most celebrated authors as well as a rudimentary outline of the literary history of France; but most of this can best be learned as an introduction to the reading of the standard writers. Good French reading books, with literary introductions to the different authors, may be used for this purpose, especially in advanced classes, with great advantage. The reading of selections which would make the pupil acquainted with the peculiar style and excellencies of Corneille, Racine, Molière, Boileau, Fénélon, etc. of the age of Louis XIV; of Voltaire, Rousseau, Montesquieu, Floriau, &c., of the philosophical century; of Chateaubriand, Béranger, Lamartine, V. Hugo, G. Sand, Guizot, Thiers, Michelet, &c., of modern times, is preferable to the exclusive reading of one or two entire works of French literature. — When colloquial exercises constitute the chief part *Colloquial* of French instruction, and to acquire fluency of speech is the *exercises.* chief aim, care should be exercised that the command of the language thus obtained may give to the pupil something more than a collection of trivial phrases and unmeaning expressions of politeness. Eminent educators have often called attention to the dangerous influence which a knowledge, so exclusively formal and without substance, may exercise upon the pupil's mind.

GENETIC METHOD, in instruction, is but another name for what is more frequently called the *developing method.* The term *genetic* implies that the mind of the pupil is to be guided by the teacher in such a way that it will be able to perceive the *genesis* of the truths communicated, that is, their development from fundamental principles; or that it will be led to construct for itself general principles from observed facts as antecedents. This method recognizes the need of a *genesis*, or development, of actual conceptions in the mind of the pupil, as the basis for every other educational process. (See DEVELOPING METHOD.)

GENIUS (Lat. *genius*, innate power or capacity, from *gignere*, to produce), as used in modern times, has been variously defined by many *Definition.* writers, who, though differing widely as to its essential quality, are agreed as to its outward, distinguishing manifestation; namely, unusual mental ability coupled always with great intuitional or creative power. Akin to *genius* are those special aptitudes which are manifested, some times at quite an early age. These, as constituting a part *Special* of the character, should be recognized by the educator; and *aptitudes.* while they should not form the basis of general training or discipline, should be allowed their specific exercise; and, in the more advanced steps of education, should become distinct objects of culture. The existence of this special talent, or of genius itself, should not be permitted to supersede the necessity of industry and application. As far as possible, the tasks imposed by the instructor should bear a proper relation to the special ability of the students, those who are of brilliant parts being required to accomplish more than those who are comparatively dull and slow to acquire. Many youths of great promise, in large schools, are often seriously injured by insufficient requirements, lapsing into sloth or bad habits by the want of full occupation. This principle is of great importance; though its application in school and college education is accompanied with many difficulties. The true educator will, however, recognize it, and allow it to guide and regulate many of his operations. The possession of the brightest genius cannot supersede the necessity of industry and study. "Invention", said Sir Joshua Reynolds, "is one of the great marks of genius; but, if we consult experience, we shall find, that it is by being conversant with the inventions of others, that we learn to invent, as, by reading the thoughts of others, we learn to think".

GEOGRAPHY (Gr. γία, γῆ, the earth, and γράφειν, to write) has in its own name a concise yet comprehensive definition. In treating of geography as a branch of elementary instruction (for such it exclusively is at the present time), we shall consider (I) what are the faculties which are specially exercised in studying it; (II) the different stages into which the instruction should be divided, and what is proper to each; (III) the age at which the study should be commenced; and (IV) the proper methods of teaching it. Geography presents to the mind conceptions of countries and *Scope.* peoples that we have never visited, analogous to those which we have acquired in relation to regions which we have actually seen. It further seeks to combine and generalize these conceptions into a systematic view of the earth as a whole, and as the abode of mankind. The fundamental conceptions, therefore, which are to be thus amplified, combined, or otherwise modified, must be based upon objective presentation. A landscape, the more varied the better, or in default of this, a good pictorial representation, as its nearest equivalent, must furnish most *First steps.* of the basic elements. The first, though limited, steps must, therefore, be made through an appeal to the *perceptive* faculties.

GEOGRAPHY

The second stage must consist in an exercise of the *conceptive* faculties in vividly recalling and combining the impressions which the objective presentation has made upon the mind. The pupil must be trained to recall the image of the mountain, the island, the forest, the placid lake, the verdant plain, or the flowing river; to see again, as it were, the tossing ocean and to hear the roar of its waves as they break upon the beach; and to picture to himself in one season of the year the aspect of nature in another. These and other analogous impressions, already obtained from physical phenomena, must furnish the indispensable basis for any true progress in geographical knowledge. But all this training is not the teaching of geography, but only the necessary preparation for it. These conceptions are to geography but as the syllables to language, or as the gamut to melody. Throughout the teaching of geography, another mental faculty, the *imagination* of the pupil, must be brought into exercise. These conceptions of phenomena and of regions that he has actually seen must now be modified, amplified, and combined, to form conceptions of phenomena and regions that he has not seen. The conception of the rivulet must be expanded to that of the mighty river; the little lake or pond must lead the mind to the broad ocean; and the little hills, to mountain ranges. The low sun and snowy fields of winter must be modified into an arctic landscape; and the verdant meadow, into the boundless prairie. When, at the proper stage, the study of maps is introduced, the discipline of the *memory* is added to that of the perceptive, conceptive, and imaginative faculties, as in remembering the location of mountains, islands, rivers, and towns, and the various facts associated with them; while an appeal is also made, with increasing frequency, to the *judgment*, in tracing the necessary relation of the location of cities to rivers and coast-lines, and in connecting the general course of a river with the elevations and slopes of the country which it drains.

Imagination to be addressed.

Memory.

II. The successive stages of geographical instruction have been already, in part, indicated. The conceptions and distinctions of mainland and island; of mountain, hill, and table-land; of lake, river, basin, valley, peninsula, and cape; of climate, vegetation, race, and other geographical elements, should first be fixed, and then the terms which embody them should be described by the pupil himself. Too much stress is usually placed upon the precise and formal definitions of these terms. Some of them, such as sea, gulf, bay, and lake, as actually used, defy all sharp differentiation; and others, such as continent and watershed, are variously used by standard authorities. It must be borne in mind that the definitions in geography have a totally distinct function from those of mathematics, grammar, and other logical or deductive sciences. In these, the correct conception of a term, such as parallelogram or adjective, is to be obtained from its definition; whereas, in geography, the definition, if required, must be developed from a correct conception of the object defined. The formal definitions of geographical terms have, indeed, their place; but this is not in the first stage of the subject. The geographical terms and their association should be followed by ideas of direction or relative position, that is, a knowledge of the cardinal points; after this, the construction and interpretation of a simple map of limited and known localities, be-

Learning of terms.

ginning perhaps with a plan or map of the school room itself, followed by a map of the immediate neighborhood, then by that of the county as it would appear if seen from a balloon. When the pupil has been thoroughly trained to understand the symbols of the map, and readily to picture to himself the things that are symbolized by the various lines, dots, and other marks, he is in possession of all the elementary ideas essential to the subject.— Either of two opposite courses may now be pursued in giving the outline of geography itself such as is usually included in a primary or elementary course for beginners. One of these plans, known as the *synthetic*, begins with the study of a map of the locality of the pupil's home or neighborhood; it takes next the map of the county, then of the state or district, and, finally, of the whole country in which the pupil resides. After this, follows the study of the simple outlines of the continent of which the country forms a part; then the outlines of the other continents or grand divisions, in some preferred order, and finally a general review, which completes and combines all that has preceded it into a brief view of the world as a whole. The other, or *analytic* system, pursues, at least in its early stages, an exactly reverse course. From the consideration of certain common phenomena and other well-known facts, the pupil is first led to form a conception of the earth as a gigantic globe or ball; then of the primary divisions of its surface into land and water; and then of the leading subdivisions of these primary elements. After learning the climatic division of the earth into zones, the pupil studies the continents, each in its turn, as in the other system. Both of these systems have their strong points, both have been successfully followed, and both have earnest advocates. Excepting in their initial and terminal stages they have much in common. One great advantage of the analytic system is, that it more readily admits the early introduction of the terrestrial globe, and requires its frequent use throughout. In no other way can certain serious misconceptions be thoroughly prevented. The use of maps of different scales, together with the inherent faults of projection, leads to erroneous ideas in regard to the relative size of countries, and to wrong conceptions of their relative positions. These first impressions are hard to correct, and, in the majority of cases, are never corrected. The globe should have the leading place in teaching elementary geography. It should be used to fix the idea of the spherical shape of the earth, its dimensions, and the division of its surface into land and water. It should give the first view of its division into continents, oceans, islands etc., and just conceptions of their relative position and magnitude. By no other means can the astronomic elements of primary geography be so simply and correctly taught; such as the causes of day and night, and of the seasons, the zones, the nature of latitude and longitude and the need of these measurements. The final stage of geography, as a branch of elementary instruction, is much more comprehensive than the preceding stages, and makes more frequent appeals to the judgment and the memory. The outline already given is to be reviewed and filled up. Political or social geography is then to be more fully and systematically taught; and the whole subject of the peculiarities and resources, together with the commercial and other relations of all the most important countries of the globe, is to be more fully shown. Geographical definitions are now desirable. These should be followed by a review of the outlines of astronomical geography, and then by a thorough training in the outlines of comparative physical geography, as furnishing the only scientific basis, and the only true principles of scientific generalization, for the facts of political geography. This training should include, at first, well-arranged exercises on simple physical maps of the hemispheres, great care being taken, at this stage, to furnish only so much of topography as is necessary for the lessons on descriptive comparative physical geography, which should immediately follow. These descriptive lessons should be brief and clear, and should substantially include the following points in their proper order: (1) a comparison of the continents or grand divisions of the land in regard to position, form, size, and principal horizontal projections; (2) the comparison and classification of islands, the chief mountain systems, table-lands, and lowland plains; (3) the oceans and ocean currents, and the great rivers and lakes; (4) climate as affected by latitude, by elevation, and by winds and ocean currents; and (5) the general distribution of characteristic plants and animals, and of the races of mankind. All, or nearly all, of these may be profitably taught simply as physical facts to be known by observation. The study of the explanatory theories belongs to a higher stage of geographical knowledge. Each of the six grand divisions should now be considered in turn; first, in relation to the leading facts of its physical geography, including its surface, drainage, climate, and characteristic plants and animals, indigenous or exotic; and secondly, on the basis of these physical facts, in relation to the separate political subdivisions, their inhabitants, towns and cities, resources, commerce, industrial development, government, and general social condition. Finally, a brief but comprehensive general review should bring out, in strong relief, the various interrelations of the different countries in regard to commerce, government, race, language, and religion.

Physical geography.

III. As a general rule, the pupil should not begin the study of geography, at least, not what may be called *map geography*, until ten or eleven years of age. There are, however, geographical lessons, of a very simple character, which may be profitably given to younger children. These should, according to the principles already stated, be pictorial and descriptive, approximating to object-lessons, in being designed to develop ideas rather than to impart knowledge. In relation to this stage of the instruction, Currie says, in *Principles of Early School Education*, "The geography of the infant school is a series of object-lessons connected by a geographical link. It but prepares materials for the formal study of geography. It may be thought that the use of the map would facilitate this instruction; but it is quite immaterial whether the map be in the school or not. It is the business of the next stage of progress *to localize* all that has been learnt; which it does by going regularly over the map, and fixing down in position the countries, which as yet are only names to the children. The utmost use of the map that should be made in the infant school is to go over with the elder infants, if time permit, at the end of their course, on a physical map of the world, distinctly outlined so as to show the features of districts, the general outline of what they have learnt". If it were not for the early period at which most

Early lessons.

children leave school, the regular study of geography might be profitably deferred considerably longer. The prevalent practice of thrusting the study of maps upon the time and attention of very young children has much to do with the general disgust of both pupils and teachers at the usual net results of its study. The introductory course should occupy from a year to a year and a half; the subsequent course, from two and a half to three years.

IV. The principles which should guide in the selection of methods of teaching this subject, have already been explained, and the difference between the synthetic and analytic systems has been defined. *Methods.* The following suggestive hints will prove valuable to practical teachers: (1) The memorizing of the details of maps without sufficient descriptive matter, will leave no permanent impression on the mind; hence, (2) let the study of the map be subordinated to that of the other important facts, such as soil, climate, productions, etc., relating to the separate countries; and (3) let these facts be presented and studied in a uniform order, so that the pupil's mind will always have a guide, both for investigation and oral description. A special order of topics for this purpose has already been suggested. It must always be borne in mind, that in proportion as the pupil becomes interested in the particular country studied, he will desire to know more of its geographical details, and will remember them longer. Hence, the *exhaustive* study of the map should not precede all other lessons. After fully locating the country to be studied, by means of its boundaries, etc., the teacher may proceed with a description of some of its most striking features, passing from these to the more minute details of topography, as they are brought out by this description, until all the topographical and descriptive details are sufficiently learned. In considering the methods to be pursued in the study of geography, reference must also be made to the necessary appliances. For the first stages of the study a simple terrestrial globe and good wall-maps are indispensable. Relief maps and relief globes, as now constructed and used, are of great value in giving correct ideas of the superficial configuration of different countries. As far as possible, each locality should have some associated idea interesting to the pupils. Whatever is taught should be frequently and systematically reviewed by careful questioning, so that the impressions made may be definite and lasting. In the first stage of geographical study, the teacher is obliged to do a large part of the work; in the later stage, the pupil should be trained to do as much as possible for himself. This subject, when properly taught, furnishes an excellent and necessary discipline for the memory. The illustrations of the text-book should be supplemented, if necessary, from other sources. Books of travel may be made one of the most powerful of auxiliaries in teaching geography. If the school possesses a cyclopædia or gazetteer, it should be used for illustration or additional facts. No element in the successful teaching of geography is of greater importance than thorough reviews. These may take any one or more of a variety of forms too well known to need description. Cartography, or the drawing of neat and minutely accurate maps, is esteemed *Map-drawing.* by many experienced teachers as a valuable adjunct in geographical teaching; yet it is at least questionable whether the large expenditure of time required is fairly repaid by the value of the results.

GEOLOGY

The necessary topography may be much more effectively memorized and reviewed by spirited exercises in drawing, or rapidly sketching, outline maps from memory, Of systems of *map-drawing*, for this purpose, there is a considerable variety, all having more or less merit; but the great *desideratum* in this part of the instruction is, that the relative sizes of countries and distances of places should, by means of it, be permanently impressed upon the memory. This constitutes what is sometimes called the *constructive method* of teaching geography; upon which much dependence is placed in the German systems of instruction. For the aid of the pupil various devices are resorted to, some using the square, others a series of triangulations, and still others a combination of these, in connection with arbitrary measures. For the literature of this subject, see *Cyclopædia of Education*.

GEOLOGY (Gr. γέα, γῆ, the earth, and λόγος, a discourse), the science which treats of the history of the earth. More exactly, it consists of a group of sciences which treat of the materials of which the earth *Definition.* is composed, and of the arrangement of these materials, whether superficial or deep-seated, and of their relations to one another; of the changes which the earth is undergoing at present, and of the series of changes through which it has heretofore passed.

The general omission of geology from the course of instruction in high schools and colleges is much to be regretted; since, whether for the purpose *Educa-* of culture or information, it has many claims to consideration, *tional* a few of which are here suggested: (1) Of all sciences it most *value.* thoroughly cultivates a habit of inductive reasoning; (2) It so completely permeates physical geography that a knowledge of its elements is essential to the intelligent comprehension of the latter; (3) It is obviously necessary and proper, while children are taught that the earth revolves around the sun, and other facts of the solar system, that they should also learn that the earth of to-day has had a long and eventful history and that the living forms upon it were not created at once as we find them now; (4) The practical applications of the truths of geology are not only of scientific interest and importance but of great general utility.

If it is true that difficulty has arisen in communicating geological knowledge, it has, probably, been owing to two causes: (1) To a hesitation in telling the whole truth, and, (2) to a misconception, in teach-
Difficulty ing, as to what really constitutes the essential part of the science.
in teaching It is customary among teachers to dwell upon the details of strata,
geology. fossils, etc., more than upon general underlying principles. The inculcation of the latter, at an early age, by reference to surrounding causes and effects, and in conjunction with the earliest lessons in physical geography, would lay a sure basis for the former, to be studied if desirable at a later date. If you wish to give a child fundamental ideas regarding valleys and mountains make him see that every rain-storm carves out, in miniature, such surface features in the sand-heap and the clay-bank; and that it requires but a sufficient increase in the number of the rain-storms to increase indefinitely the extent of their action. With a realization of the powers constantly at work producing such changes, the student will advance to an intelligent study of the rocks and of the fossils, as examples of some of the effects thus produced. See *Cyclopædia of Education*.

GEOMETRY (Gr. γεωμετρία, from γέα, γῆ, the earth, and μετρεῖν, to measure), the science which treats of the properties and relations of magnitudes. We get the elements of this science as well as the word used *Definition.* to designate it from the ancient Greeks. Etymologically, the word is synonymous with our term *land surveying*, but it does not appear that it ever had simply this signification. As far back as we can trace the history of the subject, there appears to have been a body of theoretical truths and problems designated by this term. Thus, in the time of Plato, the word γεωμετρία does not appear to have had any more specific reference to land measuring, than it has with us; for, when he spoke of God (Θεός) as *geometrizing*, he certainly had no reference to land surveying. But it is not the purpose of this article to trace the history of geometry, nor to give even a *résumé* of its truths and methods. The object is to point out its place and function in a scheme of general education, and to offer certain practical suggestions in regard to the methods of teaching it. These will be presented in connection with the following inquiries and considerations.

I. *How should this subject be approached, in the first instance, by the learner?* The proper reply to this is, he should first become acquainted *Facts* with the leading facts of plane geometry, without any attempt at *before* scientific demonstration; notwithstanding the fact that the chief *demonstra-* excellence of geometry, as a means of mental improvement, lies *tion.* in its admirable body of practical logic. It is, in part, in consequence of this very fact that the learner should have an acquaintance with the fundamental truths of the science, as facts, before he attempts to reason upon them. It must be remembered that the logical faculty is not the inventive faculty. In general, its materials must be furnished it. Especially is this true with reference to fundamental truths. The history of the development of science affords abundant proof that these truths are furnished to the logical faculty rather than *by* it. Thus, the theorems, *If one straight line meet another straight line, the sum of the angles formed equals two right angles; The sum of the angles of a triangle is two right angles; The square described on the hypotenuse of a right-angled triangle is equivalent to the sum of the squares on the other two sides; The circumference of a circle is a little more than three times its diameter*; and many others, were known to men as facts, and their practical significance was well understood, long before their logical connection, with axioms and definitions was traced. As it has been with the race, so it should be with the individual; the facts are needed as a basis for logical inquiry. We cannot reason about that concerning which we know little or nothing. Indeed, this principle has been almost universally acknowledged in the construction of our text-books on geometry upon the analytical rather than upon the synthetical model. From the time of Euclid, at least, to the present time, the custom has been to state each truth in formal proposition before attempting to demonstrate it; but this is not sufficient. The mere statement of such a truth does not give the ordinary mind a sufficiently clear and full apprehension of it to interest the attention or to guide the thought. What is needed by the individual student is exactly what was possessed by the race, as antecedent *Illustra-* to logical inquiry: he needs to know the fact, and to perceive its *tions.* practical significance, before he attempts to reason about it. For example, if the tyro has learned by trial that he cannot take three given rods and, by placing their ends together, make triangles of different forms, he is prepared to understand and reason upon the fact that *mutually equilateral triangles are equal*. Again, if he has experimented with two sets of proportional rods, and found that he can combine them only into triangles of the same shape, he is prepared to be intelligently interested in the reasoning which proves that, *if two triangles have their homologous sides proportional, they are similar*. And so of all the fundamental truths of plane geometry. Much of the superficial and merely mechanical, *memoriter* work which is done by pupils in geometry is caused by their having no adequate conception of the facts about which they are attempting to reason. Once show the pupil by measurement that the circumference of a given circle is a little over three times its diameter, and he will be induced to inquire whether it is so in another, and finally if it is true in all circles. Again, let him draw several pairs of chords intersecting in a circle, and by actual measurement find that the segments are reciprocally proportional, and his curiosity naturally prompts him to inquire why this is so. Finally, a few illustrations of the mechanical value of the truths with which they are becoming familiar will, with most pupils, give added zest to their study and acquisition. To know that the brace stiffens the frame because the angles of a triangle cannot be changed without changing the sides, while those of a quadrilateral can; to see how the carpenter can square his foundation, calculate the length of his brace or rafter, on the principle that the square on the hypotenuse is equivalent to the sum of the squares on the two other sides of a right-angled triangle; how inaccessible heights, and the distances between inaccessible objects, can be determined by the property of similar triangles — these, and the like applications of the principles he is about to investigate, give an air of practical reality to the abstract speculations of the science, which will be found exceedingly helpful and stimulating to the student.

II. *It should be borne in mind that geometry is a mechanical as well as a logical science.* No more mischievous mistake can be made than to underrate the *problems* of geometry; nevertheless this is not an uncommon practice with teachers. While some teachers permit the pupil to omit these problems in construction altogether, others allow him the almost equally pernicious habit of *describing the construction* without actually performing the work according to the description. Thus, they allow him to tell how an angle is *bisected* without requiring him actually to bisect a given angle; they accept a clumsy description of the process of inscribing a circle in a triangle, illustrated by a free-hand caricature of the thing itself, instead of requiring a neat and accurate construction upon correct geometrical principles. Now, this is geometry with the actual geometry left out. Nor is it simply that the mere mechanical part (not an inconsiderable or unimportant part) is left out; but any critical examination of such pupils will usually show that the *logical* part is also omitted; in short, that the pupil neither comprehends the nature of the process and the reasons for its several steps, nor is actually able to execute it. While it is possible for a person to have the mechanical faculty in a high degree, and tolerably well cultivated, and yet, being deficient in the logical faculty, to fail of being a good geometrician,

Use of problems.

it is equally possible, and, as the subject is too commonly taught it is quite common, to find those who have fair logical powers, or who have learned the formulas of logic, so destitute of mechanical ability or culture, that they utterly fail to appreciate the real spirit of geometry, even though they may know, and be able to demonstrate, its chief propositions. Nor are the skill and taste requisite to effect neat and accurate geometrical constructions, attainments to be despised in securing an education. Shall we study the science of form, and not cultivate taste, eye, or hand in reference to form ? Shall we call a person proficient in the science of extension and form, who cannot construct a parallelogram, and whose taste and eye are so completely uneducated, that he cannot discriminate between a right angle and an angle of 85 or 95 degrees, and who cannot, with any degree of precision, construct either? Moreover, the zest which the construction of neat and accurate figures adds to the study, and the clearness of perception which is thus induced, are most helpful. In the course here recommended, a student will never be called upon to demonstrate a proposition in plane geometry, the figure for which he cannot construct upon geometrical principles; nor, in any well-conducted class, will the pupils pass any proposition, the figures for which they have not so constructed. It is not intended that every figure used for the purpose of demonstration should be thus constructed; but it is urged that the pupil should be able to construct every figure thus, and that he should frequently be required to do this; and, moreover, it is claimed that there is a positive power to investigate geometrical truth begotten of this method. Who that has ever attained any proficiency in geometrical investigation does not know the value of an accurately constructed figure ? This is, generally, the very first step in an original investigation, the construction itself often suggesting the entire line of thought.

III. But, passing from preliminaries, suppose the student ready to commence the study of the body of geometrical propositions which make *Proper* up the *elements of geometry*, and to learn how to demonstrate *classifica-* them. What should he find presented to him ? Most assuredly, *tion.* *a well classified arrangement of the subject matter* is a prime requisite in a branch of study which enjoys the distinction of being the most perfect of the sciences. It is, however, a singular fact, that no such classification has been commonly found in our text-books. The sole principle of the arrangement in Euclid, which has prevailed for so many centuries, is to demonstrate at first such propositions as are elementary, and hence of essential use in subsequent demonstrations. Of course, such an order of sequence as this is a necessity; but is there not that in the nature of the subject matter which calls for a more scientific arrangement? We venture to suggest the following: (1) The concepts of plane geometry are the *straight line*, the *circumference of the circle*, and the *angle*; (2) The two fundamental inquiries are concerning *magnitude* and *form*, the latter of which results from *position*. Bearing these statements in mind we shall commence with the simplest concept, the straight line. But shall our first inquiry be concerning magnitude, or concerning form or position ? There are two ways of measuring a straight line: (1) the direct way, by applying one line to another, and (2) the indirect way, as in trigonometry, when, having two sides and an included angle of a triangle given, we determine the third side, etc. Now, in the first, there is little or no science, and the second is not elementary. Hence, we dismiss the question of magnitude, and turn to the question of position, which gives rise to form. Here we at once find legitimate objects of inquiry, and *the relative position of two straight lines* will be the first section. The subdivisions will be *of perpendiculars, of oblique lines, of parallels.* As these are all the positions that straight lines can occupy with reference to each other, we have exhausted this line of thought. Passing to the circumference, we dispose of the question o magnitude in exactly the same manner as we did in the case of the straight line. The direct measurement by the application of an arc involves no science; and the indirect, as when we determine the circumference from the radius, is a remote inquiry. Hence, the question of *position* recurs. Comparing the straight line and the circumference as to relative position, we find the elementary properties of chords, secants, and tangents. Comparing two circumferences as to relative position, we have external tangency, intersection, internal tangency, or one wholly interior to the other; and thus we exhaust this line of inquiry. Reaching the angle, we find that the elementary method of measuring an angle (by an arc) is the fundamental object, while the relative position of angles is an unimportant inquiry. Hence, we treat the measurement of an angle by an arc; and have the elementary propositions concerning the *angle at the center*, the *angle between intersecting chords*, the *inscribed angle*, the *angle between two secants*, etc. We thus complete the fundamental inquiries relating to the simple concepts, and proceed to treat them as combined in figures. The first inquiry now concerns the relative magnitudes of the sides and angles of a single figure; the second, the comparison of figures. Now, there are three ideas to be taken as bases of comparison; namely, (1) *equality*, (2) *similarity*, and (3) *equivalence*; out of the last of which grows the idea of *area*. Having treated these topics, we have exhausted the subject of elementary plane geometry. No other elementary inquiry can arise; and no subsequent inquiries can be carried forward except on the basis of these. Thus we have hastily sketched the outlines of a scientific arrangement; but our special purpose is to insist, that some logical order of sequence be impressed upon the mind of the student, whether it be this or some better one.

IV. *Hints concerning class-room work.* — The order of arrangement in the treatment of a geometrical proposition should be early fixed in the student's mind; namely, (1) The general statement of the proposition; (2) The illustration of this statement by reference to a particular diagram; (3) Any additional construction which may be necessary to the demonstration; (4) The demonstration proper.

Order of arrangement.

The exact language of the text-book should always be used in the statement of propositions, and in quoting definitions and all fundamental principles, unless such language is changed by the instructor or student for a particular reason; but the demonstration should not be memorized, although the general order of thought should necessarily be retained, and the spirit and style of the language be preserved. The diagram should always be constructed on the blackboard by the pupil, without prompting from any source. When the construction is complete, he should

Demonstration.

usually stand at the board, and trace the line of thought by pointing to the figure, as he proceeds in the demonstration. Some have thought it best to use the Arabic figures to designate points, lines etc., instead of the capital letters, as ordinarily found in our text-books, the purpose being to prevent mere memorizing; but in reference to this, it is to be said that, besides its exceeding inelegance, and the fact, moreover, that the capital letters are a part of the language of the science, the device is of little or no use as a preventive of memorizing. It is quite as easy for a pupil who is so disposed, to memorize by the mere position or appearance of the parts, with figures to designate them, or even without any characters attached, as by means of letters. The pupil can make as perfect a parrot-like recitation, by merely memorizing every statement as referring to certain parts of the diagram, and by using the barbarous diction, "line this", "line that", etc., which may be heard in some class rooms, as he can in any other way. Our counsel is, use the *language of the science* (the letters), and depend on something less superficial, to prevent all improper memorizing. In referring to antecedent propositions constituting the basis of the argument, it is far more important that the proposition be quoted, than that its number be given; for the latter is of no sort of use except as a mere class-room convenience, while the former method is of essential service in bringing out the argument, and also in keeping the truths of the science fresh in the mind, and familiar on the tongue. Such methods should constitute the ordinary class-room drill; but there are others which must not be neglected, nor be unfrequent. First among these is the giving of outlines of demonstrations without going through the details, and without reference to a diagram. This is one of the best tests of proficiency which can be applied, and the whole subject should be repeatedly reviewed in this way. Again, frequent reviews of groups of theorems without demonstrations are essential. Thus, the teacher may call for the propositions concerning *equality of triangles*, the elementary propositions concerning the *measurement of angles*, the propositions concerning *parallels*, etc. When a student is assigned such a topic, he should give all the facts embraced under it (definitions, propositions, corollaries, and scholiums), without being prompted. These three classes of exercises will form the staple of all class-room work. For a final review, students may be set to tracing certain lines of thought running through the whole subject. Thus, given the subject of *equality*, he will define it, distinguish it from nearly related notions, such as similarity and equivalence, show that the two latter notions make up the former, classify all the propositions of elementary geometry which relate to equality, and be able to give them with their demonstrations, pointing out any common principle which may seem to run through the demonstrations. In reference to the latter he will find that *equality* is always proved by the mere application of one figure to the other, with the modification, that in case of *equality by symmetry* the figures are divided into parts, which parts are then applied as before. In like manner, he can be set to study the subject of *similarity*. Such a study will not be merely a review of the section on *equality*, or that on *similarity*, since these ideas are the basis of the thought in many propositions where they do not constitute the main subject or purpose. In fact, it will be found that nearly one-half of the propositions of geometry involve one or the other of these notions *(equality* and *similarity)* as the basis of thought. Again he may be set to select and study the propositions relating to *form,* and then those in which *magnitude* is the object of inquiry: these two ideas dividing between them the whole domain of geometrical truth. Finally, it is of the highest importance, that, from first to last, the pupil be trained in the practical application of the abstract truths as fast as they are learned. No truth is well learned until it can be applied; and it would be quite incredible to one who has not had large observation, how fully one may appear to understand a geometrical truth, and yet be totally unable to apply it. The writer has examined in geometry hundreds of students desiring to enter college in "advanced standing", and has made this a matter of careful observation. For example, he has usually asked such students, "How do you find the area of a spherical triangle?" Generally the answer has been promptly given, "By multiplying the spherical excess by the tri-rectangular triangle"; and, quite generally, the candidate has been found able to demonstrate the proposition. But in no instance has the examiner ever found a student, who had not been trained in the practical application of the statement, able to compute the area of a triangle the angles of which are, say 110°, 94°, and 87°, on a sphere, the radius of which is 2 feet. In fact, they could tell what a tri-rectangular triangle is, what part of the sphere it is, and what the spherical excess is; but not one could actually find the number of square inches in the area of the triangle. A student may appear to have thoroughly mastered solid geometry, and yet be totally unable to solve such a problem as, To find how many barrels of water a cistern in the form of the frustum of a cone will contain. It is obvious, therefore, that the teacher of geometry should never allow his pupils to omit the practical examples.

Practical applications.

V. *Geometrical Invention.* — This term is used to designate the power to discover demonstrations of propositions or the solution of problems. Many excellent teachers quite overrate the ordinary student's power in this direction. Some have even thought, that, from the first, a pupil can be led to discover the demonstrations of all the propositions. New classes may, indeed, make commendable progress in geometry, and have put into their hands only the mere statement of propositions; but it will be found that they do not originate the demonstrations which they bring into the class; they simply look them up in other textbooks, and thus learn them. After a pupil has acquired a considerable stock of geometrical knowledge, any real test will show that original demonstrations are but slowly evolved, even of the simplest propositions. Many students have little or no capacity in this direction; and, therefore, to make it the staple of geometrical teaching, would be supreme folly. Some exercise of this kind may, and should, be given from an early stage of the study; and students may be stimulated and helped in the work, so that all the ability for such exercise, which really exists in the class, may be brought out; but, after all, there is no reasonable ground to expect that any large amount of such ability can be developed in the majority of students of elementary geometry. Certainly, this is not the purpose for which geometry holds its eminent place in the curriculum of our colleges. It is that students may learn what a logical argument is and how to frame it,

Original demonstrations.

from the study of such arguments, carefully elaborated and expressed by the ripest culture. What but the most clumsy work can be expected from the tyro in framing such arguments, if he has not had much study of the best models? To put a demonstration in good form, as well as to evolve it, is the ripest fruit of scholarship, not the daily work of beginners; the ability to do either is to be acquired, in the first instance, by a protracted and careful study of the work of masters. It is not the purpose of these remarks to discourage all attempts to secure original demonstrations, but to guard against a serious error into which enthusiastic and ambitious teachers are in danger of falling; and the conclusion is, that, for the most part, pupils must be furnished with the demonstrations of elementary geometry, either by a text-book, or by the hints of a competent and judicious teacher; and that it is best that it should be so. But let not this topic of geometrical invention be confounded with that of practical exercise in applying the truths learned. The latter is, as has been said, essential for all, but especially important for those who are dull of apprehension.

VI. Lastly, it is to be remarked that a great change has come about within the last century, in reference to the kind of demonstration which is admissible in geometry. Formerly, geometricians were totally averse to admitting any conception of *motion* or *time* into a geometrical argument. These were rigidly excluded as foreign to the subject and as defiling its purity. Both are now freely admitted. Again, the infinitesimal method was formerly as rigidly excluded, but is now coming to be admitted. These methods greatly facilitate geometrical inquiry, and are now freely used by the best writers and teachers. (See MATHEMATICS.)

Motion and time.

GERMAN LANGUAGE. The German language ranks, with the English and French, in value and importance, above all the other languages of the civilized world. It is very extensively studied in the literary institutions of every civilized country, and as a department of school and college instruction, continues to assume, from year to year, greater prominence.

Rank.

The method of studying German, in English and American universities, colleges, seminaries, and academies is about the same as that pursued in the study of French. The most important feature which broadly distinguishes the German language from the French, and which an intelligent teacher will always keep in view from the very first lesson he gives, is the close resemblance between German and English words, especially those used in common life. Many of these words are spelled exactly alike; large classes of other words show so slight a modification, that the pupils recognize them at once (as *Vater*, *Mutter*, *Bruder*, *Buch*, *Haus*), and still others present changes made according to certain laws which are easily understood, even at the earliest stage of instruction, and by the most youthful beginner (as *zehn*, ten; *Zinn*, tin; *Tag*, day; *sagen*, say). By a skillful use of this extensive resemblance of the two languages, the intelligent teacher has it in his power to give to the beginner, in a few lessons, the command of a very large number of words. The strange letters which seem to surround the first lessons in German with considerable difficulty, are quite easily learned by the aid of words which are substantially the same in German as in English. Whole German

Method of study.

sentences can, in this way, be at once understood; and when translation forms a prominent object of the study, the pupil should begin to translate from German into English, as soon as he knows the letters. For exercise in the declensions and conjugations, the selection of cognate words for the paradigms likewise facilitates the progress of the pupils. In this part of the grammar, German at once seems to the beginner to be more complicated than English, and presents to him the greatest difficulties he has to surmount; among which may be enumerated the following: (1) The noun in German has four cases, and the plural is formed in four different ways as far as its termination is concerned, besides modifying the radical vowel; (2) Adjectives and adjective pronouns are declined in three different ways; (3) The past participle generally adds the prefix *ge*, and, in compound verbs, this prefix, in many cases, is placed between the verb and the particle with which it is compounded, or the particle is detached and placed at the close of even a long sentence. In constructing exercises for the study of these differences, it will again be found a help to choose for the paradigms words similar to English words, or such as are common to both languages, so that the attention of the pupil may be concentrated upon the learning of the inflectional peculiarities. It is, however, not only the resemblance of German and English words, but also other points of similarity, in the etymology of the two languages, that should be made use of. Thus the possessive case of English nouns may be made to illustrate not only the German genitive, but the entire declension, of which the English possessive is a remnant. A reference to the plural forms *men*, *women*, *feet*, *geese*, *mice*, will explain the modification of a large number of German nouns in the plural; as will also such forms as *children*, *brethren*, and *pence*. The fact that the division of verbs into *strong* and *weak* is the same in both languages, that the formation of the principal parts of both is similar (*see*, *saw*, *seen — se-hen*, *sah, ge-sehen; love*, *loved*, *loved — lieb-en*, *liebte*, *ge-liebt*) and that even, as a general rule, the same verbs belong, in both languages, to the one or to the other conjugation, is easily comprehended even by beginners, and greatly assists them to understand the structure of the foreign language.

The comparison of the German language with the English should not be limited to the points just mentioned; but all the peculiar features of German should be noticed. In the study of any foreign language, *German* a clear understanding of the most conspicuous characteristics helps *and* to fix in the mind a clear conception of the language. Among *English.* the features of the German grammar to which special attention should be called, when they are met with for the first time, are the following: (1) The gender of nouns is arbitrary, and many nouns that are neuter in English are either masculine or feminine in German; (2) One or more long qualifying adjuncts may intervene between the article and its noun; (3) The order of sequence of auxiliary verbs is entirely reversed in subjunctive propositions; (4) Prepositions and verbs govern three different cases of the noun; (5) The object precedes the verb more frequently than in English.

The correct pronunciation of German, as of every foreign tongue, must be learned by imitating the teacher. This is especially the case with the *Pronun-* sounds that have no equivalent in English, as *ö*, *ü*, *ch*, the *ciation.* guttural *g*, short *o*, *r*, and the combinations of *sp* and *st*. Their number is comparatively small; and, if they are steadily practiced, it will require only a short time to learn to enunciate them correctly. For a full treatment of this subject, see *Cyclopædia of Education*.

GIFTS, Kindergarten, the term used by Froebel to designate the apparatus devised by him for kindergarten instruction, inasmuch as they are not used by the teacher but *given* to the children, as the *Definition.* material for interesting and instructive occupation, by the manipulation of which their faculties are unfolded in accordance with the *developing method* (q. v.). These *gifts* are grouped in sets, numbered from 1 to 20, and include the following, of which, however, Nos. 8 to 20 did not originate with Froebel directly: (1) *Six soft balls* of various *Enumeration.* colors, the object of the use of which is to teach *color* (primary and secondary), and *direction* (forward and backward, right and left, up and down); also to train the eye, and to exercise the hands, arms, and feet in various plays. (2) *Sphere, cube,* and *cylinder,* designed to teach *form,* by directing the attention of the child to resemblances and differences in objects. This is done by pointing out, explaining, and counting the sides, edges, and corners of the cube, and by showing how it differs, in these respects, from the sphere and cylinder. The manipulation by the child should, of course, precede this demonstration by the teacher. The child's self-activity will prompt it to place these forms in various positions and combinations, so as to realize in its conceptions every thing that is analogous or dissimilar in them. (3) A *large cube* divided into eight equal cubes, the object being to teach both *form* and *number,* also to give a rudimental idea of fractions. (4) A *large cube* divided into eight oblong blocks, designed to teach *number* and a simple variety of *form* (cube and parallelopiped). (5) A *large cube* divided into 27 equal cubes, three of the latter being subdivided into half cubes, and three others into quarter cubes (forming triangular prisms). This is a further continuation and complement of (3), but affording much ampler means of combination both as to *form* and *number.* (6) A *large cube* so divided as to consist of 18 whole oblong blocks, three similar blocks divided lengthwise, and six divided breadthwise, — a still further continuation of the ideas involved in (3). (7) *Triangular* and *quadrangular tablets* of polished wood, affording the means of further exercise in reversing the position of forms and combining them; and presenting, in addition, illustrations of *plane surfaces,* instead of *solids,* as in the previous gifts. This arrangement, placing the surfaces after the solids, recognizes an important principle of education, — that we should pass from the concrete to the abstract (see FORM), the square being a side of the cube, and a triangle deduced from the prism. (8) *Sticks for laying,* — wooden sticks about 13 inches long, to be cut into various lengths by the teacher or pupil, as occasion may require. These sticks, like most of the previous gifts, are designed to teach numerical proportions. The multiplication table may be practically learned by means of this gift. The forms of the letters of the alphabet, and the Roman and Arabic numerals, may also be learned. (9) *Rings for ring-laying,* consisting of whole and half rings of various sizes, in wire, for forming figures; designed to develop further ideas of form, also to afford a means for developing constructiveness of the pupils, and practice in composing simple designs. (10) *Drawing slates* and *paper,* consisting of slates ruled in squares, and paper ruled in squares, for the purpose of enabling the pupil to draw or copy simple figures, in a methodical manner, the ruling aiding them in the adjustment of proportions. (11) *Perforating paper*, ruled in squares on one side only, with perforating needles, affording more advanced practice in producing forms, and executing simple designs. (12) *Embroidering material*, to be used for transferring the designs executed on the perforating paper, by embroidering them with colored worsted or silk on card board. (13) *Paper for cutting*: squares of paper are folded, cut according to certain rules, and formed into figures. The child's inclination for using the scissors is thus ingeniously turned to account, and made to produce very gratifying results. (14) *Weaving paper*: strips of colored paper are, by means of a steel or wooden needle of peculiar construction, woven into a differently colored sheet of paper, which is cut into strips throughout its entire surface, except a margin at each end to keep the strips in their places. A very great variety of figures is thus produced, and the inventive powers of the child are constantly brought into requisition. (15) *Plaiting material*, including sets of flats for interlacing so as to form geometrical and fancy figures. (16) *Jointed slats (goniographs)*, for forming angles and geometrical figures. (17) *Paper for intertwining*: paper strips of various colors, eight or ten inches long, folded lengthwise, used to represent a variety of geometrical and fancy figures, by plaiting them according to certain rules. (18) *Paper for folding*, consisting of square, rectangular, and triangular pieces, with which variously shaped objects may be formed. (19) *Material for peas work*, consisting of wires of various lengths pointed at the ends, which are passed through peas, that have been soaked in water for six or eight hours; these are then used to imitate various objects and geometrical figures. Cork cubes are sometimes used instead of the peas, as being more convenient. (20) *Material for modeling*: modeling knives, of wood, and modeling boards, by means of which various forms are modeled in bees-wax, clay, putty, or some other soft substance. These gifts thus represent every kind of technical activity, from the mere collection of the raw material to the delicate processes of design as well as plastic art. They are designed to develop not only the constructive ability of the pupil, through his natural impulse to activity, and by the exercise of the faculty of conception, so characteristic of childhood, but by their countless combinations of color and form to lay the foundation for a complete development of the esthetic nature. They address, at once, his intellect, his emotions, and his physical activities; while, as the child works out the results himself, he gains confidence in his own ability to surmount obstacles, and thus learns an enduring lesson of self-reliance. Kindergarten gifts and occupation material suitable for schools or families, are put up in sets and sold in boxes convenient for use.

Design.

GIRLS, Education of. See FEMALE EDUCATION.

GLOBE, Artificial (Latin, *globus*), a hollow sphere, made of metal, plaster, or pasteboard, used as a model of the earth, and having delineated upon it all the various natural and political divisions of the terrestrial surface, together with the circles, etc., used in mathematical geography. Through its center, runs an iron axis the two ends of which project, and are fastened to a circle, or ring, of brass, within which the globe can be turned around. This ring, called the *brazen meridian*, is graduated so as to indicate degrees of latitude, and by rotating the globe can be made to represent the meridian of any place. The artificial globe is also usually surrounded with a broad horizontal ring of wood, called the *wooden horizon*, which has two slots in which the meridian, and with it the globe move, so that either pole may be elevated or depressed, and the horizon adapted to any place. The upper surface of the wooden horizon is divided into several concentric circles, representing degrees of amplitude and azimuth, signs of the zodiac, the points of the compass, the divisions of the year into months and days. etc. Such a globe is called a *terrestrial* globe. A *celestial* globe differs from it in representing the appearance of the starry heavens, constellations, etc., as if seen from the center of the globe. Globes of much simpler construction are made for elementary instruction.

GONIGRAPH (Gr. γωνία, an angle, and γράφειν, to write), an instrument used in kindergarten exercises and in object-teaching, to illustrate the nature and formation of angles and polygons. It consists of a series of narrow jointed slats of equal length, by the different combinations of which figures of various shapes may be formed. The number of slats, or links. varies from 3 to as many as 16, or even more. As a piece of kindergarten apparatus (*gift*), the gonigraph may be made the means of much instructive entertainment to a young child, who from its manipulation will acquire ideas of a great variety of figures. In the more advanced object-teaching, in connection with the subject of *form*, it will be found very useful, as well as attractive. Gonigraphs are usually sold in sets as a part of the apparatus necessary for kindergarten work. (See GIFTS.)

GOVERNMENT, School, like the government of a state, must be based upon the establishment of authority, which includes not only
Basis. the right to make laws, but the power, as well as the right, to execute them. These powers, in every civilized state and community, are distributed among different persons, so as to prevent centralized authority leading to despotism; but, in the little community of the school room, they must, to a greater or less extent, be possessed by one person. General rules for the management of a school, it is true, may be prescribed by the school officers to whom the teacher is amenable: but the actual government of the school, that which converts it from a chaotic, disorderly crowd of children into a regular organization, under control and discipline, must be exclusively the work of the teacher, hence called the *school-master*. Force of character in the teacher is the basis of discipline. " Divest teaching", says Kellogg, in *School Management* (1880), "of the personal force element, and of the subtle influence of the teacher, and little is left".

The character of the school government depends upon the manner as well as the degree in which the teacher's authority is established; and the influence of the school upon the intellectual and moral character of its
On what pupils will depend upon the kind of government maintained.
dependent. No school can be efficient without order, and order can only result from judicious and effective government. The latter must, in all cases, depend upon (1) the rules or requirements laid down, and (2) the manner in which they are enforced. Government is often impaired by unwise legislation — unwise in the kind of laws enacted, or in their

number. The rules made for the government of a school should be as few and as simple as possible. A multiplicity of set regulations confuses the pupils, and tends to multiply offenses. Besides, the children, *Rules.* by the habit of complying with a kind of written law, are apt to think every thing right that is not specifically forbidden, and thus fail to exercise their conscience; that is, in their attention to the *mala prohibita*, they lose sight of the *mala per se*. "If a school", says D. P. Page, "is to be governed by a code of laws, the pupils will act upon the principle that whatever is not proscribed is admissible. Consequently, without inquiring whether an act is right, their only inquiry will be, is it forbidden? Now, no teacher was ever yet so wise as to make laws for every case; the consequence is, he is daily perplexed with unforeseen troubles, or with some ingenious evasions of his inflexible code. In all this matter, the worst feature is the fact that the child judges of his acts by the law of the teacher rather than by the law of his conscience, and is thus in danger of perverting and blunting the moral sense". Government by positive enactments is, therefore, to be dispensed with as much as possible; but such rules as are made should be strictly and uniformly enforced. These rules constitute what may be called *school legislation*, and are not to be confounded with requirements of a less formal character, which the pupil's own intelligence and sense of right are to be trained to recognize without particular enunciation, nor with those moral precepts which are addressed rather to the pupil as an individual, and therefore do not directly concern the organization of the school. We here treat of school government in the strict sense of the term. In the enforcement of school legislation, however, *Enforcement.* we are to keep in view the good of the pupil as well as the good of the school, but primarily the latter. The principle is this: The school is an organization designed to be the means of affording an education to a large number of pupils, and the school laws are made to protect that organization, and render it effective in the carrying out of its proper object; hence, the welfare of the school must be paramount to that of any individual pupil. The violation of a rule may, indeed, be sometimes overlooked without injury to the offender, perhaps to his benefit; but, as such a course tends to weaken or destroy the school government, the law must be uniformly enforced. No enforcement of law can be accomplished without the punishment of the offender; hence, the kind of school punishments that are suitable under the various circumstances that arise becomes a matter for the careful consideration of the teacher. Whether in enforcing obedience to wholesome regulations, corporal punishment should be resorted to, and, if so, to what extent and in what manner, forms also an important part of the general discussion of school government. But there must be prevention as well as correction — rewards, as incentives to obedience and good conduct, as well as punishments to chastise the wrong-doer, and deter others from wrong-doing. A system of rewards has a very *Rewards.* important bearing upon school government when they are dispensed with uniformity and equity. Under this head are included merit marks, certificates and diplomas of proficiency and good conduct, and prizes. Many questions arise in connection with the administration of school government in this respect. The general efficacy and propriety of rewards cannot be doubted. They appeal to a principle of human nature universally operative. "Whatever", says Jewell, "may be possible in the mature man, in the line of that sublime abstraction, 'Virtue is its own reward', the child is neither equal to such abstractions, nor are they demanded of him".

The efficacy of school government must depend very much on the manner in which the teacher exercises the authority conferred upon him in virtue of his office. If he bases it upon force, if the language he addresses to his pupils be uniformly that of command, threatening, or angry rebuke, there will be engendered in their minds a feeling of antagonism, from which will result disobedience, and occasionally open rebellion. On the other hand, if he is kind and considerate, but at the same time firm and resolute, he will gain first the respect of his pupils and then their affection. When that is accomplished, the government of his school will be quite easy. (See AUTHORITY.) The following are wise suggestions in regard to the proper course of the teacher in obtaining and preserving the control of his school: "(1) Endeavor to convince your scholars that you are their friend, — that you aim at their improvement, and desire their good. It will not take long to satisfy them of this, if you are so in reality. (2) Never give a command which you are not resolved to see obeyed. (3) Try to create throughout the school a popular sentiment in favor of order and virtue. It is next to impossible to carry into effect, for any length of time, a regulation, however important, which is opposed to *public opinion*". Fellenberg strongly insists upon this as the most efficient means of school government. "The pupil", he says, "can seldom resist the force of truth when he finds himself condemned by the common voice of his companions, and is often more humbled by censure from his equals, than by any of the admonitions of his superiors". To the above important injunctions for the teacher should be added the following: Observe in your conduct toward your pupils a strict impartiality. Children are keen observers, and at once detect the slightest indications of favoritism; and nothing more effectually than this destroys their respect for the teacher, and undermines his authority. Tact and self-control will enable the teacher to dispense, to a very great extent, with any decided demonstration of authority. "There is", says Page, "such a thing as keeping a school *too still* by over-government. A man of firm nerve can, by keeping up a constant constraint both in himself and pupils, force a death-like silence upon his school. You can hear a pin drop at any time, and the figure of every child is as if moulded in cast-iron. But be it remembered, this is the stillness of constraint, not the stillness of activity. There should be silence in school, a serene and soothing quiet; but it should, if possible, be the quiet of cheerfulness and agreeable devotion to study, rather than the 'palsy of fear'". (See FEAR.) One of the most important means of effective school government is to keep the pupils constantly busy, to awaken in their minds an interest in their studies, to vary the exercises so as to prevent tedious monotony, to have special methods of relief, after their minds have become wearied by close attention. For this purpose, in primary schools, in which very young children are taught, movement exercises of a simple character may be resorted to; and, in all schools, vocal music, which always exerts the most pleasing and satisfactory influence. Calisthenics and gymnastics may be employed with good effect. In short, if the school is conducted in such a way as to recognize the peculiar nature, disposition, and wants of children, the school government will be found to involve but little difficulty.

GRADE (Lat. *gradus*, a step), the relative standing of schools, classes, or pupils, in a system of education. Thus education, or instruction, is designated, according to its grade, primary or elementary, secondary, and superior or higher. A course of study is divided into grades for convenience in classification, all the pupils in each class being supposed to be nearly of the same degree of proficiency. The number of grades into which a course of study should be divided is dictated by considerations of expediency and convenience. The grades, however, should be arranged so as to assign proper proportions of work for the several portions of time into which the school year, or the period of the entire curriculum, is divided. The arrangement of grades is also beneficial in definitely marking the progress of the pupil, and thus affording him encouragement to proceed by regular promotion from grade to grade. (See CLASS.)

GRADED SCHOOLS are usually defined as schools in which the pupils are classified according to their progress in scholarship as compared *Definition.* with a course of study divided into grades, pupils of the same or a similar degree of proficiency being placed in the same class. An ungraded school, on the other hand, is one in which the pupils are taught individually, each one being advanced as far and as fast as circumstances permit, without regard to the progress of other pupils. The *graded system* is thus based upon classification; and its efficacy as a system must *Grades* depend very greatly upon the accuracy with which the classifica- *and classes.* tion has been made. Grades, however, are not to be confounded with classes; the former are divisions of the course of study based upon various considerations, the latter are divisions of the school based upon uniformity of attainments. In a small school, the same number of grades may be needed as in a large school, the course of study being the same, and the promotions being made with equal frequency; hence, as the number of classes must be smaller, it will be necessary that each class should pursue two or more grades simultaneously or in succession; that is to say, the promotions from grade to grade will be more frequent than from class to class. On the other hand, in a large school, the number of classes may be greater than that of the grades, which will necessitate the forming of two or more classes, under separate teachers, in the same grade. In the management of a large school, this will be found to be better than a subdivision of the grades, requiring either an extension of the time for completing the course, or greater frequency in the promotions.

The advantages of the graded system have been thus enumerated: (1) They economize the labor of instruction; (2) They reduce the cost of *Graded* instruction, since a smaller number of teachers are required for *system.* effective work in a classified or graded school; (3) They make the instruction more effective, inasmuch as the teacher can more readily hear the lessons of an entire class than of the pupils separately, and thus there will be better opportunity for actual teaching, explanation, drill, etc.; (4) They facilitate good government and discipline, because all the pupils are kept constantly under the direct control and instruction of the teacher, and, besides, are kept constantly busy; (5) They afford a better means of inciting pupils to industry, by promoting their ambition to excel, inasmuch as there is a constant competition among the pupils of a class, which cannot exist when the pupils are instructed separately. On the other hand, many objections have been urged against the system of graded schools, chief among which is, that the interests of the individual pupil are often sacrificed to those of the many, the individual being merged in the mass.

GRADUATE (Lat. *graduare*, from *gradus*, a step or degree), to confer an academic degree, thus advancing to a higher rank in scholarship; also, to receive a degree from a college or university. A person is said to graduate when he takes a degree, and the college or university is said to graduate a student when it admits him to an honorable standing as a scholar by conferring a degree. The person who thus takes a degree, is called a *graduate*. (See DEGREES.)

GRAMMAR. The study of grammar now constitutes, in every civilized country, an essential part of the learning of languages, both the vernacular and foreign. Opinions, however, still widely differ as to the place which grammar should occupy in the study of language, the method by which it should be taught, the point of time at which it should be begun, and the amount of time which should be devoted to it. There is at present a more general agreement among educators than at any previous time, that not only is a grammatical knowledge necessary for a good command of any language, but that thorough training in the rules of grammar is one of the best means to develop the faculties of the mind, and is especially calculated to promote correct and logical thinking. (See GRAMMAR, ENGLISH; ENGLISH, STUDY OF.) For a full treatment of this subject see *Cyclopædia of Education*.

GRAMMAR, English. Probably, there is no subject that has been taught with so great a disregard of the fundamental principles of teaching as English grammar; and there is certainly none that has so imperfectly attained its practical aim — correctness in the use of language. This has arisen from two errors of procedure: (1) an attempt to teach definitions without developing in the minds of the pupils the ideas underlying them, and rules previous to an illustration of their necessity; and (2) confining the instruction to merely theoretical and critical work, without sufficient practice in the application of principles and rules to the actual use of language. The introduction of analysis was the result of an effort to reform the first of these errors; and the language-lesson system, a reaction against the second. Grammar being, distinctively, the *science of the sentence*, the preliminary step in all grammatical instruction must be, to give to the pupil a clear and correct idea of what constitutes a sentence, by presenting for his examination and analysis examples of sentences of a simple structure, by analyzing which he will easily be made to see what principal parts must enter into their composition, and how other parts are used as adjuncts. (See ANALYSIS, GRAMMATICAL.) The outline of a complete scheme of teaching grammar in all its stages is presented in the following points: (1) Principles, definitions, and rules should be progressively taught by requiring the pupil to analyze, and also to compose,

Errors.

Analysis.

System of teaching grammar.

classified sentences commencing with those of the simplest construction, and passing gradually to such as are of the most complex structure; (2) No definition or rule should be committed to memory and formally recited until the pupil, by sufficient practice, has obtained a clear conception of the office of the word defined, and the nature of the usage which the rule is intended to guide. For example, it is absurd to try to teach a child the meaning of a participle or a relative pronoun at an elementary stage of the instruction, because the structures in which alone they can occur are too complex to be understood at that stage. And it is equally absurd to require a child to commit to memory the rule, "A verb must agree with its subject or nominative in person and number", until by the comparison of a number of sentences illustrating this usage, he is made to understand what is meant by *agreement* in grammar, and how expressions may be incorrect by a failure to observe this rule. According to this method, the pupil is first made acquainted with the distinction of *subject* and *predicate*, as being the essential parts of every sentence. This forms the basis for teaching him the two parts of speech, — the verb and the noun. From this point, the sentence may be complicated by the successive insertion of modifying words, phrases, or clauses, so as to illustrate not only the nature and use of each of the parts of speech, but every peculiar structure. This may be illustrated by the following example of a sentence thus expanded: (1) *Boys learn.* (2) *The* boys learn. (3) The *studious* boys learn. (4) The studious boys learn *rapidly.* (5) The studious boys learn *their lessons.* (6) The studious boys learn their lessons *in school.* (7) The boys *and* girls learn. (8) The boys learn, *but* the girls do not learn. (9) The boys *who* study will learn. Of course, each sentence here given is only a specimen of what may be used at each step; and when these several steps have been taken, the pupil will have acquired a knowledge of the functions of the different parts of speech. Thus, in (1), he learns the noun and the verb; in (2), the article is added; in (3), the adjective; in (4), the adverb; in (5), the pronoun; in (6), the preposition; in (7), the conjunction, as a connective of words; in (8), the conjunction, as a connective of sentences; in (9), the relative pronoun. After much preliminary oral instruction of this kind the pupil may be required to learn simple definitions. Underlying the whole process, it will be perceived, is the *analysis* of the sentence, *parsing* coming in at a later stage, as the application to particular sentences, according to a given *praxis*, of the definitions and rules learned. This is the method recommended by prominent educators of the present day. "The analysis of a sentence", says Wickersham, "consists in finding its elements, or in reducing it to the parts of speech, of which it is composed. Parsing consists in finding out these parts of speech and determining their properties and relations. Both should be combined, as is the case in similar operations in other sciences. The botanist analyzes a plant, and then names and describes its several parts. The anatomist dissects a subject, and then characterizes the organs thus brought to his notice. Grammar can be studied successfully in no other way. Parsing, without a preceding analysis, can lead but to a very imperfect knowledge of the organic structure of sentences". To the value of the analytical method, Prof. Whitney thus bears witness: "Give me a man who can, with full in-

Analysis and parsing.

telligence, take to pieces an English sentence, brief and not too complicated even, and I will welcome him as better prepared for further study in other languages than if he had read both Cæsar and Virgil, and could parse them in the routine style in which they are often parsed". Parsing should not be made a routine; when it becomes such, it is worse than useless. The constant application of complicated definitions and rules derived from a language of inflections, to English words and sentences having scarcely an inflection, is to the pupil a senseless process, and must only tend to dull, instead of cultivating and sharpening, his intellectual faculties. It makes him, as has been said, a "parsing machine". The definitions and rules of English grammar should be simplified, recognizing the fact that English is not an inflectional language, except in a very few particulars; and hence, that the principles of *agreement* and *government* have scarcely any application. The multiplying of rules that regulate nothing is idle. Thus, of what use it is to cause a child to repeat, in parsing, twenty times perhaps in a single lesson, the so-called syntactical rule, "Adjectives relate to nouns and pronouns", when he has already learned as a definition that "Adjectives are words added to nouns and pronouns?" A large portion of the rules of syntax laid down in most text-books are rather a repetition of the definitions comprehended in etymology than separate rules necessary to guide us in the construction of sentences. All such needless machinery should be eliminated. The application of the terms *case*, *gender*, *person*, and all other designations of inflectional variations of words, should be kept within the narrow limits prescribed by the simplicity of the language. In most systems of grammar, however, we find these terms used in so ambiguous a way as almost hopelessly to obscure the subject and perplex the learner. Sometimes, for example, *case* is used to indicate a form or inflection, at others, a mere relation without change of form; while the fact to be taught is, that where there is no inflection there is no case. The rule that "a noun which is the subject of a verb must be in the nominative case" is, in English, useless and absurd. The senseless machinery of English grammar, as it has been generally taught, has brought the whole subject under reprobation, as being useless in an elementary school curriculum, and as superseded in that of the high school and college, by the study of Latin; while there is no doubt that college graduates, in the United States, are generally in nothing so deficient as in a practical and critical knowledge of their own language. While it is very true that the use of every language is a matter of habit rather than of rule; every writer and speaker knows, that there are myriads of instances in which the ear and the memory, however trained by habit, will not serve as a guide, and that a knowledge of the principles and usages of language in regard to nice points of construction, is indispensable. "Since language", says Currie, "is the instrument of all thought, a more commanding knowledge of it than habit alone can give must be deemed a necessity of education, and particularly of all education which pretends to cultivate the mind".

Definitions and rules.

GRAMMAR SCHOOLS, so called, not because they gave instruction in English grammar, but from the fact of their making the teaching of Latin and Greek — particularly, and sometimes exclusively, the former — their especial aim, existed in England from the earliest times. They discharged the same function as the old cathedral schools or the cloister schools of the monasteries, and were established and supported either by the endowments of benevolent individuals, or by governmental appropriations. In England, the endowed grammar schools are very numerous and many of quite ancient foundation.

Grammar schools, in the United States, were originally of the same character as in England and Scotland. The gradual development of the common-school system in the United States, joined with the partial decline of Latin and Greek as instruments of education, and the demand for studies of a more practical character, that is, more in demand as a preparation for the ordinary duties of life, have led to a different application of the term *grammar schools*. The study of English grammar having taken the place of Latin grammar in schools of an elementary grade, such schools came to be designated *grammar schools*, and the former grammar or classical schools received the name of *high schools* or *academies*. In most of the public-school systems of the cities of the Union, grammar schools are schools of a grade between the primary schools in which the first rudiments of instruction are imparted, and the high schools. Some of the grammar schools, so called, have a primary, an intermediate, and a grammar department. In these cases, the term *grammar schools* has been used with no definite idea of its propriety, except as designating a somewhat higher grade of schools than those in which the simplest rudiments of an English education are afforded; since even in these grammar schools English grammar is taught in only the higher grades or classes.

GREEK LANGUAGE, one of the two classical languages which as such constitute an important part of the course of study in all the higher literary institutions of the civilized world.

In regard to the method to be pursued in teaching Greek, there is a greater agreement among leading educators, than in respect to many other studies. It is generally admitted that the comparative difficulty *Method of* of Greek grammar, even of its first or etymological part, makes *teaching.* it desirable that all whose education is to comprehend a knowledge of this language, should begin the study at an early age, when the vigor of memory is still fresh, and its function still prevails in the course of instruction. Hamilton's and Jacotot's methods find now-a-days few followers in the teaching of Greek; and the study of grammar, with translations from Greek into English and English into Greek, chiefly occupies the attention of the beginner. It has been proposed, and sometimes attempted, to begin the teaching of the language, in accordance with the development of Greek literature, with the study of the epic and old Ionic dialects; but the old practice to make the Attic dialect the basis has victoriously maintained its traditional ascendency. Exercises in translating from the native language into Greek should not be omitted, as is frequently done; though it is well understood that, on account of the greater difficulties presented by the Greek, and the shorter time allowed for the study of it, the same proficiency in writing Greek is hardly ever or anywhere attained as in Latin. The first exercises in translating Greek into English, or any other native tongue, are now generally provided in the grammars. Where grammars are used which exclude exercises in translation, the use of a Greek reader is at once begun. In general, the use of a reader before the taking up of a particular author, is continued longer in Greek than in Latin, because of the longer time required to obtain a good knowledge of the grammatical rules in the former. When the pupil is far enough advanced to take up the reading of Greek authors, the teacher, in *Course of reading.* making the selection, should not only be careful to proceed from the easier to the more difficult writers, and to prefer the classic authors, but also to read enough of the selected work to give to the students an adequate idea of the spirit of Greek literature. The orations, philosophical dialogues, and dramas are particularly suited for advanced classes in Greek. Of course, instruction in Greek is not considered complete without the reading of, at least, one of the Homeric poems; and it is fortunate that the easy flow of the language of these poems fits them for an early stage of classic reading. Among the Greek historians, Xenophon and Herodotus fully deserve the favor of teachers and students, which they have enjoyed for centuries. In regard to Herodotus it is, however, desirable to wait until the pupils are well grounded in the Attic dialect. To include Thucydides in a regular course appears to many classical scholars objectionable, as the language is too difficult for the majority of college students, and as the gloomy period which he describes is not calculated to increase the students' interest in ancient Greece. Of the dramatic poets, Æschylus and Aristophanes are not suited for schools; and, therefore, only Sophocles and Euripides can be recommended.

GYMNASIUM (Gr. γυμνάσιον, a place for bodily exercises, from γυμνός, naked), a term applied, in ancient Greece and Rome, to schools for physical education, but in modern Germany and some other countries of continental Europe, to a class of secondary schools which hold a middle place between elementary schools and the universities. In England and the United States, in which the colleges correspond to the German gymnasia, the term gymnasium is limited to places for physical exercises.

GYMNASTICS (Gr. γυμναστική, from γυμνός, naked), a system of bodily exercises designed to develop muscular strength, and to promote general physical culture and health. In the article on *Calisthenics*, this subject has already been treated as far as it comprehends those light physical exercises which are especially adapted for females, although frequently used in the education of persons of the other sex; and, in the employment of the severer gymnastic training, there should be a careful discrimination having regard to the age and physical constitution of the pupil. Much injury may be done by requiring all the members of a school or class to perform the same exercises, more especially such as are of a violent character. Indeed, it may be doubted whether, up to the age of sixteen, for the ordinary purpose of physical development and health, boys need anything more than abundant opportunity and time for the out-door sports and recreations in which their natural activity will generally prompt them to engage. Beyond that age, gymnastic exercises, properly regulated, may be made the means of laying the foundation of permanent strength and health. Military drill is often introduced into schools and colleges, and is found an efficient substitute for gymnastic exercises, or an excellent auxiliary to them. Educators uniformly approve of this kind of exercise in boys' schools, not only as an effective means of physical culture, but as imparting habits of attention, order, subordination, and prompt obedience.

For schools of most grades, and for either sex, *light gymnastics* has been found to supply appropriate and efficient exercise. See *Cyclopædia of Education*.

HABIT, a tendency to repeat the same action, more or less unconsciously, or an inclination for the pursuits, occupations, or states to which the body or the mind has become familiar by use. Habit, as an automatic tendency, takes a wide range, not only extending over all our mental and bodily acts, but including likewise our moods of mind, our sources of indulgence, pleasure, ease, and recreation, and comprehending also, either by improvement or debasement, our entire moral and spiritual nature. The singular facility which is acquired by repeated action, in accomplishing what at first was either difficult or impossible, has never been satisfactorily explained. The fact, however, is universally recognized in the old saying, "Habit is second nature", as also in the useful educational maxim, "Practice makes perfect". "It conditions", says Rosenkranz (*Pedagogics as a System*), "formally all progress; for that which is not yet become habit, but which we perform with design and an exercise of our will, is not yet a part of ourselves." Physiologists profess to find a reason for this power of habit, in the sympathetic nerves; and some psychologists trace mental habits to the association of ideas. The extent to which habit influences the daily life of every one — even the youngest child, can scarcely be realized. Consciously or unconsciously, it enters, in some shape, into every effort at continuous action, physical or mental, and more or less controls it. From the dawn of intelligence, when the child first takes cognizance of material things, all through the period of self-education, which precedes systematic instruction, it is forming, of itself, habits of observation, comparison, and generalization, which are to constitute the basis of all subsequent intellectual activity. So is it also forming those habits which, taken together, make up what is called disposition, temper, etc. It is this tendency to contract habits which gives such plasticity to the minds and characters of youth, and which really underlies the power and office of education; for what we call training is nothing more than guiding and regulating the formation of habit.

Influence of habit.

While it is the period of formal education at which the child especially needs to be protected from the influence of habit, to some extent and in some respects, the watchful care of the educator is required even from the earliest infancy to prevent the formation of injurious and almost ineradicable habits; indeed, there is scarcely a child who, on being sent to school for the first time, will not be found to have contracted habits, both physical and mental, which the teacher will find it necessary to strive to correct. One of his most important functions will be to detect and eradicate bad habits, as a kind of morbid growth; for, like weeds, these habits not only cumber the ground themselves, but render it sterile for any other productions. For example, what can be done with that most troublesome of all cases, — a "spoiled child", until the habits of self-indulgence, self-will, wayward caprice, and despotic control of others, which characterize it, are eradicated, or superseded by other dispositions? So, too, with habits of deceit, falsehood, cruelty, and many others that are apt to spring up in even very young minds. In regard to the intellect, the

Injurious habits.

same principle holds true; for that natural development which precedes formal instruction may, indeed, be luxuriant, but cannot be regular. The mind of the most active child, under circumstances that present the very best opportunities for development, if it has been left entirely to itself, will be found to have acquired settled ways of observing, thinking, and speaking which it will be necessary to correct; and, besides, it will generally have become impulsive, impatient of any continuous attention, and prone to pass rapidly from one thing to another, in obedience to a mere momentary fancy or impulse. It will, therefore, be generally found that children, on being first subjected to regular instruction, need to have habits of attention formed, in place of those of inattention, which have been implanted by their own unconscious and unregulated activity. (See ATTENTION.) There are others, however, of a less general character which will demand special effort. As an instance, one of the earliest of these objectionable habits, and perhaps one of the most common, is the unconscious substitution in the child's mind of the symbol for the thing symbolized. This will be manifested by most children when shown, for example, the picture of a horse, and asked to state what it is. Usually the answer will be, "It is a horse", from the habit of confounding things with their representatives. Hence, the unresisting facility with which children yield their minds to mere memorizing and rote-learning, the effect of which is to confirm the bad habit referred to, and, in its final result, to extinguish intelligence and destroy mental activity. While some of the habits which demand the teacher's attention at this early stage, are common to all children, in a greater or a less degree, there are others of great variety, dependent upon either peculiar traits of character or peculiar circumstances of early life. The law of the formation of habit is *repetition* or *exercise*. This is recognized in many departments of instruction, as an indispensable

Repetition. means of imparting facility, readiness, and promptitude, without which certain accomplishments could not be made, or if made, would be comparatively useless. For example, of what value would the multiplication table be if its use required a conscious effort of mind at every application of any of its details? The same principle is illustrated by the playing upon a musical instrument, by the use of language in speaking and writing, and by the varied bodily movements needed in daily life. Good habits

Good habits. should be formed at as early a period as possible; because experience shows that, when thoroughly established in childhood or youth, they generally continue, with more or less strength, through life. Hence the importance of making those qualities and observances habitual which constitute the elements of practical success in every walk of life; such as punctuality, order, regularity, and perseverance; to which may be added neatness, courtesy, attention to the wants of others,

Correction. forbearance, and self-control. For the same reason, bad habits should be eradicated before they have reached that mature state, after which they scarcely ever entirely disappear. It is, indeed, rarely the case that thoroughly fixed habits are wholly removed; hence, the teacher should strive to counteract their evil influence, or neutralize their activity, by implanting those of a contrary nature. In dealing with the bad habits of children, the teacher should appreciate, and make due allowance for, the force of habit. He cannot uproot them at once and by violence. As time is an important element in their formation, so is it also in their eradication; and, therefore, the child is to be led along a divergent path which, by degrees, will conduct him away from the vicious impulse which, all the while, tends to overpower his best resolutions. Whatever force or coercion may be found necessary for this purpose should be gradually relaxed, till the child has formed, to some extent, the habit of self-control; which will become the foundation of most other good habits. The implanting of particular habits must not, however, be deemed the whole of moral training; there must be the culture of conscientiousness, of intelligence, of self-respect, of a constant impression and recognition of the Divine presence, and of all the other principles of human nature, by means of which it rises to the higher plane of moral responsibility, consciously exercising its own faculties, not blindly obeying habitual tendencies received from others. Properly educated, the human being, in the exercise of his own will and conscience, enlists the power of habit in support of his own moral conclusions, making a useful servant of that by which so many others are hopelessly enslaved. In this connection, Rosenkranz says, "Education must procure for the pupil the power of being able to free himself from one habit and to adopt another. Through his freedom, he must be able not only to renounce any habit formed, but to form a new one; and he must so govern his system of habits that it shall exhibit a constant progress of development into greater freedom. We must discipline ourselves, as a means toward the everchanging realization of the good in us, constantly to form and to break habits." And it is in the attainment of this grand object of self-culture, that habit may render the important aid referred to, in making the exercise of self-criticism, conscientious watchfulness of our own conduct, and obedience to the dictates of reason and religion, easy and continuous by becoming habitual. Thus it is that the man for whom education has done all that it can do, within the utmost scope of its power, truly finds habit not his master but his most useful servant and friend.

Self-control.

HALF-TIME SCHOOLS, a class of schools which, as the name denotes, hold their sessions during only one half of each day, thus affording an opportunity to a numerous class of children, employed in workshops, factories, stores, etc., to attend school without giving up their employments. They are thus kindred in object with evening schools, which in a certain sense, may be considered as half-time schools.

HARMONY in Development, as regards both the mental and bodily faculties, is now viewed by educationists as the most important aim of education. "One part of instruction", says Dittes (*Schule der Pädagogik*, 1876), "must not contradict another; nothing should be neglected, nothing exaggerated; all the faculties of the pupil should be cultivated as much as possible, and all the different objects and departments of education should receive attention, without interruption, and in due proportion. The intellect should not be favored at the expense of the moral and physical nature; and hygienic considerations should not be left out of view. The teacher should be especially careful not to accord too much time and attention to favorite branches of study." The latter is a very important admonition. Every course of study should be arranged with a view to the average condition of

All the faculties to be trained.

the growing mind and its needs; and, therefore, should comprise such a variety of subjects as will call into exercise the different mental powers, and thus become instruments in their culture and development. The scientific teacher will, however, watch for decided peculiarities *Special* of character,—special aptitudes, traits of genius, etc., and will *aptitudes.* modify his course of proceeding so as, while giving scope for the unfolding of these particular powers, or talents, not to permit them to repress the growth of other indispensable faculties. Thus, a pupil may show a special inclination and talent for drawing, which may very properly be allowed its full development; but, in doing this, the educator is not to permit all other mental or manual occupations to be neglected. Indeed, this special gift may be kept in abeyance, and stimulus applied, for a time at least, to penmanship, and to the study of language, science, or other important subjects. Some pupils, as a further example, may be too prone to the exercise of the imagination; in which case, they should be required to study science or mathematics. Others may show an almost exclusive bent for calculation or mathematical reasoning, which must, of course, be corrected by the pursuit of studies calling into exercise other powers of the mind; such as history, general literature, mental philosophy, etc. Knowledge is sometimes called the food of the mind, by the assimilation of which its various powers are nourished: hence, to continue the metaphor, there should be a due variety of this food, and the different kinds should be selected with a view to the particular condition and needs of the system which is to be supplied with nutriment. As in physical education, if a pupil manifests any signs of abnormal development or morbid growth, such, for example, as distortion of the limbs or curvature of the spine, continuous exercises and postures are prescribed to correct this tendency; so, in every department of education, a harmonious development can only result from a discriminative application of those agencies which call into active and habitual exercise the powers of mind and body. Such a development implies, too, a full recognition of all the relations and powers of the human being, embracing not only the cultivation of those capacities which concern him as an individual, but also those on which his happiness and usefulness as a social and moral being depend. How miserable is the mere student, the solitary genius, cut off from the exercise of the social sympathies and deprived of social enjoyments by a one-sided development! The educator must recognize that there is a body, a mind, and a soul to be addressed and cultivated; and that man has social, moral, and religious faculties, without the harmonious development of which he cannot properly fulfil his destiny, nor attain happiness. The special claims of particular vocations, it is said, demand one-sided culture. Of this there is no doubt; but *Special* preceding it, and hence underlying it, there should be such *vocations.* general culture as the circumstances of man, as *man*, require. Profession or business comprehends, in general, but one relation; and unfortunate, therefore, is he who can meet the demands of only that relation, unable to perform aright the domestic, social, political, and religious duties which are inseparably connected with the position of every person in this life. In order to perform these duties, every person is endowed with special faculties, which, by the want of proper cultivation in early life, or by disuse, may be so enfeebled as to be unfit for exercise; and the harmonious development of these is the only true aim of education. If all these faculties do not, at an early age, receive their due share of training, self-education, at a later period, cannot, but within very narrow limits. supply the deficiency. The individual will always find himself more or less crippled, because no self-culture can entirely supply the place of early habits. To the doctrine of harmonious development, it has *Innate en-* been objected that special innate endowments cannot be re-*dowments.* pressed by education; and to address other faculties will only result in bestowing superficial accomplishments of no practical value. Thus a youth of decided mathematical genius could never become more than an imperfect linguist; and one with special talent for language would be likely to make but indifferent attainments in science. Harmonious development, however, does not require the repression of special endowments, but the cultivation of what may be called the *general powers*, in such a way as to give support to each particular endowment. A wise educational training, commenced at the earliest childhood, and continued through each successive period of the formative state of human character, will not only fit for any particular vocation for which there may be a special bent, but will also prepare the individual for general usefulness, and render him able to enjoy the wonders of science, and the beauties of nature and art, as well as to participate in all other pleasures incident to his existence as a social and rational being.

HAZING, a term applied to the mischievous and often abusive and injurious tricks which are played by older college students upon freshmen. The term, as well as the practice, is of considerable age; but, during the last few years, much effort has been put forth by those who have the charge of higher institutions of learning to suppress the custom as demoralizing and barbarous.

HEBREW LANGUAGE, the language in which the Sacred Scriptures of the Old Testament were written, is on that account of special importance both for the Hebrew people and for Christians, more especially theologians, who desire to read the Scriptures in the original.

As the study of Hebrew, among Christians, generally is not begun until the students have obtained a good knowledge, not only of their native tongue, but also of Latin and Greek, the teacher will find it expedient to pursue a method very different from that observed in teaching young pupils the elements of Latin and Greek. The mastering of the chief rules of grammar may be expected to consume comparatively little time. As the chief purpose of nearly all students of Hebrew is to be enabled to read the Bible, it is natural that teachers should generally conform their method to that special aim. The study of the Hebrew Bible is. therefore. begun as soon as possible, and most of the grammatical peculiarities are explained in connection with reading. For a full treatment of this subject, see *Cyclopædia of Education.*

HIGH SCHOOLS, generally schools of secondary or academic instruction, corresponding, to the lower grades of the German gymnasia, but sometimes partaking rather of the character of real schools. Public high schools exist in most of the states of the Union. forming a part of the public-school system, being the connecting link between the elementary district, common, or grammar schools, and the state university, for which they perform the office of preparatory schools. Some of these schools are so organized as to comprise academic, normal, and commercial departments. In small cities and towns, high-school classes or departments, taught in the same building with the grammar schools, take the place of separate high schools. There is a great want of uniformity in the grade and character of these schools in different states and in different cities of the same state. Some are simply of a higher grade than the grammar schools; that is, they give instruction in more advanced studies; while others strictly form a part of a graded system which includes a complete representation of primary, secondary, and superior instruction.

HISTORY, as a branch of instruction, presents very many important points of inquiry for the educator. The vast field which it occupies as a realm of facts, the great difficulty in classifying these facts, and deducing from them any general principles or laws, or even in associating them so that they may be presented to the mind of the learner in groups bound together by some common relation, — these characteristics of history make it perhaps the most difficult which the educator has to deal with. This will account for the diversity of opinion as to the proper method of teaching it, as well as for the many obvious errors of method that exist. Some, indeed, have condemned it as a school study; on the ground that the mere facts of history, without the general laws which they teach, are of no account, while the study of the philosophy of history is too deep for immature minds. On this account, Prof. Bain contends that it is a subject proper only for the university. John Locke said, "As nothing teaches, so nothing delights, more than history. The first of these recommends it to the study of the grown man; the latter makes me think it fittest for a young lad". These extreme opinions arise from viewing the subject from different stand-points. There is no doubt that the study of history, like that of geography, botany, astronomy, and other school subjects may be presented to the mind of the child in such a manner as not only to be useless and distasteful, but actually injurious. As in every other subject, the educator is to consider the nature of the mind to be addressed, and the character of the study itself. Primarily, history is a narrative; and there is nothing which pleases children so much as narratives concerning things in which they take an interest, or with which they are familiar. If children, therefore, are to study history, they must first be interested in the persons and things that it refers to. Thus American children will be eager to learn about the discovery of America by Columbus, because it concerns the country in which they live; and they will be scarcely satisfied with any amount of detail in regard to the particular facts connected with that event. Columbus as a great personage will then loom up in their imagination, and their curiosity will be exerted to know something about him. This will interest them in Isabella, the good queen of Spain; and something may be said of her, and of the country to which she belonged. In this desultory way, and without any special effort to show the relations of events as to time or cause and effect, the conceptive faculty of quite young children may be addressed in teaching history, and thus their minds will be prepared for its regular study, by receiving those underlying

Educational character.

Mode of teaching history.

conceptions which are constantly needed to make formal historical narratives interesting or even understood. "The fact", says Emerson, "must correspond to something in me to be credible or intelligible". It is in reference to this principle that Wickersham remarks, "It concerns us little to know the lineage of kings and queens, the intrigues of courts, or the plans of campaigns; but it would interest us much to be told how people in past times built their houses, worked their fields, or educated their children — what style of dress they wore, what kind of food they eat, what books they read". The latter classes of facts are not, however, more interesting in themselves, but because they are more nearly related to our individual experience. Different persons will not be interested in the same class of historical facts. The soldier will attend to the military history of a country; the statesman and politician, to the political; the agriculturist, to the methods of husbandry in use; and to a numerous class of minds the dynastic history — the "lineage of kings and queens", will possess supreme fascination. All departments of history are useful in their special applications; and are of interest to those who desire to know the facts which they severally comprehend. In arranging history for educational purposes, we must consider the degree of development of the pupil's mind; and in this respect historical study may be divided into three stages: (1) The *introductory*, in which the mind of the young child has to be prepared for the study, as above indicated; (2) The *intermediate*, at which the formal study of history commences, dealing principally with facts and their obvious relations; and (3) The *advanced*, in which the higher forms of generalization are presented, constituting what has been styled the *philosophy of history*. In the first stage, what has been called the "fragments of history", that is, brief and interesting narratives, biographical sketches, etc., clothed in a simple picturesque style, should constitute the subject matter of the instruction. This may be presented in a desultory manner, without any special regard to logical or chronological order, the great object being to interest the learner by filling his mind with vivid conceptions of certain events and personages. Of course, this preliminary instruction may take a wide range, embracing the most prominent persons and events in the history of the world, and thus constituting a valuable outline, on which to base the subsequent study. But this is not so important as that, in every thing that is taught, the young pupil's experience and imagination should be addressed; that is, the facts presented to be learned should be concrete facts, not mere abstractions. Epitomes of history are valueless for this purpose, because they attempt to cover the whole ground. As has been well said by a celebrated educationist, the use of an epitome is like giving a child an "index to learn by heart".

Stages of historical study.

First stage.

In the second stage, while the same principle should be steadily kept in view, the study should become more formal and systematic. It is here that the most important questions arise for consideration. The first of these concerns the choice between a compendium of history and a series of historical text-books on different nations. The system of special national text-books grew up at a time when, from national patriotism, each country considered its own history as foremost and hence, all others as of secondary importance; and it has been fostered, in

Second stage.

the advance of historic learning, by a system of abridgments of large standard works, or by school books based, in method of treatment, upon them. But such treatment is not adapted to conditions for which the originals were not intended. Each of these special works presupposes the existence of all the others, and thus virtually depends on them for its general stand-point, and for that knowledge which is indispensable to render the narrative intelligible; and, hence, for school purposes, the abridgments are of little use, because this general knowledge cannot be supposed to exist. Besides that, the large standard works are too exclusively philosophical in their character and arrangement to admit of an abridgment for school purposes. Narrowing the field of view for the purpose of scientific investigation, such works naturally adopt largely the consecutive narrative form; but consecutive narrative is not essential when only general leading facts are to be presented, and narrative detail is unsuited to the treatment required for school instruction. There can be no perspective in such a mode of treatment. Leading facts rank side by side with subordinate ones, and the history assumes the form of dry annals. Excessive detail in historical text-books is always a fruitful source of vexation to both teacher and pupil. What is needed, for this stage of instruction, is a skillful grouping of facts, which, while it departs but little from the chronological order, shows the proper relation of events — how one brought about the other. In the history of the world, as of each separate country, and of every great event, as, for example, the Reformation, the Thirty Years' War, the Revolution in England, the American Revolution, the French Revolution, the great Civil War in the United States, there are certain conspicuous stand-points, or centers of interest, around which other events should be grouped, as dependent upon them. The same principle is opposed, in the teaching of general history, to confining the attention of the pupil exclusively to each nation in succession, throughout its entire history *(ethnographic method).* It is a well-defined feature of every historic movement that, in many of its epochs, it is carried along by some particular nation as the representative, for the time being, of some controll-

Ethnographic and grouping methods. ing idea or principle, other nations playing a subordinate part. This should be clearly brought out in the arrangement of the subject *(grouping method).* It is not always possible, however, to distinguish a single nation as holding such an undisputed prominence; but, where this question is in doubt, there is always a movement, more or less general, to which the contemporaneous nations are subject, and to which, therefore, the history of the separate nations should have a distinct reference. In the period of the Reformation, for example, it is desirable to present the nations collectively in their relation to it, the events which concern their separate existence being kept in the background. A system of instruction which presents, in succession and at widely separated intervals, the share of each particular nation in such a great movement as the Reformation, cannot possibly impress the mind of the pupil properly in regard to it. In the compilation of a compendium of history suitable for school use, a compromise is requisite between the plan of teaching the history of each nation by itself *(ethnographic method)* and that of teaching by periods or epochs, the history of each nation coming in where it belongs in the period (*synchronistic method*). The latter method, by short periods, centuries for instance, is useless for beginners, as it gives only a confused picture of the whole. In ancient history, it has *Synchro-* but a limited application; because the nations of antiquity *nistic* were essentially separate, coming on the stage at successive pe-*method.* riods, and rarely blended, to any extent, in any general movement. The ethnographic method is, therefore, the best for this department of history, but may be departed from in certain portions of it, as, for example, in the history of the states of Greece. For beginners, the ethnographic method seems to be best, at least until a good general outline has been fixed in the mind, after which the grouping method ought to be steadily pursued, but still with a constant regard to the mental advancement and maturity of the student. The *chronological method* *Chronologic* must, however, lead in every scheme of elementary historical *method.* teaching. The pupil must, above all things, attend to the order of time; or his subsequent reading and study will be greatly embarrassed. This method has been used in Germany from time immemorial, with modifications such as have been referred to, for adaption to the purposes of elementary, burgher and real schools, and gymnasia. These modifications consist chiefly in the relative prominence given to the synchronistic and ethnographic principles. Many of the school text-books on history, published in Great Britain and the United States, are based on the same system; but teachers have generally favored the ethnographic system, as less fragmentary and disjointed. For a field so vast as that of general history, it is of the highest importance that the idea of both unity and sequence should be impressed upon the pupil's mind. In the chronologic method, the perspective view which this unification of the broader parts demands, is not dependent on the special notions of any teacher or compiler, but grows up in the mind from the study of the facts themselves. In the treatment of antiquity, the history of the eastern nations precedes that of the Greeks, and the Greeks the Romans; and while teaching each in chronologic order, the other contemporaneous nations should be brought in, as episodes, at such periods and in such connections, as will best illustrate the history of the great nation which, for the time being, is controlling the affairs of the world. Egypt, Assyria, Babylon, Persia, Greece, Rome (republic and empire), may, in succession, be made the leading nation; and all the others will come in at certain periods. In the middle ages, the treatment should be analogous; there is at every period, a great tribe or nation, whether the Franks, the Saracens, the Normans, or the Germans, the history of whom, treated in its chronologic order, will absorb the remainder, except what may come in episodically. In modern history, the ethnographic principle must at first have prominence, before the pupil can study the great European movements, such as the Reformation and the Thirty Years' War, with any real satisfaction or benefit. Chiefly as episodes, in mediæval and modern history, come in certain great topics; such as the Saracenic civilization, the Byzantine culture, the Turkish ascendency, the maritime discoveries of Portugal and Spain, the Italian Renaissance, the struggle of *Syn-* the Dutch Republic, the rise of Sweden and Russia, etc. What-*chronistic* ever method may be used, *synchronistic exercises* will be *exercises.* constantly requisite to a full understanding of the relations of events. These may take the form of lists of sovereigns grouped into centuries and arranged, side by side, in perpendicular columns; or leading events arranged in the same way. After the history of any nation or period has been studied in the chronological order, various methods of arrangement may be adopted for the purpose of review, varying the sequence which has been followed in the regular lessons. Thus, the pupil may be required to state all the events connected with a particular place, or a particular individual, which he has previously learned in a strictly chronological order, or in connection with the national history. The *topical*

Topical Method. method of recitation will be found the most effective, not only for the attainment of the best results as far as history itself is concerned, but for collateral culture, particularly of expression. On account of the latter, accuracy in language should, as much as possible be insisted upon; and the pupils should be required to use their own language, instead of memorizing that of the text-book. Brief written sketches of events, personages, periods, etc., will be of great use in making this collateral culture effective, and will also afford much useful practice in other respects. — A severe and sustained drill on a single manual

Study of manual. is of great use for the strong landmarks it leaves in the pupil's mind; but, to be thoroughly effective as an educational process, it ought to be accompanied with the reading, to some extent, of auxiliary books giving interesting detail in regard to prominent points. Such a system of independent reading by the different members of a class, properly utilized, will lead to the acquisition of much interesting information, each pupil bringing his own contribution, to be offered in connection with the class exercises. Children, at an early age, with a taste for reading, will devour solid books of history, when not under compulsion; especially if they have a strong frame-work fixed in their minds for the separate facts to attach themselves to; and such reading will constitute a very important part of mental culture. — *Dates* are to some extent needed, but only in connection with the general narrative. To memorize the dates of isolated

Dates. events is worse than useless. The dates of certain great events, marking epochs, should be carefully fixed in the mind. As already said, the method pursued should be such as to keep the stream of time constantly in view; and this will render the memorizing of many dates unnecessary. Chronological relations may be better taught by means of historical charts, representing the exact position in time of every nation and event, just as a map represents countries, cities, etc., in space. These should be large enough to show clearly to the eye what is represented; and

Geography. the different nations should be marked out in strong colors. Maps, showing the states and countries, and their extent at different periods, are indispensable. These maps illustrate the relation of geography and history, and afford an indication of the extent to which geographical study is needed in connection with that of history. It is, however, desirable that all the places mentioned in history should be at least pointed out on the map.

Good historical *lectures* are eminently beneficial, in connection with regular lessons, or re-inforced by suitable class exercises. The taking of

Lectures. notes by the pupils is of little value; because such notes can concern only definite and disconnected facts which should be impressed upon the mind by the study of a compendium or by class drill; while the lecture is designed to give broad, general views of events, in their relations, and in their bearing on some great historical movement. The taking of notes by young pupils must necessarily interrupt the current of their thought, and thus mar the effect of the lecture. It is, however, in the third or advanced stage of historical study that lectures have their special place.

The *class of facts* — the kind of material — to be selected for the elementary study of history is another important consideration for the teacher, as well as for the compiler of a school compendium. *Class of facts.* There is a great diversity in this respect. In some text-books, undue prominence is given to the political and military history, every thing pertaining to social life being left out. This deprives the study of much of its strongest and best interest. The condition and progress of the people in the elements of civilization, — the industrial and fine arts, literature, education, social culture, manners, customs, etc., should be graphically sketched, in connection with the political history, which must, of course, constitute the frame-work of the whole. The office *Faculties addressed.* of history as a school study, is not only to give information in regard to the events of the past, but is to discipline the mind by cultivating and improving (1) the memory, (2) the imagination, (3) the judgment, (4) the power of expression, and (5) the moral and emotional nature. The pupil, when properly instructed, has his sympathies aroused: he applauds the noble, the patriotic, and the virtuous; he condemns the mean, the selfish, and the wicked. Every lesson teaches him by example, for it confronts him with either human virtue or human wickedness. The false tinsel of glory must not be permitted to conceal the selfishness, cruelty, and wrong of the ambitious tyrant or conqueror; and the nobleness of the martyr will not be debased because he pines in a dungeon or dies on the scaffold. Treated in the right spirit, history thus becomes a great moral teacher for pupils of every class and grade.

In the *third stage*, that of superior instruction, history has strong claims to attention. Whatever the sphere of life in which the student is to engage, *Third stage.* he should possess himself of the key to the records of the past history of mankind. History may peculiarly be called a "living study", since it draws its interest at once from the slow but certain movement of human forces, among which self-interest, will, and passion play a great part. The field is so vast, that the untrained student will be lost in the maze, and will wander about aimless and bewildered. It is the office of education to show that the elements are really simple, and to impart a system to the vast crowd of facts, by which they may become useful, by being co-ordinated. It is here, then, that history assumes whatever scientific phase it may be capable of. What has been called the *Philosophy of history.* *philosophy of history* is, in an especial manner and degree, suitable for college study, as it brings into play the higher faculties of the mind, — generalization, reason, and judgment. At this stage, we do not rest satisfied with a simple narrative of events, but we attempt to trace them to their real causes, and deduce from them those general laws on which political and social science must be based. This gives rise to various theories; as the *materialistic theory*, which supposes the co-ordinate factor in bringing about the changes in history to be the forces of material nature, acting on human character and human will; the *spiritualistic theory* which attributes to the soul of man a certain freedom of purpose and will, acting independently of its material surroundings; and the *theistic theory*, which attributes great movements and changes in the world's history to the special interposition of an overruling Providence, a Divine will, and thus makes "God in history" the supreme source of all the great events that have marked the intellectual, social, and moral progress of mankind. These theories may, however, be called the metaphysics of history; they are not essential to the investigation of the laws which constitute its philosophy; inasmuch as the generalizations upon which these laws are based, are chiefly independent of them, the course of human events, like the course of nature, being controlled only by general laws.

What has already been suggested has exclusive reference to facts, or statements of facts, accepted as such; but there is another department of *Sources of history.* history which concerns the sources of history, their nature and credibility; and this has an indisputable claim upon the attention of those who teach, and those who study history in its advanced stages. Two objects will be subserved by this: (1) The mind will acquire the useful habit of withholding its assent from all statements that are not supported by sufficient testimony; and (2) The judgment and critical faculty will receive a practical culture which must prove of great service in the further prosecution of study, and in the affairs of daily life. In the prosecution of this historical criticism, the student is invariably to consider (1) the writer or writers from whom the narration proceeds, (2) their means of information, (3) their character for sagacity and discernment, (4) their interests, associations, and affections. All these inevitably color the narrative, and hence constitute an important element to be considered in the kind and degree of credibility to which it is entitled. — In the struggle, for some time in progress, between the friends of classical and of scientific studies, history as a branch of education holds a strong and prominent position. While it is a record of the past, it is, in fact, the science of the future; and one only has to imagine the condition of the *Value of history.* world, were all its annals destroyed, to appreciate the practical value of this science. The studies pertaining to matter and force claim supreme consideration with many; and those pertaining to the mere linguistic expression of thought, often obsolete and valueless, with many others; but history deals with the facts of human intelligence and will, illustrates the principles which control the progress of mankind in all the elements of civilization, and hence assumes an office and agency in connection with human education, without which it must be measurably ineffective and imperfect. — For a full list of references see *Cyclopædia of Education.*

HOME EDUCATION is that which is carried on in the home circle, or family, as contrasted with that which is afforded by the school.
Office. Up to a certain age, and within a certain sphere, home education, or its equivalent, is not only indispensable but inevitable. The parents are the first teachers, especially the mother; and the educative influences of the nursery not only precede in time, but exceed in power,

those of the school. Here the foundation is laid on which the schoolteacher must subsequently build; and, comparatively speaking, more is accomplished in the period of earliest childhood, both in storing the mind and in forming the disposition and character, than during any equal number of subsequent years. "A child gains more ideas", says Lord Brougham, "in the first four years of his life than ever afterward". Early home education consists peculiarly in what has been called *unconscious tuition*, by means of which the plastic nature of the young child is insensibly moulded by the agencies which environ it. The mother chiefly controls these agencies, which may be enumerated as follows: (1) The affectionate tenderness which she displays, in ministering to the wants and gratifying the desires of the child, and in sympathizing with and alleviating its distresses; (2) Her behavior, as being delicate and refined, or coarse and rude, — showing self-restraint and dignity, or manifesting impulsiveness and passion; (3) The tones of her voice — sweet and tender, or harsh and dissonant, firm and decisive, or weak and yielding; (4) The expression of her face, implying similar traits; (5) The force of her will, under the intelligent guidance of educational principles and the restraints of conscience. Such are the elements of a mother's educative power, — a power the exercise of which results in forming in the child traits of character that no succeeding agency of circumstance, education, or self-discipline can entirely efface. It will be seen, from this enumeration, that the mother's influence is rather moral than intellectual; indeed, the special period of its exercise supersedes the necessity of any formal cultivation of the knowing faculties. The child, during the first few years of its existence needs little direction in this respect. Natural curiosity and innate activity constantly stimulate the growth of the mind, and fill it with those ideas which are to constitute, in succeeding years, the materials of thought. It is just as absurd to subject a very young child to formal instruction as it would be to attempt the development of its physical powers by gymnastic exercises. Watchfulness is, however, constantly required to check the formation of bad habits, which have just as strong a tendency to spring up in the young mind as rank weeds in a virgin soil. (See Habit.) The period of exclusive home education here referred to being so decisive of the future character of the child, and the mother being the first and most effective of all educators, it will be apparent that the science of education, in its most comprehensive sense, should constitute an essential part of the curriculum of every female seminary or college. Particularly should the future mother be taught to appreciate the character of the influence, in all its phases, which she is to exert; as well as to understand how to render it effectual in contributing to the future welfare of her child. The father, at a somewhat later period, but in a similar manner, is a powerful educator within the circle of home. Both by precept and example, but especially by the latter, he makes life-long impressions. In vain are precepts, however, if they are not fully supported by example. The impressions, both intellectual and moral, received by children in very many of the home circles of what are considered the better classes of society, are rather debasing than elevating. The complaint is often made by teachers that the children placed under their care are so depraved by bad home training, or in consequence of absolute neglect, that their efforts to discipline and instruct these pupils are almost useless. This is the more to be regretted, as school education can, in most cases, only supplement that of home; and because the influences that center in the latter are always more potent than those wielded by the former, chiefly because school education is primarily intellectual; whereas that of home is primarily moral. At any rate such is the fact generally.

After the period of formal instruction has arrived, the question arises in the minds of many parents, whether it is better to detain the child at home to be instructed by private tutors or to submit it to the discipline and instruction of the school. This question has been much discussed by educators. The following arguments are generally adduced to prove that the education acquired in school is to be preferred to any that is possible by private tutors at home: (1) The intellectual training is more effective; since the boy or girl coming in competition with those of the same age is stimulated to greater exertions than would be possible in any system of home instruction. As Quintilian says: "At home, the boy can learn only what is taught himself; at school, he will also learn what is taught to others. He will hear many things approved; many others, corrected. The reproof of a fellow pupil's idleness will be a good lesson to him; as will, likewise, the praise of his neighbor's industry. He will think it disgraceful to yield to his equals in age, and great honor to excel his seniors. All these matters arouse the powers of the mind; and if ambition be an evil, it is often the parent of virtue". The child educated at home can never realize the full extent of his own powers, having no standard by which to measure them. Hence, he is satisfied with meager results, at the same time that he is likely to be filled with self-conceit. It is, however, scarcely disputed that the school, as a mimic world, presents a variety of incentives which a home education could never afford; and that it is favorable to rapid mental growth. But it is its influence on the moral nature that has been chiefly called in question. Home has been depicted as the abode of purity and innocence, — of kindness, gentleness, and affection, — of courtesy and refinement, — of morality and religious influence; and such it ought to be, and it is to be hoped, often is. From such an atmosphere, the home-bred child is at once introduced into a new, and to him utterly unknown, world. Instead of sympathy, he finds, among his school-mates, indifference; instead of courtesy and kindness, a thoughtless disregard of all weakness, either of mind or body, except, indeed, to turn it into ridicule. He finds that, if he is not mindful of himself, and sufficiently self-assertive, he will be borne down in the mass. There is an antagonism — an aggressiveness in those around him that begets caution and resistance; there is a sense of danger that cultivates courage, and a matter-of-fact spirit that crushes out egotism and sensitiveness. Thus the boy, in the little world of the school, is prepared for the greater school beyond. Better, therefore, it would appear, is it to unite the education of a good school with that of a properly ordered family, in which combination the evils of school life will be neutralized by the stronger and purer influences of home. Not home *or* school, but home *and* school, constitutes the proper agency for the education of children, whether boys or girls. It

Advantages of the school.

is the opinion of some, however, that admitting the advantages, in general, of a school education, that of home generates certain peculiar traits and excellencies of character which are essential to the welfare of society.

HOME LESSONS, or Home Studies. The question whether home lessons, or home studies, should be a part of the system of instruction in schools of different grades, and if so, to what extent they should be permitted, and in what manner they should be pursued and supervised by the teacher, is one of considerable importance, which is still extensively discussed by writers on education. The need of home lessons for pupils of secondary and higher schools has never been disputed. In regard to the schools of a lower grade, many physicians have strongly objected to any kind of home lessons, as long as the children are required to spend from 4 to 5 hours a day in the school room. Their arguments are, however, chiefly directed against the length of the school sessions. From an educational point of view, it has justly been urged by recent writers, that the regulation of this matter must chiefly depend on the question, for what purpose should home lessons be given. On this point, educators, at the present time, are much more nearly agreed than formerly. No writer of note will, nowadays, maintain that home lessons should be for the mere purpose of preventing idleness — of keeping the children busy, or as a punishment for delinquencies; but it is agreed that all home studies should aim at training the pupils to self-exertion, at giving them the ability to depend upon their own efforts as students, and by degrees, to dispense with the aid of a teacher. If this principle is accepted, several corollaries are self-evident. Home lessons should not begin at too early an age. Young children need the supervision of a teacher to a much greater extent than those of a more advanced age, and are much less fitted to spend their time profitably without direct guidance. Moreover, while the school sessions for young children are as long as for older ones, the medical warning not to overwork the brain, applies with much greater force to the home lessons of the former than to those of the latter. Special care should be taken that all the children fully understand the work which they are required to perform at home, and that they are competent to do it. No child of good standing in the class should feel it necessary to apply to his parents or adult friends for help. It is especially this point that is so apt to be disregarded by teachers. Parents have a right to object to any home lesson or exercise which requires, in the case of diligent pupils, any help in addition to that of the teacher. All exercises of this kind prove a torment, and are absolutely injurious. "The school", says Diesterweg, "must teach the method of home studies. It is not enough that the home lesson be appropriate in itself; the pupil must be enabled to prepare it in a proper manner. How often poor children torment themselves where this is not taught! The teacher should show them how to memorize, how to prepare or review a lesson, how to write a composition, by previously memorizing, preparing, reviewing, etc., with them at school. Thus the teacher becomes the pupil's friend, and this is more than to be his master". Moreover, when pupils are required to write exercises at home, the teacher should faithfully correct them. The failure to do this fosters habits of carelessness. Many teachers greatly

Propriety of

Object of

Directions.

Extraneous aid.

Exercises.

err in this regard, burdening children with the task of writing pages of exercises, and correcting but few, or none, of them. Certainly, no teacher who is guilty of so serious a mistake, can be regarded as understanding the work either of instruction or of discipline.

HORN-BOOK, a book consisting of a single page, formerly used to teach children the alphabet and other simple rudiments. It was, in fact, the first page of the primer, pasted on a thin board, which terminated in a handle, and having, fastened over the printed matter, a thin plate of transparent horn, to protect it from being soiled or torn by the young learner. See *Cyclopædia of Education*.

HUMANITIES (Lat. *humaniora* or *literæ humaniores*), those branches of education or study, which are included in what is called polite or elegant learning, as languages, grammar, rhetoric, philology, and poetry, with all that pertains to what is called polite literature, including the ancient classics. The name implies that the study of these branches, in opposition to the physical sciences, which especially develop the intellectual faculties, has a tendency to *humanize* man,— to cultivate particularly those faculties which distinguish him *as man*, in all his relations, social and moral; that is, which make him a truly cultured man.

HYGIENE, School, has reference to that department of school administration, which pertains to the preservation of physical health. This *Object of* is to be distinguished from physical education, which looks rather to the special training or developing of the body; while hygienic principles and rules have for their object to preserve that condition of health in which all pupils are supposed to enter school, and, by their constant though unobtrusive influence, to make that condition permanent.

The subject of the preservation and promotion of physical health in the school involves the following considerations: (I) the character of the site on which the school building is erected; (II) the mode of *Considera-* constructing the building, as well as the location and construc-*tions* tion of the out-buildings,— water-closets, etc.; (III) the construc-*involved.* tion and arrangement of the class-rooms; (IV) the size, number, and distribution of the windows for the admission of light; (V) the mode of ventilation; (VI) the manner of heating the rooms, and the average temperature preserved in them by artificial heat; (VII) the adaptation of the school furniture to the physical wants and condition of the children; (VIII) the kind of discipline employed, in regard to hygienic principles; (IX) the degree of attention given to the personal condition of the pupils, so as to preserve cleanliness and prevent the communication of disease; and (X) the means afforded for physical exercise. Each of these will be considered in its order, according to the above enumeration.

1. Modern sanitary science, fortunately, has given such particular attention to the subjects of site and exposure, and has impressed the public *Site.* mind so thoroughly with the necessity of their healthfulness, that only willful ignorance or obstinacy will, in our day, permit a building designed for human occupancy to be placed in a manifestly unhealthy location. The healthfulness of a school site depends upon (1) the character of the soil; (2) its elevation; (3) the circumstances which facilitate or obstruct proper drainage; (4) its remoteness from any stagnant water,

or marshy ground, liable to produce malarial fevers; (5) its remoteness from any factory or establishment poisoning the air by the issue of deleterious and offensive gases; to which may be added (6) the amount of space it affords for play-grounds, so as to facilitate physical exercise.

II. The construction of the school building will depend on the number of pupils to be accommodated; the kind of school, as regards the sexes; and the grade, — whether primary, grammar, or high school. (See *School building.* SCHOOL-HOUSE.) In regard to water-closets and urinals, it is hardly necessary to say, that they should, for convenience, be as near the school-house as possible, without being near enough to allow the perception of any odor. The approaches from the school-house should be under cover, the ventilation and the supply of light should be ample. They should also be enclosed from observation.

III. *Construction and Arrangement of Class Rooms.* — This varies with the conditions under which the school-house is built. The rooms, however, should always be constructed so as to allow at least *Class rooms.* 108 cubic feet of air-space to each pupil, and 9 square feet of floor-space. The height of ceiling recommended by the best authorities is a minimum of 12 feet and a maximum of 15 feet, if the room is not very large. These provisions are absolutely necessary to furnish to each pupil the amount of air necessary for health. (See VENTILATION.)

IV. Currie, in *School Education*, remarks: "The provision for lighting a school should have two ends in view: (1) a proper amount of light, *Windows.* and (2) its just distribution. The effect either of an excess or a deficiency of light is to strain the eye and cause a depression of spirits, especially as the day advances. In regard to distribution, all the parts of the school should be equally lighted, which may be more easily done with a few judiciously placed windows of respectable size than with a number of smaller, straggling apertures. Good ways of lighting a school are these: (1) Perhaps, the best of all is when the light is admitted from the roof, as it is then steady, equable, and free from shadow. (2) The windows may be placed in the ends of the school room, or in two adjacent sides, so as to admit the light from the pupil's left. Where there are windows in front of the classes, they should be at some distance from them, and in every case they should be at such height in the walls as to remove all danger from drafts when they are opened. School windows should be of the same shape as ordinary house windows; at any rate, lattice windows, with numerous, small, lozenge-shaped panes of glass should be avoided, as the light transmitted through them is so broken as to be extremely fatiguing to the eye. (3) Each window should be fitted with blinds to moderate the intensity of light, when necessary, particularly to exclude the direct rays of the sun. If the windows are used for ventilation as well as lighting, the difficulty of using the blinds in such a case may be obviated by having a fixed Venetian blind outside the window at the top, and hanging the inside blind on a level with the bottom of it. (4) The tint of the school walls should neither be too dull, so as to absorb the light unduly, nor too glaring, so as to dazzle the eye by reflection. Of the colors commonly employed: namely, the white, the ocher, the stone color, and the lightish-brown, the last two are obviously to be preferred". If the lighting of the school room is from the roof, care should be taken that the windows or sky-lights should not slope to the south or west, as the heat and sunlight will be intolerable in hot weather, and their regulation by blinds will be difficult. If the lighting, on the other hand, is by side windows, "the height of the window sills from the floor", says ROBSON (in *School Architecture*) "should always be considerable, and the heads near the ceiling. Much of the cheerfulness of a school room, especially in a town, depends on the amount of sky which can be seen from the windows. The height of the sills from the floor, therefore, should never be less than five feet, and may be even more with advantage. This will enable the top or head to be placed nearly, if not quite, up to the ceiling, and then the upper stratum of vitiated air can be more readily removed". The importance of this subject in regard to health is very great. Liebreich, in his report to the College of Preceptors of London (July, 1872), attributes several diseases of the eye to this cause alone; and Dr. Cohn asserts that of 410 students examined by him, only one-third possessed good eye-sight, the remaining two-thirds having had their sight injured, in his opinion, by the deficient lighting of the school rooms in which they studied. A rough calculation, from researches made on the subject, gives 200 square inches of window glass as the proper number for each scholar. In the above remarks by Currie, the left side has been designated as the one from which the light should come, because this insures the fullest illumination of the page, with the least inconvenience, and the least injury to the eye. When light is admitted through the front of the room, the glare is directly in the face either of teacher or pupils, they being supposed to face each other. If it falls from behind, the shadow of the head is thrown directly upon the page; if from the right side, the shadows of the arm and hand, in the act of writing, equally obscure it. The light, therefore, should fall from the left side, and, as far as possible, from above. In evening schools, the lighting should be, as nearly as possible, equal to that by day. If gas is used, the glass cylinder with a reflecting shade is recommended, for the purpose of steadying the light and making it stronger and whiter. Ground glass shades are now generally discountenanced, their effect being to diffuse the light. For general illuminating purposes they are desirable, as in the parlor or concert room; but are out of place in the school room, or in any room where the object is to concentrate light upon a particular spot.

Mode of lighting.

V. *The Mode of Ventilation.* See VENTILATION.

VI. Many methods, based upon ingenious theories and provoking heated discussion, have been adopted to overcome the difficulties attending this subject; but it is, probably, not unfair to say that an entirely unobjectionable heating apparatus, as regards health, has yet to be devised. Wood is, of course, too dear for general use. The ordinary stove, the cellar furnace, and all devices for warming air by passing it over heated metal surfaces are now entirely discountenanced, it having been discovered that a highly poisonous gas is set free, and passes through heated metal as through a sieve. The steam coil, placed outside of the school room and heating a column of air which is drawn from the outside, and, after heating, ascends into the room, has, of late, been extensively used. At the opposite end of the room, a grate, varying in size with that of the room, is placed; the theory being that, as the heated air

Mode of heating.

ascends in one end of the room, the cool and foul air is forced out at the other through the flue of the grate, in which a fire is usually kept to facilitate the current. This method, while perhaps the least objectionable of any, has been opposed on the ground, that by it the stratum of air nearest the ceiling is kept warmest, while that nearest the floor, which should be the warmest, is least so. To obviate this difficulty, it has even been proposed to make the floor of stone and warm it after the manner of an oven, *i. e.*, by kindling a fire under it. Whatever method is adopted, however, fluctuations of temperature should, as much as possible, be avoided, and the air of the room should be kept steadily at from 65 to 70 degrees.

VII. Several diseases have been traced to faultily-constructed school furniture, chief among which is curvature of the spine, with the diseases consequent upon it. This is sometimes the result of insufficient *Furniture.* lighting; but more frequently it arises from the improper construction of the desk and seat, or the arrangement of them. (See SCHOOL FURNITURE.)

VIII. The methods of discipline which militate against bodily health are fortunately growing less in every civilized country, as more study is given to the subject of education. It may be said briefly that *Discipline.* whatever discipline tends to bodily deterioration in any way should be discountenanced, as the object of discipline is to train, not to break down. (See DISCIPLINE.) Of the errors, under the head of school management, which affect health may be mentioned those which arise from (1) *the length of the daily school session.* These errors are frequently due to the fact that courses of study are laid down first, with *School* the view of accomplishing a certain result, and the pupils' *sessions.* powers are made to conform to them. By this inversion of the natural method, sessions of five and six hours, with only slight intermissions, are sometimes ordered; this can result only in physical injury. The reversal of this, *i. e.*, a study of the child's physical necessities first, and a school course based on them, will insure the adoption of the only safe and reasonable method consistent with health. This should be so arranged, by a judicious alternation of sedentary occupations, physical exercises, and recesses, that no "violation of the primary laws of physiology", as Prof. Owen terms it, may be possible. In a room supplied with proper hygienic facilities, four hours per day is thought to be the maximum for very young pupils, and five hours for older ones. (2) *The number, length, and distribution of recesses* must vary with the different ages of the children to such an extent, that the only practicable guide for their regulation must *Recesses.* be found in the discretion of the teacher. It may be said, in general, however, that the weariness of the pupil, which is shown by his restlessness and want of attention, furnishes the best indication of the time when the ordinary text-book studies should be superseded by physical exercises, or by the absolute recreation of the play-ground. (3) *The number, length, and distribution of vacations* are, in a general way, governed by the same consideration that prescribes the number, length, and *Vacations.* distribution of recesses; namely, the freshness, both mental and physical, of the pupil, with such modifications as may be suggested by climate, prevailing contagious diseases, or other conditions. The tendency, of late years, in the United States, has been to begin the school session about the first of September, and to continue it uninterruptedly — with a slight intermission of a week during the holidays — till the following June or July. By this arrangement, a long, continuous vacation is insured during the warmest season of the year, when, it is claimed, rest is most needed. It has been objected to this, and perhaps with reason, that the heat of the summer months renders them unfavorable for that outdoor exercise which is most needed for the recuperation of the system, and that the health of pupils would be promoted rather by confining them indoors. As long, however, as the summer heats are avoided by a flight to the sea-shore or the mountains, this practice will probably prevail; and though it may be said that the poor of cities, who are by far the largest patrons of the public schools, cannot afford to leave the city for summer retreats, it must be remembered, on the other hand, that the greater prevalence of fatal diseases in cities, during the summer months, renders a vacation desirable even in their case. (4) *The regulations of the school* may, by their severity, seriously interfere with bodily health, by checking or entirely repressing that activity which is so marked a characteristic of childhood and youth. Reid, in his *Principles of Education*, says, "There is nothing in which parents are often more tyrannical and unreasonable than in expecting children to be quiet and good, and give them little trouble, when they will not put themselves to the least trouble to find suitable occupation for the active and restless faculties of their children. The trouble that a child gives to those in charge of it, should very often be viewed as an effort of nature to recall them to their neglected duty". *The degree and kind of restraint*, exercised over pupils, therefore deserve careful consideration. In this connection must be condemned all those restrictions which repress, for any considerable time, that innate activity which is a necessity of the child's very being, and the repression of which, though not immediately and actively productive of disease, becomes passively so by the condition of atrophy which it tends to produce. Want of exercise is frequently as inimical to health as excess of it. *The number and length of lessons*, also, by their excess may become physically injurious. "With young children", Currie says, "a lesson should not average in duration more than a quarter of an hour, and on no account exceed twenty minutes. It is hard enough to sustain the attention, even for this period; and no child will be able to retain more than we can tell him within it. The teacher should subdivide his lesson rather than trespass beyond this limit. Lessons of different kinds, *i. e.*, occupying different senses, should follow each other; this is a great relief. It is absurd to speak of these frequent changes as causing loss of time". Excitement and overwork, also, should be avoided. The same general directions, however, given in regard to the number and length of recesses, are applicable here. The lessons assigned by the teacher and studied in his presence may be easily directed; but those which are pursued at home should receive equal attention. (See HOME LESSONS.)

IX. Cleanliness, being a necessary condition of health, should be strenuously insisted upon. Cleanliness of the person will sometimes be found, especially in schools among the very poor, to be neglected. The danger of the outbreak of disease, or of its communication

Regulations

Restraint.

Lessons.

Personal habits.

from this source, is always great in large schools; and, therefore, the frequent use of the lavatory, in such cases, is necessary. Cleanliness of *clothing* is no less necessary to prevent the communication of disease. Realizing the neglect of a proper care of the clothing, natural to children through thoughtlessness, many school boards have made the daily dusting and brushing of clothes by the pupils a part of the school routine. In Germany, this is often insisted upon, and the necessary provision made at the expense of the school. Cleanliness of *habits* is a no less essential condition of good health, and should be watched, as far as may be, and enforced with a view to the prevention of ill health. It frequently happens that *diseases*, more or less contagious in their nature, break out in schools, and lead to the closing of the schools for a time, with sometimes more serious results. In many cases, these could have been prevented, or confined to the original case, by a proper precaution on the part of the teacher. Ophthalmia, hooping-cough, scrofula, scarlet fever, small-pox, and skin diseases, whether of the head or the body, are cases of this kind. A slight knowledge of the symptoms should apprise an intelligent teacher of the danger at once, and secure the removal of the case to the home or the hospital.

X. That exercise is one of the most effective of all agencies in preventing disease, is now generally admitted, though the excess to which it is often carried in our day has, for some time, been creating a reaction against it. The phase of the question which calls for attention here, is its use not so much as a means of development, as in promoting health. On this account, one of the most important accessories of the school-house is the *play-ground*. Whether this is used as a place for continuing the discipline of the school room, or simply as a spot where children may be absolutely free to pursue their games, its size, location, and exposure should be carefully considered.

Physical exercise.

IMAGINATION, Culture of. Imagination is the power by which conceptions, originally formed from the perception of natural objects or their representatives, are reproduced in a fictitious combination which resembles the natural. This faculty, existing as it does, in a greater or less degree, in every mind, and entering to some extent into almost every mental act, must be placed among the few great powers of the mind which demand careful cultivation. The influence of the imagination is equally felt in moral and intellectual action. By its aid, the man of science, recombining the elements gathered by an observation of the visible world around him, projects his thought into the unseen universe, and determines the existence of conditions which knowledge alone could never detect, but which observation serves only to confirm. Through the influence of imagination alone, the record of the past becomes a guide and a warning to the present. Thus, the hand of charity is opened to relieve necessities which the active exercise of this faculty pictures to us as existing in the homes of want and misery. The every-day thought of the boor, and the rare flight of the man of genius are alike indebted to its aid. The universality of its presence, therefore, and the danger attending its unregulated development, constitute its peculiar claim to attention at the hands of the educator.

Influence.

Notwithstanding this, however, the need of a systematic cultivation of the imaginative faculty seldom receives practical recognition. This is owing somewhat to the fact that the want which would be produced by its total neglect, is partly met by its indirect and irregular cultivation in the studies of any ordinary school course; but more to the hidden nature of its action, and the want of that subtle discernment necessary in the teacher to detect its influence in the mental operations of the pupil. A knowledge of its power and of the consequent need of its cultivation is derived almost entirely from our own experience. The extent, therefore, to which it influences or controls the judgment, is appreciable only in our own case, and in that only approximately; and, hence, an analysis of its effect on the thought or actions of others becomes a matter of extreme difficulty. The neglect of its cultivation in the ordinary school curriculum is productive of results hardly less pernicious than its abuse by undue stimulation; for, while by the latter the judgment and reason are subordinated, and the mind is turned from the consideration of the practical, and concentrated too exclusively upon the ideal, thus enveloping the daily concerns of life in a kind of mental mirage, which results in disappointment and discouragement when the cloud is dispersed; by the former, the dull, matter-of-fact phase of existence acquires undue prominence, to the suppression of all sentiment and that love of the beautiful which cheers and helps us to find, even in the commonest aspects and the least fortunate circumstances of life, reason for admiration and gratitude. These considerations should secure for it careful attention.

Culture.

Neglect.

The development of the imaginative faculty begins at a very early period. The consciousness on the part of the child of objects external to itself, constitutes perception. This is very soon followed by conception, which consists in taking from the object perceived a mental picture capable of reproduction at pleasure, in the absence of the original. This latter may be called the first act of the imagination — the storing of the mind with materials for future use. Simultaneously with this, or only shortly after, occurs the naming of these materials — the association of thoughts with words, with a view to their expression as language. (See INTELLECTUAL EDUCATION.) Thus far, the action of the imagination depends upon the perception of actual objects. It now remains for the imagination to use the materials already provided, by discarding the actual object, and forming, partly by the aid of words as symbols of general ideas, an ideal picture; or, independently of words, and by its own act, creating for itself scenes and images not less vivid than their tangible representatives. The work of the imagination, therefore, is complementary to that of observation. The order is, (1) perception, (2) conception, (3) imagination. The action of the latter is presupposed by that of the two former. Knowledge alone — the mere storing of the mind with facts and conceptions — would be of little value without the vivifying power of imagination. Its function is to lift the mind from the contemplation of the actual, and carry it beyond the field of mere observation, into those ideal regions where the tangible has no existence, or where its existence cannot be actually verified.

Development.

In the cultivation of the faculty of imagination, several methods are

IMAGINATION

open to the teacher, the most common of which are pictures, oral narratives, and reading, or combinations of these. In all, the attention is the principal object to be secured; since thus only can a vivid mental picture be formed, and any other is worse than useless. The picture is, of course, the surest instrument for accomplishing this result, since it is a direct appeal to the eye — the earliest and most powerful agent by which knowledge is obtained. It is desirable, therefore, that the picture should be clearly drawn or painted, and in as simple or elementary a form as is consistent with the idea of completeness. A few salient features, therefore, are all that are necessary for this purpose; since fine gradations of color or shading can be observed only at the expense of the general impression. In oral narrative, the degree to which the clearness of the general impression is produced, depends entirely upon the teacher. A warm, sympathetic nature is here the only qualification. By it he is enabled to place himself on the pupil's level, to enter into his thoughts, and by the use of figures and illustrations familiar to youthful minds, to produce a correct and precise mental image. Any other disposition than this is a decided disqualification for the cultivation of the imagination by this method. Where the picture and the oral narrative are used together, the former should not be exhibited till after the description. It should then be produced to reinforce the description and give it greater clearness; but, if it is exhibited before that time, the attention is drawn to it at once, to the neglect of the narrative. Pictures which are to be used for the purpose of illustration, should, if possible, be new to the pupil in order to produce their best effect. Of the methods mentioned, however, for the cultivation of the imaginative faculty, reading is not only the most common, but is, in most cases, indispensable. The requisites in this case, however, are still the same. The object being always to fix the attention as powerfully as possible upon a mental picture, the style should be simple and clear, but graphic and forcible, abounding in concrete terms, not in abstract phrases, and appealing to the experience of the pupil, and awakening his sympathies. An excellent test of the clearness of the mental picture formed is that of recalling at the end of the reading, the scenes, incidents, and actors in the order of their introduction or occurrence. Almost every branch pursued in the ordinary school or college course affords some opportunity for the cultivation of the imaginative faculty, but special fields for its most active exercise are found in geography, history, and poetry. Even in the teaching of subjects usually considered dry and uninteresting, there is field for the exercise of this faculty. Grammar, mathematics, political economy, and logic, if illustrated by a teacher of active fancy, can be freed, in large measure, from the abstract nature which is supposed to be essential to them, and which renders them ordinarily so uninviting. In regard to the use of fiction as an agent in the cultivation of the imagination, much discussion has arisen, the objection usually urged being that its effect is to stimulate this faculty unduly. This is probably true of one class only; namely, those in whose minds the imaginative faculty exists by nature in an abnormal degree. Where this power is deficient, it will hardly be said that the perusal of works of fiction can do more than do develop the faculty, so as to bring it into proportion with the other mental powers; while the probability is, that the result will fall short of this. In the remaining class,

Methods.

those in whom this faculty exists in a normal proportion, the evil result of stimulation produced by the reading of works of fiction, has, perhaps, been overrated. The reading alone can only serve to fill the mind with high ideals — the harm resulting has probably been produced by neglecting to provide the necessary means or occasions for an active exercise of the high and generous sentiments and resolves thus aroused. If we read continually of suffering, but never give alms, habit soon causes us to accomodate ourselves to this condition as the natural one, and the mental excitement ceases to seek any outward, active expression.

"All mere drudgery", says James Freeman Clarke, in *Self-Culture* (Boston, 1880), "tends to stupefy the imagination. And all work is drudgery which is done mechanically, — with the hand and not with the mind; when we are not trying to do our work as well as possible, but only as well as necessary. Such work stupefies the ideal faculty, quenches the sense of beauty". This is a truth of great practical significance to the teacher.

IMITATION. The possession of this important faculty, and the desire to exercise it, constitute two essential elements of all human progress.

Office. From childhood to maturity, and even beyond — as long, indeed, as the effort at self-improvement is kept up — a vast majority of the human race are employed merely in imitating the models that have been set up by individual genius, or by the accumulated wisdom and taste of ages; and their success in life is greater or less, according to the accuracy of their imitation. Especially during childhood and youth, is this faculty brought into active play. It is the necessary accompaniment and basis of instruction, the stepping-stone to all excellence. Being of so great importance, therefore, in nearly every department of education, it should receive the special attention of the teacher. — The conditions of

Conditions of success. success in imitation are chiefly two: (1) accurate observation, and (2) a retentive memory. Probably few have noticed how slightly the faculty of observation is usually exercised. This, however, may be easily illustrated. Of twenty persons listening to a speaker whose voice has some peculiar tone or inflection, it will probably be found that only half a dozen or perhaps even less will notice it, unless it is very marked; and of these, only two or three will be able to reproduce it with any degree of accuracy. How often do men differ as to the form or color of some feature in the face of an acquaintance! For example, let a draughtsman, whose attention has not previously been specially called to the object, be asked to draw a rose-leaf. The probability is, that he will confess his inability to do so though he would recognize a rose-bush without difficulty. Instances might be multiplied of the loose, general way in which this faculty is used, the result of which is, that only an indefinite impression is left on the mind, instead of an accurate picture. (See ATTENTION.) If it be granted then, that mere imitation, when uncultivated, cannot be depended on, it will probably not be denied that a good memory, and, in most cases, a certain degree of mechanical skill, is necessary, when it is cultivated, to produce the best results.

It only remains, therefore, to point out a few of the studies and pursuits in which imitation is the chief instrument, and to indicate some of the

Field of activity. methods by which it may be made most efficient. Among the first, may be enumerated writing, map-drawing, as now generally used in teaching geography, and nearly all the arts; among them, drawing, with all the professions that immediately depend upon it, as surveying, civil engineering, mechanics, architecture, together with all the natural sciences in the teaching of which, sensible objects are to be represented. In learning to speak a foreign language, also, a direct appeal is made to the faculty of imitation. Among the methods used for producing efficiency in imitation, the kindergarten system is of great value for insuring steadiness of hand and accuracy of eye. (See KINDERGARTEN.) The usual school exercises of reading, declamation, dialogues, etc., are more or less successful, according to the closeness with which the feelings and expressions of imaginary persons are imitated.

INCENTIVES, School, consist of rewards of various kinds, offered to pupils for progress in study and good behavior; such as "good tickets", certificates of merit, books, and other things awarded as premiums for excellence either in proficiency or conduct. Besides these, various expedients are resorted to for the purpose of exciting emulation, which are also to be classed among school incentives; such as giving public praise, awarding merit marks, putting the names of meritorious pupils upon a *roll of honor*, suitably embellished and framed, and hung in a conspicuous place in the school room. Daily or weekly reports to parents showing the number of merit marks received by the pupil, as compared with the full number, and thus exhibiting the standing of the pupil, are very generally used by teachers as an incentive. The dismissal of pupils from school previous to the usual time is also to be placed among the same class of incentives. To this, however, strong objection has been made, inasmuch as it seems to imply that attendance at school is burdensome and grievous, whereas it should be made pleasant and attractive; but the efficacy of this incentive, as every teacher knows, is very great, because it appeals to the natural activity of the child, upon which the confinement of school cannot but operate as a restraint, however well it may be administered; and experience has demonstrated that an occasional relief from this confinement does not, on the whole, weaken the pupil's attachment to school. All such incentives, it must be borne in mind, are of a secondary nature; and the educator should always exercise care that their influence should not be so exerted as to impair the force of higher and more enduring motives to good conduct. (See REWARDS.)

INDUCTIVE METHOD, in education, is but another name for the *developing method* (q. v.). It is so called because it is based upon the principle of logical induction, or the process of deriving general principles from an observation and comparison of individual facts. Instead of teaching definitions, principles, and rules arbitrarily, and illustrating them by facts, the teacher who uses the inductive method, calls the attention of the pupil to a sufficient number of the facts to enable him to find the principle or rule for himself. The learning of the definition, which, in the deductive method, is the first thing to be done, in the inductive method, is the last step in the process. Most text-books follow the deductive method, but the most effective elementary instruction is inductive.

INDUSTRIAL SCHOOL. The term *industrial education* is used to designate the training of pupils, not only in the common branches of instruction, but in certain industrial or business pursuits. An *industrial* *school*, in the widest sense of the word, denotes any school for teaching one or several branches of industry; but the special schools of this kind, and, in particular, those of a higher grade, are more generally comprised under the name of technical schools; and the name industrial school is usually restricted to a school for neglected children, in which training in manual labor or industrial pursuits constitutes a prominent feature of the plan of education. The common schools, however, sometimes have classes, in which children are instructed in certain industrial pursuits.

INSTRUCTION (Lat. *instructio*) is the communication of knowledge. Education trains the powers of the individual, in order that he may attain to the perfection of his being; instruction supplies him with something that is objective or external. Instruction has specially to do with the intellectual development of the child, and is an instrument in the hands of the educator, which he can wield with the greatest precision and in the most skillful manner. He may attempt to act on the feelings and the volitions; but so obscure are the operations of the soul in these regions, that he may produce exactly the opposite effect to that which he intended. But when he communicates knowledge, he knows that, if the pupil is capable and attentive, he will receive exactly that which it is intended he should receive. Moreover, knowledge stands in close relation to the feelings and volitions; and, accordingly, the teacher employs it for the purpose of influencing and directing these. Thus, it comes to pass that instruction occupies the largest part in the work of education, and constitutes that portion which can be undertaken and provided for by a community, since it can be delegated by a parent to a regularly trained teacher with the best results. Instruction is putting something into the mind; education is strengthening and developing the powers of the mind. It is plain that a teacher should put nothing into the mind which does not train and develop its powers; but as it is possible to do so, and as this frequently takes place, instruction is to be divided into educative and non-educative; and one of the most important questions which a teacher can investigate, is the nature of educative instruction. There are three qualities which attach to all educative instruction: (1) Instruction, to be educative, must follow the natural laws of the intellectual development of man. Man's intellectual life begins in the exercise of the senses. He accumulates a large number of individual observations. In these observations, like gathers to like. A child looks at a tree; and the tree produces an impression on his mind. The next day, he sees another tree; and the resemblances in this tree strike his mind, and recall the former impression. The two impressions thus unite, and form a stronger impression than either separately. Other impressions of a similar nature unite, until the child forms a definite notion of a tree. The child is thus gathering into unities the various impressions which he is continually forming; and this process continues. He learns the individual first, and groups his observations. Thus instruction, to be educative, must always proceed from the individual to the general, from the concrete to the abstract. There is no reversal of this process in education; but the process is often reversed in instruction with baneful effect. To the teacher, the general truth contains the sum of all the particulars, and he thinks he gives to the child this general truth with all its contents, when he urges it upon him, makes him commit it to memory, and frequently recalls it to his mind; but the fact is, that the child learns the general truth without the contents. He has the shell without the kernel. The result is, either that the truth lies dormant until experience gives him the particulars, and he may then recall the truth, or that the child is lulled into the belief that he has learned something when he really knows nothing, and his mind is prevented from stepping forward in that direction, by the belief that he knows the truth already. Furthermore, this non-educative instruction loses a great opportunity. If the child is allowed time, and is supplied with a sufficient number of individual instances, he is sure to make the generalization himself. Nothing imprints the truth more permanently than the discovery of it for himself, and nothing brings into play all the powers of the soul more healthily than the discovery of a truth. The teacher must, therefore, always proceed from the concrete to the abstract; but, in employing this method, he must exercise very great patience. Generalization is a slow process, somewhat uncertain in time. The child seems to be just reaching the truth, but he turns away with a bound, and he may take some time more to master it completely. Or he may, one day, have a glimpse of it, and the next, it has vanished. But, however slow or uncertain the process may be, it is the only truly educative mode of giving instruction. The teacher, like Socrates, is a maieutic artist, and he must watch carefully over the birth of a truth, not forcing nature, but giving nature every help that she will willingly receive. (2) Educative instruction arrests the atten-

Attention and interest. tion and awakens the interest of the pupil. The rule implied in this statement may be expressed in the words, that the teacher must attach the new matter to the old by a natural connection, that he must pass from the known to the unknown. The subject of attention is one that cannot be discussed here. We can note only how it is to be secured. The pupil must be on good terms with his teacher. Where there is antagonism. there can be no satisfactory attention. The pupil may, indeed, attend through fear; but fear is a weakening force; and the result is, to associate in his mind with the subject comprehended feelings of dislike and disgust, so that at the end there is no interest in the subject, but, on the contrary, a wish that he may never have to do with it again. Then, the teacher must carefully consider the state of the pupil's mind, when he commences. Probably, he has come from the play-ground. His mind is occupied with some occurrence that has taken place there, and his mind will remain occupied with it the whole hour, if the teacher does not employ means to displace it. Some little time should be given to the pupil to calm down; and then, when he is prepared to listen, the teacher should start with something that the pupil knows well and feels an interest in, and from that gradually work his way to the new matter which he has to communicate. The result of his teaching should be, that the child has a stronger interest in the subject than he had before. To rouse this interest, the teacher has to remember that every intellectual activity is closely connected with corresponding feelings and exertions, and the teacher succeeds when he makes his intellectual propositions awaken the appropriate feelings and exertions. (3) Educative instruction always keeps in view the principal aim and end of education. It always works for a purpose. The object is not to cram the pupil with a certain amount of knowledge, to give him an hour's dose of information, without regard to his whole being. It deliberately asks whether the information which is to be imparted, will fit into the harmonious development of the child's powers. It will, therefore, proportion the amount given to the healthy evolution of the child's nature. It will not look to the greatest success in the particular department, but to the greatest success compatible with the healthy action of all the child's powers.

It is not necessary, in an article like this, to go further into the questions to which the subject of instruction gives rise. They are treated in separate articles. We may, however, take a general view *Subjects of* of them: (1) We should have to treat of the subjects of in-*instruction.* struction. These may be divided into those that relate to nature, those that relate to man, and those that relate to God. The first gives us the natural sciences, — a knowledge of the earth in its present state, geology, botany, zoölogy, physics, including astronomy and chemistry. Then come the abstract subjects arising out of these: the science of numbers and of magnitude, arithmetic, algebra, and geometry. Next follows the knowledge that relates to man: physiology, psychology, and sociology; but the latter sciences cannot be taught scientifically to children. The main facts are made known concretely in literature, and therefore the pupil learns languages, — his own, modern languages, and ancient languages. Education insists that these should ultimately, and as soon as possible, pass from being mere studies of words to be a means of acquainting the pupil with the feelings, thoughts, and desires of great and good men, past and present. Closely connected with languages is the study of history; and allied to history and intermediate between the first and second classes of study, is geography, — a knowledge of the earth as it has influenced man and been used by him. The third class of subjects relate to religion; but this is closely allied to the second, and, indeed, falls properly under it; for it is the knowledge of man's relations to God. (2) We should have to inquire into the educative value of all these studies, but this inquiry belongs to the special articles. Here it has to be remarked, that none of the subjects must be entirely omitted. The mind of man must not be deliberately made one-sided. The multiplication of interest is one of the great objects of education. (3) We should have to inquire into the methods of education; and (4) into the organization, private and public, necessary to render instruction effective. All these subjects are discussed in the ordinary manuals on instruction.

INTELLECTUAL EDUCATION. The term *intellect* (Latin, *intellectus*, from *inter*, between, and *legere*, to gather, or collect) is used to denote the faculty or faculties by which man *knows*, in distinction from those of *sensibility* and *will*. In the formation of the human *Culture* character, the culture of the intellect is of subordinate impor-*of the* tance to that of the other two mental functions, — the proper *intellect.* order in this regard being (1) will, (2) sensibility, (3) intellect; for the intellect is only an instrument, the use of which must depend upon the natural strength and educational training of the other elements of human character. There is, however, without doubt, a reflex action of sound intellectual culture, by means of which the propensities and tastes of an individual are ennobled, and his moral sense strengthened. In order to direct the education of the intellect, it is necessary to understand its operations and the mode of its growth from infancy to mature age; the processes by which its powers may be guided, stimulated, and improved, and the agencies by means of which this improvement, or culture, is to be effected. The human mind acts, as it were, by separate faculties; *Faculties.* it appears to possess distinct powers. These faculties, or powers, are without doubt, intimately associated. They are but functions of a single agent; but they are functions distinct, both in their mode of operation and in the objects upon which they are exercised. To form an idea from a present object of sensation is obviously distinct from recalling that idea when the object is no longer present. This again differs essentially from the suggestion of one idea by the presence of another in some way associated with it. Again, to create from the simple impressions derived from natural objects an original picture, or series of pictures, such as those of Hogarth on canvas, or of Bunyan, in written composition, is certainly a very different process from the selection and combination of elementary propositions so as to derive from them an original principle, or truth. The mind is, nevertheless, a unit; and all its operations, of however diverse a character, may be conceived to depend, directly or indirectly, upon some rudimental process: but nothing would be gained practically by such a procedure; and, therefore, we may properly conform to the common usage in this regard, and consider the intellect as comprehending many distinct faculties, which, of course, cannot be cultivated and strengthened by the teacher without a sufficient knowledge of their respective spheres of action, their modes of operation, and the objects upon which they are specially exercised. These have been conveniently classified and designated as follows: (1) The *acquisitive faculties,* including consciousness and sense-perception; (2) The *representative faculties,* including conception, association, memory, and imagination; (3) The *elaborative faculties,* including comparison, abstraction, generalization, judgment, and reason.

The *senses,* those avenues of communication with the external world, are first to be considered, since probably ideas at first spring from sensation, which appears to be the primitive stimulus of activity *Sensation.* in the whole animal kingdom. (See SENSES.) It is, however, in no other way connected with the mind than as the means of supplying the material upon which the first mental operations are performed; and when this material is afforded, the mind as an entirely independent agent may or may not act upon it, this act being controlled by what is called *attention* (q. v.), which is only a condition of activity assumed by the mind in regard to any of the objects of sensation or consciousness.

When sensation and attention exist simultaneously, there must *Perception.* result what is called *perception,* sensation being simply the effect produced by external objects upon the bodily organs, and perception the act of the mind in becoming cognizant of it as proceeding from some cause extraneous to itself. The product of these two acts, constituting what is called *sense-perception,* would be only momentary, or would last only during the presence of the object perceived, but for the existence of a faculty by which the mind retains impressions thus made, recalls them voluntarily or involuntarily, and thus is enabled to make them the subject of independent mental action. These impressions, and in an especial manner those made through the medium of sight, become in this way a part of the mind; they are imprinted upon its very texture, as it were, like pictures upon the photographic glass. Hence the name *ideas* (from the Greek word ἰδεῖν, to see). This faculty is called *conception* (q. v.). It requires the most careful cultivation in childhood and youth; since it alone enables the mind to store up the materials of knowledge and thought in its wonderful and mysterious repository. The intellect of childhood is chiefly employed in the exercise of it — in storing up ideas, and gathering materials out of which to produce its subsequent creations, whether these are the fantastic pictures of fancy, the more regular combinations of imagination, or the sequences of ratiocination. Whatever, therefore, hinders this process, shrivels the mind and stunts its growth. Its vitality dies out for want of exercise, and torpor takes the place of elasticity and vigorous life. This is, therefore, one of the first faculties to be addressed in education. Its activity is to be fostered by supplying it with abundant food — objects on which it may be exercised, and language designed to bring into clear mental view the conceptions already acquired.—

Conception.

The next mental process to be considered is *association*. In the first stages of the mind's growth, there exists but little power of combination, certainly none of logical combination; but there is an elementary principle of intellection by which ideas tend to become linked together according to certain relations; this is called *association* (q. v.). Perhaps, the most important of the elementary associations established in regard to the conceptions is that of words or names with the conceptions of objects which they are thus made to represent. This is, without doubt, one of the earliest, as well as one of the most rudimental, of the mind's combinations. The association itself, it must be borne in mind, is all that is arbitrary; since it is not words themselves that are associated with the conceptions of the objects, but conceptions of the spoken words, formed through the medium of hearing. What is meant by asserting that the association alone is arbitrary, is that the spoken word, as an actual sense-perception, is retained and recalled by conception, and is, therefore, no more arbitrary than any other idea; but having no intrinsic relation to the conception for which it is to stand, it is associated with it arbitrarily, that is, by repeatedly bringing the two conceptions together, in accordance with that law of mental action by which ideas repeatedly brought into connection suggest each other.

Association.

Without the association of words with ideas, the mind could advance but a very few steps in its development; because, (1) it would be unable to receive any stimulus by communicating with any other minds; (2) it would be powerless to control the order in which the conceptions would present themselves to the mind, or to divest them of the vagueness of revery or dreaming; and (3) no process of thought or reasoning could be carried on without the assistance of language. This need of words is illustrated by the efforts of children to talk, and call things by names, long before the power of articulation exists, thus showing that, although they are unable to employ words for the expression of ideas, the

Language.

mind is constantly making use of them in carrying on its rudimental operations. — It is an important law that conceptions are more strongly associated when their corresponding perceptions have been associated. Thus, suppose it is desired to teach a child the meaning of the word *ship*; in other words, to associate in his mind the spoken word *ship* with the conception of the ship, so that the one will always suggest the other. If he has never seen a ship, nothing but the actual perception will suffice, and he must be taken where one may be actually seen; but if he has seen the object without learning its name, the conception may be recalled to his mind either by questioning him or by showing him a picture of it. Without doing this, the word *ship* may be repeated to him, and he may pronounce it any number of times, without learning any thing, since it would be presenting to his mind a sign without showing what it signifies. In elementary instruction, this error is quite often committed.

It is important to consider upon what fundamental or primary notion the mind proceeds in establishing the arbitrary association between things and their names; that is, between conceptions which intrinsically have no relation to each other. A slight observation will ascertain that the mind very early requires the notion of names as representatives of things, and thus comprehends the relation existing between a *sign* and the *thing signified;* not that this notion is made an object of actual consciousness or reflection, but that it is intuitively recognized by the mind, and is practically employed by the child in making known its wants or expressing its feelings. The question, "What is it?" so often heard from the lips of a young child on seeing a new object, appears generally to have reference only to this notion. The child perceives the need of affixing a name to the object in order that it may become a definite conception, as well as be prepared for expression; and when a name is given, however arbitrary or unintelligible, the inquiry proceeds no further, the child appearing entirely satisfied. It is only when the mind has made more progress in development and has acquired a knowledge of other relations, that this question can possibly have any other import. Very much of the early development of a child's mind thus consists in acquiring a knowledge of words, but, let it be carefully observed, of words only as *representatives of actual conceptions*. In this way the knowledge of things and the knowledge of words, increase *pari passu*, and the mind is prepared for operations of a more advanced character; since it is only by symbolizing individual conceptions that *generalization* can take place, that is, that individuals can be conceived with reference exclusively to certain qualities which they possess in common, and thus be arranged in classes. This office of language has been explained in the following manner by a very acute writer (H. L. Mansel): "*Intuitive generalization* consists in directing the attention, voluntarily or involuntarily, to the common features of several objects presented to us, neglecting or not perceiving those qualities which are peculiar to each. It is not a distinct cognition of the class as a class, nor of the individuals as individuals; but a confused perception of both together. To form a complete cognition of the individual. I must, by the aid of imagination, supply those distinctive features which I am unable clearly to perceive. To form a complete cognition of the class, I must separate the common attributes from their connection with a definite time and place. But how are attributes, apart from their juxtaposition in space, to be so connected together, as to constitute a single object? The head and trunk and limbs of an individual man are connected together by continuity in space, and by that continuity constitute a whole of intuition, whether distinctly recognized in that relation or not. How are the attributes of mankind in general to be separated from their position in space, and yet so united together as to constitute a whole of thought? To effect this we must call in the aid of language. The word is to thought what space is to perception. It constitutes the connecting link between various attributes — the frame, as it were, in which they are set — and thus furnishes the means by which the features characteristic of a class may be viewed apart from the individuals in which they are intuitively perceived, and combined into a complex notion or concept". In regard to the same point, Whately remarks, in *Elements of Logic*: "The majority of men would probably say, if asked, that the use of language is peculiar to man; and that its office is to express to one another our thoughts and feelings. But neither of these is strictly true. Brutes do possess, in some degree, the power of being taught to understand what is said to them, and some of them even to utter sounds expressive of what is passing within them. But they all seem to be incapable of another very important use of language which does characterize man; namely, the employment of *common terms (general terms)* formed by abstraction, as *instruments of thought*; by which alone a train of reasoning may be carried on. And accordingly a deaf-mute, before he has been taught a language — either the finger-language or reading — cannot carry on a train of reasoning any more than a brute. He differs indeed from a brute, in possessing the mental capability of employing language; but he can no more make use of that capability till he is in possession of some system of arbitrary general signs, than a person born blind from cataract can make use of his capacity of seeing, till the cataract is removed".

Next to the association of things with words as their representatives, is that founded upon a perception of *resemblance* in the objects from which
Resemblance and analogy. conceptions are derived. This, it will be perceived from what has already been adduced, takes place prior to generalization, to which it directly leads. There is, probably, no relation so obvious to a child as that of resemblance or analogy, and none that affords so much employment to its mind, or that affects it with more pleasurable emotions. This is particularly the case with the relation of analogy when found to exist between objects quite dissimilar. The facility and readiness with which very young children discern resemblances, whether they are founded upon form, color, or structure, indicate a natural aptitude of the mind to perceive the varieties of these qualities in different objects, — of these qualities especially, because they are addressed to the sight, which of all the senses gives rise to the most vivid conceptions. The varieties of color (tints), form, etc., generally have no designations in the child's mind — no symbols in language; and, therefore, cannot be made distinct objects of conception or of consciousness; and, in the earliest stages of mental development, this is not required to enable the mind to carry on its rudimental processes. Very young children can learn to classify objects with respect to their resemblances in form, color, etc.;

and to require them to do this, is one of the best exercises that can be employed to aid the development of their minds. The readiness with which children apply the same name to objects having only a general resemblance to each other in form, color, or structure, is another proof of this characteristic of the human mind. "Children", says Aristotle, "at first call every man *father*, and every woman *mother*, but afterwards they distinguish one person from another". The perception of resemblance is, thus, prior to that of difference, and, apparently, for a very good reason; since, if the reverse were the case, the mind, instead of requiring immediately words as the representatives of classes, would need a word for every object of perception, and thus could make no advancement in developing the higher faculties. This was the doctrine of Pestalozzi, and a basic principle of his system. There is no doubt that very great diversities in objects excite the attention more readily than corresponding resemblances, just as rapid transitions from one color to another, from intense darkness to a brilliant illumination, etc., produce activity in the perceptive faculties; and hence, the employment of such processes in the education of those mentally deficient; but where any two objects are placed before a child, of which the points of resemblance and of difference are equally obvious to the developed and mature mind, the child will intuitively notice the former before he will the latter. The constitution of the mind seems to necessitate this. Objects which are very unlike may, indeed, have some points of resemblance which escape the notice of a child, and which, therefore, the teacher will need to point out so as to assist in their discovery, and, in this way, to cultivate the habit of observation. The whole structure of the intellect as a thinking and reasoning apparatus seems to be based on the ready recognition of likeness and analogy in the various objects presented to the senses. Isaac Taylor remarks, in *Home Education:* "The sense of resemblance runs before the power of discriminating or designating differences; hence, it happens that by the infant and the savage the names of individuals are extended to species, and the names of species to genera". "Thus", as Mansel remarks, "by the aid of language, our first abstractions are, in fact, given to us already made; as we learn to give the same name to various individuals presented to us under slight and at first unnoticed circumstances of distinction. The name is thus applied to different objects long before we learn to analyze the growing powers of speech and thought, to ask what we mean by each several instance of its application, and to correct and fix the significance of words at first used vaguely and obscurely". The association of the conceptions as dependent

Intuitive generalization. upon an observation of resemblance, has been called *intuitive generalization*; since it does not consciously follow any process of abstraction, because, from the failure of the undeveloped mind to notice distinctions and differences, no such process is needed for the purpose. For example, a child sees a book for the first time, and learns its name, *book*; now, on seeing another book, however different from the first in size, color, etc., he invariably applies to it the term *book*; by the perception of analogy leading on to intuitive generalization. Common names are, therefore, first learned, and particular or proper names only given to such objects as are constantly presented to the mind; since, by being thus more intimately known, their distinctive peculiarities are more clearly discerned, this discernment leading to an *individualization*, as the next step in the growth or development of the mind. The operation of the sense of analogy is seen in the use of figurative, or more definitely, tropical language; and its rudimental character is illustrated by the fact that children and savages are particularly prone to the use of this language. Indeed, as before remarked, it is one of the most intense mental pleasures of the child to trace analogies in objects of considerable diversity in general appearance, and to apply such metaphorical terms as will forcibly express them. This again adds very greatly to a child's power of expression, since, without the perception of these analogies in objects, every variation would require some specific term, metaphorical names ceasing to have any meaning whatever. This characteristic of a child's mind gives to the intelligent teacher considerable resources for illustration, particularly in the use of words and their application to the objects which they represent. Thus, the term *cape* would be much better understood if its exact literal import were explained, and the analogy exhibited between the *head* and a *cape*, or *headland*. It is unfortunate that so few compound or derivative words in English are formed from the simple words of the language itself, and that recourse has been had to so great an extent to the Latin and Greek languages for a supply of such roots; since, in consequence of this, most of the words of the language are necessarily taught as arbitrary terms, which, otherwise, would be the means of stimulating mental activity in the learner. A striking contrast has very often been made, in this respect, between the English and German languages, such terms as *Regenschirm* (umbrella), *Sonnenschirm* (parasol), *Handschuh* (glove), *Fingerhut* (thimble), *einsaugen* (absorb), *durchsichtig* (transparent), etc., illustrating very clearly the fact referred to. This peculiarity of a language, in drawing almost exclusively from its own primitive words the materials for the construction of complex epithets, is also very prominent in the Greek language, and constitutes one of its excellencies. Where it exists, it must afford great facility in education, and must form the basis for processes which are impracticable where a language, such as the English, is to be employed, which derives nearly all of its abstract and scientific terms from languages not merely foreign but entirely out of use. The growth of mind in its relation to language has been here dwelt upon at some length because of its importance as a source of practical knowledge to every teacher who makes the study of mind the basis of his operations. Arbitrary rules may be laid down, and applied; but the scientific teacher who investigates the foundation of these rules in the principles of intellectual science will best know how to adapt his methods to the diversified exigencies of his work. Association as an elementary function of mind, is dependent upon a variety of circumstances other than those enumerated; as time, place, cause and effect, and design. These are, however, of secondary importance for the study of the educator.

The peculiar functions of the representative faculties, *memory* and *imagination* should receive a careful study, since they underlie many of the most important processes which he is called upon to direct.

Representative faculties. (See IMAGINATION, and MEMORY.) The elaborative faculties, comparison, abstraction, and generalization, have already been referred to in relation to the rudimental stage of their operation;

in the higher grades of instruction, they find constant exercise in the studies of mathematics and natural science, which form a part of the curriculum of every high school, college, and university. Judgment *Elaborative* and reason pass through a gradation of development from the *faculties.* most elementary to the highest stages of education.

Such is the field which a discussion of the principles of intellectual education embraces. In the practical application of these principles, the teacher is to be guided not only by a knowledge of the general *General* functions of mind and their development, but by all the pecu-*principles.* liarities of individual endowment which he may be able to discern. (See CHARACTER, DISCERNMENT OF.) He is to permit the mind to expand by its own intrinsic activities, only interposing restraining or stimulating agencies when and where he finds a tendency to abnormal or morbid growth. There are, however, special methods of operation in intellectual education, partaking more of a positive character, by means of which the teacher is directly to impart knowledge — to communicate information; and, thus, is opened up a consideration not only of the mind to be cultivated, but of the branches of knowledge to be taught, in relation to the several faculties which they tend to cultivate. (See INSTRUCTION.) In this connection, and by the use of the same guiding principles, the proper order of presenting these studies must be considered and ascertained, this order being correlated with the natural order in which the intellectual faculties are developed. (See ORDER OF STUDIES.) The final result of this department of education should be, to enable the individual, in all the circumstances of life, to exercise with efficiency and address the various intellectual faculties with which he has been endowed. (See CULTURE.)

INTEREST. To awaken an interest on the part of the pupils in the subjects of instruction should always be a prominent object of the teacher's efforts, since it is an indispensable condition of all true success. Antecedently, the young pupil feels no interest in the school studies; he neither appreciates their importance nor has any desire to acquire a knowledge of the subjects of which they treat. But the skillful teacher knows how to stimulate curiosity, and to impress upon the mind of the pupil the idea that he is acquiring knowledge, and thus to awaken an interest in the processes of instruction. When these processes are appropriate and natural, the pupil's interest is easily sustained; and it will be generally found that a flagging interest is due either to previous defective training or to the endeavor to teach subjects for which the pupil's mind is not prepared. It is a psychological axiom that the mind has no less appetite for knowledge of the right kind, than exists physically for proper food to nourish the body. It is, therefore, the office of educational science to determine the kind of mental food proper for every age, and how it should be prepared so as to stimulate, while it satisfies, the mental appetite. There should also be individual adaptation, the teacher giving whatever attention may be necessary to the special inclinations, tastes, and capacities of his pupils. (See ATTENTION.)

INTERMEDIATE SCHOOLS are schools of a grade between primary schools and grammar schools, or between elementary schools and high schools. Such schools generally constitute an important part of the graded school system. Schools of a grade between elementary schools (in

German, *Elementarschule*), and colleges and universities, are often called *middle schools* (German, *Mittelschule*).

INTERROGATION, or the **Interrogative Method,** is an indispensable means of conducting most processes of instruction; particularly those of an elementary grade. Its office is either (1) tentative, or (2) illustrative. As a tentative process, the teacher uses it to determine the quantity and the quality of the knowledge which the pupil has attained. Thus, in hearing recitations, the teacher, by means of questions, ascertains how much of the lesson previously assigned, the pupil has learned, and with what accuracy it has been learned; and on the kind of questions asked, as well as on the manner of asking them, depends the degree of skill and effectiveness of this important part of the teacher's work. The same is true, also, of the conducting of examinations by school inspectors or superintendents. The process of questioning is also tentative when used as preliminary to a course of instruction, in order to determine the amount of information, or the kind of ideas, already acquired by the pupil, either directly relating to the subject or remotely connected with it, and constituting the elementary conceptions upon which it is to be based. Instruction on every subject needs such preliminary questioning. — Interrogation is illustrative when it is used as a direct means of instruction, in order to induce the pupil to combine his ideas in such a way that he may be led to a clear conception of the truth. This was the process used by Socrates in giving instruction; and hence, it is often called the Socratic method. Great skill can be exercised by the teacher in the use of interrogation for this purpose; indeed, the art of questioning (*catechetics*) becomes a special department of the work of teaching, and has been so treated. Rules can scarcely be given for its attainment; but it may briefly be said that it depends upon (1) a thorough training of the analytic faculty of the teacher, (2) such a minute and accurate knowledge of the subject to be taught as will enable him to resolve it into its elementary principles, (3) a full appreciation of the pupil's condition of mind, both as to capacity and degree of attainment, and (4) sufficient practice in interrogation to produce facility in framing questions of every kind and form. Where these conditions exist, the questions asked will be an effective means of making every subject clear to the learner's mind. (See CATECHETICAL METHOD.)

INTUITIVE METHOD. See OBJECT TEACHING.

ITALIAN LANGUAGE. The Italian language has no claims commensurate with those of the German or the French, to a place in any regular course of instruction the object of which is general culture, and which, to that end, embraces the study of one or two modern languages. Its value for this purpose has not, however, been without advocates. Thus L. Gantter, the author of the article on the Italian language, in Schmid's *Encyclopädie* (vol. III), in discussing the relative importance of the principal modern languages for the German gymnasia, from an educational point of view, assigns the first place to English, the second to Italian, and the third to French; and he appeals to Goethe, Niebuhr, Raumer, Gregorovius, and many other celebrities to prove that the educational impulse which may reasonably be expected from a study of the Italian language and literature, would prove

Place in education.

stronger and more conducive to a general development of the mental faculties than that received from the study of French. Italian has, however, special importance for all students of music, vocal and instrumental, as well as for students of the fine arts. Music, in every country of the world, uses to a large extent technical expressions borrowed from the Italian; the Italian opera is exceedingly popular in every large city of the world, and there is no student of the fine arts who is not anxious to complete his study of Italian art in Italy. These considerations have not only created a demand for instruction in Italian, but they are sufficiently important to recommend to students of music and of the fine arts a much more general study of this beautiful language than is to be met with at present; and it is to be regretted that universities, colleges, academies, and especially female institutions of a higher grade, do not, more frequently than is the case at present, afford to their pupils an opportunity to learn this language.

Special value.

The special motives which, in a majority of cases, lead to a study of this language, naturally suggest a method of instruction different from that pursued in the teaching of French and German. The beauty of the language, which is reflected in its structure and pronunciation, and which is so intimately connected with the lofty position which Italian art has attained in the history of civilization, should be pointed out with special care. Exercises in grammar and translation will require comparatively little attention; for not only is the structure of the language unusually simple and easy, but its study is hardly ever begun until, in addition to the vernacular, the knowledge of some other language has been acquired. All the greater prominence, on the other hand, should be given to the practice of conversation; for only in this way will the pupil fully realize the superiority of the language in point of beauty and euphony, and prepare himself for a visit to the country which, more than any other, captivates the affections of every artist. The literature of Italy scarcely admits of a comparison with that of Germany or France; but the golden age of Italian literature presents names which will never fail to recommend the study of the Italian language to advanced scholars. Dante ranks with Homer, Virgil, Milton, and Goethe, as one of the greatest poets of the world, whom all civilized nations will always admire; and Italian would be studied, if it were only to read the *Divina Commedia*. See *Cyclopædia of Education*.

Characteristic.

Literature.

JUDGMENT, Training of. This department of intellectual culture needs no special attention, if the whole educational system, in other respects, is judicious and rational; *i. e.*, adapted to the individual both as to age (degree of maturity) and peculiarities of character or endowment. Where this is not the case, an efficient corrective may be applied by bringing into exercise the pupil's mental faculties in various ways and in connection with various subjects. The departure must be taken from the sphere of the pupil's experience; he must be led (1) to accurate observation of particulars — minute details; (2) to their collation, as preliminary to generalization; and (3) to their classification under appropriate heads. When general principles or rules have been established in the pupil's mind in this way, his judgment will be brought into play in the application of the principle or rule to particular objects or facts. Thus, in natural history, after the pupil has learned the characteristics of genera and species by a minute and accurate observation of individual specimens, he cannot, without an exercise of judgment, determine whether any particular specimen, previously unobserved, belongs to one or the other genus or species. He must have a clear conception of the distinguishing qualities, both of the individual and of the class, in order to determine whether the correspondence exists or not. As regards concrete objects, the judgment is exercised at a very early age, and is constantly trained more or less by every legitimate process of intellectual education; but as regards abstract truths, this faculty is one of the last to attain a full or mature development. Accuracy in judging depends very much on the mental habits formed during the period of early education. Habits of attention, careful observation, dispassionate, conscientious reasoning, and a profound and earnest love of truth, will qualify any person for the exercise of a sound judgment in regard to any subject of study or investigation. A mental character based upon such habits will be free from prejudice, and will readily learn to eliminate all passion from its intellectual processes; and, hence, its judgments being solely based upon the facts acquired, will be correct or the contrary, in proportion to the accuracy and extent of the information possessed.

KINDERGARTEN (Ger., *children's garden*), a peculiar system of education, founded by Friedrich Froebel, designed to precede all other elementary training, and to prepare the child for regular instruction by exercising all its powers so as to render it *self-active*. While the reformers of education before his time, Pestalozzi included, whose assistant he was, treated the youthful mind, more or less, as a passive recipient of truth, goodness, and beauty, it was Froebel's fundamental idea to set the child to do whatever it could be induced to do as a kind of amusement, exercising its observing faculties in connection with its playthings and games, and thus to create in it an interest in learning. He discovered, by means of half a century's attentive practice in teaching, in association with many other excellent educators, that the faculties of most children are stunted in infancy and earliest youth by the want of appropriate mental food; that every child may be developed (may develop itself) into a self-educator by appropriate amusements; and that, in this manner, pleasure may be made the most efficient instrument in the first stages of education. He studied all the plays and games in use from the most ancient times, in order to find their special adaptation to mental and bodily growth, and thus formed a complete philosophical system of early intellectual culture. This culture was to begin in the earliest years, with ball plays, accompanied by snatches of song and rhyme; later, with a sphere, a cube, and a cylinder of wood, used for various amusing exercises, and calculated to enliven the attention, and increase the self-activity of the infant. The two little books for mothers, which contain his suggestions for this purpose, disclaim any merit of invention; he considers them derived simply from a diligent observation of the methods of many excellent and successful mothers. But it was not from books alone that he intended that mothers should learn how to train their children. They were to be educated, as young children, in a *kindergarten*, and afterwards, before graduating from the upper classes, to learn the art of infant education in a model *kindergarten*. It was in this way that he hoped to render, in the course of time, all mothers true educators of infancy, the centers of happy family circles, and the priestesses of a higher humanity, so that they might be "in harmony with themselves, with nature, and with God".

But mere family education being liable to one-sidedness and exclusiveness, social education should begin early, in order to complement the former. During part of the day, the child should be in company *Social education.* with many other children of the same age, and should engage in such plays as supply, in a gradually ascending scale, proper food for the mental and bodily appetites and functions, while making the company of little ones as happy as possible. This can be done only under the guidance of a true teacher, who should be a female capable, by natural endowments and previous study, to take the place, in this respect, of the mother. The locality should be a hall in a garden, with flowers, shrubs, trees, each child having its own flower-bed, so that it may learn how to raise plants, and to enjoy nature. The playful occupations of the pupils comprise a great variety of plays in a given order which, however, should not be absolutely fixed, but should afford a healthy change, without inducing habits of imperfect attention and restlessness. None of these occupations were the invention of Froebel; they had all been practiced more or less before his time. But their combination into a harmonious whole, their adaptation for mental food in every direction, and their development in detail must be set down as Froebel's creation; and the experience had with them for more than twenty-five years, and in many hundreds of kindergartens, justifies the wisdom of the system. There is still much controversy among the followers of Froebel themselves in regard to the minor details of the system; and some improvement has been made upon his own first practical realization of the idea, which, from insufficiency of means, could not be all that he desired; but the indefinite perfectibility of the system in practical details, according to its principles, insures its progressive success.

The exercises of the kindergarten are alternately carried on in a sitting, and in a standing or walking position, for the sake of a salutary change, *Exercises.* and are partly such as can, without special training, be guided by any good teacher; namely, singing; the reciting of child-like poetry committed to memory by means of the teacher's frequent repetition; light gymnastics, marching exercises, and easy ball plays; acting the doings of men and animals; all these accompanied from time to time with song, or turned into object lessons by frequent conversation on the things mentioned or represented; also amusing employment, with playthings, called *gifts*, of which there are several sets. (See GIFTS.) The guidance of these occupations requires a practical training, on the part of the teacher, and a theoretical study which never can be too thorough, if the pupil's mental and moral development is to become what Froebel intended it to be. Each of these exercises serves a threefold purpose, — to produce forms of beauty, forms of life (such as resemble things that occur within the child's experience), and forms of knowledge (such as may lead to a knowledge of the qualities, quantities and actions of objects). The child itself is to produce these forms; the teacher is not to teach them, but to lead his pupil by suggestions conveyed in questions or conversation, so that the child may become inventive. To do this properly, Froebel has advised a method based on the *law of contraries* and their *combination into a higher unit;* but the teacher is to abstain from all learned lore — from using abstract expressions. Abstract notions and works are severely banished from the kindergarten; it is merely concrete facts, which the child can learn through the senses, and can clothe in its own language, that can become familiar to it by its own mental assimilation. Neither is discipline to be maintained by authority or by any mechanical means; but *Discipline.* by the suggestions of the teacher, and by the pupils' own absorption in the interest of their occupations. Thus children are, at an early age, enabled to discipline themselves through pleasant employment, to submit to the will of the majority of their equals, on the one hand, or to assert, on the other, their own free volition, if they can induce others to agree with them. Thus, they are to take their first lessons in moral self-government.

An objection has been urged to the general introduction of the kindergarten as being too costly; but experience has established the indisputable *Costliness.* fact, that a good kindergarten need cost no more than the best primary school. The genuine *kindergartner* — and none but such ought to be employed — can superintend more than a hundred children at a time, provided she begin with no more than twenty, adding twenty more as soon as she has a good assistant able to replace her; and again twenty more, and so on, whenever one more assistant is prepared to take her place. Such assistants may be pupils of the training or normal school classes, who wish to acquire the art of infant education, and need not be paid for their assistance. These pupil-teachers will not, of course, by merely six months' help in this way, be fully able to conduct a kindergarten independently; but they will learn enough to be valuable assistants, and to become good educators as mothers. This is not merely an economical measure but is sustained by pedagogical principles. The little pupils of a kindergarten, from four to seven years old, will form several grades, that can simultaneously be engaged only in certain occupations; while, in all others, they must be separately employed. As, then, divisions into grades are indispensable, and the principal teacher must go from one to the other, she can leave all the grades under the guidance of proficient assistants, taking the pupil teachers along from division to division, thus affording them an opportunity to witness the greatest variety of exercises possible within a short space of time, and to practice every one under her direction. Besides, she can hardly fail to receive valuable support in the singing, articulation, and gymnastic exercises, from the talents of some of her assistants. But even more important is the following consideration. It is almost impossible to carry on a genuine kindergarten successfully without the exercise of a wide-spread and lively interest in it among the women, especially the mothers, of the community. So long as they do not frequently visit the institute, they will not fully appreciate its purposes and results; they will insist that their children should begin to learn the alphabet; and, if that is not done, they will perhaps take them away to some primary school. Many *kindergartners* of our country yield to the demand of the mothers, and make the alphabet and ciphering a part of the regular kindergarten exercises; but this is a positive loss to the children.

Owing to the necessity of special skill and training in order to conduct a kindergarten efficiently, many persons who undertake this work fail, through want of preparation, to produce the results designed. *Test of efficiency.* In this way spurious kindergartens have caused much complaint, and brought considerable discredit upon the system. The test of a good kindergarten is its obvious effect upon the pupils, in exciting cheerfulness, intelligence, activity, and a fondness for the school work. If, on the other hand, the children dislike the school, it is an evidence that there is a want of tact and skill in its management. There may, indeed, exist in such a school all the occupations recommended by Froebel, and each may be used according to the established formula; but if the spirit in which the exercises are to be conducted is missing, if the treatment is mechanical, all the moral influence which should spring from the cheerful self-activity of the child, is lost. If too, the teacher shows always the calm and dignified deportment of the ordinary class disciplinarian, instead of entering with all her heart into the harmless joy from which the child's self-government is to take a fruitful growth, and calming only the troublesome excess of this mirth by now and then a look, a word, a gesture, she is not well fitted for her calling. A genuine kindergarten teacher will, like the best of mothers, take a lively interest in remedying, as far as possible, the bodily, mental, and moral defects of every child under her care,—uncleanly and disorderly habits, want of attention, stammering, color-blindness, a bad gait or posture, imperfect articulation, etc. She will, in this way, earn the gratitude of the children and their parents, and exert a great moral influence. Her efforts in this respect are, in a great measure facilitated by the pliability of the child's powers, as well as by its desire to avoid ridicule, and to enjoy the society of its comrades. Abundant experience teaches, that there need be no incurable cases of the above kind among children who have the full use of their senses; that all children may learn drawing, singing, correct enunciation, geometry, and many other arts and accomplishments that are, by common prejudice, pronounced attainable by those only who are specially gifted. It is evident, therefore, that a kindergartner can hardly be too well educated; and, also, that no education repays so abundantly its cost.—For literature of this subject, see special list in the Appendix of this work.

LANGUAGE (Lat. *lingua*, the tongue, speech), according to the ordinary acceptation of the word, is the utterance of articulate sounds for the purpose of expressing thought. This mode of expression constitutes one of the characteristic faculties of man; since no community of human beings, in historic times, has been found entirely destitute of language; and a broad line of demarcation separates every kind of human speech of which we have any knowledge from all the modes of expression used by brutes.

The development of language in a child should not outrun his mental development; it should at first follow, and subsequently accompany it. *Development.* The child, from his first infancy, has a tendency to give some kind of expression to all the emotions of his mind. At first, various movements of the body, and inarticulate sounds serve for the purpose; when the perceptions become more distinct, the child looks around for more definite expressions, and finds them in the word-language of those who surround him. If the child has sound organs of speech, the task of the educator, at first, is comparatively easy. An artificial plan is neither necessary nor practical; an occasional influence is sufficient. By hearing the names of objects, actions, qualities, circumstances, and relations, which he perceives, correctly and distinctly pronounced, the child obtains his first knowledge of words, and learns to associate them with the designated objects. The memory, without difficulty, retains a large number of words, and frequent practice soon leads to readiness of speech. Occasional conversations with the child on the objects of his attention, with little descriptions and narratives, afford him the necessary material for expressing the combinations of his thoughts, and aid in the development of his mind. Where the cultivation of speech is neglected in the education of a child, the intellectual development is likewise retarded. On the other hand, any attempt to force unduly the rapid development of speech, may lead to vain and thoughtless garrulity, or to a production of erroneous representations in the mind, which will obstruct its harmonious development. During this first stage of education, the mother is the child's natural and best teacher of language, and the language which the child thus learns has justly been called the "mother-tongue". Home education may receive a useful, and in many cases a very desirable, aid in a good kindergarten.

The instruction provided for in the common schools of modern times aims chiefly at perfecting the pupil in his vernacular language. The course of instruction to this end embraces exercises in spelling, reading, writing, definitions, composition, English grammar, elocution, etc.

Vernacular.

There is still great diversity of opinion among educators as to the best methods of teaching each of these branches, and as to the relative position which each of them should occupy in the course of studies.

Methods.

This subject is fully discussed in the special articles devoted to the branches of instruction just enumerated. All educators, however, agree in regarding it as one of the chief aims of school education to give to the pupil a good knowledge of his vernacular language, and fluency in speaking and writing it correctly. Even in those branches of study which neither solely nor chiefly aim at improving the linguistic knowledge of the pupil, as arithmetic, geography, history, etc., every educator nowadays requires that pupils shall be trained in the correction of language, and taught to avoid common errors of speech. — See MARCEL, *Language as a Means of Mental Culture and International Communication* (London, 1853); and *The Study of Languages* (N. Y., 1869); WHITNEY, *The Life and Growth of Language* (N. Y., 1875).

LATIN LANGUAGE, one of the two classical languages, which as the language of one of the greatest empires of the world, and of one of the richest of literatures, and subsequently as the official language of the Catholic church, the literary language of western Europe, and the mother of the Romanic languages, has been among the foremost agents in developing modern civilization. For a full account of its development as a branch of modern education see *Cyclopædia of Education*. We give here only a few practical suggestions as to the methods of teaching it.

Methods. However much the methods of teaching Latin may differ in certain details, no one should dispense with a thorough drilling in the inflectional part of the language and in the principal rules of syntax. Exercises in translating from Latin into English, and from English into Latin, are now quite generally connected with the very first grammar lessons. In accordance with the principles of modern educational writers, the exercises in translation are now, from the beginning, very properly given in most of the text-books in the shape of complete sentences. In the system of T. K. Arnold the inflectional peculiarities are learned gradually, as in the *Ollendorff system*, and almost the first step taken by the pupil is an exercise in construction.

The very large extent to which words of Latin origin have been received into English can be turned to great advantage by the intelligent teacher.
Relation to English. But few words will be met with in the Latin exercises, which are not etymologically related to words in the English dictionary; and a constant reference to this kinship not only facilitates the acquisition by the student of a copious Latin vocabulary, but at the same time enlarges his knowledge of English. The introduction of young students who have sufficiently mastered the elements of the language, to the Latin classics is considerably obstructed by the want of good **Need of juvenile books.** juvenile works in the literature of Rome. If that literature ever had its Barbaulds and Edgeworths, their fame has perished with their works. The books which for centuries have been the first to be read in Latin schools,—Cornelius Nepos and Cæsar, were certainly not written for boys and girls. Even in Rome, they were as little read by children of ten, eleven, or twelve years, as our children of that age are expected to read Shakespeare, Gibbon, or Macaulay; and it is, therefore, undoubtedly a pertinent question, from an educational point of view, whether it is consistent with common sense to expect English boys and girls to read and appreciate writers whom the youth of the same age in their own country would have found too difficult to understand. Various attempts have been made, in modern times, to supply this want, and to provide young Latin students with suitable reading. Sometimes modern imitations of the ancient Latin have been selected for the purpose. Such, **Text-books.** for example, is Willymot's *Century of Maturinus Corderius Colloquies*, long familiarly known in Scotland under the name of *Cordery*. Certain portions of the dialogues of Erasmus have the same object in view. As the most successful attempt of the kind, many Latin scholars regard a little work entitled *De Viris Illustribus Urbis Romæ*, and commonly known in the United States as *Viri Romæ*, by L'Homond, a French professor of the eighteenth century. This work contains the most interesting stories related by Livy, Valerius Maximus, Florus, and other eminent writers, as much as possible in the very words of those writers, and is still extensively used in the United States, Great Britain, France, and, to a less extent, in Germany. Attempts have also been made to epitomize special Latin classics for the use of young students; thus, in recent times, an epitome of Cæsar, prepared by Dr. Woodford, classical master in Madras College, St. Andrews, has been in extensive use. Many of the Latin readers also contain attempts of this kind. The reading of Latin classics constitutes the principal part of the study of Latin wherever

it is pursued, except when only the elements of Latin etymology are taught for the purpose of elucidating the structure of English. — See *Cyclopædia of Education*.

LECTURES, or **Lecture System**, a method of giving instruction by formal expositions, generally written out and read to the learners. Hence the term *lecture* (from the Latin, meaning *reading* or *something read*). Lectures are, however, quite often extemporaneous, or delivered without previous preparation of the language. The lecture differs from the lesson chiefly in dispensing with the ordinary processes of the recitation room — question and answer, repetition, etc. The learners simply listen, or take notes, while the lecturer reads or speaks, with or without illustrations by means of the blackboard, maps, pictures, apparatus, etc. Lectures, as a system of instruction, are chiefly depended on in higher education — in colleges and universities, also in technical, scientific, and professional schools, because the students are supposed to have acquired a considerable maturity of intellect, enabling them not only to receive knowledge without exercises specially designed to awaken attention or stimulate the understanding, but to exercise their own faculties in arranging it in their minds for use, — in other words, co-ordinating it with their previously acquired knowledge. They are, besides, supposed to appreciate the importance of the information communicated, so as not to need any special stimulus to self-activity. In elementary instruction, all these conditions are reversed; and, therefore, the lecture system is inappropriate at that stage. In middle schools (secondary instruction), lectures may be used with good effect, in connection, or alternation, with the ordinary recitation processes. When the material has been methodically arranged, and when the statements are definite and precise, the language simple and forcible, and the style earnest, lectures may be made to subserve a very useful purpose.

LIBERAL EDUCATION, literally, that which is suited to the condition and wants of a freeman or a gentleman, that is, extending beyond the practical necessities of life; hence, contrasted with a *practical education*, or that which is designed to fit for mechanical or business pursuits. A liberal education embraces within its scope instruction in all those branches which collectively are called *the humanities* (q. v.).

LIBRARIES constitute one of the most important instrumentalities for stimulating the intellectual improvement of the people, as well as for the mental and moral training of pupils in schools. The value of a school library will depend upon the character of the books of which it is composed, and the uses to which it is applied. A large and expensive collection of books is not needed; but the books should be instructive and interesting to children, so that through their perusal they may not only obtain useful information, but imbibe a taste for reading. By this means, an antidote may, in part at least, be applied to the influence of the trashy, exciting, and sensational literature, which so greatly abounds at the present time, and which is so apt to corrupt both the minds and morals of the young. "A library is the indispensable supplement to the systematic mental instruction given in the class-room. If, for instance, care be taken and opportunities sought during the lessons in geography, history, or in any of the departments of science, to introduce some little book from the library, and to read a few interesting paragraphs illustrating the lesson, a brief notice and commendation of the book at the close of the exercise, with a few hints as to how best to read it, will utilize many a valuable work that might otherwise remain untouched upon the shelves...... A teacher has failed in one of the most important of all his functions, if, being in possession of a good school library, he has not fixed, in at least some of his pupils, the habit and love of self-culture, by leading them to become habitual readers".

LICENSE, Teacher's, a legal permission to give instruction, generally in a public school. This license is usually conferred after examination, and attested by a certificate, either temporary or permanent, which is evidence to employing school boards that the holder is a *qualified teacher*, sometimes called a *certificated teacher*. The object of such a license to teach is to protect the interests of the community against the evils arising from the employment of incompetent persons by those who might not be able to test the qualifications of applicants, or who might, from favoritism or corrupt motives, be willing to employ as teachers persons not possessing the requisite qualifications. In the United States, the requirement that all teachers should be duly examined and licensed previous to appointment is almost universal. The practice in regard to the mode of examination, and the forms and grades of the certificate, varies considerably in the different states, for information in regard to which, see the titles of the states, respectively. In all an unqualified attestation of moral character is required, in addition to literary and professional qualifications. (See WALSH, *The Lawyer in the School-Room*, N. Y., 1871, s. v. *The Law as to the Teacher's Morality*.)

LOVE, on the part of pupils for their teacher, is one of the most essential elements of his success, just as antipathy constitutes an unsurmountable obstacle to the exertion of any important educational *Importance.* influence. The first thing, therefore, which the educator should strive to do is to win the affection of his pupils; if that is accomplished, every thing else will be done without difficulty. It is of little use to address merely the intellect of children. Their curiosity, it is true, can be excited, their attention aroused, and the faculties of their minds, to a certain extent, be developed and sharpened; but the real elements of character are behind all this; and these cannot be affected in any important degree by mere intellectual training. The heart — the sensibilities and the will — must be reached; and the key to success in this, the greatest office of the educator, is love. When love for the teacher reigns in the bosom of his pupil, there is entire confidence in him, a desire to obey him, to please him, to listen to his precepts, to imitate his example, both in words and in acts; indeed, by an inexplicable psychologic law, the pupil seems to be bound to the teacher by a kind of magnetic chain, and is subject in every *Fear.* thing to his will. Fear, on the other hand, repels, and thus prevents the operation of that influence without which educational processes are, more or less, nugatory. The fear to do wrong, and of the punishment which is to follow it, is not, however, inconsistent with a love of the teacher. (See FEAR.) The latter must make himself, and the authority which he wields, respected; or he will incur the contempt of his pupils; and this is, of course, antagonistic to love. Children naturally recognize authority, however much they may strive to evade or defy it;

and its just and rightful exercise does not interfere with their warmest affections toward parents and teachers. Hence, love is not to be inspired by making improper concessions to children, for these they construe into weakness, which they despise. Minute directions may be given for the winning of the pupil's affections, but these would be either unnecessary or futile. Love on the part of the teacher can alone produce love in the hearts of the pupils. He cannot put on a semblance of affectionate regard for his pupils; he must feel it. Children have naturally deep intuitions into character, and detect hypocrisy almost instantly; hence they at once discern whether there is any real affection in the mind of the teacher toward themselves, or only a mere pretense. Love will show itself in his appearance, his words, his manners; every tone of his voice will indicate it, if it exist, and the pleasant smile beaming habitually from his countenance will, while making his own labors pleasant and easy, make light the hardest tasks of his pupils, by exciting their ambition and determination to accomplish it. The teacher should, however, never forget the relation existing between him and his pupils. "Some teachers", says Hart (*In the School-Room*, Phila., 1868), "in avoiding a hard, repulsive manner, run to the opposite extreme, and lose the respect of their scholars by undue familiarity. Children do not expect you to become their playmate and fellow, before giving you their love and confidence. Their native tendency is to look up. They yearn to repose upon one superior to themselves".

How to inspire love.

The ability to infuse a love of study into the minds of his pupils is the characteristic of a thoroughly successful teacher. This is the basis of diligence, which is but another name for love. "There is no higher hygienic law", says Baldwin (*School Management*). "than to love with our whole soul, and to work with all our might". (See DILIGENCE.)

LYCEUM (Gr. Λύκειον, named after the neighboring temple of Apollo, Λύκειος, a surname which is differently explained by Greek etymologists), a gymnasium or public palestra with covered walks, in the eastern suburb of Athens, where Aristotle and the philosophers of his school taught. In England and in the United States, the word is not applied to any class of schools, but is sometimes given to literary associations.

MANNERS, the genuine or simulated manifestations of disposition towards each other, which occur in the intercourse of human beings. The ordinary use of the word *manners* restricts it to those personal and visible peculiarities of deportment which characterize the intercourse mentioned. The agents commonly employed for this purpose are the eye, the voice, language, and gestures. When persons are brought together without previous knowledge of each other, or with no common ground of taste or experience between them, custom has prescribed a conventional code of formal manners, characterized as etiquette, which serves to relieve the awkwardness of the situation. That this, however, is temporary in character, and not intended to survive its original uses, is evident from the fact, that after it has, in great measure, been laid aside, any attempt to revive it, as the exclusive medium of kindly expression, is regarded as a just cause for resentment. The fugitive character of mere etiquette can never constitute it an equivalent for that abiding

Definition.

Etiquette.

kindliness of disposition which finds expression in genuine politeness. Manners, therefore, are more decidedly moral in their nature than a superficial observation would lead us to suspect; hence the usual association of "morals and manners". The basis of agreeable manners is that humanity, or feeling of brotherhood, which, in a greater or less degree, pervades the human race, and which every century, by its multiplied means of communication, is tending to extend and strengthen. It is, therefore, essentially Christian; and pleasant manners may be regarded, not as an accomplishment merely, but as one of the legitimate ends of a thorough education. In social intercourse, agreeable manners are far more powerful than intellectual accomplishments; while the displeasure produced by rude manners often neutralizes moral worth, and renders mental acquisitions, however great, comparatively useless. Momentous issues — even the destiny of a lifetime — may hang upon the apparently unimportant question of manners. To educate thoroughly, therefore, and neglect the means by which that education is to be made effective, is self-evident folly. Beyond the ordinary rules of etiquette, no set rules can be given for the production of good manners; since, in addition to the moral basis above referred to, they are largely dependent upon temperament; but, no precept is half so powerful in the furtherance of this end, as the daily example of the teacher, the parents, or other persons with whom the pupil is brought into daily contact. The indirect though constant insistence upon the claims of every individual to respect and kindly attention, which results in a practical recognition of this by the pupil, together with the daily example referred to, constitute, perhaps, the most effective method for the grafting of agreeable manners on the conduct of the pupil. (See MORAL EDUCATION.)

Basis.

Force of example.

MARKING, as a means of briefly and definitely stating or registering the character of the recitations or examinations of pupils, is one of the most important of the teacher's instrumentalities, if justly and judiciously employed. Although the pupil is not to receive the impression that he is to study merely to obtain good marks, but for the benefits to be derived from the study itself; yet, in the immature development of motives in the child's mind, secondary motives or special incentives are usually indispensable, in order to stimulate to exertion or arouse ambition. These secondary incentives are to be used by the teacher with great care, avoiding excess and watching their influence upon the pupil's mind, for different dispositions are affected by them in very different ways.

Object.

Marking, in the hands of a judicious teacher, is a great help, and when kept within due limits, is as salutary to the pupil as it is useful to the teacher. Still it should never be regarded as other than an expedient, and as subordinate to the creation of the true motives. Its special value is in the definiteness with which it records (1) the character and value of the pupil's work, (2) his standing as compared with other pupils, and (3) the approval or disapproval of the teacher. This very definiteness, however, may be the means of great injury, if it is not applied with strict justice. When its application is based on correct principles or *criteria* known to both teacher and pupils, and these principles are strictly adhered to,

Special value.

How to be applied.

without the least partiality, the marking system is divested of most of the objections which have been urged against it; because, while it presents a definite recognition and reward of merit and success, it does not absolutely discourage the less deserving and talented.

An absolute standard of excellence or proficiency is, on the whole, to be preferred to a varying one; since while the latter, recognizing the diversities of talent among the pupils, and being based on the *Standard.* moral consideration of diligence and effort, is more just in itself as a criterion of merit, it nevertheless can by no means give as good satisfaction to the pupils as the former, which recognizes only the actual achievement of the pupil, without regard to diversities in intellectual endowment. The latter cannot be considered by the pupils; nor is it safe to treat one class of pupils as if they were incapacitated to perform the same tasks as their school-mates of the same grade or class, since that, in itself, would be a degradation and a discouragement. It is better to let them learn this fact by experience in competing with the more talented for the attainment of a common standard.

The teacher is not to degenerate into a mere "marking machine" in the use of this system. While employing it for the purpose of justly recording the success or failure, merit or demerit, of his pupils, *Caution* he is to encourage, to aid by explanation, sometimes specially *to the* directed to the inferior minds, and thus strive to equalize the *teacher.* difficulties to be mastered. Before all things he must study his pupils, and be guided by their respective traits of character. To this the marking should be subsidiary.

The scale most frequently adopted for marking is that of percentage, 100 indicating the highest degree of merit or excellence; and perhaps this is the most convenient for the purpose.— See BALDWIN, *Art of School Management* (N. Y., 1881).

MATHEMATICS. — The term *mathematics* is the Latin word *mathematica*, or the Greek word μαθηματικά, anglicized. The Greek word *Definition.* was derived from μανθάνω, *to learn;* whence μάθησις, *learning.* Both the Greeks and the Romans used the word *mathematica* as we do the word *mathematics.* The use of the plural form indicates that this department of human knowledge was formerly considered not as a single branch, but as a group of several branches, much as we use the phrase *the mathematical sciences.* This group of sciences is subdivided *Classi-* into *pure mathematics* and *mixed,* or *applied, mathematics.* In *fication.* this article we are concerned mainly with the former. — The *branches of pure mathematics* are *arithmetic, algebra,* the *calculus,* and *geometry.* In this classification, the *calculus* is made to include the *infinitesimal calculus,* the *calculus of finite differences,* and the *calculus of variations;* while *geometry* includes the *common* or *special geometry, general (analytic) geometry, descriptive geometry, trigonometry, conic sections,* and the new science of *quaternions.*

No attempt to give a philosophical definition of the department of knowledge embraced under the term *mathematics,* has as yet been so success-*What the* ful as to be generally accepted. The statement that "mathe-*term* matics is the science of quantity" is often flippantly repeated as *embraces.* a definition, but it can scarcely serve for that purpose. Comte defines mathematical science, as the science which has for "its object the *indirect* measurement of magnitudes, and constantly proposes *to determine certain magnitudes from others, by means of the precise relations existing between them*". It is not a little singular that, while this great thinker rules geometry out of the realm of pure mathematics, he bases his definition of the science exclusively on the geometrical conception. That he does so is especially apparent in the discussion from which he deduces the definition. Moreover, it is not clear how the abstract principles of the science can be included in this definition. Such propositions as, "The product of the multiplicand and the multiplier is equal to the sum of the products of the parts of the multiplicand into the multiplier"; "The root of the product of several quantities equals the product of their like roots"; "The bisector of any angle of a triangle divides the opposite side into segments which are proportional to the adjacent sides"; etc., are scarcely embraced in Comte's definition without an unjustifiable extension of the signification of its terms. We propose the following definition: *Pure mathematics* is a general term applied to several branches of science which have for their object the investigation of the properties and relations of quantity — comprehending number, and magnitude as the result of extension — and of form. It will be observed that this definition embraces that of Comte, inasmuch as the measurement of quantities, or the determination of unknown from known quantities, is effected by an investigation of their relations; but, on the other hand, we can scarcely say that all investigations of the relations of quantities are for the purposes of measurement, or of determining unknown quantities from known.

But the chief purpose of this article is to inquire as to the place which mathematical studies should occupy in our courses of elementary instruction.

Place in education. In such an inquiry, the leading considerations are, (I) For what purpose should these studies be pursued in such courses? (II) To what extent should they be pursued? and (III) What general principles should govern our methods of teaching?

I. Mathematical studies should be pursued in elementary schools primarily as a means of mental discipline. Notwithstanding all that Sir William Hamilton has said, and the formidable array of names which *Mental discipline.* he adduces in support of his views, it may still be claimed that there is no single line of study pursued in schools, which develops the mind in so many ways, and is so well adapted to every stage of mental growth, as mathematical studies. It has been asserted, and quite generally *Observation.* conceded, that the power of observation is not developed by mathematical studies; while the truth is. that, from the most elementary mathematical notion which arises in the mind of a child to the farthest verge to which mathematical investigation has been pushed and applied, this power is in constant exercise. By observation, as here used, can only be meant the fixing of the attention upon objects (physical or mental) so as to note distinctive peculiarities — to recognize resemblances, differences, and other relations. Now, the first mental act of the child recognizing the distinction between *one* and more than one, between *one* and *two*, *two* and *three*, etc., is exactly this. So, again, the first geometrical notions are as pure an exercise of this power as can be given. To know a straight line, to distinguish it from a curve; to recognize a triangle and distinguish the several forms — what are these, and all perceptions of form, but a series of observations? Nor is it alone in securing these fundamental conceptions of number and form that observation plays so important a part. The very genius of the common geometry as a method of reasoning — a system of investigation — is, that it is but a series of observations. The figure being before the eye in actual representation, or before the mind in conception, is so closely scrutinized, that all its distinctive features are perceived; auxiliar lines are drawn (the imagination leading in this), and a new series of inspections is made; and thus, by means of direct, simple observations, the investigation proceeds. So characteristic of the common geometry is this method of investigation, that Comte, perhaps the ablest of all writers upon the philosophy of mathematics, is disposed to class geometry, as to its methods, with the natural sciences, as being based upon observation. Moreover, when we consider applied mathematics, we need only to notice that the exercise of this faculty is so essential, that the basis of all such reasoning, the very materials with which we build, have received the name *observations*. Thus we might proceed to consider the whole range of the human faculties, and find for most of them ample

Memory. scope for exercise in mathematical studies. Certainly, the *memory* will not be found to be neglected. The very first steps in number, — counting, the multiplication table, etc., make heavy demands on this power; while the higher branches require the memorizing of formulas

Imagination. which are simply appalling to the uninitiated. So the *imagination*, the creative faculty of the mind, has constant exercise in all original mathematical investigation, from the solution of the simplest problem to the discovery of the most recondite principle; for it is not by sure, consecutive steps, as many suppose, that we advance from the known to the unknown. The imagination, not the logical faculty, leads in this advance. In fact, practical observation is often in advance of logical exposition. Thus, in the discovery of truth, the imagination habitually presents hypotheses, and observation supplies facts, which it may require ages for the tardy reason to connect logically with the known. Of this truth, mathematics, as well as all other sciences, affords abundant illustrations. So remarkably true is this, that to-day it is seriously questioned by the majority of thinkers, whether the sublimest branch of mathematics — the *infinitesimal calculus* — has any thing more than an empirical foundation, mathematicians themselves not being agreed as to its logical basis. — That the imagination, and not the logical faculty, leads in all original investigation, no one who has ever succeeded in producing an original demonstration of one of the simpler propositions of geometry, can

Induction and analogy. have any doubt. Nor are *induction, analogy*, the *scrutinizing of premises* or the *search* for them, or the *balancing of probabilities*, spheres of mental operation foreign to mathematics. No one, indeed, can claim a pre-eminence for mathematical studies in all these departments of intellectual culture, but it may, perhaps, be claimed that scarcely any department of science affords discipline to so great a number of faculties, and that none presents so complete a gradation in its exercise of these faculties, from the first principles of the science to the farthest extent of its application, as mathematics. There are, however, two respects in which, probably, special pre-eminence may be claimed for mathematics as a disciplinary study; namely, training the mind to the habit of forming clear and definite conceptions, and, of clothing these conceptions in exact and perspicuous language. This pre-eminence *Conception.* arises, in part, from the fact that, in this branch of knowledge, the terms convey exactly the same meaning to all minds. Thus, there can be no difference between the conceptions which different persons have of *five, six,* a *straight line,* a *circle,* a *perpendicular,* a *product,* a *square root;* or of the statements, that 3 *and* 5 *make* 8, that *the sum of the angles of a plane triangle is two right angles,* etc. The conception in each case is definite, and the language may be perfectly clear. That this is not so in most other sciences, no one needs to be told. Can we be sure that all have the same conception of the metaphysical terms *idea, perception, reason?* Can any one discriminate infallibly between an *adjective* and an *adverb;* between *downy, hirsute,* and *pubescent?* Are the conceptions designed to be conveyed by the terms *schistose, fissile, slaty, laminar, foliated, squamose,* so distinct that no two mineralogists will ever interchange them? Is the meaning of a Greek text always unequivocal? Is it an easy matter for any two persons to get exactly the same conception of the causes which led to a certain political revolution; can either be absolutely certain, from any language which he can use, that no one will mistake his conception? — That the habit of mind which rests satisfied only with clear and definite conceptions, and the power of speech which is able to clothe such conceptions in language perfectly unmistakable, are most important attainments, need not be argued; and these are exactly the ends which mathematical studies, properly pursued, are adapted to secure. In this hasty review, *Reasoning.* nothing has been said directly of these studies as a means of developing the *reasoning faculties,* since it is generally conceded that pure mathematics is practical logic, and that pupils, who do not learn to reason by their study of mathematics, fail of the most important end of such study.

Doubtless, the common answer to the question, Why should mathematical studies be pursued in schools, would be, *for their practical value;* *Practical value.* by which is meant, their direct application to the affairs of life, as in reckoning bills, computing interest, measuring distances, volumes, areas, etc. It is, indeed, true, that in the every-day affairs of life, to the accountant, and to the man of business, a certain amount of arithmetical knowledge is essential — that surveying, civil engineering, mechanics, navigation, geography, and astronomy, are based on geometry. But, let it be observed, that only a special few practice the arts last named, and that for the masses embraced in the former specifications, a very limited amount of arithmetical knowledge is all that they are required to apply. And still further, while it is, indeed, necessary that the business man should be able to add, subtract, multiply, divide, and compute interest, skill in these operations can never form the basis of practical success in life, except in the case of mere clerks. Many of the most sagacious business men would make wretched work with their ledger columns, and they know too well their own deficiencies to risk themselves in any important numerical computations. Indeed, the elements of practical success in life are quite other than a specific knowledge of any branch of science whatever, however indispensable a certain amount of such knowledge may be in particular callings. The conclusion, therefore, is that the important point is not, how much mathematical knowledge can be crammed into the minds of pupils, but by what methods of teaching and study such habits of mind can be secured, as will make the pupils most efficient in performing the duties of life.

II. *What place should mathematical studies occupy in the course of study?* Were we to judge from the practice of most schools, we should conclude that mathematical studies ought to occupy from one-third to one-half of the pupil's time throughout his school life, unless, indeed, a slight exception is to be made in favor of other studies for the last two years of a college course; that is, that reading, spelling, writing, geography, grammar, history, literature, rhetoric, logic, the whole domain of natural science, including the physical constitution of the human system, chemistry, languages, metaphysics, political economy,—all these, and whatever else goes to make up the furniture, and secure the discipline, of a well-cultivated mind, are only to receive as great, or at most twice as great, a part of the pupil's time, as his mathematical studies. And this is no exaggeration, as will be obvious from an inspection of the curriculum of a graded school, or college. For the first six or seven years of the ordinary graded public school course, if we include the oral lessons, in *number* and *form*, of the lowest grade, arithmetic forms one of the three main studies for the entire course; and, in not a few cases, there are two arithmetical exercises, one in mental (oral), and one in written arithmetic, or one in arithmetic and another in algebra, each day, constituting, in such cases, fully one-half of the school work.

Public school course.

High school. During the entire course of the high or preparatory school, either algebra, higher arithmetic, or geometry constitutes one of the studies, except for a part of one year; but this exception is much more than made up by the large relative amount of time which the pupil's mathematical studies usually occupy, and by the fact that not unfrequently some two of these studies are pursued at the same time. In the college course, one of the three regular studies for the first two years is, almost invariably, mathematics. So far, reference has been had exclusively to *pure mathematics,* including only arithmetic, algebra, and perhaps a little of general (analytical) geometry and the calculus. Whatever of applied mathematics, including surveying, mechanics, astronomy, etc., is to be studied, must find additional time in the course. The question then arises, can the legitimate purposes for which mathematical studies should be pursued, be secured in any less time? In order to answer this, let us observe the exact proportion of time usually given to the pure mathematics in a course of training extending through the ordinary college course. Arithmetic has from one-half to one-third of the pupil's time in the elementary schools. In the high-school or academic course, to obtain any creditable knowledge of algebra, geometry, and plane trigonometry, and to review the arithmetic, at least one-third of the time is consumed. Passing into the college with this knowledge of mathematics, the student finds one-third of the time, for the first two years, scarcely adequate to secure a respectable knowledge of higher algebra, geometry, and trigonometry, the elements of the general geometry, and the infinitesimal calculus; and

College course.

Time given to mathematics.

whatever of applied mathematics is learned, as of surveying, mathematical drawing, mechanics, astronomy, etc., must find a place in the other two years of the college course. Now, all this is simply inevitable, unless relief can be found in the course prior to entrance upon college work. If, however, the inordinate demands of arithmetic can be so abridged (see ARITHMETIC), that the grammar school course shall include, at least, eighteen months' study introductory to algebra and geometry, the high school can save this time for other studies, and also secure such thoroughness in preparation, that the student's course in college will be far more rapid and satisfactory than at present. With the quality of preparation now secured, it should be borne in mind, that the student comes to college having, it is true, been over the requisite amount, but with so little of the real strength and knowledge which that course should impart, that, if he does justice to his mathematical studies for the first two years, nearer one-half than one-third of his time is consumed upon them. By rigidly confining the study of elementary arithmetic to its proper domain, giving a year in the grammar school to an introduction to algebra, and half a year to the definitions and facts of plane geometry, the pupil may come to the high school so thoroughly prepared in the elements of the three great mathematical studies, — arithmetic, algebra, and geometry, that between two and three years in the high school will be amply sufficient to secure such further proficiency in these branches as is consistent with the course here marked out. Moreover, if the pupil's school life closes with the grammar school, the course thus secured will be of far more value to him in after life, both for practical uses and as a discipline, than the ordinary one. (SEE ARITHMETIC, ALGEBRA, and GEOMETRY.)

In the above, it will be observed, that the general geometry and the infinitesimal calculus are included in the college course. The elements of the former are usually required, although it is quite common *The calculus.* (for no good reason) to make the latter elective. By omitting the calculus, the graduate leaves college without ever having looked into one of the sublimest departments of human knowledge, or having even the remotest idea of the language and methods of the mechanics and astronomy of the day, or being able to read an advanced treatise upon any scientific subject as treated by the modern mathematician. Nor can the beauty and power of the general geometry be appreciated without a knowledge of the calculus. Thus the pupil who is allowed, at his option, to leave this out of his course, leaves college a hundred years behind his time, in one of the leading departments of human knowledge.

III. *What general principles should govern our methods of teaching mathematics?* — This topic has been quite fully treated in the separate articles ARITHMETIC, ALGEBRA, and GEOMETRY, to which reference is made.

Methods. It is proper to add here, that, from first to last, the methods should be such as will give absolutely clear perceptions and conceptions, and secure facility, accuracy, and elegance in expression. These ends are of vastly more practical importance than the mere ability "to get the answer" of special problems. The notion which prevails among some teachers, that if the pupil learns the process, and becomes expert in it, he has obtained every thing that is essential, and that, whatever of the *rationale* may be desirable will be, in some way, induced by this mechanical process, is an exceedingly vicious one. In the first place, it is far more important that the pupil should be able to comprehend the logic, and to express his ideas in intelligible language than merely to solve any number of problems, since the former ability he will have occasion to use every day of his life, while he may never need the latter at all. But we are not driven to the alternative of securing culture at the expense of mechanical skill; the very best means to acquire expertness in mathematical manipulations is that which secures the best results in culture. No greater intellectual monstrosity probably ever presents itself than he who is usually known as a mathematical genius; that is, one who has a wonderful ability to do what nobody else can do, or cares to do — to solve knotty and often senseless mathematical problems. On the contrary, the object of mathematical study should be to develop men with cultured minds, not to make them mere computing machines.

Culture.

MATRICULATE (Lat. *matricula*, a public roll or register), to admit to membership in a college or university, by enrollment.

MEMORIZING, committing to memory, or, as it is sometimes called, *learning by heart*, generally implies repetition or *rote-learning;* though it need not be without an understanding of what is memorized. The law of repetition has an important application in many processes of instruction that are addressed, wholly or in part, to the memory. The mere memorizing of words and sentences, in order to produce a show of knowledge is a great abuse. Children may, however, be required to commit to memory some statements which they do not perfectly understand, such complete understanding requiring a more mature degree of intellectual development. "No doubt", says Calderwood (*On Teaching*, Edin., 1874), "all children must commit to memory a good many things they do not rightly understand. Such storing of the memory belongs less or more to all study". This is the view also of Thring (*Education and School*, London, 1864): "There should be a clear perception how far it is wise to explain, and to proceed on the principle of making a boy thoroughly understand his lessons, and how far they should be looked on as a mere collecting of material and a matter of memory. It must be borne in mind that, with the young, memory is strong, and logical perception weak. All teaching should start on this undoubted fact. It sounds very fascinating to talk about understanding every thing, learning every thing thoroughly, and all those broad phrases, which plump down on a difficulty, and hide it. Put in practice, they are about on a par with exhorting a boy to mind he does not go into the water until he can swim." The method referred to in this citation is the other extreme from mechanical word memorizing, and while not as injurious, or as likely to be adopted, is equally unphilosophical. The extent to which memorizing is to be carried, and the branches of instruction to which it is to be applied, constitute important subjects for the exercise of the teacher's judgment and intelligence. (See CONCERT TEACHING, MEMORY, and ROTE-TEACHING.)

MEMORY is often represented as a distinct faculty of the mind; but this may do harm in education. The mind is one, and has no separate faculties distinct from each other, the term *faculty* being used merely for the sake of convenience. It is important to turn away from this mode of conception, and to look at the phe-

How to be regarded.

nomena as they arise in the mind. An object and a mind come into connection. What is the result? An impression is produced on the mind, or more correctly the mind forms an impression of the object. What becomes of this impression? A new object presents itself, and then the impression disappears before the new impression which the mind forms of the new object. Has the former impression disappeared altogether? No. We believe that, in some way or other, it still remains in the mind. If a similar object were to come before the mind, it would be conscious that it had formed an impression of it before, and the two impressions would blend into one. We have here, then, a peculiar power of *Power of the mind to retain* the mind to retain what it has once had; and this power does not apply merely to perceptions or other intellectual acts, but to feelings and desires. A longing for an object has been aroused within us. The longing is displaced for a time by some other pressing passion. But the longing is still in the mind; and when the appropriate causes of excitation occur, the longing will come back, and, it may be, blend with the new longing which helps to awaken it, or repel the new longing which has aroused it by contrast. This then is the first feature of memory. The soul has the power of retaining feelings, volitions, perceptions, and thoughts. The question has been raised, can these feelings, volitions, and thoughts entirely and absolutely vanish from the mind? A categorical answer cannot, from the nature of the case, be given to this question; but, certain facts render it likely that the mind retains every thing, and that it is merely the power of resuscitation which is defective. Many circumstances which seem to have been entirely forgotten, are, under peculiar conditions, recalled to the memory. It is said that often, when persons have been drowning, they have seen, as in a rapid vision, their past life in multitudinous details which they had entirely forgotten. People, in diseases of the brain, have remembered languages, which they had learned in early days, but which they seemed to have lost completely. Facts like these point to the indestructibility of that which has once had a place in the soul.

But, besides the power of retention, there is the other power of reproduction; and it is to this power that the educator has to direct his attention. What are the means of strengthening the reproductive *Power of reproduction.* power of the minds of children? We have to look at the conditions of its exercise; and, in this connection, we must consider the four following principles: (I) It is plain that the impression will be reproducible in proportion to the strength and vivacity with which it is first made. This strength depends partly on the natural capacity of the child, partly on whether the stimulus in the object is such as to produce a strong impression. The educational inferences from this statement are numerous. Thus it follows that wherever a real object can be presented to a child, it should be used in preference to any picture of it, and that a picture of it is better than a mere verbal description. Moreover, if more than one sense can be employed, so much the better. If any object is to be remembered, the child will remember more easily, if he can touch, smell, or taste it, as well as see it. This arises partly from the fact that these direct sensations produce strong impressions, but partly also from what we call our second principle of memory. (II)

Every means should be used to concentrate the attention on the object. If we wish to make a child remember an object, the object must be allowed to lie before the child's eye or mind for some time. In the perception of every object the process is somewhat as follows: the perception or sensation has first to displace the preceding perception or sensation. It then gathers strength and occupies for a time the whole mind. But, soon after, another object of perception or of thought presents itself; and the mind will occupy itself with this. This new perception will weaken, and finally expel, the other. Each perception is connected with two other perceptions or mental acts — with the one which it expels and the one by which it is expelled. Now, the power of reproducing the mental act depends not merely on the strength with which the act is executed at its central moment, but also on the strength of the connections which it may form with the antecedent and subsequent acts; and this strength depends partly on the time and attention with which they can be kept together in the mind; for, in every mental act, there are subsidiary simultaneous acts which scarcely reach the point of consciousness. For instance, when I examine a house, there is some slight perception of the intermediate space between me and the house, of the objects, such as trees, which may be in that space, and of the sky which is overhead. These pass from the one definite perception to the other, and in a latent state help to recall the one, when we get the other. The strength of the connection is increased, if there be a natural connection between the two mental acts, such as that of cause and effect, means and end, or if there be some points of resemblance between them, or some points of contrast. But, in all cases, time must be given to let these points of resemblance or contrast flow over, as it were, from the one to the other. The danger to which the educator is here exposed, is that of attempting to do too much and, therefore, doing what he does too hurriedly. He must be patient. He must try to intensify the impression by allowing the various senses to deal with it, and he can thus concentrate attention longer on it than he could otherwise do. And he must, as far as possible, bring only two objects or two ideas at a time before the pupil's mind. These should be held together for some time; and they should, if it is possible, be naturally connected. Of course, there are occasions in which this is neither possible nor advantageous. There are some occasions in which the teacher must pass over a good deal of matter in a short time. He does not wish his pupil to remember the whole, nor would it be good for the pupil to do so; but these cases should be limited to those of necessity. And a warning should be given against the danger of indulging too much in reading books which, awakening the interest strongly and thus disturbing the nervous system, do not demand of the reader an accurate recollection. This is specially true of novels. The frequent and rapid reading of these works, in which the reader has no stimulus and no occasion to remember the incidents accurately, fills the mind with a great number of vague memories. These memories render indistinct what ought to be distinct, for they abstract so much of the valuable power that the mind possesses for reproduction; and the habit of reading without caring to remember, is apt to transfer itself to the books and acts which ought to have the closest attention. (III) There must be frequent repetition. An object or thought is reproducible easily, when it has been made to occupy a large space in the mind. The power of reproduction is limited by time, and the mind can only reproduce within certain limits in this respect. If, therefore, an object is to be reproduced, the faded impression must be renewed; and the renewal of the impression strengthens its hold. It is thus that a fact may become indelibly imprinted on the memory. The value of the repetition cannot be overestimated, but great care must be taken not to make it wearisome. (IV) The power of reproduction greatly depends on the state of the health. That there is a very close connection between this power and the body, is proved most conclusively by the numerous instances collected by Dr. Abercrombie, in which abnormal states of the brain were accompanied by abnormal developments of memory. When, therefore, a child forgets, it must not be always attributed to carelessness. A child learns a word on Monday, and knows it with perfect accuracy; but when he comes, on Tuesday morning, to repeat it, he finds he cannot. In all probability, the impression was too weak to last a whole day, and to resist the many and more interesting ideas which have intervened; but the lesson is not lost. The original impression is there; the teacher patiently and pleasantly renews the impression; and the old blends with the new, and strengthens, until repetition fixes it in the mind forever. But it may be merely a temporary suspension of the child's power of reproduction, in consequence of illness; and there is no surer sign of latent disease than when a child, generally ready and quick, stumbles and forgets. Some physiologists go the length of affirming that, owing to the freshness of the nervous system, the exercise of the memory should be assigned to the morning; while other mental efforts, such as those of imagination, should be reserved for the evening. These four principles lead not only to the power of reproduction, but to the power of ready and accurate reproduction. In order that the memory may embrace a wide range of subjects, it is essential that the mind should devote itself to such a range of subjects. The power of reproducing a subject depends upon the frequency and strength with which it has come before the mind. It is, therefore, not quite correct to say, that a person has a good or a bad memory. Every one has many kinds of memory. If he has exercised his mind in words, he will remember words; if he has given much attention to numbers, he will remember numbers; if to any other class of ideas, he will remember such ideas. But, however great his practice in numbers may be, that practice will not enable him to remember words; and the converse is also true. The teacher must carefully exercise the pupil in each group of notions, if he expects him to remember them readily and accurately. Perhaps, one of the questions which deserve careful consideration in education is what ought to be forgotten. The human mind is limited in its range, and cannot reproduce every thing. Ought it to put into its store-house any thing that it cannot hope to reproduce? We think that it ought. Where the aim is to produce in the pupil a clear idea or notion, many particulars must be adduced which, studied attentively for a short time, will render the notion clear and distinct; but it is not necessary that the mind should retain all these particulars. This is the case, for instance, in geography. In order to form a correct notion of a country, many particulars must be carefully

Specific Memory.

What ought to be forgotten.

weighed; but, after the notion has been attained, the pupil will wisely drop a great deal of the knowledge which he has temporarily mastered, deeming it enough to know where he can get the knowledge when he wants it. Again, when the object is to inculcate a great principle of action, the same course may be pursued. If, for example, a teacher wishes to impress upon his pupils the true idea of toleration, he may choose many incidents in history to bring it home to their minds, and may go into the minutest details of these incidents in order to awaken interest; but he succeeds in his purpose, if he leaves a strong and accurate general impression, even though the pupil forgets most of the details which have been given him. The power of forgetfulness is one that can also be directed, as well as the power of reproduction. It is, indeed, true that the greater the effort to forget any thing, the more surely is it impressed on the memory; but this holds true mainly in those matters in which there is a strong personal element; and just as a man who sleeps in a room where a clock strikes can make up his mind not to take any notice of the striking of the clock in his sleep, so, in the impersonal matters of the intellect, we can make up our minds to let such and such facts fall into oblivion. Kant distinguished memory as the mechanical, the ingenious, and the judicious.

Committing to memory. The mechanical is employed when the only bond of connection is, that the two things are in the mind at the same time, the one immediately succeeding the other. This is what is called committing to memory, or learning by heart. Such kind of memory must be frequently used in early education. It is important for the teacher to note its character. It depends on simultaneity and succession, and any disturbance of these circumstances disturbs the memory.

METHODICS. See DIDACTICS.

MINERALOGY. Under the head of *mineral substances*, or those which constitute the mineral kingdom, are included all inorganic bodies; that is to say, by strict definition, all substances that are not the products of life. While in its severely scientific aspects this subject properly belongs to advanced education, as a sequel to other departments of science, yet as embracing the study of natural objects, it may, like botany, be pursued as a branch of elementary object instruction. When taught in this way, and primarily as a means of cultivating the observing faculties, the same principles should guide it as one applicable to that kind of teaching; and especially should the teacher endeavor to lead the pupil to discover for himself the qualities of every specimen examined, and impart nothing that can be thus discovered. The pupil will then search for similar specimens, and be able to write out their characteristics.

Place in education.

Schedule system. The schedule system is applicable to this subject as well as to botany. (See BOTANY.) Thus a regular formula should be adopted, noting *form, structure, cleavage, hardness, weight, color, luster,* etc.; and every term should be carefully explained as an addendum to the pupil's observation. A small cabinet of mineralogical specimens is an almost indispensable requisite for carrying on this instruction. Minerals, regarded merely as the materials of which the earth's crust is composed, offer examples of so many physical properties that come under the cognizance of the senses, either unaided or aided by the simplest experiments, that they afford excellent material for this kind of teaching.

They present these properties in the simplest conditions, uncomplicated, as in vegetable or animal materials, by the effects of vitality; and they are superior to artificial objects for objective teaching, because, if rightly used, they may be made to elucidate all that can be elucidated by the former, whilst they become, in addition, foundation stones upon which a more advanced and scientific study may be satisfactorily based. In this manner, they may be used to inculcate, in its most elementary form, a scientific method of research. Thus, by means of the physical characters of minerals, observation, accurate as far as our unaided senses can make it, and exactness of thought, and consequently of speech, may be cultivated in regard to *external form, internal structure, color, diaphaneity, luster, hardness, tenacity, fracture,* etc. Observations, elementary it is true, but still of a fundamental character, regarding *specific gravity, solubility,* and *fusibility,* may be induced by simple experiments with the balance, the test-tube, and the blowpipe. Such knowledge, acquired from the common minerals around us, will undoubtedly be a valuable stepping-stone to further acquisitions. At a later stage, if practicable, instruction in the use of the blowpipe might be made to yield a further insight into simple chemical phenomena, and, if carried far enough, might be made an excellent starting-point for systematic scientific investigation by analysis.

Objective teaching.

In connection with mineralogy, attention should be given to *lithology,* or the science of mineral aggregates, or *rocks.* This subject presents many points of interest both from a scientific and an educational point of view; and in its connections, on the one hand, with geology, and, on the other, with mineralogy, affords the materials for practical study as well as useful mental culture, thus constituting an element of both technical and liberal education. The works necessary to the general reader for reference on topics of mineralogy and lithology are few; and those only are here named that are perfectly accessible. See *Cyclopædia of Education.*

Lithology.

MISCHIEVOUSNESS, as applied to the disposition of a child, or school pupil, is the occasional transgression of an established rule in a playful spirit, but without a malicious intention. This disposition is usually the result of the union of humor, or love of fun, with sound bodily health. The exuberance of spirits thus produced generally finds vent in actions which are denominated mischievous. This spirit is so widely different from the willful breaking of rules with an evil intent, that the easy suppression of a continued exhibition of it rests entirely with the teacher; the good nature with which the mischievous act is accompanied generally causing the perpetrator to desist on a slight warning. To bring the mischievous spirit under speedy control, two qualities only are necessary in the teacher: — quick discernment of its real nature, and tact in correcting it. The want of these sometimes leads to needless irritation on both sides, and may end disastrously to the teacher's influence, and, through that, to the discipline of the school. If, on the other hand, the good humor of the transgressor is met by a similar feeling on the part of the teacher, the task of correction is usually easy, and causes no offense; while, in the end, it secures a respectful obedience on the part of the pupil. If, however, the mischievous disposition is not corrected in this way, it may lead to vicious habits, which will tend to undermine, or permanently deprave the moral character.

MODEL SCHOOLS, a term usually applied to schools of practice annexed to normal schools, or teachers' seminaries.

MODERN LANGUAGES, in the literal and widest sense of the term, are the languages now in use, in contradistinction to those which were formerly spoken, but are now extinct. Taken in this sense, the term embraces the mother-tongue, in which the home education of the child is conducted, the national or ruling language of the country, which is the medium of instruction in the schools, and the living languages of foreign nations. It is the general tendency of the age, to make a thorough knowledge of the national language the center and the chief aim of all school instruction; though it has been demanded, from an educational point of view, that wherever the mother-tongue of a large portion of the inhabitants of a country is different from that of the national language, its claims should not be ignored. The admission of modern foreign languages into a regular course of instruction is of comparatively recent date, and the credit of having first obtained this recognition belongs to the French language. Until very recently, French has enjoyed, in this respect, an acknowledged superiority over any other language of the globe; and it is but recently that English and German have to any considerable extent begun to compete with it. At present, French, English, and German are studied all over the world, as the chief representatives of modern culture. The Italian language is learned by many of the students of fine arts and of music in preference to any of the three principal modern languages; but more in courses of private instruction than in schools.

The mother tongue.

Foreign languages.

Since modern languages have come to be studied on a much more extended scale than the classical, a great variety of methods have been proposed. The authors of some of these methods are by no means distinguished for modesty, and do not hesitate to declare all former modes of instruction absolutely useless, as having been wholly superseded by their own. In most cases, they have wholly forgotten that the method of teaching and learning a modern language must, to a very great extent, be dependent upon the purpose for which it is learned. If the student chiefly aims to acquire the ability to express his thoughts in the language of another person belonging to a foreign nation, the methods which make conversation the basis of instruction will justly commend themselves to the attention of the instructor. When a foreign language is learned as a means of understanding the literature of a particular nation, an early knowledge of the inflectional part of the language, of all its peculiarities in etymology and syntax, and of its vocabulary, will be felt as an urgent want; and grammar lessons connected with translating exercises, will form the chief means of instruction. In the combination of grammar and translation, every possible method has been tried: the strictly synthetical, which starts from the parts of speech, and teaches them singly, before proceeding to a regular system of translations; the strictly analytical, which begins with the analysis of foreign sentences, and from them, by degrees, derives the knowledge of grammatical forms; and the synthetico-analytical, or analytico-synthetical, which, from the first, endeavors to combine instruction in the grammatical structure with practice in using the foreign language. Of these, the former may be said to have been

Methods.

almost entirely abandoned, the latter being the one generally preferred in schools. In regard to the arrangement of the grammatical rules, an infinite variety may be observed in the numerous grammars of modern languages. See the article on MODERN LANGUAGES in the *Cyclopædia of Education*.

MONITORIAL SYSTEM, sometimes called the *Madras system*, because it was introduced into England from Madras, by Andrew Bell; also the *Lancasterian system*, after one of its most enthusiastic advocates, Joseph Lancaster. It is, moreover, often designated the *system of mutual instruction*, because conducted on the principle of requiring the pupils of a school to teach each other. The name *monitorial instruction* is derived from the circumstance that the pupil teachers employed to carry on the system were called *monitors*. — For a full account of this system see *Cyclopædia of Education*.

MORAL EDUCATION has for its sphere of operation the culture of those principles which influence or control the voluntary action of human beings. The elements of self-control exist, in a greater
Sphere. or less degree, in every mind, as a part of its original constitution. They are distinct from its intellectual faculties, and need a special education, which is far more important than intellectual education, because it contributes in a much higher degree to the good both
Duty. of the individual and of society. The subject of moral education is *duty*, and its office is both speculative and active; that is (1) to implant correct principles of rectitude in the pupil's mind — to teach what duty is, and (2) to cultivate a desire to do what is right for its own sake — to respect duty, or moral obligation; in other words, to feel a sense of right — to listen to the voice of conscience (q. v.); to which may be added, as an important additional object, to implant in the youthful mind such *motives* as will aid the moral sense, and enable it to triumph over the natural propensities and desires, when the latter are in conflict
Means employed. with it. The means employed in moral education are the following: (1) *precepts*, addressed both to the understanding and to the conscience, the object being to enlighten the latter, which of itself does not recognize specific right and wrong; (2) *example*, appealing to imitation as well as to conscience, and enforced by the love and respect felt by the child toward its educator, leading the former to feel that whatever is done by the latter is right, and hence should be imitated (see EXAMPLE); (3) *habit*, inducing, by means of repetition, an inclination to act in the same way under the same circumstances (see HABIT); (4) *exercise*, for the purpose both of strengthening the moral feelings brought into
Exercise. play, and of forming habits. Exercise, in moral education, is just as important as in physical or intellectual education; indeed, there can be no training or culture without it; and, in carrying this on, the teacher must avail himself of every possible circumstance that arises in connection with his intercourse with the pupils, or their intercourse with each other, to give occasion for this exercise, and thus form a basis for the desired culture of the moral faculties. This culture or training must have a twofold object: (1) to cultivate virtues, and
Twofold object. (2) to correct vices. Among the former, as especially necessary, may be enumerated truthfulness, honesty, justice, candor and

modesty, kindness or benevolence, diligence, obedience to proper authority, gratitude, fidelity to every promise or trust, and patriotism; and among the latter, the opposites of these, as lying and deceit, a disposition to steal, cruelty to animals, unkindness and injustice to playmates, violence and combativeness, ill temper, anger and irritability, obstinacy, laziness, irresolution, leading to procrastination, excessive self-esteem, leading to arrogance and self-conceit, etc. These are specific qualities of character which need a particular recognition and treatment on the part of the educator; but when the moral sense has been thoroughly developed, the Christian moral principle, to do unto others as we would that they should do unto us, will comprehend, in approbation or condemnation, every class of actions, and *Moral discipline.* give the means of a just discrimination as to what is virtuous and what is vicious. But the conscience is not developed in children; and very often, not even in adults. Hence, the need of moral discipline, in order to afford to the educator the means of bringing to bear upon his pupils external restraint, as preliminary to self-restraint; for it must be borne in mind that any government that does not contemplate the cultivation of the elements of self-control can scarcely be considered as forming a part of moral education. The three elements of sensibility usually appealed to in connection with moral discipline or restraint, are fear (q. v.), hope (q. v.), and love (q. v.). (See also AUTHORITY.) The conscience being very imperfectly developed in childhood, secondary motives, such as the love of approbation, the *Secondary motives.* hope of reward, the desire to excel, may properly be appealed to, in order to promote well-doing on the part of the pupil, and thus lead to the formation of good habits. Caution should be exercised, however, in employing such incentives; and the educator should always keep in view the just limits of their use, the injurious consequences of depending too exclusively upon them, and the importance of so employing them that they may lead on to the primary motive — the desire to do right for its own sake. (See EMULATION.) The practical application of the system here briefly outlined, is attended with very great difficulty, and requires peculiar intelligence and skill on the part of the educator; and not alone this, but moral culture, involving self-control, patience, and a delicate appreciation of moral distinctions, as well as a full sympathy with the general peculiarities and wants of childhood. To this may be added, with emphasis, the ability to discern the peculiarities of individual character, as dependent on both mental and physical constitution; for the processes of moral education cannot, like many of those employed in intellectual training, be applied to children in large masses. Suitable modifications must be made in the application of general principles and rules, or much injury may be done. (See DISCERNMENT OF CHARACTER, and MORALIZING.)

MORALIZING, the formal inculcation of moral truth by means of precept, or of stories related for the sake of the moral, with the view of *Its use.* influencing conduct. This practice, common in the home circle and in the school, is the result of a consciousness on the part of the parent or teacher of a duty unperformed, the discharge of which is attempted in this perfunctory way. It is hardly necessary to say that it almost always fails; since it is either an attempt to reason with the young — a process for which their minds are not yet sufficiently mature — or an effort to impose mechanically on their minds generalizations which can only be reached naturally after the observation of many individual instances. In either case, the abstract nature of the appeal is so far beyond their powers, that the attention which is given, if indeed it is given, is only the amiable toleration of a discourse which arouses no interest. Of course, moral lessons received in such a spirit accomplish no useful purpose, if indeed they are not positively hurtful; since they tend to produce disgust for an important branch of education, which in maturer years, would be interesting. The conceptions existing in the minds of children and youth being in large measure concrete, the true method of approaching their intelligence is through concrete images. In intellectual training, this is usually done, and is always the most successful method. In one of the methods of moral training above referred to — that of moral *Moral stories* — this is attempted, and doubtless, it is supposed, with success; but it is safe to say that the interest aroused is not extended to the moral deductions drawn from the acts of the persons introduced, but ends with the acts or actors themselves. Thus the fables of Æsop are interesting to the young only as long as the men and animals are, so to speak, in motion. When the moral is reached — which is not till after the narrative has been brought to a climax, and the actors have been dismissed — their interest is at an ebb; and not till many years later is that moral brought home to them by the manifold experiences of life. This, therefore, is the peculiar value, and the only proper use, of the fables of Æsop, namely, that they present in a striking way the truth desired to be impressed on the mind, not with the design of making it immediately influential, but with an effort which, for the moment, is apparently without result — the feeling which attends the planting of a seed, *i. e.*, the certainty of future development. The mind of youth, in fact, is not given to that sober, contemplative process which we call moralizing. *Proper method.* Its natural disposition is one of gaiety, ceaseless activity, and even boisterousness. The exuberance of spirits natural to this period of life, therefore, makes the child indisposed to give patient attention to any purely speculative process of thought. That this is a wise provision of nature for the development of the physical powers, has long been recognized by observant educators; and any attempt to curb this spirit, with the view of inculcating moral truth, only inverts the natural order of development, and, in healthy children is apt to result disastrously. The only method of moral training effective with youth is that which discards formal precepts, and by restraint of actual vice, or practice of the desired virtue, engrafts it insensibly on the daily conduct. The habit of right acting is thus unconsciously acquired, but not till a much later period is the mind disposed to survey critically this action, and pass judgment upon its propriety. The maturity of the mind is an indication of the proper season for moralizing.

MUSIC. See SINGING.
MUTUAL SYSTEM. See MONITORIAL SYSTEM.

NEW EDUCATION. See EDUCATION.
NEWSPAPERS. The objection is frequently made to the character of the instruction ordinarily imparted at school, that it has little relation

to the concerns of daily life. This want of relation sprung originally from the fact that the literary class, in earlier times, was a class apart, having only slight connection with the masses who, possessing few political rights, were unworthy of consideration. The instruction given, therefore, was purposely of a kind to emphasize the exclusiveness of the educated class. Under the changed political conditions of our day, however, the tendency has steadily been to equalize the two classes in intelligence — to lift up the masses to the level of the educated, on the one hand, and, on the other, to bring the studies of the school and college more into accordance with the daily life of the majority. Traces of the original exclusiveness still remain, however, in the unpractical character of much of the instruction, imparted in school. Almost every youth, on entering upon the business of life, becomes conscious of this with chagrin. The arithmetic that he studied, for instance, seems to have little application to the concerns of daily life; the book-keeping which he mastered with so much difficulty, seems now, at this later date, to have been filled with theoretical cases which have no parallels in actual experience; even the geography, in which he attained such proficiency, has little place in his daily routine, while algebra, geometry, and many other studies, have none at all. The result is a feeling of inferiority when he is brought into contact with others of his age whose training has been entirely that of practical life, which leads him to suspect that his time has been wasted. Not till long afterwards, perhaps, does he recognize the fact that the principles on which both theoretical and practical knowledge are based, are the same, and that the ability to apply these principles was his chief want. The feeling of disappointment referred to might have been entirely removed, if, in his instruction, the teacher had kept constantly in mind, not the mental discipline alone, but the mental discipline and the adaptability to the affairs of life of the knowledge used in acquiring that discipline. One of the most useful instruments for accomplishing this double purpose is the newspaper. The arithmetic which is now taught by the use of unusual and improbable examples, could be made a living and interesting thing, by the use of problems to be found in its pages, which introduce the actual prices of articles in daily use. Interest, discount, exchange, the price of bonds and stocks, could be made so familiar to the pupil in this way, that the change from school to counting-house, which is now attended with such a want of ease and so much disappointment, would seem but the continuation of study in another class. Reading, also, if taught from the newspaper, would familiarize the pupil with the terms used in the daily conversation of professional and business men; and, through the reports of proceedings in every field of human activity, fresh interest could be aroused in studies already taken up, while attention could profitably be called to those which are ordinarily pursued in more advanced courses; and a partial preparation for them could thus unconsciously be made. Thus the study of geography would receive increased attention, if it could be connected with the reports of the interesting events from all parts of the world which are daily chronicled, by inquiring into the position on the map, population, form of government, etc., of the different countries referred to. By following, in this way, the records of campaigns and battles, a knowledge of the topography of the country could be obtained almost without effort, which would be easily retained in the memory of the most apathetic scholar; while opportunity could, at the same time, be taken for digressions into its history. Any means within the teacher's reach of divesting the studies pursued of their dry, text-book character should be taken advantage of; and this cannot be done in any way so easily as by investing them with a human interest, by showing that men and women similar to those with whom he daily associates are the actors in all these stirring events. For this purpose, hardly any medium is superior to that of the daily paper.

NORMAL SCHOOL, the name given, in the United States and in some other countries, to a school for the instruction and training of teachers, being a translation of the French term *école normale* (from the Latin *norma*, a rule or model), applied to such schools on their establishment in France. "The term *normal school*", says Hart *(In the School-Room,* Phil., 1868), "is an unfortunate misnomer, and its general adoption has led to much confusion of ideas". In England, these institutions are styled *training colleges*, and in Germany *seminaries*. Connected with these schools there are usually *model schools*, or schools of practice, in which the theoretical principles and methods taught are applied to the actual work of instruction and discipline.

The normal school is properly a professional school for teachers, and its curriculum should have strict reference to the special object of such an institution. Without this, normal schools are only such in *Special* name, as all are who permit the professional element to be *aim of* merged in those that pertain to general culture. Such culture *normal* is, of course, needed by the teacher, as it is by the lawyer, the *schools.* physician, or the clergyman, who acquires it in an academic institution — college or university; but this by no means supersedes the law school, the medical school, or the theological seminary. In like manner the normal school proper presupposes academic training, and builds upon it the special accomplishments needed for educational work. Normal instruction would be rendered more effective were this fully recognized, and a proper separation made between the academic department of such an institution and the professional department. When this distinction is not made, the latter is very apt to be overlooked; and the antiquated notion followed that all that is needed by the teacher is to know what he or she has to teach. This is overlooking entirely the science of education, now embodied in so many excellent works on the theory and practice of teaching, and on school management.

The course of instruction for normal schools should embrace (1) the history of education, including the systems or methods of distinguished educators; (2) the principles of education and instruction, de-
Course of duced from intellectual, psychological, and ethical science, (see
instruction. EDUCATION, and INSTRUCTION); (3) the art of teaching (didactics); and (4) the methods and rules of school management and discipline (school economy); besides (5) the application of these principles and methods to specific branches of knowledge, since every subject has, to a certain extent, its own system of methodics. — See BAIN, *Education as a Science* (N. Y., 1881); BALDWIN, *The Art of School Management* (N. Y., 1881); JOHONNOT,

Principles and Practice of Teaching (N. Y., 1881); KELLOGG, *School Management* (N. Y., 1880); SWETT, *Methods of Teaching* (N. Y., 1881). See references to educational authorities in the *Cyclopædia of Education, passim;* and special list of books for teachers' study, in the Appendix of this work. (See also TEACHERS' SEMINARIES.)

NUMBER is here considered as a branch of elementary or object instruction. Great importance should be placed on the means by which children acquire their first ideas of number. Since a child's knowledge of this subject begins with counting, the first exercises for teaching it should be the counting of objects. The child may first be taught to count as far as *ten* by using the numeral frame (q. v.), or buttons, pencils, the fingers, sticks, marks, or other objects. Next he should be taught to count groups of balls, buttons, sticks, or other objects, used to represent the several numbers, *one, two, three, four, five*, etc. By using the groups of objects thus counted as illustrations of the several numbers, figures may readily be taught. Let the pupil count *one* ball on the numeral frame, *one* pencil, *one* finger, *one* mark, and then show him the figure 1 to represent the number of each object. Next let him count, in groups, *two* balls on the numeral frame, *two* pencils, *two* fingers, *two* marks, etc.; then show the figure 2 as a symbol of the number of objects in each group. Afterward, require the pupil to count balls, pencils, and other objects in groups of *three*, and then show the figure 3 as the representative of the number counted in each group. In a similar manner, the several figures from 2 to 9 may be associated, and their value learned by means of counting. In order to teach children the value of the several figures by personal experience, let them count in groups *two* balls, or buttons, etc., and observe that each group contains two *ones*, — that *two* is equal to *one* and *one* more, or two *ones*. After the pupils have counted several kinds of objects in groups of *three*, lead them to notice that *one* and *one* and *one*, or three *ones*, make *three*, also that *two* and *one* make *three*. Proceeding in the same manner to count in groups *four* objects, let the pupils observe that four *ones*, or *two* and *one* and *one*, or *three* and *one*, or *two* and *two*, or two times *two*, make *four*. By means of similar exercises, the value of each number from *two* to *nine* may be thoroughly learned by children. As additional exercises, or a review of previous lessons, let the pupils count as many balls on the numeral frame, or hold up as many fingers, as the given figure represents. By this means, all the figures from 1 to 9 may be learned as symbols of numbers. In subsequent lessons, for teaching figures as representatives of numbers greater than nine, let the figures be arranged in groups as follows:

First group,   0, 1, 2, 3, 4, 5, 6, 7, 8, 9
Second group, 10, 11, 12, 13, 14, 15, 16, 17, 18, 19
Third group, 20, 21, 22, 23, 24, 25, 26, 27, 28, 29

and so on to 99. Requiring the pupils to count as many balls, or other objects, to represent in order the numbers symbolized by each of these groups, will lead them to understand the value of the numbers that are expressed with two figures. This part of the instruction may be greatly facilitated by giving the pupil several small sticks, like matches, and requiring him to count and tie in bundles as many sticks as each of the figures from 1 to 9 represents. Then to furnish the pupil with favorable opportunities of learning, by personal observation and experience, that each number represented by two figures in the second group is composed of one bundle of ten *ones*, and one or more single ones added, let him count and tie in a bundle ten sticks to represent the number 10; and then tie ten sticks in a bundle and add to it one single stick to represent the number 11, and so on to 19. Two bundles of ten sticks each may be made for the number 20, and two similar bundles and a single stick for 21; and so on to 29. In this manner, children may be taught to comprehend the value of all the simple numbers to 100. The knowledge obtained by means of the exercises described above will prepare the pupils to learn readily and intelligently both the value and the form of writing numbers through hundreds, and thereby to understand the principles of *numeration* and *notation*. See CURRIE, *Early and Infant School Education* (London); CALKINS, *New Primary Object Lessons* (N. Y., 1871).

NUMERAL FRAME. This simple apparatus has been in use for many centuries. In some form or other, it is now used for teaching number, in all parts of the world. It is sometimes employed to represent units, tens, hundreds, thousands, etc., in numeration. This use of the numeral frame renders it necessary to give artificial values to the balls on different wires; and notwithstanding that this is analogous, in order, to the arrangement of the numerical system of figures, there is danger that young children, by the use of it for this purpose, may become confused between the actual numerical value of a ball and its several artificial values. Inasmuch as numeration can be illustrated much more intelligently by the method described under *Number* (q. v.), if aided by the use of the blackboard, it is not advisable to attempt an explanation of it by the numeral frame; not, at least, until the pupils have acquired a definite understanding of the relation between the value of single figures, and their values as dependent upon their relative positions in regard to other figures. The most important uses of the numeral frame are, to teach a class of pupils to count, and to illustrate the value of numbers and figures; also to teach the first steps in adding, subtracting, multiplying, and dividing. For the first steps in adding, let the pupils add balls on the numeral frame, by *ones* as far as *ten*. When they can do this readily, let them add on the blackboard a column composed of 1s; then let them add a like column of figures on their slates. Subsequently, teach them to add balls on the numeral frame by *twos*; then to add a column of figure 2s on the blackboard; and then on their slates. When the adding of 1s and 2s has thus been learned, proceed in the same manner with *threes*, *fours*, etc. After the pupils have learned to add *threes* as above, they may be taught by these three steps to add 1s and 2s in the same column; then to add 1s, 2s, and 3s in the same column. In this manner the pupils may be taught to add readily and rapidly single columns composed of such figures as 6, 7, 8, 9. To give children an idea of subtraction, teach them to count backward on the numeral frame from ten; thus, 10, 9, 8, 7, 6, 5, 4, 3, 2, 1, 0. Subsequently, call on a pupil to hold the numeral frame, to take one ball from two balls, and tell how many remain; then one ball from three balls, etc. Proceed in a similar manner with other numbers, taking care to arrange the exercises so as to give the pupil as much actual practice as possible in taking balls or other objects from a larger number of objects. To illustrate the first ideas of multiplication to a class of young pupils, arrange the balls on the numeral frames in groups of *twos*, *threes*, etc. Place on one wire two groups of two each, and lead the pupils to perceive that they may say that, "two and two make four"; or that "two twos make four"; also that "two times two make four". Place on another wire three groups of two each, and let the pupils observe that "two and two and two make six"; or that "three twos make six"; also that "three times two are six". Proceed in a similar manner with numbers, and so arrange the exercises as to furnish the pupils as much individual practice as possible. After each step has been illustrated by the numeral frame, place figures on the blackboard to represent what has been thus taught. To illustrate the first ideas of division, arrange balls in groups of *four*, *six*, *eight*, *ten*, etc., on the different wires. Lead the pupils to see that each of these groups can be divided into groups of twos. Then require them to divide the groups thus and tell how many groups of *twos* can be made from four balls, six balls, eight balls, etc. Let the pupils also find how many *threes* there are in six, nine, twelve; and how many *fours* in eight, twelve, etc. That which is learned in each step may be represented by figures on the blackboard.— (See NUMBER.)

OBJECT TEACHING, a method of instruction in which objects are employed by means of which to call into systematic exercise the observing faculties of young pupils, with the threefold design, *Design.* (1) to cultivate the senses, (2) to train the perceptive faculty, so that the mind may be stored with clear and vivid ideas, and (3), simultaneously with these, to cultivate the power of expression by associating with the ideas thus formed appropriate language. The merit of introducing object teaching as a special method of elementary instruction, is *By whom introduced.* usually attributed to Pestalozzi; but Comenius, Locke, Rousseau, Basedow, Rochow, and others based their systems of education, more or less, upon the same principle; that is, they recognized the necessity of communicating ideas, or of affording to the mind the means to grasp ideas from objects, by actual perception, before attempting to teach the verbal expression of those ideas, and that, without such ideas, mere "book-learning" is useless. Pestalozzi appears, however, to have had only a slight knowledge of the works of those educationists. Inspired by the reading of Rousseau's *Émile* to study the phases of mental *Pestalozzi.* growth, he arrived at the conclusion that the teaching of his day was fundamentally wrong, from its violation of, or inattention to, the laws of mental development. These laws he believed to be, (1) that the knowledge of things should precede that of words, (2) that, for the acquisition of this knowledge, the only effective agents, in the first stages of mental growth, are the senses, chief of which is the eye; (3) that the first objects to be studied by the child are those immediately surrounding it, and these, only in their simplest forms and relations; and (4) that from these objects as a center, the sphere of knowledge should be widened by a gradual extension of the powers of observation to more distant objects. The first instruction, therefore, according to this plan, should consist in concentrating the attention upon concrete things, in such a way as to result in a thorough training of the observing faculties, so that the conceptions with which the mind is stored may be as well defined, and as true to nature, as possible. So impressed was Pestalozzi with the correctness, and the supreme importance, of this method, that he declared that the sum of his achievements in education was the establishment of the truth that "the culture of the outer and inner senses is the absolute foundation of all knowledge — the first and highest principle of instruction".

The failure of the first attempts of Pestalozzi and his followers, however, in the practical application of his theories, was discouraging; and the faith of the progressive educators who had accepted them as a new gospel, was seriously shaken. The reason of their failure, however, was that their practice was in conflict with the very principles which Pestalozzi had enunciated as fundamental. The human body, with which they began their instructions, is not only highly composite in its structure, and difficult of description in the language of the child, but, by its very nearness, is rendered unfit for an object of study by children, their senses being most powerfully, and, indeed, almost exclusively, turned to the observation of objects external to themselves. By attempting, therefore, to name in detail and to describe the limbs, their form, color, size, actions, and uses, the new theory was exposed to the ridicule of its enemies, and placed in serious peril. In all the Protestant countries of Europe, however, and especially in Germany, the leaven of truth contained in the principles of Pestalozzi, wrought a gradual but sure reform in the old method of instruction. — Object teaching became universal in the primary schools; and the dignity and usefulness of the teacher were increased by the very impossibility of prescribing any one method in which the principles should be applied, thus giving special prominence to the fact that the determining cause in favor of one method over another was the individual ability of the teacher. Instead of one invariable method, which might be unintelligently acquired and mechanically applied, a variety of methods now presented themselves, each dependent for its success upon circumstances. The individuality of the pupil suddenly acquired a new importance; and the teacher's individuality, also, became more than ever before an essential factor in the successful conduct of the school. For the difficult work thus foreshadowed, a long and careful preparation was necessary on the part of the student.

Why not successful.

Effect of its introduction.

The first step in this preparation was the observation of the educational work of some good teacher; then a thorough study, in the normal school, of the subjects of pedagogy, psychology, the history of education, the natural sciences, universal history, mathematics, and arts; and, finally, a course of practical teaching in trial lessons, under the supervision of model teachers and the student's own associates. Among the writers above mentioned, one of the principal points of controversy was in regard to the necessity of educating the senses. Many denied altogether this necessity, and insisted that object teaching should be reserved exclusively for exercises in using and understanding language. The senses, so they argued, take care of themselves, whenever an interest in surrounding objects is awakened by the necessities of daily life; and the common school, they said, can present but few objects of interest on which the senses can be profitably exercised. If, for instance, pictures of objects are presented — as is most frequently

Preparation required.

Points of controversy.

the case, and if these pictures are large and faithful copies of the originals — which is rarely the case — the exercise is still confined to only one sense; and experience proves that this is insufficient to awaken a lively interest. The impression made on the sight, therefore, is short-lived and feeble. If, on the other hand, the objects themselves are produced, as these are generally house utensils, or articles of school furniture, only a languid interest is aroused in the pupils' minds, because there is rarely any new feature to be observed in objects so familiar. The incentive to any observation or comparison of qualities, therefore, is utterly wanting; and any sharpening of the senses is improbable. If, on the contrary, the exercises upon objects be carried on for the purpose of enriching the child's vocabulary, and of storing his mind with just and accurate conceptions, by causing him to connect with every word its proper idea, all will have been done to benefit the pupil that can reasonably be expected. The opponents of this view, however, insisted that the use of object teaching for the exclusive purpose of the acquisition of language, would overthrow that fundamental principle of the system which discountenances mere word learning. The correct understanding and use of language, also, they thought, could be learned as well from books and conversation; while, if the child is made to understand, that to talk fluently and correctly of objects is all that is required, and that a real knowledge of those objects is of no consequence, clever talk will always be more highly valued by him than exact knowledge. According to their view, the pupil brings with him to the primary school only the raw material out of which objective knowledge and the proper use of the senses may be developed: his mental pictures are wanting in definiteness and in order. These must be taken to pieces, *i. e.*, analyzed, and recomposed, *i. e.*, synthetized, at the sight, hearing, or touch, of real objects. If the interest of the children in the exercise of the senses is lacking, it is the teacher's duty to excite it; and this should be easy with young children, if the teacher's interest in the subject is lively enough to communicate itself to them.

While the rapid progress of science and art in our day infinitely augments the mass of knowledge which it is desirable and important for every body to learn, the increasing artificiality of our daily life tends to alienate us from a spontaneous exercise of our senses; and this deficiency must be supplied by education, to enable us to compass the amount of knowledge which it is desirable to acquire. The exercise of the senses is *Education of the senses.* not only practically useful, but it is, in most cases, full of interest. To illustrate this, let pupils be asked to estimate by sight the length of a pen-holder, the dimensions of a window-pane, distances on the floor or on the ground, the weight of objects that can be held in the hand, or to distinguish shades of color, and the differences in pitch or quality of musical sounds. Such exercises are not only amusing, but useful; while, on the other hand, there is abundant evidence that the circumstances of daily life do not, of themselves, educate the senses. Thus, let a dozen countrymen be asked the length of a certain way over which they often travel, and the probability is that a dozen different answers will be given, many of them wide of the mark. Instances might be multiplied indefinitely to show that the senses are not self-educative. Some educators, while not objecting to any of the five purposes to which object lessons may be applied; namely, (1) the preparation of the pupil for serious learning; (2) the sharpening of the senses, and the exercise of all mental functions; (3) exercise in language; (4) the acquisition of knowledge; and (5) moral training; still have insisted that a distinction should be made between *object teaching* and *objective teaching*; the former comprising exercises in which the objects are taught for themselves, *i. e.*, for instruction in all the properties which are peculiar to them; the latter, for the acquisition of that generalized or fundamental knowledge which is common to many widely different objects. The former, they contended, should occupy only a part of the time during the first year or two, after which it should cease; but every branch of learning should, in turn, be treated objectively. The method of procedure should be, first, the presentation of the object. This should be analyzed by the pupils, and immediately reconstructed, the teacher supplying nothing but technical terms which are supposed to be unknown to the pupils, but guiding them by conversation to observe, compare, and reason correctly and in proper language, to rise from the single features of the object to its entirety, from similar features to generalizations, from the concrete to the abstract, from facts to laws. The opponents of this view said that the principle was good, but did not go far enough. In the first place, there is a vast body of knowledge that cannot be treated objectively. All facts, for instance, in regard to the days of the week, and the months, their names, number, etc.; many facts in regard to time, such as the number of seconds in a minute, the number of minutes in an hour, etc., the names of the seasons, the method of telling time by the clock, — these and many other necessary facts cannot be objectively presented, but must be learned arbitrarily; while, at a later period in education, there appear astronomical, geographical, and historical facts, which must simply be taken on trust, and committed to memory. In view of these things, text-books are indispensable; and all attempts to teach without them are useless, and result in a waste of precious time. While recognizing, therefore, the value of object teaching in many branches, and its pre-eminent value in a few, they assert that it has its natural limitations beyond which memorizing and an adherence to the text-book are the only proper means to be relied upon by the teacher. At the present time, this latter view — that a combination of the two methods should be employed, is in the ascendant. In Europe, especially in Germany, this reactionary movement is thought to be fostered from political and religious motives. In the United States, the demand for teachers has so far exceeded the supply from the normal schools, without a corresponding rise in salaries, that the standard of qualifications for teachers has not been maintained at the height which many educational reformers had hoped it would be. In short, the principles and system of Pestalozzi cannot be said, at the present time, to be fully carried out. Object teaching should be begun as early as possible, and in the manner of the kindergarten, and should be followed by objective and conceptive teaching, which should be carried through every branch of learning. The mental growth of pupils, however, should not be retarded by a superfluous use of this method. A safe criterion, by which the teacher may know, at any moment, whether he has made a proper use of the object method, may be found in the self-activity of his pupils, their ability to grasp, in their answers to his questions, the general fact, proposition, or law. The new method is justly called the *developing method* (q. v.), the pupils' minds being made to develop themselves, the teacher only suggesting what they are to discover. Every pupil is, as it were, to rediscover every science in the genetic method (q. v.), a difficult task for the teacher, and apparently a circuitous way for the pupil. But because of its thoroughness, it is the most rapid way of learning; and its results are indelibly fixed in the mind. This method, also, if early begun, and consistently carried out, is successful with every child, and saves precious time, which, later in life, may be devoted to those higher branches, that lie beyond the common-school course, but which are every year becoming, in many cases, highly desirable, and, in some, indispensable. The literature of object teaching is very extensive; for an enumeration of the principal works, see special list in the Appendix of this work. (See also COLOR, FORM, and NUMBER.)

ORAL INSTRUCTION is a technical term in use in the common schools of the United States to denote instruction, without text-books, in the nature and uses of common objects, and also in the elements of natural science. In a certain sense, all instruction given by the teacher *Defined.* in the class room, either to supplement the text-book, or by way of general explanation, may be said to be oral; and, considered in this sense, it belongs to every subject taught. But oral instruction, as it appears in courses of study, is limited to a distinct channel of teaching, and, therefore, is not to be confounded with general class instruction in the entire range of subjects. It is distinct from object teaching, because it is not confined to teaching through sensible objects. It deals also with more advanced pupils — those, for example, who have passed through the lowest, or primary grades, and who may be supposed to have benefited by what is known as object teaching. It has to do moreover, with elementary knowledge, and has been gradually narrowed to instruction in natural science. As might be gathered from the word *oral* its leading or cardinal idea is instruction without a text-book. The teacher is in the place of the book. The information given flows entirely from him; and the skill with which he imparts this, is the measure of his success. Closely allied in importance to the foregoing, is the principle that the instruction shall be familiar. In its methods, it must approach closely those that are adopted in *Methods.* an intelligent family circle; it must emulate the kindliness, patience, and watchfulness of a parent, or of a deeply interested friend. With a clear idea as to the kind and amount of instruction to be given at each lesson, it must avoid mere amusement and puerilities, on the one hand, and the danger of a mechanical and hard method, on the other. The test of such familiar instruction is the interest which the teacher creates and maintains; the want of life and animation on the part of the pupils is an unfailing measure of the teacher's short-coming. But instruction to be familiar must be fertile in illustration. In no part of the teacher's work is there greater need of versatility. It is in this that the vast advantage of oral teaching over that which depends on the text-book is apparent. Pliancy, variety, suitableness to the particular wants of certain pupils, or of the class as a whole, simple familiar allusions and illustrations, all come into play. If experiments are necessary, they should be always of the simplest kind, and with the commonest materials, such as nearly every child can obtain, if he can be induced to imitate the experiments. So far as objects are needed, those that are easily obtainable are to be preferred. The approach to the pupil's mind through his senses is carefully to be kept open; most constantly of all, the avenue of sight, although, of course, the other senses are not to be neglected. As a natural result of this familiar instruction, the interest of the pupils will manifest itself in inquiries, and especially in a desire to communicate the glimmerings of their own knowledge. This will render the exercise still more familiar, break down the barrier of reserve on the part of the pupils, stimulate observation and thought throughout the class, and react on the mind of the teacher, compelling perhaps new illustrations, a more carefully considered statement, or fresh investigation outside of school. From what has been stated, it will be seen that oral instruction is widely separated from lecturing. The children are brought immediately in contact with the mind of the teacher, by means of skillful questioning on his part, by requiring from them connected statements, and by stimulating them with his approval when a happy answer or statement has been made. This method never loses sight of class instruction, and, therefore, cannot be carried on without the assistance of the class. Nor is it a recitation in the generally received acceptation of the word. There is no lesson to be learned in the sense implied by a recitation, nor any to be recited. The memory is of course taxed, but it is not taxed by any lesson to be committed as a task. The measure of the pupil's interest is the measure of his acquisition. Whatever he learns is in no sense compulsory. Skillful reviewing is, indeed, used to test the hold that the oral instruction has kept on the pupil, and to supplement what has been imparted, by new or more lively illustration. But repetition, in a mechanical or rote sense, as understood to be an underlying principle in text-book instruction, is not used in oral instruction. The subjects to which oral instruction, as a special method, is usually confined, are embraced, under the head of *natural science*. While it

Natural science. does not aim to make the instruction in these subjects scientific, it does aim to impart such instruction in a methodical way, and with the most careful accuracy. Wherever classification is necessary, such classification naturally becomes more or less scientific. Whenever definitions are necessary, they must approach scientific accuracy. But the scientific nomenclature, except in those cases in which it has passed into common use, is carefully avoided. Latin or Greek terms, therefore, being burdensome to the young, however instructive to the adult, are generally to be discarded, and familiar or common names to be used. As a thorough scientific classification is not the object of oral instruction, neither does it endeavor to make the treatment of the various subjects exhaustive. It has done much of its true work when it has awakened attention, strengthened observation, led the pupils to collect illustrative objects, taught them to group and arrange what they have observed, and implanted in them a tolerably clear idea of the simpler elements of the science, to which the instruction has been confined. It has done its full work when, in addition to this, it has accustomed the pupil to express, in his own language, what he has learned and retained, without the painful halting and poverty of language so often manifest in the class room. With some approach to scientific accuracy, oral instruction may be defined as the union of conceptive and objective training. It does not *Objective* discard objective illustration, nor does it depend entirely on the *and con-* development of perception to furnish new ideas. It proceeds on *ceptice.* the principle, that, in the mind of every healthy child of eight years of age, there is a vast number of tolerably distinct conceptions, obtained through the senses, as well as from conversation, from reading, from home instruction, and from play: that these conceptions are particularly abundant in relation to natural objects; and that it is the office of the oral instructor to recognize their existence by using them to form more complex ideas, or as the nucleuses around which to arrange the new ideas imparted during instruction. As to the age when this instruction should *Age and* be given, as well as its importance, the following words of Pres-*importance.* ident Porter, in *The Human Intellect*, may be cited. "The studies which should be first pursued are those which require and discipline the powers of observation and acquisition, and which involve imagination and memory, in contrast with those which demand severe efforts and trained habits of thought. Inasmuch also as material objects are apprehended and mastered in early life with far greater ease and success than the acts and states of the spirit, objective and material studies should have almost the exclusive precedence. The capacity of exact and discriminating perception, and of clear and retentive memory, should be developed as largely as possible. The imagination in all its forms should be directed and elevated — we do not say stimulated, because in the case of most children, its activity is never-tiring, whether they be at study, work, or play. We do not say, cultivate perception, memory and fancy, to the exclusion or repression of thought, for this is impossible. These powers, if exercised by human beings, must be interpenetrated by thought. If wisely cultivated by studies properly arranged, they will necessarily involve discrimination, comparison, and explanation. To teach pure observation, or the mastery of objects or words, without classification and interpretation, is to be ignorant even to simple stupidity". Further on, the same author, in speaking of the various studies to be prosecuted in childhood says, "Natural history in all its branches, as contrasted with the science of nature, or scientific physics, should be mastered with the objects before the eye — flowers, minerals, shells, birds, and beasts. These studies should all be mastered in the spring-time of life, when the tastes are simple, the heart is fresh, and the eye is sharp and clear. But science of every kind, whether of language, of nature, of the soul, or of God, *as science* should not be prematurely taught".

ORDER, in school management, implies (1) the existence of a judicious system of regulations, and (2) a uniform and habitual observance of them by the pupils. It is one of the most important elements of a good school, since it enables the teacher to concentrate all its educative agencies without embarrassment or interruption. The characteristics of good order are (1) attention on the part of the pupils to the legitimate work of the school, (2) obedience and respect to teachers, (3) decorous deportment — the absence of tumult, rudeness, frivolity, and frolicsome actions, calculated to disturb the school, and (4) propriety and exactness in the school evolutions and drill. Order is the result of skill and tact on the part of the teacher; it cannot be fully maintained unless he is vested with suitable authority, so as to be able to correct disorder, as soon as it manifests itself. General disorder in a school can result only from bad management, indicating incompetency on the part of the teacher. "If a school be well organized", says Wickersham, "its classes well arranged, its work well systematized; if pupils be properly employed in study, in recitation, in exercise; if school-government be well understood and wisely administered, a large proportion of the offenses which now occur in school will disappear." — (See DISCIPLINE, and GOVERNMENT.)

ORDER OF STUDIES. See COURSE OF INSTRUCTION.

ORTHOGRAPHY, as a science, treats of the representation of spoken language by visible signs; it includes a systematic history of such *Of what it treats.* signs, and a discussion of the principles according to which they should be made and used. Picture writing is first used; pictures of objects are used as signs of the names of the objects, then of initial syllables in such names, and finally of elementary sounds. The pictures, meantime, are abbreviated and modified to what we call letters. The essential principle of alphabetic writing is that a perfect alphabet must have one character for each elementary sound in the language, and *Perfect alphabet.* only one. Subordinate rules are, that the characters should be easy to write and to distinguish, and shapely; like sounds should have like signs, and similar series of sounds should have analogous sets of signs; each character should be so shaped as to suggest, to some extent, the position of the organs of speech in forming the sound; derived alphabets are esteemed the better for embodying important history; all nations should use the same signs with similar values. No nation has ever made any near approach to a perfect alphabet. The growth from picture writing goes on without much guidance from ideas, and all the qualities which are merely matters of history and symmetry, are of little consequence in comparison with the essential principle of phonetic convenience. The Anglo-Saxon language was reduced to writing in Roman letters by the missionaries, who converted the people to Christianity, and *Anglo-Saxon spelling.* gave them a pretty good alphabet. The letters were used in their Roman values, or nearly so, and new characters were added for the sounds of *a* in *fat*, *th* in *their (dh)*, *th* in *thin*, and *w*. After the Norman conquest, chaos came again with Anglo-Saxon, or rather English, spelling. A large part of the words of each race of the new people were difficult for the other to pronounce. The scholars inclined to spell in the old book fashion; but the Normans dropped the special Anglo-Saxon discriminations, and left many of their own letters *Norman spelling.* standing which were not pronounced by the people; and many letters were inserted to no purpose in ill-directed attempts to represent the strange combinations. Then followed a change in the whole gamut, so to speak, of the vowel sounds. The close vowels were changed under the accent into diphthongs by taking an *a* sound before them. The old *i*, pronounced as in *machine* has thus changed to *Other changes.* *ai*, pronounced as *i* in *mine*; *u* as in *rule* has given rise to *au*, pronounced as *ou* in *house*. The open and mixed vowels have become closer: *a*, as in *far*, changing to *a* (that is, *e*) as in *fate* or *wall*, or to *o* as in *home* (A.-S. *hám*); *e* as in *they*, changing to *e* (that is, *i*) in *me;* *o* as in *foe*, changing to *oo* (that is, *u*) as in *moon* (A.-S. *móna*). Single characters have thus come to stand for diphthongs, and the long and short sounds, which go in pairs in other languages, are denoted in ours by different characters, and come from different sources. Intermediate between the old *a (far)* and *e (met)* has become established *a* in *fat, fare*; between *a (far)* and *o (note)*, *o* in *not* and *nor*, and the sounds of *u* in *but, burn*, have also arisen. All these have no special signs. Four consonants *sh, zh, th, dh* are in the same condition. The people have long since ceased to feel any necessity for keeping sounds and signs together. Changes go on without any record in the writing; etymologists slip in new silent letters, on the ground of imaginary derivations; old monsters, fertile in the popular fancy, propagate themselves in the congenial environment; and, altogether, we have attained the worst alphabetical spelling in the world. For the history of all these changes, see ELLIS's *History of English Pronunciation* (London, 1867); SWEET's *History of English Sounds* (London, 1874); HALDEMAN's *Analytic Orthography* (Phila., 1858); MARCH's *Anglo-Saxon Grammar* (N. Y., 1870); and the articles ANGLO-SAXON, and ENGLISH, THE STUDY OF, with the authorities there referred to.

Orthography, in a narrower sense, is the art of spelling correctly, according to the standard of a language. It first demands the attention of teachers as the art of inculcating the spelling of English according to the dictionaries of our language. In early times, there was no standard English spelling. The printers added or subtracted letters for convenience of spacing; the same word will be found spelt several different ways on the same page. Dr. Johnson's Dictionary (1755) was the first recognized standard. The common way of teaching spelling, is to teach from a spelling book the form and name of each of the letters of the alphabet; then to practice on combinations of the letters in pairs, naming each letter and then uttering the sound of the combination; then to practice in the same way on combinations of three letters; then on words of two syllables, and so on. These syllables and words are selected with care; similar sounds are grouped together, and the groups arranged in a progressive order of difficulty in spelling-books. The first steps of this process may be made easier by using blocks with the letters on them for the learner to name and arrange into syllables; by setting him to write the letters on the slate, on paper, or on the blackboard; by adding pictures of the objects the names of which are spelt; or by the use of rhymes, and other contrivances of artificial memory. Another method is to begin with words as wholes, and, after some progress has been made in reading in that way, to direct attention to the separate letters, their names, and sounds *(word method)*. Teachers proceeding in this way often name the letters by the sounds which they have in the word to be spelt, and not by their proper names. This is sometimes called the *phonic method*. Scholars are led on to more difficult words. Text-books of hard words, more or less classified, with rules for the most puzzling groups, are prepared, and blanks for written exercises in spelling. Some little help may be gained by rules, and mnemonic contrivances; but the standard spelling of our language is so ir-

Correct spelling.

Methods of teaching spelling.

regular, that continual practice for many years is necessary to make any approach to the mastery of it. Among the most efficient helps to the teacher is the *spelling match*, for which sides are chosen which contend for the victory. It should be noted that continual practice in reading and writing is needed, or training to spell aloud in class will not save from mistakes in writing. Further, the most important words for each person are his own vocabulary, the words which he uses in his own writing. Perfect accuracy in these is the end most to be desired in teaching. If this habit is once established, unusual words will be looked up, when the writer has occasion to use them. With all aids and arts, good spelling is one of the most rare and costly accomplishments; and, naturally, stress is laid on it as the sign of a thoroughly educated person out of all proportion to its real value. The best teachers in other respects often fail in spelling. English orthography is the opprobrium of English scholarship, and the greatest hindrance to education and to the spread of our language. Our children spend three years in learning to spell a little; while German children get further in a single year. Millions of dollars are spent every year in printing silent letters. Earnest efforts are now making for reform. The philological associations of England and America, teachers' associations, state and national, in England and America, and some state legislatures, have committees appointed on the subject. Several schemes of reform have been presented, the most important of which are those of A. J. Ellis and I. Pitman, E. Jones, A. M. Bell, and E. Leigh. Mr. Bell has invented a set of characters wholly unlike our present letters, which indicate by their form the position of the organs of speech. It can hardly come into speedy use in common books. Scholars have begun to use it somewhat in scientific treatises. (See BELL, *Visible Speech*, London, 1867.) Mr. Pitman has proposed an alphabet containing 16 new letters; and there is already quite a body of literature in that alphabet. Dr. E. Leigh has combined a phonetic print, like Pitman's, with the standard spelling. (See LEIGH, *Pronouncing Orthography*, St. Louis, 1864, and his later publications in New York.) Elementary books for schools, printed according to his system, have been used for several years in St. Louis, Washington, New York, Boston, and other cities, and are said to save much of the time usually spent in learning to read. Editions of most of the elementary books (primers, etc.) published in the United States are issued in Leigh's print. (See PHONETICS.) Mr. Ellis and Mr. Jones propose systems based on the present spelling, using always the same letters for each sound that are now oftenest used to denote it, as follows: (Mr. Jones's scheme) *a* as in *at*, *aa (father)*, *ai (aid)*, *au (taught)*, *b*, *c (cat)*, *ch (chip)*, *d*, *e (met)*, *ee (eel)*, *f*, *g (go)*, *h*, *i (in)*, *ie (pie)*, *j*, *l*, *m*, *n*, *ng (sing)*, *o (on)*, *oe (foe)*, *oi (oil)*, *oo (ooze)*, *ou (out)*, *p*, *r*, *s*, *(sun)*, *sh (ship)*, *t*, *th (their, thine)*, *u (bun)*, *ue (hue)*, *v*, *w*, *y*, *z (zeal)*. This scheme is defective in giving the letters different values in combination from those which they have when alone, and in representing so many elementary sounds by digraphs. Besides, it does not serve to bring our spelling into harmony with other languages. Its advantage is, that it can be set up from common printer's cases, and that it can be read by any one who can read the old spelling. — See *Cyclopædia of Education*.

PATIENCE, the calm endurance of necessary toil or suffering. This quality, though similar to perseverance in the prolonged effort which its exercise presupposes, differs from it chiefly in the equable temper with which that effort is made. A patient spirit is one of the most important elements in the character of a successful educator. Many occasions, indeed, will occur when patience will be the only virtue which will command success. Its cultivation, therefore, is desirable both on this account, and because of its value in mental discipline. Its possession, moreover, is necessary both to the teacher and to the pupil. To the former, it is of special use in his treatment of the varying dispositions with which he has to deal. The provocations to impatience and ill temper are so many and so constant, that, without patience, the teacher's life will be a continued series of annoyances. Impatience in children is the result either of temperament or hereditary predisposition; and, in dealing with it, the teacher should remember that nothing so tends to develop and foster it in his pupils, as a constant practical exhibition of it in his daily intercourse with them. As nothing is so infectious as ill temper, so nothing tends so rapidly to curb ill temper as that quiet forbearance which a patient spirit diffuses around it like an atmosphere. The mental powers, also, act with much greater effect when the calmness of the judgment is undisturbed by ill temper or impatience. Perseverance may, indeed, exist without patience, and to a certain extent may accomplish its objects; but it is safe to say that more than half the good results which perseverance aided by patience might accomplish, are thrown away if patience does not accompany it.

PEDAGOGY, or **Pedagogics** (Gr. παιδαγωγία, from παῖς, παιδός, a boy, and ἀγωγός, leading or guiding), the science and art of giving instruction to children, particularly in school, or as by a school-teacher (παιδαγωγός). This term is more generally used in Germany than in the United States or Great Britain, in which the theory and art of the teacher or educator is designated as *instruction* or *education;* indeed, the word *pedagogue* is, in these countries, used as a term of reproach. For information in regard to the various departments of *pedagogy*, see EDUCATION, INSTRUCTION, DIDACTICS, etc.

PENMANSHIP, writing with the pen, although the term is sometimes used to indicate any kind of handwriting, or *chirography*, the pen being the most important instrument for writing. The ability to write is one of the two fundamental characteristics of an educated person, the inability to read and write constituting what is technically called *illiteracy;* and yet, in advanced education, a legible or elegant style of handwriting is not considered of great importance; for the cases are very few in which a candidate either for admission to a college or university, or for a graduating diploma, is rejected for not being able to write; any scrawl, however illegible or inelegant, being usually accepted as evidence of such ability. The consequence is, that good penmanship has not been the distinguishing feature of college graduates, but rather the reverse. When the value of this accomplishment, in every sphere of life, is considered, it will be obvious that the policy of thus disparaging penmanship as an accomplishment of a scholar is an entirely mistaken one. It is true that it cannot be considered as an element of superior instruction; but those who have the direction of that grade of instruction, should al-

Value.

ways insist upon the completion of the inferior grades as an indispensable prerequisite for admission to higher studies. In elementary schools, penmanship constitutes a very important branch of instruction; and, in these, sufficient time should be given to it to insure, at least, a respectable degree of excellence to each of the pupils.—There are various so-called *Methods of teaching.* systems of teaching penmanship, but the underlying principles are the same in all, the difference chiefly consisting in a diversity in the arrangement of the elements of the letters, with slight modifications in their forms and mode of execution, and in the exercises for practice. In order to write well, the pupil must have (1) a thorough knowledge of the forms of the letters, and (2) a command of the pen to execute them. The two fundamental requirements must be made simultaneously, except that some previous elementary instruction and practice in drawing will aid the pupil very much in his first lessons in penmanship. In these lessons, the forms should be adapted to the pupil's untrained muscles, and should increase in complexity and difficulty *pari passu* with the training of the hand and arm. The proper position of the body and the correct mode of holding the pen are indispensable prerequisites to successful work. Lessons in penmanship also presuppose a careful analysis of the elementary forms of the letters; and, in this respect, systems greatly differ. They have, however, many points in common — indeed every thing that is essential. Commencing with straight lines, to be made at the proper slope, and with perfect parallelism, the pupil advances progressively to the *pothook*, the loop, the ellipse, as in the letter *o*, etc., till, by practicing these and their combinations, he has mastered all the *small letters* of the script alphabet, when he proceeds, in a similar manner, with the *capitals*, from which he passes to words, phrases, sentences, and paragraphs. The copybook should not be used after the pupil has become thoroughly familiar with the proper forms of the letters, and thus acquired a fair style of writing. Much time is frequently lost in compelling pupils, year after year, to write copies. Quantity as well as quality should be required; excellence in penmanship consisting both in correctness and speed of execution. Many useful exercises may be blended with practice in penmanship, as the learning of the forms used in business, such as bills, receipts, modes of superscribing and addressing letters, etc. Practice in *calligraphy*, or artistic penmanship, is also of use, but should not be carried to an extreme in schools.

PHONETICS (Gr. φωνητικά, from φωνή, voice), a term used to denote not only the science of voice-sounds (*phonology*), but the arts of *phonotypy* (printing words by their sounds), and *phonography* (writing words *Definition.* by their sounds). It is also used to designate phonetic teaching, or the practical application of phonetics. In all these cases, the use of the term *phonetic* as an adjective is more common; as, *phonetic science, phonetic print, phonetic writing,* and *phonetic teaching.* In this article, these will be severally treated in the order here enumerated.

I. *Phonology,* or *phonetic science,* is, properly, a branch of the science of *acoustics,* which embraces a consideration of the sounds used in speech, *Phonology.* as well as those used in singing, and in other departments of music. Phonology is related, on the one hand, to *physiology,* as far as the organs of speech, and their action, are concerned; and, on the other, to *philology*, being now recognized by the most eminent philologists as lying at the very foundation of that science, and hence of much greater importance than any mere orthographic etymology can be. This subject can be best presented and understood by approaching it from the side of our own language, and considering the elementary sounds of *Elementary sounds.* that language in their natural order and relations. This will lay a good foundation for the study of general phonology, and for a comparison of the sounds of all languages. The English language contains nearly all the sounds needed for a full outline of phonology; and, moreover, in Webster's and Worcester's dictionaries (now very generally accepted as standards of reference.— in the United States, universally adopted as such), there is to be found a complete analysis of these sounds — one in which they fully agree, though neither presents them in their natural order, giving them merely as the particular sounds of the letters. In arranging them according to the latest results of phonetic science, we may take these distinctions as we find them in the dictionaries, where they are correctly made: (1) the sixteen simple vowel sounds heard in the following words: fate (same as *ei* in *veil*), fat, care, far, ask, all, what (same as *o* in *not*); mete (same as *i* in *pique*), met, fin, note, whole [recognized as an English sound, but not sanctioned in orthoëpy], rude, pull, us, urn. These naturally arrange themselves in the following order, with the addition of *ü* and *ö* from the German to complete the scale:

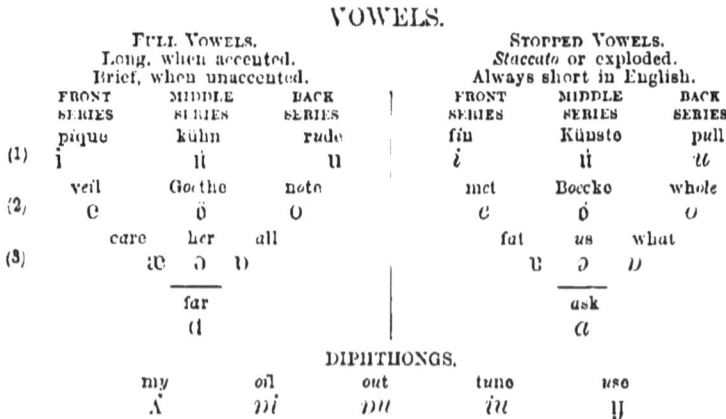

The full and stopped vowels occur in pairs, and in three corresponding series, as shown in the following table:

PHONETICS 233

No distinction is made in these tables between the sound of e in *term* or i in *girl*, and that of u in *urn* or in *furl*. These sounds, however, though kindred, are distinguishable, and are so marked by Webster, who says, "The vulgar universally, and many cultivated speakers both in England and America, give the e in such words the full sound of u in *urge*, as murcy for *mercy*, turm for *term*, etc. But, in the most approved style of pronunciation, the organs are placed in a position intermediate between that requisite for sounding u in *furl* and that for sounding e in *met*, thus making (as Smart observes) 'a *compromise* between the two'." The vowel sounds, as arranged in the above tables, may be thus described. Starting from the fundamental sound, a in *far* (or a in *ask*), they branch upward in (1) a front series, with the tongue rising upward and forward, to i in *pique;* (2) a middle series, with the tongue rising to ü, directly upward, and not pushed forward or backward; and (3) a back series, with the tongue rising upward and backward to u in *rude*. The succession in the order of the sounds as judged by the ear, corresponds to that of the movements of the tongue, as perceived by the muscular sense. The diphthongs are arranged below the simple vowels according as they terminate in the upper front vowel i or the upper back vowel u. The relations of the full and corresponding stopped vowels to each other, as affected by quantity, may be further studied by the aid of the following arrangement of words, in which they respectively occur in accented and unaccented syllables (the double letters indicating prolonged sounds):

eat	eternal	kühn	Künste	prude	prudentia
ii	i	ü	ü	uu	u

	it				wood
ĭĭ	ĭ			uu	u

mate	maternal	Goethe	Böcke	oak	location
ee	e	ö	ö	oo	o

	met				spoken
ĕĕ	ĕ			ŏŏ	o

care	clairvoyant	cur	curtail	aught	authentic
ææ	æ	ɔɔ	ɔ	ʋʋ	ʋ

	carry		curry		not
ᴂᴂ	ᴂ	ǝǝ	ǝ	ɒɒ	ɒ

	part	partake			
	aa	a			

		ask			
	aa	a			

It may be observed that the stopped vowels do not, and cannot, rise quite so high in the scale as their corresponding full vowels; but this difference is reduced to a minimum in the fundamental pair, a a, and in the lower front pair, æ v.

The following is a synoptical arrangement of consonant sounds, some German sounds being added. [a, indicates aspirates; t, subtonics; n, nasals; l, liquids; v, vowel consonants]:

CONSONANTS.

	LIP	LIP-TEETH	TONGUE-TEETH	TIP-TONGUE	TOP-TONGUE	ROOT-TONGUE
	u*p*			*t*one	*ch*in	*c*at
(*a*)	p			t	ch	c
	*b*e			*d*o	*j*ar	*g*ot
(*t*)	b			d	j	g
	*v*on	i*f*	*th*in	u*s*	*sh*e	i*ch*
(*a*)	v	f	th	s	sh	ḍḥ
	*w*ie	*v*eil	*th*is	*z*one	u*s*ual	Ta*g*
(*t*)	w	v	dh	z	zh	ǥ
	*m*e			*n*o	se*n*or	si*ng*
(*n*)	m			n	ñ	ng
				*l*et *r*a*r*e		
(*l*)				l r ɹ		
	*wh*at					*h*e
(*a*)	hw					h
	*w*e				*y*o	
(*v*)	w				y	

For an account of the development of the present method of indicating these sounds in the English language, the reader is referred to the article on ORTHOGRAPHY.

II. *Phonetic Print.* — The elementary sounds of the English language are usually represented in dictionaries by diacritical marks; but various methods of phonotypic notation, other than this, have been employed. That of Dr. Edwin Leigh has been extensively used for school purposes, and has attained a considerable degree of popularity. An ingenious system of representation approximating to the diacritical, is used in Shearer's *Combination Speller* (N. Y., 1874).

III. *Phonography*, or *phonetic writing*, in its more general sense, would include any script in which the letters are used to denote sounds; but it is now appropriated, in a special sense, to Pitman's particular system of phonetic short-hand. It can be studied in Pitman's manuals, especially those of 1860 and 1865; or as it appears in the text-books of Andrews and Boyle (Boston, 1846); Langley (Cincinnati, 1851), Graham (N. Y., 1858), Ben Pitman (Cincinnati, 1855), Marsh (San Francisco, 1868), Munson (N. Y., 1866), and E. V. Burnz (N. Y., 1872). In connection with any of these (especially those prior to 1860), Parkhurst's *Stenophonographer* (N. Y., 1852—76) can be used, and will give to the investigator, teacher, or practical reporter, the history and discussion of the various improvements, proposed or made, since 1852. — Phonography, notwithstanding its many advantages over the ordinary script, has made but little progress since that time as a general method of writing, its use, at present, being almost exclusively technical. Hence, it has not been generally introduced as a branch of instruction, except in commercial schools, or for the special purposes of preparing for the occupation of the reporter.

IV. *Phonetic teaching* now quite generally constitutes a part of the lowest grade of elementary instruction, its object being to facilitate the

teaching of children to read. (See PHONIC METHOD.) By means of phonetic exercises, the vocal organs of children are trained to clearness and correctness of enunciation, while the ear is cultivated so as to be *Methods.* able readily to distinguish sounds. At the same time, children necessarily acquire a better idea of the use of letters and of the sounds which they are employed to denote. Most educators, at the present time, recommend this mode of teaching; although there is some diversity in the manner in which it is applied. Beginning with simple words in which single letters are used to denote simple sounds, and in which no silent letters occur, the child is led to perceive the use of the letters, and to associate with them their proper sounds, the teacher passes progressively to more complex and irregular combinations, until the pupil is able to analyze words into their component sounds, and state how these sounds are represented. After such preliminary exercises, in order that the pupil may fully understand the relations of the sounds to each other, and be systematically drilled in their utterance, all the elementary sounds must be presented synoptically. This is done by phonetic charts, which should ex-
Phonetic hibit (1) a logical enumeration of the elementary sounds, illus-
charts. trated by their use in well-chosen words; and (2) the letters of the alphabet with their various sounds, and diphthongal combinations. Very many of the faults in articulation so frequently met with may be prevented or removed by persistent drilling in the elementary sounds. These phonetic drills may comprise exercises in the vowel sounds by themselves; but the consonant sounds are often most effectively practiced in combinations with vowels. In teaching persons, whether children or adults, to pronounce a foreign language, this training is indispensable. Of course, it should be preceded by a careful investigation into the particular defects which constitute what is called the "foreign accent", so that the elementary sounds involved may be made the special subject of the drill. Phonetic analysis should not cease in the lower grades, but should, at every stage, constitute a part of the regular reading or elocutionary exercises. Like the fingers of the pianist or violinist, the vocal organs need constant technical exercise in order that they may perform their office most effectively. The enunciation of the open vowel sounds constitutes a most important part of vocal training. (See VOICE, CULTURE OF THE.)

PHONIC METHOD, a term applied to a method of teaching reading, in accordance with which pupils are taught, in pronouncing words, to use the sounds of the letters, instead of their names, so that they may at once perceive the result of combination, and thus without difficulty give the correct pronunciation. For example, when the pupil is required to pronounce the word *dog*, he does not say *de-o-ge, dog*, but gives to each letter the proper sound, phonetically, and thus at once pronounces the word *dog* as the necessary product of the elements thus combined. This method is considered by teachers to possess many advantages over the old-fashioned way of compelling the pupils to learn the names of the letters of the alphabet, and then teaching them to read by spelling exercises. (See ORTHOGRAPHY.)

PHONICS. See ORTHOGRAPHY, and PHONETICS.

PHYSICAL EDUCATION may be defined as that systematic training of the bodily powers which tends to render them, in the highest possible degree efficient in their several functions. The necessity for this training is generally acknowledged, as a basis for the higher departments of education. Among the ancients — the Persians, the Greeks, and the Romans, especially, the highest respect was accorded to physical culture; and the means employed were generally well adapted to the purpose, although merely empirical; but, at the present time, the researches of science ought to supply a far better and more accurate basis for an effective system of bodily training. — Physical education looks to two objects: (1) to encourage a normal development of bodily powers; and (2) to check morbid growth. Incidentally to these, of course, the preservation of health, that is, protection against disease, is an important object; since a condition of health is the foundation upon which all physical culture must rest; indeed, if children are successfully protected from morbid influences and disturbances, normal development must result.

Definition.

Objects.

(1) The application of appropriate means to stimulate or guide the development of the bodily powers constitutes what is called *physical training*. This training may be (1) general, or (2) special. Up to a certain age, all physical exercise must have for its object general development; beyond that, the special purpose of the training must dictate the nature of the exercise to be employed. Military drill, it is true, is often employed in schools to promote general development, but there is very much required in military discipline that is quite unnecessary for ordinary physical culture. The importance of systematic exercise has been considered in the articles *calisthenics* and *gymnastics* (q. v.). Such exercise, however, must not look exclusively to muscular development; but to the prompt use of muscular power in obedience to the dictates of mind. Such power systematically exercised in any given direction becomes almost automatic, as is seen in the case of the skillful oarsman, rider, or swordsman; or in adepts in athletic games, such as those of ball and cricket. All such means of physical culture become of special value, as bringing the powers of the body under the immediate control of the will; and, hence, under the name *athletics*, they have been generally encouraged by those who have the direction of superior education. In the same category, are to be placed the exercises which regard the due development of other physical powers, as the senses, the vocal organs, the lungs, and, in a closer relation to intellectual education, the brain. Educators err greatly in forgetting that the brain is a physical organ, and that its exercise is subject to the same laws and to the same limitations as other bodily organs; and that, therefore, physical considerations should have a controlling weight in determining the means and, to some extent, the methods of intellectual training. (See BRAIN.) Many are inclined to regard the direction of physical training as unnecessary. They think that the physical powers of children and youth receive, in the instinctive and irrepressible exercises natural to that age, a sufficient education for ordinary purposes. From this view arises a neglect which is fraught with serious injury. Not only does the individual fail to act appropriately and energetically at every trying period of his life; but, in most cases, his action falls somewhat below what is required for effective results, through want of the full co-operation of the bodily powers; and, toward the close of life, decrepitude is accelerated

Physical training.

by the partial atrophy occasioned by imperfect development and by disuse.

(2) To check morbid growth or to prevent disease, careful attention must be given to the surroundings of the child, particularly in school; as *Morbid growth.* there he is subjected to constant restraint, and, hence, cannot exercise his natural instincts which would prompt him to escape from such surroundings. The preservation of children from morbid influences in school depends upon a great variety of circumstances, for a full enumeration of which, see HYGIENE, SCHOOL. The practical aim of physical education, under the influence of modern life, is almost always intellectual. Gymnastics and calisthenics, however, indirectly exert a moral influence which, of itself, makes their practice desirable. *Relation to morals.* This is that magnanimity which is produced in generous minds by the consciousness of bodily health and power, and a disposition to use that power worthily. A feeling of inferiority has always associated with it an element of immorality, which leads its possessor to acts of duplicity and meanness to preserve his equality. There is still another phase of physical education to be considered — that which relates to the joint action of the mind and body through the medium of the senses. (See EAR; EYE; and SENSES, EDUCATION OF.) The minute subdivision of *The senses.* labor characteristic of the age in which we live, by giving a utilitarian value to the cultivation of the senses is rapidly constituting this an element of increasing importance. Already, the success of numerous trades and employments is dependent upon a nicety of discrimination by means of the eye, the ear, the taste, or the touch; and the number of these is steadily increasing. The cultivation of the senses, therefore, is desirable from a merely utilitarian point of view; while for general culture, such as is required in many of the arts, its absolute necessity is manifest. Many considerations and interests, therefore, conspire to make the subject of physical education one of constantly increasing importance.

PHYSIOLOGY (Gr. $\varphi \dot{v} \sigma \iota \varsigma$, nature, and $\lambda \dot{o} \gamma o \varsigma$, discourse), the science which treats of vital phenomena — as contradistinguished from *anatomy*, which treats of the structure of living bodies and the materials of which they are composed. In the course of education, it presupposes some preliminary knowledge of chemistry, physics, anatomy, and especially of microscopic anatomy, or histology; and, in turn, it precedes the study of hygiene, or the laws of health, and that of pathology, or the science of abnormal function. As a science, physiology is of recent origin, though the name has been in use from antiquity. Like *How to be studied.* all other natural sciences, as Dalton observes, "there is only one means by which physiology can be studied; that is, by the observation of nature". It has been built up by experiment; and many of its most essential truths, and these in their practical results the most important to mankind, have been gained through vivisection. As the principal foundation of hygiene, it is obvious that its principles should be so far made an element of general education as may conduce to a just appreciation of nature's sanitary code. How this may best be accomplished *School physiology.* is a question that has hardly received the attention it deserves. School physiology, in many cases, consists of a smattering of anatomy; in others, of a still more unsubstantial fabric of information regarding function; or, in still others, of a blending of the two with hygienic doctrines, often based not on a wide conception of biological truths, but on the meager knowledge gained by personal experience. The difficulty has always consisted in attempting to build upon too narrow a foundation, and that by means of an erroneous method. Thus, the attempt is made to teach the elements of physiology without a sufficient groundwork of chemistry and physics, and exclusively from books, instead of from practical experience in the laboratory. The results have been — as those of book learning and lecture teaching in natural science, without observation and experiment, always must be — unreal and evanescent; hence, by such instruction the true nature of vital phenomena is never clearly apprehended; and the hygienic deductions are, of course, correspondingly illogical. Doubtless, a great amount of knowledge has been imparted, in these later days, to the people in general on this subject; but the advance that has been made in sanitary practice is, probably, due not so much to the results of school education, as to the improved education of medical men, and to their advice spoken and written to communities, learning by practical experience the penalty of infringing hygienic laws. The real requisite in general education on this subject appears to be, that, when a sufficient foundation has been laid, a practical course of biology *Biology.* should be employed to elucidate the general laws of life; and then the habit of scientific thought and reasoning, formed by such training, will lead to a correct application of general principles to the special conditions of human life. Some such course of biological study as *A Course of Practical Instruction in Elementary Biology*, by Huxley and Martin, might properly form a part of the curriculum of every collegiate institution; and, in all schools of a lower grade, as much preparation should be made for such a course as is practicable. Objective teaching, in outline, of anatomy, by the dissection of the lower animals, accompanied by such simple practical suggestions as arise from the interpretation of the mechanical arrangements of the body, may be early commenced; but, in all cases, this foundation should be laid systematically, with a definite end in view, and by instructors who have qualified themselves to teach, by following a complete practical course, such as is above suggested. Teaching merely from text-books and by pictures, will be almost useless, because *Text-books.* superficial; and no demonstrations, even from the best models, can ever be so effective as those from actual dissections of the lower animals. A pupil will gain a better idea of the appearances presented by his own organs, and of their own relations to one another, from seeing a demonstration of those of a rabbit or a dog, for example, than from any rigid, and necessarily unreal, model, however skillfully constructed and colored. Such models, however, admirably subserve secondary demonstrations. — For a list of works of reference, see *Cyclopædia of Education*.

PICTURES. One of the earliest efforts of the human mind, after spoken language, appears to be the communication of ideas by tangible objects. The use of pictures and images is common among sav-
Use of. ages every-where. It is no less characteristic of the infant mind among civilized races, children being not only interested in looking at pictures, but, by a natural prompting, attempting to imitate them. The

first ideas which the child takes from objects being concrete, its means of expressing them takes the concrete form — its first effort being, as near as possible, a reproduction of the objects themselves. Not till a higher development has been reached, is it fitted to make use of a system in which purely arbitrary forms are employed. This early and almost universal instinct, therefore, involving, as it must, the ability to understand ideas so communicated, suggests the peculiar fitness of this method for use in the instruction of children. This form of expression being attended with so much pleasure, it finds its natural place in the kindergarten system; and we find, accordingly, various exercises there for the employment of it. It is even extended into the ordinary school system in the shape of object lessons. But this method, useful as it is at certain stages, has its limitations. It should not be forgotten that, with children, the object itself, for purposes of instruction, is always better than any representation of it. As the picture of an animal, for instance, is only one phase of the form of that animal, and does not usually take into consideration size, color, and many other essential qualities, only a very imperfect impression can be gained from it. This fact should suggest the limitations mentioned. These have reference principally to the end to be attained, to the correctness of the picture, and the number and nature of the objects represented. As to the correctness of the picture, little need be said; as modern publications, in this respect, show a constant improvement, and leave little to be desired. The number of objects represented in each picture should be limited, single figures being, at first, given; afterwards two or three. The objects represented, also, should be familiar things, and several of a kind, inasmuch as, by the contemplation of these, the child's conceptive faculty, or imagination, and powers of generalization are exercised. In this respect, also, the right method in primers and elementary books, is, as a rule, instinctively taken — though not always. The value of this last restriction, at a later period, may be easily illustrated. If the object be to give an idea of some animal never seen — the camel, for instance — the task is made comparatively easy from the child's having seen illustrations of somewhat similar objects with which it is familiar; as the horse, cow, etc. It seizes at once upon the points of resemblance, and, immediately after, upon the points of difference, and thus makes a positive addition to its knowledge. But let the same child be confronted with a picture of a star-fish, or a printing-press, and the probability is, if it has never seen these or any similar objects, that it will get only a very imperfect idea of either. The reason is obvious. With no previous preparation, it is called upon to establish in its mind an entirely new conception, solely from the picture, without any corresponding tangible basis in its experience. The result is a thwarting of the tendency to generalization — so strong with children always — and a confusing of the mind by an indistinct conception, invariably accompanied with a loss of interest. The special uses to which pictures are put, whether as diagrams in illustration of particular studies, or as part of a higher, artistic education, need not here be considered.

POETRY, or the written expression of beauty, is an important instrument in certain departments of intellectual culture, besides aiding in the education of the emotions and sensibilities, and in the cultivation of taste. (See ESTHETIC CULTURE.) The pupil's first knowledge of written poetry is usually obtained from the school reader. The manner of its presentation there, however, is susceptible of improvement. The free use of figures of rhetoric, and of obsolete or unusual words and phrases, renders poetry inappropriate to the minds of children till after the usual modes of expression have become familiar. Its proper time for presentation, therefore, is when rhetoric is studied — that is, during the latter part of the high-school course, or in the college. Yet nothing is more common than to find a highly-involved passage from Shakespeare, or an abstruse paragraph from Wordsworth, in a reader intended for pupils of from ten to fifteen years of age. Some vague or half-considered idea that these passages are, in some way, to serve as models, by being thus presented, or are necessary for elocutionary purposes, is probably in the mind of the compiler. But what should we think of the music teacher who should present a symphony of Beethoven, as a model, to a beginner practicing the scales? The parallel case is quite as absurd. The result is bad in two ways: (1) the unintelligibility, to the child, of such a poetical selection deprives it of all use as a model; and (2) the disgust thus occasioned becomes permanent, and leads the pupil, even in manhood, to avoid a reperusal of the author thus used. How many persons, of mature years, date their dislike to Milton, for instance, from an enforced use of his works as reading or parsing exercises in early youth!

Mode of presentation.

Result.

The introduction of poetry into the school curriculum should follow the natural plan, the first poems used being exceedingly simple, containing no words beyond the vocabulary of the child, and treating of subjects and objects of every-day familiarity. An excellent plan would be to place, as an introductory lesson in reading, a paraphrase in prose of the poem to be used. In this way, the pupil, being possessed beforehand of the meaning of what he is approaching, is at liberty to give more attention to the poetical mode of expression, this being the principal thing to be considered; for, if the meaning were the principal thing, prose would be preferable — it being more direct and in more familiar language. The fact that rhythmical language is, in many cases, of assistance to the memory, indicates its peculiar fitness for certain educational purposes. By its aid, abstract truths and arbitrary rules may often be fixed in the mind, in a way not possible by any other. Moral truths, also, may often be better retained in the memory by their expression in rhythmical form. The experience of most persons will probably furnish illustrations of this fact. There appears to be a limit to this use of rhyme, however, determined partly by the nature of the things to be remembered, and partly by the esthetic effect produced by such use. It may be said, in general, that all concrete ideas and relations, — those which, upon suggestion, call up in the mind material images — do not require the aid of rhyme to fix them in the memory; while ideas and relations of an essentially abstract or arbitrary nature, are more easily retained in the memory by a rhythmical expression of them. As an illustration of a violation of the first proposition, may be mentioned a rhymed text-book on geography. In the study of geography, the definitions, descriptions, etc., being always accompanied by pictures and maps, are firmly fixed in the mind by the eye — the most effective of all the agents used in acquiring knowledge. To call in the aid

Suggestions.

Special value.

Use of rhyme.

of the ear, therefore, is superfluous, and tends, rather, to distraction. If there had been originally any vagueness of conception left by the image addressed to the eye, the ear might, with propriety, be called in to aid it; but, from the nature of things, this is impossible. The picture of a material object will always present to the mind a clearer idea of it, than any verbal description. A further objection, in this case, is *Further objection.* that the rhymed version, degenerating, as it is almost sure to do, into grotesque doggerel, familiarizes the mind of the pupil with the most degraded form of poetry, and tends to unfit it for an appreciation of the higher. In regard to the second proposition mentioned above, it may be said that we naturally seek some short, succinct form for expressing generalizations, and abstract and arbitrary relations, which shall make them convenient for use; and that form is often found. If the poetic form would enable us to remember them more distinctly, and if no objection to its use could be raised, it would be allowable; but if this form, besides adding little to our ability to remember, is open to the additional objection that it presents to the undiscriminating mind of the pupil a bad poetical model, it would seem that it ought not to be used. It can hardly be claimed that rhymed versions of the Lord's Prayer, or of the Proverbs, for instance — of the propositions of geometry, or of the rules of arithmetic, have helped us materially to learn more readily or appreciate more fully the truths contained in them. The very nature of some truths is averse to ornament; and the use of it, in such cases, should be discountenanced. A frequent result of the appreciation of the beautiful, which *Writing poetry.* underlies all poetry, is the attempt of youth sooner or later to write poetry. Every teacher's experience will supply instances of this. This inclination usually makes its appearance between the ages of 15 and 20, in minds that have a natural taste for beautiful objects, after a considerable command of language has been obtained, and before the realities of life have come to darken, with their shadows, the bright sky of youth. As not one in a hundred, however, of those who write verses, at this age, will become a poet, the teacher's course is plain. His method of cure should be, unsparing criticism, but applied in a kindly spirit. It will require only a few exposures of bad rhymes, false similes and metaphors — and of these, the most preposterous will generally be found to be the most cherished by the writer — to recall the would-be poet to a more sober and useful pursuit.

PRAXIS (Gr. πρᾶξις, from πράσσειν, to do), a particular form of exercise designed to afford practice to the pupils; as a praxis for parsing or analysis, in teaching grammar.

PREPARATORY SCHOOLS, schools for secondary instruction, in which pupils are prepared for admission to the college or university.

PRIMARY INSTRUCTION. See EDUCATION.

PRIMER (Lat. *liber primarius*, a little book containing the offices of the Roman Catholic Church, so called because used at prime — *prima hora* — the first hour), originally a small book of prayers, or for elementary religious instruction, but at the present time, an elementary reading-book of the lowest grade. The literature relating to primers, or A-B-C books, is very curious and interesting, some of these books having had great fame on account of their long and extensive use. One of the very earliest was Luther's (or Melanchthon's) *Child's Little Primer*, containing the Lord's Prayer, etc. In 1534, a *Prymer in Englyshe with certain prayers*, etc., was printed by John Byddell; and, in 1545, King Henry VIII. ordered an English *Form of Public Prayer, or Primer*, to be printed; and to be "taught, lerned, and red" throughout his dominions. Bienrod's primer, containing an illustrated alphabet, was the earliest publication of this kind in German, dating back to the middle of the 16th century. The *horn-book* was the simplest and most noted of primers. (See HORN-BOOK, and CHRIST CROSS ROW.) The *Royal Primer of Great Britain* and the *New England Primer* also had great fame.

PRIZES. See EMULATION.
PROGRAMME. See SCHOOL MANAGEMENT.
PROMOTION. See SCHOOL MANAGEMENT.
PSYCHOLOGY (Gr. $\psi v \chi \acute{\eta}$, soul, and $\lambda \acute{o} \gamma o \varsigma$, discourse), the science which treats of the human soul and its manifestations, that is, of the phenomena of intelligence, sensibility, and will. It embraces a *Definition.* consideration of all that pertains to the inner consciousness of man, whether derived from external or sensuous impression, or from the intuitions and activities of the soul itself, considered as the conscious *ego* animating, informing, and employing the material form, or body. "Psychology", says President Porter — in *The Human Intellect* (1869) — "is a science. It professes to exhibit what is actually known or may be learned concerning the soul, in the forms of science — *i. e.*, in the forms of exact observation, precise definition, fixed terminology, classified arrangement, and rational explanation". Psychology embraces a wider field of research than mental and moral philosophy, for it comprehends the whole science of human consciousness, and is concurrent with anthropology as far as the latter treats of the soul and its relations to the body. Those manifestations of intelligence which are based upon the observation of external things are the peculiar field of intellectual science, but the vast field of intuition is the peculiar sphere of psychological investigation; for it is upon a careful study of the inner perceptions and the independent activities of the soul itself, that we must rely to obtain a knowledge of its nature and its relation to the Universe and its Creator.

Education as a complete science must rest upon psychology, and can never reach its full development in theory and practice until psychological *Relation to* investigation has been carried beyond its present stage of prog-
education. ress, and has fully developed the principles needed for the construction of a complete practical system. Such a system would constitute the art corresponding to the science which President Porter in the above cited definition outlines, and would place the practical educator in possession of the principles and rules requisite for the aid and guidance of the soul in developing itself in all its relations — intellectual, ethical, and spiritual. — This subject is in this work treated in detail in separate articles. (See EDUCATION, INSTRUCTION, INTELLECTUAL EDUCATION, PHYSICAL EDUCATION, etc.)

PUNISHMENT is the intentional infliction of pain for the purpose of controlling the will, either to compel action or to restrain it. In educa-
Defined. tion this is often requisite, for the sake both of the pupil and of the school. Lawlessness would prevail were every individ-

ual allowed, without restraint, to exercise his own self-will. There must be authority, and that authority must be recognized and enforced. (See
Need of punishment. AUTHORITY.) The proper discipline of the pupils requires that they should be brought under control, either by means of agencies that will lead to self-control, as appeals to reason and conscience, or to other motives, such as the love of approbation, the desire to excel, the hope of reward, etc. Where these fail, appeal must be made to
Physical pain. the sense of fear, through the apprehension of mental or physical pain. This, as being the lowest principle to which recourse may be had, should be the last, and should always be employed by the teacher with great reluctance and with the greatest possible caution. (See FEAR.)

Where it can be made effectual, the best form of punishment is censure, which may be expressed by direct reproof, by demerit marks, or by public
Censure. disgrace. Reproof, to be effective, should be sparing, and never administered in tones of anger or irritation, as if the teacher had suffered some personal grievance, and were vindicating himself rather than pointing out and condemning the fault of the pupil. The teacher's personality must be eliminated in administering punishment, except as far as he may make apparent his sorrow that punishment is necessary, and his regret that it is his duty to inflict it. The object must be felt by the pupil to be chastisement and correction, not vindictiveness, or the desire to avenge offended dignity or authority. Constant scolding is exceedingly
Scolding. injurious to the pupil, and of no efficacy whatever; nor can the attempt on the part of the teacher be approved to wound the feelings of the pupil by satirical or sarcastic remarks; for the latter
Sarcasm. instinctively feels that this is a mean advantage taken by the teacher both of his position and of his superior ability.

Demerit marks have the advantage of definiteness in expressing, and in a way that is unanswerable, if just,— the amount of censure administered
Demerit marks. for neglect or wrong-doing; and, when these are required to be exhibited to parents, the punishment may be very severe. Forms of disgrace, humiliating positions, or badges, may be rendered exceedingly painful to some minds; while others would only be hardened by them. Extreme caution is required in employing this kind of punishment.
Forms of disgrace. The character of the pupil should be carefully studied, and the effect watched. Delicacy of feeling and self-respect in the pupil are never to be sacrificed for a temporary advantage. Detention and the imposition of tasks are also to be resorted to with care, or the school may become to the pupil a hateful place.

As to corporal punishment, the lowest form of all, there is great difference of opinion among educators regarding the propriety of ever resorting
Corporal punishment. to it in schools. D. P. Page, an educator of long experience, great moral force, and singular kindliness of nature, fully admitted the necessity of corporal punishment as a last resort. "I do not hesitate", he says, "to teach that corporal infliction is one of the justifiable means of establishing authority in the school-room. To this conclusion I have come after a careful consideration of the subject, modified by the varied experience of nearly twenty years, and by a somewhat attentive observation of the workings of all the plans which have

been devised to avoid its use or to supply its place". Horace Mann, one of the most enthusiastic advocates of moral suasion, yet recognized the necessity of corporal punishment in some cases. " Punishment", he says, "should never be inflicted except in cases of the extremest necessity; while the experiment of sympathy, confidence, persuasion, encouragement, should be repeated forever and ever". An English teacher says, "It is necessary for a child to learn that violation of law, whether of school, society, or God, brings inevitable suffering. The sense of right is so imperfectly developed in children, that one of the ways of impressing upon a child that right is right, and wrong is wrong, is by showing that suffering follows from one, enjoyment and a sense of satisfaction from the other". (*The Educational Reporter*, London, July 1., 1874.) Corporal punishment is sanctioned by Rosenkranz in *Pedagogics as a System*. "This kind of punishment", he says, "provided always that it is not too often administered, or with undue severity, is the proper way of dealing with willful defiance, with obstinate carelessness, or with a really perverted will, so long or so often as the higher perception is closed against appeal." Under peculiarly favorable circumstances, — a condition of things which may be considered ideal, that is, where the home training of the pupils of a school has been judicious and correct, where all have been taught, from their earliest years, to obey their elders and superiors; and this not by violence and severity, but with gentleness and firmness; and moreover, where the teacher or teachers of the school are gifted with the same talents for discipline, — under such circumstances, most educators would agree that a resort to corporal punishment would scarcely ever, if at all, be necessary. But such are not the circumstances under which children are instructed in school. Bain, in *Education as a Science* (1881) says: "Where corporal punishment is kept up, it should be at the far end of the list of penalties; its slightest application should be accounted the worst disgrace, and should be accompanied with stigmatizing forms. It should be regarded as a deep injury to the person that inflicts it, and to those that have to witness it, as the height of shame and infamy. It ought not to be repeated with the same pupil: if two or three applications are not enough, removal is the proper course".

As to the offenses for which corporal punishment should be inflicted, and the proper mode of inflicting it, the following suggestions (of a practical teacher) would probably meet with universal approval from those who claim that this mode of discipline is, in certain cases, indispensable: (1) It should be reserved for the baser faults. A child should never be struck for inadvertencies, for faults of forgetfulness, for irritability and carelessness, or for petty irregularities. It is a coarse remedy, and should be employed upon the coarse sins of our animal nature. (2) When employed at all, it should be administered in strong doses. The whole system of slaps, pinches, snappings, and irritating blows is to be condemned. These petty disciplines tend to stir up anger, and rather encourage evil in the child than subdue it. (3) In administering physical punishment to a child, the head should be left sacred from all violence. Pulling the hair or the ears, rapping the head with a thimble or with the knuckles, boxing the ears, slapping the cheeks or the mouth, are all brutal expedients. These irritating and annoying practices are far more likely to arouse malignant passions, than to alleviate them. (4) The temper with which you administer punishment will, generally, excite in the child a corresponding feeling. If you bring anger, anger will be excited; if you bring affection and sorrow, you will find the child responding in sorrowful feelings; if you bring moral feelings, the child's conscience will be excited. Anger and severity destroy all the benefit of punishment: love and firmness will, if anything can, work penitence and a change of conduct. See *Cyclopædia of Education*, art. CORPORAL PUNISHMENT. (See also AUTHORITY, DISCIPLINE, and GOVERNMENT.)

PUPIL-TEACHER, a term used, chiefly in England, to designate a boy or a girl employed to perform certain duties connected with the teaching and management of a school.

QUADRIVIUM. See ARTS.

READING, as the basis and instrument of all literary education, is the most important branch of school instruction. After the child has learned to talk, he may be taught to understand, and to give vocal expression to, such written language as is adapted to his degree of mental development. To do this involves an association, in the mind, *Processes.* of the printed form of the word (1) with its proper sound, or pronunciation, and (2) with the idea which it is intended to express. In teaching children to read, the first of these processes requires the principal attention; but, as progress is made, the second constantly increases in importance. The word, and not the letters composing it, is the true element in reading. No one can be said to know how to read who is obliged to stop at the word, and study its composition, before he can pronounce it. The due meaning and pronunciation of every word must be immediately recognized by the mind, without pause or hesitation, in the act of reading. But the word is made up of separate characters, representing elementary sounds; and hence arises a diversity of methods in teaching children to pronounce words. The *alphabet method*, or *A-B-C method* (q. v.), *Alphabet method.* requires that the child should learn the names of all the letters of the alphabet, and then, by means of a spelling process, learn the proper pronunciation of their combinations. This process is condemned by most teachers of the present time, as long and tedious, as well as illogical; the method most generally preferred being that denominated the *word method* (q. v.), by which the child learns at once to pronounce *Word method.* short words, and is taught the sounds and names of the letters, by an analysis of them. When the sounds of the letters are used instead of the names, the process has been called the *phonic method* (q. v.), which, in modern didactics, is most generally approved. Certainly, *Phonic method.* it is more rational to expect that a child will perceive the true pronunciation of a word through an analysis of the sounds of the letters, than by using their names, many of which afford no key to the sound. For example, if the word be *cat*, the child reaches the pronunciation at once by enumerating the sounds k-$\check{a}$-t; while by spelling, he is obliged to say *se-ā-te*, introducing sounds entirely foreign to the word. In the one case, the mental association required is simple and direct; in the other, it is complex and indirect. It is true that, by long and diligent rote-teaching, children learn to read by the latter method; but the question arises, are they not to a certain extent unfitted for other instruction by so illogical a process? Auxiliary to the *phonic method*, and, indeed, dictated by its needs, is the *phonetic method*, in which the absurd contradictions of the alphabet are removed by using the letters slightly modified, so as to have a character for each separate sound, and each sound represented by one, and only one, character. (See ORTHOGRAPHY, and PHONETICS.) These various methods are dictated by what may perhaps be called the mechanics of reading; but, in connection with that, the teacher must always bear in mind, that what the child is learning to pronounce is a symbol of thought; and, hence, at every step, the pupil's understanding is to be addressed. "Each sentence read", says JOHONNOT (in *Principles and Practice of Teaching*, N. Y., 1881), "should be the embodiment of a thought which the pupil thoroughly understands, and should be delivered precisely as it should be spoken. The practice of allowing the words, of a reading-lesson to be pronounced separately should never be permitted". Reading, as a part of education, has a twofold object: (1) to understand what is read; and (2) to give proper oral expression to it; that is to say, reading is either for the purpose of gaining information for one's self, or for imparting information to others. To teach a pupil to read properly implies far more than correct elocution. It implies the development of that judgment and spirit which, being brought to the perusal of useful books, or other reading matter, will enable the student to gather up information, and, in every available manner, make the realm of books tributary to his own mental wants. Hence, as auxiliary to reading, the proper meaning of words, phrases, and idioms must be taught; and exercises must be employed for the purpose of ascertaining to what extent the pupil has received correct ideas from what he has read. When the object is to teach the pupils elocution, the exercises should be specially adapted to that end. Thus, the pupil, having read in order to understand for himself, should be required to read the same passage for the information of his fellow pupils. For this purpose, it has been recommended, in class teaching, to permit only the pupil reading to use the book, all the others being required to listen; because, in this way, the pupils will be on the alert to hear and know the meaning of what is read, and will, besides, better appreciate the true end of reading; while, on the other hand, the one reading will endeavor to pronounce correctly, enunciate distinctly, and emphasize naturally. Reading-books should be constructed with a special reference to the accomplishment of this object; and, hence, the lessons should be adapted, at each stage, to the mental status of the pupils. Moreover, the material should not consist of mere fragments, without any logical continuity; but should be of such a character as to discipline the mind in connected thinking upon suitable subjects, and to awaken an interest in the minds of the pupils. Usually, this essential object of reading in schools is defeated by the use of extracts from essays on difficult, abstract subjects, or from authors whose style is too complex, and whose vocabulary is too ponderous for children. Simultaneous reading is commended by some teachers as an elocutionary drill, as being useful (1) to impart habits of distinctness of enunciation, (2) to remove the habit of too rapid or too slow a style of reading, (3) as means of voice culture for elocution. — (See ELOCUTION, and VOICE.)

RECESSES. See HYGIENE, SCHOOL, and SCHOOL MANAGEMENT.

RECITATION, a term used in American colleges and schools, to denote the rehearsal of a lesson by pupils before their instructor, or the repetition of something committed to memory. The manner in which the teacher should conduct the daily recitations of his class is a matter of very great importance, since apparently perfect recitations may be gone through with which not only have little educative value, but may even be productive of positive harm to the mind of the pupil. The surest guide in this respect, is that which is derived from a consideration of the essential meaning of the word education, no method of recitation having any value which does not keep constantly in view the development of the pupil's mental powers. It should always be remembered by the teacher that the supreme object of the recitation is to accustom the pupil, by daily practice, to use the faculties of which he is possessed. Many a so-called recitation results, by too much explanation on the part of the teacher, in a reversal of the functions of the teacher and the class — the former reciting to the latter, instead of the latter to the former. The passive attitude of mind in which pupils listen to a long explanation is the very attitude from which they need to be roused. There are two stages in the development of a mental power as produced by the exercises of the class room: (1) the knowing what to say; and (2) the saying of it. The first stage the pupil is supposed to have reached by the study of the lesson; the second and most important one, is not passed through by the pupil in the case above supposed. Of far greater service is it, therefore, to the pupil, to be allowed to state the result of his study in his own language, halting and imperfect though it be, than to compel him to listen to an exposition by the teacher. Under the first condition, it will be apparent, at every step, whether he really understands his lesson; and, if he does, every day will add to the copiousness of his vocabulary, and his ease of mental action, and give to his recitation its highest educative result; while, under the second — the condition of a "passive recipient", — there will always be apparent to every discerning person, an inexact apprehension of the thought presented, a certain degree of insincerity, strengthened into a mental habit through fear of ridicule, and mental powers "rusting in disuse". Even apt pupils, under such conditions, will become, at best, theorists or dreamers — critics, ready to pass judgment upon others' performances, but powerless to act for themselves. The utmost that can be claimed for this method is, that a single faculty, that of memory, has been cultivated; while this cultivation has been accomplished not only by the neglect, for the time being, of the other powers, but at their expense; since the pupil is daily becoming confirmed in the idea that they are properly exercised, and, by pursuing all future studies in the same way, acts to their permanent injury.

It is not intended by this to discountenance the explanation of those difficult points, which will always occur, sometimes through a feebleness of the pupil's understanding, and at others through a failure of the text-book to supply a link necessary to the continuity of thought. Such explanations are legitimate, and should be made in language suited to the pupil's comprehension; the most thoughtful educators agreeing in this, that one of the gravest errors on the part of the teacher is an explanation in terms so unfamiliar as to be unintelligible, or so as to leave on the mind of the pupil only a vague and unsatisfactory impression. One of the most conspicuous merits of an able teacher is his ability to explain, in concise and simple language, the difficulties which necessarily beset the paths of his pupils. But it must always be borne in mind that one of the greatest merits of a recitation is to compel the pupil to discover and present for himself the difficulties which he has encountered.

The method of *simultaneous recitation* is open to the objection that by it the errors of backward pupils — and those, therefore, who are most in need of instruction — are concealed under the readiness of the more forward. The result usually anticipated from this method, *Simulta-* i. e., a quickening of the mental powers of backward pupils *neous* under the spur of emulation, does not appear in practice. Says *recitation.* an eminent teacher, "Simultaneous recitation may sometimes be useful. A few questions thus answered may serve to give animation to a class, when their interest begins to flag; but that which may serve as a stimulant must not be relied on for nutrition. As an example of its usefulness, I have known a rapid reader tamed into due moderation by being put in companionship with others of slower speech, just as we tame a friskful colt by harnessing him into a team of grave old horses. But aside from such definite purpose, I have seen no good come of this innovation". Though this method is resorted to often from necessity in large schools, its operation should be carefully watched. It is open, also, to the objections common to all rote teaching, the answer committed to memory from the book being never so sure an indication of the pupil's apprehension of the meaning, as his answer, before the class, in his own language. This latter furnishes not only an accurate register of the pupil's real progress, but is a mental exercise of the highest value, since it leads to accuracy of conception and expression, and increases the power of continuous thinking. (See CONCERT TEACHING.)

The first requisite for skillfully conducting a recitation is a thorough preparation by the teacher for the particular lesson he is to hear, so that he may be able to follow each step taken by the pupil, and may *Prepara-* stand ready, at any moment, to supply the needed word in *tion of the* which the pupil is striving to embody his thought. This word, *teacher.* in case the pupil's conception of the idea is correct, but its expression unfamiliar, will usually be some simple generic one for which the special or technical word may properly be substituted by the teacher. Another point to be remembered is the *order in which the different parts* *Order of* of *a subject are presented.* Where these parts depend upon *presen-* each other by a natural progression, as they frequently do, a *tation.* skillful teacher will so order the recitations of a class that those parts of the subject which are the natural stepping-stones to other parts, shall be presented first, such an arrangement conducing powerfully to a correct comprehension of the subject as a whole. In some studies — in the natural and exact sciences, almost always — this method is absolutely necessary; but, while in other branches its value is not so apparent, the advantage to be derived from its adoption is generally considerable.

A thorough comprehension by the pupils of the subject under consideration will insure the maintenance of three other conditions necessary to success in teaching, and usually quite strenuously insisted on by writers on the subject; namely, *animation, attention*, and a *natural tone*. When pupils understand what they are reciting, their attention and animation are, by that fact, made certain; and a natural tone is instinctively adopted. In youth, the appetite for new truths is so eager, the exultant feeling which accompanies the conquest of difficulties is so keen, that the reflection of this in the voice and manner of the pupil is a matter of certainty. Indeed, their opposites, — inattention and want of animation, are generally considered by educational writers as an indication of a want of comprehension — as the sure test by which the teacher may, at any moment, judge of the success of his instruction. The *length of recitations* has been more carefully considered during the past few years than ever before, the weight of authority having constantly inclined to a diminution of the time considered proper for this purpose only a generation ago. Currie, for example, considers that fifteen minutes is the proper medium for classes of very young children, twenty being the maximum; while half an hour is the average for classes generally, the fixing of the attention for a longer period not being attended with profit. In classes of older children, and in advanced instruction, the time of recitation may, of course, be considerably prolonged beyond these limits, the principle, however, being still carefully observed. The following is the view of a recent writer: "The best results are secured within the following limits: (1) Primary school, from 10 to 20 minutes; (2) Grammar school, from 20 to 30 minutes; (3) High school, from 30 to 40 minutes; (4) College, from 40 to 60 minutes". — D. P. Page says on this subject: "As a motive for every teacher to study carefully the art of teaching well at the recitation, it should be borne in mind that then and there he comes before his pupils in a peculiar and prominent manner; it is there his mind comes specially in contact with theirs, and there that he lays in them, for good or for evil, the foundations of their mental habits. It is at the recitation in a peculiar manner that he makes *his mark* upon their minds; and as the seal upon the wax, so his mental character upon theirs leaves its impress behind".

RELIGIOUS EDUCATION is that which has for its special object the cultivation of that faculty of the human soul by means of which it is enabled to realize the existence and constant presence of the Deity, to know Him, and to commune with Him in worship and prayer. Some have designated this the *religious sentiment;* but strong exception has been taken to that term, as belittling the basis of religion in the human soul. An experience of human nature, in its various degrees of culture, shows that there are what may be called religious intuitions, common to all minds of whatever grade of development; but that while these may prompt to worship, yet, without religious instruction, they can lead only to superstitious and debasing practices. The religious or spiritual instinct does not necessarily involve any act of the intellect; for those whose intellectual education and endowments are quite inferior, often show a surprising degree of spiritual insight and religious fervor. This fact, however, does not supersede the necessity of appealing to the understanding in imparting knowledge of those religious truths which have been communicated by divine revelation; but,

Intellect. in receiving these truths, the intellect assumes the attitude of faith rather than of inquiry; that is to say, having become satisfied of the authenticity, or the authority, of the source whence these truths, or dogmatic teachings emanate, it does not exercise its powers to establish their validity, but only to conceive them in their true import and relations. Hence, the intellect is not to be cultivated by means

Office of religious education. of religious instruction; although its exercise cannot wholly be dispensed with. The specific office of religious education is thus twofold: (1) to cultivate the religious instincts; and (2) to impart religious truth. The one is accomplished by means of devotional exercises; the other, by dogmatic teachings. In the first stages of religious education, appropriate exercises constitute almost the only agency needed, nothing but the simplest religious truths being requisite (such as are usually contained in the catechism); but, in the more advanced period of culture, the importance of dogmatic instruction increases. Simple prayers and hymns, with just enough teaching to enable the child to realize their full significance, are the usual and the most effective means of exercising the religious faculty. It must, however, be borne in mind,

Prayers. that the mere saying of a prayer, or the singing of a hymn, will not necessarily give this exercise, any more than merely committing to memory a definition or a rule will exercise the intellect. The mechanical repetition of prayers, in religious education, is just as useless as rote-teaching in intellectual education. By an inattention to this principle on the part of parents and religious teachers, no doubt, many children become disgusted with religious devotion, while others imbibe the notion that religion is only a matter of forms and ceremonies, or the repeating of the catechism. In either case, the religious instinct becomes dormant for the want of due exercise.

The relation of moral and religious education should be carefully studied. In brief, it may be said that the former deals with the relations which mankind sustain to each other; and the latter, with those which man

Moral & religious education. as a spiritual being sustains to the Infinite Spirit, the Creator and Preserver of all things. In the one, the principle addressed is that of conscience (q. v.), the sense of right; in the other, it is the religious principle, the spiritual instinct, by which man is brought into communion with his Maker. (See MORAL EDUCATION.) In a certain sense, these two departments of education are independent, for conscience operates independently of religion; but a religious sanction is the strongest foundation for moral precepts. For this, the Christian revelation affords the fullest authority, the "first and great commandment" being to love God; and the second, "to love thy neighbor as thyself". The several departments of education are not to be divorced from one another, but all are to be carried on together, so as to produce a harmonious development of character. (See HARMONY OF DEVELOPMENT.)

In imparting religious instruction, the same principles are to be applied as in intellectual education, as far as language is the vehicle of the instruction. Very much of the religious teaching given in the *Principles & methods.* Sunday-school is of no value, because of the neglect to observe these principles. Committing to memory formulated dogmas, verses from the Bible, doctrinal lessons, etc., without any proper appreciation of their significance, can be of little service; and in some cases may do positive harm. Oral instruction plays a most important part in this kind of teaching; and Bible expositions, when clear, definite, and illustrative, always prove the most effective as well as the most attractive means of instruction. In the effort to avoid sectarianism, the secularization of the common schools in the United States has been carried to the extreme, and religious education has been too much neglected. It is well said by Baldwin, in *The Art of School Management* (N. Y., 1881), that "society in its protest against bigoted ecclesiasticism and clerical control in education, rushes to the other extreme — non-religion. All agree that sound morality must be made the very sub-basis of an educational system. But how shall we build up moral character, if we exclude from our schools God, the Bible, responsibility, future life?"

REWARDS, as an instrument of family or school discipline, are benefits or privileges conferred to incite children to well-doing. Primarily, the offer of a reward, as an incitement to effort on the part of *To what they appeal.* the pupil, appeals to *hope*, as punishment does to *fear*; but there are other elements of individual character also addressed, depending on (1) the nature of the reward offered, and (2) the individuality of the pupil. Thus, the pupil who is particularly fond of praise, if offered a valuable gift as an inducement to do right, would strive to obtain it as a striking token of his teacher's approval; while one who was naturally acquisitive, or eager for gain, would regard only the intrinsic value of the reward. Hence, in one case, the pupil's approbativeness would be stimulated; and, in the other, his acquisitiveness; but in neither would the sense *Caution.* of duty be cultivated. The necessity of exercising great care in offering rewards will, therefore, be obvious. While an appeal to hope as an incentive to do right, is in most cases, if not always, preferable to an appeal to fear; yet, it must be borne in mind that rewards as well as punishments constitute only a temporary expedient in the discipline of children, and should, as soon as possible, give place to a direct appeal to conscience, or the sense of right. (See CONSCIENCE.) When rewards are offered to a number of pupils, to be conferred upon those who excel all the others, they become *prizes*, and are liable to all the objections *Prizes and premiums.* which have been urged against the prize system; but when rewards *(premiums)*, whether gifts of money, books, pictures, or other articles of value, or merely tickets or certificates of merit, are offered to all who reach a certain specified standard of merit, either in study or behavior, these objections are obviated; as, although the mercenary spirit may still be addressed, there is not the same liability to injustice, or the same cause of envy and jealousy. Rewards may, however, consist *Privileges.* merely of special privileges conferred upon meritorious pupils; such as dismissal before the usual time for closing school, permission to occupy some post of honor or authority in connection with the management of the school or class, or to engage in some special sport or recreation planned by the teacher, as a means of encouraging well-doing. All these, doubtless, have their place in a proper scheme of school discipline; and, when used with discrimination, are beneficial.

A system of rewards has been objected to as appealing to the lower, rather than to the higher, motives; but an educator must not be led astray by any transcendental view of human nature. He must rec-*Objections.* ognize the moral imperfections of his pupil, and strive to lift him gradually to a higher plane of thought and action. In this connection, it has been properly remarked, "whatever may be possible in the mature man, in the line of that sublime abstraction, *virtue is its own reward*, the child is neither equal to such abstractions, nor are they demanded of him. They may, it is true, be gradually wrought by instruction into the body of his thought, for the sake of their ultimate effect on his principles as a man; but, embraced, as he is, in a world of perceived realities, and only capable of attaining the subtler ideals by passing to them through the fine gradations of a progressively reduced and sublimated reality, it is absurd and tyrannous to rob him of the stimulus, guidance, and aid of proper rewards as outward realities foreshadowing the ideal of absolute virtue, and rendering possible both its conception and attainment".

RHETORIC (Gr. ῥητορική, art of oratory) was originally applied to that branch of study in which students were trained for public speaking. In Greece and Rome, the orator was directly the most powerful *Province of rhetoric.* exponent of truth and opinion. As a teacher, as well as a persuader, his influence was, to a great extent, confined to his hearers; and eloquence was, therefore, in the greatest request. But, even in the writings of the three greatest of the ancient rhetoricians, — Aristotle, Cicero, Quintilian, there is evidence that rhetoric embraced compositions not intended for delivery in public. In modern times, rhetoric as an art treats of all composition, whether spoken or written. It has been well defined as the *art of discourse*, and discourse itself as "the capacity in man of communicating his mental states to other minds by means of language". It embraces poetry as well as prose "because", as Campbell says, "the same medium, language, is made use of; the same general rules of composition, in narration, description, and argumentation, are observed; and the same tropes and figures, either for beautifying or invigorating the diction, are employed by both. The versification is to be considered as an appendage rather than a constituent of poetry". In the most recent treatises on rhetoric, elocution, or the art of delivery, has been omitted. Day very justly says, "that this mode of communication is not essential. The thought may be conveyed by the pen or by the voice. Elocution, or the vocal expression of thought, is not. accordingly, a necessary part of rhetoric". In Whately's treatise (*Elements of Rhetoric*), however, a work considerably used by students, a large part is devoted to elocution.

It has often been observed that there must have been orators before there were rules in oratory; and this is often used as an argument for undervaluing the study of rhetoric, just as kindred arguments *Value as a study.* are advanced against the study of logic and grammar. But there can be no question that immense progress has been made through the critical study of writers of standard reputation by comparing, discriminating, and deciding on, their faults and graces, thus teaching us what to avoid, and what to emulate. In its best sense, rhetoric presupposes an acquaintance with logic — the science and art of reasoning; because conviction and persuasion are two of the great objects present in the minds of speakers and writers. It also requires an acquaintance with grammar, as teaching the proper arrangement of words and sentences. Rhetoric may be regarded from two points of view: (1) as a purely critical study; and (2) as the constant practice of an art. To the extent that either of these views becomes more prominent in the teacher's mind, will the character of his instruction be affected. It is quite possible to prepare students to recite well in the statement of principles and definitions; and yet the same students may be very deficient in the development or expression of spoken or written thought. In the celebrated treatise of Blair, *Lectures on Rhetoric and Belles-Lettres*, taste and style are so treated as to occupy a very large part of the subject. It is largely so with Campbell's *Philosophy of Rhetoric*. Whately drew particular attention to the subject of *invention;* but he follows style with a chapter on *elocution*. The practice, at present, which seems to be increasing in favor with teachers, is to omit elocution, or the training in mere delivery, and to extend the importance of invention even beyond that assigned to it by Whately. The two great divisions of rhetoric are thus invention and style. There can be no question as to the importance of *invention* in rhetoric. The arrangement of the thoughts according to their logical dependence must be the foundation of the art of discourse. Good thinking must always precede good writing. The office of invention is to train the pupil to habits of correct thinking. It does more than this; it seeks to supply the thought. Thus, invention is naturally divided into two parts, — the supplying of the thought, and its proper arrangement; and of these two divisions, the second is dependent on the first. It may, however, be doubted, whether invention be properly studied at the early age when pupils are usually required to study rhetoric. In many of its steps, it is essentially logical, and presupposes an acquaintance with that subject, — and this again demands some considerable maturity of mind. The preparation of arguments, or the art of influencing the will by discourse, is a power the development of which goes on past middle age; but it is a power that cannot be successfully trained in very early years. The chief danger in teaching this particular division of rhetoric, is that it may be made too scientific. There are few young minds so trained, or of such native vigor, as to be capable of dwelling long, and with benefit upon even well enunciated truths and definitions; but, even where it is insisted on and continued, the results are not always beneficial.

The second grand division of rhetoric, *style*, deals more particularly with the form of the thought. Perhaps no word has given more difficulty to define. Without speech, "thought is not possible in reality". Though so endlessly variable in its form, so subtle as almost to defy minute analysis, so subject to the moods of thought, and yet so plastic as to conform to its most sinuous and involved movements, we soon realize by a little study, how completely it is a part of the thinking. The thought and the style are thus seen to be one living body. As a subject of study, it is that part of rhetoric which has always created and maintained the greatest interest in the minds of young students. Treating of the form of the sentence, and also of its component words, it depends, to some extent, on grammar, and may be said to follow it, in a natural order of study. It is, therefore, to young minds more suitable than the other division — invention. The practice which it requires in the substitution of words, the inversion of sentences from grammatical to rhetorical forms, the use of rhetorical figures, the expansion and contraction of language, furnishes a constant stimulus to mental exertion. Such exercises in style show the student how powerfully the thought is influenced by the vehicle of thought, how it may be modified by the substitution of a clearer word, or remarkably affected by a different position of the same words.

Sentential analysis. The advantage of *sentential analysis* in the careful study of style can scarcely be overrated. The arrangement of words, phrases, and clauses, peculiar to the great English writers, affect most powerfully the turn of the thought, and are open to investigation through this analysis. The kind of sentences they use, and the variety in which they indulge, give that harmony of movement so indescribably pleasing. We, thus, see from what arise the clearness and greatness of Hume, the energy and brilliancy of Macaulay, the grace of Irving, the manly vigor of Sydney Smith, the philosophic calmness of Helps, the incomparable plasticity and fire of Byron's prose. Perhaps no part of rhetoric offers a finer field for both teacher and student than the application of sentential analysis to an investigation of the striking peculiarities in the style of great writers.

In no branch of study, is there greater necessity for abundance of practice on the part of the student. In none is there greater necessity that the student, and not the teacher, should do the chief part of the work.

Need of practice. The value of rhetoric, as a branch of study, is to be tested by its practical utility, by what it contributes towards developing clearness, force, and beauty of expression in language. Anything else, however scientific, in this branch must prove to the young student a comparatively barren and irksome task. In this light, the constant application of a few simple principles to the criticism of great writers is an admirable part of the training. In Blair's *Lectures on Rhetoric*, there is a series of papers from Addison illustrating this view; and it is to be doubted whether modern treatises on rhetoric, aiming at a more philosophic treatment of the subject, while they have gained in scientific arrangement, may not have lost some of this critical training. Accuracy, as well as force of expression, purity, propriety, grace, are, to most students, the result of constant, careful practice, combined with criticisms on distinguished writers.

ROTE-TEACHING, or Teaching by Rote (Fr. *route*, road, whence *routine*), a method of giving instruction by means of constant repetition, particularly of certain forms of speech, with little or no attention to their meaning. Hence, such teaching is often described as *mechanical*, that is, impressing the memory through the ear and the eye, but not exercising the understanding. Rote-teaching may be regarded as an abuse of the principle of repetition. (See ASSOCIATION, and CONCERT TEACHING.)

SCHOOL (Lat. *schola*, from Gr. σχολή, leisure, especially for literary studies, and hence applied to the place where such studies were pursued,— a school), a term now applied to an educational establishment, particularly of the primary or secondary grade; as a primary school, a grammar school, a high school, a classical school, etc. Schools of the secondary grade are, however, often designated *academies, seminaries,* etc. The term *school* is not applied to an institution of learning of the superior grade, but institutions for scientific or professional instruction are usually called *schools;* as theological schools, medical schools, law schools, polytechnic schools, art schools, etc.

SCHOOL ECONOMY, a general term applied to the collective body of principles and rules by which the keeping of schools is regulated. In its widest sense, it embraces all that pertains to the construction and furnishing of the school-house, the proper apparatus to be employed in carrying on the processes of instruction, the various modes of school organization and administration, including a consideration of the length and arrangement of school sessions and terms, the proper records to be kept, the course of study, programme of daily exercises, and the modes of discipline, management, and instruction.

SCHOOL FURNITURE. Under this head will be considered (1) desks and seats; (2) platform; (3) blackboard; and (4) miscellaneous furniture and apparatus.

In the matter of health, desks and seats are, perhaps, the articles of the greatest importance in the school room. Notwithstanding their importance, however, as deciding the pupil's position for several *Desks and* hours of the day, and thus determining, in a great measure, his *seats.* future health and bearing, school authorities are not yet entirely agreed as to their style, dimensions, or arrangement; each civilized country using its own, on account of some peculiar advantage, the relative value of which is determined by observation from its own stand-point. The first consideration, in the construction or arrangement of desks and seats, should have regard to their influence upon the health of the pupils; the second, to the convenience of the teacher and pupils, in the adjustability of the desk and seat for different exercises, or for purposes of school government, which last would be determined principally by the arrangement, and the means afforded for facilitating the entrance or exit of the pupils. Of the comparative advantages of different styles of desks or seats, it is not necessary here to speak, the subject being treated exhaustively in the works referred to at the end of this article. The books that have been written on this subject in different countries form almost a library of themselves. Perhaps the best form yet devised is that described in the report of M. Buisson, French commissioner to the Exposition at Vienna in 1873, which was selected for special commendation, after an examination of all the styles there presented. It is known as the Bapterosses desk and seat, from the name of the inventor, who designed it for use in his factory at Briare. It has recently been introduced into the normal school at Auteuil. The chair is single, the seat being of wood, round or square in shape, and supported by an iron leg which slides up or down in a sheath, or hollow cylinder, the base of which is firmly screwed to the floor. The leg and sheath together form the support of the seat, which is checked at any height, in its upward or downward motion, by a thumb-screw. The back of the chair is of the ordinary pattern, and is slightly inclined. The desk is stationary, and is supported by a cast-iron upright. Its upper surface is divided into two parts in the usual manner —a narrow horizontal part at the back, and a sloping part, much larger, and nearer the pupil. It is provided either with a lid which converts the desk into an ordinary box, or, if the top is not movable, with compartments which open laterally. A small leaden pipe, extending the whole length of the desk, under the horizontal part of the upper surface, serves as an inkstand. It is provided with a vent at each end, secured by a copper cap, and, opposite the pupil, is pierced to receive a small copper funnel of sufficient size to allow only the point of the pen to enter. By this arrangement, the pupil can neither dip his pen too deeply, so as to get too much ink, nor upset his inkstand. Near the foot of the leg of the desk is a foot-rest, which may be raised or lowered by the same device of slide and thumb-screw that is used for the seat. The thumb-screws used on the chair and desk are, so arranged that they cannot be turned except by a key, which is kept by the teacher. The principal advantage of this desk is, that it can be adapted to pupils of different heights; its other recommendations are obvious. An improvement, perhaps, might be made by providing the desks with two supports instead of one, thus securing a firmness which desks supported by one central pillar do not usually have. The single desk should be 2 feet long, from 25 in. to 29 in. high, and 18 in. wide; the double desk should be 4 feet long, the other dimensions being the same as those of the single desk. The seats should be from 12 in. to 16. in high. Recitation seats as well as desk seats should be provided with backs. It should not be forgotten, however, that no arrangement of desk or seat, however ingeniously adapted to the pupil's comfort, can take the place of that frequent change of position which is a necessity of his being. Of the dimensions of desks and seats, Robson says, after a careful comparison of the works of Zwey, Falk, Frey, Cohn, Kleiber, and Virchow, " The weight of opinion is to the effect that the height of the seat should correspond to the length of the scholar's leg, from the knee to the sole of the foot. There must be no stretching of muscles; therefore, the sole of the foot must rest on the floor or upon some flat surface. If the seat be too high, the swinging of the foot in the air causes a compression of the blood-vessels and nerves of the hinder part of the leg and knee; if it be too low, the thighs of the scholar are pressed against his stomach to the disadvantage of health. * * * In order to prevent the scholar's slipping forward, the seat should be slightly declined backward. The height of the desks should be so arranged, that the under part of the arm may rest comfortably on the desk-top, and that the powers of vision may not be strained, or, in other words, that the normal distance of vision may be preserved. Desks which are too low cause, by the bending of the scholar, a pressing on the chest and lower part of the body; while those which are too high cause the right shoulder to be so lifted, as to remove the upper part of the arm so far from the body, that the lower arm cannot be laid flat on the table, thereby causing the arm to be unsteady and easily tired". Much ingenuity has been exercised in devising seats capable of transformation into a variety of forms. The tendency in this respect is frequently towards a mechanism so complicated that it defeats its own object by becoming easily disarranged; and, even if this were not the case, many of the transformations will usually be found to be useless. The really desirable changes of form are very few. Says an eminent educator: "If seats could be so contrived as to remain firm when placed horizontally, to allow the pupil to lean forward easily to write upon his desk, and then could be made to have an inclination backward when the pupil desires to read or study, it would add much to his comfort in sitting, and something, perhaps, to the comeliness of his figure". Concerning the distance of the seat from the desk, a considerable difference of opinion exists, some teachers considering only one inch necessary, others as much as three. On this point Dr. Wiese says: "It is, therefore, desirable, that the inner edge of the desk should be distant from the front of the seat only about one inch". Robson says: "The scholar who sits too far from the desk, either bends too much, and thereby hurts his chest and eyes, or he glides too far forward on his seat, and so gets an unsteady position. * * * It is recommended that the vertical distance from the desk to the seat-top should be the length of the fore-arm, or one-sixth the size [height] of the body of the scholar. Too great a distance encourages crooked growth; for the scholar, while writing, has his body weighing on one arm, instead of having the arm naturally resting on his body. If the difference in height between the desk and the seat be too slight, then the chest sinks, and the back is bent out so as to encourage stooping". Of the *arrangement* of desks, many methods have been advocated, and different ones prevail in different countries; but the weight of authority seems to be in favor of seating the pupils in pairs. this method being economical as to space, and more advantageous for both teacher and pupil in the efficient carrying out of the daily exercises. Its superiority, also, in the matter of ingress and egress of the pupils is manifest. The arrangement of desks in regard to space and light has been considered in the article HYGIENE, SCHOOL. Many other considerations present themselves in this connection, the chief of which are the following: the form and height of the back of the seat; its attachment to, or independence of, the desk immediately behind it; the variation in the height of seats and desks as arranged on the same level for pupils of different sizes; the slope of the floor, or its construction in steps, for the same purpose; the movable desk or seat as compared with the stationary; the mountings of desks and seats on casters; the varying slope of the desk-top for different purposes; the space between the desks; the breadth of aisles, etc. These are all considered, however, in works specially written for the purpose; and the merits of each for different purposes are fully set forth.

Platform. The platform is now considered highly desirable, if not indispensable, in the school room. On all public occasions, whether of examination or exhibition, it is indispensable; while there are many occasions in the usual routine of the school, when it is exceedingly useful. It should be not less than 6 feet wide, and 15 inches high, and should be divided into two levels or risers. In schools in which all the exercises are conducted in one room, closets for the storing of school apparatus are often placed at each end of the platform. Recitation rooms are usually fitted up without platforms, the teacher's desk standing on the floor.

At the back of the platform, against the wall, and facing the school or class, is placed the blackboard. It should extend the entire length of the platform, should be at least 4 feet wide, and extend to within three feet of the floor. It should be provided with a frame all around, and a trough at the lower edge for the chalk, and to catch dust, and should have hooks, on which pointers may be hung. The material of blackboards is of three kinds: wood, slate, and a kind of slate-surface made to lay directly on the wall. The last, by combining in a medium the best qualities of the two others, is the most desirable. (See BLACKBOARD.)

Blackboard.

The principal consideration under the head of furniture and apparatus is not so much the comparative values of different articles, but what articles are indispensable or, at least, highly necessary. Among these, may be mentioned a clock, a small bell for the calling and dismissing of classes, chairs for visitors, closets or wardrobes, provided with wrought-iron hooks and pegs, a thermometer, sets of maps and charts, a terrestrial globe, an abacus, or numeral frame, and a collection of miscellaneous articles to be used in giving object lessons. The extent to which the articles desirable for the school room have been added to, and perfected, both in the United States and on the continent of Europe, is remarkable; the list given above, however, furnishes a tolerably complete outfit for a primary school. One consideration remains to be insisted on; namely, the exercise of good taste in the selection of furniture and articles intended to be in constant sight of the pupils. On this subject, the architect of the London School Board remarks: "The furniture of the school room should be graceful in form, and good in quality and finish. Children are particularly susceptible of surrounding influences, and their daily familiarization with beauty of form or color, in the simplest and most ordinary objects, cannot fail to assist in fostering the seeds of taste, just as daily discipline tends to promote habits of order. Furniture finished like good cabinet work is more likely to be respected, even by the mischievous school boy, than that of an unsightly or rough character". — For further information on this subject see *Cyclopædia of Education*.

Furniture and apparatus.

SCHOOL-HOUSE. — Of the first importance in any system of public instruction, is *school architecture*, including every thing that relates to the building in which the instruction is to be imparted. All matters that concern the health of the school; namely, the situation of the school-house, its furniture, the temperature of the rooms, and the means for warming, lighting, and ventilating them, are considered either in separate articles in this work, or under the head of HYGIENE, SCHOOL. It is designed here specially to treat of (I) the construction of the school-house, and (II) its internal arrangement.

I. What material should be used in the construction of a school building depends entirely upon its location and the means at command. Owing to the improved modern methods of building, wood, brick, or stone may be used indifferently, as far as healthfulness is concerned, economic considerations alone deciding which is to be employed. It may be said, in general, that these considerations point to the use of stone or brick in cities and towns, and of wood in the rural districts, except in old and thickly-settled countries where wood is scarce. The increased attention bestowed upon the appearance of the school-house at the present

Construction.

time is one of the most encouraging proofs of the general and permanent interest aroused in the welfare of schools, since purely esthetic considerations are generally the last to make themselves felt. The rudeness of the district-school building is proverbial, yet the expression of the cherished memories that cluster around it forms a part of the choicest literature of every civilized country. If the transfiguring power of early association, therefore, renders it an object of affection through life, in spite of its uncouthness, how much stronger would that affection be if the matured taste of later years confirmed the preference of childhood! Not only the testimony of eminent writers, but the unwritten experience of every observing person, bears abundant witness to the subtle and enduring influence of early associations; and now, when the subject of education is receiving so large a share of careful thought, with a view to discover all available ways to perfect its means and methods, it would seem that this powerful agent should not be neglected. Without squandering money, therefore, to make the school-house pretentious, or a perfect specimen of one of the conventional orders of architecture, pains should be taken that it should not be an offense to the eye, or out of harmony with the landscape. Since this can generally be done, also, without any, or with only slight, additional cost, the educational value, moral and esthetic, of the appearance of the school-house, may properly be included in the plans of the architect. As to the solidity of the school building in all its parts, it is not too much to say that no financial objections which would impair this, should, for a moment, be entertained. The contingencies which may happen at any moment where large numbers of children are gathered together, are so momentous in their character, as to render this imperative. The size of the school-house should be determined, of course, by the number of pupils it is intended to accommodate. An eminent authority says that, a building designed for an ungraded school to be taught by a single teacher, should contain, at least, 900 sq. ft. of floor space; being intended to accommodate from 50 to 80 pupils. In regard to the proper size of class rooms, see HYGIENE, SCHOOL.

II. Every district-school house should have a vestibule, a main room, and one or more class-rooms, unless the school is taught by only one teacher. The vestibule should be commodious, dry, well-lighted, and properly supplied with pegs for hats and outer garments, mats, wash basins, and all means for ensuring personal cleanliness. In mixed schools, it should be divided into two rooms. The best authorities are almost unanimous in the opinion that the shape of the school room proper should be that of an oblong about twice as long as broad, the size being determined by the probable attendance. The ceiling should be from 12 to 15 feet in height, the controlling consideration being that each pupil should have not less than 108 cubic feet of air space. The door and the teacher's desk should be at opposite ends of the room, the former, when practicable, at the southern extremity, the northern being without windows, and provided with a shallow platform about 15 inches high. This arrangement enables the teacher to survey the school, and is simple and convenient for examination or exhibition purposes. Very large school rooms are not expedient, experience having shown that a large number of pupils may be supervised and taught to better advantage in two rooms of medium size, the teacher having an assistant for the purpose,

Internal arrangement.

than in one large room. A separate class room is indispensable in all schools, except the smallest, the number being increased according to the size of the school. In its construction, the class room should conform proportionally to the school room, and should, if possible, be in immediate connection with it, but separable from it completely as far as noise is concerned. The teacher's room, in small schools, could be utilized as the school library, or as a temporary storing place for such delicate apparatus as required special care. Schools of other grades and sizes will, of course, require a different arrangement of rooms. Nearly every civilized country, in fact, has its own plans for the construction of school-houses, and the arrangement of school and class rooms, determined by the peculiarities of its school system, or by national characteristics. See SCHOOL FURNITURE.

SCHOOL MANAGEMENT is a department of the teacher's profession which includes (I) the organization of the school, and (II) its conduct. Under the former, must be considered (1) the classification (see CLASS); (2) the distribution, as to order and time, of the branches to be taught, (course of instruction and programme); and (3) the proper assignment of the work of instruction (in a graded school) to the several teachers, either in accordance with the class system or with the departmental system (q. v.). The conduct of the school has reference (1) to instruction, and (2) to discipline. Great care should be taken, by means of a carefully constructed programme, or daily order of exercises, to secure to each subject its proper amount of time, according to its place in the course of instruction, as well as to insure an equable advancement on the part of the pupils in each subject of the grade, as preliminary to *promotion*. The promotion of pupils is a matter of great practical importance in the management of a school. One of the most serious errors made by teachers is the too rapid advancement of their pupils. Promotions should always be based upon a careful examination; and, in a graded school, care should be taken that every grade is passed through in a legitimate manner, that is, without hurry or cramming. When the school is ungraded, the advancement of individual pupils is to be considered; but there is the same need of avoiding haste, so as to secure thorough proficiency, as the basis of promotion. *Government* is, also, an important department of school management; since, without efficient government, all attempts at effective school instruction must be fruitless. (See COURSE OF INSTRUCTION, DISCIPLINE, and GOVERNMENT.)

SCHOOL RECORDS are of great importance, both in connection with the management of the school itself, and for the purpose of affording a means of obtaining accurate and valuable returns to be embodied in a general system of school statistics. These records are, therefore, to be arranged from a twofold stand-point: (I) What are needed as auxiliary to the keeping and instruction of the school itself; and (II) What are required for a proper administration of the school laws, as well as to show the condition of the system to which the school belongs, and the progress of education in the town, city, and state in which it is located, as compared with other places.

I. For the carrying out of the first object, there should be an accurate registration of each pupil's name and age, his parents' name, the date of his admission into the school, of his successive promotion from grade to grade, and of his discharge, with the cause of the same, thus presenting a history in outline of the pupil's whole career in the school.

Register. The register kept for these items should be in such a form as to be easy of reference, either by a numerical designation of the pupils in the order of their admission, or by an alphabetical arrangement. Auxiliary to the *school-register*, there may be (in large schools, should be) an *admission book*, and a *discharge book*; the entries being first made in these books, and transferred at stated times (weekly or monthly) into *Auxiliary records.* the *register*. The *admission book* should contain a statement of the antecedents of the pupil, and the *discharge book*, the cause of his leaving the school, and his destination. There should, also, be books showing the school history of the pupil more in detail, as his daily attendance, conduct, merit and demerit marks for recitations, etc. One book, usually called the *roll book*, may be used for all these particulars, there being, in a graded school, one such book for each class, and kept by the class teacher. In this book may also be entered the place of residence of each pupil, in order to facilitate communication with the parents. The *school diary* is auxiliary to this, containing transcripts from the *roll book*, with summaries of marks and a statement of class standing, the pupil being required to take this diary home for the inspection and signature of his parents. Other records, besides those enumerated, may be kept for special purposes; but, ordinarily, these are all that are indispensably requisite to carry on the internal operations of the school.

II. The records made necessary by the provisions of law under which the school is established and supported, will vary, of course, with the nature of those provisions, and with the organization of the system to which the school belongs. But there are certain common and *Legal records.* indispensable features, inasmuch as there are facts which all school records for this purpose should aim to show, among which may be mentioned the following: (1) The number of pupils enrolled during the year; (2) The average enrollment, or "average number belonging"; (3) The number in attendance at each session of the school; and (4) the number of pupils of each grade, and of certain specified ages. — No attempt is made in this article to present the forms of these records, as there is a wide diversity of form in different places, and as the form is of secondary importance to the presenting of the required facts.

SCIENCE, the Teaching of. In this article, the treatment will refer to the teaching of science (I) as a branch of elementary instruction, and (II) as a department of higher education.

1. This subject is one into which great confusion has been introduced by the use of the words *science* and *scientific* in two different senses. In *What is science.* the strict sense of the term, the scientific knowledge of a subject is a knowledge of the laws which harmonize and explain its various phenomena. Science goes beyond mere appearances, and finds that, amidst endless variety, there is unity; and, amid apparent discord, there is harmony. In this sense, it is the highest outcome of intellectual effort. The human mind deals first with the concrete. For a long time it scarcely rises above the information of the senses. It then groups the impressions of the senses into more comprehensive unities, and in this process gains a certain power of abstraction. But science supposes

that the mind has been long practiced in that power of abstraction and generalization. It views in succession the principal facts in any department of nature as a whole, and it seeks to find the invisible order which pervades them all. In this sense of the term, also, all subjects admit of scientific treatment; as there can be no doubt that law pervades all phenomena, there must be a science of mental phenomena as well as of physical phenomena; and, therefore, no single phenomenon can exist which has not its own place in the system of the universe. But, from various considerations, the term *science* has been often restricted to the explanation of the laws which regulate matter, and this is the sense in which it is used in this article. Now it is plain that, in the strict sense of the term, children cannot be taught science. If the scientific stage is the highest in the development of the intellectual faculties, we cannot expect to find it in the school. It belongs to the university. But we may lay the foundation of it at an earlier period. Indeed, we cannot help doing something toward this work; but we may do it awkwardly and unconsciously, or skillfully and consciously. The latter is the function of the educated teacher. We must, therefore, inquire more minutely into the mode in which the foundations of science are laid. For this purpose we shall quote the words of the late Professor Payne. Science he defined as "organized knowledge", and, after explaining the meaning of *organized* in this definition, he proceeds: "Returning to the other factor of the definition, *knowledge*, we observe that there are two kinds of knowledge —

Two kinds of knowledge. what we know through our own experience, and what we know through the experience of others. Thus, I know by my own knowledge that I have an audience before me, and I know through the knowledge of others that the earth is 25,000 miles in circumference. This latter fact, however, I know in a sense different from that in which I know the former. The one is a part of my experience, of my very being. The other I can only be strictly said to know when I have, by an effort of the mind, passed through the connected chain of facts and reasonings on which the demonstration is founded. Thus only can it become my knowledge in the true sense of the term. Strictly speaking, then, organized knowledge, or science, is originally based on unorganized knowledge, and is the outcome of the learner's observation of facts through the exercise of his senses, and his own reflection upon what he has observed. This knowledge, ultimately organized into science through the operation of his mind, he may with just right call his own; and, as a learner, he can properly call no other knowledge his own. What is reported to us by another is that other's, if gained, at first-hand, by experience; but it stands on a different footing from that which we have gained by our own experience. He merely hands it over to us; but, when we receive it, its condition is already changed. It wants the brightness, definiteness, and certainty in our eyes, which it had in his; and, moreover, it is merely a loan, and not our property. The fact, for instance, about the earth's circumference was to him a living fact: it sprung into being as the outcome of experiments and reasonings, with the entire chain of which it was seen by him to be intimately — indeed, indissolubly and organically — connected. To us it is a dead fact, severed from its connection with the body of truth, and, by our hypothesis, having no organic relation to the living truths we have gained by our own minds. What I insist on, then, is, that the knowledge from experience — that which is gained by bringing our own minds into direct contact with matter — is the only knowledge that, as novices in science, we have to do with. The dogmatic knowledge imposed on us by authority, though originally gained by the same means, is really, not ours, but another's — is, as far as we are concerned, unorganizable, and, therefore, though science to its proprietor, is not science to us. To us it is merely information, or hap-hazard knowledge". — The account here given contains the very pith of the matter, and cannot be too deeply pondered and impressed on the mind; and we shall, therefore, put the same thoughts in another shape. The child

Generalization. first perceives individual objects. He notices the qualities in these objects; and, when he finds the same qualities recur in different individual objects, he naturally groups them together under the same notion or name. This is the child's first effort at generalization. (See INTELLECTUAL EDUCATION.) Now, it is plain that if he had not known the individuals, he could never have made the generalization; and that, if any one were to tell him the generalization without his having seen the individuals and noticed the similarity, the generalization

Rules for teaching science. would be of no real use to him. Out of this fact flow some of the principal rules in regard to the method of teaching science: (1) The pupil must be brought face to face with nature; he must see the individual; he must himself make the experiment. (2) He must make the generalization, himself; he must be a discoverer. It is here, however, that the skillful teacher can wisely interfere. The child, if left to himself, might be too long in making the discovery, for he might not stumble upon individuals which contain similarities. The teacher, therefore, takes care to bring similar individuals before his pupils in sufficient number. He sternly checks his own wish to shorten the work by telling the generalization; but he prepares the way for the pupil's making it by adducing instance after instance, until the similarities cannot but become visible to the pupil's mind. And this rule suggests another, — that, wherever it is possible, the pupil should be led along the road over which mankind traveled in making the discovery originally. He must, of course, commit many blunders before he reaches the truth; yet, under a skillful teacher, such a process is eminently educative. But, besides the making of generalizations, there is also the faculty of observation to be carefully cultivated. Indeed the cultivation of the faculty of observation is essentially necessary to the formation of correct generalizations. At first, the child makes his generalizations unconsciously. He sees a tree, and then another tree, and then another, and somehow they impress him as being like; but he has no accurate conception in regard to the points in which they are like. — Even when he becomes conscious of the points of resemblance in objects, he may find that the resemblances in them are on the surface, and that there are greater differences separating the objects from each other. He is now coming nearer the stage in which he can deal with a subject scientifically. For observation has to furnish, as the basis of scientific conceptions, a more accurate knowledge than that possessed by the ordinary observer. The pupil has to notice qualities which ordinarily escape observation. The teacher again must take the utmost care that the pupil has really observed the peculiarity before he tells him the special name given to it. Else the pupil's mind will be crammed with a number of technical terms of the meaning of which he probably will have no clear conception; and even should he have a clear conception of their meaning when he hears it from his teacher, he will be sure to forget it very soon. In one word, the pupil must conquer every step in science by personal observation and experience. He must find out every thing himself. The teacher has simply to arrange the order in which the facts of nature are to be presented to the pupil, and to lay before him only those phenomena which it is important for him to observe. From what has been said, it is plain that the plan of going through all the principal phenomena of a science is not to be adopted in schools. This is a method appropriate only to the last stage of scientific instruction. The teacher must select the portions of science which will be most educative; and he will treat them in such a way as to interest the pupil, and make him take an active part in ascertaining the facts of nature. At the same time, he will take care to make his various lessons bear on each other. Though he does not disclose a law, but leaves it to dawn upon the pupil's mind from the presentation of instances, he will see to it that each lesson adds to the structure which the previous one has helped to raise. He will have a fixed plan in his own mind; and he will look forward to the intellectual result which he is to produce, in process of time, by the examples and experiments which he makes the pupil observe and perform.

In all these considerations, we have been looking at science as a subject worthy of being studied for its own sake. This is unquestionably true. The intellectual powers of man are an essential feature of man's nature, and they demand exercise. This exercise is invariably accompanied by an intense pleasure. Now, the scientific knowledge of nature is eminently calculated to call the intellectual powers into activity, and therefore it opens up to man a source of pure and lasting enjoyment. But the teacher may look on the knowledge of science from other points of view. Man is corporeal, and his physical well-being depends on his coming into proper relations with physical nature. It is important for him to know these relations, and the teacher of youth will endeavor to enlighten the mind of his pupil in regard to them. At the same time, these relations are most deeply impressed on the mind, when the facts of science are taught according to the laws of education. If I inform a boy that carbonic acid gas is deleterious, the impression is of the faintest nature, and will not lead, in nine cases out of ten, to any action; but if I show the boy how to produce carbonic acid gas by the union of its component elements, that is, if I lead him to make experiments by which the truth will be forced upon his mind without my telling him that it is injurious to life; and if, in addition to this, I make him discover that he is continually exhaling this gas, he will be deeply impressed with the necessity of ventilation, and will make every effort to procure it. Then, again, nature presents herself not merely as the embodiment of law but also as the embodiment of beauty; and the teacher should, therefore, endeavor to bring out this feature occasionally. He will point, for example, to the exquisite structure of flowers; he will lead the child to feel the loveliness of landscapes; he will interest him in the habits of animals; in

Other considerations.

fact, he will try to make nature reveal herself to him in her concrete loveliness and variety.

Among the questions keenly discussed in connection with science teaching are (1) the order in which the sciences should be taught, and (2) what sciences are suitable for schools. Opinions on these subjects will necessarily differ until agreement as to the meaning of terms is reached. The fact is, as we have seen, that all the sciences call for processes of thought which can be reasonably expected only in mature minds; but it is true, at the same time, that separate facts, in all these sciences, tending toward a unity, may be discovered by a child of eleven or twelve years of age. Faraday said that chemistry could be taught to a boy of eleven; others denied that it could; and in a certain sense, both were right from their respective points of view. At the same time there is no doubt that the facts of some sciences, in the average, are much more complicated than those of other sciences; and, therefore, there is wisdom in teaching them in a certain order. Botany, for instance, is among the simplest of the sciences. It calls into play the power of minute observation. The child is interested in examining the structure of the plant and the growth of the various parts. An appeal is also made to his powers of grouping or, in other words, of classification. And the pupil has a large field in botany for these two activities. (See BOTANY.) The same is true of the other science of classification, zoölogy; but the processes are a little more complicated. It should, therefore, naturally follow botany. From these, the pupil should proceed to some department of physics, and from that, advance to chemistry. The one should go before the other, because the processes of chemical motion are much more difficult to observe accurately than those of mechanical motion. And the course of science might well end with physiology, in which many of the modes of reasoning employed are abstruse, and the student is continually liable to be misled by appearances and analogies.

Order of selection.

II. One of the most important aims of the educator is to lead man to recognize how to live most successfully for himself; to realize the responsibilities of his position, and, by seeking to comply with these responsibilities, to attain to the greatest possible happiness. In this process of education, the student must be led to recognize the material and physical conditions of his existence; to know himself, not as an independent being, but as one dependent upon the multifarious conditions of the vast scheme of nature, and as one, who, alike in what he is and in that of which he is capable, is strictly under the control of natural law. In other words, man can only know himself by comparison with other objects in nature, — can only know his powers by comparison with the forces by which other forms of matter are controlled.

An important aim.

Again, as a mere question of material prosperity, the study of natural science is forced upon our consideration. No thoughtful man wandering through the aisles of a great international exhibition can fail to see that all progress in applied science and the arts must be based, in the first place, upon an exact knowledge of natural resources, material and physical. It will be admitted that knowledge of all kinds is fundamentally based upon the evidence of our senses, but such evidence is apt to mislead, unless checked by experiment; experiment, to

Study of natural science.

be of real utility, must be exact and systematic. The reasoning that draws conclusions from such experiments must be logical; and language, at once ample and exact, is required as an implement, only of value when wielded with precision, to widen the fields of inquiry with the utmost economy of mental labor. We are compelled to make these remarks because the true importance of a scientific study of nature has not been recognized by the greater part of those who are engaged in education. A knowledge of the leading truths of natural science is, however, essential to education, (1) because of their fundamental character, and (2) because of the method by which such sciences are pursued, which method is the same as that which ought to obtain in every-action of our every-day lives. Comparing the training given by language and mathematics with that given by natural science, we see that, whilst language cultivates the memory, and mathematics trains the reasoning faculties, neither affords any means for the cultivation of observation and experiment. Turning to the natural sciences themselves, we find that the physical branches cultivate observation, experiment, and inductive reasoning; while the material branches, including the natural history sciences, cultivate especially the faculties of observation and systematic classification. But, in addition to this, from the multitudinous *data* with which the latter deal, and the impossibility of obtaining complete series of such *data*, these studies inevitably lead the inquiring mind to a constant consideration of probabilities, or, in other words, to a habit, of the utmost importance to us practically, of justly weighing circumstantial evidence. In view of the vast mass of facts accumulating more and more rapidly each day from the various fields of scientific investigation, it is impossible that any human mind can grasp all the details of even a single branch. The following considerations are, however, important in this view of education: (1) that, by experience in some two sciences, the one physical and the other relating to the forms assumed by matter, the student should learn the principles on which these natural sciences are pursued, and therefrom be able to appreciate the value of scientific training and knowledge; (2) that he should understand the general scope of the various sciences; (3) that he should be familiar with the broad generalizations of science; (4) that he should not be ignorant of such common scientific details as occur to us every day, and have an immediate and direct connection with our welfare and success in life; and (5) that he should be taught how to obtain information by reference, and how to weigh the trustworthiness of authorities. In order that the second and third of these requirements may be intelligently obtained, they must logically be preceded by the first, and simultaneously the acquisition of the knowledge implied by the fifth may well be commenced. In the physical branches of scientific inquiry, qualitative analytical chemistry theoretically best meets the requirements of the case; in the material sciences, we may select one of those which are called *natural history sciences*. Under this head, certain of the natural sciences which treat of the living forms of matter were formerly included; but the term is a most indefinite one, and must cease to be used at all, if confined to its old signification. The sciences especially included under it, botany and zoölogy, have been placed upon altogether new and broader foundations as branches of biology, so that they now cover morphological and physiological ground never contemplated in the old use of the term. There would seem to be a propriety in using the term to express that pursuit of nature which is essentially out-of-door in its character, — the study of the external relationship of beings to each other; and in this view we should certainly need to include geological investigations. At the same time, it will be apparent to every naturalist that the scope of such a term could not be rigorously defined. There can be no doubt that an out-of-door study of nature ought to be an essential element of education. It may be long before it is generally introduced into the course of school education, but it should certainly be enforced upon the community as a duty at least in home culture. It should be used to cultivate habits of close, exact and systematic observation, commenced in the field and continued in the laboratory; of judiciously collecting, carefully preserving and classifying, some one or more series of natural objects; and of referring for information not to be obtained by personal inquiry, regarding the objects observed and collected, to trustworthy sources. By well-judged, training in either botany or any one of the branches of zoölogy, the ends above indicated may be attained; whilst the general spirit of observation and inquiry in the wide field of natural science that will be encouraged, will lead to a breadth and liberality of mental tone. Nor need this general and more desultory observation be dreaded, as apt to lead to hasty, unfounded, and inexact acquirements, if the mind is duly drained, as had been suggested, in rigorous methods of thought by the exact pursuit of some special subject of scientific study. If there be any truth in the suggestions just thrown out, it will be apparent that such training in the natural history sciences cannot be commenced too early in life, because the spirit of the training is such that it should imbue the entire mental culture of the individual; and, furthermore, if this early training has been neglected, the study of science in an advanced period of education, will not be so successful, because it will lack the vivid conceptions which can only be acquired by the exercise of the observing faculties in early life. It only remains to add that, as all teaching by the very nature of these sciences must be objective, the duty of the instructor, at every stage of science teaching, is to supplement nature and not to take her place, — *Duty of the teacher.* not to impart information but to guide the pupil in the self-acquirement of knowledge. Books, similarly, are only to be permitted as dictionaries to explain such points as the pupil cannot elucidate by his own efforts. — For a valuable list of works on this subject, see *Cyclopædia of Education* and the Appendix of this work.

SCIENCE OF GOVERNMENT, the name given to a branch of instruction in primary or secondary schools, which is designed to impart to the pupils a knowledge of the political system under which they live, and to make them, as far as requisite, familiar with the different functions of government, and the mode in which they are performed. It, generally, includes a consideration of the constitution of the country or state, the qualifications and duties of the principal officers of government, the legal restrictions imposed upon citizens, and an outline of civil and municipal regulations. Many excellent treatises have been prepared for this purpose for use in elementary schools; and, there can be no question of the value of this department of instruction for all classes of pupils particularly in public schools, one of the most important objects of which is to prepare for intelligent and useful citizenship.

SECONDARY INSTRUCTION, that grade of instruction which is usually afforded in high schools, academies, etc., or in institutions above the ordinary grade of a common or primary school. This grade of instruction is intermediate between primary instruction and superior instruction, or that afforded in colleges and universities.

SELF-EDUCATION, that development of the powers which is carried on by the individual himself, without the aid of others. To a *What it is.* certain extent, this education is not only unconscious, but inevitable. The constant recurrence of like conditions or actions, the knowledge of which is conveyed to the individual by the senses, during the growth of mind and body, is always attended with an increased skill in the use of the powers of both, which, of itself, constitutes an education. *Agents.* The agents by which this knowledge is converted into an unconscious education are chiefly habit and experience; the one producing increased ease of action under like circumstances, and thus rendering the individual more capable; the other enabling him to systematize his knowledge, and to use it as an instrument for further acquisition. To determine, in all cases, just where this education ceases, and voluntary *Limit.* self-education begins, would probably be very difficult; yet, in general, it may be said that the active intervention of the will is the most obvious feature by which self-education may be distinguished. It is usually regarded as that education which is carried on intentionally, outside, or beyond the influence, of the school. Even here, however, the definition is imperfect; for it must always be difficult to estimate at its true comparative value the strength of each of two impulses which act thus at the same time and invisibly; but, probably, a truer conception of the two powers, self-education and school education, may be acquired by supposing the difference between them to be one of function rather than of degree — school education serving rather as a director or systematizer of power, while self-education must often be looked upon as identical with innate power, from our inability to separate the one from the other. We know what training the school gives; and, though we cannot analyze the results it produces with sufficient accuracy to assign to the school and to the individual the proper share due to each, we know from many comparisons made between countries with schools and those without them, that the advantage lies decidedly with the former. That the school is rather a director of power than a creator of it, is shown by contrasting the large number of men who have enjoyed its advantages without manifesting special ability afterward in any walk of life, with those who have risen to *Two kinds of education.* the highest positions without this privilege. Education is of two kinds, — practical and theoretical, the first based principally upon facts and experience, and dealing largely with human nature; the other, acquired from books, and concerning itself in great measure with abstractions and theories which, though valuable enough for purposes of general culture, are of little use in practical life, and, if exclusively pursued, produce a positive disqualification for it. Of these two kinds of education, it is hardly too much to say that the former is the more available, in the ordinary affairs of life, in a vast majority of cases. Hence, it should never be forgotten by the educator, that the facilities for mental acquisition which he offers the pupil by systematic instruction, too frequently result in vacillation, or feebleness of purpose, and are almost inevitably accompanied with a loss, on the part of the latter, of that vividness of apprehension which experimental acquaintance gives. The only amends, therefore, he can make is to render his instruction as practical, and as far removed from mere book-learning, as possible. Knowledge and rote-learning have often a wonderful resemblance, *Self-taught men.* while, essentially, they may have nothing in common. The picture of a Lincoln, hastily gathering book-knowledge by the light of the cabin fire; or of a Franklin, finding in the intervals of his work in a chandler's shop and a printing office, an equivalent for the school, should be a sufficient admonition to every teacher, that the privileges of the school room are not indispensable to the most brilliant success. It is not necessary to multiply instances of self-taught men; the ranks of greatness have been almost exclusively filled from this class. Three most valuable attributes are strengthened, if not created, by a course of *Advantages of self-education.* self-education: self-confidence, independence of judgment, and perseverance. He only who has always depended upon himself, knows accurately the limit of his powers, measures beforehand every difficulty, and does not look, at the last moment, for extraneous aid; while the habit of self-reliance thus cultivated, lays the foundation for a solidity of character which, in critical moments, is not swayed by fitful or transient influences. The third attribute, perseverance, is the necessary result of such an education. Having always been accustomed to encounter obstacles, and having always overcome them, the joy of conflict and the joy of conquest, become, to self-taught men, synonymous. The atmosphere of difficulty is as the breath of life and the result is never doubtful to those who gather strength from opposition. These are the most essential elements of success, and, in practical matters, weigh more than all the advantages of the school. On the other hand, the commonest *Disadvantages.* error of the self-taught man is a depreciation of all studies or pursuits which have no practical bearing. General culture — knowledge for itself alone, with all the pleasures and consolations which it brings — is underestimated. Accustomed always to see his thoughts followed by tangible results, the moral aspect of thought is lost sight of; and his ideal standard never rises above this utilitarian level. This narrowness of mind leads almost inevitably to a want of sympathy with liberal pursuits, and sometimes to a kind of hardness or positiveness of character which bears the appearance of arrogance. Weakness being scarcely understood by the successful, self-taught man, want of charity is a natural fruit of his habits of thought. These defects, however, are frequently removed by age; and, even at their worst, can hardly be said to be so serious as those which have been cited as incident to misdirected education in the school. Of the two kinds of education — self-education and school education, it may, therefore, be said in general, that the former is of greater value than the latter; that for all practical action in the familiar matters of daily life, all great emergencies, whether of peace or war, which require independence of judgment, promptness of decision or action, and inflexible perseverance, the self-taught man is vastly the superior; while, in purely speculative pursuits, in researches or projects undertaken without hope of immediate or material result, the man of the schools, whose education has been conducted with that broader outlook upon life which leads directly to culture solely for its own sake, manifests a far greater zeal and activity. Neither kind of education is to be commended by itself; since the deficiencies of one need to be supplied by the advantages of the other.

SEMINARY (Lat. *seminarium*) a place where seed is sown, from *semen*, seed), a term, used in education to denote an institution of learning of any grade, though oftener applied to one of secondary grade. It is also applied to certain kinds of professional schools; as a theological seminary, a teachers' seminary, etc., the idea intended to be conveyed by the term being that of preparation for subsequent usefulness.

SENSES, the Education of the. Education, through the senses, has received a great amount of attention in recent times, and a special effort to systematize it, is made in the kindergarten (q. v.); but comparatively little thought has been given to the training of the senses themselves. *Value of.* And, yet, there is ample experience to prove that much can be done in this direction. In cases where special senses have been called into the most vigorous action, they have attained capabilities which could scarcely have been dreamed of. It may not be advisable to attempt to cultivate each sense in every individual to the same degree of acuteness that has been reached in these extraordinary instances; but, there is no doubt that the neglect to train the senses, now almost universal, is not justifiable. The special attributes which we may assign to the senses, are quickness in receiving impressions, strength in taking hold of the impressions, and vivacity in noticing not merely the unity which is presented to the mind, but in remarking the various details which compose or characterize this unity. These three qualities are quite different from each other. If an object is held up before a number of children, some will be found able to form an impression of it much more quickly than others, while some will be very slow to catch a notion of it. So, again, they will differ in the strength of grasp with which they seize hold of the object. On some it will produce but a feeble impression, and that impression will, consequently, soon die away; but by others the object will be grasped firmly, and, consequently, held firmly. Many, too, that may be able to take strong impressions, may be surpassed by others of less strength in the capacity to catch the multiplicity of details which are presented to the view. In fact, the strong sense is generally absorbed in the unity; but the less vigorous notices the details along with the unity. Now, these qualities are inborn with the senses; and it is likely that the original difference, in these respects, which exists in different minds, is sufficient to account for the mental differences that ultimately appear among human beings. Circumstances will explain the rest of the phenomena; but these qualities are capable of cultivation, being intensified in proportion to the healthy exercise of the senses.

Most essential process. In attempting to train the senses, the most essential process is isolation. The blind man becomes singularly expert in the sense of touch because he brings it into continual play, and trusts much to it. He must voluntarily follow the course which necessity compels him to follow. Science has not thrown much light, as yet, on the lower senses; and, therefore, little can be done for their training. The vital sense is so closely connected with processes which take place in unconsciousness that little can be made of it. Somewhat more can be done with the senses of taste and smell. If the child were asked to *Taste and smell.* shut his eyes, and determine by taste what objects were presented to him, the sense might become much more perfect and much more useful. Attention could be called to the general harmony that exists between the taste and healthfulness of objects, and the child might thus learn, in many cases, to choose the good and reject the evil. The same remarks apply to the sense of smell; but a wider range could be given to its activities. The child, for example, might be required to determine flowers by their smells. But it is when we come to the higher senses that much can be done by isolating practice. In regard to the sense *Touch.* of touch, there are three exercises which may be usefully practiced. First, the sense of touch over the body may be rendered much more acute; and, in consequence, what are called the sensory circles, very much narrowed. Experiment has proved this fact most conclusively. Then, from touch we derive the sense of pressure. Here the child may find interesting exercise in trying to estimate the weight of an object from its pressure on the hand, or on other parts of the body. This constitutes one of the peculiar exercises of *object teaching* (q. v.). Moreover, touch gives the notion of temperature; and here again the child might be taught to come very close to the exact degree of Fahrenheit by *Hearing.* the sense of heat which he has in his touch. The training which may be given to the sense of hearing, is also various. The child might be exercised in ascertaining from what direction sounds come. He might be taught to distinguish various sounds, and, especially, musical sounds; and he might learn to analyze complex sounds. Some think, that the last exercise should always be preliminary to learning to read. Thus, the instructor utters a word, and draws the child's attention to the fact that it consists of several sounds. The child is then asked to analyze the sounds; and the child does not commence to learn to read until he is able to analyze short words into their simplest sounds. Spelling, in the sense of analyzing the sounds, according to this method, precedes reading. According to the *phonic method*, the analysis of sounds is employed to facilitate the pronunciation of words, and, hence, as auxiliary to reading. (See PHONIC METHOD.) — The sense of sight is the one through which *Sight.* education takes place most of all. It is, therefore, brought into continual activity, and thus receives greater training. In the object-teaching system, this is accomplished in various ways, but, particularly, by the use of *color* (q. v.). Distinct colors are first brought before the child's eye, and he is gradually practiced in distinguishing them, so as, ultimately, to be able to note the minutest shades of difference. Then, again, the child is taught to form from sight an accurate idea of size and distance.

The space here does not admit of more than a mere glance at this important subject; and only in connection with the training of children. But, while there is no doubt that the greatest good can be done in the earliest years, the training may profitably be continued throughout the whole period of education. The organization of methods for such training has still to be discussed by educationists. Moreover, physiologists are still in great uncertainty as to many points. Great discoveries have been recently made by the researches of Weber, Wundt, Helmholtz, and others; but we may expect still more important discoveries from the investigations now going on; and there is no doubt that such discoveries will throw light on the proper method of training the senses. — See G. WILSON, *The Five Gateways of Knowledge* (4th ed., London, 1863); WYLD, *Physics and Philosophy of the Senses* (London, 1856); JULIUS BERNSTEIN, *The Five Senses of Man* (N. Y., 1876). (See also EAR, and EYE.)

SENTENTIAL ANALYSIS. See ANALYSIS, GRAMMATICAL.

SIMULTANEOUS INSTRUCTION. See CONCERT TEACHING.

SINGING. From the days of St. Ambrose and Gregory the Great to the present age, singing-schools and classes have existed, for purposes of instruction in elementary vocal and choral exercises. The need of early training has always been recognized by the great masters as indispensable to extensive and thorough accomplishment in this art. The educational value of music, and more particularly vocal music, has been universally conceded by both theoretical and practical educators, as well as by statesmen and philanthropists. Martin Luther attached very great importance to it; and through him the choral and the special hymn were given to all the people. Subsequently, not only Germany, but Great Britain, and the United States of America, greatly encouraged the cultivation of vocal music, in its higher relations, among all classes of people. It is the opinion of some, however, that the people of the United States are a century behind the more powerful and influential of the European nations in a systematic fostering of the science and art of music by the state; but, through the more general diffusion of knowledge by means of schools, the press, and other agencies, the individual efforts of Americans are widespread, toward imparting a more thorough understanding of that which is, to the vast majority of people, an unknown language; namely, the secret of the independent reading of vocal music with facility.

The origin of the staff, and the use of the syllables *Ut, Re, Mi, Fa, Sol, La, Si*, seem to have been nearly contemporary. These, together with the clefs, notes, and chromatic signs, constitute the written language of *Language of music.* music as recognized by every civilized country; and it is not possible to change them for the letters only, valuable as these are in certain relations, without disastrously revolutionizing the whole written system of modern music, and all its magnificent accessories. Large numbers of most valuable works upon harmony, counterpoint, and orchestral effects have been written, besides innumerable scores, with all of these well known musical signs, and with the employment of the syllables *Ut, Re, Mi*, etc., as denoting absolute pitch constantly in view; and to reduce them to the dimensions of lettered signs simply, and require singers and players to translate them into music agreeable to the ear, would be an interminable and tedious task. The modern Italian method of presenting the scale through the familiar syllables *Do, Re, Mi, Fa, Sol, La, Si*, has the merit of being direct and of appealing to the ear; and it is, *Italian method.* also, quite unique, since the syllables are at once the vehicles of variations of sound required in rendering the scale, and the signs denoting absolute pitch, like the letters to the Germans and to the English. So that, by this method, the pupil has to remember only one particular syllable, either in naming a key-note or in singing it. To the Italians and to the French, and to very many others who have been taught by this method, this association of a certain syllable with a certain key-note, that particular syllable being the very vehicle for the production of the *tone* desired, is deemed, in many respects, an advantage. The fixed and immovable *Do* becomes the middle C of the system. All other *tones* of that octave, diatonic and chromatic, revolve around it, as the planets around the sun. The major scale, with its intermediate *half-tones*, becomes the nucleus of the entire tonal system. In exact proportion as the scholar acquires a thorough knowledge of the scale, by regular degrees, by intervals small and large, by chromatic as well as by diatonic progression, and by all the varieties of melodic and harmonic effect of which it is susceptible, will his succeeding study be made satisfactory and available. Multiply this knowledge of the resources of one scale within the compass of one octave by twelve, the number of independent key-notes included within the limits of the chromatic scale, and thereby are obtained the changes of progression possible in all the twelve keys, in the circle of harmony, through the transposition of the key-note. Now this may seem complicated to the uninitiated; but it is quite clear to all who have mastered the changes obtainable within the compass of one octave, and afterward have learned the rule of transposition to the succeeding eleven keys. This, indeed, is the first direct business of the faithful musical instructor and his pupils. There is no escape from traveling this well-known and well-beaten road, if accuracy and a full comprehension of the groundwork of music be really desired. In schools where the very tender age of the pupils hardly admits of any extended course of vocal musical instruction, it is now positively ascertained that the association of the sounds of the major scale with the numerals 1, 2, 3, 4, 5, 6, 7, 8, is of direct and permanent use. Practicing fragments of the major scale, ascending and descending, by regular degrees and in wider intervals, with frequent recurrence of the key-note 1 or 8, and unisonant passages, has the effect of locating the sounds of the scale in their exact order, and immediately secures the attention and the active participation of the pupils, because the order of the numerals is already familiar to them; and, in this way, each sound of the scale becomes gradually associated with its corresponding numerals. If to the use of the numerals be added that of the syllables, Do, Re, Mi, Fa, Sol, La, Si, which are more musical in themselves than the numerals, there are obtained three indicators of the different sounds of the scale; namely, the *letters*, the *numerals*, and the *syllables*, all of which are useful for special purposes: the letters, for denoting absolute pitch and the location of the key-notes, changeable only with the clefs; the numerals, for drilling in the plain sounds of the scale, and ultimately for practical use in the study of harmony, *one* and *eight* being used as key-notes in one or all of the twelve keys; and the syllables, for *sol-faing*, used according to the Italian method, C being always the fixed and immovable *Do*. It is at this point that this Italian method, which recognizes the syllables as necessary indicators of absolute pitch, and at the same time as necessary in *sol-faing* for the production of an equable and yet varied effect, differs from three other methods which are in extensive use: (1) from that of the Germans, who, with a special name for every plain sound of the scale, and for every augmented or depressed interval thereof, rely chiefly upon vocalizing with different vowels to secure accuracy in all chromatic as well as diatonic progressions; (2) from that of the United States, which quite generally, but not entirely, employs a movable *Do* as the starting-point or key-note of the major scale, the key-note for any relative minor becoming *La*; and (3) from that of the Rev. J. Curwen, the success of whose method in England has been quite remarkable, — a method, which is identical with that so extensively practiced in the United States, in the use of a movable *Do*, but which substitutes the syllable *Te* for *Si*; the names of Mr. Curwen's syllables being *Doh, Ray, Me, Fah, So, La, Te*. This method of *lettered* and *numeral* abbreviations, as substitutes for the staff, clefs, chromatic signs, bars, measures, and time-table of the present musical sign-language will be more minutely considered further on.

Use of syllables.

To return to the two methods which are chiefly employed in the United States, it is, really, very important to the beginner that he adhere to one method until it is thoroughly acquired. It is the united testimony of experienced teachers of vocal music that good readers are educated by both of these methods, provided the teacher begins, continues, and ends the work of strict reading by adopting only one method at a time. The pupil may afterward become acquainted with all other methods, and with advantage; since subsequent experience will enable him to test the merits of the method which he most thoroughly understands, and which he can make most effective. To attempt to teach, or to learn, both methods at the same time, produces a confusion of associations, and a consequent bewilderment, which should be avoided. It has been the experience of the writer to be required to teach contemporaneously according to both of these methods; and, while it must be admitted that the method which retains the immovable *Do* has a unity and consistency which demand time for their thorough appreciation and practical use, it is easier, in the first stages of instruction, to change the *Do* with each successive key-note of the entire twelve. By the former method, *Do* is invariably associated with a certain letter and a certain line or space; by the latter, *Do* becomes the key-note, or numeral *one* or *eight*, of every one of the major scales. One or the other of these ways of using the syllables being accepted, the natural and ordinary divisions of elementary vocal teaching into those of *tune, time*, and *expression* present themselves; *tune*, or *melody*, addressing itself more directly to the soul than *time* or *rhythm*, is certainly first in order in the musical education of the young. By common consent, the major scale, in great variety, is now practiced with numerals and with syllables in the primary departments of schools, as a preparation for the presentation of the staff, clefs, notes, etc., at a later period. It is a matter of no consequence whether the scale be based upon one particular line or space in preference to another, if the movable *Do* be used; but if it be the teacher's design to employ the Italian method, with its *Do* immovably fixed upon middle C, it is conducive to a clearer understanding of the subject of the *transposition* of the key-note to

Movable & immovable Do.

Order of teaching.

start from this point. If another letter be selected as the base of the scale in the earlier lessons, it is necessary to return to middle C when the subject of *transposition* is introduced, and the ordinary rules for changing the place of the key-note by help of the sharps and flats, are fully explained. After some familiarity with the sounds of the major scale is acquired, a division of the class should be made, whereby singing in two parts can be attempted. This phase of elementary vocal instruction may be postponed, in teaching children, until a considerable knowledge of the diatonic intervals of the major scale has been made familiar to them. With adults, however, the natural division of the class of mixed voices arising from the selection of the soprano, alto, tenor, and base voices, each to sing in a compact body, and in a separate location, is obviously necessary as a measure of interest and advantage to all four of these parties, after the quality of tone and compass of each voice have been ascertained. Beating time should be introduced and rigidly enforced as soon as the staff and its division into measures by bars have been explained, especially in the simpler forms of twofold, threefold, and fourfold measure. The department of *expression*, with its more apparent varieties of f, p, mf, *legato*, *staccato*, ◁═══ and ═══▷, may accompany the performance of the simplest exercises, and grow with the growth and strengthen with the strength of the pupil as he advances toward the execution of more elaborate examples in *melody*, *rhythm*, and *harmony*. They who clog the wheels of musical progress with dull and incompetent ears must gradually disappear. This is a rule without exception.

Allusion has been made to the success of the Rev. J. Curwen's *Tonic-Sol-Fa* system in England, of which Miss Sarah A. Glover, with her so-called *tetrachordal method*, was the forerunner. It is claimed *Tonic-Sol-Fa system.* that it is better suited for vocal practice than the ordinary signs, and many of Mr. Curwen's disciples consider it available for the presentation of every possible variety of music, instrumental as well as vocal. The syllables *Doh, Ray, Me, Fah, Soh, Lah, Te*, are pronounced as they are spelt, *Te* being substituted for *Si*, to avoid confusion with *So* when only the initial letter is used, as in the printed music the initial only is employed. To indicate the higher or lower octaves, figures are placed by the sides of the letters which stand for notes, as d^1, d^2, m^3, and S_2, M_2, d_2. The tune *America* is presented thus: | $d\ d\ r\ t_1$ $d\ r\ m\ m\ f\ m\ r\ d\ r\ d\ t_1$, etc. Different key-notes are announced by letter at the beginning, as key G, key A, etc. The key-note of the relative minor is always *Lah*. Changes of key are effected by what are called *bridge tones*. The note, or rather the letter indicating a certain sound, is placed side by side with the letter indicating the pitch of the letter in the key approached, and pupils are taught to think and sing the sound of the first note or letter and to call it by the name of the second. Thus $d\ r\ m\ f\ sd\ t\ d$ would show a modulation to the key of G. *Tonic-Sol-Faists* consider that this affords an easier mode of making modulations and transitions than the older system. The chromatic scale is named by adding the vowel *e* to the initial of sharped notes, and *a* (aw) to flatted notes. Thus *de, re, fe, se*, are respectively *d, r, f, s* sharp; and *ma* (maw), *la, ta*, are *m, l, t* flat. The sharp or augmented sixth of the minor scale is called *bah*, to distinguish it from *fe*, the sharp or augmented fourth of the major scale. Time and accent are indicated by measurement across the page, thus:

| : | : | : | : |

the space between one sign and the next representing the beat; the line showing the stronger accent, and the colon the weaker. Short divisions are indicated on halving the measure by one dot | . : and commas are used to divide the measure into quarters, and other divisions are similarly shown.

The method cannot easily be understood without reference to the *Tonic-Sol-Fa* arrangement, *i. e.*, the distinctive plan of teaching the musical facts indicated by the lettered notation. It is the result of laborious inquiry and experience on the part of Mr. Curwen and his fellow laborers. Great importance is attached to the doctrine of what is called *mental effect,* but which has been previously named more properly *emotional effect,* by which is meant a certain coloring or impression produced by each sound of the scale when sung slowly. Thus *doh* is considered firm; *te,* sharp and piercing; *lah,* sorrowful; *fah,* gloomy; *soh,* bright and clear, etc. Teaching by pattern is also required; the scale is taught in the following order: (1) the notes of the tonic common chord *d, m, s,* or *doh, me, soh,* and their replicates; (2) the notes of the dominant common chord *s, t, r,* or *so, te, ray;* (3) the common chord of the subdominant *f, l, d,* or *fah, lah, doh,* — which are simply the fundamental harmonics of the scale, embracing *Modulator.* all its sounds, and giving birth to the name of the system, *Tonic-Sol-Fa.* The backbone of the system, however, is the *Modulator,* without a proper use of which the method cannot be taught.

r¹	s	d		f¹			
		t	—	m	—	l — r^L	s
d¹	f						
t	m	l	=	r¹	—	s d¹	f
						t	m
l	r	s	—	DOH¹	—	f	
				TE	—	m l	r
s	d	f	ta	la			
		t₁	m	— LAH	=	r s	d
f				la so			t₁
m	l₁	r	—	SOH	—	d f	
				ba fe		t₁ m	l₁
r	s₁	d	—	FAH			
		t₁	—	ME	—	l₁ r	s₁
d	f			ma re			
t₁	m₁	l₁		RAY	—	s₁ d	f
l₁	r₁	s₁		DOH	—	f t₁	m₁
				t₁	—	m l₁	r₁
s₁	d₁	f₁					
		t₂	m	—	l₁	= r₁	s₁ d₁
f							t₂
m	l₂	r	—	s₁	—	d₁ f₁	
						t₂ m₁	l₂
r	s₂	d₁	—	f			
		t₂	—	m₁	—	l₂ r₁	s₂

This Modulator is a map of the musical sounds to be read in an ascending order, showing the scale, its minor, its chromatics, and its more closely related keys or scales. By familiarity in the use of this chart, the upward and downward motion of the notes all on one level, is gradually learned by the pupil. Syllables are used to show the length of the notes according to the French Chève system. So *taa* is the name of one beat, *taa-tai* of a half-beat, and *ta-fa-te-fe* of quarter beats. Continuations of any kind are met by dropping the consonant. *Sol-Faists* consider that the more intricate and refined of divided beats can be sooner learned in this way than in any other. But this *Tonic-Sol-Fa*-method, more than any other, requires the living teacher to illustrate the meaning of its signs; and it follows, of course, that the teacher of any particular method of imparting musical instruction will best succeed with that which he most thoroughly understands.

SOCIAL ECONOMY. The place actually held by the science of social or political economy, in modern education, presents a strange contrast with that which its importance demands. If the object of education is to fit the young to become self-supporting citizens in a progressive society, conducing at once to the happiness of all, while securing their own, then must the science whose special function is the elucidation of the conditions of man's well-being in society, rightfully claim a foremost place in every school curriculum. It is, nevertheless, to be noted that, up to the present time, instruction in this science has been limited to the few who attend colleges and universities, and to the pupils of a small number of schools, of which further mention will be made in the course of this article. A part of the difficulty popularly experienced in appreciating the proper position of this subject in the course of study appropriate to youth, is probably to be ascribed to the name, or rather to the different names which have, from time to time, been given to the science. The most appropriate term, of the many which have been suggested, will be found, on examination, to be that under which the subject is here treated, — that is, the science which treats of the manner in which are regulated the affairs that relate to man in society, a meaning fully suggested by the etymology of the words. Nevertheless, this term, as well as the allied name *political economy*, is apt to suggest to the unprepared mind a science dealing with a very different set of ideas from those of which it treats.

Place in education.

The dissatisfaction which has thus arisen with the name *social economy* has led to the attempt to adopt various other forms of expression to designate the science, of which attempts the happiest perhaps has been the proposal to call it the "science which teaches the conditions of human well-being". But this title is not without objection. In the first place, it is wanting in that terseness which is a main requirement in nomenclature; and, secondly, it is wanting in precision. This expression would logically include many other sciences; as, for instance, hygiene, a due regard to the laws of which is assuredly a condition of human well-being. If the science had to do solely with the production and distribution of wealth, the term originally employed by Adam Smith, the father of the science, namely, *the wealth of nations*, would be specially appropriate; but, even this is inadequate; for, although the laws of the production and distribution of wealth influence in a mate-

Designation.

rial degree the conditions of human well-being, the science which we have called *social economy* includes also most of the moral elements that enter into the economy of society. The diversity of names that, from time to time, have been suggested, has, not unnaturally, given rise to the idea that there must be something especially abstruse in a science the professors of which have been unable to agree even upon the name by which it should be known. The difficulty probably arises from the modern use of the term *economy*, which has, to some extent, lost its original and etymological signification. Another cause of the misapprehension of the proper place of social economy in education, arises from the intimate relations into which every person unavoidably enters with the subjects it elucidates, at nearly every instant of his industrial life; so that all persons are unavoidably possessed of some notions on the subjects of which it treats. Now, as there is an infinite number of modes of error and only one of truth, it is only by starting rightly, and proceeding, systematically or scientifically, from the known to the unknown, that error can be avoided; hence, the notions taken up in the course of practical life are, in the absence of systematic study, generally erroneous. But it is usually the most ignorant who wrangle and dictate with the loudest assumption of knowledge; and, hence, people are led to suppose that there is a difference of opinion on economic truths among the students of the science, and that, therefore, the subject must be too difficult to be understood by children. It is, nevertheless, true that, as far as regards the elements of the science, there is no more difference of opinion among those who have given systematic study to it, than there is among the students of mathematics upon the elementary principles of geometry. Another and more serious obstacle to the introduction of social economy, as a subject of instruction for the young, is the following. Owing to the extremely complex nature of human society, it is impossible to take all of its factors into account when investigating its elementary principles. But it is also true that the geometrician disregards the breadth of the line, and the mechanician the weight of the mechanical powers, when investigating the laws of magnitude in space, or the relations of forces; but as soon as the geometrician or the mathematician begins to apply the principles of his particular science to practical engineering, these discarded factors form *data* in his problems; and their effects are estimated by means of the very laws which were established while disregarding their existence. So with the laws of man in society. The laws of the production and distribution of wealth were investigated by rigorously excluding the sympathetic side of man's nature and looking upon him as purely a self-seeking being; but the principles of social economy can only be understood by regarding him from both points of view. All educators have agreed that the earlier years of youth must be directed to concrete, before proceeding to abstract, studies — to observation rather than to causation. While, speaking generally, this rule is sound, it is not to be understood as requiring the exclusion of the reasoning process from even infant minds; but, because the reasoning faculties are comparatively dormant in early youth, knowledge should be obtained through observation (as for instance in natural history); and from the facts thus obtained the child should be trained to reason logically. Now, for this purpose, social economy presents many advantages, and this hardly less as a mental discipline than for the knowledge it imparts. But the teaching of science to the very young should always be in connection with facts or subjects presented to the senses. *Advantages of the study.* For instance, suppose a lesson is to be given upon *bread* to children 8 or 9 years of age. After the children have observed those properties which are directly cognizable to the senses, the judicious teacher will proceed to the more elementary of those facts relating to it which physics, chemistry, and physiology have made known to us, and will not shrink from gradually introducing the pupils, notwithstanding their youth, to the terms used by men of science in speaking of those facts. Instruction of this kind has, for a long while, been given by the best teachers, in what are termed *object lessons;* and they have now *Taught by object lessons.* only to add the facts relating to bread which are made known to us by the science of social economy to complete their course. They will find it far easier to adopt this course with the social bearings of objects than with those which relate to physics, chemistry, or physiology, because many of the social facts will have been spontaneously and unavoidably noticed by the children themselves; and when once they perceive that what goes on around them at home, in the workshop, and in the store, has a scientific value and importance, and that an observation of surrounding facts and events can be used in school work, and have a fitting place found for it, as a help to further knowledge, their observation will be suddenly and wonderfully awakened, and fresh facts and events will be poured upon the teacher by the children themselves. By this method, long before children have passed out of the primary grades, they may have acquired a knowledge of not only the fundamental laws of the production of wealth, but morals also, as well as many of the consequences of the division of labor, and other matters connected with the interchange of commodities. At an age even earlier than that at which it is now deemed proper to commence the study of geometry, that is to say, 11 or 12 years, social economy may be taught as a special subject; but the opportunities afforded by object lessons, of observing the social aspects of the objects under consideration should always be made *A special branch.* available. In teaching social economy, as a special branch, to scholars of from 11 to 12 years of age, the subject should, as far as possible, be introduced in a manner analogous to that of object teaching. Attention should be called to the comforts enjoyed by the children, and by people in general, in the country in which they live, —things to which they have perhaps become so accustomed that they have given no thought to the means by which they have been provided at the time and place at which they are needed to be used and enjoyed. With children who have not before received any instruction in the science, some simple object of their daily use should be noticed, and its history examined, from the first preparation for the production of the raw material of which it is mainly composed, down to its distribution in the form in which it is required to be ready for their consumption. Such an examination will bring vividly before the minds of the pupils the fact that nearly all *Topics for the course of study.* the necessaries and comforts of life are produced by labor; and then the name *wealth,* by which these products of labor are to be thenceforth denoted, may be given to them. *Industry, economy*, *knowledge*, and *skill* will next be evolved as necessary to individual as well as general well-being; and the division of labor will be examined, with its resulting enormous increase in the productiveness of labor. The opportunity should then be taken to exhibit the groundlessness of prevailing prejudices in regard to the relative honor to be attached to one class of labor over another, and to point out that those by whom household labors are performed are as much engaged in the business of production as other laborers. The pupils will now be ready to observe with understanding the simpler phenomena of interchange; and then the paramount importance of honesty, truthfulness, and thorough trustworthiness on the part of all will be evolved and made apparent. While carefully avoiding all appearance of dogmatism, the teacher can hardly devote too much time to multiplying illustrations, and reviewing the investigations of the pupils, upon this head. The various forms of untrustworthiness, and the consequence thereof, should be made very clear, nor should the subject be left until the pupils have arrived at a hearty detestation, not only of unsuccessful, but still more of successful, dishonesty. The natural laws regulating the relations of *employer* and *employed* will next be studied; and, either now or at a later period, the rules of trades-unions, and the effects of strikes and of combinations, should be closely examined; nor should the subject of *wages* be left until the pupils see clearly, that the wages which they, as sellers of their labor, are destined to earn, will depend almost exclusively on the productiveness of their labor, and that all those rules of trades-unions etc. which tend to diminish the productiveness of labor, of necessity, lower also the wages of labor. The laws determining the administration of *capital* will next engage their attention; the idea of *profit* will be evolved, and its nature determined with precision; the mischievous results of combinations among capitalists, both to themselves and to the community, will be investigated, until it becomes apparent that the profit of the capitalist is the reward paid him by society for the services he has rendered, of which services it forms also, in most cases, an accurate measure.— *Property in land* will next claim attention, the justification for its adoption, as well as its just limitations, being ascertained, and the principle of *rent* determined. As the next step in the course of study, the idea of exchangeableness, and the name *value*, will be evolved. The laws which regulate value will then be investigated, and the necessity of precision, alike in ideas and the use of words, will be again impressed upon the minds of the pupils, and forcibly illustrated by as many examples as possible. It will now be time to examine into some of the means which have been adopted to facilitate interchange, among which *money* will be seen to hold a prominent place; the reasons for selecting gold or silver for money will be examined; the impossibility of fixing the relative values of the two metals, and, consequently, the want of wisdom shown in enacting laws making both metals a standard of value for the same contract, will be readily perceived; nor will it be difficult for the pupils to discern the only proper functions to be fulfilled by a mint. The causes of fluctuations in the value of money will be next investigated, and the phenomena of *price* and its fluctuations observed. The use and functions of *credit* will now be inquired into, and the unhappy consequences of its abuse traced to their source. Now, or at a later period in the course, the causes of the so-called "tightness in the money market", of business derangements, commercial crises, and of panics, will be rigidly investigated and their only remedy discerned, namely, greater trustworthiness and honesty, to be secured by the improved teaching and training of youth. The policy of laws for the recovery of debts may now be profitably inquired into, as also the function which, at best, governments may hope to perform in the economy of society. *Bills of exchange, rates of exchange*, the *par of exchange* between distant countries, *rates of interest, banks* and *banking*, may all now, in turn, be discussed, and the want of wisdom shown by legislatures in the enactment of usury laws, and of laws which attempt to control or regulate banking, may be made apparent. Paper money, and the promise made by the issuers thereof, the dishonesty evinced in breaking the promise thus made, and the duty incumbent upon those who have either dishonestly or ignorantly broken such promises, should be dwelt upon, and illustrated by examples drawn from history. *Foreign commerce* may next be illustrated, its origin and the cause of its existence observed, and the want of wisdom shown by those legislatures which have attempted improperly to interfere with it. — The proper mode of raising *revenue*, to be deduced in great part from the truths discovered when considering the phenomena of *rent* and its progressive increase, will next be investigated; and the wisest methods of expenditure, both public and private, may then be discussed. With the consideration of all these questions, and mainly in the order in which they are here sketched, the school course of study in social economy may be closed. Not, however, without warning the pupil that he has, by no means, mastered all the truths of the science, but that, if he has thoroughly assimilated the lessons he has received, they will suffice to direct his path in industrial life. The course as sketched in these pages should occupy from two to four years of the school curriculum, — two years, if the knowledge to be acquired is to be learned from books; but about four years, if the *Socratic method* be adopted by the teacher. Another method of instruction, and one which, like that already indicated, has been successfully practiced, is the division of the science into progressive problems, demonstrating these either on the Socratic plan or by a deductive process, as in the study of geometry. The former of these two plans is that chiefly followed in the admirable Birckbeck schools of London, which were founded and endowed by William Ellis, of that city, for the special purpose of introducing the science of social economy as a branch of school teaching, especially for the children of mechanics and laborers. Since the year 1848, this instruction has been continued in these schools, and their example has, at last, been followed by the London school board. — For educational literature of this subject, see *Cyclopædia of Education*, and list of educational works in the Appendix of this work.

Socratic plan.

SPANISH LANGUAGE. The Spanish language has but little claim to a place in the regular course of instruction, in schools and colleges, in comparison with the French and German languages. As Spanish, however, is not only the language of one of the nations of Europe, but is spoken in all the countries of South America, except Brazil; and also in Central America, Mexico, and even in some parts of the

United States, and is thus the vernacular language of at least 60 millions of people, practical considerations commend its study to thousands of persons, students and others, in preference to either German or French. Independently of this consideration, the Spanish language, as a school accomplishment, is not without attractions. It ranks, indeed, among the most euphonious of modern languages, being even preferred, by some linguists, to the Italian; and its literature contains many works of enduring interest and value. While the Spanish language presents a considerably larger number of non-Latin elements than either French or Italian, it deviates but little from these two sister languages in its structure and grammar. In the pronunciation of the vowels, it entirely agrees with the Italian. The two double consonants *ll* and *ñ* are peculiar to the Spanish, and of the English consonant sounds, *z* (as in *zone*) is entirely wanting. Though substantives have only two genders, masculine and feminine, the article has three, *el*, *la* and *lo*; the last, which is the neuter form, being used to change adjectives into substantives (*lo bueno*, that which is good). The Spanish is richer than either French or Italian in augmentatives and diminutives; and the reflexive form of the verb is used more extensively, perhaps, than in any other language of Europe. The subjunctive has two more tenses than the Italian or French (*amare*, future; *amara*, second conditional). In words derived from Latin, the *e* and *o* of the accented penultima have frequently been developed into *ie* and *ue*, a change which in this class of words, gives to the Spanish an undoubted superiority in euphony (Spanish *tiempo, fuerte;* French *temps, fort;* Ital. *tempo, forte*).—The proper method of teaching Spanish does not differ from that of teaching the *French language* (q. v.). A few lessons in comparative etymology will greatly facilitate the study of this as of every language. If, for instance, the pupil learns that such combinations as *cl, fl, pl*, etc. in English words of Latin origin are often changed into *ll* (*llamar*, clamor; *llama*, flame; *llano*, plain), a large number of words will, at once, be familiar to him.

SUPERIOR INSTRUCTION, a term used to denote instruction of the highest grade, or that given in colleges and universities, both in the academic course, or in special or post-graduate courses.

SUPERVISION, School, constitutes one of the most essential elements of an efficient school system. The supervision which is necessarily given by the principal of the school to the work performed by his assistants is not here referred to, but that which is usually assigned to a superintendent of schools, whose special function it is to see that every school under his jurisdiction is efficient both in discipline and instruction. As a general rule, no extensive work employing a large number of operatives, each performing certain prescribed duties, which contribute toward the accomplishment of a general result, can be carried on efficiently without constant supervision. School supervision is needed for two purposes:

Why needed. (1) to enforce the general rules and regulations prescribed by school authorities; and (2) to see that the proper methods of instruction are employed, and that the teaching is made effective. To attain these objects, the schools must be both *inspected* and *examined*. By inspection the superintendent keeps himself informed in regard to the discipline of the school and the methods of instruction employed by the teachers; by formal examinations at stated periods, he is enabled to ascertain, to a certain extent, the actual result of the teaching, that is, its effect on the pupils' minds, both as to imparting information and training. Both of these are considered indispensable. "An inspection", as defined by Superintendent Philbrick, "is a visitation for the purpose of observation, of oversight, of superintendence. Its aim is to discover, to a greater or less extent, the tone and spirit of the school, the conduct and application of the pupils, the management and methods of the teacher, and the fitness and condition of the premises. Good inspection commends excellences, gently indicates faults, defects, and errors, and suggests improvements as occasion requires. * * * An examination is different from an inspection, both in its aims and methods. An examination is a thorough scrutiny and investigation in regard to certain definitely determined matters for a specific purpose". The best methods of teaching, if not uniformly and diligently employed, will not impress the pupils' minds; and on the other hand, the pupils may gain considerable knowledge of the prescribed branches of study, but not in such a way as to cultivate proper habits of thought. Regular examinations, besides ascertaining the merits and qualifications of the teachers, afford a wholesome stimulus, when judiciously and skillfully conducted, and afford a definite aim toward which their efforts may be directed. On the other hand, if attempted by incompetent and indiscreet persons, supervision of this and every other kind may do much harm. The qualities necessary for a good examiner are well defined by Supt. Philbrick: "In the first place, he should be independent, or, to speak more precisely, he should not be dependent upon the teaching corps. He ought to have had experience in teaching; and if he has had experience in grades similar to those in which he examines, so much the better. His mind ought to be liberalized by a wide range of educational reading and study. He ought to have a good deal of practical common sense. He should be more inclined to look on the bright side of things than on the dark side. He should look sharper for merits than for demerits. He should fear only two things: he should fear to do injustice, and he should fear himself. He should be eminent for good breeding, as a guaranty of respectful treatment from teachers and pupils. And to make sure of the requisite sympathy, like Burke's lawgiver, he ought to have a heart full of sensibility. In one word, for the successful exercise of this delicate and most useful function, the very best educators are demanded". The objection has sometimes been urged against examinations of this kind, that they encourage cramming; but this will, of course, depend upon the character of the examinations themselves. — See PAYNE, *School Supervision* (Cin., 1875). (See also EXAMINATIONS.)

Qualifications of a good examiner.

SYMPATHY, an instinctive feeling of interest in, and affection for, others, which prompts a correspondence of emotions. Persons in sympathy readily discern the mental states of one another, and evince by their actions that they suffer, mentally, the same distress, and feel the same joy. It is difficult to ascertain and define the source and basis of this sympathetic relationship; but personal influence greatly depends upon it. It is natural to some persons to be in sympathy with others; they seem to exert a kind of positive influence, drawing and binding all around them to themselves. Others, on the contrary, seem to be negative in their influence; they repel instead of attracting. They are cold and indifferent to others; or, if otherwise, unconsciously show that their apparent interest is feigned, not felt, proceeding from a sense of duty, not from natural warmth of feeling. The teacher, above all others, should be sympathetic, because so much of his success depends upon personal influence. He should habitually strive to cultivate this quality, feeling assured that the measure of his professional skill and efficiency is the degree of sympathetic regard with which he inspires his pupils. (See ANTIPATHY, and LOVE.)

TEACHER, a person who assists another in learning, that is, in acquiring knowledge or practical skill. A school-teacher's office is, for the most part, confined to aiding the pupil in acquiring knowledge, with the twofold object of (1) mental discipline, and (2) imparting valuable information. Which of these is to be considered of primary importance depends upon the grade of the instruction and the subject taught. Although teaching is only a part of education, the teacher should be an educator, since he is required to perform an office which bears an important relation to the general development, or education, of the child; and, consequently, he should clearly understand the nature of that relation. In other words, no person can be merely a teacher; he must, to be truly efficient, educate while he teaches. Indeed, he cannot but do so. His example, and his personal influence of every kind, will necessarily educate — will tend to form, permanently, the character of his pupil, either for good or evil. This consideration should determine the qualifications of the teacher, which should not consist merely in scholarship, book learning, or intellectual culture, but that assemblage of personal qualities and accomplishments (including scholarship) which will render his influence in every respect effective and salutary. The requirements of a successful teacher, independent of intellectual accomplishments are thus summarized in a recently published work: "(1) The teacher must love his work. (2) He must understand, and sympathize with, the motives which govern humanity — especially children. (3) The whole scope of his intercourse with his pupils must be to secure their co-operation and thus develop self-government. (4) He must plan to interest his pupils. (5) He must give them constant employment. (6) He must conduct his work with the utmost system. See KELLOGG, *School Management* (N. Y., 1880). (See DIDACTICS, EDUCATION, and INSTRUCTION.)

TEACHERS' INSTITUTE, the name given, in the United States, to an assemblage of teachers of elementary or district schools, called together temporarily for the purpose of receiving professional instruction. Such meetings are held under the direction of the school authorities, usually the state, county, or town superintendent; and quite often there is a provision of law requiring the teachers employed in the common schools to attend, and permitting a continuance of their salaries during such attendance. A teachers' institute is usually conducted by an experienced teacher, having special skill for the work. This requires a good knowledge of the practice and theory of teaching, especially as applied to the ordinary branches of common-school education; it also needs ability as a lecturer. Teachers' institutes are designed to serve as a substitute for, or as complementary to, normal instruction; and as such they constitute a valuable agency in connection with a system of common-school instruction. — See BATES, *Method of Teachers' Institutes* (N. Y.); and *Institute Lectures* (N.Y.); FOWLE, *The Teachers' Institute* (N.Y.); PHELPS, *The Teachers' Hand-Book* (N. Y.).

TEACHERS' SEMINARIES. Schools for the education and training of teachers are called *teachers' seminaries* in Germany, Russia, Finland, Norway, Sweden, Denmark, and the German cantons of Switzerland; *training schools*, in Austria and the Netherlands; *preparatory schools*, in Hungary; and *normal schools*, in France, Great Britain, Italy, Spain, Portugal, Greece, Roumania, the French cantons of Switzerland, and the United States. In Great Britain, the name *training college* is very generally used. (See NORMAL SCHOOL.)

TEMPER, the disposition or constitution of the mind, in relation particularly to the affections and the passions. Good temper implies a serenity of mind, and a natural or habitual cheerfulness, which is not easily disturbed. It is opposed to peevishness and sullenness, which seem to be characteristic of certain minds. As good temper predisposes to docility, so ill-temper is directly antagonistic to it; hence, the educator must cultivate the former in the mind of his pupil, and strive to eradicate the latter. In dealing with this fault, the utmost patience is requisite; since any exhibition of ill temper on the part of the educator will, from the force of example, as well as from the additional irritation caused by it, aggravate the difficulty, and foster the natural failing in the pupil's mind into a confirmed vice. Allowance must always be made for the natural peculiarities of children; since these cannot be immediately or forcibly repressed, but must, by careful training, be brought under self-control, which is one of the earliest lessons to be taught, but one of the last objects attained in education. Discouragement may sometimes take the form of ill temper; and, in such a case, the teacher must make concessions, and give special attention to remove the feeling and restore confidence. A violent, irascible, or stubborn temper in the pupil is to be met with calmness and firmness on the part of the teacher; and very often the marked contrast between his manner and that of the pupil will serve to recall the latter to himself, and excite in his mind a feeling of shame at his haste or violence. Nothing will tend so strongly as this to cure the vice, since it really leads the child to punish himself for his fault. Ill temper that takes the form of obstinacy, is the most difficult to deal with; and it is this that Locke reserves as the special and only case for the use of the rod. A resort to this should not, however, be hastily made, and will scarcely ever be needed, if the circumstances admit of persistent discipline of another kind by the educator. In school, unfortunately, this is not always the case, the teacher being obliged promptly to choose between the immediate conquest of his stubborn pupil, or the disorganization of his school. (See PUNISHMENT.)

TEXT-BOOKS, for educational purposes, are books designed to be used by pupils in connection with the instruction given by the teacher. Their purpose is threefold: (1) to aid the teacher, by affording to the pupil independent sources of information and instruments of study; (2) to aid the pupil, in acquiring habits of self-reliance in study; and (3) to enable the pupil to learn how to use books, as a means of self-culture. These objects dictate the mode of constructing school text-books; and should all be carefully kept in view by the teacher in the selection of books, so that they may be suited to the mental status and grade of culture of his pupils in regard to the following points: (1) language and style; (2) arrangement of topics and general treatment of the subject, and (3) adaptability to the time and general opportunities of the pupil. The object of using text-books is often entirely defeated by a disregard of the first of these points. A text-book written in a style beyond the capacity of the pupil is not only useless, but positively injurious; since the pupil either becomes disgusted with the study and neglects it altogether, or he commits to memory the language of the book, under the impression that he is acquiring knowledge; and thus his mental habits are seriously, if not permanently, vitiated. — The following cautions should be particularly observed by teachers in the use of text-books: (1) the book should not be permitted to supersede the teacher, its use being always preceded, accompanied, and supplemented by oral instruction; (2) it should never be paramount, in the pupil's mind, to the subject, the impression being constantly inculcated by the teacher that it is the subject that is studied, and that the book is only an instrument of the study, or an auxiliary to it; (3) it should not be allowed to supersede the necessity of acquiring knowledge, as far as possible, by personal experience, particularly in elementary education. In advanced instruction, it will always be found that those will use text-books most effectively who have acquired the most knowledge without them. (See ORAL INSTRUCTION.)

TOPICAL METHOD. See CATECHETICAL METHOD.

TRAINING, a department of education, in which the chief element is exercise, or practice; the object being to impart practical skill, or facility in any bodily or mental operation. No teaching can be effectual that is not supplemented by training; that is to say, not only is the understanding of the pupil to be addressed, but the principle of *habit* is to be appealed to. (See HABIT.)

UNIVERSITY, a name first given, in the middle ages, to institutions for superior instruction. In the second half of the 12th century, a free union of students of medicine was formed in Salerno (1150), and another of students of law in Bologna (1158). The students had equal rights with the professors in these unions; which soon attracted such crowds that, in Bologna, the studies of medicine and theology were added; and, in Salerno, those of law and philosophy. This was the origin of the modern European university. At the university of Bologna, as well as at the universities of Padua and Naples, which were early established, the study of law remained predominant, ecclesiastical and secular law (*decreta* and *leges*) being eagerly studied in order to obtain high offices in church and state. In Paris, a university arose from the cathedral school, and as the chief seat of scholasticism, soon attained the rank of the foremost university of western Europe. The formation of *nations* and of faculties exerted a decisive influence upon the further development of the university. As scholars from all parts of the Christian world flocked to Paris in large numbers, and the government of the state took no notice of them, they found it necessary to form national groups for the purpose of self-government. Thus, the four *nations* of the Gallicans (including

Spaniards, Italians, Greeks, and Orientals), the Picards, the Normans, and the English (including Germans and Northmen) were formed. The formation of special faculties was caused by the Mendicants' orders, which early recognized the importance of the rising university, and, as teachers of theology and ecclesiastical law, assumed, in regard to the *nations*, an independent position. In consequence of the complications which were produced by their teaching, the professors of theology (about 1270), and, somewhat later, those of medicine and of ecclesiastical law, formed a union, and in this way organized three distinct faculties. The faculties represented, therefore, special sciences; while the four *nations*, as a continuation and enlargement of the former cathedral school, represented the *trivium* and the *quadrivium*, or the preparatory sciences. Following, at length, the example of the other faculties, the *nations* gradually transformed themselves into the faculty of the liberal arts, which, for a time, occupied a position inferior to that of the older faculties. These developments made the university of Paris the great literary center of Europe; and, at times, it was attended by more than 20,000 students. See *Cyclopædia of Education*.

VENTILATION. Probably no subject connected with the improvement of schools has, of late years, been more fully and earnestly discussed than that of ventilation. Unfortunately, however, the results reached have by no means corresponded in importance to the length or vigor of the discussion. Notwithstanding the minute and elaborate experiments made by modern science on this subject, it is hardly too much to say that the only point of agreement is, that ample ventilation is of paramount importance in the economy of the school room. Any recommendation of particular methods of effecting this, or any appeal to statistics or experimental details, becomes at once the occasion for fresh dispute. The subject will be considered here under the following heads: (I) The conditions favorable to proper ventilation; (II) The methods employed to utilize those conditions; (III) Some of the ways in which ventilation is prevented.

I. Under this head, will be considered (1) the sources from which a proper supply of fresh air for the school room is to be obtained, and the quality of air so obtained; and (2) the determination of the quantity needed by each pupil for purposes of respiration. That the great reservoir of the outer air which surrounds the school room is the only proper source of supply for the lungs of its inmates, requires no demonstration; *Fresh air.* the only question being that which concerns its purity. The direct and intimate connection which has been ascertained to exist between the air which we breathe and the blood, has been found to extend to the brain, and healthful intellectual activity and pure air are now almost convertible terms. Whatever causes, therefore, tend to vitiate the air surrounding the school building should be carefully eliminated. (Concerning the proper site of the school building, as regarded from a sanitary stand-point, see HYGIENE, SCHOOL.) Another cause which, in certain sites, and, at certain seasons of the year, in any site, may affect the quality of the air introduced into the school-room, is the height above the ground from which it is drawn. The danger to be apprehended from malarial fever, one of the most insidious foes of the human race detected by modern sanitary science, has led recent writers on the subject of ventilation to recommend that the inlet for fresh air be placed as high as possible, so that the lower stratum of air — that near the ground or from the cellar — be not admitted.

Much of the difficulty which attaches to the subject of ventilation, arises from the fact that medical men who have given special attention to the matter, are by no means agreed as to the amount of pure air needed by each person for purposes of respiration; their estimates of the number of cubic feet of space required by each pupil in the school room where the ventilation is ample, varying from 300 to 1,200. From a comparative examination of various estimates, it appears that the average amount of fresh air required by each individual hourly is at least 1,000 cubic feet. In school rooms provided with adequate means of ventilation, this requires, according to most sanitarians, at least 300 cubic feet of space for each pupil. This, though hardly above the minimum, exceeds, probably, in a majority of cases, the most liberal allowance made by those school officers who pride themselves on their generosity in this respect. Usually, the allowance is less than 110 cubic feet. The quantity of air, also, admitted by the ventilating apparatus, bears a constant relation to the size of the room. Says Dr. A. N. Bell on this point, "The smaller the space, the greater the necessity for, and the larger the opening required for, the admission of fresh air. * * * It has been calculated that, with ordinary exposure, an open space equal to 5 inches in the square, will admit the passage of 2,000 cubic feet hourly; this, of course, implies that there should be an equal amount of open space for the escape of the air displaced".

Cubic feet of space.

II. In considering the different methods of ventilation, attention should, at the same time, be given to the method of warming the school-room; since the two subjects are almost inseparably connected. The entrance of warm air into a room for breathing purposes, is inevitably attended by, and naturally suggests, a corresponding exit of vitiated air, and points unmistakably to the resulting current as the most efficient means for ventilation. If the question were merely that of determining the easiest way of replacing a certain amount of impure, by a corresponding amount of pure, air, the problem would be one of easy solution; since the difference of temperature which generally exists between the outer air and that of the school room furnishes the condition most favorable to ventilation, the only agent needed being a connection between the two, which is readily supplied by an open door or window. In summer, this method, which may be called the natural one, is in almost universal use, and is accompanied generally with satisfactory results. In winter, however, the violent displacement of one atmosphere by the other, which results from the greater difference in their temperature, and which immediately begins when a connection is made between them, makes itself felt in the shape of dangerous drafts. The problem for the inventor, therefore, is how to produce this change of air without any perceptible draft; and to this additional condition, is to be attributed the practical failure of so many ingenious devices which, in theory, are admirable. One of the simplest and most effective methods of ventilation is used in connec-

Methods of ventilation.

tion with the method of warming described under the head of school hygiene. (See HYGIENE, SCHOOL.) It consists of a chimney with two flues, one for the fire, the other for ventilation. The latter is separated from the former by a partition of metal which becomes heated by the air from the fire, and, by warming the column of air in the ventilating flue, causes it to ascend, tending thus to produce a vacuum, which the vitiated air of the room flows in to fill. The ventilating flue has two registers, one near the floor, the other near the ceiling, both of which can be controlled at pleasure. A more economical method consists in making a ventilating flue only, but making it sufficiently large to permit the passage of the stove pipe along its middle line, while leaving considerable air space around the latter. By extending the stove pipe to the top of the house, the heat of the stove is used, as in the previous case. If the room is warmed by an open fire, the increase in the amount of fuel used should be charged to the account of ventilation, and the additional expense incurred should not be regarded as a violation of the laws of economy, but rather as an observance of the provisions of that true economy which does not look for immediate and petty results, but is fundamental in its action, and conducive to the permanent benefit of teacher and pupil. For combined ventilating and warming purposes, in small school rooms, the open grate fire has many advantages; but, of course, it should be carefully screened. For more elaborate methods of ventilation, with modifications to suit circumstances, see the works quoted in the Appendix of this work, in which the subject is exhaustively treated.

111. The great importance of effective ventilation, to which it is exceedingly probable that the public mind is not yet sufficiently aroused, and *Obstructions and defects.* the practical difficulty which attends it when any but the simplest means and appliances are used, render it necessary to make some mention of the ways in which proper ventilation is thwarted, even when it is apparently provided for. These are principally two: (1) a ventilating apparatus, originally inadequate in size, or, if adequate, the ineffective working of it, through frequent derangement; (2) the overcrowding of the school room after the originally liberal estimates for air supply, based on a smaller number of pupils, have been made. Insufficient apparatus, from either the first or second cause mentioned above, is one of the commonest difficulties with which intelligent school officers have to contend; so easy is it for any one, in the absence of decidedly bad results, to lose sight of the essential conditions of a healthy school room, and so clamorous is the tax-payer usually for smaller demands upon his purse. In the compromises which generally follow these contests between the pocket and the lungs, it is too often found that the greater concessions have been made by the latter. In the second case — that of overcrowding — the same deleterious effects follow, insufficient air space being the evil in both. Even intelligent teachers are, in this way, frequently deceived. The number of pupils is increased so gradually that the evil is for a long time unsuspected, and not till its effects have declared themselves in some unmistakable, and perhaps fatal, manner, is attention called to the probable cause. As has been said, the air provided for breathing purposes should be drawn from out-of-doors, at a height above the ground sufficient to preclude all danger from exhalations, and should

be introduced into the room at the opposite end from that at which the impure air passes out, and at the top of the room, but in such a way as to prevent drafts. This is best done by providing a number of small apertures, the air from which passes through the vitiated air of the room in numerous small currents which are imperceptible, and which cause the fresh air to be evenly diffused. If warmed by a cellar furnace, it should not be introduced into the room by floor registers, since these are always, more or less, traps for dust, which thus, in some shape, is liable to be taken into the lungs. The ventilating apparatus should not only be sufficiently large at the outset, but should be thoroughly tested before it is introduced, so as to ascertain whether its working sustains the theory of its construction, and should be carefully examined, from time to time, with the view to secure its constant efficiency. — For literature of this subject, see the Appendix of this work.

VOICE, Culture of the. The human voice may be considered as the audible expression of the mental and physical characteristics of its possessor; and, therefore, no means employed in the varied processes of education are of more importance than those that have regard to its culture. Its powers are often widely misunderstood and misapplied, sometimes abused and destroyed. In the very beginning of education, large numbers of boys, in addition to marked inherited peculiarities, such as defective ears, weak lungs, asthmatic and husky bronchial tubes, contracted chests, elongated palates, and inflamed, swollen tonsils, are permitted to indulge in the pernicious habit of loud shouting and hurrahing, and in the baneful and distressing use of the chest tones, so frequently heard in the singing of male pupils. Every boy should be made to understand that if he thus abuses his voice, he must not expect to overcome his constitutional defects, or retain a tone which, even by assiduous practice, will become agreeable to his audience, in reading, declamation, or vocal music. Girls, while in many instances they have all the inherited disadvantages above referred to, present, through their more delicate organization and guarded habits, far more promising material for the production of purely musical effects. Parents and teachers may well take warning, also, in the education of either boys or girls, against a long-continued strain upon their vocal chords. Many a young voice has been completely ruined by this untimely forcing of the powers of the youthful candidate for declamatory or musical honors. A child five years of age, for example, is placed on a chair, to amuse a large audience by speaking or singing in a forced utterance, and with an unnaturally loud chest tone, entirely beyond its years, or powers of endurance. Such a tax upon its vocal chords, if long continued, is exceedingly injurious. The medium or falsetto tone, that most mellow, most musical, most sweet and expressive part of the female voice, or of the unchanged voice of the boy, gradually deteriorates, and is finally lost by this injurious process. The remedy for

Remedy. this destruction lies in the early protection of the health, and in the careful use of the young voice, at home, in school, in the church, and wherever there is any danger of this overstraining of its powers. The vocal exercises should be within a limited compass, — neither too high nor too low. All forcing of the voice should be positively forbidden and avoided; and each lesson should come to a close without fatigue.

Margin notes: Injury to the voice.

An easy and systematic mode of breathing should be an early acquisition, since it lies at the foundation of all success in singing, as well as in speaking. Tone, of itself, being nothing more nor less than breath, or air in motion through contact with a sonorous body, it is important to know, to some degree at least, the character of the organs which enter into the production of vocal tone. All cultivated speakers and singers are conscious of a thorough employment of the abdominal muscles, and of those of the diaphragm, in order to secure complete control of the breath. *Inhaling*, however, may be carried to excess, a result well known to professional dramatic vocalists, who often protect themselves against rupture by wearing shoulder braces, trusses, and abdominal supporters. *Exhaling* involves that careful use of the diaphragm, which keeps the intercostal nerves and muscles in a state of tension, in order that the lungs may have their fullest play. To know when and where to inhale and to exhale, is as necessary to the speaker, in his written or extemporaneously delivered sentences, as it is to the singer, in the enunciation of his musical phrases; and, in such case, it assumes the dignity of consummate art, — an indispensable and prime necessity to the conscientious interpreter of either classic language or classic music. Without case, sustained repose, and a method made effective through long habit, in the management of the breath, all subsequent attention to details in the art of speaking or singing is measurably lost. Demosthenes, with pebbles in his mouth, declaiming to the winds and waves on the sea shore, and Braham, lifting up his voice amid the hills and forests of Northumberland, may profitably be remembered and imitated by all students who desire to remedy defects, and to acquire new breathing power. — A graceful attitude, and thorough skill in the proper use of the breath being gained, the close sympathy always existing between the bronchial tubes and the stomach next demands attention. A rapid and complete digestion is esteemed by all intelligent persons the greatest of physical blessings; and to no one is it a more necessary condition of success than to the public speaker or singer. So important is this to the professional vocalists, that those times, in the daily routine of duty, which find the lungs and bronchial tubes freest from the oppression arising from sympathy with the stomach, in its process of digestion, should be selected for practice. Proceeding upward toward the organs of articulation, we arrive at the trachea, or windpipe, the larynx, and the pharynx. It is a prolific subject of discussion among speakers and singers, whether the character of the tone depends as much upon the size of the lungs, the bronchial tubes, the windpipe, the larynx, and the pharynx, as it does upon the condition of the muscles and nerves, and more remotely still upon the general organization, temperament, will, and endurance of the speaker or singer. It is surprising to notice the compass and the variety of tone which the larynx can produce, by using the vowels alone. Beginning with the lowest sounds of the base voice, and ascending in regular order through its limits, of one and a half or two octaves; through the compass of the baritone, with a similar register, though somewhat higher in pitch; and, successively, through the registers assigned to the tenor, contralto, mezzo-soprano, and soprano voices, there is embraced a compass of four octaves of available tones susceptible of cultivation to an almost infinite degree of excellence. Bass voices confine themselves mainly to the use of the chest tones throughout their entire register; but the barytones, by a prudent use of the somber tone, and of the medium register, greatly increase the pure quality and flexibility of the higher portions of their voices. For the orator or declaimer, there is no quality of tone comparable to that of the orotund base or barytone voice; and, in the oratorio and opera, it is assigned to characters of inherent dignity and force. The tenor voice, un-

Tenor. doubtedly, demands a combination of native and acquired qualities, which, in some countries, are exceedingly rare. In its uncultivated state it is thin, reedy, and somewhat nasal; but steady, persevering practice upon the open vowels *ah, oh,* and *oo*, soon corrects this defect, and renders the tenor, of all male voices, the most tender and expressive. Great care should be exercised by tenor voices, lest the clear *timbre* of the chest tone be carried too high, thereby crushing out the delicacy of the real medium register, which is the most flexible and available part of the tenor voice.

Contralto & soprano. The contralto, mezzo-soprano, and soprano voices encounter a similar difficulty, at the very outset of their practice, in combining the chest with the falsetto or medium voice. While this difficulty occurs in the higher register of the male voice, it is found in the lower register of the female voice, and presents obstacles in the way of cultivation, which nothing but long and persistent practice can overcome, though the strain upon the nervous system is far less than that experienced by the male voice. The contralto yields to no other female voice in depth and richness of tone, as is clearly evident after listening to singers like D'Angri and Alboni. Naturally not so flexible as the soprano or mezzo-soprano, it is yet endowed with a wonderful power in causing effects replete with the most ardent passion, and with the most noble womanly feeling. There is a great temptation to abuse the lower register of the contralto voice by indulging in the disagreeable habit of forcing the chest tones to a point bordering upon masculineness, if not positive coarseness. The practice of descending runs, diatonic and chromatic, using the medium, veiled, or somber tone, will gradually change this objectionable habit. There are not wanting cases, also, of contralto voices which have been destroyed by attempts to cultivate the tone and compass of the soprano, — a process absurd and unnatural to the last degree. Notwithstanding the efforts of some late authors to ignore the division of the female voice into at least three different registers, namely, the chest, the medium or falsetto, and the head; these registers are now generally recognized by the highest and most competent authorities. Elaborate methods

Methods of development. and studies for the development of the contralto, mezzo-soprano, and soprano voices have been devised with these three divisions constantly in view. Some even assert that there are five distinct registers, requiring as many different modes of producing the tone, — a condition of the larynx and pharynx suggesting an expertness in the management of the voice which may well be deemed bewildering. It is, however, too certain to admit of a doubt, that the voices of the most accomplished female vocalists living have been trained by recognizing this division into the chest, medium or falsetto, and head registers, and are, moreover, preserved in their wonted availability by adhering to the same method. Allusion has been made above to the pharynx, or arched chamber

immediately back of the palate, which is a most important modifier of the voice in its passage from the larynx, and the expansion and contraction of which gives greater or less volume of tone, especially if the root of the tongue be not artificially enlarged, so as to produce an impure *throatiness* of tone, frequently heard in voices imperfectly cultivated and badly managed. To know the important influence of a healthly pharynx under complete control, it is only necessary to compare the voice of one possessing it, to that of a vocalist suffering with a cold in the head, or with a catarrhal affection and swollen tonsils. The difference in the clearness of the vibrations, and in the diffusive character of the tone, is very perceptible and marked. A clear knowledge of the organs which are employed in producing a vocal tone, and of the proper combination of the registers to secure power, purity, and equality throughout the entire vocal compass being gained, the organs of articulation present themselves for particular consideration; and this leads directly to the subject of musical elocution. System and facility in breathing, the employment of all the proper organs, in their healthy condition, for the production of a pure tone, expertness in reading music, and the minutest attention to attitude and gesture, will all fail to produce an impression worth remembering, unless a true conception of the meaning of the words and music, a bold enunciation, a distinct articulation, a well-rounded phrasing, and an accurate intonation be added to the acquirements of the finished vocalist. *Conception* relates to both words and music. If it be necessary for the speaker to study well the signification of words, in order to get at the true meaning of the poet, it is even more necessary for the singer to do so; since the effect of melody and harmony upon all persons, is such as to deprive them, measurably, of the power, for the time being, of judging of the signification of words. The singer who rests upon the simple effect of his melody, is certainly as weak as the speaker who relies upon his manner of uttering fine language, rather than upon the strength of the ideas involved. A true conception, it is hardly necessary to add, is the rarest of possessions among modern vocalists. *Pronunciation*, in its musical connection, not only implies that enunciation, or careful throwing out of each syllable and word which good speech and declamation require, but also that which, not particularly recognizing the inflections of reading or declamation, is entirely absorbed in the far more permeating channel of sound, a melody or recitative song according to a given key or scale. Dr. Rush alludes to this as the special advantage which the singer has over the speaker. Slowness and quickness of utterance are also controlled, to so great a degree, in music, by the relations of the notes, the bar, the fractional measure-marks, and words indicating varieties of movement, that there is left less liberty to the singer than to the speaker, in many respects. But such curtailment of liberty (which liberty, by the way, is often a clog to inexperienced speakers), and, by consequence, greater concentration upon the characteristics of the melody, only tie the singer to a more vivid conception of the subject, and to a more distinct pronunciation of the words. For the correction of marked inelegancies of pronunciation, whether of foreign or native growth, no means are so effective as the careful study of the classic languages, together with the study of the principal modern languages taught by native professors. Of these latter, the Italian is most musical in itself, and, therefore, is most useful to the musical student, whose pronunciation of his native language, particularly if he be English or German, will be vastly improved by often reading and singing in the most euphonious of modern languages. Of distinct *articulation*, it may in general be said, that the vowels only are sung while the consonants are articulated; in other words, that the vowels are *sung*, and the consonants are *spoken*. In vocalizing alone, the larynx, obedient to the mind and will, performs unassisted, save by the lungs, trachea, pharynx, and diaphragm, all those changes which promote power, purity, sweetness, and flexibility of tone. Some slight changes in the position of the jaws, tongue, and lips are necessary in vocalizing with *ah*, *ee*, *oh*, and *oo*; but only the consonants, as initial, intermediate, or final letters, require a constant and vigorous use of the tongue, teeth, and lips, which are the chief agents in acquiring an effective articulation. Full respirations should be the rule, and partial respirations the exception. In plain music, where one or two notes are appropriated to a syllable, the article should not be separated from the noun or qualifying adjective, nor the adjective from the noun, by a separated breathing; nor should the syllables of a word be separated. Long diatonic or chromatic runs, *arpeggios*, trills, and *cadenzas*, must, however, be executed with an unbroken continuity of the musical phrase. The orotund *basso* or barytone, as well as the rich and deep contralto, require to be particular in their articulation, in order to be heard, since the very fullness of their voices produces a resonance not easily overcome in large assembly rooms. Good *phrasing* implies good singing; such a knowledge of the composer's idea on the part of the singer, as shall not mar, to say the least, either the poetic or musical symmetry of what is sung. The singer should be able to analyze the phrases he sings, in order that, in melodic and harmonic construction, he may discover where they begin, how they progress, and where they end. But, if he cannot do this, he should be able, intuitively to grasp a musical passage to the fullest extent of its melodic proportions, and spontaneously to present it with such accessories as shall make it appear his own. All the bright coloring which may be imparted by a vivid conception, a good pronunciation and articulation, will be seriously dimmed by defective phrasing. Last, but by no means least, there must be the accurate *intonation* which is the result of a correct ear. Some persons do not hear correctly, concords becoming to them discords. Whether it be a local difficulty of the tympanum, or, as is more probable, a rigidity of the entire organization and sluggishness of temperament, the fact is obvious that defective ears are by no means uncommon; and, of course, to imitate musical sounds with the voice, in such cases, is an impossibility. The commonness of the defect increases, as we descend in the scale of social being, particularly where, in addition to poverty and moral degradation, there is superadded the prolific cause, absence of youthful opportunities of hearing music well sung or played. Could all classes, without exception, be gladdened, when young, by hearing music correctly sung and played, the number of those who pass through life unmoved "by the concord of sweet sounds", would be much diminished. It is important, also, that the sounds heard by children, be correct both as to

Phrasing.

Intonation, correct ear.

melody and rhythm, if it be expected that such children, when grown, shall have a so-called good ear for music. In remarking upon articulation, the value of the vowel sounds *ah, ee, oh,* and *oo* was noticed; and it is known that a thorough scale, and rhythmical use of these, combined with all the consonants as initial and final letters, will not only develop a more distinct articulation, but also a purer, more effective, and manageable tone. For standard authorities, on this subject, see *Cyclopædia of Education.*

WORD METHOD, a term applied to the analytic method of teaching children to read. The process consists of using short words instead of letters in the first lessons, the pupil learning to recognize and pronounce these words, and sometimes to read easy sentences, before learning the names of the letters. When a sufficient number of words have been learned, the pupil is shown their composite character, and taught the names and sounds of the letters which form them, thus learning the alphabet. In this process, care should be taken to select appropriate words, and present them in a progressive manner, as: *cat, rat, hat, mat, — man, fan, can, — dog, log,* etc. The pupil, in this way, perceives the power of each letter, and soon learns to spell and pronounce words, after which the synthetic method may be employed. (See ALPHABET METHOD.)

WORDS, Analysis of. The analysis or resolving of words into their elementary parts, is an important branch of the study of languages, the native as well as foreign. In ordinary school parlance, this branch is sometimes styled *etymology,* since the analysis comprehends not only an explanation of the meaning of each of the parts of a word — both root and affixes, but a knowledge of the derivation of these. For elementary school purposes, however, it should be borne in mind that the latter is of secondary importance. In the study of the native tongue, it will be acknowledged, the importance of training pupils to analyze compound and derivative words can hardly be overestimated. The fact that *Value of the study.* the English language derives about one-half of the words in ordinary use from the Latin, renders exercises in word analysis, of far greater necessity for the study of English, than for that of most other languages. That, without being trained in this analysis, pupils will scarcely be able to grasp the true meaning of English words, probably no experienced teacher, at present, will be inclined to dispute. To very many of the pupils who are merely drilled in spelling and reading, the force even of the most common Anglo-Saxon prefixes, like *a, be, en,* etc., and of suffixes, like *dom, hood, ship,* etc., must remain unknown. How many, for example, will be able to infer the meaning of *for* or *fore* in *forswear* and *forego*? The knowledge of the Latin prefixes and suffixes, even in the words of ordinary life, will be acquired with still greater difficulty by pupils not sufficiently trained in word analysis. On the other hand, only a slight knowledge of the simplest Latin prefixes, as: *ad, con, pre, pro, sub,* etc., affords a key to the distinctive meaning of a large number of words. It is, therefore, a matter of gratification to find that, at present, this branch of study is scarcely ever entirely omitted from the common-school course of instruction.

In regard to the method of teaching word analysis, it may justly be said that there are few subjects taught in elementary schools to which the fundamental principles of the developing method can so easily, and with so much advantage, be applied as to this. At whatever *Methods of teaching.* stage of the pupil's progress the instruction may begin, provided a knowledge of reading and writing has been acquired, the number of words already learned, will be found ample for the first and easiest exercises. Hardly any arbitrary memorizing is needed, since, if the teacher follow a natural course, he will only have to develop the knowledge already in the child's mind. Thus, children, even in the lowest grades, knowing the meaning of words like *teacher* and *preacher*, will not find the least difficulty in understanding that *er*, in both these words, means *one who*, and in perceiving that these words mean, respectively, *one who teaches*, and *one who preaches*. Nine-tenths of a class of pupils, of ordinary intelligence, will now readily find, among the words they are accustomed to use, several others in which the suffix *er* has the same meaning. They will not only fully comprehend this initiatory lesson, but they will feel a manifest delight that one simple explanation has so greatly added to their knowledge of the meaning of words. The intelligent teacher will not fail to perceive that the more closely he is able to accomodate his teaching to the knowledge of the words which belong to the pupils' own vocabulary, the more rapid will be their progress, and the more intense will be the interest which they will take in the new study. It is obviously a point of great importance that the first examples of prefixes or suffixes that are presented, should fully illustrate their general meaning. Thus, the word *teacher* would be a better selection for this purpose than *grocer;* sailor, better than *tailor;* and *repay*, better than *receive*. In the further progress of the study, it is important that the most common prefixes and suffixes should be learned before those of rarer use. It shows a great lack of pedagogical tact in a teacher to drill his pupils on *preter, subter*, and *retro*, before they know the meaning of *sub, con*, and *in*. A more difficult stage of this branch of study, is that which *Latin roots.* treats of the Latin roots, and their use in English words. Here, also, a strict adherence to the principle that we should proceed from the "known to the unknown"— from an analysis of what is already in the pupil's mind to that which is new, will guide the teacher with unerring certainty on the right path. For example, a judicious teacher who desires to familiarize his pupils with the derivates from the Latin root *duc* or *duct* (from *duco*), will not, at first, select such words as *induct, inductire, superinduce*, etc., or even words like *adduce, conduce, deduce*, before his pupils have learned to analyze words of a more obvious meaning; as *introduce, produce, reduce, aqueduct, viaduct*, etc. What is here meant is, that the first lessons in this kind of analysis should concern only those words the meaning of which may readily be explained by showing the meaning of their parts. In every subject of instruction, the order of presenting the various matters which are to be learned by the pupil, is of vital importance; but in none is it more essential than in the etymological analysis of words. The numerous class of words which cannot be explained, except by the history of their formation (such as *ambition, candidate, chancellor, peculiar;* also *sycophant, gazette, quarantine*, *Greek roots.* etc.) should be reserved for a higher grade of this study. The analysis of words derived from the Greek, should follow that of words derived from Latin roots; and the discussion of the etymological affinity of the words of different languages should be reserved for that stage of the course of studies which comprehends comparative philology. — For list of works on this subject, see Supplementary List in the Appendix. (See also ENGLISH, THE STUDY OF.)

ZOÖLOGY (Gr. ζῶον, an animal, and λόγος, a discourse) treats of the structure, classification, habits, etc., of animals. It is an important branch of descriptive natural science, or natural history, and usually forms a part of the course of study in various grades of schools. In elementary instruction, it constitutes, with its sister science, botany, one of the most effective and available subjects for training the observing faculties; and, hence, is often comprised in the course of instruction prescribed for common schools. This subject has peculiar attractions for children; since, as is well known, they invariably manifest a deep interest in animal life. The principles by which the teacher should be guided in giving instruction in this, as in other branches of natural science, have been to some extent explained in previous articles. (See ASTRONOMY, and BOTANY.) In teaching zoölogy, care must be particularly taken to exhibit as much as possible the natural objects themselves; and, in elementary teaching, this comes first. That is to say, the pupils are not to be required to commit to memory dry definitions and formulated statements; but their minds should be brought in contact with the living realities. In this way an interest in the study will be created without which no real progress can be made. After a considerable amount of discursive observation, so that the child's mind has become stored with conceptions, a more systematic treatment may be commenced, approaching the elements of classification, the pupil being gradually made to perceive the distinctions upon which the classification depends. In order to fix these destinctions in the mind, well-known animals may be taken as types: as (class 1) *man, monkey, bat, cat, rat, horse, deer, cow, whale*; (2) *eagle, parrot, canary, rooster, ostrich, snipe, duck*; (3) *turtle, alligator, rattlesnake, frog*; (4) *perch, cod, shark*, etc.; (5) *bee, butterfly, beetle*, etc.; (6) *spider, crab*; (7) *squid, snail, oyster*; (8) *starfish, jellyfish, coral*. Thus the classes, orders, and genera may be illustrated very clearly, and in an interesting manner.

At first it is better to use the simple English vocabulary than to trouble the mind of the young pupil with the difficult, and to him unmeaning, scientific terms; as *four-handed* instead of *quadrumana*, *gnawers* for *rodentia*, *scratchers*, for *rasores*, *two-winged* for *diptera*, etc. In this elementary instruction, it is not necessary that the classification should include species and variety, in some cases not even genera; but in describing an animal it is proper to require the pupil to mention the *class*, *order*, *family*, and *genus*, and in this order.

Great care should be taken, as in all science teaching, to have the pupil depend as much as possible upon his own observation for the facts used; and, as in botany, the schedule system may have a modified or limited application in teaching this subject. Microscopic examinations of a simple kind may also be resorted to in order to increase the interest of the pupil, and kindle a desire for closer research.

In the higher grades of instruction, the three different departments of the science — morphology, physiology, and distribution, should systematically be treated. In every grade of instruction, however, the teacher or professor cannot too closely follow the principle laid down by Huxley: "The great business of the scientific teacher is to imprint the fundamental, irrefragable facts of his science, not only by words upon the mind, but by sensible impressions upon the eye, and ear, and touch of the student, in so complete a manner, that every term used, or law enunciated, may afterwards call up vivid images of the particular structural, or other, facts which furnished the demonstration of the law, or the illustration of the term". Moreover, every teacher should bear in mind that a good share of his own knowledge should be at first-hand — acquired by his own observation, not simply gleaned from books — or he will not succeed in awakening an interest in the minds of his pupils. The proper method of teaching this subject has been clearly shown by one of its greatest masters. See HUXLEY, *On the Study of Zoölogy*, in *The Culture demanded by Modern Life*. (N. Y., 1867.) (See SCIENCE, THE TEACHING OF.)

Higher instruction.

APPENDIX.

A SELECT LIST OF

EDUCATIONAL WORKS,

ENGLISH, FRENCH, AND GERMAN,

ARRANGED BY

W. H. PAYNE, M. A.,

PROFESSOR OF THE SCIENCE AND THE ART OF TEACHING

IN THE UNIVERSITY OF MICHIGAN.

"A true university in these days is a collection of books."
CARLYLE.

"If the soul of a library be its librarian, its heart is the catalogue." *Gentleman's Magazine.*

"If you are troubled with a pride of accuracy, and would have it taken completely out of you, print a catalogue."
STEVENS.

CONTENTS.

I. WORKS OF REFERENCE.
II. ALLIED SCIENCES.
III. GENERAL EDUCATION.
IV. SPECIAL EDUCATION.
V. SCHOOL ECONOMY.
VI. HISTORY OF EDUCATION.
VII. MISCELLANEOUS EDUCATIONAL LITERATURE.

NOTICE.

This List purposely omits works that are out of print, or are privately printed, or otherwise difficult to obtain. On the other hand it is intended to enumerate — within its limited compass — publications now in the market that are of sufficient merit and importance. It will be revised for future editions, and the undersigned publishers will, therefore, be obliged for the suggestion of corrections and additions.

E. STEIGER & CO.

THE DICTIONARY OF EDUCATION AND INSTRUCTION

I. WORKS OF REFERENCE.

Bibliographies, Catalogues, Cyclopædias, Dictionaries, Hand-Books and Text-Books of Education.

Henry Barnard. *Library of Practical Pedagogy.* 8vo. 10 vols. — *National System of Education.* 8vo. 10 vols. — 400 Treatises on Educational Subjects. —
 For prices address HENRY BARNARD, 28 Main St., HARTFORD, Conn.

J. B. Basedow's *Elementarwerk. Ein encyclopädisches Methoden- u. Bildungsbuch für alle Kindererziehung und den Jugend-Unterricht in allen Ständen.* 8vo. Stuttgart. $2.00

H. Beyer's Bibliothek pädagogischer Classiker. *Sammlung der bedeutendsten pädagogischen Schriften älterer und neuerer Zeit. Unter Mitwirkung mehrerer Schulmänner und Gelehrten neu hrsg. v. FRDR. MANN.* Parts 1—98. 8vo. Langensalza. Each $0.20

Dictionnaire de Pédagogie *et d'Instruction Primaire.* Redigé par T. BUISSON. Parts 1—85. 8vo. Paris. Each $0.20
 Now in progress of publication in parts. The work will probably comprise six volumes of about 1000 pages each, and will be the most valuable of its kind ever published. Contains a bibliography of French educational works.

Adf. Diesterweg's *Ausgewählte Schriften,* hrsg. v. EDU. LANGENBERG. 8vo. 4 vols. Frankfurt a. M. $5.50

F. A. W. Diesterweg. *Wegweiser zur Bildung für deutsche Lehrer. In neuer zeitgemässer Bearbeitung hrsg. von dem Curatorium der Diesterweg-Stiftung.* 8vo. 3 vols. Essen. $7.70

Education and General Philology. *A Classified Descriptive Catalogue of American, British, German, French, and other Foreign Publications on Education and General Philology; together with Works of Reference, Teachers' Hand-Books, etc., exclusive of Text-Books.* Edited by E. STEIGER. 8vo. N. Y. $0.10 net.

Encyclopädie d. gesammten Erziehungs- und Unterrichtswesens, bearbeitet von einer Anzahl Schulmänner und Gelehrten, hrsg. unter Mitwirkung v. PALMER u. WILDERMUTH, v. K. A. SCHMID. 8vo. 11 vols. Gotha. $55.75

H. Kiddle and A. J. Schem. *The Cyclopædia of Education: A Dictionary of Information for the use of Teachers, School Officers, Parents, and Others.* 8vo. N. Y. Cloth. $5.00. Sheep. $6.00
 An educational library in itself, invaluable to every progressive teacher.

—— *The Dictionary of Education and Instruction; A Reference Book and Manual on the Theory and Practice of Teaching, for the use of Parents, Teachers, and Others; based upon the Cyclopædia of Education.* 12mo. N. Y. Cloth. $1.50

—— *The Year Book of Education for* 1878. 8vo. N. Y. Cloth. $2.00
—— *The Year Book of Education for* 1879. 8vo. N. Y. Cloth. $2.00

Pädagogische Bibliothek. *Sammlung der wichtigsten pädagogischen Schriften älterer und neuerer Zeit. Im Verein mit Gesinnungsgenossen hrsg. v. K. RICHTER.* 8vo. Parts 1—93. Leipzig. Each $0.20

Real-Encyclopädie des Erziehungs- und Unterrichtswesens *nach katholischen Principien. Unter Mitwirkung von geistlichen und weltlichen Schulmännern für Geistliche, Volksschullehrer, Eltern und Erzieher bearbeitet von H. ROLFUS u. A. PFISTER.* 8vo. 4 vols. Mainz. $10.30

K. A. Schmid. *Pädagogisches Handbuch für das Haus, die Volks-, Bürger-, Mittel- und Fortbildungsschule. Auf Grundlage der "Encyclopädie des gesammten Erziehungs- und Unterrichtswesens" in alphabetischer Ordnung bearbeitet.* 8vo. 2 vols. Gotha. $8.45
 " A vast mine of information on everything connected with education ". QUICK.

G. E. Schott. *Handbuch der Pädagogischen Literatur.* 8vo. 3 Parts. Leipzig. $2.20

Steiger's *Educational Directory for* 1878. 8vo. N. Y. Limp Cloth. $1.50

August Vogel. *Systematische Encyclopädie der Pädagogik. Ein Wegweiser durch das gesammte Gebiet der Erziehung. Mit ausführlicher Angabe der Literatur.* 8vo. Eisenach. $1.50

THE DICTIONARY OF EDUCATION AND INSTRUCTION

II. ALLIED SCIENCES.

Anthropology, Ethnology, Ethics, Linguistics, Metaphysics, Psychology, Physiology, Sociology, Political Economy.

John Abercrombie. *The Philosophy of the Moral Feelings*, edited and adapted to the use of schools by JACOB ABBOTT. 12mo. N. Y. Cloth. $0.90

—— *Inquiries concerning the Intellectual Powers*, edited and adapted to the use of schools by JACOB ABBOTT. 12mo. N. Y. Cloth. $0.90

Aristotle. *The Rhetoric and Poetics, and Nicomachean Ethics.* BOHN'S translations. 2 vols. London. Cloth. Each $2.00

Alexander Bain. *The Senses and the Intellect.* 8vo. N. Y. $5.00

—— *Mind and Body. The Theories of their Relation.* 12mo. N. Y. Cloth. $1.50

—— *The Emotions and the Will.* 8vo. N. Y. Cloth. $5.00

S. P. Bates. *Lectures on Mental and Moral Culture.* 12mo. N. Y. Cloth. $1.50

Fr. E. Beneke. *The Elements of Psychology, on the Principles of Beneke, Stated and Illustrated in a Simple and Popular Manner* by G. RAUE. Fourth ed. by JOHANN GOTTLIEB DRESSLER. Translated from the German. 8vo. Oxford. Cloth. $3.00
Commended by Dr. DONALDSON.

Julius H. Bernstein. *The Five Senses of Man.* 12mo. N. Y. Cloth. $1.75

H. T. Buckle. *History of Civilization in England.* With a complete Index. 2 vols. 8vo. N. Y. Cloth. $4.00

S. Butler. *Unconscious Memory: A Comparison between the Theory of Dr. EWALD and "The Philosophy of the Unconditioned"* of Dr. EDWARD V. HARTMANN. *With translations from these Authors, and Preliminary Chapters bearing on Life and Habit, Evolution Old and New, and Mr.* CHARLES DARWIN'S *edition of Dr.* KRAUSE'S *"Erasmus Darwin."* 8vo. London. Cloth. $3.00

W. B. Carpenter. *Principles of Human Physiology.* By H. POWER. 8vo. Illustrated. London. $11.20

—— *The same.* New American from 8th London ed. Illustr. 8vo. Philadelphia. Cloth. $5.50 Leather. $6.50

S. T. Coleridge. *Aids to Reflection in the Foundation of a Manly Character.* 12mo. London. Cloth. $2.10
—— —— 12mo. N. Y. Cloth. $1.50

And. Combe. *The Principles of Physiology applied to the Preservation of Health, and the Improvement of Physical and Mental Education.* Illustr. 18mo. N. Y. Cloth. $0.75

Victor Cousin. *Course of the History of Modern Philosophy.* 2 vols. 12mo. N. Y. Cloth. $4.00

F. W. Farrar. *Chapters on Language.* 8vo. London. Cloth. $2.80

Joseph Marie de Gerando. *Histoire comparée des systèmes de philosophie, considérés relativement aux principes des connaissances humaines.* 2e partie: *Histoire de la philosophie moderne à partir de la renaissance des lettres jusqu'à la fin du 18. siècle.* 4 vols. 8vo. Paris. $8.60

F. Guizot. *History of Civilization.* 2 vols. 12mo. N. Y. Cloth. $4.00
—— —— 3 vols. London. Cloth. $3.75

E. Haeckel. *Freedom in Science and Teaching.* 12mo. N. Y. Cloth. $1.00

H. Hallam. *Introduction to the Literature of Europe in the Fifteenth, Sixteenth, and Seventeenth Centuries.* 2 vols. 8vo. N. Y. Cloth. $2.50
—— *A View of the State of Europe during the Middle Ages.* 2 vols. 8vo. N. Y. Cloth. $2.50

W. Hamilton. *Lectures, embracing the Metaphysical and Logical Courses.* 2 vols. 8vo. N. Y. Cloth. $7.00
The best system of psychology, for the scientific study of education, with which I am acquainted.

Mark Hopkins. *An Outline Study of Man.* 12mo. N. Y. Cloth. $1.75

W. S. Jevons. *Elementary Lessons in Logic, Deductive and Inductive.* 16mo. London. Cloth. $0.90
—— *The Principles of Science. A Treatise on Logic and Scientific Method.* 8vo. London. Cloth. $2.75

Krauth-Fleming. *Vocabulary of the Philosophical Sciences.* 12mo. N. Y. Cloth. $3.50
Invaluable to students of philosophy and educational science.

THE DICTIONARY OF EDUCATION AND INSTRUCTION

Albert Lemoine. *L'Habitude et l'Instinct. Étude de Psychologie Comparée.* 16mo. Paris. $0.90

G. H. Lewes. *Problems of Life and Mind.* 5 vols. 8vo. Boston. Cloth. $14.00
—— *Physiology of Common Life.* 12mo. 2 vols. N. Y. Cloth. $3.00

Sir John Lubbock. *The Origin of Civilization, and the Primitive Condition of Man.* 12mo. N. Y. Cloth. $2.00

J. M'Cosh. *Intuitions of the Mind, inductively investigated.* 8vo. N. Y. Cloth. $3.00

H. Longueville Mansel. *Metaphysics; or, the Philosophy of Consciousness, Phenomenal and Real.* 12mo. N. Y. Cloth. $1.75

C. Marcel. *The Study of Languages brought back to its true Principles.* 12mo. N. Y. Cloth. $1.25

H. Maudsley. *The Physiology and Pathology of the Mind.* 8vo. 2 vols. N. Y. Cloth. $4.00
—— *Body and Mind; an Inquiry into their Connection and Mutual Influence, especially in reference to Mental Disorders.* With Appendix. 12mo. N. Y. Cloth. $1.50

J. S. Mill. *A System of Logic.* 8vo. N. Y. Cloth. $3.00

G. Moore. *Power of the Soul over the Body, in relation to Health and Morals.* 12mo. N. Y. Cloth. $1.00

J. D. Morell. *History of Modern Philosophy.* 8vo. N. Y. Cloth. $3.50

Noah Porter. *The Human Intellect.* 8vo. N. Y. Cloth. $5.00

J. Ray. *Mental Hygiene.* 16mo. Boston. Cloth. $1.50

H. Spencer. *The Study of Sociology.* 12mo. N. Y. Cloth. $1.50

W. Thomson. *Outline of the necessary Laws of Thought.* 12mo. N. Y. Cloth. $1.50
One of the best introductions to logic.

R. C. Trench. *On the Study of Words.* 12mo. N. Y. Cloth. $1.25

F. Wayland. *The Elements of Political Economy.* 12mo. N. Y. Cloth. $1.75
—— Abridgment for schools and academies. 16mo. N. Y. Cloth. $0.70

Richard Whately. *Elements of Logic.* 12mo. N. Y. Cloth. $0.75

W. D. Whitney. *The Life and Growth of Language.* 12mo. N. Y. Cloth. $1.50

G. Wilson. *The Five Gateways of Knowledge.* 12mo. London. $0.40

R. S. Wyld. *Physics and Philosophy of the Senses.* 12mo. London. Cloth. ($3.00) reduced to $1.50

E. L. Youmans. *The Culture demanded by Modern Life.* 12mo. N. Y. Cloth. $2.00

III. GENERAL EDUCATION.

Philosophy of Education. Science and Art of Teaching (Pedagogy and Didactics). Special Didactics. Home Education and Self-Education.

1. Philosophy of Education.

Alexander Bain. *Education as a Science.* 12mo. N. Y. Cloth. $1.75
"Signalons au premier rang les essais de pédagogie psychologique, les articles récemment publiés par M. BAIN." COMPAYRÉ.
A text-book in the Science of Teaching, in the University of Michigan.

F. A. P. Barnard. *Early Mental Training,* and HENFREY's Lecture on the *Educational Claims of Botanical Science,* contained in "*The Culture demanded by Modern Life*". By E. L. YOUMANS. 12mo. N. Y. Cloth. $2.00

H. Barnard. *English Pedagogy — Old and New: or, Treatises and Thoughts on Education, the School, and the Teacher. First Series: Ascham to Wotton. — Second Series: Arnold to Wolsey.* 8vo. Hartford. Cloth. Each $3.50
—— *American Pedagogy: Contributions to the Principles and Methods of Education.* 8vo. Hartford. Cloth. $3.50
—— *German Pedagogy: Views of German Educators and Teachers on the Principles of Education, and Methods of Instruction for Schools of different Grades.* 8vo. Hartford. Cloth. $3.50

THE DICTIONARY OF EDUCATION AND INSTRUCTION

H. Barnard. *Aphorisms and Suggestions on Education and Methods of Instruction — Ancient and Modern.* 8vo. Hartford. Cloth. $3.00

These books, and others that will be named, are republished from *Barnard's American Journal of Education*, a periodical that can not be too highly commended.

E. Barth. *Ueber den Umgang. Beitrag zur Schulpädagogik.* 8vo. Langensalza. $0.55

G. Baur. *Grundzüge der Erziehungs-Lehre.* 8vo. Giessen. $2.20

Beesau's *Spirit of Education.* 12mo. Syracuse. Cloth. $1.25

F. E. Beneke. *Erziehungs- und Unterrichtslehre. Neu bearbeitet und mit Zusätzen versehen v. J. G. DRESSLER.* 8vo. 2 vols. Berlin. $4.40

C. W. Bennett. *Education Abroad.* 12mo. Syracuse. $0.25

C. Beyer. *Erziehung zur Vernunft. Philosophisch-pädagogische Grundlinien für Erziehung und Unterricht.* 8vo. Wien. $1.10

J. S. Blackie. *On Education.* 8vo. London. $0.40

Ernst Böhme. *Des Sohnes Erziehung. Pädagogische Briefe an eine Mutter.* 12mo. Dresden. $0.85

K. Bormann. *Ueber Erziehung und Unterricht.* 8vo. Leipzig. $1.10

—— *Pädagogik für Volksschullehrer, auf Grund der allgemeinen Bestimmungen vom 15. October 1872, betreffend das Volksschul-, Präparanden- und Seminarwesen, bearbeitet.* 8vo. Berlin. $1.50

W. Braubach. *Fundamentallehre der Pädagogik oder Begründung derselben zu einer strengen Wissenschaft.* 8vo. Giessen. $0.60

Buell's *Elements of Education.* 12mo. Syracuse. $0.15

E. H. Clarke. *The Building of a Brain.* 16mo. Boston. Cloth. $1.25

—— *Sex in Education. A fair Chance for Girls.* 16mo. Boston. Cloth. $1.25

G. Combe. *On Education.* 12mo. N. Y. Cloth. $5.00

Johann Amos Comenius. *Pädagogische Schriften. Uebersetzt und mit Anmerkungen und des Comenius Biographie versehen von TH. LION.* 16mo. Langensalza. $1.10

—— *Ausgewählte Schriften. Mutterschule, Pansophie, Pangnosie, etc. Uebersetzt und mit Erläuterungen versehen von Jr. BEEGER und J. LEUTBECHER.* 8vo. Leipzig. $1.10

Johann Amos Comenius. *Grosse Unterrichtslehre. Aus dem Lateinischen übersetzt und mit Anmerkungen versehen von Jr. BEEGER und FRL. ZOUBEK.* 8vo. Leipzig. $1.30

"As a school reformer he was the forerunner of Rousseau, Basedow, and Pestalozzi, suggested a mode of instruction which renders learning attractive to children by pictures and illustrations, and wrote the first pictorial school-book". *New Amer. Cyclopædia.*

W. J. G. Curtmann. *Lehrbuch der Erziehung und des Unterrichts.* 8vo. 2 vols. Leipzig. $2.80

B. G. Denzel. *Einleitung in die Erziehungs- und Unterrichtslehre für Volksschullehrer.* 8vo. 3 vols. With 5 plates. Stuttgart. $4.00

Frdr. Dittes. *Grundriss der Erziehungs- und Unterrichtslehre.* 8vo. Leipzig. $1.10

—— *Methodik der Volksschule. Auf geschichtlicher Grundlage.* 8vo. Leipzig. $1.35

—— *Schule der Pädagogik. Gesammt-Ausgabe der Psychologie und Logik, Erziehungs- und Unterrichtslehre, Methodik der Volksschule, Geschichte der Erziehung und des Unterrichts.* 8vo. Leipzig. $3.70

J. Donaldson. *Lectures on Education in Prussia and England.* 8vo. Edinburgh. Cloth. $1.40

Mrs. E. B. Duffey. *No Sex in Education; or an equal chance for both boys and girls.* 16mo. Philadelphia. Cloth. $1.00

F. A. Ph. Dupanloup. *De l'Éducation.* 8vo. 3 vols. Paris. $3.50

—— *Die Erziehung. Aus dem Französischen übersetzt.* 8vo. 3 vols. Mainz. $4.25

R. L. and M. Edgeworth. *Treatise on Practical Education.* 12mo. N. Y. Cloth. $1.50

Edward Everett. *Importance of Practical Education and Useful Knowledge; being a Selection from his Orations and other Discourses.* 12mo. N.Y. Cloth.$1.50

F. W. Farrar. *Essays on a Liberal Education.* 8vo. London. Cloth. $3.00

J. Foster. *Essays on the Evils of popular Ignorance.* 12mo. N. Y. Cloth. $1.25

O. S. Fowler. *Education and Self-Improvement.* Illustr. 12mo. N. Y. Cloth. $3.50

A. H. Francke. *Schriften über Erziehung und Unterricht. Bearbeitet und mit Erläuterungen versehen von KARL RICHTER.* 8vo. 2 vols. Langensalza. $2.20

Th. Fritz. *Esquisse d'un système complet d'Instruction et d'Éducation et de leur histoire.* 8vo. 3 vols. Strasbourg. $4.50

H. Gräfe. *Allgemeine Pädagogik. In drei Büchern.* 8vo. 2 vols. Leipzig. $4.40

—— *Deutsche Volksschule, oder die Bürger- u. Landschule nach der Gesammtheit ihrer Verhältnisse. Nebst einer Geschichte der Volksschule. Ein Handbuch für Lehrer und Schulaufseher. Neu bearbeitet von J. Chr. Gottlob Schumann.* 8vo. 3 vols. Jena. $5.35

Frdr. Froebel. *Gesammelte pädagogische Schriften.* Hrsg. v. Wich. Lange. 8vo. 2 vols. in 3 divisions. Berlin. $8.80

Separately:
I. 1. *Aus Froebel's Leben und ernstem Streben. Autobiographie und kleinere Schriften.* With portrait. $2.60
I. 2. *Ideen Froebel's über die Menschenerziehung und Aufsätze verschiedenen Inhalts.* With 3 plates. $2.95
II. *Die Pädagogik des Kindergartens. Gedanken F. Froebel's über das Spiel und die Spielgegenstände des Kindes.* With 4 pages of music and 16 plates. $3.30

John Gill. *Systems of Education: A History and Criticism of the Principles, Methods, Organization and Moral Discipline Advocated by Eminent Educationists.* 8vo. London. Cloth. $1.00

J. B. Graser. *Divinität oder das Princip der einzig wahren Menschenerziehung zur festen Begründung der Erziehungs- und Unterrichtswissenschaft.* 8vo. 2 vols. Bayreuth. $3.60

A. W. Grube. *Pädagogische Studien und Kritiken für Lehrer und Erzieher. Vermischte Aufsätze aus den Jahren 1845—1860.* 8vo. Leipzig. $1.65

—— *Neue Folge. Studien und Kritiken für Pädagogen und Theologen.* 8vo. Leipzig. $0.75

—— *Von der sittlichen Bildung der Jugend im ersten Jahrzehend des Lebens. Pädagogische Skizzen für Eltern, Lehrer, etc.* 8vo. Leipzig. $0.75

—— *Blicke in's Triebleben der Seele. Psychologische Studien für angehende Pädagogen und Psychologen, wie auch für gebildete Väter und Freunde der Seelenkunde überhaupt.* 8vo. Leipzig. $1.10

W. N. Hailmann. *Lectures on Education.* 12mo. Milwaukee. $0.25

—— *Erziehungs-Grundsätze für Schule und Haus.* 12mo. Milwaukee. $0.25.

Ph. Gilb. Hamerton. *The Intellectual Life.* 8vo. Boston. Cloth. $2.00 Part III. (Of Education) is especially valuable.

—— *Higher Education.* 12mo. N. Y. Cloth. $1.00

Elizabeth Hamilton. *Letters on the Elementary Principles of Education.* 32mo. 2 vols. London. Cloth. $1.60

Sir William Hamilton. *Discussions on Philosophy and Literature, Education and University Reform.* 8vo. N. Y. Cloth. $3.00

Contains the famous essay on the value of mathematical studies.

John Hecker. *Scientific Basis of Education.* 8vo. N. Y. Cloth. $2.50

J. F. Herbart. *Pädagogische Schriften in chronologischer Reihenfolge.* Hrsg. v. O. Willmann. 8vo. 2 vols. Leipzig. $5.50

Herm. Hoffmeister. *Comenius und Pestalozzi als Begründer der Volksschule.* 8vo. Berlin. $0.55

—— *Examen-Katechismus.* III. *Pädagogik. Ein Repetitionsbuch für Abiturienten, Schulamts-Candidaten und Aspiranten der Mittelschullehrer- und Rectoratsprüfung.* 8vo. Berlin. $0.95

F. D. Huntington. *Unconscious Tuition.* 12mo. Syracuse. $0.15

This essay is an educational classic.

Thos. H. Huxley. *Lay Sermons, Addresses and Reviews.* 12mo. N. Y. Cloth. $1.75

Imm. Kant. *Ueber Pädagogik. Mit Einleitung und Anmerkungen von Otto Willmann.* 8vo. Leipzig. $0.40

Jos. Kehrein. *Handbuch der Erziehung und des Unterrichtes zunächst für Seminarzöglinge und Elementarlehrer. Nach dem Tode des Verfassers bearbeitet v. A. Keller.* 8vo. Paderborn. $1.00

L. Kellner. *Kurze Geschichte der Erziehung und des Unterrichtes mit vorwaltender Rücksicht auf das Volksschulwesen.* 8vo. Essen. $0.75

—— *Zur Pädagogik der Schule und des Hauses. Aphorismen, Schulaufsehern, Lehrern und Eltern gewidmet.* 8vo. Essen. $0.70

—— *Volksschulkunde. Ein Hand- und Hülfsbuch für katholische Seminare, Lehrer und Schulaufseher.* 8vo. Essen. $1.10

—— *Die Pädagogik der Volksschule und des Hauses in Aphorismen.* 8vo. Essen. $0.55

THE DICTIONARY OF EDUCATION AND INSTRUCTION

L. Kellner. *Pädagogische Mittheilungen aus den Gebieten der Schule und des Lebens. Mit besonderer Rücksicht auf die Fortbildung der Volksschullehrer in den Conferenzen.* 8vo. 2 parts. Essen. $1.50

Frdr. Körner. *Unterrichts- und Erziehungskunst nach physiologisch-psychologischen Gesetzen und den Forderungen des Culturlebens. Für Eltern, Lehrer und Freunde einer zeitgemässen Volksbildung.* 8vo. Pressburg. $2.75

Ernst Laas. *Die Pädagogik des Johannes Sturm. Historisch und kritisch beleuchtet.* 8vo. Berlin. $0.75

Wich. Lange. *Knospen, Blüthen und Früchte erziehlichen Strebens. Pädagogische Anregungen.* 8vo. Hamburg. $1.55

Emile de Laveleye. *L'Instruction du Peuple.* 8vo. Paris. $2.50

G. E. Lessing. *The Education of the Human Race. Translated by F. M. Robertson.* 8vo. London. Cloth. $1.25

J. Leutbecher. *Joh. Amos Comenius' Lehrkunst.* 8vo. Leipzig. $0.45

John Locke. *Some Thoughts concerning Education. With Introduction and Notes by Rev. R. H. Quick.* 12mo. Cambridge. $1.40
"Almost all the influence which England has had on the theory of Education must be attributed to Locke alone." QUICK.

L. C. Loomis. *Mental and Social Culture.* 12mo. N. Y. Cloth. $0.75

Horace Mann. *Thoughts selected from the writings of* HORACE MANN. 12mo. Boston. Cloth. $1.25
—— *Lectures and Annual Reports on Education.* 8vo. Boston. Cloth. $3.00
As an exposition of a body of sound public school doctrine, these lectures are unequalled in the whole range of our educational literature.

E. D. Mansfield. *American Education.* 12mo. N. Y. Cloth. $1.50

T. Markby. *Practical Essays on Education.* 8vo. London. Cloth. $2.00

Ira Mayhew. *Universal Education: Its Means and Ends.* 12mo. N. Y. Cloth. $1.75

J. Milton. *Treatise of Education.* 24mo. N. Y. $0.25

M. de Montaigne. *Works. Comprising his Essays, Journey into Italy, and Letters; with Notes from all the Commentators, Biographical and Bibliographical Notices, etc., by* W. HAZLITT. 8vo. Philadelphia. Cloth. $3.50
(Paternal Affection; against Idleness; of Lyars; of Pedantry; Custom and Law; of the Education of Children; of Anger.)
"An admirable resume of all that has been settled in regard to educational aims up to the present time." *Cyclopædia of Education.*

A. Oppler. *Three Lectures on Education, delivered before the College of Preceptors.* Revised and enlarged. 8vo. London. Cloth. $1.80

Joseph Payne. *The Science and Art of Education.* 12mo. N. Y. Paper. $0.15; Cloth. $0.40
—— *Lectures on the Science and Art of Education, with other Lectures and Essays. Edited by* JOSEPH F. PAYNE. *With an Introduction by Rev. R. H.* QUICK. 8vo. Portrait. London. Cloth. $3.60
Joseph Payne was one of the first educators of this century; and this volume is one of the most valuable contributions ever made to our educational literature.

J. H. Pestalozzi's *Sämmtliche Werke. Gesichtet, vervollständigt und mit erläuternden Einleitungen versehen v.* L. W. SEYFFARTH. 8vo. 18 vols. Brandenburg. $13.45
—— *Ausgewählte Werke. Mit Pestalozzi's Biographie hrsg. v.* FRDR. MANN. 8vo. 4 vols. Langensalza. $2.75
—— *Lienhard und Gertrud. Ein Buch für das Volk.* 16mo. Leipzig. $0.40; Cloth. $0.60
—— *Auszug in einem Bande. Von* L. W. SEYFFARTH. 8vo. Brandenburg. $0.90
—— *Wie Gertrud ihre Kinder lehrt. Mit einer Einleitung: Johann Heinrich Pestalozzi's Leben, Werke und Grundsätze. Einleitung und Commentar v.* K. RIEDEL. 8vo. Leipzig. $0.75

Mrs. A. H. L. Phelps. *The Educator; or, Hours with my Pupils.* 12mo. N. Y. Cloth. $1.50

W. F. Phelps. *What is Education?* 12mo. N. Y. Paper. $0.10

Richard Quain. *On Some Defects in General Education.* 8vo. N.Y. Cloth. $1.25

A. W. Raub. *Plain Educational Talk with Teachers and Parents.* 12mo. Philadelphia. Cloth. $1.50

Hugo Reid. *Elementary Treatise on Principles of Education.* 12mo. London. $2.00

Ernest Renan. *La Part de la Famille et de l'Etat dans l'Education.* 12mo. Paris. $0.20

Jean Paul F. Richter. *Levana, or, The Doctrine of Education.* 12mo. Boston. Cloth. $2.00

Pädagogische Bibliothek. *Sammlung der wichtigsten pädagogischen Schriften älterer und neuerer Zeit. Hrsg. v.* KARL RICHTER. 8vo. Parts 1–93. Leipzig. Each $0.20
(I. Pestalozzi; II. Salzmann; III. Comenius; IV. Montaigne, Rabelais; V. VI. Francke;

VII. Pestalozzi; VIII. Rousseau; IX. Locke; X. Kant; XI. Comenius; XII. Campe; XIII. XIV. Herbart; XV. Salzmann; XVI. Vives.

G. A. **Riecke.** *Erziehungslehre.* 8vo. Stuttgart. $1.55

Carl **Rosenkranz.** *The Science of Education: or, Pedagogics as a System. Translated from the German by* ANNA C. BRACKETT. 8vo. St. Louis. Paper. $1.00; Cloth. $1.50
The text-book in the department of Pedagogics in the University of Missouri.

—— *Die Pädagogik als System. Ein Grundriss.* 8vo. Königsberg. $1 35

J. J. **Rousseau.** *Emil, oder Ueber die Erziehung.* Deutsch von H. DENHARDT. 16mo. 2 vols. Leipzig. Cloth. $1.10

—— *Emile, ou de l'Education.* 16mo. Paris. $1.05
"Perhaps the most influential book ever written on the subject of education." QUICK.

—— *Emilius and Sophia: or, A New System of Education.* 12mo. 4 vols. London. About $4.50
"C'est de l'Angleterre (Locke) qu'est venu le premier germe de l'EMILE; c'est en Allemagne que l'EMILE a porté tous ses fruits bons ou mauvais". COMPAYRÉ

C. G. **Salzmann.** *Noch etwas über die Erziehung.* $0.40. — *Ameisenbüchlein.* $0.40. — *Ueber die wirksamsten Mittel, Kindern Religion beizubringen.* $0.55. 8vo. 3 parts. Leipzig. $1.35

Frdr. **Schleiermacher.** *Erziehungslehre.* Hrsg. v. C. PLATZ. 8vo. Leipzig. Cloth. $1.85

K. A. **Schmid.** *Aus Schule und Zeit Reden und Aufsätze.* 8vo. Gotha. $1.50

—— *Pädagogisches Handbuch für das Haus, die Volks-, Bürger-, Mittel- und Fortbildungsschule. Auf Grundlage der Encyklopädie des gesammten Erziehungs- und Unterrichtswesens in alphabetischer Ordnung bearbeitet.* 8vo. 2 vols. Gotha. $10.65

C. Chr. G. **Schmidt.** *Ueber Erziehung. Nach den Aussprüchen der heiligen Schrift, den Werken Jean Paul's, Schleiermacher's u. A., sowie nach eigener Erfahrung.* 8vo. Leipzig. $0.55

K. **Schmidt.** *Buch der Erziehung. Die Gesetze der Erziehung und des Unterrichts, gegründet auf die Naturgesetze des menschlichen Leibes und Geistes. Briefe an Eltern, Lehrer und Erzieher.* With woodcuts. 8vo. Cöthen. $2.20

C. F. **Schnell.** *Zur Pädagogik der That. Praktische Punkte der Erziehung und Bildung, nebst Anhang, Schulgesetze betreffend.* 8vo. Berlin. $1.10

J. Chr. Glob. **Schumann.** *Leitfaden der Pädagogik für den Unterricht in Lehrerbildungsanstalten.* 1. *Die systematische Pädagogik und die Schulkunde.* 8vo. Hannover. $0.90

—— II. *Geschichte der Pädagogik.* $0.90

—— *Pädagogische Chrestomathie. Eine Auswahl aus den pädagogischen Meisterwerken aller Zeiten für die pädagogische Privatlectüre mit Einleitungen und Anmerkungen versehen.* 1. *Die pädagogischen Meisterwerke des orientalischen Alterthums und der alten Griechen.* 8vo. Hannover. $1.10

L. **Schwenke.** *Erziehung und Unterricht; Pädagogische Aussprüche für Eltern, Lehrer und Erzieher.* 8vo. Leipzig. $0.95

E. **Schwab.** *School-Garden: a practical contribution to the Subject of Education.* 12mo. N. Y. $0.50

Jules **Simon.** *L'Ecole. Nouvelle édition mise au courant des dernières statistiques et de l'état actuel de la législation.* 18mo. Paris. $1.25

—— *La Réforme de l'enseignement secondaire.* 18mo. Paris. $1.25

Herbert **Spencer.** *Education: Intellectual, Moral and Physical.* 12mo. N. Y. Cloth. $1.25
A work of great ability, written from the *laissez faire* point of view. It magnifies the part played by Nature in education, but observes the influence of human art. It is suggestive and worthy of study; but unless studied critically, it is misleading.

J. G. **Spurzheim.** *Education: its Element; Principles founded on Nature of Man.* 12mo. N. Y. Cloth. $1.50

Ludwig **Strümpell.** *Psychologische Pädagogik.* 8vo. Leipzig. $2.00

Thos. **Tate.** *The Philosophy of Education.* 12mo. London. Cloth. $2.60

G. **Thaulow.** *Hegel's Ansichten über Erziehung und Unterricht.* 8vo. 3 vols. Kiel. $5.20

D'Arcy W. **Thompson.** *Day Dreams of a Schoolmaster.* 12mo. London. Cloth. $2.50

—— *Wayside Thoughts on Education.* 12mo. Edinburgh. Cloth. $2.40

E. **Thomson.** *Educational Essays.* Edited by Rev. D. W. CLARK. 12mo. Cincinnati. Cloth. $1.50

E. **Thring.** *Education and School.* 8vo. London. Cloth. $1.75

Isaac **Todhunter.** *The Conflict of Studies, and other Subjects connected with Education.* 8vo. London. Cloth. $2.50

THE DICTIONARY OF EDUCATION AND INSTRUCTION

J. J. Wagner. *Philosophie der Erziehungskunst.* 8vo. Leipzig. $1.05
Th. Waitz. *Allgemeine Pädagogik und kleinere pädagogische Schriften.* Hrsg. v. O. WILLMANN. 8vo. Braunschweig. $3.70
F. G. Welch. *Moral, Intellectual and Physical Culture.* 12mo. N. Y. Cloth, $1.75
Wm. Whewell. *Of a Liberal Education in General, and with Particular Reference to the Leading Studies of the University of Cambridge.* 8vo. London. Boards. $2.00
J. F. T. Wohlfarth. *Pädagogisches Schatzkästlein.* 8vo. Leipzig. $1.10
T. Ziller. *Vorlesungen über allgemeine Pädagogik.* 8vo. Leipzig. $2.05
——— *Grundlegung zur Lehre vom erziehenden Unterricht. Nach ihrer wissenschaftlichen und praktisch-reformatorischen Seite entwickelt. Mit Sachregister.* 8vo. Leipzig. $3.85
——— *Die Regierung der Kinder. Für gebildete Eltern, Lehrer und Studirende bearbeitet.* 8vo. Leipzig. $0.90

2. Science and Art of Teaching. (Pedagogy and Didactics.)

J. Alden. *Outlines on Teaching.* 12mo. N. Y. $0.40
Roger Ascham. *The Scholemaster.* With copious notes and a glossary by J. E. B. MAYOR. 12mo. London. $2.40
"I had rather have thrown ten thousand pounds into the sea than have lost my Ascham." QUEEN ELIZABETH.
"It contains, perhaps, the best advice that was ever given for the study of language." Dr. JOHNSON.
"Roger Ascham * * * one of those men of genius born to create a new era in the history of their nation * * * the venerable parent of our native literature." D'ISRAELI.
Ascham's complete Works. 12mo. London. 4 vols. $8.00
J. Baldwin. *Art of School Management.* 12mo. N. Y. Cloth. $1.50
Henry Barnard. *American Pedagogy: Education, The School and the Teacher, in American Literature.* 8vo. Hartford. Cloth. $3.50
——— *Elementary and Secondary Instruction in the German States. (National Education. Part I.)* 8vo. Hartford. Cloth. $5.50
——— *Elementary and Secondary Instruction in Switzerland (each of the 23 Cantons), France, Belgium, Holland, Denmark, Norway and Sweden, Russia, Turkey, Greece, Italy, Portugal, and Spain. (National Education. Part II.)* 8vo. Hartford. Cloth. $5.50

Henry Barnard. *English Pedagogy: Education, The School and The Teacher in English Literature.* First Series. 8vo. Hartford. Cloth. $3.50 — Second Series. 8vo. Hartford. Cloth. $3.50
——— *French Teachers, Schools and Pedagogy — Old and New.* 8vo. Hartford. Cloth. $3.50
——— *German Pedagogy: Education, The School and The Teacher in German Literature.* 8vo. Hartford. Cloth. $3.50
W. Bornemann. *Lehrpläne für den Unterricht in den Realien nebst methodischen Winken und Regeln für sämmtliche Schulsysteme.* 8vo. Kreuznach. $0.25
S. S. Boyce. *Hints toward a National Culture for Young Americans.* 12mo. N. Y. Paper. $0.25; Cloth. $0.50
E. Brooks. *Normal Methods of Teaching.* 12mo. Philadelphia. Cloth. $1.75
H. Calderwood. *On Teaching: Its Ends and Means.* 16mo. N. Y. $1.00
Jas. Currie. *The Principles and Practice of Common School Education.* 12mo. Edinburgh. Cloth. $2.40
G. F. Dinter. *Die vorzüglichsten Regeln der Pädagogik, Methodik und Schulmeisterklugheit.* 8vo. Neustadt. $0.25
H. Dunn. *Principles of Teaching.* 12mo. London. Cloth. $1.40
E. Eggleston. *Counsel for Teachers.* 12mo. Chicago. Paper. $0.30
Frederick C. Emberson. *The Art of Teaching. A Manual for the use of Teachers and School Commissioners.* 8vo. Illustr. Montreal. Cloth. $0.50
J. G. Fitch. *Lectures on Teaching delivered in the University of Cambridge during the Lent Term,* 1880. 8vo. Cambridge. Cloth. $1.75
Text-Book in the Art of Teaching in the University of Michigan.
H. Graefo. *Allgemeine Pädagogik.* 8vo. 2 vols. Leipzig. $3.60
J. Fr. Herbart's *pädagogische Schriften, In chronologischer Reihenfolge herausgegeben mit Einleitung, Anmerkungen und comparativem Register versehen v.* OTTO WILLMANN. 8vo. 2 vols. Leipzig. $5.50
A. Holbrook. *Normal Methods of Teaching.* 12mo. N. Y. Cloth. $1.50
J. H. Hoose. *On the Province of Methods in Teaching.* 12mo. Syracuse. Cloth. $1.00
Julia Ward Howe. *Sex and Education. A Reply to Dr.* CLARKE's *"Sex in Education."* 16mo. Boston. Cloth. $1.25
J. Hughes. *Mistakes in Teaching.* Syracuse. $0.50

J. Jacotot. *Enseignement Universel.* 1. Mathématiques. 2. Epitome de Mathématiques à l'usage des élèves de l'enseignement universel. II. Langue Maternelle. 8vo. Paris.
Joseph Payne was a disciple of Jacotot. His system will repay a careful study.

James Johonnot. *Principles and Practice of Teaching.* 12mo. N. Y. Cloth. $1.50

A. M. Kellogg. *The New Education; School Management.* 16mo. N. Y. $0.75

H. Kern. *Grundriss der Pädagogik.* 8vo. Berlin. $1.85

H. Kiddle, Tho. Harrison, and Norman A. Calkins. *How to Teach. A Manual of Methods for a Graded Course of Instruction: embracing the Subjects usually pursued in Primary, Intermediate, Grammar and High Schools, also Suggestions relative to Discipline and School Management. For the use of Teachers.* 12mo. Cincinnati. Cloth. $1.25

G. V. Le Vaux. *Science and Art of Teaching.* 12mo. Toronto. Cloth. $1.25

A. Liese. *Lehrpläne für die ein- und mehrklassige Volksschule.* 8vo. Neuwied. $0.45

J. L. Ludwig. *Grundsätze und Lehren vorzüglicher Pädagogiker von Locke bis auf die gegenwärtige Zeit.* 8vo. 3 vols. Bayreuth. $4.95

Arch. Maclaren. *Training, in Theory and Practice.* 12mo. Illustr. N. Y. Cloth. $2.25

H. Maudsley. *Sex in Mind and Education.* 16mo. N. Y. Paper. $0.25

Fr. Denison Maurice. *Learning and Working. Six Lectures on the Foundation of Colleges for Working Men.* 8vo. London. Cloth. $2.00

Hugh Miller. *My Schools and Schoolmasters; or, the Story of my Education.* 12mo. N. Y. Cloth. $1.50

J. Ogden. *Science of Education and Art of Teaching.* 12mo. Cincinnati. Cloth. $1.50

H. Orcutt. *Teacher's Manual.* 12mo. Boston. Cloth. $1.00

D. P. Page. *Theory and Practice of Teaching.* 12mo. N. Y. Cloth. $1.50

Joh. Heinr. Pestalozzi. *Lienhard und Gertrud. Bearbeitet und mit Anmerkungen versehen von* KARL RICHTER. 8vo. Leipzig. $0.55

—— *Lienhard und Gertrud. Ein Buch für das Volk. Herausgegeben von* L. W. SEYFFARTH. 8vo. Brandenburg. $3.70

Joh. Heinr. Pestalozzi. *Wie Gertrud ihre Kinder lehrt. Erläutert und mit Anmerkungen versehen von* ALB. RICHTER. 8vo. Leipzig. $0.75

W. F. Phelps. *The Teacher's Handbook for the Institute and Class-Room.* 12mo. N. Y. Cloth. $1.50

Mrs. A. H. L. Phelps. *The Discipline of Life, or Ida Norman.* 12mo. N. Y. Cloth. $1.75

—— *The Educator: or, Hours with my Pupils.* 12mo. N. Y. Cloth. $1.50

—— *The Student: or, Fireside Friend. With an Appendix on Moral and Religious Education.* 12mo. N. Y. Cloth. $1.50

A. Potter and G. B. Emerson. *The School and the Schoolmaster: Manual for Teachers, Employers, etc.* 12mo. N. Y. Cloth. $1.50

K. Richter. *Die Reform der Lehrerseminare nach den Forderungen unserer Zeit und der heutigen Pädagogik. Gekrönte Preisschrift.* 8vo. Leipzig. $1.50

H. Schiller. *Ueber die pädagogische Vorbildung zum höheren Lehramt.* 8vo. Giessen. $0.40

E. Seguin. *Report on Education.* 12mo. Milwaukee. Cloth. $1.50

E. A. Sheldon. *Lessons in Objects, graded series, designed for children between the ages of six and fourteen years; containing also Information on Common Objects.* 12mo. N. Y. Cloth. $1.75

—— *A Manual of Elementary Instruction, for the use of Public and Private Schools and Normal Classes. Containing a graduated course of Object Lessons for training the senses and developing the faculties of children.* 12mo. N. Y. Cloth. $1.75

N. Sizer. *How to Teach according to Temperament and Mental Development.* 12mo. N. Y. Cloth. $1.50

Herbert Spencer. *Education: Intellectual, Moral and Physical.* 12mo. N. Y. Cloth. $1.25

Alb. Stöckl. *Lehrbuch der Pädagogik.* 8vo. Mainz. $1.80

Isaac Stone. *Complete Examiner; or, Candidate's Assistant. Prepared to aid Teachers in securing Certificates from Boards of Examiners, and Pupils in preparing themselves for Promotion, Teachers in selecting Review Questions in Normal Schools, Institutes, and in all Drill and Class Exercises.* 12mo. N. Y. Cloth. $1.25

Dav. Stow. *Training System in Glasgow Model Schools.* 8vo. London. Cloth. $2.60

H. Strelow. *Der Volksschullehrer, wie er ist und wie er sein soll.* 8vo. Löbau. $0.30

L. Strümpell. *Die Pädagogik der Philosophen Kant, Fichte, Herbart.* 8vo. Braunschweig. $1.15

John Swett. *Methods of Teaching. A Hand-Book of Principles, Directions, and Working Models for Common school Teachers.* 12mo. N. Y. Cloth. $1.50

J. R. Sypher. *Art of Teaching School: Manual of Suggestions.* 12mo. Phila. Cloth. $1.50

J. P. Wickersham. *Methods of Instruction, or, that part of the Philosophy of Education which treats of the Nature of the Several Branches of Knowledge, and the Method of Teaching them.* 12mo. Phila. Cloth. $1.75

3. Special Didactics.

E. A. Abbott. *How to Write Clearly.* 16mo. Boston. Cloth. $0.60

—— *How to Parse.* 16mo. Boston. Cloth. $1.00

A. M. Bacon. *A Manual of Gesture. With 100 Figures, embracing a complete System of Notation, with the Princip'es of Interpretation, and Selections for Practice.* 12mo. Chicago. Cloth. $1.75

W. W. Davis. *Suggestions of Teaching Fractions.* 16mo. Syracuse. Paper. $0.25

A. Douai. *A Reform of the Common English Branches of Instruction.* 12mo. N. Y. Boards. $0.30

J. G. Fitch. *The Art of Questioning.* 12mo. N. Y. Paper. $0.15

Wm. Ellis. *Education as a means of preventing Destitution; with Exemplifications from the Teaching of the Condition of well-being and the Principles and Applications of Economical Science.* 8vo. London. $1.60

L. T. Fowler. *Manual of Oral Instruction for Graded Schools.* 4to. San Francisco. $0.75

Ed. Frankland. *How to teach Chemistry. Hints to Science Teachers and Students. Being the Substance of Six Lectures delivered at the Royal College of Chemistry, June, 1872. Summarized and edited by* GEORGE CHALONER. 12mo. Phila. Cloth. $1.25

J. E. Frobisher. *Voice and Action. A new and practical system on the culture of Voice and Action, and a complete analysis of the Human Passions, with an appendix of Readings and Recitations, designed for Public Speakers, Teachers, and Students.* 12mo. N. Y. Cloth. $1.25

A. A. Griffith. *Lessons in Elocution and Drill Book for Practice of the Principles of Vocal Physiology, and for acquiring the Art of Elocution and Oratory, comprising all the Elements of Vocal De'ivery and Gestures for Schools, Colleges, the Pulpit, and Private Learners.* 12mo. Chicago. Cloth. $1.50

Thomas Hill. *The True Order of Studies.* 12mo. N. Y. Cloth. $1.25

J. H. Hoose. *Studies in Articulation.* 12mo. Syracuse. Paper. $0.30

M. E. Lilienthal and Robt. Allyn. *Things Taught; Systematic Instruction in Composition and Object Lessons.* 16mo. Cincinnati. Paper. $0.25

Francis A. March. *Method of Philological Study of the English Language.* 12mo. N. Y. Paper. $0.60; Cloth $0.75

E. A. Sheldon and E. H. Barlow. *Teacher's Manual of Instruction in Reading, designed to accompany Sheldon's Readers.* 12mo. N. Y. Cloth. $1.00

I. Stone. *The Teacher's Examiner.* 12mo. N. Y. Cloth. $1.25

J. Swett. *Questions for Written Examinations; Aid to Candidates for Teacher's Certificates.* 12mo. N. Y. Cloth. $1.00

4. Home Education and Self Education.

Frdr. Ascher. *Briefe an meinen Sohn. Anleitung zur Selbsterziehung.* 12mo. Berlin. Cloth. $1.10

—— *Die Erziehung der Jugend. Ein Handbuch für Eltern und Erzieher.* 8vo. Berlin. $1.10

W. H. Bacon. *Parental Training.* 16mo. Phila. $0.70

Mrs. J. Bakewell. *Mothers' Practical Guide.* 18mo. N. Y. $0.60

J. R. Beard. *Self-Culture. A Practical Answer to the Questions: What to learn? How to learn? When to learn? The whole forming a complete Guide to Self-Instruction.* 3d edition. 12mo. Manchester. Cloth. $1.50

L. Besser. *Das Werden und Wachsen unserer Kinder. Ein Buch über Kindespflege.* 12mo. Berlin. $0.95

THE DICTIONARY OF EDUCATION AND INSTRUCTION

John Stuart Blackie. *On Self Culture, Intellectual, Physical, and Moral. A Vade Mecum for Young Men and Students.* 16mo. N. Y. Cloth. $1.00

A. v. Bohlen. *Das Buch der Mutter für Haus und Erziehung.* With illustr. 8vo. Berlin. $1.50

F. Bridges. *Hints to Mothers on Home Education. A popular Epitome of such Points in Physiological Science as bear upon the Moral and Physical Training of Youth.* 8vo. London. Cloth. $1.50

J. F. Clarke. *Self Culture.* 12mo. Boston. Cloth. $1.50

J. A. Comenius. *Die Mutterschule. Auf's Neue hrsg. von* H. SCHRÖTER. 8vo. Weissenfels. $0.40

W. J. G. Curtman. *Lehrbuch der Erziehung und des Unterrichts. Ein Handbuch für Eltern, Lehrer und Geistliche.* 8vo. 2 vols. Leipzig. $2.80

Thos. DeQuincey. *Letters to a Young Man, and other Papers (Rhetoric, Style, etc.).* 16mo. Boston. Cloth. $1.25

A. Döllen. *Der erste Unterricht. Ein Rathgeber für Eltern, die ihre Kinder selbst für die Schule vorbereiten wollen.* 8vo. Dorpat. $1.65

G. Cary Eggleston. *How to Educate Yourself. A complete Guide to Students showing How to Study, What to Study, How and What to Read.* 12mo. N. Y. Cloth. $0.75

J. Fölsing. *Erziehungsstoffe für Familien und Kleinkinderschulen.* 8vo. Darmstadt. $2.05

—— *Die Menschenerziehung, oder die naturgemässe Erziehung und Entwickelung der Kindheit in den ersten Lebensjahren. Ein Buch für das Familienleben und Kleinkinderschulleben.* 8vo. Leipzig. $1.10

O. S. Fowler. *Memory and Intellectual Improvement applied to Self-Education and Juvenile Instruction.* 12mo. N. Y. Cloth. $1.25

—— *Education and Self-Improvement Complete. Comprising Physiology, Animal and Mental; Self-Culture and Perfection of Character; including the Management of Youth; Memory and Intellectual Improvement.* 12mo. Cloth. $3.50

J. M. de Gerando. *Self-Education.* 12mo. Boston. Cloth. about $3.00

J. C. A. Heinroth. *On Education and Self-Formation, based upon Physical, Intellectual, Moral, and Religious Principles.* 12mo. London. Cloth. $2.25

H. Herzog u. K. Schiller. *Das Kind. Anleitungen zur rationellen physischen Erziehungsweise und Winke zur Entfaltung des Seelenlebens der Kinder. Für Mütter und ihre erziehenden Stellvertreterinnen.* 8vo. Wien. $1.50

H. Klencke. *Die Mutter als Erzieherin ihrer Töchter und Söhne zur physischen und sittlichen Gesundheit vom ersten Kindesalter bis zur Reife. Ein praktisches Buch für deutsche Frauen.* 8vo. Leipzig. Cloth. $2.65

M. S. Kübler (Frau SCHERR). *Die Schule der Mutter. Ein Hand- und Hülfsbuch für Mütter und Erzieherinnen.* With illustr. 8vo. Leipzig. $4.40

H. Martineau. *Household Education.* 18mo. Boston. Cloth. $1.25

J. McCrie. *Autopædia; Personal Education for Young Men.* 8vo. London. Cloth. $4.90

Wm. Mathews. *Getting on in the World; or, Hints on Success in Life.* First and Second Series. 8vo. London. Cloth. $1.40

—— *The same.* 12mo. Chicago. Cloth. $2.00

H. Meier. *Das Kind in seinen ersten Lebensjahren. Skizzen über Leibes- und Geistes-Erziehung. Deutschen Müttern gewidmet.* 8vo. Leipzig. $0.75

S. Neil. *Culture and Self-Culture.* 8vo. London. Paper. $0.40

K. Oppel. *Das Buch der Eltern. Praktische Anleitung zur häuslichen Erziehung der Kinder in allerlei Geschlechts vom frühesten Alter bis zur Selbstständigkeit.* 8vo. Frankfurt a.M. $2.35

Hiram Orcutt. *Parent's Manual. Home and School Training.* 12mo. Boston. Cloth. $1.25

Miss J. Pardoe. *Parental Instruction for Young Persons.* 12mo. N. Y. Cloth. $0.75

B. Sigismund. *Kind und Welt. Vätern, Müttern u. Kinderfreunden gewidmet.* 1. *Die 5 ersten Perioden des Kindesalters.* 8vo. Braunschweig. $1.10

Samuel Smiles. *Self-Help Library.* Consisting of *Life of George Stephenson, Industrial Biography, Brief Biographies and Self-Help.* 4 vols. 16mo. Philadelphia. Cloth. $ vol. $1.25; $ set in box $5.00

S. Stern. *Die häusliche Erziehung.* 8vo. Leipzig. $1.50

I. Taylor. *Home Education.* 8vo. London. Cloth. $2.00

Th. D. Woolsey. *Helpful Thoughts for Young Men.* 12mo. Boston. Cloth. $1.25

IV. SPECIAL EDUCATION.

Primary, Secondary, and Higher Instruction. The Kindergarten. Commercial, Military, Naval, Industrial, and Technical Education and Schools; Art Education and Schools. Normal Instruction and Schools; and Teachers' Institutes. Schools for the Blind, Deaf and Dumb, and Imbecile, and Reform Schools. Education of Women or Female Education. Physical Education. Moral and Religious Education; Sunday Schools.

1. Primary, Secondary, and Higher Instruction.

F. Adams. *The Free School System of the United States.* 8vo. London. $3.60

Matthew Arnold. *Popular Education in France, with Notices of Holland.* 8vo. London. Cloth. $4.20
—— *A French Eton; or, Middle-Class Education and the State.* 8vo. London. Cloth. $1.00
—— *Higher Schools and Universities in Germany. With a new Preface comparing the Policy of the Prussian Government towards Roman Catholic Education and Roman Catholicism with that of the English Government in Ireland.* 8vo. London. Cloth. $2.50

W. H. Bainbrigge. *Early Education. Being the Substance of four Lectures delivered in the Public Hall of the Collegiate Institution.* 12mo. Liverpool. Cloth. $1.00

J. L. Bashford. *Elementary Education in Saxony.* 8vo. London. $0.40

Anna Lætitia Barbauld. *Early Lessons for Children.* 12mo. London. $0.60

Henry Barnard. *Primary Schools and Elementary Instruction: Object Teaching and Oral Lessons on Social Science and Common Things, etc. (Papers for the Teacher. Second Series.)* 8vo. Hartford. Cloth. $3.50
—— *Superior Instruction in different Countries.* Revised Edition, 1874.
Part I. *Universities in Germany, Italy, France, Belgium, Holland, Denmark, Sweden, Russia, Greece, Spain, Portugal.* 8vo. Hartford. Cloth. $3.50
Part II. *Universities in Great Britain.* 8vo. Hartford. Cloth. $3.50

A Bohlmann. *Vollständiger Lehrplan nebst Pensenvertheilung und Lektionsplänen für eine ungetheilte einklassige Volksschule.* 8vo. Leipzig. $0.40

Chas. A. Bristed. *Five Years in an English University.* 12mo. N. Y. Cloth. $2.25

J. Breiden. *Theoretisch-praktische Anleitung für den Anschauungsunterricht.* 8vo. Essen. $0.30

W. Burton. *The Culture of the Observing Faculties.* 16mo. N. Y. Cloth. $0.75

Norman A. Calkins. *Primary Object Lessons, for Training the Senses and Developing the Faculties of Children. A Manual of Elementary Instruction for Parents and Teachers.* Re-written and enlarged. 12mo. N. Y. Cloth. $1.25

Jas. Currie. *Principles and Practice of Early and Infant School Education.* 12mo. Edinburgh. Cloth $2.00

J. H. Deinhardt. *Der Gymnasial-Unterricht nach den wissenschaftlichen Anforderungen der jetzigen Zeit.* 8vo. Hamburg. $1.65

Ed. Davies. *Intermediate and University Education in Wales.* 8vo. London. $0.40

Denzel's *Entwurf des Anschauungsunterrichts in katechetischer Gedankenfolge.* Practisch ausgeführt von C. WRAGE. 8vo. Altona. I. Cursus $0.55; II. Cursus $1.65

Friedrich Dittes. *Methodik der Volksschule.* 8vo. Leipzig $1.35

Fel. A. P. Dupanloup. *The Child.* Translated by KATE ANDERSON. 12mo. Boston. Cloth. $1.50

G. M. Dursch. *Pädagogik, oder Wissenschaft der christlichen Erziehung auf dem Standpunkte des katholischen Glaubens.* 8vo. Tübingen. $3.00

J. E. Erdmann. *Vorlesungen über akademisches Schulleben und Studium.* 8vo. Leipzig. $2.20

F. W. Farrar. *On Some Defects in Public School Education. A Lecture delivered at the Royal Institution, February 8th, 1867.* 16mo. London. Paper. $0.40

THE DICTIONARY OF EDUCATION AND INSTRUCTION

H. Feix und F. Jung. *Durch die Heimath. Umschau in Haus, Schule, Garten, etc. Ein Beitrag zur Erweiterung des sinnlichen und sittlichen Vorstellungskreises unserer Kleinen.* 8vo. Wiesbaden. $0.90

B. Fohmann. *Der sinnliche und religiössittliche Anschauungsunterricht als Lehrstoff zu elementarischen Sprach-, Denk- und Stylübungen nach bewährten Grundsätzen für deutsche Elementar- und Volksschulen.* 8vo. Stuttgart. $1.10

G. Fröhlich. *Die Volksschule der Zukunft ein Ideal für die Gegenwart. Ausführlich dargestellt.* 8vo. Jena. $0.85

J. H. Fuhr und J. H. Ortmann. *Der Anschauungs-Unterricht in der Volksschule. Oder: Anschauen, Denken, Sprechen und Schreiben zur Begründung der Realien des Styls und der Grammatik.* 8vo. 4 parts. Dillenburg. $3.25

John Gill. *The Art of Teaching Young Minds to Observe and Think.* 12mo. London. $0.80

—— *Systems of Education. A History and Criticism.* 12mo. London. Cloth. $1.00

Ed. Günther. *Kurzer Wegweiser für Lehrer, stotternde Kinder zu heilen.* 8vo. Neuwied. $0.55

F. Harder. *Theoretisch-praktisches Handbuch für den Anschauungsunterricht. Mit besonderer Berücksichtigung des Elementarunterrichts in den Realien.* 8vo. Altona. $2.20

Thomas Hughes. *Tom Brown's School Days at Rugby.* 12mo. Boston. Cloth. $1.00

L. T. Knauss. *Das erste Schuljahr ohne Lese- und Schreibunterricht oder Darstellung eines Anschauungs-Unterrichts, der den gesammten Schulunterricht begründet.* 8vo. Stuttgart. $1.50

Simon S. Laurie. *On Primary Instruction in relation to Education. With an Appendix on "Secondary Instruction".* 8vo. London. Cloth. $1.80
"Of the highest possible interest, and affords solutions of many psychological problems that are still debated among the learned in such matter." *Westminster Review.*

G. Luz. *Der Anschauungsunterricht für die untern und mittlern Klassen der Volksschule.* 8vo. Wiesensteig. $1.05

L. Meyer. *Die Zukunft der deutschen Hochschulen und ihrer Vorbildungsanstalten.* 8vo. Breslau. $0.40

C. F. v. Nägelsbach. *Gymnasial-Pädagogik.* 8vo. Erlangen. $0.90

John Henry Newman. *Idea of a University: considered in Nine Discourses, Occasional Lectures, and Essays.* 8vo. London. Cloth. $2.80

Olin's *College Life; Its Theory and Practice.* 12mo. N. Y. Cloth. $1.50

Alexandre Ott. *Un Mot sur l'Instruction primaire. L'ancien Régime, la Révolution, l'Epoque actuelle.* 8vo. Nancy. $0.80

J. H. Pestalozzi. *Buch der Mütter, oder Anleitung für Mütter, ihre Kinder bemerken und reden zu lehren.* 8vo. Leipzig, 1803. About $0.50

K. Wm. Piderit. *Zur Gymnasialpädagogik. Schulreden.* Hrsg. v. Alb. FREIBE. 8vo. $1.85

Noah Porter. *The American Colleges and the American Public. With afterthoughts on college and school education.* 12mo. N. Y. Cloth. $1.50

K. Richter. *Der Anschauungsunterricht in den Elementarklassen. Nach seiner Aufgabe, seiner Stellung und seinen Mitteln dargestellt. Gekrönte Preisschrift.* 8vo. Leipzig. $1.05

J. H. Rigg. *National Education in its Social Condition and Aspects and Public School Education. English and Foreign.* 8vo. London. Cloth. $3.60
—— *History and Present Position of Primary Education in England.* 12mo. London. Paper. $0.25

C. L. Roth. *Gymnasial-Pädagogik.* 8vo. Stuttgart. $1.65

P. Rousselot. *Pédagogie à l'usage de l'enseignement primaire.* 18mo. Paris. $1.25

K. A. Schmid. *Die modernen Gymnasialreformer.* 8vo. Stuttgart. $0.20

Edmond Schmidt. *L'Instruction primaire à la Campagne en Lorraine, il y a cent ans. d'après l'enquête de 1779.* 8vo. Paris. $0.40

K. Schmidt. *Gymnasialpädagogik.* 8vo. Gotha. $1.65

W. Schrader. *Erziehungs- und Unterrichtslehre für Gymnasien und Realschulen.* 8vo. 2 vols. Berlin. $3.85

W. F. L. Schwartz. *Der Organismus der Gymnasien in seiner praktischen Gestaltung.* 8vo. Berlin. $1.35

Ernst Senckel. *Die Schulsparkassen. Eine Denkschrift.* 8vo. Berlin. $0.40

Sir J. K. Shuttleworth. *Public Education as affected by the minutes of the Committee of Privy Council from 1846 to 1852.* 8vo. London. Cloth. $3.60
One of "the most important works on English education known to me". DONALDSON.

S. H. Taylor. *Classical Study.* 12mo. Andover. Cloth. $2.00

—— *Method of Classical Study.* 12mo. Boston. Cloth. $1.25

O. F. Thwing. *American Colleges: their Students and their Work.* 16mo. N. Y. Cloth. $1.00

F. Wiedemann. *Der Lehrer der Kleinen. Ein praktischer Rathgeber für junge Elementarlehrer, überhaupt aber ein Buch für Alle, welche sich für die Erziehung der Kleinen interessiren.* 8vo. Leipzig. $1.10

A. S. Welch. *Object Lessons.* 12mo. N. Y. Cloth. $1.00

Wm. Whewell. *On the Principles of English University Education.* 12mo. London. Cloth. About $1.25

A. Wittstock. *Ueber die Gründung pädagogischer Facultäten an den Universitäten.* 8vo. Bleicherode. $0.30

2. The Kindergarten.

Henry Barnard. *Kindergarten and Child Culture Papers.* 8vo. Hartford. Cloth. $3.50

Adf. Diesterweg. *Der Unterricht in der Klein-Kinder-Schule, oder die Anfänge der Unterweisung und Bildung in der Volksschule.* 8vo. Bielefeld. $0.55

Adolf Douai. *The Kindergarten. A Manual for the Introduction of Fröbel's System of Primary Education into Public School's, and for the Use of Mothers and Private Teachers.* With 16 plates. 12mo. N. Y. Cloth. $1.00

A. S. Fischer. *Der Kindergarten. Theoretisch-praktisches Handbuch.* With woodcuts and 10 plates. 8vo. Wien. $1.35

Friedrich Fröbel. *Die Pädagogik des Kindergartens. Gedanken Friedrich Fröbel's über das Spiel und die Spielgegenstände des Kindes.* With 4 pp. of Music and 16 plates. 8vo. Berlin. $3.30

—— *Manual pratique des jardins d'enfants, à l'usage des institutrices et des mères de famille, composé sur les documents allemands par J. E. Jacobs de Mme. la baronne de Marenholtz-Buelow.* With 85 engravings and several pages of Music. 8vo. Bruxelles. $3.70

Herm. Goldammer. *Friedrich Fröbel, der Begründer der Kindergarten-Erziehung. Sein Leben und Wirken.* 8vo. Berlin. $0.75

Herm. Goldammer. *Le Jardin d'enfants. Dons et Occupations à l'usage des mères de famille, des salles d'asile et des écoles primaires. Avec une introduction de Mme. la baronne de Marenholtz-Buelow. Traduit de l'allemand par Louis Fournier.* 120 plates. 8vo. Berlin. Paper. $3.70; cloth. $4.40

—— *Der Kindergarten. Handbuch der Fröbel'schen Erziehungsmethode, Spielgaben und Beschäftigungen. Nach Fröbel's Schriften und den Schriften der Frau B. v. Marenholtz-Billow bearbeitet. Mit Beiträgen v. B. v. Marenholtz-Buelow.* 8vo. 2 vols. Berlin. $3.60. Cloth. $4.70

I. *Fr. Fröbel's Spielgaben für das vorschulpflichtige Alter.* With 60 plates. Cloth. $2.60

II. *Fr. Fröbel's Beschäftigungen für das vorschulpflichtige Alter.* With 60 plates. Cloth. $2.10

Goldammer-Reffelt. *Die Einordnung des Kindergartens in das Schulwesen der Gemeinde. Nach H. Goldammer mit Rücksicht auf amerikanische Verhältnisse dargestellt von H. Reffelt.* 12mo. N. Y. Paper. $0.15

Joseph Gruber. *Die Pädagogik des Kindergartens und der Bewahranstalt.* With 16 plates. 8vo. Leipzig. $0.75

W. N. Hailmann. *Four Lectures on Early Child Culture.* 12mo. Milwaukee. Paper $0.25; Flexible Cloth $0.40

—— *Kindergarten Culture in the Family and Kindergarten: A complete Sketch of Fröbel's System of Early Education, adapted to American Institutions. For the use of Mothers and Teachers.* Illustrated. 12mo. Cincinnati. Cloth, net $0.75

Handbook for the Kindergarten. With plates. 4to. Springfield. Paper. $1.00

Alex. Bruno Hanschmann. *Friedrich Fröbel. Die Entwickelung seiner Erziehungsidee in seinem Leben.* 8vo. Eisenach. $2.60

—— *Das System des Kindergartens nach Fröbel. Für Mütter und Kindergärtnerinnen.* 12mo. N. Y. $0.15

Eleonore Heerwart. *An Abstract of Lessons on the Kindergarten System given to the senior Students of the Training College, Stockwell.* 12mo. London. Paper. $0.50

James Hughes. *The Kindergarten; its Place and Purpose. An Address.* 12mo. N. Y. Paper. $0.12

Der Kindergarten in Amerika. *Entstehung, Wesen, Bedeutung und Erziehungsmittel des Fröbel'schen Systems und seine Anwendung auf häusige Verhältnisse. Für Eltern, Lehrer und Kinderfreunde kurz dargestellt.* 12mo. N. Y. Paper. $0.15

Aug. Köhler. *Die neue Erziehung. Grundzüge der pädagogischen Ideen Fr. Fröbe's und deren Anwendung in Familie, Kindergarten und Schule.* 12mo. N. Y. Paper. $0.15

—— *Die Praxis des Kindergartens. Theoretisch-praktische Anleitung zum Gebrauche der Fröbel'schen Erziehungs- und Bildungsmittel in Haus, Kindergarten und Schule.* 8vo. 3 vols. Weimar. $5.10
(1. With 18 plates. $1.70; II. With 40 plates. $1.70; III. With 2 plates. $1.70)

Maria Kraus-Boelte. *The Kindergarten and the Mission of Woman; my Experience as Trainer of Kindergarten Teachers in this Country.* An Address. N. Y. Net $0.06

—— **and John Kraus.** *The Kindergarten Guide. An Illustrated Hand-Book designed for the Self-Instruction of Kindergartners, Mothers, and Nurses.*
No. 1. $0.35; cloth $0.65 — No. 2. $0.70; cloth $1.00 — No. 3. $0.50; cloth $0.80 — No. 4. $0.70; cloth $1.00 — No. 5. $0.70; cloth $1.00

Matilda H. Kriege. *The Child, its Nature and Relations. An Elucidation of Fræbel's Principles of Education. A free rendering of the German of the Baroness* MARENHOLTZ-BÜELOW. 12mo. N. Y. Cloth, gilt top. $1.00

—— *Friedrich Frœbel. A biographical Sketch.* With portrait. 12mo. N. Y. Paper $0.25; cloth $0.50

Mary J. Lyschinska. *The Kindergarten Principle; its Educational Value and Chief Applications.* 12mo. London. Cloth. $1.80

B. von Marenholtz-Bülow. *The New Education by Work, according to Fræbel's Method.* Translated by Mrs. HORACE MANN, with the assistance of LEOPOLD NOA. 12mo. Camden. Net $0.75

—— *Reminiscences of Friedrich Frœbel.* Translated by Mrs. HORACE MANN. With a Sketch of the Life of Friedrich Frœbel by EMILY SHIRREFF. 12mo. Boston. Cloth. $1.50

—— *Das Kind und sein Wesen. Beiträge zum Verständniss der Fröbel'schen Erziehungslehre.* 8vo. Berlin. $1.10

B. von Marenholtz-Bülow. *Die Arbeit und die neue Erziehung nach Fröbel's Methode.* 8vo. Cassel. $1.65

C. Mayo. *Lessons on Objects in a Pestalozzian School.* 12mo. San Francisco. Cloth. $1.75

Eliz. Mayo. *Practical Remarks on Infant Education, for the Use of Schools and Private Families.* 12mo. London. $0.50

Bertha Meyer. *Von der Wiege bis zur Schule an der Hand Frdr. Fröbel's.* 8vo. Berlin. $0.85

Lina Morgenstern. *Das Paradies der Kindheit. Eine ausführliche Anleitung für Mütter und Erzieherinnen, Friedrich Fröbel's Spiel-Beschäftigungen in Haus- und Kindergarten praktisch auszuüben.* With 150 woodcuts. 8vo. Leipzig. $1.65; cloth $2.05

C. B. Morehouse. *The Kindergarten: its Aims, Methods, and Results. A practical Explanation of the System of Frœbel.* Illustrated. 12mo. N. Y. Paper. $0.25

Joseph Payne. *The Science and Art of Education* (a Lecture), *and Principles of the Science of Education, as exhibited in the Phenomena founded on the unfolding of a Young Child's Powers under the Influence of Natural Circumstances.* 12mo. N. Y. Paper $0.15; cloth $0.40

—— *Frœbel and the Kindergarten System of Elementary Instruction.* 12mo. N. Y. Paper. $0.15

—— *A Visit to German Schools. With discussions on the Kindergarten.* 12mo. London. $1.80

Elizabeth P. Peabody. *Guide to the Kindergarten and Intermediate Class. And Moral Culture of Infancy.* By MARY MANN. Revised Edition. 12mo. N. Y. Cloth. $1.25

—— *Education of the Kindergartner.* A Lecture. 12mo. N. Y. Paper. $0.25

—— *The Nursery.* A Lecture. 12mo. N. Y. Paper. $0.25

W. F. Phelps. *Pestalozzi.* 12mo. N. Y. Paper. $0.10

—— *Frœbel.* 12mo. N. Y. Paper. $0.10

H. Pösche. *Frdr. Fröbel's entwickelnderziehende Menschenbildung.* 8vo. 2 parts. Hamburg. $0.90

—— *Frdr. Fröbel's entwickelnd-erziehende Menschenbildung (Kindergarten-Pädagogik) als System. Eine umfassende wortgetreue Zusammenstellung.* 8vo. Hamburg. $1.65

THE DICTIONARY OF EDUCATION AND INSTRUCTION

Joh. Fr. Ranke. *Aus der Praxis für die Praxis in Kinderstube und Kleinkinderschule.* 8vo. Elberfeld. $0.40

Johannes and Bertha Ronge. *A practical Guide to the English Kindergarten, for the use of Mothers, Governesses, and Infant-Teachers, being an exposition of Fræbel's System of Infant-Teaching, accompanied with a great variety of Instructive and Amusing Games, and Industrial and Gymnastic Exercises.* With numerous Songs set to Music and arranged for the Exercises. With 71 lithographic plates. 4to. London. Cloth. $2.10

Frdr. Seidel. *Katechismus der praktischen Kindergärtnerei.* With 35 illustr. 16mo. Leipzig. $0.45

Emily Shirreff. *The Kindergarten. Principles of Fræbel's System and their Bearing on the Education of Women. Also, Remarks on the higher Education of Women.* 8vo. London. Cloth. $1.25

Edward Wiebe. *The Paradise of Childhood. A Manual for Self-Instruction in Fr. Fræbel's Educational Principles, and a practical Guide to Kinder-Gartners.* With 74 plates. 4to. Springfield. Paper. $1.50; cloth $2.00

3. Commercial, Military, Naval, Industrial and Technical Education and Schools; Art Education and Schools.

Henry Barnard. *Military and Naval Schools in France, Prussia, Bavaria, Italy, Russia, Holland, England, and the United States.* 8vo. Hartford. Cloth. $5.50

— *Science and Art. Systems, Institutions, and Statistics of Scientific Instruction, applied to National Industries in different Countries.* Vol. I. 8vo. Hartford. Cloth. $5.50

G. Coulie. *The Education of Boys for Business. Being practical Suggestions to Parents on the Education of their Sons for commercial Life.* 12mo. London. Cloth. $1.60

E. Dürre. *Pädagogisches Wanderbuch. Reisebericht über Industrie-, Strick- und Nähschulen, ihre Methode, Organisation und Erweiterung, nebst kurzer kritischen Beleuchtung der Strohflechterei.* 8vo. Gotha. $0.60

J. Langl. *Modern Art Education.* 12mo. Boston. Cloth. $0.75

H. R. Palmer. *Music-Class Teaching.* 12mo. Cincinnati. $0.50

Elizabeth P. Peabody. *The Identification of the Artisan and Artist the proper object of American Education.* Illustrated by a Lecture of Cardinal WISEMAN, on the *Relation of the Arts of Design with the Arts of Production.* With an Essay on FRŒBEL'S *Reform of Primary Education.* 8vo. Boston. Paper. $0.20

Walter Smith. *Art Education, Scholastic and Industrial.* Illustr. 8vo. Boston. Cloth. $5.00

C. B. Stetson. *Technical Education: What it is and what American Public Schools should teach. An Essay based on an Examination of the Methods and Results of Technical Education in Europe, as shown by Official Reports.* 16mo. Boston. Cloth. $1.25

Thos. Twining. *Technical Training. Being a suggestive sketch of a National System of Industrial Instruction, founded on a general diffusion of Practical Science among the people.* 8vo. London. Cloth. $4.50

4. Normal Instruction and Schools; and Teachers' Institutes.

Henry Barnard. *Normal Schools, and other Institutions, Agencies and Means designed for the Professional Education of Teachers.* 8vo. Hartford. Cloth. $5.50

S. P. Bates. *Institute Lectures on Mental and Moral Culture.* 12mo. N. Y. Cloth. $1.50

— *Method of Teachers' Institutes, and the Theory of Education.* 12mo. N. Y. Cloth. 0.75

H. G. Brzoska. *Die Nothwendigkeit pädagogischer Seminare auf der Universität und ihre zweckmässige Einrichtung.* 8vo. Leipzig. $1.50

H. Deinhardt. *Ueber Lehrerbildung und Lehrerbildungsanstalten.* 8vo. Wien. $0.20

F. A. W. Diesterweg. *Zur Lehrerbildung.* 8vo. Frankfurt a. M. $0.20

— *Pädagogisches Wollen und Sollen. Dargestellt für Leute, die nicht fertig sind, aber eben darum Lust haben, nachzudenken.* 8vo. Frankfurt a. M. $0.90

— *Wegweiser zur Bildung für deutsche Lehrer.* 8vo. 3 vols. Essen. $7.70

W. B. Fowle. *Teachers' Institute; or, Familiar Hints to Young Teachers.* 12mo. N. Y. Cloth. $1.25

T. Grünewald. *Wie erhält sich der Lehrer den idealen Schwung und die Begeisterung für seinen Beruf?* 8vo. Lüneburg. $0.20

F. Leutz. *Die Theorie und Praxis des pädagogischen Unterrichts an den deutschen Schullehrer-Seminarien.* 8vo. Karlsruhe. $0.50

C. Nohl. *Pädagogische Seminarien auf Universitäten.* 8vo. Neuwied. $0.55

W. F. Phelps. *Teacher's Hand-Book for the Institute and the Class Room.* 12mo. N. Y. Cloth. $1.50

E. B. Pusey. *Collegiate and Professional Teaching and Discipline.* 8vo. N. Y. Cloth. $1.00

Wm. Russell. *Normal Training.* 12mo. Hartford. Cloth. $1.50

5. Schools for the Blind, Deaf and Dumb, and Imbecile; and Reform Schools.

T. R. Armitage. *The Education and Employment of the Blind. What it has been, is, and ought to be.* 8vo. London. Cloth. $1.00

H. Barnard. *Reformatory and Preventive Agencies.* 8vo. Hartford. Cloth. $5.50

— *Tribute to Gallaudet; with History of Deaf-Mute Instruction and Institution.* 8vo. Hartford. $0.50

Mary Carpenter. *Reformatory Schools, for the children of the Perishing and Dangerous Classes, and for Juvenile Offenders.* 8vo. London. Cloth. $2.00

T. Guthrie. *Ragged Schools.* 12mo. N. Y. Cloth. $1.00

M. Hill. *Anleitung zum Sprachunterricht taubstummer Kinder.* 8vo. Essen. $1.35

Wm. H. Latham. *First Lessons for Deaf-Mutes.* 16mo. Cincinnati. Paper. $0.30

H. P. Peet. *Course of Instruction for Deaf and Dumb.* 16mo. N. Y. Part I. Cloth. $0.75; Part II., not published; Part III. Paper. $1.00

Isaac Lewis Peet. *Language Lessons, Designed to introduce young learners, deaf-mutes and foreigners, to a correct understanding and use of the English Language.* 12mo. N. Y. Cloth. $1.25

Ed. Rössler. *Beiträge zur Förderung des Taubstummen - Bildungswesens.* 8vo. Leipzig. $0.75

Alexandre Rodenbach. *Les Aveugles e, les Sourds-Muets. Histoire, instruction éducation, biographie.* 2e édition, revue, corrigée et augmentée d'un alphabet des sourds-muets et deux fac-similes. 12mo. Tournai. $0.60

Jos. Ruppert. *Ueber Erziehung, Unterricht und Versorgung der Blinden.* 8vo. München. $0.30

Ludwig v. St. Marie. *Der Blinde und seine Bildung.* 8vo. Leipzig. $0.25

E. Seguin. *Idiocy, and its Treatment by the Physiological Method.* 8vo. N. Y. Cloth. $5.00

— *Traitement moral, Hygiène et Education des Idiots et des autres enfants arriérés ou retardés dans leur développement, agités de mouvements involontaires, débiles, muets non sourds, bègues, etc.* 12mo. Paris. $2.10

Henr. Söder. *Die Methodik des Sprach-Unterrichts in Taubstummen-Anstalten.* 8vo. Hannover. $0.40

6. Education of Women, or Female Education.

Aimé-Martin. *The Education of Mothers of Families; or, the Civilization of the human race by Women.* 12mo. London. Cloth. $2.00

"Ce sont les femmes qui font et défont les nations."   SAINT PIERRE.

Mme. Cl. Beaudoux. *La Science maternelle; ou éducation morale et intellectuelle des jeunes filles.* 12mo. Paris. $1.40

Anna C. Brackett. *The Education of American Girls, considered in a Series of Essays.* 12mo. N. Y. Cloth. $1.75

Edu. Cauer. *Die höhere Mädchenschule und die Lehrerinnenfrage.* 8vo. Berlin. $0.40

Edward H. Clarke. *Sex in Education; or, A Fair Chance for the Girls.* 16mo. Boston. Cloth. $1.25

A statement of the physiological argument against co-education.

A. Dammann. *Die deutsche Bürger-Mädchenschule. Ein vollständiger Unterrichtsplan. Mit besonderer Benutzung der einschlägigen Literatur.* 8vo. Berlin. $1.00

Darwin's u. Hufeland's *Anleitung zur physischen und moralischen Erziehung des weiblichen Geschlechts.* Hrsg. v. F. A. AMMON. 8vo. Leipzig. $0.40

Emily Davies. *The Higher Education of Women.* 12mo. London. Cloth. $1.40

THE DICTIONARY OF EDUCATION AND INSTRUCTION

Fr. Fénélon. *De l'Education des Filles.* 12mo. Paris. $1.20

F. J. Günther. *Briefe an eine Mutter über die wichtigsten Mängel in der jetzigen Erziehung der Töchter höherer Stände.* 8vo. Bielefeld. $1.50

Harriet Martineau. *Household Education.* 12mo. Boston. Cloth. $1.25

J. S. Mill. *On Liberty; The Subjection of Women.* 8vo. N. Y. Cloth. $2.50

Hannah More. *Strictures on the Modern System of Female Education; with a View of the Principles and Conduct prevalent among Women of Rank and Fortune.* 2 vols. 12mo. London. Cloth. $4.00

J. Orton. *Liberal Education of Women.* 12mo. N. Y. Cloth. $1.50

Mrs. A. H. L. Phelps. *Fireside Friend; or, Female Student: Advice to young Ladies on Education.* 12mo. N. Y. Cloth. $1.50

J. Preis. *Die beste Ausstattung für junge Damen.* 8vo. Brieg. $1.50

K. v. Raumer. *Die Erziehung der Mädchen.* 8vo. Gütersloh. $0.90

Miss E. M. Sewell. *Principles of Education drawn from Nature and Revelation, and applied to Female Education in the upper Classes.* 12mo. N. Y. Cloth. $2.00

Emily Shirreff. *Intellectual Education and its Influence on the Character and Happiness of Women.* 12mo. London. Cloth. $2.40

Augustin Thery. *Conseils aux mères sur les moyens de diriger et d'instruire leur filles, à l'usage des mères, des institutrices et des maîtresses de pensions.* 12mo. 2 vols. Paris. $2.40

John Todd. *The Daughter at School.* 12mo. Northampton. Cloth. $1.50

7. Physical Education.

Cath. E. Beecher. *Physiology and Calisthenics in Schools and Families.* Over 100 Illustr. 16mo. N. Y. Cloth. $1.00

H. Klencke. *Schul-Diätetik. Praktische Gesundheitspflege in Schulen und Gesundheitslehre für Knaben und Mädchen in der Schulzeit. Ein Buch für Unterrichtsbehörden, Schulvorstände, Lehrer und Eltern.* 8vo. Leipzig. $0.70

Chas. Kingsley. *Health and Education.* 12mo. N. Y. Cloth. $1.75

Gius. Lauri. *Manuale di ginnastica educativa ad uso delle scuole elementari maschili e femminili.* 4. Macerata. $0.90

Dio Lewis. *New Gymnastics for Men, Women and Children.* Illustr. 12mo. Bost u. Cloth. $1.50

Archibald Maclaren. *A System of Physical Education, Theoretical and Practical.* With Illustrations. 12mo. London. $2.25

E. Paz. *La Gymnastique obligatoire.* 12mo. Paris. $0.40

—— *La Gymnastique raisonnée, moyen infaillible de prévenir les maladies et de prolonger l'existence.* 8vo. Paris. $1.75

Aug. Ravenstein. *Volksturnbuch, im Sinne von Jahn, Eiselen und Spiess.* 8vo. Frankfurt a. M. $2.95

C. J. Robinson. *Hand-Book of the Physical Training in Schools, including full Directions for a Variety of Calisthenic Exercises. Adapted to Classes of all Grades, and to Social and Individual Practice.* 16mo. San Francisco. Paper. $0.75

Math. Roth. *Gymnastic Exercises according to Ling's system.* 12mo. London. $0.50

R. Schenström. *Réflexions sur l'Education physique et les Mouvements corporels à l'occasion du projet de loi sur la Gymnastique scolaire obligatoire dans les écoles de France.* 8vo. Paris. $0.75

D. G. M. Schreber. *Aerzliche Zimmergymnastik, oder System der ohne Geräth und Beistand überall ausführbaren heilgymnastischen Freiübungen.* 8vo. Leipzig. Boards. $1.10

R. Th. Trall. *The Illustrated Family Gymnasium.* 12mo. N. Y. Cloth. $1.50

J. Madison Watson. *Manual of Calisthenics: A systematic Drill-Book without Apparatus, for Schools, Families, and Gymnasiums.* With music to accompany the Exercises. 8vo. Illustr. N. Y. Cloth. $1.20

—— *Hand-Book of Calisthenics and Gymnastics: A Complete Drill-Book for Schools, Families, and Gymnasiums.* With music to accompany the Exercises. 8vo. Illustr. N. Y. Cloth. $2.00

8. Moral and Religious Education; Sunday Schools.

Jac. Abbott. *The Teacher. Moral Influences employed in the Instruction and Government of the Young.* 12mo. Illustr. N. Y. Cloth. $1.75

J. Abercrombie. *The Philosophy of the Moral Feelings, with Additions by* Jacob Abbott. 12mo. N. Y. Cloth. $0.90

—— *Culture and Discipline of the Mind, and other Essays.* 12mo. Edinburgh. Cloth. $1.40

Amos Bronson Alcott. *Record of a School, exemplifying the Principles and Methods of Moral Culture.* 16mo. Boston. Cloth. $1.50

F. Beard. *The Blackboard in the Sunday-School. A Practical Guide for Superintendents and Teachers.* 12mo. N. Y. Cloth. $1.50

Cath. E. Beecher. *The Religious Training of Children in the Family, the School, and the Church.* 12mo. N. Y. Cloth. $1.75

C. Bray. *Education of the Feelings, a Moral System for Secular Schools.* 8vo. London. Cloth. $1.00

N. C. Brooks. *School Manual of Devotion. For Daily Exercises consisting of Selections, Hymns, and a Form of Prayer.* 18mo. N. Y. Cloth. $0.75

—— *Scripture Manual; or, Religious Exercises for the Morning and Evening of each Day in the Month. For Academies, Schools, and Families.* 18mo. Phila. Cloth. $0.75

And. Combe. *A Treatise on the Physiological and Moral Management of Infancy. For the Use of Parents.* 18mo. N. Y. Cloth. $0.75

W. F. Crafts. *Childhood. The Text Book of the Age. A Book for Parents, Pastors, and Sunday-School Teachers.* 12mo. Illustr. Boston. Cloth. $1.50

—— *Through the Eye to the Heart, or, Eye-Teaching in the Sunday School.* Revised Edition, with Illustrations for the International Lessons for 1877. 12mo. Paper. $0.50; cloth $1.00

F. Dittes. *Naturlehre des Moralischen und Kunstlehre der moralischen Erziehung.* 8vo. Leipzig. $0.55

M. G. Dursch. *Pädagogik oder Wissenschaft der christlichen Erziehung, auf dem Standpunkte des katholischen Glaubens dargestellt.* 8vo. Tübingen. $3.00

B. W. Dwight. *Higher Christian Education.* 12mo. N. Y. Cloth. $1.50

Ed. Eggleston. *The Manual. A Practical Guide to the Sunday-School Work.* 32mo. Chicago. Paper, $0.30; cloth, $0.75

A. M. Gow. *Good Morals and Gentle Manners for Schools and Families.* 12mo. Cincinnati. Cloth. $1.25

D. S. Gregory. *Christian Ethics; or, The True Moral Manhood and Life of Duty.* A Text-Book. 12mo. Phila. Cloth. $1.50

A. W. Grube. *Von der sittlichen Bildung der Jugend im ersten Jahrzehend des Lebens.* 8vo. Leipzig. $0.90

William T. Harris. *Moral Education in the Public Schools.* A Paper. 24 pp. $0.06

J. S. Hart. *The Sunday-School Idea; consisting of an Exposition of the Principles which underlie the Sunday-School Cause, and setting forth its Objects, Organization, Methods, and Capabilities.* 12mo. Phila. Cloth. $1.50

Excelsior, or Essays on Politeness, Education, and the Means of Attaining Success in Life. Part I. For Young Gentlemen, by T. E. Howard. — Part II. For Young Ladies, by a Lady (R. U. V.) 12mo. Baltimore. Cloth. $1.50

Chr. Palmer. *Evangelische Pädagogik.* 8vo. Stuttgart. $2.65

E. P. Peabody. *Record of Mr. Alcott's School exemplifying the Principles and Methods of Moral Culture.* 16mo. Boston. Cloth. $1.50

Mrs. Lincoln Phelps. *The Student; or Fireside Friend; with an Appendix on Moral and Religious Education.* 12mo. N. Y. Cloth. $1.50

Cath. A. Sedgwick. *Morals of Manners; or, Hints for our Young Folks.* 16mo. N. Y. Cloth. $0.60

Fz. Splittgerber. *Die moderne widerchristliche Pädagogik, nach ihren Bahnbrechern Rousseau und Basedow vom Standpunkte des Evangeliums aus dargestellt und beurtheilt.* 8vo. Leipzig. $0.75

J. Stadlin. *Die Erziehung im Lichte der Bergpredigt.* 8vo. Aarau. $1.30

J. Todd. *The Sabbath-School Teacher. Designed to aid in elevating and perfecting the Sabbath-School System.* 12mo. Northampton. Cloth. $1.50

V. SCHOOL ECONOMY.

School Laws; School Architecture; School Hygiene; School Furniture and Apparatus; School Supervision, Discipline, and Management; School Libraries and Museums; Teachers' Manuals.

Jac. Abbott. *Gentle Measures in the Management and Training of the Young, or the Principles on which a firm Parental Authority may be established and maintained without violence or anger, and the Right Development of the Moral and Mental Capacities be promoted by methods in harmony with the Structure and Characteristics of the Juvenile Mind. A Book for the Parents of Young Children.* 12mo. N. Y. Cloth. $1.75

—— *The Teacher. Moral Influences employed in the Instruction and Government of the Young.* 12mo. N. Y. Cloth. $1.75

E. Ackermann. *Das Ehrgefühl im Dienste der Erziehung.* 8vo. Eisenach $0.20

Charles F. Adams, Jr. *The Public Library and the Common Schools: Three Papers on Educational Topics.* I. *The Public Library and the Public Schools;* II. *Fiction in Public Libraries, and Educational Catalogues;* III. *The New Departure in the Common Schools of Quincy.* 16mo. Boston. Paper. $1.25

A. B. Alcott. *Record of a School.* 16mo. Boston. Cloth. $1.50

H. Barnard. *American Graded Public Schools, with Plans of School-Houses and Equipment and Regulations for Schools in Cities.* 8vo. Hartford. Cloth. $3.50

—— *School Codes: Constitutional Provisions respecting Education, State School Codes, and City School Regulations.* 8vo. Hartford. Cloth. $3.00

—— *School Architecture: Principles, Plans and Specifications for Structures for Educational Purposes.* 8vo. Hartford. Cloth. $5.00

C. W. Bardeen. *Common School Law. A Digest of the Provisions of Statute and Common Law as to the Relations of the Teacher to the Pupil, the Parent and the District. With four hundred references.* 16mo. Syracuse. $0.50

A. J. Bicknell. *School Houses and Church Architecture.* 4to. N. Y. Cloth. $3.00

J. R. Blackiston. *Hints on School Management.* 12mo. London. Cloth. $0.75

Buckham. *Hand-books for Young Teachers.* I. *First Steps.* 16mo. Syracuse. Cloth. $0.75

F. Buisson. *Devoirs d'Écoliers Américains, récueillis à l'Exposition de Philadelphie* (1876). 16mo. Paris.

Lyman Cobb. *The Evil Tendencies of Corporal Punishment as a means of Moral Discipline in Families and Schools, examined and discussed.* Part I. *Objections to the use of the Rod.* Part II. *Substitutes for, and Preventives of the use of the Rod.* 8vo. N. Y. 1847. About $2.00

The whole book deserves study, though Part II. is particularly valuable.

H. Cohn. *Die Schulhygiene auf der Pariser Weltausstellung,* 1878. 8vo. Breslau. $0.55

J. C. Dalton. *A Treatise on Physiology and Hygiene; for Schools, Families, and Colleges.* 18mo. Illustr. N. Y. Cloth. $1.50

E. W. DeGraff. *The School-Room Guide, embodying the Instruction given by the Author at Teachers' Institutes in New York and other States, especially intended to assist Public School Teachers in the Practical Work of the School-Room.* 16mo. Syracuse. Cloth. $1.50

M. et Mme. Delon. *Méthode intuitive, exercises et travaux pour les enfants selon les méthodes et les procédés de Pestalozzi et de Frœbel.* With 24 lith. plates. 8vo. Paris. $2.45

Theodore Dwight, Jr. *The School-Master's Friend, with the Committee-Man's Guide; containing Suggestions on Common Education, Modes of Teaching and Governing, arranged for ready Reference; Plans of School-Houses, Furniture, Apparatus, Practical Hints and Anecdotes on Different Systems, etc. For daily use in Common Schools; also Directions to Committee-men and Trustees of Schools, and Friends of Education, on the Means of improving Schools this Year.* Plates. 12mo. N. Y. 1835. About $1.50

THE DICTIONARY OF EDUCATION AND INSTRUCTION

S. F. Eveleth. *School-House Architecture. Designs for School-Houses, with Perspectives, Elevations, Plans, Sections, Details, and Specifications, all drawn to working scale, with methods of Heating and Ventilation.* 4to. N. Y. Cloth. $4.00

F. Falk. *Die sanitäts-polizeiliche Ueberwachung höherer und niederer Schulen und ihre Aufgaben.* 8vo. Leipzig. $0.90

J. Frey. *Der rationelle Schultisch als das hauptsächlichste Verhütungsmittel der schlechten Brustentwickelung, der schlechten Haltung und der Rückgratsverkrümmung.* With 8 plates. 8vo. Zürich. $0.55

A. Freimund. *Ueber körperliche Züchtigung beim Unterricht.* 8vo. Leipzig. $0.40

John Gill. *Introductory Text-Book to School Education, Method, and School-Management.* 8vo. London. Cloth. $1.20

J. S. Hart. *In the School-Room; or, Chapters in the Philosophy of Education.* 12mo. Phila. Cloth. $1.25

A. Holbrook. *School Management.* 12mo. Cincinnati. Cloth. $1.50

Fr. S. Jewell. *School Government: A Practical Treatise, presenting a Thorough Discussion of its Facts, Principles, and their Applications; with Critiques upon Current Theories of Punishment, and Schemes of Administration.* 12mo. N. Y. Cloth. $1.50

J. Johonnot. *School Houses.* 8vo. N. Y. Cloth. $3.00

P. W. Joyce. *A Hand-Book of School Management and Methods of Teaching.* 12mo. London. $0.80

C. Kehr. *Die Praxis der Volksschule. Ein Wegweiser zur Führung einer geregelten Schuldisciplin und zur Ertheilung eines methodischen Schulunterrichts für Volksschullehrer und für Solche, die es werden wollen.* 8vo. Gotha. $1.50

John Kennedy. *The School and the Family; The Ethics of School Relations.* 12mo. N. Y. Cloth. $1.00 Abounds in good sense and in practical suggestions.

C. Klett. *Der Lehrer ohne Stock. Gegen die körperliche Strafe in der Schule.* 8vo. Stuttgart. $0.30

G. Köpp. *Illustrirtes Hand- und Nachschlagebuch der vorzüglichsten Lehr- und Veranschaulichungsmittel aus dem Gesammtgebiete der Erziehung und des*

Unterrichts für Fachleute an Lehranstalten und Instituten jeder Art, insbesondere an Volksschulen, Fortbildungsschulen, höheren Bürgerschulen, Lehrerseminarien, Realschulen, Gymnasien, etc. With 576 woodcuts. 8vo. Bensheim. $2.75

F. Küchler. *Die Reform unserer Volksschule in hygienischer Richtung.* 8vo. Bern. $0.25

L. W. Leeds. *A Treatise on Ventilation. Comprising Seven Lectures delivered before the Franklin Institute, showing the great want of improved methods of Ventilation in our buildings, giving the chemical and physiological process of respiration, comparing the effects of the various methods of heating and lighting upon the ventilation, etc.* 8vo. Illustr. N. Y. Cloth. $2.50

D. F. Lincoln. *School and Industrial Hygiene.* 16mo. Phila. Paper. $0.50 Should be studied by every teacher.

Horace Mann. *Lectures and Annual Reports on Education.* New Edit. 8vo. Boston. Cloth. $3.00

F. Migerka. *Das Unterrichtswesen in den Vereinigten Staaten.* 8vo. Wien. $0.60

T. Morrison. *Manual of School Management.* 12mo. Glasgow. Cloth. $1.60

John F. Moss. *Handbook of the New Code of Regulations, 1880; and other Official Instructions, Orders, and Circulars, of the Education Department.* 12mo. London. $0.80

Felix Narjoux. *Règlement pour la construction et l'ameublement des maisons d'école, arrêté par le Ministre de l'Instruction Publique, suivi d'un commentaire et des plans explicatifs.* 8vo. Paris. $0.75

F. M. Norman. *The Schoolmaster's Drill Assistant: A Manual for Elementary Schools, Boys', Girls', or Mixed; by aid of which any Teacher may easily Drill his or her own Scholars. Being Military Drill simplified and adapted for School use; with Class Drill, Dual Desk Drill, and other useful Exercises, specially prepared for Schools.* Illustr. 12mo. London. Cloth. $0.80

Charles Northend. *The Teacher's Assistant, or Hints and Methods in School Discipline and Instruction; being a Series of Familiar Letters to one entering upon the teacher's work.* 12mo. N. Y. Cloth. $1.50

321

W. H. Payne. *Chapters on School Supervision. A practical Treatise on Superintendence; Arranging Courses of Study; The Preparation and Use of Blanks, Records, and Reports; Examinations for Promotions, etc.* 12mo. Cincinnati. Cloth. $1.25

Jas. Pillans. *Rationale of Discipline in the High School of Edinburgh.* 8vo. Edinburgh. Cloth. $2.00

L. A. Prevost-Paradol. *Du Rôle de la Famille dans l'Éducation.* 8vo. Paris. $0.90

Ambroise Rendu. *Code universitaire ou lois, statuts et règlements de l'Université de France jusqu'au 1er janvier 1846.* 8vo. Paris. $4.50

A. Riant. *Hygiène Scolaire, Influence de l'École sur la Santé des Enfants.* 18mo. Paris. $1.05

—— *L'Hygiène et l'Éducation dans les Internats, Lycées, Collèges, Pensionats, Maisons d'Éducation, Écoles Normales, Écoles Spéciales, Universités, etc.* 8vo. Paris.

E. R. Robson. *School Architecture. Practical Information on the Planning, Designing, Building, and Furnishing of School-Houses.* 8vo. Illustr. London. Cloth. $6.30

S. Roggero. *Le nostre scuole considerate in relazione coll' igiene e colla morale.* 8vo. Viterbo. $0.90

N. W. T. Root. *School Amusements; or, how to make the school interesting.* Embracing simple rules for military and gymnastic exercises, and hints upon the general management of the school-room. 12mo. N. Y. Cloth. $1.00

M. Mc.N. Walsh. *The Lawyer in the School-Room. Comprising the Laws of All the States on important Educational Subjects.* 12mo. N. Y. Cloth. $1.00

An admirable book.

W. H. Wells. *The Graded School. A Graded Course of Instruction for Public Schools; with copious practical Directions to Teachers, and Observations on Primary Schools, School Discipline, School Records, etc.* 12mo. N.Y. Cloth. $1.00

J. P. Wickersham. *School Economy. A Treatise on the Preparation, Organization, Employments, Government, and Authorities of Schools.* 12mo. Phila. Cloth. $1.50

G. Wilson. *A Handbook of Sanitary Science.* 12mo. London. Cloth. $3.40

L. Wintrebert. *Consultation hygiénique à propos de la Construction et de l'Ameublement d'une École primaire à Lille.* 8vo. Paris. $0.55

A. Wolpert. *Theorie und Praxis der Ventilation und Heizung.* 8vo. 2 vols. Braunschweig. $7.35

W. T. Wylie. *Lessons and Prayers for the School-Room.* 8vo. Philadelphia. Cloth. $3.00

T. Ziller. *Die Regierung der Kinder.* 8vo. Leipzig. $0.75

VI. HISTORY OF EDUCATION.

Histories; Biographies and Memoirs; Descriptions of Educational Systems; Catalogues and Reports.

H. André. *Nos Maîtres, hier. Études sur les progrès de l'éducation et sur les développements de l'instruction populaire en France, depuis les temps les plus reculés jusqu'à J. J. Rousseau.* 16mo Paris. $1.25

—— *Nos Maîtres, aujourd'hui. Études sur les progrès de l'éducation, les méthodes et les établissements de tous les degrés en France depuis J. J. Rousseau jusqu'à nos jours.* 12mo. 2 vols. Paris. $1.75

M. Arnold. *Higher Schools and Universities in Germany.* 8vo. London. Cloth. $2.00

H. Barnard. *German Teachers and Educational Reformers; Memoirs of Eminent Teachers and Educators with contributions to the History of Education in Germany.* 8vo. Hartford. Cloth. $3.50

—— *French Teachers, Schools, and Pedagogy — Old and New.* 8vo. Hartford. Cloth. $3.50

—— *English Teachers, Educators, and Promoters of Education.* 8vo. Hartford. Cloth. $3.50

—— *American Teachers, Educators and Benefactors of Education.* With Portraits. 8vo. 5 vols. Hartford. Per vol. $3.50

THE DICTIONARY OF EDUCATION AND INSTRUCTION

H. Barnard. *Pestalozzi and Swiss Pedagogy; Memoir, and Educational Principles, Methods, and Influence of* JOHN HENRY PESTALOZZI, *and Biographical Sketches of several of his Assistants and Disciples; together with Selections from his Publications, and Accounts of Schools and Teachers in Switzerland.* 8vo. Hartford. Cloth. $3.50

A. Beer u. F. Hochegger. *Die Fortschritte des Unterrichtswesens in den Culturstaaten Europa's.*

I. *Das Unterrichtswesen in Frankreich und Oesterreich.* 8vo. Wien. $4.40

II. 1. *Das Unterrichtswesen Russlands und Belgiens.* 8vo. Wien. $1.85

II. 2. *Das Unterrichtswesen der Schweiz.* 8vo. Wien. $2.60

E. Biber. *H. Pestalozzi and his Plan of Education; an Account of his Life and Writings, with copious Extracts from his Works.* 8vo. London. Cloth. About $2.20

E. Biot. *Essai sur l'Histoire de l'Instruction Publique en Chine et de la Corporation des Lettrés, depuis les anciens temps jusqu'à nos jours.* 8vo. Paris. $3.60

Ed. Bock. *Der Volksschul-Unterricht.* 8vo. Breslau. $2.20

J. Boehm. *Geschichte der Pädagogik mit Charakterbildern hervorragender Pädagogen und Zeiten. Als Commentar zu seiner "Kurzgefassten Geschichte der Pädagogik."* 8vo. 2 vols. Nürnberg. $2.95

Wm. Oland Bourne. *History of the Public School Society of the City of New York.* 8vo. N. Y. Cloth. $5.00

Joh. Bruestlein. *Luther's Einfluss auf das Volksschulwesen und den Religionsunterricht.* 8vo. Jena. $0.75

G. Bruckbach. *Wegweiser durch die Geschichte der Pädagogik.* 8vo. Leipzig. $0.55

Augustin Cochin. *Pestalozzi. Sa Vie, ses Oeuvres, ses Méthodes d'Instruction et d'Education.* 12mo. Paris. $0.50

E. Celezia. *Storia della Pedagogia italiana da Pittagora ai di nostri.* 8vo. Milano. $2.00

C. Compayré. *Histoire critique des Doctrines de l'Education en France depuis le seizième siècle.* 8vo. 2 vols. Paris. $4.45

"Le livre de M. COMPAYRE est certainement un des plus complets et des plus intéressants qu'on puisse lire."

Revue des Deux Mondes.

V. Cousin. *On the State of Education in Holland, as regards Schools for the Working Classes and the Poor.* 12mo. London. Cloth. About $3.00

—— *Report on the State of Public Instruction in Prussia.* 12mo. London. About $2.00

These reports led to a reorganization of the school system of France, and had a marked influence on the educational policy of this country.

F. Cramer. *Geschichte der Erziehung und des Unterrichts im Alterthume.* 8vo. 2 vols. Elberfeld. $6.60

—— *Geschichte der Erziehung und des Unterrichts in den Niederlanden während des Mittelalters, mit Zurückführung auf die allgemeinen literarischen und pädagogischen Verhältnisse jener Zeit.* 8vo. Elberfeld. $1.85

Frdr. Dittes. *Geschichte der Erziehung und des Unterrichtes.* 8vo. Leipzig. $1.10

J. Donaldson. *Lectures on the History of Education in Prussia and England, and on kindred Topics.* 12mo. Edinburgh. Cloth. $1.40

A book of great value.

M. Duschak. *Schulgesetzgebung und Methodik der alten Israeliten, nebst einem geschichtlichen Anhang und einer Beilage über höhere israelitische Lehranstalten.* 8vo. Wien. $1.35

Educational Code of the Prussian Nation. With its Present Form. 18mo. London. $1.00

W. Everett. *On the Cam. Lectures on the University of Cambridge in England.* 12mo. Cambridge. Cloth. $1.00

W. Fraser. *The Life and Educational Principles of David Stow, Esq., Founder of the Training System of Education. With portrait.* 8vo. London. Cloth. $2.50

Th. Fritz. *Esquisse d'un Système complet d'Instruction et d'Education, et de leur Histoire.* 8vo. 3 vols. Strassburg. $4.50

Fred. J. Furnivall. *Education in Early England. Some Notes used as forewords to a Collection of Treatises on "Manners and Meals in Olden Times", for the Early English Text Society.* 8vo. London. $0.40

M. Giordano. *Dell' istruzione pubblica in Italia nei suoi rapporti economici, morali e religiosi. Osservazioni e proposte.* Parte I. 16mo. Napoli. $0.75

THE DICTIONARY OF EDUCATION AND INSTRUCTION

James Grant. *The History of the Burgh Schools of Scotland.* 8vo. London. Cloth. $3.70

W. N. Hailmann. *Twelve Lectures on the History of Pedagogy*, delivered before the Cincinnati Teachers' Association. 12mo. Cincinnati. Cloth. $0.75

W. T. Harris. *Annual Reports of the Schools of St. Louis.* 8vo. St. Louis. Cloth. Each $1.50

These Reports are among the most valuable educational documents published in this country.

Ja. Morgan Hart. *German Universities; A Record of Personal Experience and a Critical Comparison of the System of Higher Education in Germany with those of England and the United States.* 12mo. N. Y. Cloth. $1.75

W. B. Hazen. *The School and the Army in Germany and France. With a Diary of Siege Life at Versailles.* 12mo. N. Y. Cloth. $2.50

H. Heppe. *Das Schulwesen des Mittelalters und dessen Reform im sechzehnten Jahrhundert.* 8vo. Marburg. $0.55

C. Hippeau. *L'Instruction Publique en Angleterre.* 12mo. Paris. $0.50

—— *L'Instruction Publique dans les Etats du Nord, — Suède, Norwége, Danemark.* 12mo. Paris. $1.40

—— *L'Instruction Publique en Allemagne.* 12mo. Paris. $1.25

—— *L'Instruction Publique aux Etats-Unis.* 12mo. Paris. $1.40

—— *L'Instruction Publique en Italie.* 12mo. Paris. $1.25

—— *L'Instruction Publique pendant la Révolution.* 12mo. Paris. $1.40

All the books on education written by this author are trustworthy and valuable.

John S. Hittell. *A Brief History of Culture.* 12mo. N. Y. Cloth. $1.50

V. A. Huber. *The English Universities.* An abridged translation edited by F. A. Newman. 8vo. 3 vols. London. Cloth. About $12.00

G. P. R. James. *On the Educational Institutions of Germany.* 12mo. London. Cloth. About $3.00

Education in Japan. A Series of Letters addressed by prominent Americans to Arinori Mori, Japanese Minister. 12mo. N. Y. Cloth. $1.50

Thomas Jefferson and J. C. Cabell. *Letters on Early History of the University of Virginia.* 8vo. Richmond. Cloth. $5.00

Sophia Jex-Blake. *A Visit to some American Schools and Colleges.* 8vo. London. Cloth. $1.75

F. E. Keller. *Geschichte des preussischen Volksschulwesens.* 8vo. Berlin. $2.95

C. Kehr. *Geschichte der Methodik des deutschen Volksschulunterrichts. Unter Mitwirkung einer Anzahl Schulmänner.* 8vo. 3 vols. Gotha. $6.60

L. Kellner. *Erziehungsgeschichte.* 8vo. Essen. $2.95

Frdr. Körner. *Geschichte der Pädagogik von den ältesten Zeiten bis auf die Gegenwart. Ein Handbuch für Geistliche und Lehrer beider Confessionen.* 8vo. Leipzig. $1.50

Herman Kruesi. *Pestalozzi: His Life, Work, and Influence.* With portraits and illustr. 8vo. Cincinnati. Cloth. $2.25

Ja. Leitch. *Practical Educationists and their System of Teaching.* 12mo. Glasgow. Cloth. $3.00

(Locke; Pestalozzi; Bell; Lancaster; Wilderspin; Stow; Spencer.)

Letters from Hofwyl by a Parent on the Educational Institutions of Fellenberg. 12mo. London. Cloth. $2.25

Contains a series of letters written by M. C. Woodbridge, and originally published in the *Annals of Education.*

Fred. Lorenz. *The Life of Alcuin.* Translated by Jane Mary Slee. 12mo. London. $0.75

Horace Mann. *Annual Reports on Education from 1839 to 1848.* 8vo. Boston. Cloth. $3.00

Mrs. Horace Mann. *The Life of Horace Mann. By his Wife.* 8vo. Boston. Cloth. $3.00

Baroness Marenholtz-Buelow. *Reminiscences of Frederic Fræbel.* Translated by Mrs. Horace Mann. 12mo. Boston. Cloth. $1.50

H. Mascher. *Das deutsche Schulwesen nach seiner historischen Entwickelung und den Forderungen der Gegenwart. Vom Standpunkte der Staats- und Gemeindeverwaltung, sowie der Nationalökonomie dargestellt und beleuchtet.* 8vo. Eisenach. $1.50

J. M. D. Meiklejohn. *An Old Educational Reformer; — Dr. Andrew Bell.* 12mo. London. Cloth. $1.40

Everardo Micheli. *Storia della Pedagogia italiana dal tempo dei Romani a tutto il secolo XVIII.* 16mo. Torino. $1.50

324

J. Michelet. *Nos Fils.* 8vo. Paris. $1.25 (Livre III; Rabelais; Montaigne; Comenius; The Jesuits; Port Royal; Fénelon; Locke; Rousseau; Pestalozzi; Frœbel.)

Frédéric Monnier. *L'Instruction Populaire en Allemagne, en Suisse et dans les Pays Scandinaves.* 8vo. Paris. $2.65

J. Morley. *Rousseau.* 8vo. 2 vols. London. Cloth. $9.00

—— *Struggle for National Education.* 8vo. London. Cloth. $1.20

J. Bass. Mullinger. *The Schools of Charles the Great and the Restoration of Education in the Ninth Century.* 8vo. London. Cloth. $3.00

John Henry Newman. *Historical Sketches of Universities.* 12mo. 3 vols. London. Cloth. $6.30

Jules Paroz. *Histoire Universelle de la Pédagogie.* 16mo. Paris. $1.50

For a work in small compass, this is the best History of Education within my knowledge.

W. H. Payne. *A Short History of Education: being a reprint of the article "Education" from the ninth edition of the Encyclopædia Britannica.* 16mo. Syracuse. Cloth. $0.50

F. W. Pfeifer. *Die Volksschule des 19. Jahrhunderts in Biographien hervorragender Schulmänner.* 8vo. Nürnberg. $3.40

Philobiblius (Dr. L. P. Brockett). *History and Progress of Education.* 12mo. N. Y. Cloth. $1.50

R. H. Quick. *Essays on Educational Reformers.* 12mo. Cincinnati. Cloth. $2.00

(Schools of the Jesuits; Ascham, Montaigne, Ratich, Milton; Comenius; Locke; Rousseau's Emile; Basedow and the Philanthropin; Pestalozzi; Jacotot; Herbert Spencer; Thoughts and Suggestions about Teaching Children; Some Remarks about Moral and Religious Education; Appendix.

Josiah Quincy. *A History of Harvard University.* 8vo. 2 vols. Boston. Cloth.

S. S. Randall. *History of the Common School System of the State of New York.* 8vo. N. Y. Cloth. $3.00

K. von Raumer. *Geschichte der Pädagogik vom Wiederaufblühen klassischer Studien bis auf unsere Zeit.* 8vo. 4 vols. Gütersloh. $9.15. Singly: I. *Das Mittelalter bis zu Montaigne.* $2.00 — II. *Vom Tode Baco's bis zum Tode*

Pestalozzi's. $2.30 — III. *Unterricht.* $2.65— IV. *Die deutschen Universitäten.* $2.20

Copious translations from this work are to be found in BARNARD'S *American Journal of Education.*

J. E. T. Rogers. *Education in Oxford: Its method, its aids and its rewards.* 12mo. London.

E. Sassi. *L'istruzione pubblica in Torino dal medioevo ai tempi nostri. Con note e documenti.* 8vo. Torino. $1.35

H. I. Schmidt. *History of Education, ancient and modern.* 18mo. N.Y. Cloth. $0.75

K. Schmidt. *Die Geschichte der Pädagogik dargestellt in weltgeschichtlicher Entwickelung und im organischen Zusammenhange mit dem Culturleben der Völker. Vermehrt und verbessert von* WICH.LANGE. 8vo. 4 vols. Cöthen. $11.00 Singly: I. *Geschichte der Pädagogik in der vorchristlichen Zeit.* $2.20 — II. *Geschichte der Pädagogik in der christlichen Zeit.* $1.85 — III. *Geschichte der Pädagogik von Luther bis Pestalozzi.* $2.95 — IV. *Geschichte der Pädagogik von Pestalozzi bis zur Gegenwart.* $3.30 — (*Geschichte der Erziehung und des Unterrichts. Für Schul- und Predigtamtscandidaten, für Volksschullehrer, für gebildete Eltern und Erzieher übersichtlich dargestellt.* Hrsg. von WICH. LANGE. 8vo. Cöthen. $1.50

J. K. Shuttleworth. *Four Periods of Public Education,* 1832, 1839, 1846, 1862. 8vo. London. Cloth. $4.90

J. H. Smart. *Indiana Schools and the Men who have worked in them.* 12mo. Cincinnati. Cloth. $1.00

Goldwin Smith. *The Reorganization of the University of Oxford.* 16mo. London. $0.80

A. P. Stanley. *Life and Correspondence of Thomas Arnold.* 8vo. 2 vols. N.Y. $2.50

Howard Staunton. *The Great Schools of England. An Account of the Foundations, Endowments, and Discipline of the chief Seminaries of Learning in England.* 8vo. London. Cloth. $3.00

Heinrich Steffens. *German University Life. The Story of my Career as a Student and Professor. With Personal Remembrances of Goethe, Schiller, Novalis, and Others.* Translated by W. L. GAGE. 12vo. Phila. Cloth. $1.25

THE DICTIONARY OF EDUCATION AND INSTRUCTION

A. Stöckl. *Lehrbuch der Geschichte der Pädagogik.* 8vo. Mainz. $3.10
Karl Strack. *Geschichte des deutschen Volksschulwesens.* 8vo. Gütersloh. $2.05.
W. B. S. Taylor. *History of the University of Dublin: Its Origin, Progress, and Present Condition.* Illustr. 8vo. London. Cloth. $2.50
And. Ten Brook. *American State Universities; their Origin and Progress. A History of Congressional University Land-Grants; a particular Account of the Rise and Development of the University of Michigan; and Hints toward the Future of the American University System.* 8vo. Cincinnati. Cloth. $3.50
Augustin Thery. *Histoire de l'Education en France, depuis le Ve siècle jusqu'à 1858.* 8vo. 2 vols. Paris. $4.20
E. B. Tylor. *Primitive Culture.* 8vo. 2 vols. N. Y. Cloth. $7.00

A. Vogel. *Geschichte der Pädagogik als Wissenschaft.* 8vo. Gütersloh. $2.75
G. A. Walton. *Report of Examinations in Norfolk County, Mass.* 8vo. Boston. Paper. $0.50
Adalb. Weber. *Die Geschichte der Volksschulpädagogik und der Kleinkindererziehung, mit besonderer Berücksichtigung der Letzteren. Ein Handbuch für Lehrer und Lehrerinnen, sowie zum Gebrauche in Seminarien.* 8vo. Eisenach. $1.85
L. Wiese. *Das höhere Schulwesen in Preussen. Historisch-statistische Darstellung, im Auftrage des Ministers der geistlichen, Unterrichts- und Medicinal-Angelegenheiten herausgegeben.* With illustr. 8vo. 3 vols. Berlin. $14.60
— *German Letters on English Education. Written during an Educational Tour in 1876.* 8vo. London. Cloth. $2.60

VII. MISCELLANEOUS EDUCATIONAL LITERATURE.

Educational Periodicals. Proceedings of Educational Associations; Mixed Educational Writings; Reviews.

1. Educational Periodicals.

(The figures — e. g. 4|8 — denote the number of issues per year, and the size of these.)

Allgemeine deutsche Lehrerzeitung. BERTHELT. Leipzig. 52|4. $2.40 net.
American Journal of Education. BARNARD. 4|8. Hartford. $1.00
The *American Journal of Education* — from 1856 to 1880 — consists of 30 volumes (over 25,000 pages), with 800 wood cuts of structures for educational purposes, and 130 portraits of eminent educators and teachers. Cloth. $135; half goat, $164. Single vols., cloth. $5.00; half goat, $5.50
A complete set of this *Journal* is invaluable. It is a mine of information on educational topics of every sort: historical, biographical, practical, statistical. American subjects are copiously treated. The various works published by Mr. BARNARD are made up of selections from his *Journal*. Unfortunately, the same matter is made to do service under different titles; so that for educational libraries, the more economical plan is to buy a complete set of the *Journal* rather than the republications under special titles.
American Journal of Education. MERWIN. 12|4. St. Louis. $1.00
Bulletin Officiel de l'Instruction Primaire du Département de la Seine. 12|8. Paris. $2.00
Canada Educational Monthly. ADAM. 12|8. Toronto. $1.50

Canada School Journal. 12|4. Toronto. $1.00
Centralblatt für die Unterrichts-Verwaltung in Preussen. 12|8. Berlin. $2.10 net.
Common School Teacher. CRISLER and FIELDS. 12|8. Bedford. $1.00
Cornelia. Zeitschrift für häusliche Erziehung. PILZ. 10|8. Leipzig. $1.35 net.
Le Courrier de l'Enseignement Libre. 12|8. Paris. $3.60
Eclectic Teacher. CHASE and VANCE. 12|8. Lexington. $1.00
L'Ecole Laïque. Revue hebdomadaire de l'Instruction populaire et laïque. Sr. MARTIN. 52|8. Paris. $2.40
L'Ecole Nouvelle. Revue de l'Education intégrale, scientifique, industrielle, artistique et de la réforme pédagogique. FRANCOLIN. 12|8. Paris. $2.10
Education. BICKNELL. 6|8. Boston. $4.00
L'Education. Journal des Ecoles primaires. 52|8. Paris. $3.00
Educational Journal of Virginia. FOX. 12|8. Richmond. $1.00
The Educational News. A Weekly Record and Review. 52|4. Edinburgh. $2.00 net.
Educational Times, and Journal of the College of Preceptors. 12|4. London. $2.00 net.

326

THE DICTIONARY OF EDUCATION AND INSTRUCTION

Educational Weekly. WAGGONER. 52|4. Chicago. $2.50
Educationist. HOSS. 12|8. Topeka. $1.00
Die Erziehung der Gegenwart. SCHRÖDER. 12|4. Dresden. $1.20 net.
Erziehungs-Blätter. KLEMM. 12|4. Milwaukee. $2.00
Indiana School Journal. BELL. 12|8. Indianapolis. $1.50
L'Instruction Publique. Revue des lettres, sciences et arts. BLOT. 52|4. Paris. $7.20
Iowa Normal Monthly. 12|8. SHOUP. Dubuque. $1.00
La Jeune Mère, ou l'Education du premier age. Journal illustré de l'enfance. BROCHARD. 12|8. Paris. $2.40
Journal des Instituteurs et des Bibliothèques Publiques Scolaires. 52|8. Paris. $2.40
Journal Général de l'Instruction Publique. 12|8. Paris. $6.00
Journal of Education, New England and National. BICKNELL. 52|2. Boston. $2.50
Journal of Women's Educational Union. SHIRREFF and BARTLEY. 12|8. London. $2.00 net.
Kindergarten, Bewahranstalt und Elementarklasse. KÖHLER. SCHMIDT. SEIDEL. 12|8. Weimar. $1.00 net.
Kindergarten Messenger and the New Education. HAILMANN. 12|4. Syracuse. $1.00
Louisiana Journal of Education. LUSHER and ROGERS. 12|8. New Orleans. $1.00
Magazin für Lehr- und Lermittel. SCHRÖDER. 24|4. Leipzig. $1.20 net.
Manuel Général de l'Instruction Primaire, journal des Instituteurs et des Institutrices. 52|8. Paris. $2.40
Maryland School Journal. NEWELL and EDWARDS. 12|8. Baltimore. $1.25
New York School Journal. KELLOGG. 52|2. N. Y. $1.50
Normal Teacher. SHERRILL. 12|8. Danville. $1.00
Ohio Educational Monthly and National Teacher. HENKLE. 12|8. Salem. $1.50
Organ der Taubstummen- und Blindenanstalten. MATTHIAS. 12|4. Friedberg. $1.35 net.
Pacific School and Home Journal. LYSER. 12|8. San Francisco. $2.00
Pädagogische Blätter für Lehrerbildung. KEHR. 6|8. Gotha. $3.60 net.
Pädagogisches Archiv. KRUMME. 10|8. Stettin. $4.80 net.

Pädagogium. Monatschrift für Erziehung und Unterricht. DITTES. 12|8. Leipzig. $3.60 net.
Parents' and Teachers' Monthly. CLINE, WILLIAMSON, HARDIN. 12|8. Louisville. $1.00
Pennsylvania School Journal. WICKERSHAM. 12|8. Lancaster. $1.50
Der praktische Schulmann. RICHTER. 8|8. Leipzig. $3.00 net.
Primary Teacher. SHELDON. 12|8. Boston. $1.00
The Princeton Review. 6|8. New York. $2.00
This Review is noticeable for the high quality of its papers on educational subjects.
Repertorium der Pädagogik. HEINDL. 12|8. Ulm. $1.75 net.
Revue de l'Enseignement Secondaire Spécial et de l'Enseignement Professionel. 12|8. Paris. $2.60
Revue des Deux Mondes. 24|8. Paris. $13.75 net.
Questions of national education are discussed with great clearness and ability in the pages of this Review.
Revue Internationale de l'Enseignement. DREYFUS-BRISAC. 12|8. Paris. $7.20
Revue Pédagogique. HANRIOT. 12|12 Paris. $2.70
Rheinische Blätter für Erziehung und Unterricht. (Founded in 1827 by A. DIESTERWEG.) LANGE. 6|8. Frankfurt. $2.40 net.
Rundschau über das Unterrichtswesen aller Länder. KONZE u. KLOSE. 24|8. Berlin. $3.60 net.
The School Board Chronicle. An Educational Record and Review. 52|4. London. $1.75 net.
School Bulletin and New York State Educational Journal. BARDEEN. 12|4. Syracuse. $1.00
Texas Journal of Education. HOLLINGSWORTH. 12|4. Austin. $2.00
Wisconsin Journal of Education. WHITFORD. 12|8. Madison. $1.00
Zeitschrift für das Gymnasialwesen. HIRSCHFELDER u. KERN. 12|8. Berlin. $6.00 net.
Zeitschrift für die Oesterreichischen Gymnasien. TOMASCHEK. 12|8. Wien. $7.20 net.
Zeitschrift für weibliche Bildung. Centralorgan für deutsches Mädchenschulwesen. SCHORNSTEIN. 12|8. Leipzig. $3.60 net.
Zeitung für das höhere Unterrichtswesen Deutschlands. WEISKE. 52|4. Leipzig. $2.40 net.

2. Proceedings of Educational Associations; Mixed Educational Writings; Reviews.

American Institute of Instruction. Lectures. Boston. 1830–1880. Each about $1.00. Price variable according to scarcity of volumes.

C. W. Bardeen. *Common School Law for Common School Teachers. To which are added the Questions given at the New York Examinations for State Certificates.* 16mo. Syracuse. $0.50

H. Barnard. *Compulsory School Attendance.* 12mo. Hartford. Cloth. $1.00

—— *Official Reports — as Superintendent of Common Schools in Connecticut,* 1 vol.; *as Commissioner of Public Schools, R. I.,* 1 vol.; *as National Commissioner of Education,* 3 vols. Each volume, 8vo. Cloth $4.50

The Bible in the Public Schools. Arguments in the case of John D. Minor et al. v. The Board of Education of the City of Cincinnati et al., in the Superior Court of Cincinnati; with the Opinion and Decision of the Court. 8vo. Cincinnati. $2.00

—— *Arguments of Messrs. Ramsey, Sage, and King in the above case in favor of the use of the Bible.* 8vo. Cincinnati. $0.50

—— *Arguments of Messrs. Stallo, Hoadly, and Matthews in the above case against the use of the Bible.* 8vo. Cincinnati. $0.50

—— *Opinion and Decision of the Supreme Court of Ohio in the above case.* 8vo. Cincinnati. $0.25

Goold Brown. *Grammar of English Grammars.* 8vo. N. Y. Sheep. $6.25

Chas. L. Brace. *The Dangerous Classes of New York, and Twenty Years' Work among them.* 12mo. N. Y. Cloth. $2.50

Classical Studies. By a Scotch Graduate. 12mo. N. Y. $1.50

Conférences pédagogiques de Paris en 1880. Rapports et procès-verbaux. 12mo. Paris. $0.75

Victor Cousin. *Lectures on the True, the Beautiful, and the Good. Translated by Wight.* 8vo. N. Y. Cloth. $2.00

Chas. Dickens. *Schools and Schoolmasters. Edited by T. J. Chapman.* 12mo. N. Y. Cloth. $1.25

R. Dulon. *Aus Amerika über Schule, deutsche Schule, amerikanische Schule, und deutsch-amerikanische Schule.* 8vo. Leipzig. $1.65

A. du Mesnil. *Congrès international de Bruxelles. Lettre à M. Jules Ferry, ministre de l'instruction publique et des beaux-arts.* 8vo. Paris. $0.75

Jahrbuch des Vereins für wissenschaftliche Pädagogik. 1880. Zeller. 8vo. Langensalza. $1.85

G. Jost. *Les Congrès des Instituteurs allemands.* Paris. 12mo. $0.75

Horace Mann. *Annual Reports on Education from 1839–1848.* 8vo. Boston. Cloth. $3.00

—— *Lectures and Annual Reports on Education.* 8vo. Boston. Cloth. $3.00

A. D. Mayo and T. Vickers. *The Bible in the Public Schools.* 12mo. N. Y. Paper. $0.25

National Educational Association. Addresses and Journal of Proceedings. 1858–1880. Each $2.00

Some of the best specimens of American pedagogy are to be found in these volumes.

Pädagogisches Jahrbuch. 1880. 8vo. Wien. $1.10

Pädagogischer Jahresbericht von 1879. Dittes. 8vo. Leipzig. $3.70

Plato. *The Republic.* 16mo. London. Cloth. $1.25

"C'est le plus beau traité d'éducation qu'on ait jamais fait." Rousseau.

The Regents' Questions. 1866 to 1876. *Being the Questions for the Preliminary Examinations for admission to the University of the State of New York, prepared by the Regents of the University. Compiled by D. J. Pratt.* 18mo. Syracuse. $1.00

Regents' Reports on the Academies and Colleges of New York together with the *Proceedings* and *Addresses* at the Annual Convocations. By far the most complete and detailed educational reports ever published. 1837–1876. 8vo. Albany. Price variable according to scarcity of volumes.

S. Smiles. *Thrift.* 12mo. N. Y. Cloth. $1.25

Should be on every teacher's desk for occasional reading.

Meta Wellmer. *Deutsche Erzieherinnen und deren Wirkungskreis.* 8vo. Leipzig. $0.75

L. Wiese. *Verordnungen und Gesetze für die höheren Schulen in Preussen.* 8vo. 2 vols. Berlin. $3.70. — Singly: I. *Die Schule.* $1.85. II. *Das Lehramt und der Lehrer.* $1.85

—— *Deutsche Briefe über englische Erziehung, nebst einem Anhang über belgische Schulen.* 8vo. Berlin. $1.00

NOTICE.

It is due to Prof. PAYNE to state here that, in addition to the publications mentioned in the List, a number of books of the highest importance were originally enumerated by him; the fact, however, that they are out of print and difficult to obtain dictated their omission from the present list, which is designed to be practically available, in that the publications mentioned therein are such as can easily be obtained through any bookseller.

Copies of old and valuable educational publications needed for libraries may, however, be obtained frequently from dealers in second-hand books, and the undersigned — having direct connections with all countries — offer their services in procuring such, and invite the filing of lists of publications thus desired second-hand as opportunity may offer.

To the statement elsewhere made that this list is to be revised for future editions, we will here add that Prof. PAYNE proposes also to give suggestions for the formation of the best selection of 20, 50, or 100 volumes of educational and reference books for the use of teachers*); and we shall be glad to transmit to him for consideration the opinions which practical educators, librarians, and others may see fit to express to us on the blank form issued for that purpose.

E. STEIGER & CO.

---

*) In 1880, Prof. PAYNE recommended the following List of "Ten Books for Teachers":

1) *The Cyclopædia of Education.* $5.00. — 2) LAURIE's *Primary Instruction.* $1.80. — 3) QUICK's *Educational Reformers.* $2.00. — 4) PAGE's *Theory and Practice.* $1.50. — 5) CURRIE's *Common School Education.* $2.40. — 6) DONALDSON's *Lectures on Education.* $1.40. — 7) BARDEEN, *Common School Law.* $0.50. — 8) CALKINS' *Primary Object Lessons.* $1.25. — 9) KENNEDY, *School and Family.* $1 00. — 10) HUNTINGTON's *Unconscious Tuition.* $0.15.

THE DICTIONARY OF EDUCATION AND INSTRUCTION

NEWCOMB'S
MATHEMATICAL COURSE.

ALGEBRA.   GEOMETRY.
(Ready.)   (Ready.)
TRIGONOMETRY.   ANALYTICAL GEOMETRY
(In press.)   (In preparation.)
CALCULUS.

By SIMON NEWCOMB, Prof. of Mathematics U. S. Navy, Member of the National Academy, Corresponding Member of the Institute of France, Supt. American Ephemeris and Nautical Almanac, Author of Newcomb's Astronomy *(American Science Series)* etc., etc.

☞ *A copy of the Algebra or Geometry for examination with view to introduction mailed post paid to teachers for 95 cents.*

GARDINER'S HISTORIES OF ENGLAND,
EUGÈNE'S FRENCH GRAMMAR AND LESSONS,
THE AMERICAN SCIENCE SERIES,
HANDBOOKS IN SCIENCE, LITERATURE, ART AND HISTORY,
FREEMAN'S HISTORICAL COURSE.
BAIN'S ENGLISH GRAMMAR,
CHAMPLIN'S YOUNG FOLKS' CATECHISM OF COMMON THINGS, AND YOUNG FOLKS' ASTRONOMY,
BOREL'S GRAMMAIRE FRANÇAISE.
GASC'S FRENCH DICTIONARIES,
PYLODET'S FRENCH COURSE,
SAUVEUR'S MÉTHODE NATURELLE.
WHITNEY'S GERMAN COURSE,
WHITNEY'S GERMAN DICTIONARY,
OTTO'S GERMAN AND FRENCH COURSES,
KLEMM'S LESE- UND SPRACHBÜCHER,
HENESS' NATÜRLICHE METHODE,
STERN'S STUDIEN UND PLAUDEREIEN,

And numerous other educational works. Catalogue Free.

HENRY HOLT & CO., 12 East 23d St., NEW YORK

EDUCATIONAL BOOKS.
SUPLÉE'S TRENCH ON WORDS.
By RICHARD CHENEVIX TRENCH, D.D.
FROM THE LATEST REVISED ENGLISH EDITION. WITH AN EXHAUSTIVE ANALYSIS, ADDITIONAL WORDS FOR ILLUSTRATION, AND QUESTIONS FOR EXAMINATIONS.

By THOMAS D. SUPPLÉE.
1 Vol. 400 pages. Net price $1.00.

The advantages claimed for it, over all other editions, are as follows:
1. A complete and exhaustive analysis of the revised text has been added.
2. A set of questions has been prepared, designed not only to call forth the facts stated by the author, but also to follow up lines of thought suggested by him.
3. At the end of each lecture a list of words has been added, illustrating its various topics, and intended to encourage original research on the part of the pupil.

Copies for examination sent post paid — on receipt of 75 cents.

THE ÆNEID OF VIRGIL
Translated into English Verse (Scott's Ballad Metre).
By JOHN CONINGTON, M.A., of Oxford.
1 vol., crown 8vo, 506 pages. Retail price $2.00. *Price to Students $1.50.*

Just Published:
ARMSTRONG'S
PRIMER OF UNITED STATES HISTORY
for School and Family Use.
With 6 new and beautifully colored Maps, from original drawings.
1 vol. Square 16mo. Cloth. Price 50 cents.

THE UNABRIDGED STUDENT'S HALLAM.
FOR USE IN COLLEGES AND SCHOOLS.
1. **THE MIDDLE AGES.** Europe during the Middle Ages. The revised and corrected edition. 2 vols., cr. 8vo. $2.50. (*Price for use as text-books, 83 cents per volume.*)
2. **THE CONSTITUTIONAL HISTORY OF ENGLAND,** from the Accession of Henry VIII. to the death of George II. Including Mr. Hallam's Supplemental Volume of Revision up to 1848. Indispensable to Students. Complete in 2 vols. cr. 8vo. $2.50. (*Price for use as text-books, 83 cents per volume.*)
3. **INTRODUCTION TO THE LITERATURE OF EUROPE** in the 15th, 16th, and 17th Centuries. Revised and corrected edition. Compl. in 2 vols., cr. 8vo. $2.50. (*Price for use as text-books, 83 cents per vol.*)
4. **MAY'S CONSTITUTIONAL HISTORY OF ENGLAND,** since the Accession of George III., 1760—1860. *With a new Supplementary Chapter, 1860—1871.* By THOMAS ERSKINE MAY. 2 vols. $3.50. (*Price for Students, $1.16 per vol.*) "May" is a continuation of and uniform with Hallam
Copies sent by mail post paid — on receipt of Price by the Publishers.

A. C. ARMSTRONG & SON, Publishers, Booksellers, Importers,
714 Broadway, NEW YORK

THE DICTIONARY OF EDUCATION AND INSTRUCTION

STANDARD TEXT BOOKS.

The American Educational Series.

This justly popular Series of Text-books is noted for its freshness, completeness, admirable gradation, and the beauty and substantial nature of its manufacture. It comprises a full and thorough course of study, from the simplest Primer to the most advanced Mathematical and Scientific work. Among which are:

Sanders' Union Readers,
American Educational Readers,
Swinton's Supplementary Readers,
Swinton's Word-book Series,
Swinton's Geographies,
Robinson's Mathematics,
Kerl's Grammars,
Webster's Dictionaries,
Gray's Botanies,
Spencerian Copy-Books,
Bryant & Stratton's Book-Keeping,
Wilson's Histories,
Swinton's Histories,
Fasquelle's French Course,
Woodbury's German Course,
Wells' Science,
Eliot & Storer's Chemistry,
Dana's Geology,
Silliman's Phys. and Chem.,
White's Industrial Drawings,

And many other well-known works.

☞ CATALOGUES and Circulars, descriptive of THE AMERICAN EDUCATIONAL SERIES OF SCHOOL AND COLLEGE TEXT-BOOKS, mailed free to any address.

IVISON, BLAKEMAN, TAYLOR & CO., Publishers,
753 and 755 Broadway, NEW YORK.

D. APPLETON & CO.'S
EDUCATIONAL PUBLICATIONS.

APPLETONS' SCHOOL READERS,
Consisting of Five Books.
By *WM. T. HARRIS*, Supt. Public Schools, St. Louis; *ANDREW J. RICKOFF*, Supt. of Instruction, Cleveland, O.; *MARK BAILEY*, Instructor in Elocution, Yale College.

Appletons' First Reader. Small 4to, 90 pp.
Appletons' Second Reader. 12mo, 142 pp.
Appletons' Third Reader. 12mo, 214 pp.
Appletons' Fourth Reader. 12mo, 248 pp.
Appletons' Fifth Reader. 12mo, 471 pp.

APPLETONS' GEOGRAPHIES.
AMERICAN STANDARD SERIES.

Another Signal Improvement.

The remarkable success which Appletons' Readers have attained, is due to the fact that no effort or expense was spared to make them not only mechanically superior, but practically and distinctively superior in their embodiment of modern experiences in teaching, and of the methods followed by the most successful and intelligent education of the day.

We now offer a new series of Geographies, in two books, which will as far excel all geographical text-books hitherto published as our Readers are in advance of the old text-books in Readers.

THE SERIES.

Appletons' Elementary Geography.
Small 4to, 108 pages.
Appletons' Higher Geography. Large 4to, 128 pages.

THE MODEL COPY-BOOKS.
In six Numbers. With Goodman's Sliding Copies.

The Primary Copy-Books. Model Series. with Wakeman's Detachable Sliding Copies. Six numbers.

KRÜSI'S DRAWING SERIES.
Easy Drawing Lessons, for Kindergarten and Primary Schools. Three parts.
Synthetic Series. Four Books and Manual.
Analytic Series. Four Books and Manual.
Perspective Series. Four B'ks and Manual.
Advanced Perspective and Shading Series. Four Books and Manual.

Industrial Courses in Textile Designs, Outline and Relief Designs, Mechanical Drawing, and Architectural Drawing.

STICKNEY'S LANGUAGE SERIES.
Child's Book of Language. A Graded Series of Lessons and Blanks, in Four Numbers. I. Stories in Pictures; II. Studies in Animals; III. Studies in Plants; IV. Studies of Words. Teachers' Edition.

Letters and Lessons in Language. A sequel to "The Child's Book of Language."

These are charming books for awakening and developing thought and for acquiring the fluent use of language.

WE PUBLISH ALSO:

CORNELL'S GEOGRAPHIES; APPLETONS' ARITHMETICS; QUACKENBOS'S HISTORIES; GRAMMARS, AND RHETORIC; BALLARD'S WORDS, WORD-WRITER, AND PIECES TO SPEAK; PRIMERS OF SCIENCE, HISTORY, AND LITERATURE; YOUMANS'S BOTANIES AND CHEMISTRY; MORSE'S ZOOLOGY; LECONTE'S GEOLOGY; HARKNESS'S LATIN SERIES NEW GRAMMAR nearly ready; HADLEY'S GREEK, ETC., ETC., ETC., all of which are among the most popular and successful text-books of the day.

Our list embraces standard works representing every department of study from the Kindergarten to the University.

Catalogues, price lists, and "Educational Notes" sent free on application, and the most favorable terms made for first introduction.

D. APPLETON & CO., Publishers,
NEW YORK, BOSTON, CHICAGO, SAN FRANCISCO.

THE DICTIONARY OF EDUCATION AND INSTRUCTION

Four Valuable Books for Teachers.

SPENCER.

Education:
Intellectual, Moral and Physical.
By HERBERT SPENCER,
AUTHOR OF "A SYSTEM OF SYNTHETIC PHILOSOPHY."
One volume, 12mo, 283 pages .... Price, $1.25.

CONTENTS: I. What Knowledge is of Most Worth? II. Intellectual Education; III. Moral Education; IV. Physical Education.

VOLUME XXV. "INTERNATIONAL SCIENTIFIC SERIES."

BAIN.

Education as a Science.
By ALEXANDER BAIN, LL.D.,
PROFESSOR OF LOGIC IN THE UNIVERSITY OF ABERDEEN.
One volume, 12mo, 453 pages .... Price, $1.75.

CONTENTS: I. Scope of the Science of Education; II. Bearings of Physiology; III. Bearings of Psychology; IV. Terms explained; V. Education Values; VI. Sequence of Subjects: Psychological; VII. Sequence of Subjects: Logical; VIII. Methods; IX. The Mother Tongue; X. The Value of the Classics; XI. The Renovated Curriculum; XII. Moral Education; XIII. Art Education; XIV. Proportions, Appendix, Further Examples of the Object-Lesson, Passing Explanations of Terms.

JOHONNOT.

Principles and Practice of Teaching.
By JAMES JOHONNOT.
One volume, 12mo, cloth, 396 pages..Price, $1.50.

CONTENTS: I. What is Education; II. The Mental Powers: their Order of Development, and the Methods most conducive to Normal Growth; III. Objective Teaching: its Methods, Aims, and Principles; IV. Subjective Teaching: its Aims and Place in the Course of Instruction; V. Object Lessons: their Value and Limitations; VI. Relative Value of the Different Studies in a Course of Instruction; VII. Pestalozzi, and his Contributions to Educational Science; VIII. Froebel and the Kindergarten; IX. Agassiz: and Science in its Relation to Teaching; X. Contrasted Systems of Education; XI. Physical Culture; XII. Æsthetic Culture; XIII. Moral Culture; XIV. A Course of Study; XV. Country Schools.

BALDWIN.

Art of School Management.
A Text-Book for Normal Schools and Normal Institutes. A Handand Reference-Book for Teachers, School-Officers and Parents.
By J. BALDWIN,
PRESIDENT OF THE STATE NORMAL SCHOOL, KIRKSVILLE, MO.
One volume, 12mo, 504 pages .... Price, $1.50.

CONTENTS: I. Educational Instrumentalities; II. School Organization; III. School Government; IV. Course of Study and Programme; V. Study and Teaching; VI. Class Management and Class Work; VII. Management of Graded Schools; VIII. Grading, Examinations, Records, and Reports; IX. Professional Education; X. Educational Systems, Educational Progress, and School Supervision.

D. APPLETON & CO., Publishers.

NEW YORK, BOSTON, CHICAGO, SAN FRANCISCO.

THE DICTIONARY OF EDUCATION AND INSTRUCTION

Educational Publications.

Abbott's Abercrombie's Intellectual Philosophy. Inquiries concerning the Intellectual Powers and the Investigation of Truth. By JOHN ABERCROMBIE, M. D. With additions by Jacob Abbott. 12mo, 90 cents.

Abbott's Abercrombie's Moral Philosophy. The Philosophy of the Moral Feelings. By JOHN ABERCROMBIE, M. D. With additions by Rev. Jacob Abbott. 12mo, 90 cents.

Adams's New Arithmetic. Revised edition. By DANIEL ADAMS, M. D. 12mo, 65 cents.

Adams's Improved Arithmetic. An Improved edition of Adams's New Arithmetic (first published in 1827), rewritten in a style much condensed. With additions by Daniel Adams, M. D. 12mo, 65 cents.

Addicks's Elementary French. An elementary practical book for learning the French language. By Mrs. ADDICKS. 12mo, cloth, 60 cents.

Coffin's Conic Sections. Elements of Conic Sections and Analytical Geometry. By Prof. J. H. COFFIN. 8vo, cloth, $1.35.

Dymond's Moral Philosophy. Essays on the Principles of Morality, and on the Private and Political Rights and Obligations of Mankind. By J. DYMOND, 12mo, cloth, $1.10.

Kirkham's Grammar. English Grammar for the use of Schools. By SAMUEL KIRKHAM. 12mo, 60 cents.

Lovell's United States Speaker. Exercises in Elocution, for Colleges and Schools. By JOHN E. LOVELL. 12mo, $1.25.

Lovell's New School Dialogues. Dramatic Selections for Schools and Families. By JOHN E. LOVELL. 12mo, $1.25.

Northend's Little Speaker. Prose, Poetry, and Dialogues, for Primary Classes. By CHARLES NORTHEND. 18mo, cloth, 50 cents.

Northend's American Speaker. Exercises for Declamation in Schools. By C. NORTHEND. 12mo, 85 cents.

Northend's School Dialogues. One hundred and twenty Selections for Schools. By C. NORTHEND. 12mo, 85 cents.

Olmsted's School Astronomy (Snell). A Compendium of Astronomy, for Schools. By Prof. OLMSTED. A new edition, revised by Prof. Snell. 12mo, $1.

Olmsted's College Astronomy (Snell). An introduction to Astronomy, for college students. By Prof. OLMSTED, Yale College. Third stereotype edition. Revised by Prof. Snell, Amherst College. 8vo, $2.

Olmsted's College Philosophy (Snell). An introduction to Natural Philosophy, for college students. By Prof. OLMSTED. New stereotype edition. Prof. Snell's second revision. 8vo, $3.12.

Parker's Natural Philosophy. First Lessons in Natural Philosophy. By R. G PARKER. 16mo, 50 cents.

Parker's Natural Philosophy (Plympton). A Compendium of Natural and Experimental Philosophy. By RICHARD G. PARKER. A thorough revision, with additions, by G. W. Plympton. 12mo, $1.50.

Preston's Book-keeping. A System of Book-keeping by Double and Single Entry, with a complete treatise on Equation of Payments. By LYMAN PRESTON. Revised and enlarged edition. Royal 8vo, $1.65.

Scott's Manual of United States History. A Manual of History of the United States, with the Constitution and Declaration of Independence; with questions. For the use of Schools. By DAVID B. SCOTT. A new edition. 55 cents.

Scott's Review History. A Short Outline History of the United States, for review grades and beginners in the study. By DAVID B. SCOTT, JR. 12mo, cloth, 70 cents.

Underhill's New Table-Book. The Arithmetical Primer; or, New Table-Book. By DANIEL C. UNDERHILL. 36 pp., 18mo, paper, 4 cents; half bound, 8 cents.

Whelpley's Compend of History. A Compend of Universal History. By SAMUEL WHELPLEY. Revised by Joseph and Samuel Emerson. 12mo, $1.35

Zachos's New American Speaker. Oratorical and Dramatical Pieces, Soliloquies, and Dialogues, for schools and colleges. By J. C. ZACHOS. Large 12mo, $1.65.

Copies mailed upon receipt of printed price.
A liberal discount to the Trade.   Special terms for introduction.

COLLINS & BROTHER, Publishers, 414 Broadway, NEW YORK

The Monthly Index

To the current Periodical Literature of the World, in English, except Fiction.

The only Publication of the kind in the World.

Useful to

Teachers, Students, School Officers, Libraries, Clergymen, Lecturers, Physicians, Lawyers,

To all Literary and Professional Workers, to all who read the Magazines and Periodicals of the Day.

An invaluable assistant to those who desire to keep up with the times. — *Southern Collegian.*
Of great convenience to readers and writers. — *New York Times.*
Something that students and periodical readers have long needed. — *The Methodist.*

Price $1.00 per year; 10 Cts. per copy.

Published at the Office of

THE AMERICAN BOOKSELLER, 10 Spruce St., NEW YORK.

The American Bookseller.

A semi-monthly journal, devoted to the interests of book buyers and book readers, containing complete lists of the new books as soon as published; announcements of all books in press; pithy, descriptive and critical notices and reviews; and literary news of all sorts.

A very agreeable literary companion. Every teacher would find it entertaining and useful. — *Iowa Journal of Education.*
Of interest to all fond of the latest literary news. — *Louisville Courier-Journal.*
No one can keep thoroughly posted on the new books of the day without it. — *Journal of Progress.*
It furnishes just such news as we have often looked for, but have been unable to find. — *Tufts Collegian.*
One of the most useful and carefully prepared guides to book-buying is THE AMERICAN BOOKSELLER, brought out under the auspices of the American News Company. Its articles are well prepared, and its summaries invaluable. Every number presents new improvements. — *N. Y. World.*
Gathers together and gives us more literary information than any similar publication we have. — *Philadelphia Morning Post.*
It is a careful and faithful record of everything concerning publishers, books, and authors, and one of the most useful and interesting publications of its kind. — *Philadelphia City Item.*

Price $1.00 per year; 5 Cts. per copy.

Published by THE AMERICAN NEWS COMPANY,

at 10 Spruce St., NEW YORK.

THE DICTIONARY OF EDUCATION AND INSTRUCTION

College Text-Books.

BOWSER'S ANALYTIC GEOMETRY.
12mo. Cloth. $1.75. To Teachers $1.40.
AN ELEMENTARY TREATISE ON ANALYTIC GEOMETRY, embracing Plane Geometry, and an Introduction to Geometry of Three Dimensions, by EDWARD A. BOWSER, Professor of Mathematics in Rutgers College.

BOWSER'S DIFFERENTIAL AND INTEGRAL CALCULUS.
12mo. Cloth. $2.25. To Teachers $1.80.
AN ELEMENTARY TREATISE ON THE DIFFERENTIAL AND INTEGRAL CALCULUS, with numerous examples, by EDWARD A. BOWSER, Professor of Mathematics in Rutgers College.

PLATTNER'S BLOW-PIPE ANALYSIS.
Third Edition. Revised. 568 pages. 8vo. Cloth. $5.00.
PLATTNER'S MANUAL OF QUALITATIVE AND QUANTITATIVE ANALYSIS WITH THE BLOWPIPE. From the last German Edition, revised and enlarged. By Prof. TH. RICHTER, of the Royal Saxon Mining Academy. Translated by Professor H. B. CORNWALL; assisted by JOHN H. CASWELL. With eighty-seven wood-cuts and Lithographic Plate.

NAQUET'S LEGAL CHEMISTRY.
Illustrated. 12mo. Cloth. $2.00.
LEGAL CHEMISTRY. A Guide to the Detection of Poisons, Falsification of Writings, Adulteration of Alimentary and Pharmaceutical Substances; Analysis of Ashes, and Examination of Hair, Coins, Fire arms, and Stains, as Applied to Chemical Jurisprudence. For the Use of Chemists, Physicians, Lawyers, Pharmacists, and Experts. Translated, with additions, including a list of Books and Memoirs on Toxicology, etc., from the French of A. NAQUET. By J. P. BATTERSHALL, Ph. D., with a Preface by C. F. CHANDLER, Ph.D., M.D., LL.D.

PLYMPTON'S BLOW-PIPE ANALYSIS.
12mo. Cloth. $1.50.
THE BLOW-PIPE: A Guide to Its Use in the Determination of Salts and Minerals. Compiled from various sources, by GEORGE W. PLYMPTON, C. E., A. M., Professor of Physical Science in the Polytechnic Institute, Brooklyn, N. Y.

PYNCHON'S CHEMICAL PHYSICS.
New Edition. Revised and enlarged. Crown 8vo. Cloth. $3.00.
INTRODUCTION TO CHEMICAL PHYSICS: Designed for the Use of Academies, Colleges and High Schools. Illustrated with numerous engravings, and containing copious experiments, with directions for preparing them. By THOMAS RUGGLES PYNCHON, M. A., President of Trinity College, Hartford.

ELIOT AND STORER'S QUALITATIVE CHEMICAL ANALYSIS.
New Edition. Revised. 12mo. Illustrated. Cloth. $1.50.
A COMPENDIOUS MANUAL OF QUALITATIVE CHEMICAL ANALYSIS. By CHARLES W. ELIOT and FRANK H. STORER. Revised, with the co-operation of the Authors, by WILLIAM RIPLEY NICHOLS, Professor of Chemistry in the Massachusetts Institute of Technology.

RAMMELSBERG'S CHEMICAL ANALYSIS.
8vo. Cloth. $2.25
GUIDE TO A COURSE OF QUANTITATIVE CHEMICAL ANALYSIS, ESPECIALLY OF MINERALS AND FURNACE PRODUCTS. Illustrated by Examples. By C. F. RAMMELSBERG. Translated by J. TOWLER, M. D.

ATTWOOD'S PRACTICAL BLOW-PIPE ASSAYING.
12mo. Cloth. Illustrated. $2.00.

EXPERIMETAL ORGANIC CHEMISTRY.
FOR STUDENTS. By H. CHAPMAN JONES. 16mo. $1.00.

PRESCOTT'S PROXIMATE ORGANIC ANALYSIS.
12mo. Cloth. $1.75.
OUTLINES OF PROXIMATE ORGANIC ANALYSIS, for the Identification, Separation, and Quantitative Determination of the more commonly occurring Organic Compounds. By ALBERT B. PRESCOTT, Professor of Organic and Applied Chemistry in the University of Michigan.

PRESCOTT'S ALCOHOLIC LIQUORS.
12mo. Cloth. $1.50.
CHEMICAL EXAMINATION OF ALCOHOLIC LIQUORS. A manual of the Constituents of the Distilled Spirits and Fermented Liquors of Commerce, and their Qualitative and Quantitative Determinations. By ALBERT B. PRESCOTT, Professor of Organic and Applied Chemistry in the University of Michigan.

PRESCOTT'S AND DOUGLAS' QUALITATIVE CHEMICAL ANALYSIS.
Third Edition. Revised. 8vo. Cloth. $3.50.
A Guide in the Practical Study of Chemistry and in the Work of Analysis.

MOTT'S CHEMISTS' MANUAL.
8vo. 650 pages. Cloth. $6.00.
A PRACTICAL TREATISE ON CHEMISTRY (Qualitative and Quantitative Analysis), Stoichiometry, Blow-pipe Analysis, Mineralogy, Assaying, Pharmaceutical Preparations, Human Secretions, Specific Gravities, Weights and Measures, etc., etc. By HENRY A. MOTT, Jr., E. M., Ph.D.

BEILSTEIN'S CHEMICAL ANALYSIS.
12mo. Cloth. 75c.
AN INTRODUCTION TO QUALITATIVE CHEMICAL ANALYSIS. By F. BEILSTEIN. Third edition, translated by I. J. OSBUN.

CALDWELL AND BRENEMAN'S CHEMICAL PRACTICE.
8vo. Cloth. 188 pages. Illustrated. New and enlarged edition. $1.50.
MANUAL OF INTRODUCTORY CHEMICAL PRACTICE, for the Use of Students in Colleges and Normal and High Schools. By Prof. GEO. C. CALDWELL and A. A. BRENEMAN, of Cornell University. Second edition, revised and corrected.

PRESCOTT'S QUALITATIVE CHEMISTRY.
12mo. Cloth. $1.50.
FIRST BOOK IN QUALITATIVE CHEMISTRY. By ALBERT B. PRESCOTT, Professor in University of Michigan.

Copies sent by mail, post-paid, on receipt of price.

D. VAN NOSTRAND, Publisher,
23 Murray and 27 Warren Streets, NEW YORK

WEBSTER'S UNABRIDGED DICTIONARY.

The following from page 1161, shows the value of the Illustrative Definitions in Webster.

Sale of Webster's is 20 times as great as the sale of any other series of Dictionaries. — 32,000 Webster's Unabridged have been placed in the Public Schools of the United States, and Recommended by State Supt's of Education in 36 States, by 50 College Presidents.

1, flying jib; 2, jib; 3, fore-top-mast-stay sail; 4, fore-course; 5, foretop sail; 6, foretop-gallant sail; 7, fore-royal; 8, fore sky-sail; 9, fore-royal studding sail; 10, foretop-gallant studding-sail; 11, foretopmast studding-sail; 12, main-course; 13, maintopsail; 14, maintop-gallant sail; 15, main-royal; 16, main sky-sail; 17, main royal studding-sail; 18, main top-gallant studding-sail; 19, maintop-mast studding sail; 20, mizzen-course; 21, mizzen-top sail; 22, mizzen-top-gallant sail; 23, mizzen-royal; 24, mizzen sky-sail; 25, mizzen-spanker.

New Edition of WEBSTER, has 118,000 Words, 3000 Engravings, 4600 New Words and Meanings, Biographical Dictionary of over 9700 Names.
Published by G. & C. MERRIAM,
SPRINGFIELD, Mass.

WEBSTER'S is the Dictionary used in the Government Printing Office, January, 1881. — Every State purchase of Dictionaries for Schools has been of Webster. — The School Books used in the Public Schools of the U. S. are mainly based on Webster.

UNIVERSITY SERIES OF TEXT-BOOKS.

Newest,
Brightest,
Best.

Maury's Geographies.
Holmes' Readers.
Venable's Arithmetics.
Gildersleeve's Latin, &c.

Venable's Easy Algebra.
Maury's Revised Manual.
Gildersleeve's Latin Grammar.

It can be safely said that Maury's Geographies, Gildersleeve's Latin and Venable's Easy Algebra are skillfully adapted to the most interesting and most thorough modes of instruction. Of this, thousands of letters and testimonials from all parts of the country leave no room for doubt. Samples: Easy Algebra, 55 cents; Latin Primer, 65 cents; Revised Manual of Geography, $1.20. Send for Circulars.

PUBLISHED BY THE

UNIVERSITY PUBLISHING COMPANY,
19 Murray St., NEW YORK.

THE DICTIONARY OF EDUCATION AND INSTRUCTION

EXCELLENT BOOKS FOR TEACHERS.

SUPPLEMENTARY READING.

AMERICAN POEMS. Selections of entire Poems from the works of LONGFELLOW, WHITTIER, BRYANT, HOLMES, LOWELL, and EMERSON. With Biographical Sketches, and Notes explaining the Historical and Personal Allusions. 463 pages, $1.25. Teachers' price, 95 cents.

AMERICAN PROSE. Selections from the works of HAWTHORNE, IRVING, LONGFELLOW, WHITTIER, HOLMES, LOWELL, THOREAU, EMERSON. With Introductions and Notes. $1.25. Teachers' price, 95 c.

A book of entire stories, sketches, and essays, embracing some of the best specimens in these departments of American Literature.

BALLADS AND LYRICS. Selected by HENRY CABOT LODGE. $1.25. Teachers' price, 95 cents.

A very attractive collection of about one hundred and fifty of the best ballads and lyrics, placed generally in chronological order, beginning with "Chevy Chase", and coming down through the long line of English and American poets to the present time.

POETRY FOR CHILDREN. Edited by SAMUEL ELIOT, LL.D., late Superintendent of Public Schools, Boston. 16mo, 327 pages, illustrated with sixty original designs by the best artists, $1.00. Teachers' price, 75 cents.

A delightful book of the best short poems in English and American Literature, such as children will read with equal profit and satisfaction.

LONGFELLOW LEAFLETS. Selections from the works of HENRY WADSWORTH LONGFELLOW. With illustrations. 12mo, 50 cents. Teachers' price, 40 cents.

These "Leaflets" comprise short poems and a few prose passages from Longfellow's writings. They are bound in a pamphlet, and are also put up in a box in single leaves for distribution and use in schools.

SIX STORIES FROM THE ARABIAN NIGHTS. Edited by SAMUEL ELIOT, LL.D., late Superintendent of Public Schools, Boston. With new and beautiful illustrations, by the best artists and engravers. 60 cents. Teachers' price, 45 cents.

SIX POPULAR TALES. Two Series. Fully illustrated. Also **SELECTED POPULAR TALES.** 20 cents each. Teachers' price, 15 cents.

HOUSEHOLD EDUCATION. By HARRIET MARTINEAU. "Little Classic" style, 18mo, $1.25. Teachers' price, $1.00.

An exceedingly wise and helpful book for teachers. It discusses the best methods of developing and training all the powers, physical, intellectual, and moral; emphasizes the importance of habit; and, in short, abounds in excellent suggestions which will help many teachers in difficult and perplexing situations.

ON THE THRESHOLD. By T.T. MUNGER. 16mo, gilt top, $1.00. Teachers' price, 80 cents.

A book of thoroughly sensible, judicious, sympathetic, helpful essays on Purpose, Friends and Companions, Manners, Thrift, Self-Reliance and Courage, Health, Reading and Intellectual Life, Amusements, and Faith. Teachers will find it an excellent book to put in the hands of their older pupils.

"This book touches acts, habits, character, destiny; it deals with the present and vital thought in literature, society, life; it stimulates one with the idea that life is worth living; there are no dead words in it." *New York Times.*

The chapter on "Reading" is one of the best, wisest, and most discriminating of all that we have read on that topic. — *Lutheran Observer* (Philadelphia).

BOOKS. An Essay. By R. W. EMERSON. One of the best and most suggestive essays ever written by Mr. Emerson, or written on the important subject of Books. This essay, with eight other essays by Mr. Emerson on Culture, Behavior, Beauty, Art, Eloquence, Power, Wealth, and Illusions, forms a "Modern Classic" volume. 75 cents. Teachers' price, 60 cents.

WORDS AND THEIR USES. By RICHARD GRANT WHITE. New and revised edition. 12mo, $2.00.

We take leave of this interesting volume with thanks to the author for the valuable service which he has rendered to the English language in pointing out the abuses to which it has been made subject, and the errors which are of common occurence in its colloquial and literary use. — *New York Tribune.*

EVERY-DAY ENGLISH. By RICHARD GRANT WHITE. 12mo, $2.00.

A book of great value to all who appreciate accuracy and fitness in the use of language. It treats many points in speech, writing, grammar, and special words and phrases, and is written with so much humor that it is as entertaining as it is useful.

For sale by Booksellers. Sent, post paid, on receipt of price by the Publishers,

HOUGHTON, MIFFLIN & COMPANY, BOSTON, Mass.

THE DICTIONARY OF EDUCATION AND INSTRUCTION

STANDARD LITERATURE AND ART.

SELF-CULTURE. By JAMES FREEMAN CLARKE. 12mo. $1.50.
"Twenty-two Lectures full of the ripe experience, profound wisdom, broad views and beautiful religious spirit, which makes Dr. Clarke one of the foremost men of his day." *Saturday Evening Gazette.*

SKETCHES AND REMINISCENCES OF THE RADICAL CLUB. 12mo. $2.00.
A work of over 400 pages, prepared under the direction of Mrs. JOHN T. SARGENT, and containing choice gleanings from the discussions and conversations on philosophy, religion and literature, which have been held at the Chestnut Street Radical Club, by many of the foremost thinkers of America. The words of Bartol, Weiss, Everett, Emerson, Channing, Frothingham, Hedge, Fiske, Alcott, James, Cranch, Higginson, and other leaders in religious and philosophical thought.

A HAND-BOOK OF LEGENDARY AND MYTHOLOGICAL ART. By CLARA ERSKINE CLEMENT. Profusely illustrated, and with a complete index. Fourteenth edition, revised and enlarged. Crown 8vo, cloth, $3.00.

PAINTERS, SCULPTORS, ARCHITECTS, ENGRAVERS, AND THEIR WORKS. A Hand-book, with many illustrations and monograms. By CLARA ERSKINE CLEMENT. Seventh edition, revised and enlarged. Crown 8vo, cloth, $3.00.

OUR POETICAL FAVORITES. Edited by Rev. A. C. KENDRICK, D.D. Household Edition. First, Second, and Third Series, each complete in one volume, and sold separately. 12mo. $2.00 @ volume.
This admirable collection of choice poetry is equal to the great single-volume collections, and much more convenient to handle. The flower of American and British poesy is included in these volumes, with several grand translations from the Latin, French, and German.

ASPECTS OF GERMAN CULTURE. A volume of Essays and Criticisms. By G. STANLEY HALL, Ph.D., Harvard University Lecturer on Contemporary German Philosophers and on Pedagogy. 12mo, $1.50.
Twenty-eight chapters on varying phases of German life, thought, and theories; on Lasalle, Herman Lotze, Hegel, Hartmann; on pessimistic ethics, spiritualism, hypnotism, and æsthetics; on the new Cultus war, the latest works on German philosophy, the study of psychology; on the Passion Play, and the Leipsic fair.

THE TRIP TO ENGLAND. By WM. WINTER. Illustrated by JOSEPH JEFFERSON. $2.00.
"England in a drop of honey." — *Harper's Magazine.* "A delicious view of England." — *Scribner.* "As sweet and pure as sincere." — *Atlantic.*

HELIOTYPE ENGRAVINGS.

The **Heliotype** is a photo-mechanical print, in which the precision and absolute fidelity of photography is combined with the permanent qualities of ordinary printing. Nearly 300 choice and selected engravings, worth from ten to fifty dollars each, have been copied by this process with unerring exactness. They are printed on the very best heavy bevelled plate paper, each one being 19x24 inches in size, equally adapted for framing or portfolio. The works of the best engravers have thus been duplicated, and the most celebrated and fascinating pictures of the most celebrated artists of ancient and modern times; and these exquisitely delicate masterpieces are sold for FIFTY CENTS EACH.

Catalogues given or sent free on application. — These books are for sale by all Booksellers, or will be sent post paid, on receipt of price, by the Publishers.

JAMES R. OSGOOD & CO., 211 Tremont Street, BOSTON

SCHOOL AND COLLEGE TEXT-BOOKS.

HOW TO WRITE CLEARLY.

Rules and Exercises on English Composition. By the Rev. Edwin A. Abbott, M.A., Head Master of the City of London School. 16mo. Cloth. Price 60 cents.

HOW TO PARSE.

An Attempt to apply the Principles of Scholarship to English Grammar. With Appendixes in Analysis, Spelling, and Punctuation. By the Rev. Edwin A. Abbott, M.A., Head Master of the City of London School. 16mo. Cloth. Price $1.00.

ENGLISH LESSONS FOR ENGLISH PEOPLE.

By the Rev. Edwin A. Abbott, M.A., Head Master of the City of London School, and J. R. Seeley, M.A., Professor of Modern History in the University of Cambridge. Part I., Vocabulary. Part II., Diction. Part III., Metre. Part IV., Hints on Selection and Arrangement. Appendix. One vol. 16mo. Cloth. Price $1.50.

HOW TO TELL THE PARTS OF SPEECH.

An Introduction to English Grammar. By the Rev. Edwin A. Abbott, D.D., Head Master of the City of London School; Author of "How to Write Clearly", "How to Parse", "English Lessons for English People". American Edition. Revised and Enlarged by Prof. John G. R. McElroy, A.M., of the University of Pennsylvania. 16mo. Cloth. Price 75 cents.

SANSKRIT AND ITS KINDRED LITERATURES.

Studies in Comparative Mythology. By Laura Elizabeth Poor. 16mo. Cloth. Price $2.00.

The Buffalo *Courier* says: "The book, of course, is an elementary one, but it must be valuable to the young student who desires to get a complete view of literature and of the reciprocal relations of its various divisions. It can hardly fail to interest the reader in the new science of which it gives results, and lead him to more exhaustive studies for himself. If such a work could be made a school text-book it would give pupils a long start in their pursuit of a correct and systematic knowledge of language and literature."

MÆTZNER'S ENGLISH GRAMMAR.

An English Grammar: Methodical, Analytical, and Historical. With a Treatise on the Orthography, Prosody, Inflections, and Syntax of the English Tongue, and numerous Authorities cited in Order of Historical Development. By Prof. Mætzner, of Berlin. Translated from the German, with the sanction of the author, by Clair James Grece, LL.B., Fellow of the Philological Society. 3 vols. 8vo. Cloth. Price $15.00.

A PARAGRAPH HISTORY OF THE UNITED STATES.

From the Discovery of the Continent to the Present Time. With Brief Notes on Contemporaneous Events. Chronologically arranged. By Edward Abbott. Square 18mo. Cloth. Price 50 cents.

A PARAGRAPH HISTORY OF THE AMERICAN REVOLUTION.

By Edward Abbott. 18mo. Cloth. Price 50 cents.

The above books are in use in a great many schools and academies throughout the United States and Canada. On application, we will be pleased to submit terms for Examination and Introduction.

ROBERTS BROTHERS, 299 Washington St., BOSTON, Mass.

STEIGER'S French Series.

AHN'S French Primer. By Dr. P. HENN. Boards $0.25. (Great care has been bestowed upon the typographical execution of this little book, the perplexing difficulty of the *silent* letters being alleviated by the use of distinguishing outline and hairline type.

AHN'S French Reading Charts. 20 Plates with Hand-book for Teachers. By Dr. P. HENN. $1.00. These Wall Charts are printed in very large type, the *silent* letters being shown by outline type cut expressly for the purpose.)

The same. The 20 Plates mounted on 10 boards. $3.75 net. Mounted on 10 boards and varnished. $5.00 net.

(**AHN'S French Primer** and **French Reading Charts** may be advantageously used as an introductory course to any *French Grammar*.)

AHN'S Practical and Easy Method of Learning the French Language. By Dr. P. HENN. First Course. (Comprising a fundamental Treatise on French Pronunciation, French and English Exercises, Paradigms, and Vocabularies.) Boards $0.40.

*Key to same. Boards $0.25 net.

AHN'S Practical and Easy Method of Learning the French Language. By Dr. P. HENN. Second Course. (Comprising a Series of French and English Exercises, Conversations, Elements of French Grammar with Index, and full Vocabularies.) Boards $0.60.

*Key to same. Boards $0.25 net.

AHN'S Practical and Easy Method of Learning the French Language. By Dr. P. HENN. First and Second Courses, bound together. Half Roan $1.00.

AHN'S Elements of French Grammar. By Dr. P. HENN. Being the Second Part of *AHN-HENN'S Practical and Easy Method of Learning the French Language.* —Second Course—printed separately. Boards $0.35

AHN'S First French Reader. With Foot-notes and Vocabulary. By Dr. P. HENN. Boards $0.60; Half Roan $0.80.

AHN'S First French Reader. With Notes and Vocabulary. By Dr. P. HENN. Boards $0.60; Half Roan $0.80.

These two editions of one and the same book differ solely in the typographical arrangement of Text and Notes. In the latter the Notes are given separately on the pages following the 75 pieces of Text; in the former each page has at its bottom exactly so much of the Notes as is needed to explain the French Text above. In respect to Vocabulary, etc., both editions are alike.

*Key to **AHN'S First French Reader**. By Dr. P. HENN. Boards $0.30 net.

AHN'S Second French Reader. With Foot-notes and Vocabulary. By Dr. P. HENN. Boards $0.80; Half Roan $1.00.

AHN'S Second French Reader. With Notes and Vocabulary. By Dr. P. HENN. Boards $0.80; Half Roan $1.00.

*Key to **AHN'S Second French Reader**. By Dr. P. HENN. Bds $0.40 net.

AHN'S French Dialogues. Dramatic Selections with Notes. Number One. (Specially suitable for young ladies.) Boards $0.30; Cloth $0.40.

AHN'S French Dialogues. Dramatic Selections with Notes. Number Two. (Specially suitable for young gentlemen.) Boards $0.25; Cloth $0.35.

AHN'S French Dialogues. Dramatic Selections with Notes. Number Three. Specially suitable for young ladies.) Boards $0.30; Cloth $0.40.

Additional volumes of this Series of French Dialogues, which fully meet the requirements of advanced students, are in press, and will shortly be published.

AHN'S Manual of French Conversation. In press.

Collegiate Course.

C. A. SCHLEGEL. **A French Grammar.** For beginners. Half Roan $1.50.

C. A. SCHLEGEL. **A Classical French Reader.** With Notes and Vocabulary. Half Roan $1.20.

[* These *Keys* will be *supplied to teachers only* upon their direct application to the publishers.]

STEIGER'S German Series.

AHN'S German Primer. Edited by W. GRAUERT. Boards $0.45.

AHN'S German Reading Charts. 25 Plates with Hand-book for Teachers, By Dr. P. HENN. $1.00.
The same. The 25 Plates mounted on 13 boards. $4.50 net. Varnished $6.00 net.

AHN'S German Script Charts. 4 Plates mounted on 4 boards, varnished $1.25 net.

AHN'S First German Book. By Dr. P. HENN. (Exercises in Reading, Writing, Translation, and Conversation. Printed in bold type and containing a very large amount of German Script. Designed for the lowest two grades.) Boards $0.25.

AHN'S Second German Book. By Dr. P. HENN. (Exercises in Reading, Writing, Translation, and Conversation. Containing much German Script. With Dialogues, Paradigms, Vocabularies [with the pronunciation of all German words], Conversational Exercises, Uncommon Styles of German Type, and Specimens of German Business Handwriting.) Boards $0.45, Half Roan $0.60.

These two books together form:
AHN'S Rudiments of the German Language. By Dr. P. HENN. First Course. Boards $0.65, Half Roan $0.80.
Key to same. Boards $0.25 net.

AHN'S Third German Book. By Dr. P. HENN. Boards $0.45, Half Roan $0.60.
Key to same. Boards $0.25 net.

AHN'S Fourth German Book. By Dr. P. HENN. Boards $0.60, Half Roan $0.80.
Key to same. Boards $0.25 net.

AHN'S Rudiments of the German Language. By Dr. P. HENN. Second Course. (This contains AHN-HENN'S Third and Fourth German Books together.) Boards $1.00, Half Roan $1.25.

AHN'S Complete Method of the German Language. By Dr. P. HENN. (AHN-HENN'S First, Second, Third, and Fourth German Books together.) Strongly bound in Half Roan $1.75.

AHN'S Synopsis of German Grammar. By Dr. P. HENN. Boards $0.60. Half Roan $0.80.

AHN'S First German Reader. With Notes and Vocabulary. By Dr. P. HENN. Boards $0.60, Half Roan $0.80.
The same. With Foot-notes and Vocabulary. Boards $0.60, Half Roan $0.80.
Key to same. Boards $0.30 net.

AHN'S Second German Reader. With Notes and Vocabulary. By Dr. P. HENN. Boards $1.00, Half Roan $1.20.
The same. With Foot-notes and Vocabulary. Boards $1.00, Half Roan $1.20.
Key to same. Boards $0.50 net.

AHN'S German Dialogues. Dramatic Selections. Number One. Boards $0.25, Cloth $0.35.

AHN'S Rudiments of the German Language. (Old Edition of 1870.) Boards $0.35.

AHN'S Method of Learning the German Language. Revised by GUSTAVUS FISCHER. First Course, Boards $0.50.—Second Course, Boards $0.50. — Both Courses bound together, Half Roan $1.00.
Key to same. Boards $0.30 net.

AHN'S New Practical and Easy Method of Learning the German Language. With Pronunciation by J. C. OEHLSCHLÆGER. Edition of 1873. First Course. (Practical Part.) Boards $0.60.—Second Course. (Theoretical Part.) Boards $0.40.

AHN'S First German Reader. With Notes by W. GRAUERT. Boards $0.50. — Second German Reader. With Notes and Vocabulary by W. GRAUERT. Boards $0.70.—The two Readers bound together, Half Roan $1.20.

Key to AHN-GRAUERT'S First German Reader. Boards $0.30 net. — to Second German Reader, Boards $0.35 net.

AHN'S German Handwriting. With Notes by W. GRAUERT. Boards $0.40.

AHN'S Manual of German Conversation. Revised by W. GRAUERT. Cloth $1.00.

AHN-OEHLSCHLÆGER'S Pronouncing Method of the German Language. Designed for Instruction in Schools, and for Private Study. (Edition of 1880.) First Course: *Exercises, Reader, Pronouncing Vocabularies, Conversations, Collections of Words, etc.* Boards $0.80, Half Roan $1.00. — Second Course: *Synopsis of German Grammar.* Boards $0.40, Half Roan $0.60. —Both Courses bound together, Boards $1.15, Half Roan $1.40.
Key to same. Boards $0.40 net.

GRAUERT'S Manual of the German Language. First Part, Boards $0.40. — Second Part, Boards $0.40. — Both together, Boards $0.70, Half Roan $0.90.

Collegiate Course.

SCHLEGEL'S German Grammar for Beginners. Half Roan $1.25.

SCHLEGEL'S First Classical German Reader. With Notes and Vocabulary. Half Roan $1.00. — *Second Classical German Reader.* With Notes and Vocabulary. Half Roan $1.50.

[* These *Keys* will be supplied to teachers only upon their direct application to the publishers.]

E. STEIGER & CO., 25 Park Place, NEW YORK

German in the Public Schools.

The AHN-HENN German Course with its **alternating exercises for translation** meets the expectations of the friends of German instruction, while at the same time it answers the objections of all opponents.

The AHN-HENN books **combine all the qualities** needed to make the **study of German easy** and **popular**, and for this reason the series has been adopted for use in the Public Schools of very many of our leading cities. No other method enables School-Boards to retain the study of German without an accompanying increase of expense and **no other method** can present so many acceptable arguments in favor of the continued study of the language in the **Public Schools.**

I prefer AHN's method, because it introduces the learner to language before it discourages him with the complicated difficulties of technical grammar. This method has reason and nature on its side, and is growing in favor among progressive educators. In —— —'s books this method seems to be reversed, and the young learner is precipitated at once into the intricacies of grammar. The exercises in the AHN books seem to me to be far more practical and satisfactory than those given by ——.

The exercises in AHN's books in letter-writing, business forms, advertisements, German script, etc., are very valuable. These matters are almost entirely omitted in ——'s books. For these and other reasons I decidedly prefer the AHN series.
(J. M. B. SILL, Supt. of Schools, Detroit, Mich.)

We have been using the AHN-HENN German series for some three years. Our children are doing excellent work in the language by the use of this series.
(W. W. JAMIESON, Supt. of Schools, Keokuk, Iowa.)

It gives me great pleasure to certify to the uniform excellence of AHN-HENN's French and German text-books after a use of them since their first publication. I recommend them unhesitatingly as the best books for class use.
(J. C. JONES, Supt. of Schools, East Saginaw, Mich.)

We, last year, began the introduction of your German series — the AHN-HENN method — and we are so pleased with it that we shall, as fast as we can work out the old books, substitute this. Thus far the series has given eminent satisfaction.
(CHAS. C. SNYDER, Supt. of Schools, Freeport, Ill.)

We use your AHN-HENN series of German Books. I consider it the best course for our Public Schools. (THOS. W. HUBBARD, Supt. of Schools, Perrysburg, O.)

I desire to tell you of my own free will that I have used the AHN-HENN German Course over two years and that I consider it without a rival as a text-book for common schools. (WM. MC K. BLAKE, Supt. of Schools, New Castle, Ind.)

We are using very successfully AHN-HENN's German Method, which we prefer to any other work we have seen.
(W. W. SHARPE, Prin. Orwell Normal Institute, Orwell, O.)

We have concluded to use AHN's German Series in the Mansfield Normal College. The books are prepared on a rational basis, and merit a general introduction. (J. FRAISE RICHARD, President Mansfield Normal College, Mansfield, O.)

Many similar testimonials have been sent to the Publishers. More significant, however, is the fact that after several years' trial the AHN-HENN German Text-books are being used **in constantly increasing quantities** in the Public Schools of New York, Hoboken, Buffalo, Cleveland, Sandusky, Detroit, San Francisco, Rochester, Hartford, Dubuque, Louisville, Galena, Davenport, Kansas City, La Crosse, Elmira, Pittsburg, Elizabeth, Newark, Wheeling, Worcester, Indianapolis, as also in those of hundreds of smaller cities, **other books** being **discarded** entirely.

STEIGER'S Latin Series.

AHN'S Latin Grammar. By Dr. P. HENN. With References to the Exercises in the *First, Second,* and *Third Latin Books.* Boards $0.80; Cloth $0.90.

AHN'S Latin Wall Charts. By Dr. P. HENN. 22 Plates, in Sheets $1.50; mounted on 22 Boards $6.00.

AHN'S First Latin Book.* (Rules and Exercises mainly on *Nominal Inflection.*) By Dr. P. HENN. Boards $0.60; Cloth $0.70.

AHN'S Second Latin Book.* (Rules and Exercises mainly on *Verbal Inflection.*) By Dr. P. HENN. Boards $0.80; Cloth $0.90.

AHN'S Latin Vocabulary for Beginners. *Methodical and Etymological. With a Collection of Latin Proverbs and Quotations.* By Dr. P. HENN. (To be used with the *First* and *Second Latin Books.*) Boards $0.60; Cloth $0.70.

AHN'S Third Latin Book.* (Rules and Exercises on *Syntax* and Latin Composition.*) By Dr. P. HENN. Boards $0.80; Cloth $0.90.

AHN-HENN'S First Latin Reader. (*De septem regibus Romanorum,* from LIVY.) With Notes, Vocabulary, and References. To be used with the *Second Latin Book.*) Boards $0.70; Cloth $0.80.

AHN-HENN'S Second Latin Reader. With Notes and References. (To be used with the *Third Latin Book.*) In press.

* The *Keys* to the *First Latin Book, Second Latin Book,* and *Third Latin Book* intended as aids in dictation exercises, etc., will be supplied to teachers only upon their direct application to the publishers.

☞ Thorough Study of Latin made easy. ☜

Most Latin grammars now in use task the beginner with a mass of grammatical detail which is worse than useless, a bar to progress all the more irritating because unnecessary. Hence the wide-spread demand for a grammar *that contains every thing of importance* for all learners, including those who contemplate a collegiate course of study, while it *studiously omits matters of disputed usage,* the study of which will offer no difficulty whatever to the college-student, to whom they properly belong *AHN'S Latin Grammar* and the other books of this *Latin Course* are the realization of this view, and particular attention is invited to the following distinctive features:

1. The best Orthography is exhibited; Quantity is marked throughout, besides Syllabification and Accent in paradigms.

2. Etymology is carefully treated. Without being cumbersome, this *Course* is believed to be more full and complete, especially in the illustrative examples in Declension and Conjugation than any other Latin grammar now in use. On these points a comparison will show how simple, practical, and clear it is.

3 The Derivative Endings (Word-formation) are thoroughly illustrated and classified.

4. Syntax is logically treated in every part. Though brief, it is very comprehensive and so clear in its statements that this subject, generally considered so difficult, is easily understood. The construction of Prepositions, commouly left to the Dictionary, receives here, for the first time, the attention that is its due in a school grammar.

5. The clear and compendious description of the Metres, and especially the full Alphabetical Index of Subjects are very important.

6 The usefulness of these books is increased by judicious typographical arrangement.

AHN'S Latin Course furnishes an excellent preparation to any of the Latin grammars used at College, the difficulties in which will be mastered all the better when the groundwork has been securely learned from the *AHN Course.*

Particular attention is invited to the *Wall Charts* and the *Vocabulary* which are unique, and may be used advantageously also in connection with any other Latin Course. The *First, Second,* and *Third Latin Books* offer an abundance of Exercises for double translation, of which the teacher may use all, or a portion only, as his judgment or other circumstances may dictate. The Vocabularies in these three books contain every Latin and English word occurring in the exercises. The *Readers* furnish the best classic Latin.

The books are printed in large, clear type, and issued in superior style, at low prices. Favorable terms for introduction and exchange. Specimen copies sent to teachers upon receipt of half the advertised price.

E. STEIGER & CO., 25 Park Place, NEW YORK

Samples of Type used in the *AHN-HENN Latin Course*.

467. All words which may be grouped into one family so as to associate their meaning are said to have a common ground-form or **Root**. Thus:

ăcŭō, -ĕrĕ, *to whet* ăcŭs, -ūs, *a needle*
ăcūtŭs, -ă, -ŭm, *sharp* ăcĕr, -rĭs, -rĕ, *sharp*
ăcūmĕn, -ĭnĭs, *acuteness* ăcerbŭs, -ă, -ŭm, *sharp*
ăcĭēs, -ēī, *an edge* ăcĭdŭs, -ă, -ŭm, *sour*

may all be retraced to the ROOT AC.

468. The **Stem** must be distinguished from the **Root**. The stem is that part of the word which remains after taking away the *Inflections*, as: ăcŭ-ĕrĕ, *to whet*, **stem** ăcŭ.. Again, the root is that part of the word which remains after taking away the *Suffix;* thus the verb-stem **ăcŭ** belongs to the **root** AC.

927. Horace uses the Hexameter in his Epistles and Satires. The Odes include nineteen varieties of strophe, viz.:

1. **Alcaic Strophe,** consisting of:

   Two Greater Alcaics ... *923.* 10
   One Trochaic Dimeter with anacrusis ...
   One Lesser Alcaic ... *923.* 9

   Justum ét tenácem própositi virúm
   Non cívium árdor práva jubéntiúm
   Non vúltus instántis tyránni
   Ménte quatít solidá neque Aúster.

From Vocabularies to *Third Latin Book*.

ă, ăb (with abl.), *from, by*
abdĭtŭs, -ă, -ŭm, *hid*
abdōmĕn, -ĭnĭs (n.), *the abdomen*
abdūcō, abduxī, abductŭm, abdūcĕrĕ, *to carry away; to take*
ăberrō, -āvī, -ātŭm, -ārĕ, *to go*
ăbhinc, *ago* [*astray*

the abdomen, abdomen
to abet, adjuvare
ability, facultas
to be able, posse, quire; *not to be able*, nequire
an abode, domicilium

From Index to *Latin Grammar*.

advenīre, with in & acc., 690
adventu, abl. of *time*, 673
Adverbial accusative, 586; phrases, 431
ADVERBS, 32, 424–446; derivation of, 425–434; from adjectives of the 1st & 2d decl., 425; of the 3d decl., 426; of *time*, 437; of *manner*, 438; of *order*, 242; numeral, 241; of *place*, 436; used as *prepositions*, 436; comparison, 440–442; with **gen.**, 566. c; correlative, 439; position, 562
Adversative conjunctions, 451, 853

THE DICTIONARY OF EDUCATION AND INSTRUCTION

German, French, and Latin Dictionaries.

W. O. Elwell's New and Complete Dictionary of the German and English Languages. Remodelled and greatly improved. (With the pronunciation according to the method of J. E. WORCESTER.) 2 parts in 1 vol. 12mo. Half Morocco, $2.50

F. E. Feller. New Pocket Dictionary, English and German, to which is added a Pocket Companion for Travellers, containing a Collection of Conversations, etc. 2 parts in 1 vol. 32mo. Cloth, $1.10
—— The same, bound in 2 vols. Cloth, $1.40

F. and J. G. Flueqel. Practical Dictionary of the English and German Languages. 2 vols. 8vo. Half Morocco, $6.45

Chr. F. Grieb. Dictionary of the English and German Languages, to which is added a Synopsis of English words differently pronounced by different Orthoëpists. 2 vols. 8vo. Half Morocco, $7.00

J. H. Kaltschmidt. New complete Dictionary of the English and German Languages. (With German pronunciation of the English words — for Germans.) 2 parts in 1 vol. 8vo. Half Morocco, $3.50

F. Koehler. English-German and German-English Dictionary. (With German pronunciation of the English words.) 2 parts in 1 vol. 8vo. Half Morocco, $2.95

F. Koehler. Pocket Dictionary of the German and English Languages. 2 parts in 1 vol. 24mo. Cloth, $0.75

Koehler and Witter's New German-English and English-German Pocket Dictionary. (With English pronunciation of the German words.) 2 parts in 1 vol. 24mo. Half Roan, $1.50

J. C. Oehlschläger. English-German and German-English Pocket Dictionary. (With English pronunciation of the German words.) 2 parts in 1 vol. 24mo. Half Roan, $1.50
—— The same. (With German pronunciation of the English words.) 2 parts in 1 vol. 24mo. Half Roan, $1.50

J. F. L. Tafel and L. H. Tafel. New English-German and German-English Pocket Dictionary. (With pronunciation of the German and the English words.) 2 parts in 1 vol. 24mo. Half Roan, $1.50

Thieme-Preusser. A New and Complete Critical Dictionary of the English and German Languages. (With pronunciation of the English words.) 2 parts in 1 vol. 8vo. Half Morocco, $4.25

J. E. Wessely. German-English and English-German Pocket Dictionary. 2 parts in 1 vol. 16mo. Cloth, $0.85

For Dictionaries of the German Language by EBERHARD, GRIMM, HEYSE, HOFFMANN, PETRI, SANDERS, WEBER, WEIGAND, WENIG, and others see STEIGER's Catalogue "German Language."

F. E. Feller. New English and French Pocket Dictionary. 2 parts in 1 vol. 32mo. Cloth, $0.85

Fleming and Tibbins. Large English-French and French-English Dictionary. 4to. 2 vols. Half Morocco, $24.00

Wm. James and Molé. Dictionary of the English and French Languages. 2 parts in 1 vol. 16mo. Half Morocco, $2.60

Spiers and Surenne's Complete French and English, and English and French Dictionary. (With pronunciation of the English and the French words.) 8vo. Half Morocco, $4.50

Spiers and Surenne's Standard Pronouncing Dictionary of the French and English Languages. 2 parts in 1 vol. 12mo. Half Roan, $2.25

J. E. Wessely. French-English and English-French Pocket Dictionary. 2 parts in 1 vol. 16mo. Cloth, $0.85

A Complete Dictionary, English, German, French, for the Use of the three Nations. 3 parts in 1 vol. 8vo. Half Morocco, $3.30

F. E. Feller. New Pocket Dictionary, English, German, and French, containing all the Words indispensable in daily Conversation; admirably adapted for the Use of Travellers. 3 vols. Cloth, $1.90

Pocket Dictionary of Technical Terms used in Arts and Manufactures. Abridged from the Technological Dictionary of RUMPF, MOTHES, and UNVERZAGT. With the Addition of Commercial Terms. 3 vols. 16mo. Paper, $3.00; Half Morocco, $6.00

Technological Dictionary in the English, German, and French Languages. Containing about 76,000 technical terms and locutions employed in Arts, Trades, and Industry in general. By A. TOLHAUSEN. 3 vols. 12mo. Paper, $8.80; Half Morocco $12.40
Each volume sold separately. Paper, @ $2.95; Half Morocco, @ $4.15

Chas. Anthon's Latin-English and English-Latin Dictionary. 2 parts in 1 vol. 12mo. Sheep. Net $2.50 (including Postage $2.92)

Chas. Anthon's Latin-English Dictionary. 12mo. Sheep. Net $2.05 (including Postage $2.40)

A New Dictionary of the Latin and English Languages. With an Appendix of Latin Geographical, Historical, and Mythological Proper Names. 16mo. Cloth, $0.85

Kaltschmidt's Dictionary, English-Latin and Latin-English. 2 parts in 1 vol. 8vo. Cloth. Net $1.80 (including Postage $2.16)

Wm. Smith's English-Latin Dictionary. To which is added a Dictionary of Proper Names. 8vo. Sheep. Net $4.40 (including Postage $4.67)

Any of these Dictionaries will be mailed upon receipt of price.

E. STEIGER & CO., 25 Park Place, NEW YORK

THE CYCLOPÆDIA OF EDUCATION:
A DICTIONARY OF INFORMATION
FOR THE USE OF
TEACHERS, SCHOOL OFFICERS, PARENTS, AND OTHERS.

This important work, which was first issued in 1877 after three years of laborious and careful preparation, has secured an acknowledged position as the one standard educational authority in the English language. The simple fact that this is the first and only publication of its kind in English literature, sufficiently indicates the difficulty of its preparation. It is due to the fortunate association of the editors, Mr. HENRY KIDDLE and Prof. ALEX. J. SCHEM, who were pre-eminently fitted for this work, and regarded it truly as a labor of love, that this *Cyclopædia* at once gained universal recognition — not only in this country but also in Europe, and notably at the *Exposition Universelle* at Paris, 1878, where it was decreed a Medal, while the honorary degree of *Officier d'Académie* was awarded to Mr. KIDDLE by the University of France.

Each year has served to give the *Cyclopædia* still greater prominence and to strengthen the position it has attained. Official endorsements have been added to private and public recommendations, which are all the more indicative of the real merit of the work, as they are the result of a careful study and constant use of the *Cyclopædia* as an educational help. From present indications it is confidently expected that, in time, a copy of the *Cyclopædia of Education* will be purchased by or for each teacher, or that one at least will be provided for every school building in the United States.

"No professional teacher can afford to be without it."
(*Pennsylvania School Journal.*)

"Such a work as this is the living educator; it will do for general education what the dictionary does for the language. It is a work which for many years will lead and control our public and private schools." (*N. Y. Daily Times.*)

"The facts are there in wonderful fullness; but thoughts, opinions, and suggestions are there also, and the critic tries in vain to strike some educational theme upon which no light is thrown in the compact pages of the *Cyclopædia*."
(*Brooklyn Times.*)

"The work is a monument no less of the publisher's enterprise than of the talent and perseverance of its editors." (*Philadelphia Inquirer.*)

"The work ought to, as of course it will, find a place on the shelves of every public school and library in the land. We wish that some of our generous laymen would provide a copy for each of our educational institutions, for it is simply invaluable." (*Christian Leader.*)

"The *Cyclopædia of Education* should be in every library."
(*Popular Science Monthly.*)

"Indispensable to every class of book buyers and book readers."
(*Christian Standard.*)

"It has a living interest to persons in every walk of life."
(*St. Louis Republican.*)

THE DICTIONARY OF EDUCATION AND INSTRUCTION

"This is a magnificent book in every respect — in the value and accuracy of the information it contains, its substantial binding, fine calendered paper, and elegant, clear typography. The external appearance of the work is highly creditable to that careful and enterprising publisher, E. Steiger of New York."
(*Teachers' Journal.*)

"Nearly the whole nation is engaged in the cause of education, and has to rejoice in the publication of a work like this *Cyclopædia*...... We regard it as a treasure to our schools and families, and we congratulate Mr. Steiger upon his enterprise and success. It must have a large sale." (*The Library Table.*)

"We have a very strong conviction that no volume of equal value to the cause of education has ever been produced in the English language. If there be a teacher or school-officer in the land, who is henceforth ignorant upon any subject pertaining to his work, he or she will be without a justifiable excuse. The information needed is compressed within the covers of this book, and the book itself can be had at a price that is within the means of every person fit to be entrusted with the responsibilities of a school, or a system of schools. It should become a text-book in normal schools, and a reference-book in every family where there are children to be educated, or parents to learn their duties in connection therewith." (*The Educational Weekly.*)

"The work is altogether undoubtedly the most valuable contribution to the Science of Education which has yet appeared in our language. The English teacher, as well as the American, will find in it a store-house of compact and well ordered information on an immense variety of educational topics and there are few subjects pertaining to his work on which he will not find some light thrown, and few points in practical teaching on which he will not discover something worth consulting in its pages." (*The Educational Times*, London.)

"America has done what Britain ought long ago to have accomplished. It has added to the scholastic library the *Cyclopædia of Education*."
(*The School*, London.)

"The first Cyclopædia of Education published in the English language, constructed after careful examination of *all* cyclopædias and histories of education, besides general cyclopædias, etc., in English and other languages. Its design is to be comprehensive and complete, within a moderate compass; that like a dictionary, it should be on every teacher's desk and, while supplying information should also *stimulate the pursuit of it*....To sum up, many subjects are dealt with which will be found treated in the ordinary works of reference, but here they are taken from the *educational point of view*. The teacher has in one moderate-sized volume matter of a special character, which, being buried, as it were, in bulky works of reference and in the languages of foreign countries, has, until now, been out of most persons' reach." (*The Publishers' Circular*, London.)

"I have placed it at the head of my list of 'Valuable Books for Teachers'."
(A. B. LEMMON, State Supt. of Public Instruction, Kansas.)

"In no other work is so much useful information comprised in such a convenient form." (LEON. TROUSDALE, State Supt. of Public Schools, Tennessee.)

"The *Cyclopædia of Education* is a scholarly and valuable work which deserves a place in the library of every educator and every school."
(B. G. NORTHROP, Secretary State Board of Education, Connecticut.)

"I find it singularly accurate and very comprehensive in both the range and treatment of subjects. I wish it could be in the hands of every teacher in Kentucky." (H. A. M. HENDERSON, State Supt. of Public Instruction, Kentucky.)

"The book is in every way an honor to the profession. It will make its place, for, like the pioneer edition of Webster's Unabridged, 'it comes to stay'."
(J. P. WICKERSHAM, State Supt. of Public Instruction, Pennsylvania.)

"I take great pleasure in commending the *Cyclopædia of Education* as a very valuable work to Educators and to all persons interested in the work of Education. The information which it contains is not ordinarily accessible in any other form. The work is in constant use in my own office and will, I hope, have a wide circulation."
(WM. C. WHITFORD, State Supt. of Public Instruction, Wisconsin.)

THE DICTIONARY OF EDUCATION AND INSTRUCTION

"I hope the year 1878 will find your excellent *Cyclopædia* introduced into our schools. I do not see how it could be improved and it, certainly, fills a great want."   (E. S. CARR, State Supt. of Public Instruction, California.)

"We, the undersigned, Teachers of Randolph County, Ind., after a practical test of the *Cyclopædia of Education*, do most heartily recommend it to our fellow teachers as a work of superior merit. We have never referred to it in vain for information upon any subject connected with our work in the school-room, literary meeting, or township institute. Indeed, we have found it a complete library in one volume. Broad in its compass, philosophic in its arrangement, authentic in its data, and unsurpassed in its mechanical finish, it comes as a strong stay and support to the weary but zealous teacher."
J. M. BRANSON — A. GILLISPIE — A. CANFIELD — J. L. MILLS — W. W. FOWLER — S. P. GLUNT — O. L. HARBOUR — T. S. SPENCE — J. W. WILLS — W. T. DAVIS — M. C. GAFFEY — FREMONT GARRETT — D. S. GRAHAM — H. D. GOOD — O. P. MCCABE — D. W. MOTE — A. GADDIS — C. H. ALLEN — J. W. DENNEY.

"In looking through the *Cyclopædia* I have been much pleased in noticing the amount of valuable and interesting information contained therein and have so expressed myself to our Brothers and to others as occasion presented."
(Brother PAULIAN, Provincial Visitor Brothers of the Christian Schools, in the United States.)

"The *Cyclopædia of Education* is a most valued and valuable book, a real Treasury of Knowledge and has been in constant requisition since it arrived. In this superficial age when the teacher's office and labors are so little understood, the *Cyclopædia* is indeed a most useful and necessary work."
(Sister LUCINA, Superior of St. Vincent's Academy, St. Louis, Mo.)

"The *Cyclopædia of Education* having been my handbook for the last year, I am prepared to speak cordially of its merits.
No teacher of to-day has a right to gain all his professional experience by blundering, isolated experiments upon the minds placed in his care. It is his duty to seek of the past at least three things: what has been thought, — what has been planned and attempted, — what has been the result of experiment. The *Cyclopædia* has never failed to answer these questions and I have often been surprised to find that which I had read a volume to learn, clearly and systematically stated here upon a single page.
This work should be the **corner-stone** of every teacher's professional library, while no man should undertake the responsible duties of a school officer without having thoughtfully studied the leading articles."
(G. S. ALBEE, President State Normal School, Oshkosh, Wis.)

☞ Agreeing with the above and with hundreds of similar opinions of the highest American and foreign authorities, the *Educational Weekly* (November, 1880), the *School Bulletin* (December, 1880), and other periodicals have recommended the *Cyclopædia of Education* as **the very first** in a List of "Ten Books for Teachers" which List was, moreover, formed by a selection from **more than 200** educational works.

The *Cyclopædia of Education* is issued in one large octavo volume of about 900 pages, in the styles and at the prices which follow, viz.:
In paper Cover, uncut edges $4.00 (also in 4 divisions at $1.00 each); bound in Cloth $5.00 — and uniform with the volumes of *Appleton's American Cyclopædia*, in Library Leather $6.00; in Half Morocco $7.00; in Half Russia, extra gilt $8.00; in Full Morocco, or Full Russia, with gilt edges $10.00.

This work will be forwarded promptly upon receipt of price.

E. STEIGER & CO., 25 Park Place, NEW YORK.

Steiger's Free Educational Bureau

has been established for the purpose of assisting Teachers and Kindergartners in their efforts to obtain positions, **saving them**, however, the usual **'Registration Fee'** and **the percentage upon their salaries** which it is customary to pay — when engaged — to the Agent or person through whom the position has been obtained.

The organization of this **Free Educational Bureau** was intended to be but another step in the series of services which it is Mr. STEIGER's desire to render in behalf of the interests of Education, and the very general manner in which Teachers as well as Principals, and also Parents, have availed themselves of the facilities thus offered, is sufficient proof of the need of an Establishment conducted on such principles; its prompt efficiency has been fully acknowledged, and is being gratefully appreciated and remembered. But while Mr. STEIGER takes pleasure in thus offering his aid, he trusts, on the other hand, that he will be saved unnecessary labor, and that neither his own nor his assistants' time will be occupied in attending to personal calls. A clearly-written statement setting forth what is desired by, and what are the qualifications of, the applicant is, in most cases, the best introduction, and of more real value than a personal interview and a verbal application.

The Application Forms (with **transcripts** of testimonials and photograph attached) are filed in the Office of **Steiger's Free Educational Bureau**, and Principals of Educational Institutions, upon calling, are given access to these files, after an inspection of which they will be able to make their selection, to enter into *direct* communication with applicants, and to conclude arrangements with them — without incurring any monetary obligation to Mr. STEIGER.

On the other hand, Principals residing at a distance, who can not personally inspect the files, should indicate upon the Blank Forms furnished for that purpose, what they expect from the Assistant they wish to engage. Reference will then be made to the files, and the names of such applicants as seem best suited for the position, will be sent to the Principal, who is thus placed in *direct* communication with available Teachers, and can effect the desired arrangement without other intervention.

In consequence of the extensive information in regard to nearly all the Schools and Educational Institutions of this country, and of Canada, which is in the possession of this **Free Educational Bureau** — in the form of circulars, catalogues, reports, and special particulars — Mr. STEIGER is enabled to offer advice respecting the choice of schools for the education of children. Information can also be given concerning the Universities, and the leading High, Special, and Private Schools of Europe.

Parents and Guardians who wish to avail themselves of the facilities offered by this **Bureau** for the selection of a Tutor or Governess for home instruction will be accommodated in the same manner as Principals. The Blank Forms furnished should be carefully filled out with a distinct statement of the qualifications which are considered necessary and the nature of the service desired. Upon the receipt of such application, Mr. STEIGER will examine the files of the **Bureau** and communicate a select list of names to each inquirer. The concluding arrangements will, however, be left entirely to the Parents or Guardians themselves.

E. STEIGER, 25 Park Place, NEW YORK.

THE DICTIONARY OF EDUCATION AND INSTRUCTION

Kindergarten
Material, Gifts, and Occupations.
The Most Complete Assortment

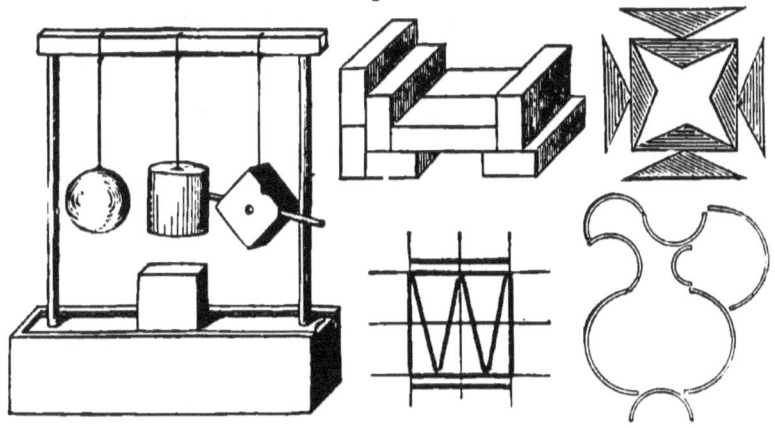

carefully manufactured according to the directions of the highest authorities of

☛ **the genuine Frœbel System.** ☚

Full illustrated Catalogue sent free upon application.

Most favorable Terms.

Full Assortment of Kindergarten Publications in English, German, and French.

E. STEIGER & CO., 25 Park Place, NEW YORK

THE DICTIONARY OF EDUCATION AND INSTRUCTION

Text-Books and Aids to Teachers.

NET PRICES: *when sent by mail, one-tenth of the net price should be added for postage.*

Supplementary Reading.

Graded Supplementary Readers. Prepared for use in Schools by Prof. TWEED, late Supervisor of Boston Public Schools. Six Parts ready.
Nos. 1 & 4 for 1st Year. Primary.
" 2 & 5 for 2d " "
" 3 & 6 for 3d " "
Brown paper covers, per dozen, $0.48.
Without paper covers " " 0.36.

Cambridge Series of Information Cards. For Upper Classes in Schools. First seven numbers now ready.
Price, per Dozen, $0.24.
By mail, " " 0.36.
1. Sugar. By W. J. ROLFE, A.M.
2. The Yosemite Valley. By A. P. PEABODY, D.D.
3. The English Language. By W. J. ROLFE, A.M.
4. The Sphinx at Mt. Auburn. By N. LINCOLN.
5. The Employment of Time. By CHARLES SUMNER.
6. The Sun as a Worker. By W. J. ROLFE, A.M.
7. About Combustion. By W. J. ROLFE. A.M.

Geographical Plays. For Young Folks at School and at Home. By Miss JANE ANDREWS, author of "Seven Little Sisters", "Each and All", etc. Very entertaining and instructive. May be used for Supplementary Reading, or Review Exercises in Geography.
Price, each, $0.12.
United States. Europe.
Asia. Africa.
Australia and the Isles of the Sea.
The Commerce of the World.

Young Folks' Book of American Explorers. By Col. T. WENTWORTH HIGGINSON. Illust. 16mo. $1.20

Stories of American History. By N. S. DODGE. Illust. School edition. 16mo. $0.50.

The Seven Little Sisters who live on the Round Ball that floats in the air. By Miss JANE ANDREWS. Illust. School edition. $0.50.

Each and All; or, How the Seven Little Sisters Proved their Sisterhood. By Miss JANE ANDREWS. Illust. School edition. $0.50.

Text-Books.

Young Folks' History of the United States. By Col. T. WENTWORTH HIGGINSON. With more than 100 Illustrations. $1.20.

Campbell's Hand-Book of English Synonyms. With an appendix showing the correct use of prepositions, also a collection of Foreign Phrases. By L. J. CAMPBELL. 32mo. Cloth. $0.50.

Pronouncing Hand-Book of Words often Mispronounced. By RICHARD SOULE and LOOMIS J. CAMPBELL. School edition. $0.30.

Arithmetical Primer. By A. G. METHFESSEL. Paper. 4to. $0.12.

Art; Its Laws, and the Reasons for them. Collected, considered, and arranged for General and Educational purposes, by SAMUEL P. LONG. With steel plates and wood engravings. $1.60.

Arithmetic for Young Children. By HORACE GRANT. American edition. edited by WILLARD SMALL. $0.30.

Hand-Book of English Literature. Intended for the use of High Schools, as well as a Companion and Guide for Private Students and for General Readers. By FRANCIS H. UNDERWOOD, A.M.
American authors, Crown 8vo. $2.00.
British authors, Crown 8vo. 2.00.

Hand-Book of Punctuation and other Typographical Matters. For the use of Teachers, Authors and Printers, by MARSHALL T. BIGELOW, Corrector at University Press, Cambridge. Cloth. $0.40.

Advanced Readings and Recitations. Compiled by Austin B. FLETCHER, A.M., LL.B., Professor of Elocution, Boston University. Cloth. $1.20.

Prof. L. B. Monroe's Humorous Readings in Prose and Verse, for Home, School, and Public Readings. 12mo. $1.20.

Monroe's Miscellaneous Readings. 12mo. $1.20.

Monroe's Dialogues and Dramas. In Prose and Verse. 12mo. $1.20.

Monroe's Young Folks' Readings, in Prose and Verse. $1.20.

Full Catalogues of our Publications furnished on Application.

LEE AND SHEPARD, Publishers, BOSTON

www.ingramcontent.com/pod-product-compliance
Lightning Source LLC
Chambersburg PA
CBHW031427230426
43668CB00007B/466